Incarceration
he Eva Braun
To Consider

p xviii in introduction

ALLEGORY AND EVENT

A STUDY OF THE SOURCES AND SIGNIFICANCE
OF ORIGEN'S INTERPRETATION OF SCRIPTURE

R. P. C. HANSON, D.D.

*Senior Lecturer in Christian Theology
in the University of Nottingham*

With an Introduction by
JOSEPH W. TRIGG

Westminster John Knox Press
LOUISVILLE • LONDON

First published simultaneously in Great Britain by SCM Press, London and in the United States by John Knox Press, Richmond, Virginia.

Cover design by Mark Abrams

Published by Westminster John Knox Press
Louisville, Kentucky

This book is printed on acid-free paper that meets the American National Standards Institute Z39.48 standard. ⊚

PRINTED IN THE UNITED STATES OF AMERICA

02 03 04 05 06 07 08 09 10 11 — 10 9 8 7 6 5 4 3 2 1

Library of Congress Cataloging-in-Publication Data

Hanson, R. P. C. (Richard Patrick Crosland), 1916–
    Allegory and event : a study of the sources and significance of Origen's interpretation of Scripture / R. P. C. Hanson ; introduction by Joseph W. Trigg.
        p. cm.
    Originally published: Richmond: John Knox Press, 1959. With new introd.
    Includes bibliographical references and indexes.
    ISBN 0-664-22444-X (alk. paper)
        1. Origen.   2. Bible—Criticism, interpretation, etc.—History—Early church, ca. 30-600.   3. Allegory.   I. Title.

BS500 .H33   2002
220.6'092—dc21   2002028896

CONTENTS

INTRODUCTION

Joseph W. Trigg

AT its publication in 1959, *Allegory and Event* was the first scholarly and comprehensive study of Origen's biblical interpretation in English. It has not been superseded.[1] Nonetheless, the intervening time has seen a burgeoning interest in Origen and his biblical interpretation. That time has also seen the emergence of radically new perspectives in biblical hermeneutics. To appreciate this book fully we need some understanding of Hanson, of the questions he was dealing with and the assumptions he made, and of how subsequent studies have modified the way we look at Origen and at the Bible.

Richard Patrick Crosland Hanson

R. P. C. Hanson was a fine scholar, conversant with Origen's works as they have come down to us in the original Greek and early Latin translations as well as with the whole body of Greco-Roman religious and philosophical literature from the early Christian centuries. He was a committed Christian for whom Origen's biblical interpretation raised living issues of faith. He was also a man of strong views who did not hesitate to express them. Anglo-Irish by heritage and education, Hanson had already served as a priest in Irish and English parishes before writing this book.[2] In 1970 he would take one of the most difficult pastoral assignments in the Anglican Communion, becoming Bishop of Clogher, a diocese straddling the border of Northern Ireland. Seeking to ameliorate the bitterness of the troubles, Hanson promoted warm relations with Roman Catholics as well as with Protestants of other denominations. Although his

---

[1] The most serious work in English prior to Hanson that deals with Origen's biblical exegesis is Robert M. Grant's *The Letter and the Spirit* (New York: Macmillan, 1957), a work that shows how allegory was developed by Greek authors and mediated to Christians through Hellenistic Judaism. After Hanson, two excellent works, both discussed below, that deal with aspects of Origen's interpretation are Robert M. Grant's *The Earliest Lives of Jesus* (New York: Harper & Brothers, 1961) and Karen Torjesen's *Hermeneutical Procedure and Theological Method in Origen's Exegesis* (Berlin: Walter de Gruyter, 1986).

[2] For information about Hanson's life I am indebted to Benjamin Drewery ("R. P. C. Hanson: A short biographical memoir," in *Scripture Tradition and Reason, A Study in the Criteria of Christian Doctrine: Essays in Honour of Richard P. C. Hanson*, ed. Richard Bauckham and Benjamin Drewery [Edinburgh: T. & T. Clark, 1988], pp. 3–12).

Protestant credentials were well in order—in 1948 he had, along with Reginald Fuller, published *The Church of Rome: A Dissuasive*,[1] and he had spoken at a meeting called in 1950 to protest Pius XII's recent proclamation of the Dogma of the Assumption—he still, to his credit, ran afoul of the Loyalist Orange Order. After he denounced its Protestant bigotry, an effective ministry was no longer possible for him. Leaving Ireland, he spent the rest of his career primarily as a teacher and scholar at the University of Manchester but remained active pastorally as assistant bishop in the Dioceses of Chester and Manchester.

In addition to his work on Origen, Hanson made contributions to the study of early British Christianity, notably in *Saint Patrick: His Origins and Career*, published in 1968.[2] There he argued that our only valid sources are the saint's two genuine writings, which he himself would edit in the French series, Sources Chrétiennes,[3] along with the slender information we can glean from contemporary writings and from archeology about Britain in Patrick's time. From these sources, however, he drew a convincing portrait of Patrick as a flesh-and-blood human being, a winsome figure equally accessible to Protestants and Catholics.

He also traced the development of the doctrine of the Trinity in his last and most ambitious book, *The Search for the Christian Doctrine of God: The Arian Controversy*, published in 1988.[4] There he examined the development of the doctrine of the Trinity in the crucial period between the Councils of Nicea in 325 and Constantinople in 380. He presented the reception of the Nicene Creed not as a heroic conflict between orthodoxy and state-supported heresy but as a genuine search to which all parties involved made contributions and in which the eventual outcome only gradually became clear. In both works Hanson challenged prevailing views still tinged with nineteenth-century Romanticism by freshly examining the actual historical evidence.

Origen, however, first and most fully engaged Hanson's scholarly interest. In 1954 his first academic book, *Origen's Doctrine of Tradi-*

---

[1]Richard P. C. Hanson and Reginald H. Fuller, *The Church of Rome: A Dissuasive* (London: SCM Press, 1948).

[2]Richard P. C. Hanson, *Saint Patrick: His Origins and Career* (Oxford: Oxford University Press, 1968).

[3]See Saint Patrick, *Confession et Lettre à Coroticus*, ed. and trans. with intro. by Richard P. C. Hanson and Cécile Blanc, Sources Chrétiennes 249 (Paris: Cerf, 1978).

[4]Richard P. C. Hanson, *The Search for the Christian Doctrine of God: The Arian Controversy, 318–381* (Edinburgh: T. & T. Clark, 1988).

tion, examined how Origen related the Bible to the church's rule of faith. There he discussed how Origen taught a secret tradition, a notion he took from two Alexandrians who had already set forth learned, Platonizing interpretations of the Bible: Clement of Alexandria, with whom he probably studied himself, and the first-century Jewish philosopher Philo. Hanson argues that Origen borrowed directly from Clement "the doctrine of Reserve," a "tendency to allot to the uneducated simple believers a kind of faith which is not fully faith but has in it an ingredient of fear which is wholly absent from the faith of the Christian intellectual."[1] Unlike Clement, though, Origen did not appeal to a succession of teachers mediating this secret tradition from Jesus himself. Rather, "the only indispensable source of tradition is the Old and New Testaments," and "there is no evidence for a source of doctrine independent of the Bible."[2] Origen's rejection of claims to an oral tradition met Hanson's approval, but he castigated Origen's actual exegetical methods as "tortuous twistings of meaning" and "gross violations of the original intention of the Biblical text" that "derive much more obviously from non-Hebraic and non-Biblical sources."[3] His attitude towards Origen's thought could be sarcastic and dismissive; by means of allegory, he claimed, "the balloon of Origen's speculation may soar sublimely or extravagantly into the upper air of philosophical irrelevance."[4] In the opening chapters of *Origen's Doctrine of Tradition*, Hanson set forth the chronology of Origen's life and works and laid down his reasons for giving preferential treatment to those of Origen's writings that have survived in Greek over those that survive in early Latin translations. Since Hanson did not lay these foundations again in *Allegory and Event*, it may be helpful to summarize information Hanson presupposes.

Origen, Sign of Contradiction

Origen was born around A.D. 185,[5] to parents who must have been well-to-do and devout Alexandrian Christians like those for whom

---

[1] Richard P. C. Hanson, *Origen's Doctrine of Tradition* (London: SPCK, 1954), p. 88.
[2] Ibid., pp. 182, 191.
[3] Ibid., p. 104.
[4] Ibid., p. 188.
[5] I follow the reconstruction of Origen's life in Pierre Nautin's *Origène: sa vie et son œuvre* (Paris: Beauchesne, 1977), which differs only in details from the outline Hanson gave in *Origen's Doctrine of Tradition*.

Clement of Alexandria wrote his *Paedagogus*, a work that provides instruction on such matters as how to deal with servants and what symbols to use on a signet ring. His upbringing in a cosmopolitan city that had long been a preeminent center of learning gave Origen an extraordinary grounding in the literary, philosophical, and religious thought of his time. His education taught him the Christian Scriptures alongside the standard Hellenistic curriculum, which consisted of the study of Greek literature along with mathematics and astronomy. When around 203 his father died as a martyr during a persecution under Septimius Severus, his property was confiscated and his family left without resources. With the assistance of a wealthy Christian woman, who also patronized a gnostic teacher, Origen was able to further his studies, becoming a *grammateus*, a teacher of Greek literature. It seems that he also studied philosophy from Ammonius Saccas, a Platonist who also taught Origen's younger contemporary, Plotinus. He probably studied as well under Clement of Alexandria and, probably through Clement, he became familiar with works of Philo. He also sought help with Hebrew and insights from Jewish exegetical traditions from at least one Jewish teacher.

A second period of persecution, some years after his father's death, provided Origen with his lifelong identity as a Christian teacher. At a time when the Alexandrian church was under attack, persons interested in Christianity sought out the young Christian *grammateus* for catechetical instruction. He risked his life to oblige them. Adopting a rigorous asceticism and abandoning his teaching of Greek literature, he devoted himself to studying and teaching the Bible. A rich Christian layman, Ambrosius, whom Origen had won away from Gnosticism, eventually became his lifelong friend and patron, providing him means and encouragement to write. Nonetheless, as Origen's fame spread among Christians and pagans alike, his relations with Demetrius, the Bishop of Alexandria, deteriorated. This is almost certainly why, in 231, Origen left Alexandria to settle in Caesarea Maritima in Palestine, where he had already been ordained as a presbyter by Bishop Theoctistus. In Caesarea he continued to teach and to publish, becoming one of the most prolific authors of antiquity. He also preached and, on at least two occasions, was called in as a doctrinal authority in the heresy trials of bishops. He had extensive intellectual relations with Caesarea's flourishing Jewish community. He died around 253 as a result of injuries sustained in 251 under torture during the Decian persecution.

Only a fragment of Origen's oeuvre survives, about half of that in ancient Latin translations. Even so, far more of his works remain to us than those of any Christian author of the ante-Nicene period. His most massive work, the *Hexapla*, has almost totally disappeared. It was a word-for-word comparison of the various Greek translations of the Old Testament. His remaining works belonged to four genres: learned treatises arranged in books (*tomoi*), homilies, dialogues, and letters. Most of the treatises are multivolume scriptural commentaries, usually expounding a biblical book sequentially, verse by verse. We possess some complete books of his commentaries on John and Matthew in the original Greek and parts or abridgments of his commentaries on the Song of Songs, Matthew, and Romans in Latin translations. Other commentaries, including his massive works on Genesis and the Psalms, survive only in disconnected fragments, if at all. Other treatises dealt with particular theological topics: eight books, *Against Celsus* (or *Contra Celsum*), refuted a pagan attack on Christianity; four books, *On First Principles* (which Hanson refers to by the Greek title, *Peri Archon*); and books entitled *On Prayer*, *An Exhortation to Martyrdom*, and *On the Passover*. Twenty homilies on Jeremiah and one on 1 Samuel survive in Greek and 184 more on various books (all from the Old Testament except for a series on Luke) in Latin translations. The two letters by Origen that survive intact also deal, to a large extent, with biblical interpretation. Hanson was able to use the one surviving dialogue, the *Conversation with Heracleides*, which had been discovered in 1941 at Tura, near Cairo. Other works found with it, extracts in Greek from Origen's *Commentary on Romans* and two treatises, *On the Passover*, were edited too late for him to take them into consideration.[1] Hanson also does not take into consideration Jerome's *Tractates on the Psalms*, which have been recognized as the translation and adaptation of a series of Origen's homilies.[2] On the other hand, we now consider spurious some fragmentary comments on the Revelation to John that Hanson considered genuine.[3] Hanson's taking (or not taking) these works into account would not have altered any of his conclusions.

[1] Jean Scherer, ed., *Le Commentaire d'Origène sur Rom. III.5 –V.7 d'après les extraits du Papyrus N° 88748 du Musée de Caire et les fragments de la Philocalie et du Vaticanus Gr. 762* (Cairo: Institut Français d'Archéologie Orientale, 1957); and Octave Guérand and Pierre Nautin, eds., *Origène sur la Pâque: Traité inédit publié d'après un papyrus de Toura* (Paris: Beauchesne, 1979).

[2] Vittorio Peri, *Omelie origeniane sui Salmi* (Rome: Bibliotheca Apostolica Vaticana, 1980).

[3] See Nautin, *Origène*, p. 449.

Origen was the most creative and influential Christian thinker between the New Testament and Augustine, but, as Hanson's friend Henri Crouzel aptly described him, Origen was, in the phrase from Luke 2:34, like a "sign that will be contradicted."[1] The fundamental criticism of Origen, beginning during his own lifetime, was that he used allegorical interpretation to provide a specious justification for reinterpreting Christian doctrine in terms of Platonic philosophy. Ultimately, this charge led the Emperor Justinian to insist on Origen's condemnation as a heretic by the Second Council of Constantinople in A.D. 553, an action that resulted in his rejection by Eastern Orthodoxy and in the destruction and loss of most of his works. The medieval Latin tradition was kinder to his memory, so many works, including, fortunately, *Peri Archon*, survived in Latin translations.

In *Peri Archon* Origen sought to fill in the gaps in the church's rule of faith as it had been transmitted from the apostles. The rule of faith, provided, as Hanson himself would write in a subsequent book, *Tradition in the Early Church*, "what the church conceived as 'the main body of truth' (to use Irenaeus's phrase) . . . a key to what the Church thought the Scriptures came to, where it was, so to speak, that their weight fell, what was their drift."[2] *Peri Archon* dealt with those aspects of theology that Origen identified as most vital for the attainment of spiritual perfection. These are, by his account (*Peri Archon* 4.2.7) the doctrines of God, of the nature and work of Christ, of the nature of rational creatures (including angels and demons as well as human beings) and their fall and redemption, of the world and why it exists, and of the nature of evil. Since, as Origen understood it, the rule of faith itself included the doctrine that the Scriptures have a spiritual sense, *Peri Archon* also includes an extended discussion of biblical interpretation. Because of its importance to his overall scheme, Origen also included an extended treatment of free will, considered both from philosophical and biblical perspectives. In the process, Origen sought to refute positions he considered heretical, specifically those of Valentinus and Marcion. The subsections on biblical interpretation and on free will are the only parts of *Peri Archon* to survive in Greek.

[1] Henri Crouzel, "Signum qui contradicetur," in *Origen*, trans. Henry Worrall (San Francisco: Harper & Row, 1989), p. xi.
[2] Richard P. C. Hanson, *Tradition in the Early Church* (Philadelphia: Westminster Press, 1961), p. 128.

In his exposition of the doctrine of God, Origen argues that God (the Father), is one and utterly simple and, hence, incorporeal. God's Son or Word, having his own individual existence (Gk. *hypostasis*) mediates between God's simple unity and the complex multiplicity of the cosmos. Various aspects (*epinoiai*) of the Son meet the needs of rational beings at every level of distance from God. A third divine hypostasis, the Holy Spirit, inspires and sanctifies those rational beings that have become children by adoption through the Son. Although the Son and Holy Spirit receive their being from the Father, the ultimate source of all existence, they did not come into existence in time and so are coeternal with the Father. At a lower level of being are created rational beings (*logikoi*), which were created to know and enjoy God. Almost all of these beings, however, have fallen to some degree or another from their original unity with God. The material world was created by God as a means whereby some of these rational beings—now called souls (*psuchai*) because of their having cooled (*psuchesthai*) from their original ardor for God—will freely choose to return to him. In Origen's thought God's divine plan of salvation (*oikonomia*) embraces not only the cosmos as a whole but also each individual rational being; God providentially arranges circumstances so that those beings that have fallen will repent and return freely to God. In this process, more advanced rational beings assist those less advanced. These include the angels, who do not require material bodies; the stars, clothed in ethereal bodies and witnessing by their ordered movements to the divine order; and human spiritual teachers. Adverse powers, the demons, who have fallen too far for material bodies to be helpful, oppose the soul's progress. One rational being, the soul of Christ, did not fall at all but, by its steadfast devotion, became utterly united with the Logos. The preexistent soul of Christ became the means whereby the Logos was united, in the incarnation, with a full human being in such a way that the properties of his divinity became those of his humanity and vice versa. Origen's eschatology involved the return of created order to a state like that which it had originally, with all rational creatures united to God. In such a state the embodiment that we now experience as a result of the fall will no longer be necessary. He expected that this process would take many successive world-ages.

According to Hanson's contemporary, Henry Chadwick, "no discussion of Origen can proceed far without coming back to the perennial problem of his orthodoxy."[1] Such doctrines as the eternal generation of the Son and the communication of properties between the divine and human natures of Christ provided the foundation for orthodox doctrine as it came to be defined in the fourth and fifth centuries. Other aspects of the theology set forth in *Peri Archon* were problematical in his time or later. Origen knew he was opposing the beliefs of most Christians in his own time (whom he referred to as "the simple") when he rejected eternal damnation and when he taught that the resurrection could not entail the reanimation of our earthly bodies. Objections soon arose also to his notion of the soul's preexistence and of the animation of the stars. Such ideas may have been what Hanson had in mind when he wrote that Origen's thought could soar into philosophical irrelevance. With the development of Trinitarian doctrine, Origen was also accused of a heretical subordination of the Son and Holy Spirit to the Father. Furthermore, accusers of Origen united in denying that allegory could give access to a hidden, secret doctrine. That Origen's work could be so fundamental to the development of Christian thought but so difficult to assimilate in its entirety gives him a unique status, simultaneously at the center and at the margin. The fourth-century Latin scholar Jerome exemplifies the ambivalence this odd status produced. Jerome modeled his life on Origen, translated many of his works, and freely borrowed from Origen in works he published as his own. Yet Jerome, who had called Origen "the church's teacher after the Apostle [Paul],"[2] would later spare no effort to expose him as a heretic. The source of Origen's heresy, on this interpretation, was his uncritical acceptance of philosophical doctrines derived from Plato, which he read into the Bible by means of allegory. This is probably still the way Origen is understood by many theologians—Catholic, Protestant, and Orthodox. To a large extent, it is the way Hanson understood Origen when he wrote *Allegory and Event*.

If Origen has never lacked detractors, he has rarely lacked defenders. Most, like Jerome's contemporary and erstwhile friend, Rufinus of Aquileia, acknowledge the validity of officially received

---

[1] Henry Chadwick, *Early Christian Thought and the Classical Tradition: Studies in Justin, Clement and Origen* (Oxford: Oxford University Press, 1966), p. 96. For Chadwick, this problem does not reflect as badly on Origen as it does on the notion of orthodoxy.

[2] Jerome, *On Hebrew Names*, Preface (*PL* 23.772b). All translations are mine unless otherwise indicated.

orthodoxy and seek to justify Origen in its terms. Such an approach became easier as churches assimilated the teaching of nineteenth-century theologians such as Friedrich Schleiermacher and John Henry Newman that Christian doctrine was not an unchanging apostolic deposit but rather the product of gradual historical development. In the 1930s, a number of Roman Catholic theologians indebted to Newman promoted a rehabilitation of Origen. Von Balthasar launched this effort with a lengthy and learned article, "Le Mysterion d'Origène," published in 1936 and 1937.[1] In 1942 Daniélou and de Lubac helped launch the French text and translation series, Sources Chrétiennes, in order to make Greek Christian spiritual writers, especially Origen, accessible to the French-speaking public.[2] In 1948 Daniélou published Origène, an influential overview of Origen's life and work.[3] Such scholars argued that those who condemn Origen as a heretic do not understand him. Origen admittedly set forth positions inconsistent with later orthodoxy. These should be understood, though, as innocent speculations on the part of a loyal son of the church at a time when orthodoxy was not yet defined. They stressed that Origen was critical in his stance toward Greek philosophy and always gave priority to the teachings of the Bible as the church had received them. Like Newman himself, Daniélou and de Lubac became cardinals in their old age after spending most of their lives under Vatican suspicion; it would almost seem as if they wanted to make Origen one of their number. The indefatigable Henri Crouzel, author of a bibliography now in three volumes and of many other works on Origen,[4] and a Jesuit like Daniélou, de Lubac, and (originally) von Balthasar, has maintained their perspective down to our time. (Hanson and Crouzel became warm friends, and Hanson would dedicate The Search for the Christian Doctrine of God to him.[5])

[1] Hans Urs von Balthasar, "Le Mysterion d'Origène" in Recherches de science religieuse 26 (1936): 512-62 and 27 (1937): 38-64.
[2] See Étienne Fouilloux, La collection "Sources chrétiennes" Editer les Pères de l'Eglise au XXe siècle (Paris: Cerf, 1995).
[3] Jean Daniélou, Origène (Paris: La Table Ronde, 1948).
[4] His works are too numerous to list. They include Bibliographie Critique d'Origène (The Hague: Martinus Nijhoff, 1959), which appeared in the same year as this book; Bibliographie Critique d'Origène: Supplément I (The Hague: Martinus Nijhoff, 1982) and Supplément II (Turnhout: Brepols, 1996), and one work that has been translated into English, Origen: The Life and Thought of the First Great Theologian, trans. A. S. Worrall (San Francisco: Harper & Row, 1989).
[5] A phrase in Hanson's dedication alludes playfully to a sense of proprietorship Crouzel would develop: "Origenis illius celeberrimi strenuo defensori" (strenuous defender of his most famous Origen).

x   INTRODUCTION

Event or Allegory?

When Hanson wrote, the principal books on Origen's biblical interpretation were Daniélou's *Sacramentum Futuri* and de Lubac's *Histoire et esprit*, both published in 1950.[1] Daniélou argued that what
he called a "typological" interpretation of the Old Testament, in
which events under the Old Covenant prefigured events under the
New, was integral to Christian teaching in the first four centuries.
Furthermore, such interpretation was a prolongation of the messianic typology of the prophets and of the apostolic preaching.
Daniélou noted Origen's tendency to apply this typological interpretation to the individual soul. Thus, for example, the manna the
Israelites ate in the wilderness is a type of Christ and its adaptation
to the individual tastes of those who eat it prefigures Christ's adaptation to the needs of particular souls.[2] The implication of Daniélou's
work was that such typology, as practiced by Origen among others,
was a legitimate way of understanding the Bible that developed
within the Judeo-Christian tradition. In *Origène*, Daniélou had
already argued that such typology in the church's common catechetical tradition was Origen's fundamental approach to exegesis,
although, out of concern to make use of every possible resource for
understanding Scripture, he also drew on other exegetical traditions.
These included rabbinic Jewish exegesis, the exegesis of Philo, and a
gnostic exegesis concerned with angelic powers and eschatology.[3]
Daniélou did not consider Greco-Roman philosophical allegory
among the principal sources of Origen's exegesis. In his discussion of
Philo, Daniélou stresses the Jewish roots of his interpretation,
although he does admit only some "slippage" from Semitic to Hellenistic symbolism.[4]

In *Histoire et esprit*, de Lubac forthrightly defended Origen, beginning his work with a chapter responding to accusations against him.
De Lubac presented Origen as someone who genuinely sought to
defend and explain the church's faith. He pointed to Origen's own
frequent description of himself as a "man of the church"; his almost
complete lack of references to pagan authors outside the *Contra Cel-*

[1] Jean Daniélou, *Sacramentum Futuri: Études sur les origins de la typologie biblique*
(Paris: Beauchesne, 1950), and Henri de Lubac, *Histoire et esprit: L'intelligence de l'écriture d'après Origène* (Paris: Aubier, 1950).
[2] Daniélou, *Sacramentum Futuri*, p. 199.
[3] Daniélou, *Origène*, pp. 175–98.
[4] Ibid., p. 185.

sum; and his condemnations of heretics, idolaters, and philosophers.[1] He also pointed to Origen's moving expressions of devotion
to the incarnate Christ, which exhibit "a nobility of tone that makes
one think of Pascal."[2] He convincingly sought to clear Origen of
charges that he relativized the importance of the death of the incarnate Word on the cross as a once-and-for-all saving act, what we
would call a historical event: "It does not follow that in his eyes the
drama of salvation, as the whole Bible presents it, appears at all as a
sort of sensible reflection of a drama in which the essential action
will be played out in celestial or supercelestial regions. . . . For him
the redemptive act is unique and it is that of Calvary."[3]

When dealing with Origen's exegesis, de Lubac minimized or
explained away wherever possible Origen's often expressed disdain for
the letter of the Bible, which de Lubac identifies as "history" ("*l'histoire*"). Origen, he argued, "spiritualizes" history "or, if one likes, he
interiorizes it, but he by no means destroys it," and he "spiritualizes
the whole Scripture for the use of the Christian soul without taking
away anything from history."[4] Rather Origen's exegesis is "an effort to
seize the spirit in history or to assure the passage from history to
spirit."[5] Such spiritual exegesis depends on history: "Every symbolic
construction, with its interiorizations, its spiritual digressions, does
not evacuate the narrative. It is not even indifferent to it, as Philo's
allegorism could be. It is built, in principle, on its basis."[6] Thus, far
from distorting the Christian message, Origen's "extraordinary apti-
tude for spiritualizing everything" is "even more evangelical than
Alexandrian."[7] De Lubac also cleared up a long-standing source of
misunderstanding with the vital observation that Origen's interpretation of Scripture is not univocal: "What it is important to remember
is that one sense (*intelligence*) does not prevent another sense, because
Wisdom, which is one in itself, prepares itself for a multiplicity of par-
tial and various meanings."[8] Thus an allegorical interpretation does
not automatically negate interpreting a passage as a factual account of
actual events or as commandment intended to be observed.

[1] De Lubac, *Histoire et esprit*, pp. 56–57.
[2] Ibid., p. 58.
[3] Ibid., p. 290.
[4] Ibid., pp. 20, 112.
[5] Ibid., p. 278.
[6] Ibid., p. 245.
[7] Ibid., p. 137.
[8] Ibid., p. 140.

De Lubac did not find Origen's exegesis flawless. He believed that Origen was led astray by widely shared assumptions that even the smallest detail in the text is there for a reason and that whatever is in the Bible must be worthy of God. Furthermore, Origen's characteristic procedure of bringing together similar concepts from throughout the Bible in order to illuminate a particular text often failed to take into account original context or development of ideas. He also conceded that Origen failed to recognize characteristically Semitic modes of thought and expression and lacked the historical sense that would have enabled him to recognize the development of religious concepts in ancient Israel, so that "the domestic life of the Patriarchs becomes an institute of spiritual philosophy."[1] However, he shared such a deficient historical sense with all other commentators prior to the nineteenth century.

De Lubac's case would have been more persuasive if Origen, in what he actually wrote, did not lend himself so often and so easily to the kinds of misunderstanding that he, de Lubac, deplored. *Allegory and Event* makes this abundantly clear. De Lubac would also have been more persuasive if he did not give the impression of blurring the concept of "history." Although he admits that Origen did not and could not have had a modern concept of history, in practice he acts as though Origen, when he used the word *historia*, meant much the same things by it that a modern theologian would. In fact, *historia*, as Origen used it, means not so much "history," in any of the senses we use the word in English, but "narrative" or "story line." (The French word *histoire* includes this range of meaning.)

Both Daniélou and de Lubac wished to counter a standard criticism of Origen since early times: that he reinterpreted the Bible in terms of a platonic worldview. Adolf Harnack had reiterated this criticism in his magisterial *History of Dogma* and had extended it into an indictment of early Christian doctrine as a whole. Although Daniélou and de Lubac rejected Harnack's conclusion, they accepted his assumption, now discredited, that Greek and Hebrew (or Greek and biblical) thought are distinct and antithetical. Thus they seemed to believe that by demonstrating the continuity of Origen's exegesis with earlier Jewish and Christian interpretation, they obviated charges, current already during Origen's own lifetime, that he made use of an allegorical method taken from Greek philosophy.

[1] Ibid., pp. 248–49.

christian biblical exegesis begins with Origen.

In the face of the evidence, their position now seems either tendentious or naïve.

Even in its title, *Allegory and Event* lays down a challenge to *Histoire et esprit*, implying that Hanson is a plainspoken Englishman like George Orwell who will call things by their real names. His book builds a refutation of what we have seen to be de Lubac's fundamental point: "If the contention of Bigg, Cadiou and de Lubac, however, means that the allegorical sense in Origen's exposition has any necessary or justifiable connection with the literal sense, then any impartial reader surveying the evidence in these pages will see that this is untrue."[1] Furthermore, Hanson rejects the claim of Daniélou and de Lubac that Origen simply continues methods already developed in the Judeo-Christian tradition. Hanson argues that Origen practiced an Alexandrian allegory derived ultimately from platonic and stoic philosophy. Unlike typology, this Alexandrian allegory is fundamentally unhistorical; in fact, "[i]ts ultimate aim is to empty the text of any particular connection with historical events."[2] Although he does not here discuss the problem of Origen's orthodoxy beyond an occasional insinuation that the incarnation plays a smaller role in Origen's thought than it should, Hanson evidently does not share Daniélou's and de Lubac's positive evaluation of Origen's theology. Even so, he readily acknowledges Origen's genius: "He brought the touch of a master to what had hitherto been nothing much more than the exercise of amateurs. . . . In this sense we may say that Christian biblical exegesis begins with Origen."[3] He also praises him for his "unfailing humility," the "sweet reasonableness" in his handling of texts, and his "sophisticated attitude towards the Bible's presentation of scientific facts."[4] At the same time, he attacks Origen's threefold interpretation, looking for a message in the text for the body, for the soul, and for the spirit as "arbitrary fancy" and "largely a façade or a rationalization whereby he was able to read into the Bible what he wanted to find there."[5] In contrast to de Lubac, he argues that "[i]n history as event, in history as the field of

---

[1] See in *Allegory and Event* below, p. 242. The other references are to Charles Bigg, *The Christian Platonists of Alexandria*, 2nd rev. ed. (Oxford: Oxford University Press, 1913), and René Cadiou, *La jeunesse d'Origène: Histoire de l'école d'Alexandrie au début du IIIe siècle* (Paris: Beauchesne, 1935).
[2] See in *Allegory and Event* below, p. 63.
[3] Ibid., p. 360.
[4] Ibid., pp. 183, 178, and 224.
[5] Ibid., pp. 257 and 258.

Reading thoughts that are hrs own

God's self-revelation *par excellence*, Origen is not in the least inter-ested."[1] Even though he is admittedly a great pioneering interpreter, Origen "never quite" gives the impression that he has put himself into the minds of the biblical authors, but "on countless occasions gives the opposite impression, that he is reading into the mind of the biblical author thoughts which are really his own."[2] This is a serious shortcoming indeed, because, Hanson writes, "[p]resumably the guiding principle in all exegesis of both Old and New Testaments will remain indefinitely the question of what any given text meant when it was first written or uttered to the first audience for which it was intended."[3] The reason for these failings, Hanson argues, is Ori-gen's method: "Allegory, . . . instead of ensuring that he would in his exegesis maintain close contact with biblical thought, rendered him deplorably independent of the Bible."[4] Hanson's verdict is therefore negative. Origen's presuppositions are too different from ours to give his interpretation lasting value:

series of oracles that or may not have connectn w/ each other.

> Generally, Origen assumed that the Bible was an oracular book; that is to say, it consisted of a vast series of oracles which might or might not have some connection with each other, but which each in its own right had some divine or mysterious truth to convey. This is a conception which, since the arrival of historical criticism, had to be entirely abandoned and is, as far as one can prophesy, never again likely to be revived.[5]

New Perspectives

Origen studies have flourished since *Allegory and Event* was published, although most of this work is in languages other than English. Inter-national Origen Colloquia have gathered every four years since 1973—Hanson hosting the third at the University of Manchester in 1985—and Crouzel's bibliography actually shows more entries after 1959 than before. Italian scholars have recently published the first Origen dictionary[6] and are working on a concordance. The first

[1] Ibid., p. 276.
[2] Ibid., p. 363.
[3] Ibid., p. 368.
[4] Ibid., p. 371.
[5] Ibid., p. 367.
[6] Adele Monaci Castagno, ed., *Origene Dizionario: la cultura, il pensiero, le opere* (Rome: Città Nuova, 2000).

Origen conference saw papers by Marguerite Harl and Gilles Dorival that marked major advances in our understanding of the form and
intention of *Peri Archon*. They established that *Peri Archon* fit into
the established genre of a philosophical treatise on what was then
called "physics," a discipline that embraced divine and spiritual as
well as what we would call "physical" reality.[1] This confirmed and
explained an underlying structure of the work already noted by
Basilius Steidle in 1941.[2] Although divided for practical reason into
four books, *Peri Archon* actually consists of two cycles of treatises.
The first cycle descends the hierarchy of being from God the Father
through the demonic powers opposed to God and explains the creation of the material world and its ultimate destiny. The second cycle
deals with specific issues in the same order, ending with a treatise on
biblical interpretation.

Another major advance in Origen studies came in 1977 with the
publication of Pierre Nautin's *Origène: sa vie et son œuvre*.[3] Its rigorous
analysis brought our understanding of the sources of information
about Origen to a new level. Nautin's reconstruction of Origen's life
and work on the basis of this analysis was necessarily tentative, but the
general outline, if not all the details, has been generally accepted.
Nautin demonstrated the role that tension with established church
authorities played in shaping Origen's life and provided strong evidence that *Peri Archon* was written while he was in his forties and so
could not be dismissed as a youthful extravagance.

Since Hanson wrote *Allegory and Event*, Origen's biblical interpretation has been the focus of considerable attention. *Allegory and
Event* was one of a spate of books that appeared around the same
time. Hanson used Robert M. Grant's *The Letter and the Spirit*, which
appeared in 1957, to buttress his contention that Origen's allegory
had Greco-Roman sources.[4] Jean Pépin's *Mythe et Allégorie*, which
appeared in 1958, evidently too late for Hanson to take it into consideration, would have further strengthened this case. Although
dealing relatively little with Origen, Pépin's work is of fundamental

---

[1] Gilles Dorival, "Remarques sur la forme du Peri Archon," and Marguerite Harl,
"Structure et cohérence du Peri Archon" in *Origeniana*, pp. 11–45. Marguerite Harl's
article is reprinted in Marguerite Harl, *Le déchiffrement du sens: Études sur l'herméneutique
chrétienne d'Origène à Grégoire de Nysse* (Paris: Études Augustiniennes, 1993), pp. 225–46.
[2] Basilius Steidle, "Neue Untersuchungen zu Origenes 'Peri Archon'" in *Zeitschrift
für die neutestamentliche Wissenschaft und die Kunde der älteren Kirche* 40 (1942 for 1941):
236–43.
[3] See above, p. iii, n. 5.
[4] See above, p. i, n. 1.

importance for our understanding of the theoretical basis for allegory in pagan, Jewish, and Christian traditions and for the ways pagan philosophical allegory influenced Christian biblical interpretation. Implicitly refuting Daniélou and de Lubac, who treated Origen's allegory as if its sources were almost wholly Jewish and Christian, *Mythe et Allégorie* and a subsequent book, *La tradition d'allégorie de Philon d'Alexandrie à Dante*, treated allegory as a technique common to all three traditions.[1]

In the same year that *Allegory and Event* appeared, Henri de Lubac published two of an eventual four volumes of *Exégèse Médiévale*, now being translated into English.[2] De Lubac treats the fourfold spiritual exegesis of the Bible, which he traces through the Latin Middle Ages into the Renaissance, as the central Christian spiritual tradition and presents Origen's work as translated into Latin (not the controversial *Peri Archon* but the homilies and the *Commentary on the Song of Songs*) as its principal inspiration. The contrast with Hanson's appraisal of Origen could not be greater. De Lubac argued that fourfold spiritual exegesis promoted the church's spiritual life by providing an ongoing and genuine encounter with the inspired biblical text. De Lubac did not claim that we can now resume doing exegesis as Origen did, but he considered the separation of exegesis from spirituality that largely characterizes modern Christianity as a serious loss.

Robert M. Grant's *The Earliest Lives of Jesus*, published in 1961, established that Origen's relationship to history was more complicated than either Hanson or de Lubac had thought. Grant demonstrated that Greco-Roman rhetoricians such as Theon and Dio Chrysostom developed and employed sophisticated methods for testing the verisimilitude of historical events. Such historical criticism belonged to the study of literary texts the ancients knew as "grammar." He further showed how Origen used these methods of historical criticism to deal with the historical issues raised by the differences

---

[1] Jean Pépin, *Mythe et Allégorie: Les origins grecques et les contestations judéo-chrétiennes* (Paris: Études Augustiniennes, 1958; rev. ed. 1976) and *La tradition d'allégorie de Philon d'Alexandrie à Dante: Études historiques* (Paris: Études Augustiniennes, 1987). Henry Chadwick exhibits much the same approach in a magnificent article, "Pagane und christliche Allegorese" (in Henry Chadwick, *Antike Schriftauslegung* [Berlin: de Gruyter, 1998], pp. 1–23).

[2] Henri de Lubac, *Exégèse Médiévale: Les quatre sens de l'Écriture* (Paris: Aubier, 1959 [vols. 1 and 2]; 1961 [vol. 3]; 1964 [vol. 4]). So far the first two volumes have appeared in English as *Medieval Exegesis: The Four Senses of Scripture*, vol. 1, trans. Mark Sebanc (Grand Rapids: Eerdmans, 1998), and vol. 2, trans. E. M. Macierowski (Grand Rapids: Eerdmans, 2000).

between the Gospel accounts of the life of Jesus, especially the differences between John and the Synoptics. Origen accepted the general outline of Jesus' life common to all four Gospels; he affirmed
that Jesus Christ was the Word incarnate who was born of a human
mother, gathered and taught disciples, performed miracles, died on
the cross, and rose again. At the same time Origen upheld a theory,
enunciated in *Peri Archon* 4.2.9, that the Holy Spirit deliberately
"interwove" falsehoods into otherwise true biblical narratives,
including the Gospels, in order to pique the curiosity of more pene-
trating readers and to spur them to seek the deeper, spiritual significance of the events described. An example comes in Book 10 of his
Commentary on John, where Origen compares the inconsistent
accounts of the cleansing of the Temple and concludes—using
historical-critical arguments much like those of D. F. Strauss, the
pioneer of historical criticism of the Gospels—that the event never
took place. This theory enabled Origen to concede to Celsus that the
Gospel accounts were not consistent and to argue that this was a
deliberate strategy on the part of the evangelists. Grant concludes
that "[p]erhaps it should be said that [Origen] is not interested in history as such but in the use of historical methods."[1] Origen did not use
allegory per se to evacuate "history," in the sense of "significant factual events," from certain biblical narratives; he used "history" in the
sense of "historical criticism" to do the job.

The mid-1980s saw another spate of works of lasting value. In
1983, Sources Chrétiennes published an edition with introduction,
translation, and notes of the passages on scriptural interpretation in
the *Philocalia*, an ancient collection of selected passages from Origen's works. The volume also included an edition by Nicholas de
Lange of Origen's *Letter to Julius Africanus*, a work in which Origen
marshaled critical arguments supporting the authenticity of the story
of Susanna in the book of Daniel. Harl's introduction provides what
is still the best overall discussion of Origen's scriptural interpretation.[2] In addition, Harl's articles on Origen's exegesis over the sev-
enties and eighties, collected in *Le déchiffrement du sens*, provide
exquisite insight into his methods.[3] An excellent history of patristic
exegesis, Manlio Simonetti's *Lettera e/o allegoria: Un contributo alla
storia dell'esegesi patristica*, published in 1985, presented Origen's

[1] Grant, *The Earliest Lives of Jesus*, p. 114.
[2] *Philocalia 1–21* (SC 302; Paris: Cerf, 1983), pp. 42–157.
[3] See above, p. xv, n. 1.

work as central to early Christian biblical interpretation. Origen, he argued, "made biblical hermeneutics into a true and proper science and in this sense conditioned in a decisive manner all successive Patristic exegesis, even . . . that of his adversaries."[1] Simonetti points out that Origen, largely in response to Gnosticism, was the first Christian interpreter to have included the entire Bible within the scope of his exegesis, rather than isolated proof texts, and to have used the entire Scripture for interpreting any individual part. Without assuming that Platonism is inconsistent with Christianity, Simonetti shows how Origen's "science" of hermeneutics is grounded in a coherent, platonic understanding of reality, in which allegory enables the interpreter to move into a deeper level of reality. He stressed, nonetheless, that Origen's "science" also has as its basis a rigorous, philological approach to the text using the techniques of Hellenistic grammar. Paradoxically, in light of that school's hostile stance toward him, Origen's philological rigor was a major influence on the later Antiochene school of interpretation that rejected allegory. Simonetti also drew attention to the principle of "usefulness" (Gk. ōpheleia) in Origen's work, the principle that in Scripture every word must be spiritually useful to the interpreter. Karen Torjesen's *Hermeneutical Procedure and Theological Method in Origen's Exegesis*, published in 1986, explained in detail the way Origen made Scripture useful. She showed how Origen's scriptural interpretation functioned as a pedagogy of the soul, enabling the human soul to ascend what she referred to as the "ontological gradient" between life in the flesh and the Father.[2]

Bernhard Neuschäfer's *Origenes als Philologe* appeared in 1987.[3] Neuschäfer documented Origen's massive use of the full range of techniques belonging to ancient "grammar," the disciplined approach to literary texts developed, to a large extent, in Hellenistic Alexandria. Neuschäfer showed, first, how Origen's pioneering work in textual criticism (Gk. *diorthōtikon*), best known from his *Hexapla*, which compared the Septuagint text to the Hebrew itself and other Greek translations, made use of these techniques. He then showed in detail how Origen used the four procedures ancient grammarians

---

[1] Manlio Simonetti, *Lettera e/o allegoria: Un contributo alla storia dell'esegesi patristica* (Rome: Institutum Patristicum «Augustinianum», 1985), p. 73.

[2] Karen Jo Torjesen, *Hermeneutical Procedure and Theological Method in Origen's Exegesis* (New York: Walter de Gruyter, 1986).

[3] Bernhard Neuschäfer, *Origenes als Philologe* = Schweizerische Beiträge zur Altertumswissenschaft 18, 2 vols. (Basel: Friedrich Reinhardt, 1987).

referred to as exegesis proper (*exēgētikon*). These are the explanation of words (*glōssēmatikon*), the study of the events described (*historikon*), the use of figures of speech (*technikon*), and the study of style (*metrikon*). He concluded by demonstrating how Origen relied on principles of Hellenistic grammar to explain the meaning and application of the text—the discipline ancient grammarians knew as "judgment" (*krisis*). Origen drew from this discipline his emphasis on the importance of determining the character (*prosōpon*) from whose perspective any particular passage is written and the general principle of using passages from throughout the Bible to illuminate other passages, an application of the long-established principle of "clarifying Homer out of Homer." Although Hanson and others recognized Origen's indebtedness to ancient grammar, Neuschäfer demonstrated how thorough and pervasive that indebtedness was.

Since *Allegory and Event* appeared, there have also been a number of studies of Origen's interpretation of particular books. Maurice F. Wiles suggested in *The Spiritual Gospel: The Interpretation of the Fourth Gospel in the Early Church* that Origen's exegesis was well fitted for the interpretation of the Gospel of John. Guido Bendinelli finds in Origen's *Commentary on Matthew* the influence of contemporary philosophical commentaries in addition to those of grammarians.[1] Hermann Josef Vogt also dealt with Origen's interpretation of John and Matthew in *Origenes als Exeget*.[2] Marie-Josèphe Rondeau investigated Origen's exegetical work on the Psalms in her magisterial work demonstrating the theological significance of the grammatical concept of *prosōpon*, entitled *Les commentaries patristiques du Psautier (IIIe–Ve siècles)*.[3] Other works by Maurice Wiles, Peter Gorday, Francesca Cocchini, and Theresia Heither have focused on Origen as an interpreter of Paul.[4] Heither, in particular, values Origen's

---

[1] Maurice Wiles, *The Spiritual Gospel: The Interpretation of the Fourth Gospel in the Early Church* (Cambridge: Cambridge University Press, 1960); Guido Bendinelli, *Il Commentario a Matteo di Origene: L'ambito della metodologia scolastica dell'antichità* (Rome: Institutum Patristicum Augustinianum, 1997).

[2] Hermann Josef Vogt, *Origenes als Exeget* (Paderborn: Schöningh, 1999).

[3] Marie-Josèphe Rondeau, *Les commentaires patristiques du Psautier (IIIe–Ve siècles)*, vols. 1 and 2 = *Orientalia Christiana Analecta* 219 and 220 (Rome: Pont. Institutum Studiorum Orientalium, 1982 and 1985).

[4] Maurice F. Wiles, *The Divine Apostle: The Interpretation of St. Paul's Epistles in the Early Church* (Cambridge: Cambridge University Press, 1967); Peter Gorday, *Principles of Patristic Exegesis* (New York and Toronto: Edwin Mellen, 1983); Francesca Cocchini, *Il Paolo di Origene: Contributo alla storia della recezione delle epistole paoline nel III secolo* (Rome: Edizione Studium, 1992); and Theresia Heither, *Translatio Religionis: Die Paulusdeutung des Origenes* (Cologne and Vienna: Böhlau Verlag, 1990).

interpretation of Romans because it provides an alternative to the Augustinian interpretation that has long dominated Western theology. In 1993 the Sixth International Origen Colloquium focused on Origen's biblical interpretation and its legacy. Its sixty-one presentations, published as *Origeniana Sexta*, provide an overview of current scholarship. So do articles on Scripture, on method, and on individual books of the Bible in the new *Origene Dizionario*.[1] In general, Origen scholarship since *Allegory and Event* appeared in 1959 has shown more appreciation and understanding of Origen as a man of his time and less concern for defending or attacking his orthodoxy.

Hanson and Biblical Interpretation Today

By contrast to these relatively subtle changes of emphasis in Origen scholarship, the years since *Allegory and Event* appeared have seen a radical transformation in approaches to biblical interpretation. In 1959 Hanson could take for granted a broad agreement that the interpreter's task was to ascertain "the question of what any given text meant when it was first written or uttered to the first audience for which it was intended." Such an assumption was fundamental to the historical-critical method that had a near monopoly on serious biblical scholarship. The historical-critical method came into prominence at the same time when scientific developments, culminating in Darwin's theory of evolution, had made it impossible for thinking Christians to maintain that the opening chapters of Genesis provided a factual account of actual events. At the same time, scholars such as D. F. Strauss or Julius Wellhausen also made it impossible to ignore the internal inconsistencies within the Bible itself. By Hanson's time this method had enabled scholars to gain considerable understanding of the development of the biblical text and of the origins of Judaism and Christianity. As a result, biblical scholars with academic credibility abandoned any notion that the Bible was without error. In this context, an appealing way to maintain traditional reliance on the Bible as a source of religious authority was to see it not as an infallible record of actual events but as a privileged historical source for the understanding of the saving acts of God in history. Whether or not they saw the Bible as a source of historical informa-

[1]Gilles Dorival and Alain le Boulluec, eds., *Origeniana Sexta: Origène et la Bible/Origen and the Bible: Actes du Colloquium Origenianum Sextum, Chantilly, 30 août–3 septembre 1993* (Louvain: Peeters, 1995). Also see above, p. xv, n. 1.

tion thus became an implicit criterion for evaluating biblical interpreters like Origen from earlier periods.

Hanson accepted this criterion, as did de Lubac and Daniélou.
Nonetheless, he differed from the French Jesuit scholars not only in
his belief that Origen fundamentally evacuated the Bible of history,
but also, at least implicitly, in his appraisal of typology. Pointing out
that so-called "typology"—the concept that events in the Old Testament foreshadow those of the New—was fundamental in the New
Testament itself and in the subsequent Christian tradition, Daniélou
and de Lubac argued for its consistency with our modern understanding of the Bible. This is so because real, historical events necessarily underlie it. They defended Origen as a practitioner of this,
fundamentally Christian, typological method and sought to shield
him from accusations that he was a Platonist who disregarded history
by interpreting the events of biblical history as symbols pointing to
a deeper, timeless reality. In the process, they downplayed his
indebtedness to Greek philosophical allegory. Nonetheless, Hanson
would maintain that, if the task of a biblical interpreter is to use the
Bible to reconstruct the actual history of God's saving acts, simply
conceding that events occurred is not enough. Real historical study
entails ascertaining with reasonable accuracy the original intention
of the ancient author or speaker whose words are recorded in the
biblical text. For this purpose, we need to enter the ancient author's
mental world. Interpretations of any particular passage in the light of
other passages in Scripture are genuinely respectful of history only
to the extent that the ancient author would have taken such ideas
into consideration. If de Lubac and Daniélou want to defend Origen
as an author who respects history, they must do so in terms of history as we understand and practice it. That, Hanson argues in this
book, is a case they cannot make.

For that purpose such works are not likely to be very helpful in
ascertaining the original author's intentions, since neither Origen nor
any other patristic interpreter was especially concerned to do so.
They often seem incapable of conceiving of an anachronistic interpretation, but they themselves were primarily concerned with "usefulness," that is, reader response, not with authorial intention. Most
would have agreed with Augustine that "[w]hoever actually finds [in
Holy Scripture] a message useful for building up [the double love of
God and neighbor], even if he has not said what the writer can be
proved to have intended in that place, has not made a pernicious

error, nor is he lying in any way."[1] Premodern interpretations are, from Hanson's perspective, worse than useless. The biblical interpreter encounters the text not just as words on a page but also through the mediation of a living tradition of Christian thought, art, and worship that still pervades Western culture. For example, Milton's *Paradise Lost* follows this cultural tradition when it does not distinguish the creation narrative in Genesis 2–3 from the quite different story in Genesis 1 and reads Genesis 3 as the account of a battle between God and Satan and of the fall of humanity from a condition of original innocence and immortality. Likewise, Christmas celebrations still follow this cultural tradition when they harmonize birth narratives of Luke 1–2 with the corresponding chapters of Matthew and further elaborate them with apocryphal stories; three named kings following the star of Bethlehem troop into the stable once the shepherds have left. Those premodern authors who contributed to the construction of the Western cultural tradition's understanding of the Bible—and no one contributed to it more than Origen—thus made legitimate interpretation harder. The modern interpreter must develop a mental discipline that deliberately excludes tendencies to harmonize one passage with another in order to purge the legacy of their misguided efforts.

Frances M. Young recently observed, concerning *Allegory and Event*, that "the standard English account of Origen's exegesis virtually organizes the material around the view that Origen never really understood the Bible because he sat too loosely to history. Since that book was written, the shift in biblical studies has helped us to recognize that concern about 'history' has a very modern ring."[2] Today no scholar could assume a general consensus that ascertaining "what any given text meant when it was first written or uttered to the first audience for which it was intended" is the only valid purpose of biblical interpretation. For one thing, it is not clear just whose original intention should determine the text's meaning. Redaction critics force us to recognize that, even if we seek to reconstruct the authentic message of Jesus as he intended it to be understood, we must also take into consideration the intentions of those persons, whether we call them evangelists or anonymous redactors, who assembled the Gospels as we have them. Much the same applies to Moses, assuming

[1] Augustine, *De Doctrina Christiana* 1.36.40.
[2] Frances M. Young, *Biblical Exegesis and the Formation of Christian Culture* (Cambridge: Cambridge University Press, 1997), p. 3.

there was such a person, and to the prophets. In response, to some extent, to this uncertainty, canonical critics make the books of the Bible as we now have them—rather than presumed sources such as Q or J, E, D, and P—the object of their study.

In the now flourishing study of the Bible as literature, the Bible as received in the Western tradition is precisely what is relevant. Given that, at least since Origen—and, if Simonetti is to be believed, to a large extent because of him—the Western tradition has read the Bible as a single, unified book, it makes sense, from a literary perspective, to study it that way, disregarding the different intentions and views of the biblical authors. As Northrop Frye put it, "'[t]he Bible' has traditionally been read as a unity, and has influenced Western imagination as a unity."[1] Furthermore, Frye points out that a common set of symbols—the grist for Origen's allegory—provide a literary justification for studying the Bible as a whole. Likewise historians of Judaism and Christianity have exhibited a burgeoning interest not in how the Bible's constituent parts were originally intended but in how they have been received. Thus, for example, Jeremy Cohen's history of one verse, Gen. 1:28, has provided fresh and surprising insight into what we would now call environmental ethics in the Jewish and Christian traditions, and James Kugel has shown us how traditional exegesis itself creates traditions.[2] Kugel also shows how early interpretation can be understood on its own terms without being found wanting by the standards of our time. This increasing interest in works as received has been encouraged by a postmodern ethos that makes authorial intention more problematical by denying outright that it has a privileged role in determining the meaning of the text and by making us aware of the ambiguities and cross purposes authors themselves bring to their works.

Even as scholars have become more open to studying the Bible as it has been received and to getting beyond authorial intention as their sole criterion, the assumption that we actually can determine authorial intention has become increasingly problematical. In the light of postmodernism, historians have become more aware of the

[1] Northrop Frye, *The Great Code: The Bible and Literature* (New York: Harcourt Brace, 1982), p. xiii.

[2] Jeremy Cohen, *'Be Fertile and Increase, Fill the Earth and Master It': The Ancient and Medieval Career of a Biblical Text* (Ithaca, N.Y.: Cornell University Press, 1992); James L. Kugel, *The Bible As It Was* (Cambridge, Mass.: Harvard University Press, 1997) and *Traditions of the Bible: A Guide to the Bible As It Was at the Start of the Common Era* (Cambridge, Mass.: Harvard University Press, 1999).

through an encounter the text.

contextual spiritual transformation

impossibility of getting beyond their own subjectivity, if only because our fundamental assumptions in approaching any work are so much a part of us that we are unaware of them. Postmodernists also offer new perspectives on what Origen was doing. In 2002, John David Dawson's book *Christian Figural Reading and the Fashioning of Identity* sought to vindicate Origen's biblical hermeneutics against three critics—Daniel Boyarin, Erich Auerbach, and Hans Frei—from a postmodern standpoint. Dawson takes a fresh tack in arguing that we can best understand Origen not as someone concerned to find meaning in a text (a characteristically modernist preoccupation) but as someone who seeks a continuing spiritual transformation through an encounter with the text.[1] His critique of modernism thus converges with the work of Simonetti and Torjesen, who identify "usefulness" as fundamental to Origen's interpretation.

Once historians become aware of the inescapability of subjectivity, patristic biblical interpretation takes on new value. Ancient interpreters may offer us the possibility of genuine insight into ancient texts not because they lack presuppositions, as if that were possible, but because their presuppositions are not the same as ours. Julia Annas's recent book *Platonic Ethics: Old and New* argues that ancient interpreters of Plato may be helpful in this way, not the least because they lack our modern presupposition that we can find a development in Plato's thought.[2] She does not argue that ancient commentators are right and modern commentators wrong, but rather that taking ancient interpreters seriously enables us to see aspects of Plato that we would otherwise miss and enables us to question our own assumptions. Theresia Heither takes this approach to Origen's *Commentary on Romans*, valuing Origen because he does not assume that the epistle is about justification by grace. Such new perspectives allow a new appreciation for what Origen was about.

When a work like *Allegory and Event* has dominated its field, it is inevitable, after forty years or so, that subsequent scholars will have defined their own positions in opposition to it. Frances M. Young does so in *Biblical Exegesis and the Formation of Christian Culture*, one of the best recent books on patristic exegesis. Forthright as he was, Hanson made himself an easy target. His weaknesses are obvious: his

[1] John David Dawson, *Christian Figural Reading and the Fashioning of Identity* (Berkeley: University of California Press, 2002).
[2] Julia Annas, *Platonic Ethics: Old and New* (Ithaca, N.Y.: Cornell University Press, 1999).

inability or unwillingness to enter sympathetically into Origen's thought, his tendency to be dismissive and hypercritical, and his assumption that there is only one valid way to do biblical interpretation. No Origen scholar today would uphold his critique as he wrote it. At the same time it would be difficult to refute Hanson's objections to de Lubac: that Origen did not consistently maintain and had relatively little concern for the factuality of the events related in the Bible and that he took his allegorical method largely from Greco-Roman sources. With the appearance in English of de Lubac's *Exégèse Médiévale*, Hanson's corrective is needed. That said, what makes *Allegory and Event* still valuable now is not the way Hanson evaluates Origen, or even the way he corrects de Lubac, but the way he brings us into Origen's world. Origen himself compared the Bible to the storehouse in the palace of a rich and powerful king, a place with many different rooms full of gold, silver, precious stones, pearls, purple garments, and diadems.[1] We might say the same thing of Origen's exegesis. By virtue of his thorough knowledge of the palace, Hanson exposes to us the treasures of Origen's thought. For this reason, *Allegory and Event* remains a work that any student of Origen's thought or of ancient biblical interpretation must take seriously. *Allegory and Event* also testifies to Hanson's high critical intelligence, his splendid linguistic abilities, his sheer capacity for painstaking work, and his admiration for these same qualities in Origen. Such capacities are as relevant now as they were when this book was first published, even if we may think that Origen's interpretation has more usefulness than Hanson, with his presuppositions, was able to see.

[1] Origen, *Commentary on Romans* 5.1.

This book is dedicated with admiration
and gratitude to my wife,
who during the years when it was being composed
continually encouraged me,
helped me with no small part of the work,
and took on her shoulders more than
her fair share of domestic labour
in order to leave me free to write.

PREFACE

ABOUT fifteen years ago I picked up in the library of the Theological Society of the University of Dublin a copy of Armitage Robinson's edition of the *Philocalia*. I read it and found it intensely interesting; but it started in my mind the question: Has the interpretation of the Bible as it is practised today anything seriously in common with the interpretation of the Bible as Origen, and indeed as the early Church generally, practised it? I resolved in any time available to me to begin reading in order to gain material by which I could supply the answer to this question. At that time and in that country the word 'research' did not exercise the magic influence in evoking financial aid, securing expert supervision and obtaining rare books which it exercises in this country today. I worked entirely without aid except that of a good old-fashioned classical education (for which I can never be sufficiently grateful to the school and university which supplied it) and a persistent interest in the subject. It proved in the course of many laborious hours a subject well worth pursuing. The firstfruits of this labour was *Origen's Doctrine of Tradition*, which was published in 1954. *Allegory and Event* is the final harvest. At least I can say that I have answered the original question to my own satisfaction.

I should make it clear that my definitions of typology and allegory are those which will be met early in the first chapter, viz:

> *Typology is the interpreting of an event belonging to the present or the recent past as the fulfilment of a similar situation recorded or prophesied in Scripture.*
>
> *Allegory is the interpretation of an object or person or a number of objects or persons as in reality meaning some object or person of a later time, with no attempt made to trace a relationship of 'similar situation' between them.*

It should also be made clear that all the translations into English from any other language in this work are my own translations, except for a few cases where I have indicated the translator. I have been particularly anxious to avoid filling the book with 'translator's English', which is a type of lame and stilted writing to be found in particular abundance among translators of theological works. I have therefore not hesitated to employ translations which are nearer paraphrases than literal renderings, in order to convey the proper impression at the expense of the literal meaning. Usually in such cases I have given the original words in brackets or footnote.

As will be seen from the bibliography, I have used Stählin's text for most of my quotations from Clement of Alexandria. But I know from experience that Stählin's edition is not easily accessible to those who cannot afford large libraries of their own or who do not live near well-stocked public libraries, so in most of my quotations I have added the reference in Migne. When quoting from Commentaries on the Psalms I have used the enumeration of the English versions, not that of the Septuagint.

I have been able only at the last minute to obtain (through the kindness of my friend, the Rev. J. N. Birdsall of the University of Leeds) a copy of J. Scherer's edition of the Greek fragments of Origen's *Commentary on Romans*, some more of which were recently discovered at Toura. I have marked with an asterisk the passages referred to in this book which appear to be confirmed by these Greek fragments; but the fragments are relatively so few that the hope concerning them expressed on p. 163 of this book must be regarded as disappointed, and the fact that a passage cited from the *Commentary on Romans* does not appear in Scherer's edition must not necessarily be thought to throw doubts on its authenticity.

My warm thanks are due to Miss Jean Cunningham, of the Student Christian Movement Press, for valuable aid in checking references, and to my wife for assistance in the task of compiling indices.

R. P. C. HANSON

University of Nottingham
September 1958

PART ONE

The Sources of Christian Allegory

I

Jewish Allegory

IN their interpretation of Scripture the ancient Rabbis held a doctrine of what we would now call plenary or verbal inspiration. They regarded the Hebrew Scriptures as coming from heaven, they treated them as if they were dictated, indeed as if they were pronounced, by God himself. The composition of the Scriptures is generally attributed by them to the Holy Spirit of God, and they speak of the Spirit as uttering certain texts.[1] There are even a few examples of the practice, followed later by almost all the Christian Fathers, of dividing up a passage in Scripture (usually in the Psalms or the Song of Solomon) among different divine speakers.[2] Their attitude to the patriarchs was, of course, completely uncritical. They envisaged Abraham and the other patriarchs as keeping the whole Law, having either discovered it by their own efforts, or enjoyed a revelation about it from God.[3] The Fathers of the Christian Church, therefore, were not the first to create in their imaginations a fantastic Utopia, compounded of much later conceptions of the ideal, for the patriarchs to inhabit. Similarly, Moses was regarded as the author of the Pentateuch and the fountain of all law. Some authorities claimed that he wrote the account of his own death, weeping as he wrote, though others held that Joshua wrote the narrative of Moses' end.[4] All approved decisions of the oral law, *halakoth*, even though actually made by Rabbis, were attributed to Moses and assumed to derive from him by a continuous oral tradition, and this applied even to minute grammatical points. Once a law was called '*halakah* given to Moses from Sinai',[5] it was implicitly received, and, once rabbinical decisions were thus denominated, controversy about them ceased. In spite of some extravagant statements, however, the words of the written Torah were ranked above the oral law. The words of Rabbis or scribes

[1] J. Bonsirven, *Le Judaisme Palestinien au Temps du Jesus-Christ*, I, ch. V, p. 259.
[2] Bonsirven, *Exégèse Rabbinique et Exégèse Paulinienne*, pp. 172 f.
[3] *Judaisme*, I, p. 251.
[4] *Ibid.*, p. 260. Philo follows the more fanciful version, *De Vita Mosis* II.291.
[5] הלכה למשה מסיני

needed a *hizzûq*, that is a confirmation by specially strong arguments, whereas the Torah had no such need. Certain prescriptions, too, even though they were called *halakoth*, were described as flying in the air, or as mountains suspended by a hair, because of their lack of Scriptural support.[1] The Rabbis' estimate of the prophets was only lower than their estimate of Moses. The prophets did not indeed enjoy Moses' experience of speaking to God face to face, but God did put his Spirit in their mouths, and with the cessation of prophecy the Rabbis believed that the appearance of the Holy Spirit in Israel had ceased. The function of the prophet was above all to predict the future.[2]

In handling the text of Scripture the Rabbis began invariably from the literal meaning,[3] and with subtlety and acuteness derived from it the last ounce of possible meaning, comparing other texts to illuminate it, reconciling apparently contradictory texts, and deriving all sorts of conclusions, often fantastic ones, from it. They are much concerned to explain the reasons for such things as the existence of several accounts of the same event and to draw far-reaching conclusions from such apparently trivial points as that God spoke on several occasions to Moses and Aaron and on even more to Moses alone, and so on.[4] This is no doubt the reason why several Christian Fathers, particularly Origen, persistently accuse Jewish exegesis of an opaque literalism. Justin Martyr, who as a native of Samaria, is likely to have known more than most Christian writers about Judaism,[5] is the first to voice this complaint. He accuses the Rabbis of teaching that God has hands and feet and fingers and a soul,[6] and of confining themselves to feeble and pedestrian explanations of the Law and neglecting more important and interesting points,[7] and brands their explanations of the embarrassing fact that the patriarchs had more wives than one at the same time as 'designed for the souls of clodhoppers and men destined for corruption'.[8]

In regard to the Greek translation of the Hebrew Scriptures, two different attitudes can be detected among the Rabbis. One of them

[1]Bonsirven, *Judaisme*, I, pp. 270–2.
[2]*Ibid.*, pp. 255 f.
[3]כמשמע, which Bonsirven aptly translates *prout sonat*.
[4]*Ibid.*, pp. 296–8.
[5]He shows, for instance, in *Dial.* 137.2, quite a detailed knowledge of how and when in their liturgy Jews anathematize Christians, and in *Dial.* 122.1 and 123.1 he uses the word γηόρα instead of διάσπορα for the Dispersion.
[6]*Dial.* 114.3.
[7]*Dial.* 112.4.
[8]πρὸς τὰ χαμαιπετῆ καὶ τὰ διαφθορᾶς παθῆ.

LXX viewed as evil.

reproduces the legend of the production of the LXX in its most embroidered form; the other disparages the whole event, saying that the day on which the elders translated the Torah for King Ptolemy was as evil for Israel as the day on which the golden calf was made, or that when the LXX was produced darkness lay on all the world for thirty days as a punishment. One Rabbinic view can even be detected which tries to mediate between the two extremes, by passing the favourable judgement on the LXX but assigning the damning verdict to another (purely imaginary) translation.[1] Justin makes the childish accusation that the Jews suppressed in their copies of the Hebrew Scriptures the passages found only in the LXX;[2] but he does sometimes, after registering a protest, face facts and argue from a reading based on the Hebrew rather than the Greek text.[3] It is evident that by the middle of the second century no Christian could persuade a Jewish scholar to regard the Greek Old Testament as an authoritative text.

We might be surprised that the Rabbis, writing in the tradition of so careful an adherence to the literal text, should admit any deviation into a typological or allegorical interpretation. And yet it is undoubtedly the truth that Rabbinic or Jewish (as contrasted with Alexandrian) interpretation is one of the main sources of Christian allegory. That Jewish Messianic expectation included an expectation of what we might call fulfilled typology is evident from an interesting passage in Strack-Billerbeck.[4] The Rabbis conceived of Israel's redemption in the Messianic Age as foreshadowed in every detail by the redemption from Egypt as its type. As Israel was delivered in one night, so will Israel be delivered in one night in the Messianic times. The days of the Messiah would be forty years, as Israel was chastened forty years in the Wilderness (this from Rabbi Akiba). As Israel was fed with rich food in the Wilderness, so will God feed them at the Last Time. As God took vengeance on the Egyptians at the Exodus, so will he take vengeance on Edom (Rome) at the Messianic time; he will bring upon them frogs, flies, all sorts of beasts, plague, scab, hail, locusts, darkness; and he will slay their firstborn. Though in Egypt Israel went out in haste, at the Messianic Deliverance she will not go out in haste nor flight, but God will go before her. As the first deliverer (Moses) revealed himself and then hid himself, so will the last deliverer, the Messiah. And the deliverer will lead them out of the land into the wilderness of Judah and

---

[1] SB IV, Part I, Exkurse 15, p. 414, v, w, and x.
[2] E.g. *Dial.* 73.1–4; 120.5.
[3] E.g. *Dial.* 131.1.
[4] SB I, pp. 85–8, on Matt. 2.15 ('Out of Egypt have I called my son').

later redemption would do as the deliverance from Egypt

cause them again to dwell in tents, and whoever believes in him will remain in life, but whoever does not will go to the nations of the world and they will kill him. At the end God will reveal himself to them and cause manna to come down for them. Just as Moses took his wife and sons and made them ride on an ass, so will the last deliverer come riding on an ass. As the first deliverer brought bread down from heaven, so will the last, and as the first caused water to spring forth, so will the last. Pharaoh's daughter fostered him who was to bring vengeance on her father; so the King the Messiah who will bring vengeance on Edom (Rome) will dwell with them in the city (i.e. Rome). As God sent deliverance through two saviours (Moses and Aaron) to the tribes at the Exodus, so he will at the end (through Elijah and the Messiah).

This is obviously the sort of interpretation which we recognize in the New Testament and in the Christian Fathers as typology, but it is a very primitive and simple typology. We might describe it, from its pattern of the recurrence in the future of an event connected with a crisis of redemption in the past, as 'similar situation' typology.[1] It is noticeable that many of the instances of Rabbinic interpretation given by Strack-Billerbeck (not all of which have been reproduced here) show that the Rabbis can use Old Testament texts quite as wildly and with quite as little respect for their original meaning as the Christian Fathers, with this significant difference, that the Rabbis always seem to relate the text (however fantastically) to the historical crisis in the past as foreshadowing the final crisis in the future. Strack-Billerbeck, for instance, cite a Targum on Job[2] which refers Job 30.4 ('They pluck saltwort from the bushes') to the forty years' period of affliction of the children of Israel in the Wilderness, when they were compelled to eat thornbushes instead of edible plants. Origen might have referred the same text to the necessity of penitence for the Christian in his journey towards perfection. To anyone reading a Targum, indeed, this tendency of the Rabbis to relate all texts to the great historical crises of Israel in the past is continually impressive.

We can probably find more information about 'types' in ancient Jewish interpretation of the Hebrew Bible if we examine certain early Christian sources. D. Kaufmann, in an article in the *Revue des Études Juives*,[3] explored the motifs of early Christian funerary art in order to

---

[1]Woollcombe (*Essays on Typology*, pp. 42 ff.) calls this sort of interpretation *recapitulative* typology, but fails to realize that it has a pre-Christian origin.
[2]SB I, p. 87.
[3]'Sens et origine des symboles tumulaires de L'Ancient Testament dans l'art chrétien primitif', *REJ* XIV.

discover 'whether there already existed, even in Judaism, which is, to be sure, the source of Christianity, a range of images, a closed circle of types, which could have been employed in the liturgy'.[1] The material handled by the author of this article is of great interest, but he suffers from a disinclination to see in this early Christian art any Christological significance, which we today might well consider unreasonable. There are for instance on many early Christian tombs representations of Adam and Eve, and several examples of them show the two figures (Adam holding a sheaf and Eve a lamb) accompanied by a third who is undoubtedly intended for Christ. If we must see in these last examples an interesting illustration of early Christological interpretation of the Old Testament, it is difficult to deny the same significance (as Kaufmann is anxious to do) to the representations of Adam and Eve alone.[2]

However, without going further into the question of whether these scenes are Christological or not, Kaufmann makes it clear that a number of themes representing miraculous deliverances wrought by God can be detected as occurring frequently in these funerary monuments. Noah and the ark form one, as 'the first example in history of a miraculous deliverance by God',[3] and another is the sacrifice of Isaac,[4] and another the crossing of the Red Sea (a very frequent theme in the Jewish liturgy); there are a few examples too of the rain of quails, the manna, the cluster of grapes brought back by the spies, and the pillar of cloud.[5] The picture of Moses striking water out of the rock appears very often, occasionally accompanied by a picture of Moses receiving the Law and of the people revolting against Moses, and sometimes embellished by Moses being represented without sandals (where probably the story of the Burning Bush has exercised an attraction). Kaufmann observes that the miracle of the water struck from the rock is an obvious example of answered prayer, and that it is so used in the Jewish liturgy 'in prayers for rain and in those which are called *hoschanot*'.[6] The picture of David and Goliath appears on a few sarcophagi.[7] The ascension of Elijah is often depicted.[8] The picture of Jonah, represented as undergoing his various adventures, thrown into the sea, swallowed by the sea-monster,

[1] *Ibid.*, p. 35.
[2] *Ibid.*, pp. 38 f.
[3] *Ibid.*, p. 43.
[4] *Ibid.*, p. 47. In this case Kaufmann displays the same reluctance to see a Christological meaning. Cf. H. J. Schoeps, *Aus Frühchristlicher Zeit*, p. 231, and the whole of Section 2 (Paulus und die Aqedath Jischaq), pp. 229–38.
[5] 'Sens et origine des symboles', p. 221.
[6] *Ibid.*, p. 224. But he refuses to see Christological significance in the scene.
[7] *Ibid.*, pp. 224 f.
[8] *Ibid.*, pp. 224 f.

sitting under the booth and the gourd, and disconsolate at the withering of the gourd, is very frequent indeed in all types of early Christian art. No doubt Kaufmann is right in seeing in Jonah an outstanding example of a miraculous deliverance from death.[1] The three young men in the fiery furnace, sometimes accompanied by an angel, are well attested in the catacombs and frequent on sarcophagi.[2] They no doubt were used from early times as an example of miraculous deliverance from death. The same may be said of the picture of Daniel in the lions' den (with or without an apocryphal accompaniment of Habbakuk), which occurs frequently in the catacombs, even among the earliest paintings, and on sarcophagi and other funerary monuments.[3]

Ezekiel's vision of the resurrection of dry bones in the valley never appears anywhere in the catacombs, but it is found very occasionally on funerary monuments. The significance of this in suggesting the general resurrection is obvious, and it is interesting that the theme appears in the Jewish liturgy for 'the Haftara of the Sabbath of the Feast of Passover'.[4] It is not certain that Job appears in the paintings of the catacombs, but he does appear in a few sarcophagi. His significance is uncertain. Is he, in view of Job 19.25 f., a witness to the Resurrection, or is he there because of Job 1.22, which plays an important part in the Jewish funeral liturgy?[5] There are also some examples in the catacombs and sarcophagi and other monuments of representations of Tobias and the fish, of Susanna and the elders, and of scenes from the Apocryphal Daniel. These can all be reasonably explained as examples of deliverances by God.[6]

We can then make a list of the most important and most widespread scenes which appear in early Christian funerary monuments:

Noah in the ark.
The sacrifice of Isaac by Abraham.
The miraculous spring of Moses.
Israel's crossing of the Red Sea.
The ascension of Elijah.

[1]'Sens et origine des symboles,' pp. 228–33. But it is hard to believe, in view of Matt. 12.40 and Eph. 5.14, that Kaufmann is justified in denying that Jonah is also here a type of the Resurrection; the ascension of Elijah indeed probably serves the same purpose.
[2]Ibid., pp. 234–7.
[3]Ibid., pp. 237–9.
[4]Ibid., pp. 226–8.
[5]Ibid., pp. 233 f. Or is he conceivably there as the vanquisher of the serpent? See below, p. 18.
[6]Ibid., pp. 239–41. We are reminded by the appearance of Susanna here of the way Hippolytus dealt with this story in his Commentary on Daniel. See below, p. 114.

The deliverance of Jonah.

The three young men in the furnace.

Daniel in the den of lions.[1]

The question is at once raised by this list, Why did the early Christians largely confine themselves to this limited and by no means self-explanatory range of types? Kaufmann answers this by saying that this list of types came from the Jewish liturgy. He gives evidence of the existence in Jewish rites of a type of prayer which might be called 'Who didst hearken to',[2] for it consists of a list of examples of answered prayer headed by this formula (a form which we shall find Lundberg calling *exauditi*),[3] all taken from the Old Testament. He finds a late and much altered version of this in a section of the *Ordo Commendationis Animae* in the Roman breviary, the earliest extant example of which comes from the ninth century, which exhibits the formula, *Libera, Domine, animam eius sicut liberasti* x *de* y. No example which Kaufmann can cite exactly reproduces the list which can be derived from the funerary monuments, but he reasonably claims that this is because the 'funerary canon' is earlier than any other similar formula.[4]

This is impressive evidence for the suggestion that early Christian typology is in part derived from Jewish liturgical typology. We can in fact find much earlier literary evidence to support this 'canon' or limited list of types derived by Kaufmann from early Christian funerary monuments. One piece of this is supplied by Hippolytus' *Commentary on Daniel*, where the author in his elaboration of the text of Daniel represents the three young men as reminding each other of God's classic acts of deliverance in the past, his deliverance of 'our forefather' from the hand of Pharaoh,[5] of the deliverance at the Red Sea, of the parting of Jordan, and of the sparing of Rahab the harlot during the massacre at Jericho.[6]

sparing of Rahab

A much fuller and more striking piece of evidence is supplied by the Clementine Liturgy in the *Apostolic Constitutions*.[7] This liturgy forms a part of the work (VIII.5–14) which is not dependent (as other parts of the *Apostolic Constitutions* are) on the *Didascalia Apostolorum*. The liturgy was probably never in use as a liturgy, but is merely a compila-

[1] *Ibid.*, p. 242.

[2] So *Anglice*, but Kaufmann calls it *Mi Scheâna* (מי שענה).

[3] See below, p. 66.

[4] *Ibid.*, pp. 245–53.

[5] Moses perhaps; the editor Lefevre cites Ex. 18.4 and Deut. 7.8; but it could mean Israel generally, or even Joseph.

[6] *Comm. on Dan.* II 19.5.

[7] Daniélou has called attention to this in his *Sacramentum Futuri*, pp. 98 f.

tion of liturgical formulae made by the same hand as made the interpolations in the letters of Ignatius, that of an Arian writer living at the
end of the fourth or the beginning of the fifth century, who used as his
basis perhaps a Syrian type of liturgy.[1]

The passage of particular interest to us occurs in the long prayer of
the anaphora designed to be made by the bishop celebrating the Eucharist.
The prayer as a whole is written in ornate and rather inflated Greek and
consists of a recapitulation of God's mercies. In the latter part of it
however the language becomes noticeably simpler and plainer, and the
prayer becomes little more than the rehearsal of a number of 'types'
taken from the Old Testament. First of all are mentioned God's acceptance of Abel and rejection of Cain, and his acceptance of Seth and
Enoch and translation of Enoch. Then after a few more lines occurs a
long series of what we might call 'Who didst hearken to' types. God is
invoked as he who:

> rescued Noah from the flood (making an end and a beginning),[2]
> snatched Lot from the destruction of Sodom,
> rescued Abraham from his ancestral impiety,
> prepared Melchisedek as high-priest of God's worship,
> manifested Job as conqueror of the serpent, primal source of evil,[3]
> made Isaac a son of promise,
> made Jacob a father of twelve children and his descendants into a
>   multitude and brought them into Egypt,
> rewarded Joseph's self-control by giving him rule in Egypt,
> fulfilled promises by rescuing the ill-treated Hebrews from Egypt.

Then after a few more preparatory clauses God is invoked as he who:

> manifested Moses as the giver of a written law,
> glorified Aaron and his descendants with the priesthood,
> punished sinful and received repentant Hebrews,
> chastised the Egyptians with ten plagues,
> brought the Israelites across the sea,
> drowned the pursuing Egyptians,
> sweetened the bitter water with a stick,
> produced water from a rock,

---

[1]See F. E. Brightman, *Liturgies Eastern and Western*, I, pp. 17 f.; Benedict
Steuart, *The Development of Christian Worship*, p. 52.

[2]τέλος and ἀρχή; see below, p. 69.

[3]ἀρχέκακου, obviously by then a conventional epithet for the Leviathan in Job;
it occurs in a fragment of Origen on Job, Pitra, *Analecta Sacra* .II, p. 386; cf.
Comm. on Rom. V 10.

rained manna from heaven and quails for food from the air,
maintained a light, and a pillar of cloud by day for shade,
manifested Joshua as leader and destroyed the seven nations of
   Canaan through him,
cleft Jordan and dried up the rivers of Etham,[1]
destroyed walls without machines or men's hands.

Several points combine to suggest that these are in fact types derived
from a Jewish liturgy: the change of style, the absence of an obviously
Christological reference in the types,[2] the resemblance to the lists both
of the funerary monuments and of Hippolytus' *Commentary on Daniel*,
and the reference at the very beginning to God's acceptance of Abel and
of Enoch, a feature paralleled in Aphraates, whose Jewish affinities are
unmistakable;[3] Aphraates groups together God's making of the world,
his creation of man, his acceptance of Abel, his translation of Enoch,
his choosing of Abraham, his conversing with Moses, his speaking
through the prophets and his sending of Christ into the world.

It looks very much, then, as if there were already in existence before
the birth of Christianity a list, or several lists, of types, references to
saving or miraculous events ordained by God and recorded in the
Hebrew Scriptures, and that these types were used in Jewish liturgy. If
we allow this it is almost impossible to refuse the conclusion that these
types were used and adapted by Christians from the earliest times, and
that we have in fact here one source of Christian typology. But typology
is presumably not exactly the same as allegory, and we have yet to show
that Jewish typology was likely to become either Jewish or Christian
allegory by its own development apart from other influences.

We can in fact see Jewish typology at one point beginning to melt
into Jewish allegory, and that at a time earlier than any example of
typology we have yet considered. In this case the material is supplied
by the Dead Sea Scrolls and the documents associated with them. One of
these Scrolls, which is usually called the *Habakkuk Commentary*,[4] consists of a number of glosses on the first two chapters of the book of

---

[1]So the LXX translates Ps. 74.15: נַחֲרוֹת אֵיתָן ('mighty' or 'everflowing
rivers').
[2]In the clause referring to Abraham there is indeed the addition 'and revealed
to him thy Christ', but this suggests no more than a working over of an already
existing Jewish model.
[3]See the Epistola Interrogatoris preceding Aphraates' *Demonstratio* I (De
Fide), col. 4. The Epistle is probably by Aphraates himself.
[4]Translated into English by Millar-Burrows in his book *The Dead Sea Scrolls*,
pp. 365–70.

Habakkuk explaining how, in the writer's opinion, the utterances of the prophet have been or are being fulfilled in the history and vicissitudes of the sect to which the writer belongs. On several occasions this identification of the fulfilment of prophecy (itself closely resembling typology) seems to pass over into allegory. On Hab. 1.6 ('For lo, I am rousing the Chaldaeans, that bitter and hasty nation'), the comment runs, 'This means the Kittim, who are swift and sure in battle', etc.[1] On Hab. 1.15 ('Therefore he sacrifices to his net . . . and burns incense to his drag'), the writer comments, 'This means that they sacrifice to their standards, and their weapons of war are the objects of their worship.'[2] And on Hab. 2.17 ('For the violence done to Lebanon will cover thee; the destruction of the beasts shall make thee afraid'), the writer gives the interpretation, 'for Lebanon is the Council of the Community and beasts are the simple ones of Judah, the doers of the Law.'[3] Dupont-Sommer is probably going too far when he describes the exegesis of this *Habakkuk Commentary* as 'purely and entirely allegorical'. It would be more accurate to say that in this work we can see how the conviction that prophecy has been fulfilled is beginning to melt into allegory proper. It is all the more significant to our search for the sources of Christian allegory that this work is probably the earliest commentary on any part of the Hebrew Scriptures in existence; it may date from the middle of the first century B.C.

An even more striking example of the same process is supplied by the work called *The Damascus Document*, or the *Zadokite Fragment*, which comes from much the same period. It was discovered in 1896 in the geniza of a Karaite synagogue in Old Cairo and an English translation of it has been published, with an introduction and notes, by R. H. Charles.[4] Its exact date is uncertain. The outside limits are 106 B.C., when the Book of Jubilees, to which this work refers, was published, and A.D. 70, for it is obvious that the Temple was still standing when this work was written. Charles is anxious to narrow this dating to between 63 or 57 B.C., when Roman rule, to which a reference is probably made in x.1, may be said to have begun, and A.D. 70. He even suggests that it is possible that we can restrict the date still further to between 18 B.C., when Alexander and Aristobulus, sons of Herod by the last representative of the Maccabaean royal house, Mariamne, returned from Rome to

[1] *The Dead Sea Scrolls*, p. 365.
[2] *Ibid.*, p. 367.
[3] *Ibid.*, p. 370.
[4] *The Apocrypha and Pseudepigrapha of the Old Testament in English*, II, pp. 785–834. He calls it 'Fragments of a Zadokite Work'.

Palestine, and 8 B.C., when both men were put to death by their father Herod; but this dating depends upon the hypothesis that the expectation found in this work of the Messiah 'from Aaron and from Israel' (ii.10; viii.2; ix.10, 29; xv.4; xviii.8) attached itself to one of these two young men. Dupont-Sommer dates the work about 45 B.C.[1]

This *Damascus Document* is distinguished by the high value it attaches to the prophets alongside the law, and contains many examples of the application of passages in the Hebrew Scriptures (the Pentateuch as well as the prophets) to the contemporary situation, such as we have already found in the *Habakkuk Commentary*. Early on (i.9, p. 801) a prophetic passage (Hos. 4.16) is referred to the religious corruption prevailing in Judaea about 200 B.C., and a little later (vi.1, p. 808) the writer states that Ezek. 44.15, with its mention of 'the priests and the Levites and the Sons of Zadok', was fulfilled, for 'the priests are the penitents of Israel who went forth out of the land of Judah; and the Levites are they who joined them. And the Sons of Zadok are the elect of Israel called by the Name'. All these names are groups connected with the sect, established at one point of its history at Damascus, from which this document emerges. Almost immediately after this passage occurs another one (vi.9–11, p. 809) which describes the words of Isa. 24.17, referring to 'fear, the pit and the snare', as fulfilled in the misdoings of the contemporary Pharisees, each of these threats being interpreted as meaning various sins. Again, in another passage (viii. 5–9, pp. 812 f.) the writer quotes his own version of Num. 21.18 and then interprets it:

> ' "A well the princes digged
> The nobles of the people delved it
> By order of the Lawgiver."
>
> The well is the Law, and they who digged it are the penitents of Israel . . . and the Lawgiver is he who studies the Law. . . . And the nobles of the people are those who came to dig the well by the precepts in which the Lawgiver ordained that they should walk throughout the whole period of wickedness.'

Finally, the ninth chapter of the work exhibits two examples of the same type of interpretation. In the first (ix.4–9, p. 816) the writer quotes Amos 5.26 f. as 'And I will cause to go into captivity Siccuth your King and Chiun your images (the star of your god which you made for your-

[1]See Charles, *op. cit.*, pp. 785–8; Dupont-Sommer, *The Dead Sea Scrolls*, pp. 54–60.

typology

selves) beyond Damascus,' and Amos 9.11 is quoted as 'And I will raise
up the tabernacle of David that is fallen.' The two passages are then
allegorized thus: The tabernacle is the books of the Law, David is the
Congregation, Chiun the images are the books of the prophets, the Star
is he who studied the Law. In the second passage (ix.20, p. 818) Deut.
32.33 is allegorized so that the dragons mean the Kings of the Gentiles
and the venom of asps 'the head of the Kings of Javan' (according the
Charles, *in loc.*, the successors of Alexander in Egypt and Syria who
invaded Palestine).

It is evident that in this document we have an example (perhaps the
earliest known clear example) of typology—the interpreting of an event
belonging to the present or the recent past as the fulfilment of a similar
situation recorded or prophesied in Scripture—slipping gradually into
allegory, that is to say the interpreting of an object or person or a number
of them as in reality meaning some object or person of a later time, with
no attempt made to trace a relationship of 'similar situation' between
them.[1] In the *Damascus Document* ix.4–9, for instance, the only connection between the Tabernacle, David, Chiun and the Star mentioned in
Amos on the one hand, and on the other the books of the Law, the congregation, the books of the prophets and him who studied the Law, is
that both groups were connected with Damascus. In ix.20 the connection between the dragons and the venom of Deuteronomy and kings of
the Gentiles and of Javan is purely arbitrary. It is noteworthy too that
there are no reasons for believing that this allegorizing has been influenced by any Hellenistic tradition of allegorizing. It seems to be a
purely native product of Palestinian Judaism, nothing but a natural
development from the practice of seeing the fulfilment of the prophetic
Scriptures in contemporary events. 'We arrive then at the conclusion,'
says Daniélou,[2] '. . . that the exegesis of the Old Testament in primitive Christianity consists of the development of Jewish exegesis, such as
can be found in the last books of the Old Testament and the literature
of pre-Christian Judaism. But Christianity fills exegesis with an entirely
new content when it sees in it the figure of the reality of Christ.' And he
suggests elsewhere that a passage in Justin's *Dialogue* linking texts in
the Old Testament where the Messiah is described as a Stone, such as
the account of the stone cut out without hands in Daniel and the narrative of Joshua using flint knives for circumcision, relies upon a Rabbinic

[1] This is the distinction between typology and allegory which will be consistently maintained throughout this work. For a very similar distinction, see Lampe
in *Essays on Typology*, pp. 30–33.
[2] *Sacramentum Futuri*, p. 103.

haggadah which originally connected these passages. Trypho, Justin's Jewish opponent in the *Dialogue*, seems to recognize and in a sense accept these texts.[1]

But it must be pointed out that hitherto we have not established quite as wide a claim as Daniélou makes here. The material hitherto discussed has suggested strongly that the roots of Christian typology, of the sort of exegesis of the Hebrew Scriptures which we find abundantly in the New Testament, lie in Jewish typology, and we have shown how easily early Jewish typology can merge into simple allegory. But we have done little to show that Christian allegory, which is found, though not abundantly, in the New Testament, and which is a characteristic feature of all Christian exegesis after the New Testament, derives from or is strongly influenced by Jewish allegory. It is significant (though this point has entirely escaped Daniélou's extensive and usually shrewd gaze) that those forms of Jewish typology most closely resembling early Christian typology, the forms of the *Habakkuk Commentary* and the *Damascus Document*, do not derive from strictly Rabbinic circles, but rather from those quarters where a lively Messianic expectation is to the fore[2] and where the emphasis is laid upon the prophetic rather than the legalistic aspect of the Hebrew Scriptures.

When we approach, as we now must, the subject of Rabbinic allegory, we are on a very thorny path.[3] Bonsirven remarks[4] that there is even a controversy as to whether the Rabbis really did allegorize or not. Certain exegetes are called *dôrŝé reŝûmôt* and *dôrŝé hamûrôt*;[5] they claim that the words of Scripture are signs and symbols figuratively meaning something else than their literal meaning, and that some texts in Scripture should not be taken literally. About the etymology and the exact meaning of these two titles for these exegetes there is considerable dispute. J. Perles, in an article written some time ago in the *Revue des*

---

[1]*Ibid.*, p. 187. The passage in the *Dialogue* is 36.1; Daniélou compares Philo, *De Leg. Alleg.* II.86, where the word ἀκρότομος is applied to σοφία, perhaps recalling a similar haggadah on Isa. 28.16. Daniélou makes a similar suggestion on p. 211.

[2]A document which is apparently a list of Messianic proof-texts used by the Qumrān Community has in fact turned up. It includes Deut. 18.18 conflated with 5.28 f.; 33.8–11, and Num. 24.15–17. See C. T. Fritsch, *The Qumrān Community*, p. 46; J. M. Allegro, *The Dead Sea Scrolls*, ch. X; and T. H. Gaster, *The Scriptures of the Dead Sea Sect*, pp. 353 f.

[3]As well as the authorities referred to below, see also R. B. Tollinton, *Selections from the Commentaries and Homilies of Origen*, pp. xxx–xxxiii; and J. Daniélou, *Origène*, pp. 176–9. I greatly regret that I have been unable to procure either E. Heinemann's *Altjudaische Allegoristik* or E. Goppelt's *Typos*.

[4]*Judaisme*, I, pp. 298 f.

[5]דרשי חמורות and דרשי רשומות.

Études Juives,[1] claims that the phrases *dôrŝé reŝûmôt* and *dôrŝé hamûrôt* mean the same thing, 'those who allegorize', and that these are identical with people named in other phrases as 'those who explain by a parable'.[2] He quotes[3] Rabbi Johanan ben Zakkai (a contemporary of Philo) as uttering some allegorizations, and Rabbi Akiba[4] as saying that reading the 'books of the allegorists' (*Siphre Hamîram*) is as harmless as reading letters. The books of the allegorists, in fact, were regarded as not in any way authoritative, but not as heretical. Strack-Billerbeck[5] translate *dôrŝé reŝûmôt* as 'expounders of interpretations' and *dôrŝé hamûrôt* as 'expounders of difficult passages', or possibly 'expounders of pearls'. J. Z. Lauterbach, on the other hand, in an article in the *Jewish Quarterly Review*[6] maintains that the two groups were originally quite different and represented distinct traditions of interpretation, but were confused by later tradition. He finds a quite new etymology for *dôrŝé hamûrôt*, rejecting all others, and interpreting the phrase to mean 'the seekers (by allegory) of the real intention behind the Law'.[7] This school, he thinks were allegorists certainly, but, in distinction from the *dôrŝé reŝûmôt*, they tended to make the commandment insignificant in comparison with the fulfilment of its intention.

The difficulty, it is clear, lies not in determining whether there were Rabbinic allegorists or not, but in deciding whether those who appear to be allegorists were using allegory in its proper and full sense. Most of the authorities are very cautious about admitting that the Rabbis reached anything as developed as the sort of allegory employed by the Christian Fathers. Strack-Billerbeck call attention to the evidence for an opposition to allegorizing in the saying of Rabbi Eleazar of Modiim (ob. *c.* 135) that 'whoever expounds meanings in the Torah which do not agree with the Halakah has no part in the age to come'.[8] Marcel Simon[9] allows that the sources of the spiritualizing interpretation of the Scriptures of some church Fathers, such as Justin, are undoubtedly Jewish. The doctrine,

[1] J. Perles, 'Études Talmudiques', on the רשומות דרשי, in *REJ* III (1881), pp. 109–20.

[2] דרשי במין חומר and דרשי במין חשל. The phrase ספרי המירם he thinks to mean 'books of the allegorists'.

[3] *Ibid.*, pp. 110 f.　　[4] *Ibid.*, p. 112.　　[5] SB III, p. 388.

[6] 'The Ancient Jewish Allegorists in Talmud and Midrash', *JQR* (NS) I.

[7] *Ibid.*, pp. 503–10.

[8] SB III, p. 399. Strack-Billerbeck think that the passage has been worked over by writers later than Rabbi Eleazar and that all that the Rabbi may originally have meant was a condemnation of him 'who uncovers his face against the Torah', i.e. handles the Torah in an impudent, disrespectful way; but they admit that the Rabbi may in fact have been condemning contemporary allegorizers.

[9] *Verus Israel*, pp. 178 f.

God alone has authorized – It is not for him to question.

Allegory applying to those texts, which taken literally

found in Justin as well as in several others, Origen included, that noth-ing in the sacred text is fortuitous and that the smallest number or letter is significant, is a Jewish doctrine. But Simon emphasizes that the Rabbis made only a modest and prudent use of allegory in its strict sense. 'Halachic exegesis' of the Pentateuch, he believes, was entirely excluded (though we shall shortly see evidence to modify this conclu-sion). 'As for the Torah and the commandments, you must not interpret them by the method of *maschal* (parable)', said Rabbi Eleazar.[1] The tendency was to confine allegory to those texts which, taken literally, appeared unsatisfactory, and the Rabbis never claimed, according to Simon, that the literal sense in any passage should be abandoned. Bon-sirven himself stresses the comparative rarity and insignificance of Rabbinic allegorization.[2]

On the question of whether this Rabbinic method of interpretation so much resembling allegory owed anything to, or can be associated with, the Alexandrian tradition of allegorizing as found in writers such as Philo, a tradition which has very marked affinities with Stoic or Hellenistic allegorizing, opinions are sharply divided. Strack-Billerbeck[3] distinguish firmly between Palestinian or Rabbinic allegorizing and Alexandrian allegorizing. Rabbinic allegory is characterized by the fact that it never for a moment impugns the validity of the literal sense. Behind Alexandrian allegory lies the assumption that the allegorical sense is the deeper, more important one, to which the literal is only the shell or outer part. This thought is almost entirely foreign to Palestinian exegesis. To it the literal sense alone is sanctioned. God has ordained; it is not for the Jew to question why, but to obey, for that is what his heavenly Father has commanded him as a member of the chosen race, and God has annexed to his command a reward. To such a tradition of exegesis, allegorization can never be anything but superfluous and un-authorized. There are only two cases, Strack-Billerbeck state, in the whole of Rabbinic literature, in which allegorization of the Alexandrian sort seems to be referred to, and in both the Rabbis set their faces firmly against it. These two cases are discussions dealing with two texts, the passage in Deut. 22.6 forbidding the Jew to take both the mother-bird and her young when she is found sitting on her nest, and the com-mandment of Lev. 22.28 forbidding to kill either cow and calf or ewe and lamb on the same day. The Rabbis firmly discouraged anybody from

[1]Simon is here relying upon Bonsirven, *Exégèse Rabbinique*, p. 207.
[2]*Ibid.*, pp. 246–51.
[3]SB III, pp. 397–9.

Behind allegory – the assumption that the deeper meaning is the more important.

taking these two examples as illustrations of the mercy of God, or as indications that God's lovingkindness is his leading and dominant characteristic, indications that might be expressed in such a prayer as one beginning, 'Thou that dost care for the bird's nest, care for us and have mercy upon us.' The Rabbis insist that this is just a commandment of God to be obeyed because it is a commandment, and for no other, ulterior, speculative or philosophical reason. They take exactly the same line on the command not to slay the cow and calf, etc., on the same day.

Other scholars, however, emphasize the affinity between Palestinian and Alexandrian Jewish allegory, and suggest that the former owes much to the latter. Zöllig, for example, declares that allegorism arose among the Jewish scholars of Alexandria who were influenced by Platonic ideas, and that they were taught this method by pagan allegorizations of Homer.[1] Lauterbach thinks that the dôrše hamûrôt were in fact the Alexandrian Jewish allegorizers, who were ready to abandon the literal meaning of the Law in favour of the spiritual.[2] Büchsel, the author of the article on ἀλληγορέω in Kittel's Wörterbuch, is even more emphatic. The Palestinian Rabbis certainly used allegory, he says, and the distinction between their use of it and that of the Alexandrian Jews is only relative, not absolute. They were less skilled, less indiscriminate, less regular in their use of it than the others, but they did use it, even on the Pentateuch. It will not do, he holds, to distinguish Alexandrian allegorism as being indifferent to the historicity of the Old Testament narratives, whereas Palestinian allegorism believed in their literal truth. The only distinction is that the Alexandrians welcomed Greek culture and its criticism of such things in the Scriptures as anthropomorphisms, whereas Palestinian scholarship did not; yet neither of even these statements he believes to be accurate without qualification.[3] It is, in his view, very probable indeed that allegory among Palestinian Jews arose under Greek influence derived through Alexandrian Jewry. 'Even though independent beginnings for it among the Biblical scholars of Palestine may be visible, it nevertheless most probably first came to maturity through Greek influences which arrived through Alexandria.'[4]

But it is time that we ceased canvassing the opinions of others and looked at the examples of allegory or alleged allegory themselves. They

[1]Die Inspirationslehre des Origenes, p. 120. It is doubtful, however, if Zöllig (who on the subject of his thesis is well-informed, judicious and worth reading) knew much about Jewish exegesis.
[2]'The Ancient Jewish Allegorists', JQR (NS) I, pp. 525 f.
[3]TWNT I, p. 262 f.   [4]Ibid., p. 263.

are surprisingly abundant. Rabbinic allegory, according to Bonsirven, takes three forms: interpreting a legal or historical passage in a figurative or moral way; seeing in certain objects, persons or historical events symbols of spiritual realities, particularly of the Torah and of the cult; and recognizing in the Bride and Bridegroom of the Song of Solomon the figures of Israel and of God. In this same passage Bonsirven gives examples of this allegorization of the Pentateuch. The bitter wood and the water and other elements are often interpreted as the Torah; the branches of the vine (Gen. 40.10) signify the Torah or the patriarchs. Three interpretations of Rabbi Ismaël,[1] called 'interpretations in the manner of parable,' are quoted. In these the phrase from Ex. 21.19 'to walk abroad upon his staff' is interpreted to mean 'in full health'; the phrase from Ex. 22.2, 'if the sun be risen upon him', is allegorized as 'if he knows that he goes in peace'; and the phrase from Deut. 22.17, 'they shall spread out her garment', is taken to mean 'they shall expose her doings openly like a garment'.[2] Strack-Billerbeck give several more examples of allegorizations of the Law.[3] Rabbi Johanan ben Zakkai (ob. c. A.D. 80) in one of his allegorical interpretations explains that the reason why no iron tool was to be used in building the altar (Deut. 27.5) was because swords, the symbol of punishment, are made of iron, and it is not fitting that such things should be associated with the means of reconciliation between God and Israel. Again Rabbi Acha (c. A.D. 320) said that the names of the tribes were written on the stones of the High Priest's breastplate (Ex. 28.9 ff.) because though all God's people are a royal priesthood it is impossible for all to approach the altar, so that by means of this breastplate it was as if all approached God when the High Priest approached the altar. In a later work[4] Bonsirven adds several more examples of allegorization of legal or juridical texts, of which two may be given here. Rabbi José the Galilean[5] interpreted Lev. 19.14 ('Thou shalt not place a stumbling block before a blind man') to mean that if somebody asks you whether the daughter of so and so is fit to marry a priest you are not to reply that she is if in fact she is not. And the physical fear before the battle mentioned in Deut. 20.8 was interpreted

---

[1]This (according to Bonsirven, *Judaisme*, I, pp. xxxi and xxxiii) can be either Ismaël b. Elisa (ob. 135), Tannaite second generation, or Ismaël b. José, Tannaite fourth generation, presumably to be dated two generations later than the other, c. 180.
[2]*Ibid.*, pp. 298 f. Compare the same writer's *Exégèse Rabbinique*, p. 237. The last three examples are also cited in SB III, pp. 392 f.
[3]*Ibid.*, pp. 388–90.
[4]*Exégèse Rabbinique*, pp. 225–33. The examples given here come from pp. 228 f.
[5]In *Genesis rabba in loc.*, 20.7, p. 191: his date is about A.D. 110.

by the same Rabbi[1] to mean fear arising from the consciousness of
having transgressed the law.

Strack-Billerbeck give examples of two more kinds of allegorization
of the law. The first kind is allegory based on the interpretation of one
text by another, occurring next to it in a biblical passage though often
quite unconnected with it.[2] For instance, Deut. 24.6 forbids a man to
take the upper or lower millstone in pledge. The *Jerusalem Targum* I
interprets this as meaning that no one is to cast a spell on the bride or
bridegroom on their wedding night. At first sight this seems sheer
arbitrary allegory, but in fact the connection is quite easily explicable.
The verse before this one (Deut. 24.5) deals with the freedom from
National Service allowed to a man who has only just married; add to
this the text 'Then let my wife grind unto another, and let others bow
down upon her' (Job 31.10), and the similarity of the word meaning
'take in pledge' (חבל) to the word meaning 'cast a spell on' (חבר), and
the allegorization becomes understandable. This allegorization may go
as far back as Rabbi José the Galilean. Another example of this kind is
the interpretation of the text which Paul in fact allegorized in I Cor. 9.9
—'Thou shalt not muzzle the ox when he treadeth out the corn' (Deut.
25.4). The *Jerusalem Targum* I interprets this as meaning that a sister-
in-law left childless and a widow shall not be held to be bound to a
Levirate marriage with a surviving brother of her husband if he is a
leper or in other ways unsuitable. The explanation of this allegorization
lies in the next verse (Deut. 25.5) which deals with Levirate marriage.
Strack-Billerbeck emphasize that these allegorical interpretations are
not intended to annul the literal meaning of the law; on the contrary,
they are only used to give Scriptural support to already established
observances.

The other kind of allegory of the law mentioned by Strack-Billerbeck[3]
consists of the most fanciful identifications of various persons and
objects mentioned in the law with various empires, such as those of
Babylon, Persia, Greece and Rome, and also with Israel and with God.
These interpretations always depend upon a supposed third term
common to both original and interpretation found in some other text
and very often involving a play on words. Of these, Strack-Billerbeck
say 'allegorizations of the law of this sort have no connection with the
ordinance involved at all. They represent in the last resort a harmless
homiletical play of fancy.'[4]

---

[1] In *Sota* 8.5.   [2] SB III, pp. 391 f.
[3] *Ibid.*, pp. 393–6.   [4] *Ibid.*, p. 393.

So far we have encountered no very convincing evidence that in Rabbinic allegory Christian allegory has one of its sources, though the material hitherto surveyed is not without parallels in Christian exegesis. But when Bonsirven gives us examples of the allegorization of passages which are historical or pseudo-historical narrative, we are nearer the mark. First of all we may note some Rabbinic allegorizations of names.[1] The *dôršé rešûmôt*, we are told,[2] dealing with the text 'Amalek came to attack Israel at Rephidim' (Ex. 17.8), interpreted this word to mean 'relaxing of hands' (*rephayôn yâdaim*), because all the Israelites had neglected the law, and so the enemy attacked them. Again the text of Gen. 38.14, 'She sat at the entrance of Enaim,' was allegorized to mean that she sat at the gate to which all eyes are directed (i.e. heaven), with a play, as in the other example, on the meaning of the word.[3] And on the text, 'They departed for Succoth' (Ex. 12.37), Rabbi Eliezer said that Succoth was simply a place, but Rabbi Akiba said that Succoth was nothing else except the clouds of glory, citing Isa. 4.5 f.[4] Again some Rabbis interpreted the account of the sweetening of the waters by a tree (Ex. 15.25) as meaning the law, and the light referred to in Deut. 33.2 as the Torah; and Rabbi Joshua explained to the proselyte Aquila that in the text, 'If God will give me bread to eat and clothes to wear' (Gen. 28.20) 'bread' means the law and 'clothes' means the prayers of the faithful Jews.[5] Rabbi Johanan saw a symbol of the sufferings of the Messiah in the text, 'And Boaz said unto her, Come hither and eat of the bread and dip thy morsel in the vinegar' (Ruth 2.14), citing Isa. 53.5.[6] Several second-century Rabbis indulged in a thoroughgoing allegorization in all its details of Pharaoh's dream (Gen. 40.9 ff.).[7] These are undoubtedly allegorizations applied to passages contained in narrative, rather than in the law proper. There is, however, little tendency (with the possible exception of Rabbi Akiba's explanation of Succoth)

[1] For further information on this subject, see my article, 'The Interpretations of Hebrew Names in Origen', *Vig. Chr.* X.
[2] *Mekhilta* of Simeon b. Yohai *in loc.*, p. 83. Lauterbach also cites this example in 'The Ancient Jewish Allegorists', *JQR* (NS) I, pp. 313–15.
[3] *Genesis rabba* 85.7, on Gen. 38.14, p. 1041.
[4] *Mekhilta* on Ex. 12.37, p. 48. These last three examples are given by Bonsirven, *Exégèse Rabbinique*, pp. 233 f.; and also by Daube, *The New Testament and Rabbinic Judaism*, p. 30.
[5] *Genesis rabba* 70.5, p. 802; Bonsirven, *op. cit.*, p. 237. Compare Lauterbach, 'The Ancient Jewish Allegorists', *JQR* (NS) I, p. 311, where he cites the interpretation of Ex. 15.25 and adduces in comparison Philo's treatment of the passage in *De Post. Caini* 157 and *De Mig. Abrahami* 36 f., where he interprets 'tree' as meaning 'virtue' and 'waters' as meaning 'mind'.
[6] *Ruth rabba* 5.6, on Ruth 2.14; Bonsirven, *op. cit.*, p. 239.
[7] *Hullin* 929; Bonsirven, *op. cit.*, p. 241.

[margin annotations: from the text? Allegorizing — finding a deeper meaning than it's searching for or adding a deeper meaning?]

to explain away the historicity of episodes so treated. The most usual aim seems to be to modify or even explain away something apparently shocking, or to give a *raison d'être* for some apparently meaningless name or detail.

Bonsirven gives us examples also of Rabbis allegorizing passages in the third division of the Hebrew Scriptures, the Writings. Rabbi Bibi interpreted Eccles. 11.1, 'Cast thy bread upon the waters, for thou shalt find it after many days,' so that casting bread meant giving alms and the waters meant the Torah.[1] The text Eccles. 10.1, 'Dead flies cause the ointment of the perfumer to send forth a stinking savour,' was interpreted by Rabbi ben Azzai of a single sin losing great benefits, and by Rabbi Akiba of the man who has not enough merits to incline the balance of judgement in his favour, and the *dôršé rešûmôt* interpreted the text similarly.[2] A gnomic passage, though it is not in the Writings, 'Blessed are ye that sow beside all waters, that send forth the feet of the ox and the ass' (Isa. 32.20), was thoroughly allegorized in all its details by Rabbi Johanan, speaking in the name of Rabbi Simeon b. Yohai.[3]

In these allegorizations of details in historical narratives we are evidently approaching nearer Christian allegory, especially in Rabbi Johanan's almost Christological interpretation of Ruth 2.14. Daube, who cites this last example, in his book *The New Testament and Rabbinic Judaism*, reminds us that the Rabbis, even those of the first two or three Christian centuries, were often ready to see allusions to the Messiah or the Age to Come in almost any part of the Hebrew Scriptures.[4] The examples given by him from their interpretation of the Book of Ruth are illuminating, even though we suspend judgement as to whether this sort of exegesis can be called allegorizing or not. The life of Ruth is often taken by Rabbis to prefigure Messianic events.[5] The sentence in Ruth 2.14, 'and she did eat, and was sufficed, and left thereof' was interpreted to mean that she ate in this world, was sufficed for the days of the Messiah, and left thereof for the Age to Come.[6] Or it can be taken of David and be interpreted as a prophecy of David eating in this world, his eating for the days of the Messiah, and his eat-

---

[1] *Eccles. rabba* in Eccles. 11.1. *Exégèse Rabbinique*, pp. 241 f.
[2] *Eccles. rabba* in Eccles. 10.11. *Exégèse Rabbinique*, pp. 242 f.
[3] *Baba qamma* 17a; *Exégèse Rabbinique*, p. 243. Bonsirven records other allegorizations of Ps. 68.14, of Eccles. 8.15 and 11.6, and of Prov. 28.19 on pp. 244 f.
[4] Part I of his book (pp. 1–51) is called 'Messianic Types', but these types are not exactly the types of typology or allegory; except for the examples set out below most of his types are little more than subjects of Midrash.
[5] *The New Testament and Rabbinic Judaism*, p. 30.
[6] *Babylonian Shabbath* 113b; *Ruth Rabba* on 2.14, *Yalqut ad loc.*; Daube p. 47.

ing for the Age to Come. And Daube tells us that a Rabbi Johanan or Jonathan of the third century was able to list ten different allegorical interpretations of this sort.[1]

Two more considerable pieces of evidence, however, have still to be added before we can gain a properly informed view of the question. The first piece of evidence is the case made by Lauterbach for his view that allegorization was well known at a very early period among the Rabbis and that it later (perhaps as early as the third century) was deliberately discouraged as tending towards a spiritualization of history and as playing into the hands of the Christians. This case Lauterbach supports with a good deal of material.[2] He produces every single example of the interpretations of the *dôršé rešûmôt* that he can find, and to every single example he can give a parallel in the works of Philo. This does not lead him to argue that the allegorists were influenced by Philo, but 'that Philo was influenced by the Palestinian allegoristic interpreters of the Scriptures . . . as his rules of allegorical interpretation were composed of the rules applied by the Palestinian teachers as well as the rules applied by the Stoic philosophers. . . . In the *Dôršé Rešûmôt* we recognize, therefore, the oldest Palestinian allegoristic interpretation of the Scriptures.'[3]

The examples which he gives[4] are certainly very striking, and go far to bear out his contention. For instance, Deut. 28.66 runs, 'And thy life shall hang before thee.' The *dôršé rešûmôt* said (*b. Berakot* 249) that this verse applies to the man who lets his *Tefillin* (phylactery) hang, meaning, to the man who allows his religious beliefs to be uncertain. Philo interprets this same passage (*De Post. Caini* 24) in much the same way of a man who is uncertain or careless about his religious opinions. Again the verse 'And they went three days in the wilderness and found no water' (Ex. 15.22) is interpreted by the allegorists[5] to mean that they found no law or religious instruction, with a comparison of Isa. 55.1. Philo sometimes interprets 'water' thus. In *De Leg. Alleg.* II. 84-6 he interprets the phrase in Deut. 8.15, 'who brought thee forth water' to mean the bringing forth of the divine Word. Christian readers will inevitably be reminded of the fourth chapter of St John's Gospel. Another passage, commenting on Gen. 50.24 which contains the phrase

---

[1]*Op. cit.*, p. 48.
[2]'The Ancient Jewish Allegorists', *JQR* (NS) I, pp. 291-333.
[3]*Ibid.*, p. 328.
[4]We have seen two of them already, p. 29, notes 2 and 5.
[5]*Mekhilta* of Rabbi Ismael and *Mekhilta* of Rabbi Simeon and b. *Baba Qamma*; 'The Ancient Jewish Allegorists', p. 310.

פְּקֹד יִפְקֹד ('God will surely visit you') runs: 'The *dôrĕ̆ rĕšûmôt* said that there was a tradition among the Israelites in Egypt that the one who will come and speak words beginning with פקד (Ex. 3.16) is the true redeemer, and he will deliver them.'[1] Lauterbach points out that it was a rule of allegorical interpretation applied by Philo to derive a certain meaning from a word apparently superfluous. This is what the allegorists are doing with the word פקד here. Indeed, it might be added that they are, like any Christian father, putting a Christological interpretation of a far-fetched sort on a passage in the Pentateuch. Later Lauterbach collects examples of allegorical interpretation of the manna by the allegorists. They are obscure and have probably been confused by later tradition, but they still constitute interesting evidence.[2] Philo more than once interprets manna as the Word or the Wisdom of God.[3] A saying of Rabbi Akiba (*Yoma* 75a) was to the effect that the manna was what angels ate (Ps. 78.25) meaning probably spiritual food. A saying in *Yoma* 75 states that the manna caused the sins of Israel to become white (Ex. 16.31). Another saying (*Mekhilta Way.*, ed. Weiss, 59b) runs 'manna was like the words of the *Haggada* which attract the heart of man'; this interpretation is attributed in *Yoma* 75 to *Aḥerim* (others), which may mean the allegorists. Christian readers are again reminded of the Fourth Gospel, this time of the sixth chapter.

Lauterbach believes that the *dôrĕ̆ ḥamûrôt* must be distinguished from the *dôrĕ̆ rĕšûmôt*, and that their interpretations differ from those of the other group, inasmuch as they tended to make the commandment appear insignificant in comparison with the fulfilment of its intention.[4] One example of the interpretations of this group may be given: 'The *dôrĕ̆ ḥamûrôt* said that Anah was a bastard, and therefore he brought bastard creatures into the world.'[5] This is an intepretation of Gen. 36.24, 'Anah that found the mules in wilderness, as he fed the asses of Zibeon his father', and it presupposes a knowledge of a Midrashic tradition that Zibeon became the husband of his own mother and that Anah was the result of this union. Lauterbach thinks that the allegorists are here following an exegetical rule of Philo that when the literal meaning of a Scriptural passage conveys a trivial or unworthy thought an allegorical meaning should be given to it, and they find unsatisfactory

[1] *Midrash Hagadol* (ed. Schechter), p. 769; 'The Ancient Jewish Allegorists', pp. 317 f.
[2] 'The Ancient Jewish Allegorists', pp. 324–8.
[3] *Quod Deterius* 118; *De Leg. Alleg.* II.86.
[4] 'The Ancient Jewish Allegorists', pp. 503–10.
[5] From *b. Pesaḥim* 549; the passage is discussed in 'The Ancient Jewish Allegorists', pp. 513 f.

the literal meaning of the apparently trivial statement about Anah's discovery of the mules in the wilderness.

Lauterbach gives several more examples of the interpretations of the *dôršê hamûrôt*.[1] He claims that in each one of these examples the allegorists, once they had explained the meaning of the law, thought its actual observance a matter of indifference. He goes on to suggest[2] that the *dôršê hamûrôt* were in fact Alexandrian exegetes who, though themselves influenced by Palestinian exegetical traditions, did have some influence in Palestine. This is an interesting suggestion, though not much more than a matter of conjecture.

The other considerable piece of evidence which we must take into account in order to estimate properly Rabbinic allegory is the undoubted fact that from an early period the Rabbis unreservedly encouraged the allegorization of the Song of Solomon. It is evident that even as early as the first Christian century allegorization of the Song of Solomon was usual in Rabbinic arguments. Bonsirven[3] cites Rabban Gamliel (in *Sanhedrin* 90b) as relying on the text, 'Thy mouth is like the best wine which goeth down smoothly for the beloved, gliding through the lips of those that are asleep' (S. of S. 7.9) to support the belief in a resurrection from the dead. This was a subject of argument between Pharisees and Sadducees, and therefore presumably the saying must be placed before A.D. 70, perhaps no later than 66. Not much later than this must be placed a passage in II (4) Esdras. R. H. Charles[4] says that the part of the book from which this passage comes is from the source called the Salathiel Apocalypse, which can be dated from internal evidence thirty years after the Fall of Jerusalem, i.e. A.D. 100, though the whole work may not have appeared till A.D. 120. It was originally written in Hebrew, though the best form of it now is in Latin. The passage (II (4) Esd. 5.25 f.) runs thus:[5]

> 'Out of all the flowers of the world hast thou chosen thee one lily; out of all the depths of the sea hast thou replenished for thyself one river; out of all the cities that have been built hast thou sanctified Sion unto thyself; out of all the birds that have been created hast thou called for thyself one dove.'

[1]'The Ancient Jewish Allegorists', pp. 513–29; most of these are reproduced in either Bonsirven, *Judaisme*, or SB; in particular he reproduces five sayings of Rabbi Johanan b. Zakkai, one of which we have already looked at (see above, p. 27).
[2]*Ibid.*, pp. 525 f.
[3]*Exégèse Rabbinique*, pp. 63 f.
[4]*The Apocrypha and Pseudepigrapha of the Old Testament in English*, Vol. II, p. 542.
[5]*Ibid.*, p. 571. Charles' note is on the same page.

A.E.—B

In his note on this passage, Charles points out that the lily and the stream and the dove come from S. of S. 2.2; 4.15, and 2.14 respectively, and that this is an unmistakable allegorizing of these terms to mean Israel.[1]

In an article in *Recherches de Science Religieuse* Bonsirven has collected many examples of Rabbis allegorizing this book, beginning with Rabbi Johanan b. Zakkai and Rabbi Akiba.[2] Bonsirven divides the interpretations of the Song of Solomon into three categories: those who interpret the theme as the love of God for Israel and of Israel for God; those which see in the book a symbolic account of the Exodus from Egypt; and those which apply the images of the poem either to the theocratic institutions or to traditional doctrines.[3] Here is an example of the first category, from Rabbi José ben Hanina (mid-third century A.D.); it is an interpretation of S. of S. 6.2a, 'My beloved is gone down to his garden, to the beds of spices'; ' "My beloved" is the Holy One, blessed be He!; "in his garden", that is the world; "to the beds of spices", that is Israel.' Then he interprets 'to feed in the gardens and to gather lilies' (S. of S. 6.2b): ' "To feed in the gardens", that is the synagogues and the schools; "to gather lilies", that is to raise (from the dead) the righteous who are in Israel.'[4] When therefore the first Christian writers to write commentaries on the Song of Solomon, Hippolytus and Origen, allegorized it quite freely (though in quite different ways),[5] they had behind them not only a Christian tradition of interpreting this book allegorically[6] but also a Jewish one, and it is difficult to imagine that the Christian tradition owed nothing to the Jewish.

In the face of all this evidence it seems impossible any longer to doubt

---

[1] I would venture to suggest that we can in fact identify an allegorization of a passage in the Song of Solomon coming from a period a little earlier than this document in Rev. 3.20, which looks like a Christological interpretation of S. of S. 5.2.

[2] J. Bonsirven, 'Exégèse Allégorique chez les Rabbins Tannaites', *RechSR* XXIV, pp. 35–46. The material of this article, and of its predecessor under the same title in *RechSR* XXIII (pp. 513–41), is reproduced almost untouched in Bonsirven's later book *Exégèse Rabbinique*, pp. 214 ff.

[3] 'Exégèse Allégorique', pp. 38–43.

[4] *Ibid.*, p. 38.   [5] See above, pp. 115–7.

[6] Harnack (*Die Kirchengeschichtliche Ertrag der Exegetischen Arbeiten des Origenes*, II, pp. 20 f.) observes that in his interpretation of this book Origen certainly owed something to previous expositors, for in *Comm. on S. of S.* II, he gives four different interpretations of the significance of the 'steed' in S. of S. 1.9, all of them Christian. And W. Völker (*Das Vollkommenheitsideal des Origenes*, pp. 104 f., and especially p. 104 n. 3 and p. 105 n. 1) describes Origen's imagery of the soul as reminiscent of Gnostic, and particularly of Valentinian, language (cf. *ibid.*, pp. 114 f.). It is possible therefore that some Gnostic scholars had written commentaries on this book. After all, the first extant commentary on any book of the New Testament was written by a Gnostic, Heracleon.

that there was a lively and full-blooded tradition of allegorizing in existence in the Palestinian Judaism of our Lord's day, and that Christian allegory owes its origin mainly to this tradition. The only alternative is so to restrict the meaning of 'allegory' as to reduce it almost to insignificance. We have found evidence of the existence, not merely of allegory used to explain apparently irrational and trivial points in the law, but of allegory used indiscriminately on all parts of Scripture, with the aim more often than not of deriving from them the doctrine dear to the allegorist's heart. We have found evidence of Messianic allegory among the Rabbis, and, both parallel with this and earlier than it, of a Messianic typology, which is beginning to blend into allegory. It is true that Strack-Billerbeck and Bonsirven sound notes of caution and warn us that there is evidence of allegory being deliberately restricted and even frowned upon among the Rabbis; it is true that most of the evidence (though not by any means all) comes from a period well after the time of the earthly life of Jesus and the writing of the New Testament. But if we ask ourselves the question, was this allegory a late phenomenon, not to be attributed to the Rabbis of the first century, and widely practised only later; or was it an early phenomenon, well known, widely accepted and frequently practised in the first century, and afterwards discouraged by the Rabbis of the second or third and later centuries?—there can be only one answer. Everything suggests that it was an early phenomenon, later discouraged. By the third century Jewish scholarship is, to those Christian writers who are acquainted with it, a byword for its literalism and dislike of allegory.[1] By the third century it must have become perfectly clear that it was mainly by her use of typology and allegory that the Christian Church was able successfully to retain the Hebrew Scriptures among her holy books. Lauterbach's hypothesis, that allegory was at an early period widely used in Palestinian Judaism, but was later officially discouraged, is almost irresistible.

To the question whether this Palestinian allegory was in its turn borrowed from the Alexandrian tradition of allegory (which itself is generally assumed to derive from the Stoic, Hellenistic tradition of allegory), or not, it is not easy to return so confident an answer. Lauterbach suggests that Philo (the great exponent of Alexandrian allegory) was influenced by a previously existing Palestinian tradition of allegory.

[1]See Harnack, *Der Kirchengeschichtliche Ertrag*, II, p. 83 n. 3 where several references in Origen's works to this point are given. The Jews will give no reason for their observances, but only *ita visum sit legislatori*. No Jewish school of thought with which Origen was in touch was willing to allegorize.

Büchsel confidently asserts that the contrary was the case, and that Palestinian allegory must be attributed to the influence of Alexandrian, and so ultimately of Hellenistic allegory. We cannot indeed answer this question fully until we have explored further this Alexandrian tradition of allegory. And no doubt during the first Christian century the situation was more fluid than it was two centuries later when Judaism had closed its ranks against the danger of Christianity, or as it is in the conceptions of analytically-minded modern scholars; Rabbinic Judaism, prophetic Judaism and Hellenized Judaism were more freely mixed and more open to influences from each other than was the case later on. But in spite of all these considerations I cannot help concluding that Lauterbach's case seems stronger than Büchsel's case, and that the Palestinian allegory which we have been considering owed little to the exotic influence of Alexandria and much to its own native soil. The fact is that we can account for the origin and development of Palestinian allegory without finding the necessity of calling in Alexandria to provide a source for it. The *Habakkuk Commentary* and the *Damascus Document* provide enough evidence to account for the emergence of this phenomenon independently of any other tradition of allegory. That there were in a sense two other traditions of allegory (Alexandrian and Hellenistic) contemporary with Palestinian allegory is not, when we come to think of it, a very remarkable coincidence, especially when it can be shown that these two traditions as well as possessing points of resemblance with the other did in some important respects differ from it.

Christian allegory is essentially an allegory of realization, of types finding their consummation and oracles their fulfilment and events their ordained re-enactment, just as Christian eschatology is an eschatology that largely has happened or is happening. This is one reason why the early Christians apparently found it so easy to interpret their Scriptures in an allegorical or typological way. In their view, what was to happen *had* happened, and each detail could be found foreshadowed in the Scriptures if the Christian set about finding it in the right way. But the methods and the types and the tradition for this allegory were already there in Palestinian Judaism.

2

Alexandrian and Hellenistic Allegory

'THE home of Christian allegory was Alexandria,' says R. H. Snape;[1] and as we turn our attention to the task of examining whether this sweeping statement is accurate, we find ourselves studying that extensive field of thought where Jewish and Hellenistic thought meet. It would not therefore be out of place to consider the origin and use of some of the Greek terms employed to describe allegory by authors writing in this tradition and by others.

The first known use of ἀλληγορία or its cognates apparently occurs very early, in a fragment of the Stoic philosopher Cleanthes, quoted by Apollonius the Sophist,[2] coming from perhaps the third century B.C. On the word *moly*, known to English readers from Tennyson's line describing the Lotus-Eaters as 'propped on beds of amaranth and moly', Apollonius says, 'Cleanthes the philosopher says that Reason is indicated allegorically, by which the impulses and passions are mollified.'[3] But we cannot be sure that the presence of the word 'allegorically' in this sentence is not due to Apollonius rather than to Cleanthes, and we can in fact find no occurrence of this root in Greek literature for about two centuries after Cleanthes' day. It is therefore rather more likely that

---

[1] *A Rabbinic Anthology*, by C. G. Montefiore and H. Loewe, Excursus II, 'Rabbinical and Early Christian Ethics', by R. H. Snape, p. 619.

[2] *The Fragments of Zeno and Cleanthes*, ed. A. C. Pearson (London, 1891), frag. 66, p. 293, quoting p. 114 of Bekker's edition of Apollonius' *Lexicon Homericum*. Cleanthes almost certainly lived from 331 to 232 B.C. (Pearson, *op. cit.*, pp. 1 and 35) and Apollonius lived in the first or second century A.D. For further information on this subject see the Loeb edition of Philo's works, edited by F. H. Colson and G. H. Whitaker, Vol. I, Introd., pp. xiii–xiv; G. W. Butterworth, *Origen on First Principles*, Introd., pp. xxx–xxxvi; R. B. Tollinton, *Selections from the Commentaries and Homilies of Origen*, Introd., pp. xxx–xxxiii; Büchsel in the article on ἀλληγορέω cited above, *TWNT* I, pp. 261, 264; C. Spicq, *L'Épitre aux Hébreux*, I, p. 63, n. 6; H. J. Rose, *A Handbook of Greek Literature*, pp. 391 f.; W. Rhys Roberts, *Demetrius on Style*, p. 264; H. N. Bate, 'Some Technical Terms of Greek Exegesis', *JTS* XXIV, pp. 59–66; W. B. Stanford, *Greek Metaphor*, pp. 22–5; K. J. Woollcombe, in *Essays on Typology*, pp. 50–52; R. M. Grant, *The Letter and the Spirit*, pp. 1–30, 121–3.

[3] μῶλυ· Κλεάνθης δὲ ὁ φιλόσοφος ἀλληγορικῶς φησι δηλοῦσθαι τὸν λόγον, δι' οὗ μωλύνται αἱ ὁρμαὶ καὶ τὰ πάθη.

the first occurrence of this root is to be found in a number of writers who were all roughly contemporary in the first century B.C. An obscure but interesting writer who, significantly enough, comes from Alexandria, in giving a number of model letters for Egyptian literary aspirants, describes one which he calls an 'allegorical' letter.[1] The author of a book *On Style* of about the same period uses the words 'allegory' and 'allegorically'.[2] Philodemus, a writer on mainly rhetorical subjects of about the same period, uses the word as almost a synonym for 'metaphor'.[3] Cicero (*Orat.* 94) quotes the word in Greek as a figure of speech, so that it must have been in common use well before his time. The verb, 'to allegorize' (ἀλληγορεῖν) is first found in Philo (*passim*) and in St Paul (Gal. 4.24).[4] We can collect some early definitions or descriptions of allegory. The author of the model letters defines an allegorical letter as one written 'when we want only the person to whom we are writing to understand, and we indicate a meaning different from the thing said', and one of his examples is distinctly reminiscent of a threatening letter.[5] Demetrius in *On Style* commends allegory as a useful way of conveying meaning darkly, and especially menacing meaning, and quotes the threat of Dionysus the Syracusan tyrant to the men of Sicilian Locri, 'Their crickets will chirp on the ground' (i.e. not on the trees, for their territory will be laid waste).[6] H. N. Bate quotes an unnamed source which describes this figure of speech as 'making one sort of statement instead of another or subtly introducing an unusual meaning'.[7] Quintilian (*c.* A.D. 95) refers to the figure (VIII.6.44; IX.2.46) and defines it as 'sustained metaphor' (μεταφορά continuata). Heracleitus, the first-century A.D. author of the book *Quaestiones Homericae*, defines the term

---

[1] ἀλληγορικός; Τύποι Ἐπιστολικοί, a work wrongly ascribed to Demetrius Phalereus, edited by V. Weichert, sec. 15, p. 8. Weichert dates this author between the first century B.C. and the middle of the first A.D., and earlier rather than later in that period. I do not think that anybody has previously noted this early occurrence of the word.

[2] Demetrius, *On Style*, ed. W. Rhys Roberts. The author is not Demetrius Phalereus, though its author may have borne the very common name of Demetrius (Introd., pp. 49–64). ἀλληγορία occurs in sections 99–102 (p. 118) and 151 (p. 142), ἀλληγορικῶς in 243 (p. 180).

[3] Philodemus, *Volumina Rhetorica* (ed. S. Sudhaus) IV. 2, col. 3.22 (Vol. I, p. 164) where Philodemus describes ἀλληγορία as a τρόπος; *ibid.*, 14.24 (p. 174) where ἀλληγορίαις is a synonym for μεταφόραις; and col. 22.25 (p. 181) where it is possible that he divides ἀλληγορίαι into three sorts, αἴνιγμα, παροιμία and εἰρωνεία; but, as there are seventeen illegible lines between the word and the mention of these three varieties, we cannot be sure of the author's meaning.

[4] ἅτινά ἐστιν ἀλληγορούμενα· αὗται γάρ εἰσιν δύο διαθῆκαι.

[5] Τύποι Ἐπιστολικοί 15, p. 8.

[6] οἱ τέττιγες αὐτοῖς ἄσονται χάμοθεν, *On Style* 99–102 (p. 118); cf. 243 (p. 180).

[7] ἕτερα ἀνθ' ἑτέρων ἀγορεύων ἢ καὶ ἀλλόκοτα ἐπεισφέρων.

carefully: 'That is called allegory which, as the name implies, says one thing but means something other than what it says.'[1]

Philo and Heracleitus are the first authors to use the noun in the meaning of 'figurative interpretation of an authoritative text', and not long after them Josephus. A century later Plutarch gives us some interesting information about the word's development. He says in *Audiendis Poetis* 4(19e) that what used to be called ὑπόνοια is now called ἀλληγορία. In his *De Iside et Osiride* he twice distinguishes sharply his own interpretation of traditional legends from that of the allegorizers. 'For those who believe that by Hades is meant the body when the soul in it is insane or intoxicated allegorize meanly,' he says.[2] He prefers to interpret Hades as Dionysus. And later[3] he discusses the people whom he calls 'the simplest sort'. These are people who want to allegorize the Egyptian gods Osiris, Iris and Typhon to mean the Nile, the earth, the sea, etc. just as the Greeks allegorize Kronos to mean time, Hera to mean air, and the birth of Hephaistos to mean the change of air into fire. Plutarch's comment on these interpretations is: 'These can be called external as they simply present the ordinary account (of their subjects).'[4] He himself prefers to interpret these gods as philosophical terms. We can find the same disparagement of allegory used in some restricted sense in Josephus, who, in *Contra Apionem*, refers to 'the futile devices of allegories', though elsewhere he is quite ready to treat Scripture in an allegorical manner.[5] It looks therefore as if the word ἀλληγορία and its cognates came into use in the first Christian century in the special sense of figurative interpretation of authoritative Scripture or tradition, and by the end of the second was being even further restricted to some special sort of such interpretation. Clement of Alexandria reproduces the ingenious rationalization given by the earlier writer Aristobulus of the descent of the Lord upon Mount Sinai for the Giving of the Law and describes it as 'allegory of the Bible',[6] a term which, as far as we know, Aristobulus did not use.

Philo (as has already been said) uses ἀλληγορία or its cognates

---

[1] ὁ γὰρ ἄλλα μὲν ἀγορεύων τρόπος, ἕτερα δὲ ὧν λέγει σημαίνων ἐπωνύμως ἀλληγορία καλεῖται, Heracleitus, *Quaestiones Homericae* 22, p. 32.

[2] Plutarch, *De Is. et Os.* 28, 362AB.

[3] *Ibid.*, 32 f., 363D–64A.

[4] ταῦτα μὲν οὖν ἔξωθεν εἰρῆσθαι κοινὴν ἔχοντα τὴν ἱστορίαν. For a fuller account of Plutarch's allegory, see below, pp. 60–62.

[5] τὰς ψυχρὰς προφάσεις τῶν ἀλληγοριῶν, Josephus, *Contra Apionem* II.255 (p. 283). The context suggests that he is referring to the contemporary attempt to rehabilitate pagan religion by allegorizing its myths.

[6] ἡ κατὰ τὴν γραφὴν ἀλληγορία, *Strom.* VI.3.32 (PG 9.249,252). For Aristobulus, see below, pp. 41 f.

several times. He wrote for instance, three books called *The Allegorizing of the Laws* (concerned rather with re-interpreting historical narrative than allegorizing legal ordinances). He describes the story of the Fall in Genesis as, not a mythical invention, but 'an example of types calling for allegorical interpretation'.[1] On Gen. 39.1 ff. he points out that those who prefer the literal sense to the allegorical will be faced with an apparent contradiction if they observe that Pharaoh's head cook, Potiphar, had a wife, but yet was a eunuch.[2] And in *De Posteritate Caini* he concludes that we must adopt 'the way of allegory dear to the natural philosophers'.[3] It is significant that he associates the practice of allegory with this class of scholarship. Similarly Aristobulus before him had urged the Ptolemy to whom he addressed his work, when faced with anthropomorphic descriptions of God in the Scriptures, to 'adopt philosophical interpretations'.[4] In another passage Philo, after giving a description of the altar of sacrifice, says, 'This is the literal account, but the intellectual interpretation must be observed by the rules of allegory.'[5]

But the more usual word employed by Philo to denote allegory is ὑπόνοια. He says, for instance, that nobody should, admitting the superficial interpretation of a passage, attribute undiscriminatingly his own lack of subtlety to the Law, but should observe carefully the enigmatic meaning conveyed through ὑπονοιῶν and so understand the passage clearly.[6] We have seen that Plutarch tells us that what used to be called ὑπόνοια was in his day being called allegory; Plutarch himself in his *De Iside et Osiride* uses ὑπονοία to mean the reminders or hints of her sufferings which the goddess Isis is said to have included in her rites and also to denote the interpretation given to explain why Egyptians carry out various customs about donkeys.[7] But Philo can also

---

[1] ἔστι δὲ ταῦτα οὐ μύθου πλάσματα, οἷς τὸ ποιητικὸν καὶ σοφιστικὸν χαίρε γένος, ἀλλὰ δείγματα τύπων ἐπ' ἀλληγορίαν παρακαλοῦντα κατὰ τὰς δι υπονοιῶν ἀποδόσεις, *De Opificio* 157—a passage remarkable for its use of three interesting words, ἀλληγορία, τύπος and ὑπόνοια, as well as for the disparagement of μῦθος.

[2] *De Leg. Alleg.* III.236: τοῖς γὰρ τὰ ῥήματα τοῦ νόμου πραγματευομένοις πρὸ ἀλληγορίας ἀκολουθήσει τὸ δοκοῦν ἀπορεῖσθαι.

[3] Or 'men of science', φυσικοῖς ἀνδράσιν, 7. Cf. *De Abrahamo* 99, where he says that he knows some φυσικοί allegorize Abraham's concealment from Pharaoh of Sarah's relationship to himself, and, Philo adds, οὐκ ἀπὸ σκόπου.

[4] Eus. *PE* VIII 10.2 (376B) where a fragment of Aristobulus is reproduced. The Greek is φυσικῶς λαμβάνειν τὰς ἐκδοχάς.

[5] *De Spec. Leg.* I.287; the phrase is τοῖς τῆς ἀλληγορίας κανόσιν, but this does not, I think, imply that there is a fixed set of rules for allegory which Philo feels bound to follow.

[6] *Quod Deterius* 155; cf. *De Agric.* 131ff., *Quis Rer. Div. Heres* 289, et al.

[7] *De Is. et Os.* 27, 361E, and 32, 363D.

use to describe allegory the word 'symbol',[1] a word also employed by Justin in a not dissimilar sense.[2] Occasionally Philo will use the word τροπικός to describe allegory,[3] a root used before him in the same sense by Pseudo-Aristeas.[4] Only very rarely does Philo use the word τύπος or its cognates for allegory, though Josephus in his allegorization of the tabernacle and its furniture uses a phrase with a cognate of this word in it.[5] The reason for the sparseness of the use of τύπος is no doubt because Philo's lack of interest in eschatology or Messianic expectation precludes his developing a typology. This brief survey should make it clear enough that, except for the word *allegory* itself, Alexandrian Jewish scholars neither inherited nor themselves formed a range of technical terms in which to express their allegory. That was a task left for the Alexandrian Christian scholars to accomplish.[6]

It would, however, be a mistake to assume that Philo was the first of the Alexandrian Jews to allegorize. In fact he stood almost at the end of a long tradition of allegorizers who wrote as Jews for Gentile ears. The earliest of whom we can find any trace is Aristobulus.[7] He was a Jew of Alexandria who wrote a book called Περὶ τῶν ἱερῶν νόμων ἑρμηνείας, addressed to one of the Ptolemies. His date cannot be fixed with certainty, but he probably wrote his work, which is known only through fragments quoted in later writers, before Pseudo-Aristeas' *Letter*, for his version of the story of the first Greek translation of the Torah does not seem to owe anything to that of Pseudo-Aristeas.[8] He attempts to interpret the historical narratives in the Pentateuch philosophically or

[1] E.g. *De Spec. Leg.* I.200; λόγος ὁ διὰ συμβόλων; *ibid.*, II.29: θεωρίαν τὴν διὰ συμβόλων; *De Praem. et Poen.* 61: σύμβολον διανοίας ἀφανοῦς.
[2] *Apol.* I. 55.1: the crucifixion was spoken of in the Scriptures συμβολικῶς; 55.2: the Cross is the greatest σύμβολον of all, being found as a shape in all sorts of ways, as a mast, as a ploughshare, etc.
[3] E.g. *De Leg. Alleg.* II.14; *De Josepho* 125.
[4] *The Letter of Aristeas* 150, p. 545.
[5] *Antiquities* III.180, p. 7: εἰς ἀπομίμησιν καὶ διατύπωσιν.
[6] For a full account of ancient exegetical terminology, see R. M. Grant, *The Letter and the Spirit*, pp. 120–42.
[7] For information on Aristobulus see *Eus.HE* VII.32.16 f., pp. 250 f.; Eus.*PE* VII.13.7 (323D); 14.1 (324A); VIII.9.38–10.17 (376D–78B); XIII.11.2–12.15 (664B–68C); Clement of Alexandria, *Strom.*I.22.150, PG 8.893; VI.3.32, PG 9.249–52; W. Knox, *Saint Paul and the Church of the Gentiles*, p. 68; H. Chadwick, *Origen: Contra Celsum*, p. 226, on *Contra Celsum* IV.51; Pauly Wissowa, *Real-Encyclopädie der Altertumswissenschaft* II, pp. 918 f., article by Gercke.
[8] See Eus.*PE* XIII.12.2 (664B). In *HE* VII.32, which is mainly a long extract from the Περὶ τοῦ Πάσχα of Anatolius, a third-century bishop of Laodicea, Eusebius' language seems to imply that Aristobulus wrote before Pseudo-Aristeas, whom Eusebius also mentions in this passage. Eusebius' chronological estimate of Aristobulus is however in other respects hopelessly unreliable. H. Chadwick (*op. cit.*) suggests that Aristobulus is a name pseudonymously assumed by the writer to enhance the reputation of his work.

A.E.—B*

scientifically, that is by interpreting or allegorizing them into philosophical or scientific truths. In two extracts he claims that a doctrine of the Peripatetics about wisdom can be found in the Proverbs of Solomon, and that Plato and all the Greek philosophers and poets had found their ideas in Moses' works.[1] Two more passages from his work deal more directly with the text of Scriptures. In both Aristobulus is concerned to explain away anthropomorphic descriptions of God to be found in the Bible. They are worth examining in detail.

In the first extract[2] Aristobulus urges the king to whom he addresses his work, when he reads certain passages in the Scriptures, 'to adopt philosophical interpretations', and thus achieve the proper understanding about God 'and not to lapse into a legendary and anthropomorphic conception of him'.[3] Moses often by using language apparently referring to quite different subjects is really 'describing natural phenomena and the way that important matters are designed'.[4] To those who do not possess the capacity of understanding but pay attention only to what appears in writing, the grandeur of such passages is lost. Then Aristobulus gives examples of how to interpret passages such as these. References to God's hands in the Scriptures signify his power and references to his standing mean his ordering of the universe. The extract ends with a rationalization of the account in Exodus of God's descent upon Mount Sinai at the giving of the law. Aristobulus insists that this descent was not spatial, for God is everywhere, and during the period of the Law-giving he was seen as fire by the Jews everywhere, not just in one place. Further, the fact that though the fire burnt it did not consume anyone and though the trumpet blew there was nobody blowing it shows that these things were taking place 'by a divine device',[5] and that God was merely 'manifesting his grandeur everywhere without human aid'. Philo imitates this passage when he says[6] that God's voice at Sinai was not a real voice, but he produced a miraculous voice equally clear to those who were near and to those who were far away, 'an invisible resonance more wonderful than all instruments, adapted to heavenly harmonies'.[7] The second extract from Aristobulus refers to the verse in Gen. 2.2 which says that God rested on the seventh day. This does not mean, Aristobulus insists, that God did nothing, but it

[1] Eus. *PE* VIII.14.1 and 11.2–12.8 (386A, 379B–82B).
[2] *Ibid.*, VIII.10.1–17 (377A–78B).
[3] ἐκπίπτειν εἰς τὸ μυθῶδες καὶ ἀνθρώπινον κατάστημα.
[4] φυσικὰς διαθέσεις ἀπαγγέλλει καὶ μεγάλων πραγμάτων κατασκευάς.
[5] θείᾳ κατασκευῇ.
[6] *De Decalogo* 33.
[7] ἦχον ἀόρατον πάντων ὀργάνων θαυμασιώτερον ἁρμονίαις τελείαις ἡρμοσμένον.

Anthropomorphism – the attribution
of human characteristics to
God –

means that God established order permanently throughout the universe.[1]

The Scriptural interpretation of Aristobulus is obviously trembling
on the verge of allegory even if it has not yet quite reached it. It is a
surprising fact that his is the earliest text we possess which practises
allegory, or near-allegory; no Hellenistic allegorizer's work has survived
except in the smallest fragments of a period as early as this. Yet we must
agree that Aristobulus is borrowing his allegory from Hellenistic models.
He uses the word φυσικῶς of his interpretation; his aim is to explain
away anthropomorphisms in the Scriptures which would be repellent
to the ears of people educated in Greek philosophy. His interpretation
does not in the least resemble Rabbinic, or indeed New Testament,
allegory. It is worth noting too that, as far as we know, he did not
attempt to explain away the Jewish law by allegory.

This cannot be said of the next Alexandrian writer who claims our
attention, Pseudo-Aristeas. His *Letter of Aristeas* is a short historical
romance giving a spirited but largely fictitious account of how the
Pentateuch was translated into Greek at the command of the second
Ptolemy, and includes the description of the visit of an embassy from
Ptolemy to the High Priest at Jerusalem, and what they saw there. Most
scholars agree that the book dates from about 100 B.C. In the course of
his work the author causes one of the characters in his story to discourse
about the Mosaic law. He remarks that the legislation of Moses is
generally regarded 'superstitiously',[2] meaning, presumably, that most
Jews accept it as an arbitrary command, without knowing the real
reason for the various ordinances. Then a little later[3] he tells us why
Moses gave these laws: 'He arranged the whole generally with an equal
regard for philosophical principles, for they were planned by a single
controlling purpose; and each individual regulation concerning the
things from whose use we refrain and the things which we do use has a
deep reason.' An example of this is given in Lev. 11.29, which forbids
the eating of the weasel and the mouse. We can approach the understanding of this if we realize first that certain birds which the Jews are
allowed to eat are gentle and do not prey on others, whereas other birds
which they are forbidden to eat are fierce and predatory; this is a lesson
to the Jews to be gentle and controlled in their conduct and not to

---

[1]Eus.*PE* XIII 12.9–12 (667A–C). Cf. Philo *De Opificio* 13; Origen, *Fragment
on Genesis* (*PG* 12.97).

[2]*Letter of Aristeas* 129, p. 542; δεισιδαιμόνως is the word used.

[3]*Ibid.*, 143–50, pp. 544 f.; 'philosophical principles' translates τὸν φυσικὸν
λόγον.

indulge in arrogant violence. This sort of interpretation he calls τροπο-λογῶν. Again, the commandment found in Lev. 11.3 permitting the eating of those animals that divide the hoof and chew the cud means that Jews must always consider carefully and discern wisely about God's works and especially about human nature itself.[1] These examples help us to understand the prohibition of eating the weasel and the mouse. It is really a warning against various types of evil men. The weasel 'conceives through the ears, but brings forth by the mouth', and this is reproduced in the conduct of the 'weasel' kind of men; 'what they receive through hearing they give body to (σωματοποιήσαντες) by speech'.[2] The mouse presumably stands for men whose behaviour in some way resembles that of mice. And the author adds, in a manner reminiscent of the Rabbinic approach to the Bible, 'Nothing that is set down throughout Scripture is a matter of chance or of legend.'[3]

This kind of interpretation presents us with unmistakable allegory and the biblical texts are allegorized, not into Messianic prophecies nor types of the Law, but into moral examples and exhortations. We shall find exactly the same treatment of the Law in Philo, and later still in the *Epistle of Barnabas*, in Clement of Alexandria and in Origen; but this is the first known appearance of such an interpretation, and it is remarkable that in effect it empties the régulation of its literal force, making this merely the outward pretext for an inner moral meaning. At the same time the author applies the same word (φυσικῶς) to his interpretation as do Aristobulus and Philo, and this is probably his way of acknowledging his debt to Hellenistic allegory.

That there were other allegorizers of Scripture before Philo as well as Aristobulus and Pseudo-Aristeas is certain. We have already seen[4] that Philo betrays acquaintance with 'natural philosophers' (φυσικοί) who allegorize Abraham's encounter with Pharaoh over the concealment of Sarah's relationship. He also gives an alternative allegorization of Joseph's adventures with Pharaoh, very much in his own tradition, reading into the story information about the mind, the love of pleasure, the body, and so on; but it is not Philo's own.[5] In another place[6] he

[1]*Letter of Aristeas*, 153–61, pp. 545–7. Philo borrows and improves upon this allegorization in *De Agric.* 131 ff. and in *De Spec. Leg.* IV. 109, where he interprets the two different sorts of animals as two necessary processes in apprehending wisdom.
[2]*Ibid.*, 163–6, p. 547.
[3]*Ibid.*, 168, p. 548: οὐδὲν εἰκῆ κατατέτακται διὰ τῆς γραφῆς οὐδὲ μυθωδῶς.
[4]See above, p. 40 n. 3.
[5]*De Josepho* 151 ff.
[6]*Quis Rer. Div. Heres* 280 f.

gives us a wealth of allegorizations, all suggested by other people, of the phrase 'thy fathers' in the text 'Thou shalt depart to thy fathers' (Gen. 15.15); some people say it means the sun, the moon and the stars, some the archetypal ideas (in Plato's philosophy), others the four elements of the world. It is obvious that the allegorization of Scripture is a firmly established tradition in Philo's *milieu* by Philo's day, and it is interesting that those allegorizations tend to transmute the words of the biblical text into either philosophy or natural science, not into references to the Law and the chosen people, or into Messianic prophecies, as we should expect had Philo and his predecessors been influenced by the Rabbinic, presumably Palestinian, tradition of allegorizing.

Philo actually names two sources of allegorical interpretation besides himself. He tells us that the Essenes, that remarkable sect with which many scholars are inclined to connect the Dead Sea Scrolls, practise allegory, perhaps inheriting it from an older tradition.[1] And he also mentions, and much more fully, the Egyptian Jewish sect of the Therapeutae, to whom he devotes his work *De Vita Contemplativa*, as indulging in allegory. 'For they search the Holy Scriptures,' he says, 'and they expound their philosophy in their ancestral tradition, that is by allegory, for they hold that the meaning of the literal interpretation is symbolic of a hidden meaning which is brought to light by figurative interpretations.'[2] And later in the same work[3] he says that at the meetings held by the Therapeutae for Scripture reading and edifying homily on the reading, 'the expositions of the Holy Scriptures are made in a figurative way by means of allegories; for these men think that the whole of the Law is like a living person and that the literal text presents the body, but the hidden meaning lying below the text presents the soul.' One is tempted to see in this alleged allegorizing of the Essenes the survival into Philo's day of the allegory or near-allegory which we have found in the *Habakkuk Commentary* and the *Damascus Document*, and indeed Dupont-Sommer affirms confidently that this hypothesis is true.[4] Philo's reference, however, is vague enough for us to need caution in agreeing with this view. The scriptural interpretation of these two documents, allegorical though it may be, is widely removed from Alexandrian or

[1] *Quod Omnis Probus Liber Sit* 82. His words are τὰ γὰρ πλεῖστα διὰ συμβόλων ἀρχαιοτρόπῳ ζηλώσει παρ' αὐτοῖς φιλοσοφεῖται. Here αρχ. ζηλ. may mean 'emulating the tradition of the past' (as the Loeb editor, F. H. Colson, translates it) or 'with an ardour worthy of the men of old'.

[2] *De Vita Contempl.* 28 f. The last phrase is in Greek σύμβολα . . . ἀποκεκρυμμένης φύσεως ἐν ὑπονοίαις δηλουμένης.

[3] 78; the words for allegory in this passage are δι' ὑπονοιῶν ἐν ἀλληγορίαις.

[4] A. Dupont-Sommer, *The Dead Sea Scrolls*, p. 26.

Philonic allegory, and Philo is capable of reading into the tradition of scriptural exegesis of the Essenes his own conceptions of what exegesis should be. On the practice of the Therapeutae, however, we may trust Philo, for he must have known them well, living as he did in the same country with them, and there can be little doubt that this sect was a nursery of Alexandrian allegory. This fact alone should deter anybody who was inclined to see the Therapeutae as an Egyptian branch of the sect of the Dead Sea Scrolls. It can readily be seen, then, that allegory of the Hebrew Scriptures in the Alexandrian manner had a considerable history behind it when Philo learned it, and that it was distinguished by an attempt to discover a 'real' or truer or profounder meaning behind the text of the Pentateuch (we have no clear evidence for its attempting to allegorize other parts of Scripture). In view of this well-rooted tradition the theory of Lauterbach, that the *dôrśé hâmurôt* were no more or less than the school of Alexandrian allegorists who tended to belittle the literal meaning of the Law in comparison with its deeper 'philosophical' meaning, becomes attractive, even though it cannot be regarded as established.

Philo is the most confident and the most elaborate and prolific exponent of Alexandrian allegory whose works have come down to us. But even he shares many traits in biblical exegesis with the Palestinian Rabbinic tradition. He is convinced, for instance, that there is nothing superfluous or accidental in the Scriptures. 'Observe every subtle point,'[1] he says, 'for you will find nothing stated accidentally'; and elsewhere he tells us that Moses does not add a single superfluous word.[2] He often follows the Rabbinic practice of finding all the occurrences in the Pentateuch he can of a single word or phrase and interpreting them all together.[3] And he argues in a most Rabbinic way from the juxtaposition of texts. On the text in Ex. 2.23, 'And it came to pass in the course of those many days, that the king of Egypt died: and the children of Israel sighed by reason of the bondage,' Philo assumes that there is a relation of cause and effect between the two statements: 'In its literal sense the passage exhibits no consistency, but the logical connection in it is discovered when it is taken of the powers that are in the soul.'[4] We

[1] *De Leg. Alleg.* III. 147; πᾶσαν τὴν λεπτολογίαν is his phrase. Cf. H. A. A. Kennedy, *Philo's Contribution to Religion*, p. 37; C. Spicq., *L'Épître aux Hébreux*, I, Introduction, pp. 62 f.; R. M. Grant, *The Letter and the Spirit*, pp. 31–40.
[2] *De Fug. et Invent.* 54; cf. *Quod Deus Immut.* 140 ff.
[3] E.g. his collecting all the references to 'firstfruits' which he can find, in the *De Sacrificiis Abelis et Caini*.
[4] *Quod Deterius* 95.

*Philo - because Moses is a prophet
of God, he can attribute no error.*

have seen the evidence produced by Lauterbach that Philo in many cases followed Rabbinic rules of exegesis.[1] To Philo, Moses was a prophet, and therefore inerrant. 'For the prophet is an interpreter of God, who oracularly produces (ὑπηχοῦντος) the words within him, and to God we can attribute no error.'[2] But for him the text endowed with such an inspiration as this was not the Hebrew but the Greek version of the Pentateuch which he knew, and which he assumed to be the original version produced by the Seventy Translators in the reign of Ptolemy Philadelphus.[3] In his description of the production of this version he follows the *Letter of Aristeas* fairly closely, insisting upon the miraculous agreement of the translators and the word-for-word exactness of the translation. He says that those who know both Greek and Hebrew describe the translators, because of their faithful reproduction of the spirit of Moses' writing, 'not as interpreters but as past-masters and prophets'.[4] He bears out this uncritical trust in the accuracy of his Greek version as he expounds individual passages. In connection with a discourse on happiness he observes that Moses often describes happiness and the fruits of happiness by a single word ὁλοκαρπώματα ('wholefruits', to translate it literally).[5] F. H. Colson, in a note on this passage,[6] points out that Philo is fond of quoting this word, which occurs only three times in the LXX, and then only as a variant for 'burnt offerings' (ὁλοκαυτώματα; but ὁλοκάρπωσις occurs more often). Neither of these Greek words ever translates any word in Hebrew but one, meaning 'burnt offering', yet Philo stresses the significance of the meaning 'fruit' in this word. Similarly in commenting upon the word which the LXX uses to translate the Hebrew word for cakes in Gen. 18.6, ἐγκρυφίας (literally 'hidden things', perhaps because they were buried in ashes for cooking), Philo lays full emphasis on the meaning 'hidden', though no such meaning appears in the original Hebrew word: 'For it is written, "Make ἐγκρυφίας," because the

[1]See above, pp. 31–3. For evidence that Philo was influenced by contemporary Midrash, see my *Origen's Doctrine of Tradition*, pp. 146–8.
[2]*De Praem. et Poen.* 55.
[3]Cf. Kennedy, *op. cit.*, p. 30.
[4]ἱερόφαντας καὶ προφήτας, *De Vita Mosis* II.40. This alone should suggest strongly that Philo knew virtually no Hebrew, for he obviously does not count himself as among these judges. I have in fact found no satisfactory evidence that Philo knew Hebrew (that he gives etymologies that imply a knowledge of Hebrew only indicates that he used other people's collections of name-interpretations) and a certain amount of evidence that he did not. See *De Sacrif. Abelis et Caini* 17 (derivation of Esau); *De Post. Caini* 124 f. (derivation of Seth); *De Mutatione Nominum* 107 (derivation of Baal-peor).
[5]*Quod Omnis Probus Liber Sit* 69.
[6]Loeb, IX, p. 511.

holy supernatural (μύστην) Word concerning the Unoriginate and his powers must be hidden, since it is not permitted to everybody to guard the treasury of divine rites.'[1] The city Pithom (Ex. 1.11) he reproduces as πειθώ (persuasion) and takes it to mean 'speech to which persuasion is attached'.[2]

Philo, as we have seen, constantly allegorizes this, for him, inspired text. He uses his allegory to produce statements about psychology or morals, suggested by his individual blend of Platonism, Stoicism, and Judaism. Most of the material which he finds in Genesis for instance, in his De Legum Allegoria I he transmutes into statements about 'conception', 'mind', and 'perception'.[3] Whenever he finds the word 'woman' in the text he is inclined to interpret it as 'sense perception';[4] and Egypt for him is the country of the body, in contrast to the soul.[5] Judah and Issachar are allegorized into the man who is thankful to God and the man who does practical deeds of virtue.[6] Pharaoh is 'the atheistic and pleasure-loving disposition',[7] or the man who causes various good qualities to disintegrate.[8] The incest of Lot's daughters with their father represents Counsel and Consent making their father Mind drunk with folly and from Mind producing unlawful offspring.[9] Occasionally this passion for allegorizing leads Philo into exposition which is not only fanciful but preposterous. He takes Jethro in his words to Moses when he paid him a visit (Ex. 18) to have advised Moses to leave the Law and devote himself to very unjust arbitration in Lawsuits;[10] and he regards all the honours that Pharaoh gave Joseph (Gen. 41) as symbols of degradation, whereas the necklace and the seal which Judah gave Tamar (Gen. 38) he takes to be signs of beauty and order.[11]

Philo's methods of allegory, then, are not dissimilar from the methods of the Rabbinic Palestinian schools, nor indeed from those of the prophetic allegorizers or typologists of the Habakkuk Commentary and the Damascus Document, and no doubt owed something to at least the former of these two traditions of allegory. But it is important to note

---

[1] De Sacrif. Abelis et Caini 59 f. In 62 and 86 Philo similarly treats the word as it occurs in Ex. 12.39 and Num. 11.8.

[2] De Somniis I. 77. Cf. his allegorization, involving the meaning 'double', of the LXX word δίδυμοι in Deut. 25.11 f., a meaning quite absent from the original Hebrew word, De Spec. Leg. III. 179.

[3] De Leg. Alleg. I. 25–27.

[4] De Leg. Alleg. III.49 is only one example among many.

[5] De Agric. 88.   [6] De Leg. Alleg. I.80.   [7] De Leg. Alleg. III.212.

[8] De Sacrif. Abelis et Caini 69.

[9] De Post. Caini 175 f.

[10] De Mutatione Nominum 104.

[11] De Somniis II.43 ff. But in De Josepho 149 f. he seems to take the awards made to Joseph by Pharaoh as good and honourable.

that the *results* of Philo's allegory are quite different from the results of either of these two traditions. The psychological, moral or philosophical truths which he extracts from Scripture by the use of allegory are easily distinguishable from the sort of doctrine which the other two traditions derive by the use of allegory, and the two types of doctrine have little or nothing in common. The great difference between Philo and Jewish allegorizers of other traditions is, as has already been mentioned, that Philo exhibits no typology whatever. He does indeed say that Abraham is a type (χανών) for good proselytes,[1] and speaks of Moses as a type (χανών) for rulers,[2] and would no doubt have agreed that other Old Testament characters, such as Joseph, were similarly types or paradigms of particular virtues. But this is obviously not typology in the sense in which the word has hitherto been used in this work; there is no question in those types of interpreting an event of the present or recent past as fulfilling a similar situation recorded or prophesied in Scripture.[3] Philo is little interested in Messianic expectation and not at all in eschatology. He is not even much interested in historical events, for his attitude to history is ambiguous.

[margin: Biblical characters as types of paradigms of virtue]

It is obvious that there are many narratives and incidents in the Old Testament which Philo takes as historical, even though he only reluctantly concedes their historicity or regards the allegorical meaning of the events as more important than their actual occurrence.[4] In his account of the births of Ishmael and of Isaac, for instance, he takes careful notice of the literal details of the biblical narrative and does his best to reconcile apparent inconsistencies,[5] and he reluctantly agrees that Samuel did have an historical existence: 'Samuel was indeed perhaps a human being, but he is set before us not as a composite being (sc. of body and soul) but as mind which rejoices in the worship and service of God alone.'[6] On the subject of the Tower of Babel he is equivocal. In one of his works[7] he begins by saying that the narrative of the happenings at Babel is attacked on two grounds: first that it is a legend because the story has obvious parallels in Greek myths; secondly because confusion of tongues did not succeed in curing the sin of the peoples—quite the contrary. Philo's reply to these accusations is that you must not take the superficial interpretation, but you must allegorize the story. Later

[margin: describing to others some human beings God-like characters Tion]

---

[1]*De Virt.* 219.   [2]*Ibid.,* 70.
[3]For a very useful note on 'type' in Philo see Woollcombe, *Essays on Typology,* pp. 60–63.
[4]On this subject see Kennedy, *Philo's Contribution to Religion,* pp. 32–6, 39.
[5]*De Sobrietate* 6–9.
[6]*De Ebrietate* 144; cf. *De Somniis* I.254.
[7]*De Confusione* 1–15.

[margin annotations: "shadow", "literal meanings. shadows of the real substance", "literal(ism)", "Abraham", "Terah the personification of the principle of self-knowledge"]

in the same work, however (190) he tells us that some people, who follow only the surface meaning, think that this narrative does no more than give the origin of the Greek and barbarian languages. 'I would not blame such people, for perhaps they too are using a true argument,' he says. But he would exhort them to use allegory also, for 'the literal meanings of the oracles are as shadows of the real substances'. This is, indeed, to acknowledge the historicity of the incidents, but at the same time to disclaim any significance for that historicity. The same suggestion that the event happened historically but is only significant for its allegorical meaning is found in his remark on Terah leaving Chaldaea and migrating to Haran: this was related, he says, 'not that we might learn, as we might from an historical writer, that some people became emigrants, left their ancestral land and inhabited another as if it was their native country, but for the sake of a most profitable doctrine and the sort of one which a man should not ignore'.[1] Later in the passage he compares Terah to Socrates, but he immediately adds, 'but Socrates was a human being, whereas Terah was the personification of the principle of self-knowledge set before us'[2]—a phrase which almost suggests to us that he did not think of Terah as an historical person at all.

On other occasions he will extol both literal and allegorical meaning together. He remarks of the narrative of Jacob at Bethel (Gen. 28), 'Our admiration is extorted, not only by the lawgiver's allegorical and philosophical teaching, but by the way in which the literal narrative inculcates the practice of toil and endurance.'[3] In his book on the subject of Abraham this comes out particularly clearly. After describing Abraham's migration from Chaldaea, he says: 'The migrations set forth by the literal text of the Scriptures are made by a man of wisdom, but according to the laws of allegory by a virtue-loving soul in its search for the true God.'[4] Later he explains that 'I have employed both interpretations, the literal as applicable to man and the allegorical as applicable to the soul, and have shown both the man and the intellectual interpretation to be worth investigating'.[5] This is the way in which in this book he treats all the incidents connected with Abraham and the other patriarchs; first he describes the literal story at length, drawing edifying lessons from it, and then he allegorizes it.[6] In his lives of Joseph and of Moses, which are clearly intended mainly for non-Jews and are among

---

[1] *De Somniis* I.52; cf. *De Sobrietate* 33.
[2] αὐτὸς ὁ λόγος ὁ περὶ τοῦ γνῶναί τινα ἑαυτὸν προκείμενος.
[3] *De Somniis* I.120.   [4] *De Abrahamo* 68.   [5] *Ibid.*, 88.
[6] Cf. *ibid.*, 114–244.

the most readable of Philo's works, he pays particular attention to
the literal sense. Indeed in his account of the plagues of Egypt and
the destruction of the Egyptians he almost entirely eschews allegory.[1]

But against such instances as these where Philo concedes to the
literal meaning a value, whether he does so freely or reluctantly, can be
cited many more where he rejects or derides the literal meaning. This is
particularly evident in his treatment of what we would now call the
'myths' of Genesis, the stories of the creation and fall. Moses writes that
God made the world in six days, Philo tells us, not because God had
need of time (it is more likely that he made everything in one act), but
'because the things which were created needed order'.[2] The making of
woman from man's rib is, in Philo's view, too irrational to be literally
true: 'the literal meaning in this passage is legendary;' it must be allegorized.[3] And the statement in Gen. 2.8 that God placed in Eden the
man whom he had made is interpreted by Philo entirely psychologically,
to the effect that 'trainings in and exercises of the virtues belong to
rational beings only'.[4] Similarly he thinks that the tree of life and of the
knowledge of good and evil is not intended to be taken literally, but is
designed for allegory.[5] In dealing with the serpent which tempted Eve
(which he identifies with the serpent of Gen. 49.17) he says that taken
literally these things are 'like bogies and monsters', but 'in the allegorical
interpretation the legendary part disappears altogether.'[6]

But these stories, which we ourselves might today call 'myths', are
not the only narratives in the Old Testament whose historical truth
Philo rejects. A long list of incidents whose historicity he cannot accept
can be compiled: the slaying of Er related in Gen. 38.7;[7] Jacob's sending
of Joseph to find his brethren;[8] the command to the host of Israel to
reduce its numbers before battle;[9] the massacre of three thousand men

---

[1] Cf. *De Josepho* 5–27; *De Vita Mosis* I.96–190.
[2] *De Opificio Mundi* 13; *De Leg. Alleg.* I.2; cf. Aristobulus' fragment in Eus.
PE XIII. 12.9–12 (667A–C), by which Philo was doubtless influenced, and
Origen, *Comm. on Gen.* fragment, *PG* 12.97, which is certainly influenced by
Philo's passage.
[3] *De Leg. Alleg.* II.19.
[4] *De Plantatione* 41 f.
[5] *De Opificio* 154; cf. *De Plantatione* 32–9.
[6] *De Agric.* 96 f. On the other hand, in *De Virt.* 37 a reference to Adam seems
to regard him as an historical figure; cf. Bonsirven, *Judaisme* I, p. 261.
[7] *De Leg. Alleg.* III.69.
[8] *Quod Deterius* 13–15: Jacob could not have sent his son on such an errand
because he was a rich king and had plenty of servants to send.
[9] *De Agric.* 146–58: the command could not be intended literally, because it
would be incongruous and impracticable.

by the Levites at Moses' command;[1] the flood, which is simply the letting loose of a flood of sin;[2] the story of Hamor, Shechem and Dinah;[3] the intercourse of Abraham and Hagar and the genealogy of the sons of Nahor;[4] the destruction of Sodom;[5] the turning of Lot's wife into a pillar of salt;[6] the promise to Abraham that his descendants would rule 'from the river of Egypt to the great river Euphrates;[7] the sevenfold vengeance vowed upon the slayer of Cain;[8] and the phrase addressed to Abraham (Gen. 15.15), 'thou shalt go to thy fathers'.[9] In view of this evidence we may feel that the conclusion that Philo has only enough sense of history to preserve the bare essentials of God's acts in history[10] is conceding too much. Philo has virtually no sense of history.

Philo's love of allegory has of course its effect upon his attitude to the Torah. In his *De Migratione Abrahami* he explains himself. The Law, he says, is only an outward symbol of intellectual things; circumcision, for instance, is an outward symbol of the duty of excising passion from our lives. But this does not mean that we should not keep the Law. Just as we must look after the body because it is the house of the soul, so we should keep the Law, as the outward embodiment of its inner meaning.[11] To this principle he adheres fairly consistently throughout his works, emphasizing strongly the allegorical meaning of each commandment, but seldom actually declaring that the commandment was not intended to be kept literally. He allegorizes the commandment that the Nazirite should not touch a corpse (Num. 6.6) to mean that he must not let an evil thought defile his mind,[12] and indeed he treats similarly almost every ordinance which he has to deal with in his three books called *The Allegorizing of the Laws*. On the other hand, in his three books of *The Special Laws* he usually does not allegorize the laws he here so

---

[1]*De Ebrietate* 69: 'The priests do not of course, as some people think, kill human beings, rational animals composed of body and soul, but they cut off everything which is proper and welcoming to the flesh from their own minds.' We shall find Origen using precisely this interpretation later; see below, p. 266.

[2]*De Confusione* 23–5.   [3]*De Mig. Abrahami* 223–5.

[4]*De Congressu* 12, 43 ff.

[5]*Ibid.*, 109: 'when apparently the land of Sodom was doomed to be burnt, but in fact the soul which is destitute of good and blind in its rational faculty.'

[6]*De Fug. et Invent.* 121: when Moses was recounting this incident he was οὐ μυθοπλαστῶν, ἀλλὰ πραγμάτων ἰδιότητα μηνύων, which does not mean that it is literally true, but that Philo's *allegory* of it indicates precisely a real fact.

[7]*De Somniis* II.255; this does not mean an extent of country but the better part of ourselves.

[8]*Quod Deterius* 167; Philo cannot make sense of the Greek version and so assumes that the passage must be allegorized.

[9]*Quis Rer. Div. Heres* 277 ff.; Abraham had deliberately left the home of his fathers, so the phrase must be allegorized.

[10]C. Montdesert, *Clement d'Alexandrie*, p. 170.

[11]*De Mig. Abrahami* 93.   [12]*De Leg. Alleg.* I.17.

fully surveys, or does so only occasionally and in a separate section, but rather rationalizes their literal sense. Still even here we do sometimes find allegory, and in one case, that of the woman who grasps the genitals of her husband's adversary in a fight (Deut. 25.11 f.), he explicitly suggests that the penalty—that the woman's hand shall be cut off—is not to be taken literally.[1] The distinction between the animals who chew the cud and who part the hoof, which we have already seen occupying the attention of Pseudo-Aristeas,[2] causes Philo to say that he does not know how its literal meaning can be defended, so clearly does it call for allegory.[3] He is similarly baffled by the regulations in the Law about the disposal of the intestines of the animal sacrificed; he says that if intellectual people examining the passage 'find a more convincing reason, they will benefit themselves' and him. But he can see no alternative to allegorization.[4]

Philo's use of allegory, then, marks him and the tradition in which he stands as taking an attitude to the Old Testament Scriptures in several important points quite distinct from that of Palestinian Judaism. Philo used allegory not only to emancipate himself from the literal meaning of the text, but also from its relation to history, and also to some extent from the obligation to observe the Jewish Torah in full.[5] We know of almost no direct successors to Philo; with him, as far as we know, the line of Alexandrian Jewish thought ended. Pharisaic Judaism took over the direction of Jewish thought after the fall of Jerusalem, and in its schools a speculative, Hellenistic Judaism was impossible. The heirs of Philo's system—in its own way a noble and admirable system—were the theologians of the Christian Church.

We should perhaps make an exception to this last statement to allow for the case of Josephus. He does not have occasion during his works to refer to allegory often, but it is evident that he did believe in allegorizing the Scriptures in an Alexandrian or Hellenistic way, as one would expect of an Hellenized Jew who was acquainted with Alexandria and knew of Philo and respected him. At one point in his *Antiquities* he expatiates upon the virtues of Moses as a lawgiver. Other lawgivers, he

---

[1] *De Spec. Leg.* III.179. We have met already another such instance in *De Agric.* 146–58, where the command of Deut. 20.5–7 is regarded as not intended literally.
[2] See above, p. 44. The *Epistle of Barnabas* deals with this too.
[3] *De Agric.* 131.   [4] *De Spec. Leg.* I.214.
[5] I cannot, however, agree with Woollcombe (*Essays on Typology*, p. 54), when he distinguishes Rabbinic allegory from Alexandrian by the fact that the Rabbis 'used the actual text'. Philo was almost superstitiously anxious to preserve the actual text.

shameful mistakes of lawgivers

says, relied upon legends and made shameful mistakes. But Moses 'in some passages produced elegant riddles, in others profound allegories, but whatever required to be spoken plainly that he declared literally'.[1] In another passage he says that he believes that Moses 'engaged deeply in natural philosophy',[2] and in another that those who want to know the cause of each point in Moses' work would find that 'the investigation is deep and very philosophical'.[3] Later still in this work Josephus gives an explanation of the significance of the array of the tabernacle and of the High Priest, in which each detail is taken to symbolize some point of natural science.[4] Each point is there 'as an imitation and representation of the universe' (εἰς ἀπομίμησιν καὶ διατύπωσιν τῶν ὅλων, 180). The part of the tabernacle open to all represents the earth and sea, the part reserved for God only the heavens (181). The twelve loaves of the shewbread represent the twelve months of the year (182). Other details are taken to represent the four elements (183), the pole, lightnings and thunders, the sun's rays (184), the ocean, the sun, the moon (185), and the stars of the zodiac (186). It is interesting to find a third author of the Alexandrian tradition besides Philo and the author of the Epistle to the Hebrews interpreting this passage of Scripture. Philo's allegorization (of which Josephus is probably independent) is mainly concerned with natural science, but also introduces philosophy and psychology (*De Vita Mosis* II. 71–135). The author to the Hebrews evidently intends to resolve the details of the passage into a realized Christian eschatology very different from Philo's ideas.[5] But Josephus reads into it the sort of material that we might expect to meet in Heracleitus' allegories of Homer. One conclusion which might be drawn from this interesting variation is that there were more schools of thought than Philo's to be encountered in the Alexandrian tradition, and that we need not therefore assume the dependence of the author to the Hebrews on him.

We have seen that Aristobulus and Philo claim that in allegorizing they are imitating the people whom they call 'natural philosophers' (οἱ φυσικοί) and we have been from time to time during this survey

---

[1]*Antiquities* I.22, p. 7; 24, p. 7: τὰ μὲν αἰνιττομένου τοῦ νομοθέτου δεξιῶς, τὰ δ' ἀλληγοροῦντος μετὰ σεμνότητος, ὅσα δ' ἐξ εὐθείας λέγεσθαι συνέφερε, ταῦτα ῥητῶς ἐμφανίζοντος.
[2]*Ibid.*, I.18, p. 6: ἐπὶ τοσοῦτον φυσιολογίας κεκοινώνηκεν.
[3]*Ibid.*, I.25, p. 7: πολλὴ ἡ θεωρία καὶ λίαν φιλόσοφος. It is interesting to note that H. N. Bate ('Some Technical Terms of Greek Exegesis', *JTS* XXIV, p. 69) says that in the Christian Platonists of Alexandria θεωρία is almost equivalent to ἀλληγορία.
[4]*Ibid.*, III.179–87, pp. 172–4.
[5]See below, pp. 89 f.

aware that there did exist an Hellenistic tradition of allegorizing, distinct from both the Jewish Palestinian and the Alexandrian traditions. That this Hellenistic tradition exercised an important influence upon the thought of the ancient world is evident. Porphyry, indeed, the philosophical enemy of Christianity who flourished during the second half of the third century, attributes all Origen's allegorizing to an unwarrantable plagiarism of Hellenistic allegory. 'Having learnt from these [i.e. the Greek philosophers] the figurative interpretation used in the mystery religions of the Greeks, he applied it to the Jewish Scriptures.'[1] E. de Faye agrees with Porphyry,[2] and G. L. Prestige supports him.[3] We must therefore examine, even though briefly, this tradition of allegorizing.

It is a surprising fact that though the practice of allegorizing an authoritative text had begun at least three hundred years before Philo's day and probably much earlier, his writings are the first extensive example of it that we possess, and the chief non-Jewish examples of allegorizing that have survived are either contemporary with Philo (Heracleitus) or later than his day (Plutarch and Porphyry). In spite of this state of affairs, nobody would today attempt to argue that Hellenistic allegory was an imitation of Alexandrian allegory,[4] and we can in fact recover a few traces of the long tradition of Hellenistic allegory that had existed before Philo's day. Porphyry (on *Iliad* XX.67) alleged that Theagenes of Rhegium, a grammarian who flourished about 529–522 B.C., was the first to allegorize Homer. But J. Tate[5] thinks that Pherecydes of Scyros (about 600 B.C.) allegorized earlier than he. Hermias, the Christian apologist who so amusingly caricatures the opinions of the ancient philosophers, says that Pherecydes maintained that Zeus was the air, Chthonia the earth and Kronos time.[6] In *Contra Celsum* VI.42, Origen says that Celsus procured from Pherecydes his opinion that the words of Zeus to Hera (*Iliad* XV.18) are the words of God to matter. Tate suggests that the earliest philosophers having expressed their philosophical opinions in mythical form, it then followed that the mythical

---

[1] Quoted in Eus. *HE* VI.19.8.
[2] E. de Faye, *Origène, sa Vie, son Œuvre, sa Pensée*, pp. 85–95; these pages are a good account of Hellenistic allegory, though, as will be seen, I cannot agree with all the conclusions drawn in them.
[3] G. L. Prestige, *Fathers and Heretics*, pp. 56 f.
[4] For information on this subject see J. Tate, 'The Beginnings of Greek Allegory', *CR* XLI, pp. 214 f.; 'Plato and Allegorical Interpretation', *CQ* XXIII, pp. 142 ff. and XXIV, 1 ff.; W. B. Stanford, *The Ulysses Theme*, pp. 36 f., 121, 125–7.
[5] 'The Beginnings of Greek Allegory', pp. 214 f.
[6] Hermias, *Irrisio Gentilium Philosophorum* 12, p. 654.

language of Homer and Hesiod might contain philosophical opinions.
The great century of allegorical interpretation, however, was the
fifth before Christ. Anaxagoras declared that the subject of Homer's
poetry was 'virtue and justice'. His disciple Metrodorus of Lampsacus
developed this theme to an extreme and read subjects of natural philosophy into Homer; indeed he allegorized away the very existence of
Homer's gods and goddesses. He said that Agamemnon was the *aither*,
Achilles the sun, Helen the earth, Paris the air, Demeter the liver,
Dionysus the spleen, and Apollo the gall. Democritus of Abdera was
one of the first to use etymologies in allegorizing, a practice discussed
and rejected by Plato in the *Cratylus*, but taken up later vigorously by
the Stoics. 'It is at all events clear,' says Tate, 'that the practice had
become exceedingly common before Plato had begun to write.'[1] The
word used by Plato and everybody else for about two centuries after his
day for allegory was ὑπόνοια, which Tate admirably translates 'undersense'.[2]

It has been generally assumed that the use of allegory by the Stoic
philosophers who flourished during the fourth and third centuries
before Christ was employed in order to vindicate Homer from the
aspersions cast upon him by Plato. Tate disputes this view and believes
that these philosophers allegorized Homer because they thereby found
support for their theories in an authoritative body of writings which
were at the time widely regarded as almost infallible, without feeling
themselves under any particular necessity of defending Homer.[3] However that may be, there is no doubt that these Stoic philosophers did
allegorize Homer, in order to derive Stoic philosophy from his text.
Indeed Stanford says that 'through their ingenious use of allegorical
interpretation, the Odyssey became a kind of Pilgrim's Progress'.[4] One
example of this, Cleanthes' treatment of the word *moly*, we have seen
already.[5] It is difficult to glean much more information from the scanty
references in antiquity to this subject. But Cornutus, a philosophical
writer of a *De Natura Deorum* and an *Ars Rhetorica* of the first century
after Christ, tells us that Cleanthes referred the twelve labours of Her-
cules to God, that is to say that he interpreted them as giving us information about the nature of God, and that as Cleanthes did not believe
in the existence of any God except the Stoic deity he consequently pro-

---

[1]'Plato and Allegorical, Interpretation', *CQ* XXIII, pp. 142 f.
[2]*Ibid.*, p. 145.
[3]See Tate's two articles referred to above, *passim*.
[4]*The Ulysses Theme*, p. 121.
[5]See above, p. 37.

duced allegorical etymologies of all the other gods mentioned in Homer except Zeus to show that they were originally something else than gods.[1] The Demetrius who wrote the book *On Style*, though he wrote perhaps as much as three centuries after Cleanthes, gives us an interesting example of allegorization of Homer which may date from a much earlier period. Demetrius has no particular philosophical axe to grind, and he gives it only in order to illustrate a point in his discourse about style in rhetoric. Supplications, he says, are always long-drawn-out and slow, and this is what Homer meant when he wrote the lines (*Iliad* IX.502):

'Supplications are of course the daughters of mighty Zeus;
They are lame and shrivelled and squinting in their eyes.'[2]

Cornutus himself seems to have revived an 'etymological' method of allegorizing Homer in the first century, in imitation of the Stoic allegorists of some centuries earlier.[3]

Roughly contemporary with him was Heracleitus, whose work, the *Quaestiones Homericae*, survives and enables us to obtain the first, and almost the only, extended view of Hellenistic allegorizing of Homer.[4] We have already had occasion to note his admirably careful definition of allegory.[5] He illustrates this definition by referring to Archilochus' famous figure of the Ship of State.[6] It is obvious that he is influenced by the practice of contemporary mystery-religions, for he tries to justify his allegorizing by reference to 'the mysterious principles which form the religious instruction on the secret rites'.[7] As he develops his method of allegorizing the text of Homer it becomes obvious that he is transforming the poem, if not into a highly metaphorical chat about the

---

[1] *The Fragments of Zeno and Cleanthes*, frag. 62, p. 291; cf. frag. 54, p. 286.
[2] Demetrius *On Style* 7 (p. 70). The Homeric lines run thus:
καὶ γάρ τε Λιταί εἰσι Διὸς κοῦραι μεγάλοιο,
χωλαί τε ῥυσαί τε παραβλῶπες τ' ὀφθαλμώ.
The editor, Rhys Roberts, suggests that this sentence may be an interpolation because of its abruptness, but is far from confident about this opinion, which seems to me to be an unjustified one.
[3] See Tate, 'Plato and Allegorical Interpretation', *CQ* XXIV, p. 2.
[4] Heracleitus is otherwise unknown. The latest author cited by him is Alexander of Ephesus, so he is usually placed in the Augustan or Neronic period; he probably represents the close contact that prevailed in the first century B.C. between the scholarship of Alexandria and of Pergamum. See Pauly-Wissowa, *Real-Encyclopädie der Altertumswissenschaft* II, pp. 508–10, article 'Heracleitus' by Reinhardt. Büchsel (ἀλληγορέω, *TWNT* I, p. 260) also mentions the allegorizing of the Pergamene school.
[5] See above, p. 38 f.
[6] *Quaestiones Homericae* 5, p. 6. The reference is to Archilochus' poem beginning: Γλαῦκ' ὅρα, βαθὺς γὰρ ἤδη κύμασιν ταράσσεται πόντος.
[7] *Ibid.*, 6, p. 10: ἐκ τε τῶν μυστικῶν λόγων οὓς αἱ ἀπόρρητοι τελεταὶ θεολογοῦσιν.

weather, at least into a rationalistically conceived scientific and historical account of the siege of Troy. References to Apollo are interpreted as in reality a description of the epidemic that befell the Greek troops; the arrows shot by the god and the references to Hera fit into the design of describing a summer pestilence, and so on. His object is apparently to explain away anything that is theologically shocking.[1] 'We have demonstrated,' he says, 'that this first example of allegory is not a description of the futile wrath of Apollo in a fit of temper, but a scientific account based on the observation of nature.'[2] It is obvious that he is motivated in explaining away awkward passages by a desire to defend Homer against his detractors, among whom he mentions Zoilus of Amphipolis and Plato.[3]

He allegorizes the embarrassing passages of the poet into either psychological or scientific statements. The account in the *Iliad* of Athene restraining Achilles by pulling his hair is really a psychological account of the state of Achilles' mind.[4] The story of how the gods plotted to bind Zeus is, taken literally, inexpressibly shocking: 'There is one remedy for this irreverence, if we can show that the story is an allegory.' And so the next few passages are devoted to explaining that the incident is really an account of the interaction of air and water.[5] A reference to Dionysus in the *Iliad* is allegorized into some agricultural instruction and a poetical expression into an astronomical lesson.[6] 'Homer is therefore,' he says, 'a painter as it were of human experiences as he clothes allegorically our experience with the names of gods';[7] and after a vast deal of allegorizing of the designs on Achilles' shield, mainly in an astronomical sense, he produces this sentiment which may strike us as remarkably like many of Origen's utterances: 'If anyone will take the trouble to penetrate further into the Homeric mysteries and gaze upon his supernatural wisdom (ἐποπτεῦσαι τὴν μυστικὴν αὐτοῦ σοφίαν) he will realize how profound a philosophy is contained in the apparent irreverence.'[8] The use of the language of the mystery-religious to describe the results of allegorizing Homer is significant, and we cannot help finding a very familiar ring in it. With Moses substituted for Homer, this sentence could have come straight from the pen of Philo or of Clement of Alexandria or of Origen. Finally Heracleitus

[1] *Quaestiones Homericae* 6–15, pp. 10–24.
[2] *Ibid.*, 16 f., p. 25: φυσικῆς θεωρίας φιλοσοφοῦσαν ἔννοιαν.
[3] *Ibid.*, 14, p. 22. But he can also cite Plato's myth of the charioteer (*Timaeus* 90A) in order to support his resort to allegory, 17, pp. 26 f.
[4] *Ibid.*, 17, pp. 26 f.
[5] *Ibid.*, 21 f., pp. 31 f.
[6] *Ibid.*, 35 f., pp. 51–3.
[7] *Ibid.*, 37, p. 53.
[8] *Ibid.*, 53, p. 75.

devotes the last quarter of his work to allegorizing the Odyssey. The whole wandering of Odysseus is an allegory, describing the ills into which man's life can fall, for Odysseus is only 'the self-expression of every virtue'.[1]

It looks, then, as if Heracleitus, however his contemporary Cornutus may have used allegory, himself employed it with a definitely apologetic purpose, in order to defend Homer against his detractors, and that he was encouraged in this course by the practice of the mystery-religions of his day, which in some way gave him authority for allegorizing. We can find the same tendency in Philo.[2] It is congruous with this that what we know of the Hellenistic allegorizers of the next century suggests that they were more interested in allegorizing contemporary religious customs and traditions than in allegorizing Homer. Maximus of Tyre, though he did not exactly allegorize popular religion, spiritualized it; he held that poets are only philosophers expressing their message in myths, and that it would be a mistake to take the narratives of poets literally.[3] Numenius the Pythagorean is referred to by Origen as allegorizing the sayings of the prophets.[4] Some passages of Numenius are preserved in Eusebius.[5] They do not indeed give us an example of Numenius allegorizing the prophets, but one of them says that the most reputable of the nations have customs and beliefs whose principles are manifestly in agreement with Plato,[6] and he instances the Brahmins, the Jews, the Magi and the Egyptians. He is obviously attempting to elaborate a syncretistic religion with a Platonic basis. But another passage does give us the remarkable statement, 'What is Plato but Moses writing Attic Greek?'[7] It is difficult to see how he could have reached this extraordinary conclusion unless he had allegorized the Pentateuch.

Celsus, the anti-Christian author who wrote his book *A True Account* about the year 170, indulged in allegory. Origen in his *Contra Celsum* on

[1]*Quaestiones Homericae* 70, p. 91: πάσης ἀρετῆς καθάπερ ὄργανον.
[2]For Philo's use of the language of the mystery-religions, see *Origen's Doctrine of Tradition*, pp. 54 f.
[3]For Maximus of Tyre, see de Faye, *Origène*, II, ch. XI, pp. 157–64; Daniélou, *Origène*, p. 104.
[4]*Contra Celsum* I.15; cf. IV.51; V.58. He was probably a contemporary of Marcus Aurelius. See H. Chadwick, *Origen, Contra Celsum*, p. 17. I cannot see what support Chadwick has for saying that the passage of Numenius preserved in Eusebius is probably the one referred to in *Contra Celsum* I.15. See also R. Cadiou, *La Jeunesse d'Origène*, pp. 172 f.
[5]Eus.*PE* IX 7 f. (411CD).
[6]IX.7 (411C): τὰς δὲ ἱδρύσεις συντελουμένας Πλάτωνι ὁμολογουμένως.
[7]IX.6.9 (411A): τί γάρ ἐστι Πλάτων ἢ Μωσῆς ἀττικίζων; The epigram is quoted earlier by Clement of Alexandria, *Strom.* I.22.150, *PG* 8.893.

two occasions describes Celsus as allegorizing,[1] and on the second occasion gives quite a long quotation from Celsus' book. Celsus is allegorizing the embarrassing passage in *Iliad* XV.18–24 in which Zeus describes how he punished Hera and Hephaestus; Zeus is God and Hera is matter and the whole affair is an account of God ordering chaos.[2] Celsus mentions Heracleitus and Pherecydes as interpreting Homer in this way, and he goes on to allegorize the robe of Athene which was carried ceremoniously in the annual procession of the Panathenaea at Athens, and attributes this opinion to Pherecydes. In this same work Origen makes several references to the contemporary custom of allegorizing Hesiod, the legends of Egyptian religion,[3] the stories about Dionysius current in the Dionysiac mysteries,[4] and the Greek myths;[5] though he obviously does not think that these legends deserve allegorizing, he will use them to justify his own allegorizing of biblical stories. It is probably this sort of interpretation that Josephus alludes to so contemptuously when he speaks of 'the futile devices of allegories'.[6]

The great exponent of allegorizing contemporary religion in the second half of the second century, and the chief source of information on it, is Plutarch, and in particular his interpretation of the cult and legends connected with Isis and Osiris.[7] We have already seen that in this work he rejects what he calls allegorizing[8] as the correct way of dealing with cult and legend. It is pretty clear that what he means is that he would disallow the type of allegorizing which Aristobulus, Pseudo-Aristeas, Philo and Josephus call 'physical' allegorizing,[9] the turning of the material to be allegorized into what we could call a scientific treatise dealing with the sea, the air, fire, the planets and so on. He rejects with equal indignation the books of Euhemerus, who had his own way of accounting for the traditional gods; Plutarch describes these as 'volumes of incredible and unreal legend'.[10] He prefers to interpret the customs and observances of the priests of Isis and of Egypt generally in a moralistic manner reminiscent of Pseudo-Aristeas.[11] 'Plutarch,' says Tate,

---

[1] III.43 and VI.42. See above, p. 55.
[2] Chrysippus is alluded to in *Contra Celsum* IV.48 as making the same identification of Zeus and Hera.
[3] IV.38.   [4] III.23; IV.17.   [5] V.29; VIII.66–8.
[6] *Contra Apionem* II.255 (p. 283). See above, p. 39.
[7] For another account of this work see de Faye, *Origène*, II. ch. VIII, pp. 115–22.
[8] See above, p. 39.
[9] See above, pp. 40, 42 f., 54.
[10] *De Is. et Os.* 23, 360A.
[11] E.g. *ibid.*, 3–7, 352B–3D. He has a liking for etymological interpretations, e.g. 3, 352B; 10, 355A; 14, 356DE; 29, 362B (where he first rejects an etymology by a certain Phylarchus), *et passim*.

'rejects the allegorical interpretation of poetry, but is anxious that the right morals should be derived from the myths.'[1] But Tate is inaccurate when he goes on to say that he concentrated on types (τύποι in the Philonic sense of exemplary characters) and rejected the undersenses (ὑπόνοιαι). Plutarch, as we have already seen, uses undersenses quite freely.[2] It would be more correct to say that Plutarch accepts an undersense but rejects an allegory, meaning by the latter word an interpretation into some 'physical' statement dealing with phenomena which we would now describe as fit for scientific investigation. He himself prefers to produce an undersense which is in fact a philosophical rather than a strictly scientific statement. When he has rejected the allegorical interpretation of 'the simplest sort' of people in their attempt to explain the gods Osiris, Isis and Typhon, he gives his own interpretation: Osiris is 'the principle and power of moistness, substance causative of birth and seed'; Typhon is 'everything which is dry and fiery and generally parching and contrary to moistness', and so on.[3]

His attitude to the literal meaning of the legends is uncompromising. They cannot be literally true. In the worship of Isis there is 'nothing irrational nor legendary nor caused by superstition'.[4] 'But when you hear the stories which the Egyptians tell about the gods, about wanderings and dismemberings and many other such experiences, you must remember what has been said above, and not imagine that any one of these things were done in the way in which it is described as occurring.'[5] And when he has related at great length the extremely legendary story of Isis and Osiris, he describes it as 'feeble legends and futile inventions' in its literal sense, and says that the reader will naturally assume that these legends are not to be taken literally.[6] In one place he distinguishes between the two meanings of an Egyptian custom whereby the people eat fish on a particular day while the priests abstain from it. One meaning is 'sacred and additional', the other 'obvious and superficial'.[7] But he does not use the word 'legend' (μῦθος) in a wholly pejorative sense, as all the Christian Fathers do with one consent. 'So the legend in this case,' he says, writing of the story of Isis and Osiris, 'is an indication of

---

[1] 'Plato and Allegorical Interpretations', *CQ* XXIV, p. 7 n. 4.
[2] See above, p. 39, on *De Is. et Os.* 27, 361E, and 32, 363D.
[3] *Ibid.*, 32 f., 363D–64A.
[4] *Ibid.*, 8, 353E: οὐδὲν ἄλογον οὐδὲ μυθῶδες οὐδ᾽ ὑπὸ δεισιδαιμονίας.
[5] *Ibid.*, 11, 355B.
[6] *Ibid.*, 20, 358EF; the phrase quoted is μυθεύμασιν ἀραίοις καὶ διακένοις πλάσμασιν.
[7] *Ibid.*, 7, 353D; the phrases are δύο λόγους . . , τὸν μὲν ἱερὸν καὶ περιττόν . . . ὁ δὲ ἐμφάνης καὶ πρόχειρος.

a lesson which reflects a meaning referring to something else.'[1] He describes his rationalizing of these folk-legends as 'the lesson attached to the legend',[2] and elsewhere says that 'we must use legends not as a straightforward account,[3] but accept that which is useful in each according to whether it is likely' (κατὰ τὴν ὁμοιότητα).

The history of allegorical interpretation of Homer and of contemporary religious traditions does not end with Plutarch, but for the purposes of our survey we need not follow it further. The practice began with the attempt of the philosophers of the fifth century B.C. to turn the myths of Homer and Hesiod into philosophy. It was eagerly adopted, in spite of Plato's discouragement, by the Stoics of the fourth and third centuries before Christ, who saw in it a means of gaining the support of authoritative Scripture for their systems. In the first century B.C. and the first A.D. allegory seems particularly to have been used by those who were known as 'the physicists' (οἱ φυσικοί), and in particular by Heracleitus, who used this device of transmuting poetry into scientific statements in order to vindicate Homer from his detractors. In the second century A.D. allegory was described, as far as we can discover, indifferently as either 'undersense' or 'allegory', in spite of Plutarch's attempt to confine the latter term to the discovery of 'physical' facts in the traditional material. It was by then being extensively used to defend traditional religion against rationalistic attacks, and perhaps in the latter part of the century against specifically Christian attacks, upon it. By the third century at latest it had become almost part of the intellectual atmosphere in which educated men moved, in a position perhaps comparable to that held by the theory of evolution in our day.

This Hellenistic allegory was characterized by being entirely unhistorical; it took no account at all of the historical situation, and very little of the original meaning, of the material allegorized. It was not only arbitrary; it required no sense of history at all; the results of its allegorization were general statements of a philosophical or psychological or scientific nature. What we have called typology was wholly unknown to it.

In spite of the remarkable historical accident that the first extensive examples of this allegory are found, not in Hellenistic, but in Jewish writers, Aristobulus, Pseudo-Aristeas and Philo, it is clear that we must conclude that Alexandrian allegory was derived from Hellenistic. Per-

---

[1] De Is. et Os. 21, 359A: οὕτως ὁ μῦθος ἐνταῦθα λόγου τινος ἔμφασίς ἐστιν ἀνακλῶντος ἐπ᾽ ἄλλα τὴν διάνοιαν.
[2] Ibid., 36, 365C: ὁ προστιθέμενος τῷ μύθῳ λόγος.
[3] Ibid., 58, 374E: χρηστέον τοῖς μύθοις οὐχ ὡς λόγοις πάμπαν οὖσιν.

haps it would be more accurate to say that Alexandrian allegory was imitated from and inspired by Hellenistic. Aristobulus, Pseudo-Aristeas, Philo and Josephus all betray by their use of the word 'physical' that this is the source of their inspiration. Josephus, indeed, directly reproduces a 'physical' type of allegory very like that of Heracleitus, or of the people whom Plutarch calls 'the simplest sort'. Pseudo-Aristeas and Philo are not so directly comparable with the Hellenistic allegorizers, partly because of their specifically Jewish concern to allegorize the Torah. Philo is perhaps most like the Stoic allegorizers, or indeed Plutarch himself, because he is determined to extract from the given text his own particular philosophy. But though he is imitating Hellenistic allegory, his imitation is modified by the fact that he is a Jew. He is not uninfluenced by rules of Rabbinic exegesis which he has inherited; he is cautious in his statements about the Torah; and he has a respect for the letter of his text greater even than that which Heracleitus has for his. Indeed, it should be recognized that a comparison of either Alexandrian or Christian allegory with the allegory of writers like Plutarch or Maximus of Tyre or Numenius is severely limited by the fact that the former were allegorizing an authoritative text (as the Stoics and Heracleitus were), whereas the latter were allegorizing a large, loosely connected, not very well defined *corpus* of traditional legends, myths and customs. In such a case the comparison cannot lead us very far, certainly not as far as scholars such as de Faye would have us think.

But Alexandrian allegory has in all its forms one feature in common with Hellenistic allegory; it is unhistorical. It does not use typology. Its ultimate aim is to empty the text of any particular connection with historical events. Even in the matter of allegorizing the Torah we can safely conclude that the Alexandrian allegorists saw no profound significance in its literal meaning, however cautiously they may have expressed their conviction. Philo can see no point in history as history; to him it is simply so much material to be allegorized into philosophy, just as Heracleitus can see no point in the literal meaning of Homer's description of the quarrels of gods and goddesses, and Plutarch discourages belief in the literal meaning of the legends about Isis and Osiris.

We have therefore found sufficient evidence to conclude that Alexandrian allegory was derived from Hellenistic allegory, but none whatever to suggest that Palestinian allegory, the sort of allegory that we considered in the first chapter, was derived from Hellenistic allegory. The two types of allegorical tradition seem quite distinct. The Palestinian is full of typology, closely linked with historical events, unenterprising in its speculation and motivated by either Messianic eschatological expectation or an intense devotion to the Torah. Hellenistic allegory is quite unhistorical, it knows nothing of typology, it is unrestrained in its speculation, where it touches the Torah it is designed to emancipate from a literal observance of it, and it is motivated by a desire to read various types of Greek philosophy into the given text or to remove difficulties which offend philosophy in it. The only reliable piece of evidence that Palestinian allegory is indebted to Hellenistic is that they were contemporary in the same civilization, but this is not a very remarkable coincidence. Hellenistic allegory in fact was born at least three centuries before Palestinian, they belong to two quite different cultural traditions, and we can account for their historical origins quite independently of each other. It would even be an exaggeration to say that the two traditions met in the work of the Jewish writers of Alexandria, for there is no strong evidence that these writers were influenced by Palestinian allegorical tradition. Their lukewarm attitude to the observance of the Torah, to Messianic expectation and to eschatology would anyway be likely to preclude this. Whether these two allegorical traditions, Palestinian and Hellenistic, met in early Christianity, and in particular in the literature of the New Testament, is another matter.

3

Allegory in the New Testament

W E have so far refrained from using one source of information about the origins of Christian allegory, a source which is obviously of the greatest importance, and that is the New Testament itself. It has indeed been frequently claimed that the practice of allegorizing the Scriptures is part of the earliest tradition of the Church. Clement of Alexandria and Origen regard it as part of the Church's rule of faith.[1] De Lubac indeed quotes with approval Newman's sentiment: 'the destiny of the mystical interpretation and that of orthodoxy are bound up together.'[2]

That the writers of the New Testament used typology in interpreting the Hebrew Scriptures is evident from almost every page of their work; it has been the task of a number of recent works of scholarship to elucidate the typological patterns in the minds of the evangelists, or at least in the minds of the scholars themselves.[3] We can in fact go a little further back than the text of the New Testament and find in some cases that a mass of typological material already existed before the New Testament writers used it. The First Epistle of Peter is particularly illuminating for this subject. Of this C. H. Dodd says, 'An already accepted tradition of scriptural interpretation lies behind this Epistle.'[4] P. Lundberg in an interesting study of baptismal typology[5] has endeavoured to explore this previously existing tradition of interpretation. He believes that we can distinguish two sorts of prayer in early baptismal liturgies, the type-prayers for transformation and the paradigm-prayers for deliverance.[6] The main scriptural examples of transforma-

[1]See H. de Lubac, *Histoire et Esprit*, pp. 65 f., and *Origen's Doctrine of Tradition*, pp. 63 f., 82, 101–5.
[2]De Lubac, *op. cit.*, p. 104. Cf. Zöllig, *Die Inspirationslehre des Origines*, pp. 122 f.
[3]See the works of Dr Austin Farrer and the recent volume *Studies in the Gospels* (ed. D. Nineham).
[4]*According to the Scriptures*; he is referring particularly to I Peter 1.22–2.10.
[5]*La Typologie Baptismale dans L'ancienne Église.*
[6]*Ibid.*, pp. 10–63.

A.E.–C

tion used in the type-prayers are the flood, the crossing of the Red Sea, the miracle at Marah, the water struck from the rock, the miracle at Horeb, the stories connected with Elijah, the miracle at Cana, and the baptism of Jesus.[1] Another series of such types of transformation consists of the separation of the earth and sea at the creation, the miracles at Marah, at Horeb, at Cana, the walking of Jesus on the water, the Baptism of Jesus, the curing of Naaman, the healing of the man blind from birth, and the blood and water flowing from Jesus' side.[2] The paradigm-prayers for deliverance derive originally from a Jewish type of prayer which we have already glanced at.[3] The Christian form of these, which Lundberg distinguishes usefully by the name of *exauditi*, begins with some such formula as 'Thou who didst (bring the people over the Red Sea, preserve Daniel from the lions, etc.)', or 'He who (healed the paralytic man, raised from the dead the son of the widow of Nain, etc.)'. They were originally used as a type of prayer over catechumens, designed to conjure out of them the power of the evil spirit, and were only later used as a prayer for blessing the water in baptism. Though they occur in baptismal liturgies they were not originally prayers calling upon the Holy Spirit to bless the water, but derive from Jewish liturgical paradigms of people whose prayer was answered by God. The main Christian examples of *exauditi* are Elijah, Enoch, Mordecai, Judith, Judas Maccabaeus, Elisha, Daniel, the three holy children, Jonah, Susanna and the elders, Lazarus, Jairus' daughter, the paralysed man, the man born blind, the multiplication of the loaves, the miracle at Cana, the stater in the fish's mouth. The Jewish precedents for this sort of prayer use as examples Abraham on Mount Moriah, Israel at the Red Sea, Joshua at Gilgal, Samuel at Mizpah, Elijah on Mount Carmel, Jonah in the belly of the whale, David and Solomon at Jerusalem, Moses saved from Pharaoh, Daniel, and the three holy children.[4]

A parallel to these lists can be found in I *Clement* (9–12, 17, 18). We have already seen similar lists in Hippolytus, in the Clementine Liturgy of the *Apostolic Constitutions*, and in early Christian funerary art.[5] We can indeed add a little to the last item in these sources for early Christian typology by giving the statistics for the occurrence of biblical scenes in

[1] These examples are taken from Greek, Syrian, Coptic, Ethiopian and Armenian liturgies, *La Typologie Baptismale*, p. 19.
[2] These types are provided by the Bobbio Missal, the Gelasian and Gregorian Sacramentaries and the Ambrosian Missal, *ibid*., p. 27.
[3] See above, pp. 15–19.
[4] *Ibid*., pp. 34–6.
[5] See above, pp. 14–19. We shall see further parallels in Origen later.

the art of the catacombs; the scenes, with the number of times they occur are: Moses striking the rock (68); Jonah (57); Daniel in the lions' den (39); Noah and the ark (32); the sacrifice of Isaac (22); the three holy children (17); the raising of Lazarus (53); the feeding of the five thousand or the four thousand (35); the healing of the paralysed man (20); the figure of the Good Shepherd (114). It is noteworthy that the Passion, Resurrection and Ascension appear to be entirely neglected in early Christian art.[1]

It is clear then that there existed in the early Christian Church a corpus, more or less definitely limited, of types taken from the Old Testament and used for illuminating the Christian gospel; this corpus must have been in large part inherited from Jewish liturgical forms, though it would necessarily have been added to and modified to meet the needs of preaching the gospel of the Christian church. Further, Christian typology must have had from the beginning a peculiar character of its own, in that it was a *fulfilled* typology, that is to say, it saw each of the Old Testament types as ultimately no more than prophecies or pointers to the reality which had taken place in the Christian dispensation. Lundberg brings out this point when he discusses that passage in I Peter where the author uses the (doubtless traditional) type of the flood to illuminate Christian Baptism.[2] In this passage, Lundberg points out, Baptism was the *antitype* of the flood, and he contrasts Heb. 9.24, where the statement is made that Christ has not entered a sanctuary made with hands, the *antitype* of the true sanctuary. The two authors are using the word *antitype* in different senses. To the author of Hebrews, '*antitype* means that which is inferior and imperfect in comparison with the type.'[3] But in I Peter, *antitype* cannot have this meaning, because Christian Baptism, which is called the *antitype*, is obviously intended to be the reality and fulfilment. These two uses, Lundberg thinks, betray two different conceptions of typology. The typology of Hebrews, which is ultimately Platonic, 'uses categories of a spatial order and subdivides reality into a sensible world and a world of ideas'; in the Petrine typology 'it is the categories of time which are most important.

[1] This information is taken from R. L. P. Milburn, *Early Christian Interpretations of History*, p. 204 n. 3, who is himself relying upon Wilpert, *Die Malereien der Katacomben Roms* I (Freiburg im Breisgau, 1903).
[2] I Peter 3.19–21, and especially the words ὃ καὶ ὑμᾶς ἀντίτυπον νῦν σώζει βάπτισμα. The passage in Lundberg, *La Typologie Baptismale*, is pp. 110 f.
[3] Lundberg compares *II Clement* 14.3, ἡ γὰρ σάρξ αὕτη ἀντίτυπός ἐστιν τοῦ πνεύματος. But I doubt if this is a satisfactory parallel. See also a long note on this word in J. H. Bernard, *Studia Sacra*, pp. 26–34: he does not distinguish between the use in *II Clement* and that in Hebrews, and is anxious to interpret the use in I Peter 3.21 as identical with that of Hebrews. See below, p. 102.

The past and present are presented as a limited period in which events and persons are examples, determined according to the will of God, which prefigure that which will take place in the future.' And later Lundberg aptly defines the word τυπικῶς ('by way of example') in I Cor. 10.11 thus: 'That which happened to the generation of the wilderness has a typological meaning, that is to say that the events and facts quoted in this passage are exemplary warnings of that which will take place at the end of the ages.'[1] This typological conception, and this particular type of the flood, Lundberg considers to have been known in the Christian church before they were used by the author of I Peter. He devotes a long section of his work[2] to showing that behind the earliest Christian ideas about Baptism and early liturgical types of Baptism and language used about it lie even earlier, perhaps pre-Christian, conceptions of the kingdom of the Dead, usually conceived as a sea and associated with the flood. He also suggests that the thought of Baptism as a journey across this Sea of the Dead in the boat of the Church (inevitably likened to the ark) was very early indeed.

He then in the light of these previously existing ideas about Baptism proceeds to a very careful study of I Peter 3.18–22.[3] He concludes that the passage assumes already the existence in the Christian community of a typological comparison between those who were baptized into Christianity and those who survived the flood; Noah is here thought of as having almost gone under, after 'the Jewish legend according to which Noah did not enter the ark until the water had reached his knees'.[4] Lundberg assumes the existence also of a similar traditional type representing Baptism as the *descensus* of the Christian into the waters of the kingdom of Death, as Christ descended into them. Further, Christ is conceived as preaching to the spirits in prison as Noah preached to his wicked contemporaries at the time of the flood. He remarks that these conceptions, which he calls 'a realist and sacramental conception given by tradition',[5] have been to some extent moralized or spiritualized by the author of I Peter, who describes Baptism as 'not the putting away of the filth of the flesh but an approach to God based on a good conscience'.[6] The fact that there is no immediately obvious connection between the act of Baptism and the approach to God based on a good conscience suggests that this sentence is an interpretation of the author

---

[1]*La Typologie Baptismale*, p. 135.   [2]pp. 64–98.   [3]*Ibid.*, pp. 98–116.
[4]*Ibid.*, p. 112; cf. I Cor. 10.1: διὰ τῆς θαλάσσης.
[5]*Ibid.*, p. 115.
[6]3.21; this seems to be the best translation of the Greek οὐ σαρκὸς ἀπόθεσις ῥύπου ἀλλὰ συνειδήσεως ἀγαθῆς ἐπερώτημα εἰς θεόν.

of the Epistle. 'We can then establish,' says Lundberg, 'that a baptismal conception of a moral kind could be formed even on the foundation of a realist and sacramental conception given by tradition. This traditional conception evidently represents a very old element in the whole nexus of the baptismal ideas of the primitive Christian community.'[1] For us it is particularly interesting to note that this looks very like a primitive form of allegorizing applied to a traditional type on the part of the author of I Peter.

Daniélou in his work *Sacramentum Futuri* has examined the typology of Noah in the early Church very fully.[2] He shows that the most primitive typology of Noah was an eschatological one, Noah the survivor of a world catastrophe being regarded as the type and warning of the cosmic catastrophe at the Judgement; this typology can be found, not only in Matt. 24.38 f., 42, and in I and II Peter, but in *I Clement*, Justin, Irenaeus, Ephrem, and Gregory of Elvira.[3] This typology Daniélou thinks to be originally Jewish and pre-Christian: 'We are brought therefore once again, as far as the traditions about Noah are concerned, into primitive Christianity, to conceptions which derive from the Pharisaic background of the apocalypses, with which the Epistles of Peter, the eschatological discourse, the Epistle of Clement, Justin and Irenaeus have contacts.'[4] There were however other typologies of Noah and the flood. Noah, for instance, was thought of as a type of Jesus the End and the Beginning (τέλος-ἀρχή), based on the significance of the number of souls saved from the flood, eight to correspond to the eighth day (the last and first and day of resurrection). Noah and the flood were thought of (as we have seen) as a type of Baptism, or (the sacramental and eschatological interpretations combined) as a type of eschatological deliverance effected in Baptism.[5] There are in typologies of this sort really three stages: Noah, in the Old Testament, prefiguring; Christ in the New Testament, the reality, fulfilling; the Christian in sacramental imitation configured to Christ reproducing the experience.[6] This is a pattern which we shall find repeated in Origen with significant transmutations. This typology of Noah is developed in Tertullian and others

---

[1]*La Typologie Baptismale*, p. 115.
[2]See Book II, ch. II, 'Noé et le Déluge: Déluge, Baptême, Jugement chez les Pères de L'Église', pp. 69–85.
[3]*Ibid.*, pp. 69–74.
[4]*Ibid.*, p. 70. But his identification on the same page of the 'presbyters' referred to by Irenaeus as 'not the authorities of the church but the "ancients" in its strict sense, the Palestinian Jewish circles which were the first disciples of the Lord and were impregnated with Judaism' seems to me doubtful.
[5]*Ibid.*, pp. 75–7.
[6]*Ibid.*, p. 76.

into the traditional picture of the ark as symbolic of the Church which saves Christians from the storm or flood of death.[1]

Lundberg later examines another piece of baptismal typology to be found in the New Testament, the comparing of Baptism to the people of Israel crossing the Red Sea. He suggests, very convincingly, that behind many baptismal phrases using this type is the very old idea already mentioned of Baptism as a descent into the Sea of the Dead or the kingdom of the Dead and a survival of it, or a victorious walking over it, following the *descensus* and victory of Jesus.[2] The obvious passage in the New Testament to illustrate this subject is I Cor. 10.1 f. Paul, he thinks, inherited the conception of the crossing of the Red Sea as a crossing of the Sea of the Dead, and himself added the thought that this experience was a going through the Sea of the Dead *with Christ*, a being drowned in it as Christ was buried.[3] Lundberg thinks that Rev. 15.2 ff. has a similar typology behind it. The victors stand beside (that is on the far side of) the Sea of the Dead (which is not just glass, but glass mingled with fire). He suggests too that Revelation models its seven plagues, seven trumpets and seven vials upon a section of the Book of Wisdom (chapters 11–19) which draws out the close correspondence between the seven plagues afflicting the Egyptians and the benefits enjoyed by God's people at the time of the Exodus. The Book of Wisdom, indeed, gives an eschatological character to these events: 'For the whole creation was again remodelled in each of its species.'[4] This thought may be taken up in the words of Rev. 21.1, 3, 'And I saw a new heaven and a new earth: for the first heaven and the first earth are passed away; and the sea is no more,' etc. Lundberg also seeks to show that the crossing of Jordan by the people of Israel was thought of in Christian typology as a foreshadowing of Christian Baptism, though there is no very obvious passage in the New Testament to illustrate this, and Lundberg can find no convincing evidence in Christian (as distinct from Gnostic) sources that Jordan was identified with the Sea of the Dead.[5]

There is one more example of baptismal typology to be found in early Christian literature, and that is Baptism considered as a walking on or finding of the Cross in the water, a conception which Lundberg calls

[1]*Sacramentum Futuri*, pp. 81–5.
[2]*La Typologie Baptismale*, pp. 116–35.   [3]*Ibid.*, pp. 135–45.
[4]Wisd. 19.6: ὅλη γὰρ ἡ κτίσις ἐν ἰδίῳ γένει πάλιν διετυποῦτο. The reference which Lundberg finds to the Sea of the Dead in Wisdom is in 19.7, ἐξ ἐρυθρᾶς θαλάσσης ὁδὸς ἀνεμπόδιστος, where the last word suggests the mass of water (or sometimes river of fire) which bars the way to Paradise or to the holy city.
[5]*La Typologie Baptismale*, pp. 146–66.

lignum sacramenti, taking the phrase from Augustine. One of the earliest exponents of this type is the author of the *Epistle of Barnabas*. The texts from the Old Testament which this Epistle cites to illuminate Baptism are at first sight bewildering.[1] They consist of Jer. 2.12 ff. (the children of Israel have left the fountain of living waters and made broken cisterns for themselves), Isa. 16.1 ff. (which he cites in the form 'Surely my holy mountain of Sion is not a forsaken rock' etc.); Isa. 45.2 f. ('I will go before thee and make the rugged places plain: I will break in pieces the doors of brass' etc.); Isa. 33.16 ff. ('He shall dwell on high; his place of defence shall be the munitions of rocks; his bread shall be given him; his waters shall be sure'); Ps. 1.3–6, which the author paraphrases (11.8) as 'Blessed are those who have hoped in the cross and gone down into the water'. Then he quotes the unplaceable text, 'And the land of Jacob was praised above every other land.'[2] The writer's comment on this sentence is, 'He glorifies the vessel of his spirit.' The next text is a mixture of Dan. 7.10, with its reference to the sacred stream of fire, and Ezek. 47.1, 7, 12 which mention the sacred waters, the trees by the river and the fruit of the trees; to this mixture the author of the Epistle adds the apocryphal words (as perhaps a Targum on the last sentence of Ezek. 47.12), 'and whosoever eats of it shall live for ever.'

This at first sight extraordinary collection of proof-texts for Christian Baptism Lundberg explains convincingly by showing that in the writer's mind is the thought that the Baptism of Jesus was a *descensus* in which he broke the power of death and the devil, and provided a Cross, or wooden causeway, or else a rock, by which those who are baptized into him can cross the Sea of Death.[3] The Baptism of Jesus must presumably here mean not only his Baptism by John in Jordan, but his whole experience of Passion, Death, and Resurrection, as it does in Mark 10.38 and Luke 12.50. Lundberg points out that the writer begins his section on Baptism with the words, 'Let us inquire whether it was the Lord's concern to show beforehand concerning the water and the Cross.'[4] The reference to the living water and broken cisterns in Jeremiah is clear enough. The passage from Isaiah is taken as forecasting the firm footing which the baptized will find amidst the waters of death; their 'waters will be sure' because the baptismal water will be transformed by the Cross. The

[1] *Epistle of Barnabas* 11.1–11.
[2] καὶ ἦν ἡ γῆ τοῦ Ἰακὼβ ἐπαινουμένη παρὰ πᾶσαν τὴν γῆν, *Barnabas* 11.9.
[3] *La Typologie Baptismale*, pp. 178–84.
[4] Ζητήσωμεν δὲ εἰ ἐμέλησεν τῷ Κυρίῳ προφανερῶσαι περὶ τοῦ ὕδατος καὶ τοῦ σταυροῦ, *Barnabas* 11.1.

forbidden to Adam.

eat of fruit

writer's comment on Ps. 1 speaks for itself. The apocryphal sentence glossed with the words 'He glorifies the vessel of his spirit' may refer to the idea that the Christian becomes the temple of the Holy Spirit at Baptism.[1] The final testimony derived from Ezekiel and Daniel is produced to emphasize the theme that the baptized person has been transported to Paradise by Baptism and that he can eat fruit that was forbidden to Adam.

Lundberg sees this theme of the Cross found in the water in a number of other passages in early Christian literature, in Justin, *Dial.* 86 and 138.2, in Ignatius, *Ephesians* 18.2[2] and 9.1,[3] in Melito's *Homily on the Passion*,[4] and in several other writers.[5]

We must not of course assume that these types were the only pictures used by the early Church to illuminate its conception of Baptism. There is some rather disconcerting evidence to the contrary. A baptistery chapel discovered at Dura on the Orontes, to be dated before 260 and possibly before 232, has the following scenes depicted on its walls: the Wise and Foolish Virgins (or possibly Christ's tomb); Peter trying to walk on the water; the healing of the paralysed man; Adam and Eve; and the Good Shepherd. There is no representation of Noah in the flood, nor of the crossing of the Red Sea, nor of the Jordan.[6] On the architrave of what is probably the baptistery of the Christian basilica recently excavated at Ostia (built perhaps as early as the fourth century) is the inscription, *In Christo Geon Fison Tigris Eufrata Christianorum sumite fontes.* Conversely, we can find examples of early Christian writers who deal quite fully with the Exodus and the crossing of Jordan, but do not link it with Baptism at all, such as Irenaeus in his *Demonstration of the Apostolic Preaching* and Clement of Alexandria.[7]

It is evident, then, that behind much early Christian writing, and certainly behind the text of the New Testament, there lies a corpus of traditional typology, originally inherited from or imitated from Jewish liturgical expressions, but multiplied and developed by the conviction of the early Christians that the type had been fulfilled, the prefigure-

---

[1] But for a different interpretation of this odd passage see below, p. 98.
[2] ὁ γὰρ θεὸς ἡμῶν Ἰησοῦς ὁ Χριστὸς . . . ὃς ἐγεννήθη καὶ ἐβαπτίσθη ἵνα τῷ πάθει τὸ ὕδωρ καθαρίσῃ.
[3] The famous passage describing the Cross as the machine that lifts us on high to be made stones of God's building.
[4] ἐγώ, φησίν, ὁ Χριστός, ἐγὼ ὁ καταλύσας τὸν θάνατον . . . εἰς τὰ ὕψη τῶν οὐρανῶν, 102, p. 163.
[5] *La Typologie Baptismale*, pp. 191–3.
[6] Milburn, *Early Christian Interpretations of History*, p. 99.
[7] Irenaeus, *Dem.* 46; for Clement see Daniélou, *Sacramentum Futuri*, pp. 191–200. See also below, p. 112.

ment had been transformed into reality, in the life, death, and resurrection of Jesus Christ. We have only explored a small part of that corpus, the typology of Christian Baptism, but it has been enough for us to conclude that though such an interpretation of the Old Testament may well have given rise to allegory, in its early stages it did not do so very profusely. We have found only one example of anything that we could confidently call allegory, the interpretation contained in I Peter 3.21, and nothing whatever (not even the chapter of the *Epistle of Barnabas* which we have examined) to suggest that this sort of typological interpretation gave rise to allegorizing of an Alexandrian sort.

But besides typology of this sort there was another way of interpreting the Hebrew Scriptures current in the early Church, distinct from typology though liable to blend with it, and that is the finding in the Old Testament of proof texts to show that the prophecies of the Scriptures had been fulfilled in Jesus Christ. It is *a priori* highly likely that we shall find allegory employed somewhere in this tradition of interpretation, if we are to judge by the close analogy provided by the *Habakkuk Commentary* and the *Damascus Document*. In two works Rendel Harris attempted to explore this tradition of interpretation.[1] He set out to show that underlying many works of Christian antiquity was a *Book of Testimonies* containing a collection of passages of the Old Testament grouped under different headings designed to demonstrate to the Jews that Jesus was the Christ and the Son of God. The main works drawn on to support this hypothesis are the *Epistle of Barnabas*, Justin Martyr's *Dialogue*, Athanasius' *De Incarnatione*, Cyprian's *Testimonia*, Irenaeus' *Demonstration of the Apostolic Preaching*, Cyril of Jerusalem's *Catechesis*, Gregory of Nyssa's *Testimonia adversus Judaeos*, Novatian's *de Trinitate* and Lactantius' *Divine Institutes*. The second part of Harris' work tried to show that just such a *Book of Testimonies* underlay most of the documents of the New Testament. The Old Testament passages included in this hypothetical book are mostly of a prophetical rather than of a precisely typological character, and may be easily sampled by a reading of the *Dialogue*. Some of them suggest that allegory of a primitive, Palestinian kind, reminiscent of that of the *Habakkuk Commentary* and the *Damascus Document*, was being used on the Old Testament. If Harris' claims for this collection are valid, then it must represent very early interpretation indeed and could reproduce in part pre-Christian Messianic proof texts. The more commonly used proof-texts are these:

[1] *Testimonies* by Rendel Harris. The parts written in even cloudier English than the rest are by Vacher Burch.

A.E.–C*

study these

1. Gen. 49.10 f. (Jacob's prophecy about Judah).
2. Num. 24.17 (Balaam's forecast of the star arising out of Jacob).
3. Ps. 110 ('Before the day-star I begat thee', only found in the LXX).
4. Isa. 7.14 (the virgin who is to conceive).
5. Isa. 11.1 (a Messianic passage).
6. Isa. 8.14 and 28.16 (the reference to the Stone with many other 'Stone' texts).
7. Isa. 63.9 (the angel of God's presence; LXX version).
8. Zech. 11.12 f. (the pieces of silver).
9. Mal. 3.1 (the forerunner).
10. Deut. 28.66 ('Thy life shall hang before thee').

Some of these (notably Nos. 2, 6, and 10) demand a form of allegory for their Christological interpretation, such as we have already encountered in Rabbinic sources and in the Dead Sea Scrolls documents. But it is clear that most of these proof-texts suggest that a Christian rather than a pre-Christian mind assembled them; in particular those which rely on a Greek version of the Old Testament can be neither pre-Christian nor indeed the product of the very early Aramaic-speaking church. They show no signs of Alexandrian influence at all.

C. H. Dodd, in his book *According to the Scriptures*, has given good reason for being cautious about accepting Rendel Harris' hypothesis of the existence at a very early period, before even the New Testament was written, of a *Book of Testimonies*.[1] It is very odd that no author mentions the book (with the possibility of Papias forming an exception) until the time of Cyprian, and indeed that the book is not in the Canon. The main argument of Harris is that the common citation of variants differing from the LXX, the common citation of passages in the same combination, and the recurrence of groups of passages connected by such a key word as *stone* demand that we shall assume a common written source for all these phenomena; but Dodd points out that, with the single exception of the passages referring to the Stone, these passages are not in fact to be found in so widespread a range as to be very impressive. In his conclusions[2] he rules out the hypothesis of such a Book of Testimonies existing when the New Testament was being written. The most that can be said, he thinks, is that a certain method of interpreting the Old Testament was early established. This method involved the

[1]*Op cit.*, pp. 23–6.   [2]*Ibid.*, pp. 126 f.

selection of certain passages as particularly significant. These passages (which were sections, not mere verses) were usually understood as a whole, and if detached lines or verses were quoted they were regarded as pointers to the whole context.

Dodd's own list of Testimonies (even though he does not believe that they were collected into a book) is particularly interesting as affording us an opportunity of judging whether the use of proof-texts by the writers of the New Testament, themselves probably standing in a tradition of using such texts, involved the use of allegory or not. Dodd gives a list of fifteen passages from the Old Testament, the use of which in his view gives us ground 'for believing that New Testament writers were working upon a tradition in which certain passages of the Old Testament were treated as "testimonies" to the Gospel facts'.[1] The list runs thus:

1. Ps. 2.7 ('Thou art my son').
2. Ps. 8.4–6 ('What is man?').
3. Ps. 110.1 ('The Lord said unto my Lord').
4. Ps. 118.22 f. ('The stone which the builders rejected').
5. Isa. 6.9–10 (the blinding of the eyes of Israel).
6. Isa. 53.1 ('Who hath believed our report?').
7. Isa. 40.3–5 (the voice crying in the wilderness).
8. Isa. 28.16 (the foundation stone laid in Sion), conflated with Isa. 8.14 (the stone of stumbling).
9. Gen. 12.3 ('In thee shall all the tribes of the earth be blessed'), conflated with Gen. 22.18 ('In thy seed shall all the nations be blessed').
10. Jer. 31.31–4 (the new covenant).
11. Joel 2.28–32 (the pouring out of the spirit on all flesh).
12. Zech. 9.9 ('Rejoice greatly, O daughter of Sion').
13. Hab. 2.3 f. ('The righteous will live by faith').
14. Isa. 61.1 f. ('The Spirit of the Lord is upon me').
15. Deut. 18.15, 19 (the coming of the prophet like Moses).

It is remarkable that in only two items on this list can we confidently see allegory at work. Nos. 4 and 8, with their reference to the Stone, could have been used by Christians only by employing a Rabbinic form of allegory upon the passages which allude to the Stone. Rendel Harris finds a similar interpretation in the *Epistle of Barnabas*, Cyprian's *Testi-*

---

[1] *According to the Scriptures*, p. 57. The list of fifteen passages is given on pp. 31–57.

monia and the *Dialogue between Athanasius and Zacchaeus*, as well as in several other Fathers.[1] The only other possible allegorization in this list provided by Dodd is in No. 6, where the sentence, 'Unto whom hath the arm of the Lord been revealed?' might have been taken as allegorically predicting the Christ; several Fathers, notably Irenaeus, take this expression as denoting Christ, and we cannot absolutely exclude it from the mind of the New Testament writers who use this text. But there is no convincing proof that the writers of the New Testament intended to allegorize here, and it is wiser to conclude that they did not. Even if we count this as an allegorization, the meagre evidence for allegory afforded by this list is most remarkable, and suggests that allegory did not figure largely in the Scriptural interpretation of the Church in very early times.

Whether Jesus himself spoke allegories we cannot know. The Gospels of Mark (4.14–20), of Matthew (13.18–23) and of Luke (8.11–15) attribute to him an allegorical interpretation of the parable of the Sower, and the Gospel of Matthew allegorical interpretations of the parables of the Wheat and the Tares and of the Drag-net (13.36–43, 49). But many scholars would regard these as secondary interpretations produced in the early Church and not the words of the Master himself. The parable of the Wicked Husbandmen (Mark 12.1–9, parallels Matt. 21. 33–41, Luke 20.9–16) could perhaps be described as an allegory, and if we choose to identify contemporary political figures in the characters appearing in some other parables we could perhaps regard them as semi-allegorical.[2] But there is no evidence whatever that Jesus ever interpreted the Hebrew Scriptures allegorically, unless we are to count the reference to 'the stone which the builders rejected' placed at the end of the

[1] *Testimonies* II, pp. 19 f., 60 f.
[2] Daniélou (*Sacramentum Futuri*, pp. 246 f.) cites a passage from Origen's *Hom. on Luke* XXXIV, which Origen describes as coming from one of the *presbyteri*, interpreting the parable of the Good Samaritan allegorically; the injured man is Adam; Jerusalem is Paradise; Jericho is the world; the bandits are hostile powers; the Samaritan is Christ; the wounds are disobedience; the ass is Christ's body; the inn is the Church; the Samaritan's promise to return is the Parousia. This interpretation is found in Irenaeus (*Adv. Haer.* III.18.2), and Daniélou suggests that *presbyteri* here means, not merely 'the men of old', but 'the presbyters', the group of immediately post-apostolic bearers of tradition referred to by Papias, Irenaeus and Clement of Alexandria, and conjectures that this interpretation of the parable may go back in some form to Jesus himself. I know of no other instance where Origen uses οἱ πρεσβύτεροι in this special sense, and the suggestion that this interpretation was one intention in our Lord's mind in his producing of the parable of the Good Samaritan I cannot regard as worthy of serious consideration. Cf. Harnack, *Der Kirchengeschichtliche Ertrag der exegetischen Arbeiten des Origenes*, II, pp. 27 f. See also R. M. Grant, *The Letter and the Spirit*, p. 43.

parable of the Wicked Husbandmen by the Synoptic Evangelists (Mark 12.10, Matt. 21.42, Luke 20.17, 18). But this is a very slight foundation upon which to build a general theory of a dominical precept ordaining allegorizing of the Scriptures, such as the Fathers hold.

The existence of allegorical interpretations of some of the parables of Jesus in the Gospels does, however, show that allegory was in the mind of the earliest Christians. The tendency of the writers of the New Testament Epistles, and particularly St Paul, and of the author of Revelation, to see almost every passage in the Old Testament as speaking of Christ in some way would encourage the growth of allegory, and so would the habit of envisaging Christ as being in some mode present under the old covenant during the critical period of the Exodus and the wandering in the Wilderness. When St Paul says that God spoke to Abraham about Christ (Gal. 3.16) or that Christ was the rock that followed the children of Israel in the Wilderness (I Cor. 10.4), or that when Moses turned to face the Lord in the tabernacle, the Lord was the Spirit of Christ (II Cor. 3.7–17), or that Moses wrote in Deuteronomy about justification through faith in Christ (Rom. 10.6–9), he is moving in a world of interpretation where the appearance of allegory sooner or later is almost inevitable. The same is true of the thought of the early Christian hymn embedded in Eph. 5.14, 'Awake, thou that sleepest, and arise from the dead, and Christ shall shine upon thee', which deliberately recalls Jonah 1.6, 'What meanest thou, O sleeper? Arise, call upon thy God, if so be that God will think upon us', taking it as a prophecy of the Resurrection,[1] and of the use by the author of Revelation of Isa. 63.1–6 as a prophecy of the Crucifixion (Rev. 14.19 f.; 19.13, 15), and of a great number of other passages in the New Testament.

But though as one reads the New Testament one feels that allegory is a very likely device for the authors to use, it very rarely becomes explicit in the text. We have seen something like an allegorization in I Peter 3.21, and perhaps in the references to the Stone mentioned in

---

[1] NT: ἔγειρε ὁ καθεύδων, καὶ ἀνάστα ἐκ τῶν νεκρῶν, καὶ ἐπιφαύσει σοι ὁ Χριστός. LXX: τί σοι ὁ ῥέξων; ἀνάστα καὶ ἐπικαλοῦ τὸν θεόν σου, ὅπως διασώσῃ ὁ θεὸς ἡμᾶς. This is not a particularly striking parallel in the Greek, but if we assume that the Jonah text was read in Hebrew by the original author of the hymn, and that the word for 'think upon' (תְשׁ) was mistaken for a similar word meaning 'to be smooth or shiny' עָשׁוּ, which occurs in Jer. 5.28) we can then imagine that the text appeared to the writer of the hymn in the form of 'What meanest thou? Arise, thou that sleepest, call upon thy God, perhaps thy God shall shine upon us.' In that case it would become highly probable that the author of the hymn was regarding these words as a prophecy of the Resurrection. For the Book of Jonah as a source of proof-texts for the Resurrection see Matt. 12.39 f.

Isaiah and in the Psalms as foreshadowing Christ. And it has been suggested that Rev. 3.20 ('Behold, I stand at the door and knock; if any man hear my voice and open the door, I will come in to him') is an allegorization of S. of S. 5.4 f. ('My beloved put in his hand by the hole of the door . . . I rose up to open to my beloved').[1]

The letters of St Paul, however, are a more hopeful quarry for those who are looking for allegory in the New Testament. De Lubac indeed regards all Paul's references to the spirit being preferable to the letter as equivalent to a justification of the practice of allegorizing the Torah, an interpretation which certainly commended itself to Origen, but would find favour with very few modern New Testament scholars.[2] Others are more cautious, and cite a short list of passages in St Paul where he can confidently be said to be allegorizing.[3] These passages we must now examine.

I Cor. 5.6–8, the passage likening Christians who have been rid of the old leaven of evil, to the Unleavened Bread of the Passover celebration, and Christ to the Passover Lamb sacrificed for them. It is difficult to describe this as an example of direct allegory, because for one thing we cannot precisely determine the text of the Scriptures allegorized. It is more likely to be an interpretation of the Unleavened Bread and the Lamb associated with the Passover Meal, given in a well-established tradition of such interpretation. Paul is, as it were, a Christian Rabbi interpreting in advance for his Christian converts, in response to their unspoken question, 'What mean ye by this service?', the constituents of the meal in a Christian sense.[4]

I Cor. 9.8–10, the passage where Paul interprets the words of Deut. 25.4, 'Thou shalt not muzzle the ox when he treadeth out the corn', to mean that the Christian community have the responsibility for supporting the apostle who brought them into the Christian fold. This looks very like Rabbinic allegory; indeed it is from this text that Strack-Billerbeck begin their account of allegory among the Rabbis. It is noteworthy that Paul says that the text in Deuteronomy could not be taken literally: 'Doth God care for oxen, or saith he it altogether for our sakes? For our sakes no doubt this is written.' Is this reminiscent of Philo, who evacuates the commandment of its literal meaning? But then the allegoriza-

---

[1]See above, p. 34 n. 1.   [2]*Histoire et Esprit*, pp. 69–73.
[3]Bonsirven, *Exégèse Rabbinique*, pp. 309 f., suggests II Cor. 3.13–4.6; Gal. 4.21–31; and I Cor. 9.8–10. Büchsel, ἀλληγορέω, *TWNT* I, pp. 263 f., suggests I Cor. 5.6–8; 9.8–10; 10.1–11; Gal. 4.21–31.
[4]See J. Jeremias, *The Eucharistic Words of Jesus*, pp. 34 f. Woollcombe, however, treats this passage as a full allegory (*Essays on Typology*, p. 55).

example of that a text that cannot be taken literally

tions in the Jerusalem Targum are very reminiscent of the kind of interpretation found in this text, and the *dôrĕé hamûrôt* may have been ready to deprive the commandment of its literal meaning.[1] Again, Paul here allegorizes into neither moral exhortation nor philosophical speculation, as the Alexandrian tradition would. He is so much convinced that the Scriptures of the Old Covenant prefigure the New, even to quite trivial circumstances, that he cannot believe that this ordinance about an ox can be intended to be taken literally, but concludes that it refers to the liability of the people of the Messiah, when he comes, to support the Messiah's apostles. Paul is certainly allegorizing as a Rabbi of the sect of the Nazarenes, and not as an Alexandrian philosopher.[2]

I Cor. 10.1–11. That this is a piece of Pauline typology is obvious. Whether we can class it as allegory is another question. It is obvious that Paul is here elaborating his conviction that the situations which occurred and the events which took place during the critical period of the Exodus and wilderness wanderings were being repeated in some sense in the experience of the contemporary Church, and especially in the administration of the sacraments. So far we have only 'similar situation' typology; that is presumably what St Paul meant by 'examples' (τύποι, I Cor. 10.6).[3] The only possible instance of allegory that I can find here is the phrase 'and the rock was Christ' (v.4). This would certainly be allegory if it meant 'the rock described in Ex. 17 signified or predicted Christ', as, for instance, the Fathers of the Church say that the Stone referred to by Isaiah was a prophecy or figure of Christ. But it is much more likely that Paul here means that the rock really *was* Christ; the word *was* (ἦν) is expressed in the Greek. That is to say, he believed that the Messiah was in some form present with the people, who were all the time in their ultimate significance the Messiah's people, during this critical period in the wilderness, for salvation and for judgement, just as in II Cor. 3.17 he expresses his belief that 'the Lord' to whom Moses turned when he entered the tabernacle, and contact with whom caused Moses' face to shine, was the Spirit. In that case, this would not be an allegory at all, but an example of Paul's tendency to read back, so to speak, the Messiah into the Old Testament. For Paul, when Moses

---

[1] See above, pp. 32 f.

[2] A very similar piece of interpretation is found in I Cor. 14.21 f., where Paul takes the passage Isa. 28.11 f. as a prediction of the glossolalia which is to take place in the Messianic community. But as this (in spite of Paul's referring to the text as 'the law') is more like a direct identification of the fulfilment of prophecy than an allegorization, I have not considered it in the text.

[3] Cf. Lundberg's explanation of τυπικῶς quoted on p. 68.

wrote 'rock' he meant Christ present then and there, not a figure or forecast or symbol of Christ, except in as far as a name is a symbol. *II Cor. 3.13–4.6.* Here we are faced with very much the same difficulty of distinguishing typology from allegory as in the last passage.[1] Once again Paul is envisaging a situation described in the Old Testament, in this case the necessity imposed upon Moses of putting on a veil when he turned to the people after communing with God, presumably in the tabernacle (Ex. 34.29–35), as both prefiguring and repeated in a situation occurring under the New Dispensation, in this case the possibility open to Christians of seeing God's light reflected in Christ.[2] It is another, though admittedly a remoter and more complicated, example of 'similar situation' typology, and we can no more describe the phrase 'now the Lord is the Spirit' (II Cor. 3.17) as allegory than we can describe the phrase 'and the rock was Christ' as allegory.

Gal. 4.21–31. This well-known passage comparing Ishmael and Isaac to the old and the new covenants is explicitly and undisguisedly allegorical, for when Paul has said that Abraham has two sons, one from the slave woman, 'according to the flesh', and one from the free woman, as a 'result of a promise' (v. 23) he comments 'and these events are allegorically stated'. 'Which things contain an allegory' of the RV and 'Now this is an allegory' of the ARSV seem to me not very accurate, because Paul does not in fact use the word *allegory* (ἅτινά ἐστιν ἀλληγορούμενα, not ἅτινά ἐστιν ἀλληγορία). It is a very complicated and, one must confess, unconvincing allegory, not easily worked out, because one is uncertain how far Paul is allegorizing Ishmael and how far Hagar, and whether he is not in fact confusing the two allegories, and because he hardly works out at all the other allegory of Isaac and Sarah. Presumably one may elaborate Paul's thought in some such way as this:

Hagar = Sinai = the political Jerusalem.
   Ishmael = the old covenant = contemporary Judaism.
Sarah = Jerusalem which is above (= the Christian Church ?).
   Isaac = the new covenant = contemporary Christians.

There is nothing in the member of this parallelism headed by Sarah to correspond to the identification of Hagar and Mount Sinai (a *tour de*

---

[1]For a comment on the meaning of this passage see my article 'Moses in the typology of St Paul', in *Theology* XLVIII, pp. 174–7.
[2]'Just as the people of Israel could have seen God's light reflected in Moses' face, but for the veil, so Christians today, possessing the Spirit, see God's light reflected in Christ, and the apostle ministers God's light to his converts.' (R. P. C. Hanson, *II Corinthians*, pp. 39 f.).

force which may derive from some piece of etymological Midrash otherwise unknown to us). The exact meaning of 'Jerusalem which is above' (ἡ ἄνω Ἰερουσαλήμ, v. 26) is obscure; the phrase could perhaps mean 'the new Jerusalem' and recalls the picture of the New Jerusalem coming down from heaven in Revelation.[1] It is perhaps either a heavenly, real church (in some sort of contrast to an empirical, earthly church), a concept for which there is some little support in Rabbinic sources,[2] or the Christian Church regarded in its heavenly aspect, considered purely in the light of its divine destiny.

That this is allegory is certain. Is it Alexandrian allegory? In favour of this suggestion is the use of the verb ἀλληγορέω which, as we have seen,[3] is nearly the earliest use of the verb traceable anywhere, and, along with Philo's use, the earliest use of it in the sense of allegorizing the Scriptures of the Old Testament. At first sight too in favour of this view we might adduce the contrast between the son born 'according to the flesh' (κατὰ σαρκά) and the son born 'as a result of a promise' (δι' ἐπαγγελίας), assuming that this is an echo of the Alexandrian tendency to substitute a philosophical or moral meaning for the literal one. But in fact this would be a wrong surmise, because by his contrast between 'according to the flesh' and 'as a result of a promise' Paul does not mean that Ishmael was a real man of flesh and blood whereas Isaac was a philosophical or theological symbol and no more, but that Ishmael was born as a result of normal human motives and intentions, what the Fourth Evangelist calls 'of the will of the flesh' (John 1.13), whereas Isaac was born (really born, of flesh and blood) as a result of a divine promise.[4] The contrast between the political Jerusalem and the Jerusalem which is above is at first sight nearer to Philonic allegory at least. But even here the resemblance will not stretch very far, for there is no reason for thinking that Paul regarded the political Jerusalem as a mere earthly symbol of a philosophical reality, which would be the Philonic interpretation of it.[5] The political Jerusalem to Paul was an outward

[1]The passage is Rev. 21.2 ff.; cf. Heb. 12.22; *II Clement* 14.1–5. Polycarp (*Philippians* 3.3) seems to take it as meaning Christian faith, conceived both subjectively and objectively.

[2]Bonsirven, *Judaisme*, II, ch. XV, p. 112, mentions a notion sporadically occurring among the Rabbis that the Temple is the image and earthly counterpart of the heavenly temple and its services. He describes it as a 'traditional idea', and cites also Wisd. 9.8 and II Baruch 4.6; 59.4, 8.

[3]See above, p. 38.

[4]If we are to see any analogy intended here between the birth of Isaac and the birth of Jesus (which is of course far from certain), it would suggest that Paul did not know of the Virgin Birth, because there is no doubt that he believed that Abraham was the father of Isaac.

[5]See above, pp. 49–52.

Hagar — an allegorical rejection by God of the Jewish race? (handwritten annotation)

sign and summary of what he conceived to be an historical event, or at any rate an event involved in history, the rejection by God of the Jewish race as the exclusive object of his choice. He regarded Hagar as an allegorical prefigurement in the Scriptures of this rejection.

Against these arguments in favour of this passage representing an allegory in the Alexandrian tradition must be set the fact that the only other unusual word employed in the passage to expound the allegory (συστοιχεῖ, v.25, RV 'answereth to', ARSV, 'corresponds to') is not particularly Alexandrian, but is used by Aristotle and Polybius and other Greek writers, usually in a mathematical or astronomical context. Again if we apply the test which our examination of allegory so far has shown to be the most satisfactory for determining the character of any piece of allegorization, and ask, 'Into what does Paul allegorize this text?' we shall find no evidence of Alexandrian influence. Paul is not here trying to emancipate the meaning of the passage from its historical content and transmute it into a moral sentiment or a philosophical truth, which is the almost invariable function of Alexandrian allegory. He is doing what he is doing in his scriptural expositions of I Cor. 9 and 10 and II Cor. 3, though, as has been said, in a more remote and speculative and a more complicated way. He is envisaging a critical situation which took place under the Old Covenant (or, to be strictly accurate, before it but in prefiguration of it) as forecasting and repeated by a situation under the New Covenant. The 'similar situation' typology has here been strained and distorted in an unconvincing but highly Rabbinical fashion into allegory; that is all.[1] The fact that Paul can use the verb ἀλληγορέω and expect to be understood does not mean that he had been influenced by the Alexandrian method of allegory, but that the practice of allegorizing was much more widespread among Rabbis trained in a Palestinian tradition in Paul's day than has hitherto been realized, or than later Rabbinic literature was willing to admit. After all, the Christians to whom Paul was writing this letter may well have included Jews imbued with some of the learning of the Rabbinic schools conducted in the Palestinian tradition, but were most unlikely to have counted among their number men trained in the scholarship of Alexandria. It seems reasonable to conclude, then, that St Paul was quite

[1] Cf. the appropriate remark of Lampe on the passage: 'It is a picturesque and valuable sermon-illustration, designed for a limited purpose of apologetic; it does not advance or clinch his argument' (*Essays on Typology*, p. 35). Woollcombe effectively contrasts Philo's allegory of the same incident (*De Congressu* 23) with St Paul's (*ibid.*, p. 53). R. M. Grant also comments upon this passage, which is one of those that cause him to conclude that St Paul 'combines Rabbinic and Hellenistic Jewish exegesis' (*The Letter and the Spirit*, pp. 48 f., 54).

ready to use allegory, and even to use it in order to evacuate the ordinances of the Torah of their literal meaning on occasion, but that he employed this allegory in a Palestinian rather than an Alexandrian tradition, and that in practice the bent of his thought lay so much towards
typology rather than what we should strictly call allegory that he had in
the course of his extant letters few occasions to indulge in allegory. His
motives for using it were, as far as we can discover, far from being those
of the Alexandrians, and especially Philo, who wanted by allegory to
avoid the necessity of taking historical narrative seriously; Paul on the
contrary used allegory as an aid to typology, a method of interpreting
the Old Testament which, however fanciful some of its forms may be,
does at least regard history as something meaningful. It is significant
that there is no typology in Philo whereas Paul is full of it.

There remains one document which we would *a priori* expect to
display examples of allegorization, even if no examples appeared in elsewhere in the New Testament, and that is the Epistle to the Hebrews.
That this work is Alexandrian there can be no shadow of doubt. Its use
of the Book of Wisdom, its style and vocabulary, the Platonic influence
which it betrays, all stamp it as unmistakably coming from an Alexandrian *milieu*. We might therefore expect from it not only allegory, but
allegory in the Alexandrian tradition. The fact that, in spite of statements to the contrary by eminent scholars,[1] there is virtually no allegory
of any sort in the book, and absolutely no Alexandrian allegory, is a most
remarkable one, and demands that we shall spend some time considering this question. Necessarily bound up with the subject is the decision
as to whether the author of the Epistle is directly indebted to Philo or
not. If he is not indebted, his avoidance of allegory is explicable enough,
though still a little surprising. If he is indebted to Philo, and especially
if he is deeply indebted for ideas and vocabulary, then his eschewing of
allegory becomes almost incomprehensible.

It would be very unwise to approach this subject without taking
account of a recent work upon the Epistle to the Hebrews by C. Spicq,
written with immense erudition and a most impressive capacity for marshalling argument, a work which every scholar must respect even though
he may not agree with all its conclusions.[2] Spicq is convinced that the
author of the Epistle knows Philo's work thoroughly and has been profoundly influenced by it, even though on occasion he deliberately dissents

[1] E.g. de Faye, *Origène*, I, p. 94.
[2] C. Spicq, *L'Épître aux Hébreux*: I; ch. III, 'Le Philonisme de L'Épître aux
Hébreux', pp. 39–91, is the part that concerns us here.

from it. Spicq bases his argument partly upon the vocabulary and
style and partly upon the stock of ideas which he believes the authors to
have in common, and in a thorough and painstaking study, more exhaustive probably than any that has hitherto been undertaken on the subject, he makes a case for his point of view which at first sight is a very
convincing one. If his arguments have here to be summarized arbitrarily
it is not out of disrespect for their cogency, but because to do otherwise
would be to allow this subject to grow out of proportion to the whole
investigation of the sources of Christian allegory. I believe that Spicq's
arguments fall on each occasion just short of conviction, and that to
accept his conclusion brings us into greater difficulties than to
reject it.

A priori considerations can never be decisive in matters of scholarship, but they have their place and in this question they are of particular
significance. We must remember how devoid we are of other literature
besides Philo's works to compare with the Epistle to the Hebrews in
matters of style and vocabulary. Unless we are to count the works of
Josephus (whose evidence seems, if anything, to count against Spicq's
thesis), absolutely no literature of Alexandrian Judaism survives outside Philo within a century before or after Philo's time. Two works of
Alexandrian Christianity of about that period, as we shall see, do survive, and they tell against Spicq's contention; but no work of Alexandrian Judaism is extant. To take a parallel from English literature: if
the works of John Donne and besides that only George Herbert's
Country Parson survived of all the English literature of 1600–50, would
we not inevitably conclude, on grounds of style, vocabulary and common ideas, that George Herbert had been profoundly influenced by
John Donne? But a greater acquaintance with the literature of the period
assures us that in fact he was not noticeably influenced by Donne. This
should warn us to be cautious about allowing arguments from style and
vocabulary to influence us in a case where we have so little knowledge of
what vocabulary and style was common to all Alexandrian literature of
the period and what was peculiar to Philo.

Again, the chronological demands made by the theory that the
author of the Epistle to the Hebrews was influenced by Philo, though
not impossible, are distinctly exacting. I assume that the Epistle was
written before the destruction of the Temple in A.D. 70, for two reasons.
In the first place, the passage 6.1–6 seems to me only explicable if we
are to agree that the Epistle was written to Christians who had been
Jewish proselytes before their conversion to Christianity. The little

summary in vv. 1 f. gives a picture of the teaching which the Jewish proselyte would receive:

repentance from dead works (=renunciation of Gentile immorality),

faith in God (=monotheism),

teaching of washings[1] (=purifications),

laying on of hands (i.e. what can be touched and what not, cf. Col. 2.20–22 and perhaps Mark 7.1–6),

resurrection from the dead ⎫(which would both form part of
everlasting judgement ⎭ Pharisaic teaching to proselytes).

That the author calls this teaching 'the first principles of Christ'[2] is very natural, for to all early Christians Judaism, especially since it professed to be grounded on the Old Testament, formed the first principles of their doctrine. They began by proving Christ from the Jewish Scriptures, they took over almost unaltered Jewish traditional morality, they were convinced that the religious institutions of Judaism were meant to point to Christ, and who is more convinced of this than the author of Hebrews? But if this Epistle is destined for proselytes become Christian, it is wiser to place it early rather than later within the period that the other evidence allows. In that case, it is better to interpret the ambiguous passage 9.6–10 as betraying the fact that the Temple was still standing rather than suggesting the contrary; v. 8 (τοῦτο δηλοῦντος τοῦ πνεύματος τοῦ ἁγίου μήπω πεφανερῶσθαι τὴν τῶν ἁγίων ὁδὸν ἔτι τῆς πρώτης σκηνῆς ἐχούσης στάσιν)[3] suggests that the outer court is not still standing, but the present tense in v. 9 (καθ᾽ ἣν δῶρά τε καὶ θυσίαι προσφέρονται) suggests as strongly that the sacrificial ritual is being carried on still in the writer's day. Anyway it is very difficult to believe that had the Temple already been destroyed the writer would not have used so very weighty an argument in the development of his thesis that the point of the Temple ritual is now lost, and have referred explicitly to this event. But if we are to place the composition of the Epistle before A.D. 70, to be on the safe side we should say before A.D. 66; the author must have had time to become soaked in Philo's thought and language, to transpose them into a Christian key and to write this letter before 66. We do not know when exactly Philo ceased

---

[1] βαπτισμῶν; cf. the βαπτισμοῖς of 9.10 which undoubtedly refer to Jewish practices.

[2] τὸν τῆς ἀρχῆς τοῦ Χριστοῦ λόγον, v. 1.

[3] But the words ἐχούσης στάσιν could mean 'possessing status or authority (from God)' and not 'still standing'.

writing; it was certainly at some point after 41, when presumably the *Legatio ad Gaium* was written, and quite possibly much later than this date, perhaps as late as 50 or 55. The possibility of his influencing the writer of Hebrews is not ruled out, but it is distinctly restricted.

Thirdly, we must consider the differences from Philo in the realm of ideas, apart from that of style and vocabulary, exhibited by the author of Hebrews. One obvious difference is that the author of Hebrews is full of Messianic expectation, whereas Philo has almost none. And—connected in fact with this point—the thought of Hebrews is eschatological through and through, whereas eschatology is virtually absent from Philo's thought. Again, the author of the Epistle, like all the writers of the New Testament, pays a great deal of attention to typology, what we have called 'similar situation' typology, whereas there is no trace of typology of this sort in Philo.[1] Further, the approaches to the law of the two writers are quite different. To Philo the law must be allegorized into psychological or philosophical truths; where its ordinances are not obviously rational their literal sense must be dissolved into some meaning quite alien to the original one, though it is right to observe the commandments of the Torah for the sake of convention and tradition.[2] The author of Hebrews also sees no real point in observing literally the Torah, but for quite different reasons. For him, the law has been evacuated of an authority which it for a time possessed by the crisis brought about by the arrival of the Messiah, and its true significance can now be seen to lie in its prefiguring of that crisis and of its consequences and accompanying circumstances. These seem to me to be two quite incompatible attitudes to the Law, differing on the vital point of the Law's authority. In their use or avoidance of allegory, too, the authors differ. Philo uses allegory as a great part of his philosophical system, or at least of his philosophical method. There is only one solitary example of allegorizing in Hebrews, and that is when he gives an allegorical etymology for the name Melchizedek (7.2), an allegorization so simple and obvious that though Philo reproduces it also we cannot call it characteristically Alexandrian, much less characteristically Philonic. Otherwise the Epistle gives no sign of allegory, not even of the Pauline, not even of the Rabbinic type; there are more instances in Paul's epistles, indeed, than there are in the Epistle to the Hebrews.[3]

---

[1] See above, pp. 48 f.   [2] See above, pp. 52 f.
[3] It must be admitted that Spicq entirely agrees that the Epistle to the Hebrews contains no allegory; indeed, he does not even mention the allegory of Melchizedek. On the other hand Lampe (*Essays on Typology*, p. 34) describes as typology the whole treatment of Melchizedek.

And finally, in consequence of this, the attitudes to history of these two authors are totally opposed, in spite of what Spicq says at the end of his chapter on the subject.

It is therefore reasonable to approach Spicq's arguments with the conviction that the *onus probandi* should be upon those who maintain a connection between the Epistle to the Hebrews and the works of Philo. Spicq labours, quite successfully, to prove that the two authors have a common vocabulary.[1] But this proves no more than that the two authors come from the same literary and intellectual *milieu*, and from about the same period, a fact of which nobody can have any doubt. Until we can find some more works besides Philo's of the same period and provenance this argument must as a rule fall short of conviction. There are, however, a number of resemblances of vocabulary and treatment which call for particular attention.

Spicq's assertion that the passage in Hebrews describing the character of the Word of God (4.12 f.) is dependent upon Philo's language about the Logos falls far short of proof.[2] The Word, says Hebrews, 'is living, and active, and sharper than any two-edged sword, and piercing even to the dividing of soul and spirit, of both joints and marrow, and quick to discern the thoughts and intents of the heart'. Spicq can produce instances of a 'living word' in some Philonic passages, and reference to the word as 'the cutter' (ὁ τόμευς; the word in Hebrews is τομώτερος), and he finds the thought expressed more than once in Philo that the Word can discern and divide. Further, he can find the word used by Hebrews for 'laid open' (τετραχηλισμένα) in Philo's vocabulary. From a purely linguistic point of view, however, this evidence is not as impressive as it at first sight appears. The verb τραχηλίζω is, as Spicq admits, found in Josephus and in Plutarch, and we have not enough evidence to declare that any word used by an Alexandrian writer of that period is unusual. Again, Philo does not give us an example of what is perhaps the oddest phrase of all, the statement that the Word can divide 'soul and spirit, joints and marrow' (ἁρμῶν καὶ μυελῶν). Further, we can produce at least two passages from the Old Testament which may well be behind this passage of Hebrews, rather than Philo. The first is the passage (strange to say not mentioned by Spicq) in Wisd. 18.15 f., describing the slaying of the Egyptians' first-born:

'Thine all-powerful Word leapt from heaven out of the royal throne,
A stern warrior, into the midst of the doomed land,

[1] *L'Épitre aux Hébreux*, pp. 39–50.   [2] *Ibid.*, pp. 51 f.

Bearing as a sharp sword thine unfeigned commandment;
And standing it filled all things with death.'

The second passage is one brought forward by Rendel Harris in his *Testimonies*, Part II.[1] He suggests that the reference in Heb. 4.12 to the Word being sharper than a two-edged sword is really based upon the passage in Josh. 5.2 where Joshua (who of course is a type of Jesus to the author of Hebrews) is commanded to make 'stone swords from a very sharp stone'.[2] Harris compares Justin Martyr, *Dial.* 113 ff., where the same text occasions a discourse of Jesus and the new circumcision. 'The process of inspection of the Logos . . . is the new circumcision *of the heart*, the thoughts and intents of the heart. . . . The sharp instrument of circumcision is the Logos.'[3] Justin (*ibid.*, 115 ff.) proceeds to move on from Joshua-Jesus the War-leader to Joshua-Jesus the High Priest, of Zech. 3. This connection, Harris thinks, is to be found also in the Epistle to the Hebrews and accounts for the writer speaking in the next chapter of Christ as High Priest. It is perhaps significant that just before the passage about the sharpness of the Logos the Epistle has been comparing Jesus and Joshua and maintaining that whereas Joshua under the old dispensation did not give the people rest, Jesus-Joshua under the new does. Here is an explanation of Heb. 4.12 f. which may well be regarded as subtler and more convincing than Spicq's theory that it represents a borrowing from Philo.

The passage in Hebrews referring to the immature or unitiated disciple (5.11–6.6) Spicq thinks strikingly reminiscent of Philo's language throughout his works concerning the same subject.[4] But the only significant word used in common by the two writers on this subject is 'without experience' (ἄπειρος). As Spicq himself points out, both St Paul (I Cor. 3.2) and the author of I Peter (2.2) use language of much the same sort in comparing immature Christians to children fed with milk or soft food.[5] In this passage Hebrews is reminding the Christians to whom the letter is addressed of their situation of comparative ignorance when they were proselytes of Judaism and not Christians. Now that they have become baptized Christians ('enlightened', φωτισθέντας,

[1] pp. 54 f.
[2] This is a literal translation of the LXX μαχαίρας πετρίνας ἐκ πέτρας ἀκροτόμου, which Harris suggests is echoed by the τομώτερος ὑπὲρ πᾶσαν μάχαιραν δίστομον of Heb. 4.12.
[3] *Ibid.* Admittedly, the reference to joints and marrow is not elucidated by this explanation.
[4] *L'Épître aux Hébreux*, pp. 55–7.
[5] So does Ignatius, *Trallians* 5.1.

an obvious reference to Baptism), and are communicants ('have tasted
of the heavenly gift', a reference to the Eucharist which has nothing to
do with alleged parallels from Philo), and stand consciously within the
crisis and the new dispensation brought about by the coming of the
Messiah ('were made partakers of the Holy Ghost and have tasted the
good word of God and the powers of the age to come'), there can be no
falling back. The Epistle may well be using the Alexandrian way of
putting things, though not necessarily the Philonic, but the two authors
in using rather similar language are in fact writing about two quite
different things; Philo is using the ideas of the mystery-religious to
describe the initiation into his own particular philosophical system,
whereas the author of Hebrews is thinking in terms of sacraments as
embodiments of realized eschatology.

Again the fact that both authors speak of an Old Testament character
as being 'without mother' (ἀμήτωρ), Philo of Sarah (*De Ebrietate* 61),
Hebrews of Melchizedek (7.1–3), is certainly striking. But might not
this be simply an example of both authors applying the same Rabbinical
rule of exegesis? That both authors present the same obvious etymology
of Melchizedek is, as we have seen, not surprising. Spicq admits[1] that
the two make quite different uses of the figure of Melchizedek.

The treatment of the typology of the Epistle to which his discussion
of Melchizedek leads Spicq is not an altogether satisfactory one. Agreeing that there is no allegory to be found in the Epistle, he quotes[2] a
passage from a book called *Dieu nous parla*[3] which makes a sharp distinction between typology and allegory; typology, says this author, takes
into consideration the intention of the original writer and carries it out,
whereas allegory ignores this and is only concerned with the ideas and
intentions of the allegorist; typology is ultimately divine, allegory is
ultimately human. The usefulness of this distinction seems to me very
doubtful; many examples of early Christian typology can hardly be
called divine, and typology has always a tendency to slip over into
allegory. But this distinction leads Spicq to an assertion which reveals
what seems to me a significant misunderstanding of the typology of the
Epistle to the Hebrews. He says that the author 'refuses to reveal the
correspondences between the old and the new cult', a matter in which
he is more reserved than the authors of the *Epistle of Barnabas* and
Revelation.[4] Now, it is true that we are not told what 'the things in the

[1]*Op. cit.*, p. 61; his discussion of Melchizedek covers pp. 59–61.
[2]*Ibid.*, p. 61 n. 3.
[3]By S. Javet (Paris 1945), pp. 67 f.
[4]Spicq. *op. cit.*, p. 62.

heavens' were of which the ordinances and apparatus of the old sacrificial system were patterns or copies or shadows (8.5; 9.23). But it is
clear enough from other passages in the Epistle what it was that the
author thought such things as these to reflect—the crisis brought about
by the coming of the Messiah, its consequences and circumstances. The
sabbath ordained by the Torah (and therefore presumably the laws
referring to it) were a prefigurement of the rest which the Christian now
enjoys in Christ (4.11). The 'heavenly gift' of manna in the wilderness
was a prefigurement of the 'Christian Eucharist (6.4). The dreadful
accompaniments of the law-giving at Sinai were a prefigurement of the
situation which Christians now enjoy, association with 'the city of the
living God, the heavenly Jerusalem, thousands of angels, the general
assembly and church of the first-born . . . God the Judge of all, the
spirits of just men made perfect, and the mediator of a new covenant,
Jesus' (12.18–23). The murder of Abel calling for vengeance was the
prefigurement of the Crucifixion of Jesus bestowing reconciliation
(12.24). Though he uses Platonic phraseology and even Platonic ideas,
the author of Hebrews envisages the Old Testament types as being
fulfilled, not in moral sentiments (Pseudo-Aristeas and the *Epistle of
Barnabas*), not in philosophical truths (Philo), but in realized eschatology, just as Paul and the author of the Fourth Gospel do. The failure
to realize this point considerably impairs Spicq's argument that the
Epistle to the Hebrews is really Philonism, less Philonic allegory.[1] Their
difference on this point reveals a wide and significant diversity which is
not to be mitigated by some similarity of vocabulary.

The similarity of ideas, rather than merely of vocabulary, which
Spicq claims to trace in the two authors, presents a much more cogent
argument.[2] But even here his arguments give rise to doubts. He maintains, for instance, that the author of the Epistle to the Hebrews has
taken the attributes ascribed to Moses by Philo and has attributed them
to Jesus; that he has applied to Jesus the Philonic concept of God as
Leader of his people; and that he has borrowed the Philonic doctrine
of the priesthood as an intercessory instrument in order to apply this
also to Jesus.[3] But the more the Philonic application of the concept
alleged to be borrowed differs from the application of it in Hebrews the
less likely it is that the author of Hebrews in fact borrowed it. In Philo's

[1] R. M. Grant, who concludes, against Spicq, that the allegorization of
Hebrews is wholly Philonic, has also failed to see this point (*The Letter and the
Spirit*, pp. 54–6).
[2] *L'Épitre aux Hébreux*, pp. 64–91.
[3] *Ibid.*, 64–9.

view Moses, though a hierophant, is still no more than a man. In Hebrews Jesus Christ is a heavenly being who has taken human nature upon himself. He is of course the Leader of God's people, because, as St Paul also believes (and in e.g. I Cor. 10.1–11 and II Cor. 3.12–4.6 declares), and as the author of Stephen's speech in Acts 7 probably believes, the Messiah appeared on occasions to Israel in his pre-incarnate existence. He intercedes precisely (as the Epistle to the Hebrews carefully explains) as the Jewish priesthood did *not* intercede, and as Paul in Rom. 8 describes Christ as interceding. If we did not have Philo's works, we could without grave difficulty describe all these doctrines as contemporary Rabbinic doctrines Christianized and clothed in Alexandrian language. As we possess Philo's books, we are tempted to conclude that the Epistle to the Hebrews was influenced by Philo. But need we yield to this temptation?

Spicq suggests that the author of Hebrews transfers the attributes of the Philonic Logos to Christ as Logos.[1] Between the relatively primitive Logos-doctrine of the Book of Wisdom and the highly developed Logos-doctrine of Philo, was there absolutely no intermediate development? Did the history of the Logos-doctrine leap immediately from one to the other? Surely not. There must have taken place a considerable intermediate development which is now lost to us in the interval (perhaps as long as 100 years) that separated the writer of Wisdom and Philo. It is more likely that the Logos-doctrine of Hebrews, which is not one of its more prominent features, represents a Christianization of a pre-Philonic stage of the doctrine.[2]

It is true that both authors speak of two sorts of temple and sanctuary, one made by hands and one divine or ideal. The buildings referred to in the legislation of Moses were in Philo's thought perfect copies (τύποι) intended to mean, when transmuted by allegory, the incorporeal archetypal images of Plato. To the author of Hebrews the patterns or copies (τύποι) were incurably imperfect, and the realities which they prefigured were not Platonic images but Christian realized eschatology. Hebrews never uses *archetype* (ἀρχέτυπος); Philo never uses *antitype*

---

[1] *Op. cit.*, p. 70.
[2] I omit mention in my text of Spicq's argument (*op. cit.*, pp. 71 f.) about the doctrine of remission of sins in the two authors. Hebrews (7.26) says that the Jewish High Priest cannot be perfect, whereas Philo says that he is perfect; Hebrews says unconditionally that Jewish sacrifices could not remit sin but only served to bring it again to remembrance, whereas Philo says that the sacrifices of the wicked serve to bring sin to remembrance but those of good people really remit sins. Far from concluding from this as Spicq does, that Hebrews is deliberately correcting Philo, I deduce that on both these subjects Hebrews takes an independent and wholly different attitude to Philo.

(ἀντίτυπος, cf. Heb. 9.23 f.). To the author of Hebrews, the true Temple of God was the Messiah, the Word in whom God tabernacled, on whom the Spirit rested, and the tabernacle and the Temple made with hands were only a prefiguring of this. We can find precisely the same doctrine (with the same reference to the pattern, τύπος) underlying Acts 7.44, 48, a passage which nobody has ever (as far as I know) attributed to Philo's influence. The chief coincidence of vocabulary between Philo and Hebrews upon this point is the use of the word ὑπόδειγμα (for I cannot allow that the use of τύπος is significant at all), and this is not at all a remarkable one.[1]

Spicq next turns to the treatment of faith and the interpretation of the lives of the patriarchs in both these authors.[2] In this we find what appears to be a contradiction unrecognized by Spicq. He compares two sayings, one from each author:

'By faith we understand that the worlds were framed by the word of God, so that what is seen hath not been made out of the things which do appear' (Heb. 11.3).

'The things that appear are the clearest proof of the creation' (Philo, *De Opificio Mundi* 84).[3]

Anybody can see that the meaning 'faith' in the first quotation and the meaning 'proof' in the second, though they are both represented by the same word in Greek (πίστις), express two quite different conceptions. I cannot see how anybody can conclude, on this evidence, that one author is indebted to the other for his doctrine of faith, even though both use the phrase 'the things that appear' (τὰ φαινόμενα), which is almost a Platonist technical term.

Spicq has an important point in his favour when he shows that the thought of the patriarchs, and especially of Abraham, as strangers and sojourners, and as making a pilgrimage, occurs in both writers, and that both writers say that God had promised Abraham a city (πόλις, Heb. 11.10; Philo *De Leg. Alleg.* III.83). But the thought of Abraham and the other patriarchs as strangers and sojourners is already found in Gen. 23.4, and the actual phrase 'strangers and pilgrims' (ξένοι καὶ παρεπί-

---

[1]Cf. *I Clement* 5.1; 6.1; 46.1; 55.1; 63.1, where on each occasion the word is used, not in the stricter sense of 'earthly pattern' as Hebrews uses it, but in the more general sense of 'pattern', even though Clement obviously knows the Epistle to the Hebrews.

[2]*Op. cit.,* pp. 76–84.

[3]In Greek: Hebrews: πίστει νοοῦμεν κατηρτίσθαι τοὺς αἰῶνας ῥήματι θεοῦ, εἰς τὸ μὴ ἐκ φαινομένων τὸ βλεπόμενον γεγονέναι. Philo: πίστις δὲ τῆς ἀρχῆς ἐναργεστάτη τὰ φαινόμενα.

δῆμοι, Heb. 11.13), presumably from a Greek version of Gen. 23.4, is not found in Philo. The use by both of the word 'sojourn' (παροικέω and its cognates) merely means that both are reproducing Gen. 26.3. That the theme of Abraham and his descendants as sojourners was used in contemporary theological literature independently of Philo is shown by Acts 7.4, 6. It is possible that the coincidence of both mentioning that God promised Abraham a city is accounted for by both authors assuming (perhaps following a Rabbinical tradition) that Abraham bought Mamre or part of it (Gen. 23). In fact Philo's interpretation of the significance of Abraham's departure and sojourning is entirely different from that of the Epistle to the Hebrews. To Philo it means that the soul must free itself from passions and bodily encumbrances; to the author of Hebrews it means that the promises of God would be fulfilled with the Messiah and his dispensation. The same entire difference of content applies to the resemblance (not a very striking one) of the use in the two authors of the phrase 'outside the camp' (ἔξω τῆς παρεμβολῆς, Heb. 13.13, Philo, De Gigantibus 54, both reproducing Lev. 16.27). The number of genuine similarities, too, to the long list of biblical characters found in Heb. 11 is surprisingly small, considering that we are comparing one chapter of Hebrews with thirty-seven books of Philo. If I tried hard enough I could probably parallel out of all the works of Shakespeare the list of pagan gods in Milton's Ode to the Nativity, but that would be no argument at all that Milton was indebted to Shakespeare for his list.

Finally, there are two very questionable statements in the closing pages of Spicq's argument. The first is that both authors regard history as nothing but 'a theme for speculation and moral teaching'.[1] This is wholly to misunderstand the attitude to history of the Epistle to the Hebrews; it is in fact this misunderstanding which continually throws doubt on Spicq's thesis, for all its apparent strength and thoroughness. The doctrine in Hebrews that the patriarchs and great men and women of faith under the old dispensation 'apart from us should not be made perfect' (11.40) means that the author is subordinating the whole Old Testament Heilsgeschichte to the epoch when the Messiah arrived, the Son of God incarnate. This is different toto caelo from, is in fact the direct contradiction of, Philo's resolute abandonment of the significance of history, as demonstrated most clearly in his use of allegory.

The second questionable statement is found in Spicq's assertion that both Philo and the author of Hebrews are alike in their preference for

[1] Op. cit., p. 85.

'an entirely spiritual cult'.[1] Though both turn their backs upon the Jewish sacrificial system, this resemblance is purely superficial. Philo does indeed desire to spiritualize and moralize the cult as far as he dare. But the author of Hebrews is steeped in the thought of sacrifice, the supreme, final sacrifice, made upon Calvary. He does not make the slightest attempt to moralize or allegorize this. And it is shortsighted to conclude that the Epistle to the Hebrews makes no reference to sacraments, just because his mention of the word 'baptism' on both occasions (6.2 and 9.10) refers to Jewish ceremonies. In his sixth chapter ('those who were once enlightened and have tasted of the heavenly gift', v.4) and in his tenth ('having . . . our bodies washed with pure water', v.22, cf. I Peter 3.21) he makes what appear to be clear references to the sacraments of Baptism and of the Eucharist.

In short it seems to me that the distinctive vocabulary and, to a smaller extent, the distinctive ideas of this Epistle reminiscent of Philo can be better explained by assuming that Philo and the author of the Epistle to the Hebrews were using a common Alexandrian Jewish stock of vocabulary and perhaps of ideas, rather than by concluding that Hebrews is directly influenced by Philo. Spicq's arguments, impressive and scholarly though their presentation is, envisaging Philo's whole syncretism of Judaism and Greek philosophy as virtually arising *de novo*, in the ultimate analysis fall short of conviction.

This survey of the scriptural interpretation of the Epistle to the Hebrews has discovered three points of coincidence in interpretation between the Epistle and another part of the New Testament, Acts 7.1–53, Stephen's Speech before the Sanhedrin. The Speech, like the Epistle, emphasizes the transitoriness of the state of Abraham and his descendants, even in the land which God gave them; Acts 7.3–5 emphasizes this, and especially in the words, 'And he did not give him an inheritance in it, not even a foothold, and he promised to give it for a possession to him and his seed after him, though he had no child'; in other words, God encouraged Abraham to look for another country, that is, an heavenly. There is probably also here a desire to allegorize the land to mean Christ, a conception which we shall find useful later for explaining a difficult passage in the *Epistle of Barnabas*.[2] Again, it is quite possible (though this point is, I admit, questionable) that the author of the Speech, like the author of the Epistle, envisages Christ as present with the people of Israel in the critical moments of their history under

[1] *Op. cit.*, p. 86.
[2] See below, p. 98.

the old dispensation. This may be the reason for the mention of the angel who appeared to Moses 'in a flame of fire in a bush' (ἄγγελος ἐν φλογὶ πυρὸς βάτου, 7.30, 35), who is also described as 'the voice of the Lord' (φωνὴ Κυρίου, 7.31). It also may account for the mention of the 'angel who spoke to him [Moses] in Mount Sinai' when Moses was 'in the church in the wilderness'.[1] Thirdly, the Speech, like the Epistle, almost certainly envisages two Temples, one a building made with hands (χειροποιήτοις, 7.48), after the pattern (τύπος, 7.44) which Moses saw on Mount Sinai, the other the Messiah, in whom God dwells as his true tabernacle (cf. John 1.14) and Temple (cf. John 2.17-22).

The fact is that the whole of Stephen's Speech is full of typology which is just ready to slip over into allegory, that is to say move from representing 'similar situation' typology to an identification of an object or a person in the Old Testament as prefiguring Christ, arbitrarily made without any attention to historical situation. Christ is seen prefigured in the Inheritance, the Seed, the Land; perhaps even the place-names Emmor and Sychem are intended for etymological allegory (7.16). Jacob is a type of Christ, and so is Moses; the correspondences between the career of these two figures and that of Christ (especially in the case of Moses) are worked out in some detail. Joshua is a type of Christ. The Tabernacle and the House of God are types of Christ. Only by interpreting the Speech in this way can any sense be made either of the charge made against Stephen at his trial (Acts 6.13 f.) or of his own summary at the end of his Speech (Acts 7.51, 53).[2]

In view of this evidence it becomes very likely that this Speech must be allowed an Alexandrian provenance, and regarded as a separate source, independent of the other early speeches in Acts. We shall see in the next chapter that the speech has two interesting points of resemblance to the *Epistle of Barnabas*, a document whose Alexandrian origin cannot be doubted, and this brings the suggestion of the Alexandrian character of Stephen's Speech almost to a certainty. It is most interesting to find another very early example of Christian theology in the Alexandrian tradition in the New Testament, and to observe that it gives no signs either of characteristically Alexandrian allegory or of Philonic influence. It suggests that there was an Alexandrian tradition of

---

[1]Acts 7.38: ὁ γενόμενος ἐν τῇ ἐκκλησίᾳ ἐν τῇ ἐρήμῳ μετὰ τοῦ ἀγγέλου τοῦ λαλοῦντος αὐτῷ ἐν τῷ ὄρει Σινᾶ. But the phrase in 7.53, εἰς διαταγὰς ἀγγέλων, is against this interpretation.

[2]For a fuller treatment of Stephen's Speech, drawing out all its typology, and suggesting that in fact the author does mention Jesus, see my article 'Studies in Texts, Acts 6.13 f.' in *Theology* L, pp. 142-5.

theological writing independent of Philo though contemporary with him. It also suggests that while allegory was a well-known device during the period that the New Testament was being written, and indeed the use of it to set aside the literal meaning of the Torah was quite common, the influence of specifically Alexandrian allegory, the allegory of Pseudo-Aristeas and Philo, was not at all strong, and that it would be most unwise to attribute to this Alexandrian allegory the origin of either Jewish or early Christian allegory. It would for the same reasons be utterly unreasonable to imagine these two types of allegory as having arisen, even remotely and indirectly, from the influence and example of pagan allegory.

4

The Development of the Allegorical Tradition

I T would not be appropriate within the limits of this study to consider all the Christian literature which survives for the period
between the writing of the New Testament and the work of Origen.
We will confine ourselves to what appear to be representative or particularly significant works, and especially to those which profess to be
interpreting the Old Testament. The *Epistle of Barnabas*, a book whose
baptismal typology we have already considered,[1] will provide a good
starting-point for this investigation. That this work is Alexandrian is
scarcely open to doubt. Its use of the word *gnosis* to mean scriptural
interpretation suggests this strongly;[2] so do its coincidences with the
Epistle to the Hebrews, whose arguments it reproduces without quoting
the text.[3] Even more decisive, however, is the Epistle's attitude to the
Jewish ceremonial law. Here the author takes exactly the line of Pseudo-
Aristeas, and on two points positively reproduces the arguments of that
work. The categories of animals mentioned in the Law, says *Barnabas*,[4]
are really categories of behaviour. The pig means careless, extravagant
behaviour. The eagle, vulture and hawk mean predatory and anti-social
behaviour. Three sorts of fish[5] mean cursed and impious people. The
hare means sensual behaviour. The hyena means licentious people. The
weasel means women 'who behave lawlessly with the mouth' (τὴν
ἀνομίαν ποιούσαις ἐν τῷ στόματι, 10.8) because the weasel conceives through the mouth. The commands to eat animals that cleave the
hoof and chew the cud mean, in the former case, 'that the righteous
makes his journey (περιπατεῖ) even in this world and expects the holy

---

[1]See above, pp. 70–72. For an illuminating and useful account of exegesis in
this period, written from a slightly different point of view, see R. M. Grant,
The Letter and the Spirit, pp. 58–84.
[2]*Epistle of Barnabas* 6.9; 9.8; 10.10; 19.1. See *Origen's Doctrine of Tradition*,
pp. 68 f., for an elaboration of this point, and for the Epistle's peculiar relation
to the works of Clement of Alexandria.
[3]E.g. the contrast between Moses as a servant (θεράπων) who received and
Jesus as the Lord (Κύριος) who gave, reminiscent of Heb. 3.1–6, where the same
word (θεράπων) borrowed by both from Num. 12.7, appears (*Barnabas* 14.4);
and the attitude to the Temple (*Barnabas* 16.1).
[4]The passage dealing with this subject is 10.1–12.
[5]σμύραινα, πώλυπα, σήπια, unknown to our Pentateuch.

A.E.–D

aeon', and in the latter, 'people who put into practice whatever distilla-
tion of word they have received in the heart' (τῶν μελετώντων ὃ ἔλαβον
δίσταλμα ῥήματος ἐν τῇ καρδίᾳ, 10.11).[1]

It is particularly interesting, then, in view of the Alexandrian character of the *Epistle of Barnabas* to find in it several coincidences with
Stephen's Speech in Acts. The most interesting is the allegorization of
the Land as a forecast of Christ. *Barnabas* interprets 'the good land' of
Ex. 33.1, 3 to mean Christ in the flesh. 'You must hope in him who is
destined to be manifested to you, Jesus,' is how the author interprets
this text.[2] And later this interpretation gives us in all probability the
reason for the curious comment of the author upon the apocryphal text
which he quotes, 'And the land of Jacob was praised above all the earth';
'he glorifies the vessel of his spirit,' the author's gloss on this text,
probably means that the Land is the body of Christ.[3] The same theme
probably accounts for the emphasis upon the Land in Acts 7.3–5. Again
Barnabas emphasizes the mysterious coincidence of the name which
Moses gave to Joshua with the name of the Saviour (12.8). We may
suspect the same theme in the phrase in Acts 7.44 f., 'The tabernacle
. . . which our fathers also succeeded to and transported with Joshua
at the disinheriting of the nations (of Canaan)', for the last words could
be interpreted to mean 'with Jesus at his acquisition of the Gentiles'.
Certainly in later times, especially in the work of Justin,[4] this argument
from the coincidence of the names was widely drawn. Thirdly, the
Epistle of Barnabas, as we have seen, maintains that the Temple was
never intended to be more than a prefiguring of the Messiah: 'Further,
I will tell you about the Temple, how deceived were the miserable
people who put their hope in the building, and not in their God who
made them to be the real temple of God.'[5] This is almost certainly the
theme also of Acts 7.44–51, with perhaps the difference that whereas
Barnabas sees that which was prefigured in the Temple as the Christian
Church, the author of Stephen's Speech sees it as the Messiah. But in
view of the readiness of the authors of the New Testament to pass from
one conception to the other, this is not a serious difference.[6]

---

[1]The interpretation of the predatory birds and of the weasel are direct reproductions from Pseudo-Aristeas 153–61. See above, pp. 43 f.
[2]6.8 f.   [3]See above, p. 72.   [4]See below, p. 106.
[5]16.1; the rest of the chapter develops this theme.
[6]This incidentally might supply one more example to the list of resemblances
of the *Epistle of Barnabas* to the Fourth Gospel compiled by J. N. Sanders in his
The Fourth Gospel in the Early Church, pp. 14 f. They are not, as I am sure
Sanders would admit, a very impressive array of coincidences, even when this
one is added.

We are justified, then, in classing the Epistle to the Hebrews, Stephen's Speech in Acts, and the *Epistle of Barnabas* together as productions of Alexandrian Christianity. Is *Barnabas* a wholly Alexandrian work showing, as far as allegory is concerned, no sign of Palestinian influence? The evidence does not justify us in saying this. In the first place, the *Epistle of Barnabas* shows no sign of influence from Philo whatever.[1] The allegorizations of the ceremonial law found in *Barnabas* are either borrowed directly from or modelled upon the allegory of Pseudo-Aristeas. Indeed we know that Barnabas did not reproduce the Philonic allegory of the animals that cleave the hoof and chew the cud; Philo interprets the two different sorts of animals as two necessary processes in apprehending wisdom; *Barnabas* interprets them as two different ways of behaving.[2] In the second place, there are also typological interpretations and allegorizations in the *Epistle of Barnabas* which are not specifically Alexandrian but rather Palestinian in character. We have already examined the baptismal typology of this author, which is a case in point.[3] There is also the author's allegorization of the ordinance (which cannot be found in any extant version of the Pentateuch) directing that the wool bound round the scapegoat shall be placed in a thorny shrub; this, he says, is a type, made for the Church, of Jesus (τύπος ἐστιν τοῦ Ἰησοῦ τῇ ἐκκλησίᾳ θέμενος), because those who want to reach him must endure tribulation.[4] Again there is the famous interpretation of the 318 souls circumcized by Abraham as a prediction of the Cross, of which the author is inordinately proud in spite of his affectation of modesty.[5] These interpretations are not characteristically Alexandrian; Philo, for instance, though he shows a little interest in the significance of numbers, nowhere, as far as I know, translates numbers into letters in order to secure a suitable allegorization. There is also the remarkable comment in the *Epistle of Barnabas* on the sabbath. The sabbath, he says, is really a prophecy of God's finally winding up everything at the last day; his making the world in six days means that he will complete all in 6,000 years; the seventh day means the return of the Son for judgement.[6] This eschatological interpretation is not Alexandrian, and not even remotely Philonic.

---

[1] The statement of R. H. Snape (*A Rabbinic Anthology*, Excursus II, 'Rabbinic and Early Christian Ethics', p. 619) that 'there are coincidences of interpretation between Barnabas and Philo which show the immediate connexion between Christian and Hellenistic Judaism', is, as far as I know, wholly unjustified.
[2] Philo, *De Agric.* 131 ff., and *De Spec. Leg.* IV.109; see above, p. 44, n.1.
[3] See above, pp. 70–72.
[4] 7.11.   [5] 9.8.   [6] 15.1–9.

The date of the *Epistle of Barnabas* must, I believe, be placed early rather than late within the possible limits.[1] The fact that it quotes a saying which also appears in II Peter 3.8, 'one day is with the Lord as a thousand years, and a thousand years as one day' (15.4), does not compel us to place *Barnabas* later than II Peter, because it is perfectly possible to imagine this saying as one current widely in the Church well before the writing of II Peter. The fact that it reproduces (18–21) the primitive, wholly ethical, very Jewish document, 'The Two Ways', which also appears in the *Didache*, need not compel us to place *Barnabas* late either; on the contrary, it would be a relief from many points of view to envisage the *Didache* as a first-century rather than a second-century work. The first seventeen chapters of *Barnabas* obviously come from an Alexandrian source, but they show no signs of a Philonic influence, and they also display several points consistent with what we know of the earliest, Palestinian, Christian tradition of interpretation. It is reasonable to conclude that in this work we have an example of Palestinian Christian typological argument and tradition modified by Alexandrian Christian influence, and that it is one of a group of three such documents, with the Epistle to the Hebrews and Stephen's Speech in Acts, which we should place in the second half of the first century. None of these works are indebted to Philo, whose influence upon Christian allegory did not make itself felt for a century after the appearance of these documents.

Apart from the *Epistle of Barnabas* allegory is not at all a prominent feature of the literature of the sub-apostolic period. The *First Epistle of Clement* is full of Scriptural allusions and 'types' in the Philonic use of the word as examples (instances of envy, of obedience, etc.), but there is very little typology[2] and we can identify with confidence only two examples of allegory proper. The first of these is the author's notable interpretation of Rahab's scarlet thread: 'And they further gave her a sign that she should hand a scarlet thread out of her house, thereby prefiguring (πρόδηλον ποιοῦντες) that through the blood of the Lord

---

[1]It knows of the destruction of the Temple (4.14 οὕτως ἐνκαταλελεῖφθαι αὐτούς). But the fact that it does not quote Hebrews suggests that we must not place this work long after 70; by about 96 I *Clement* can quote Hebrews freely as an authoritative document, so that presumably by then it was quite a widely-known work. The author of *Barnabas* may of course have known Hebrews without quoting it.

[2]We may perhaps classify as typology the statement (3.1) that Deut. 32.15 ('Jeshurun waxed fat and kicked', etc.) has been fulfilled (ἐτελέσθη τὸ γεγραμμένον) in the self-confidence of the church of Corinth after a period of prosperity. It would however be rather more accurate to describe this as fulfilled prophecy.

there shall be deliverance to all who trust and hope in God. You see, beloved, that there was not only faith but also prophecy in the woman' (13.7 f.). The other example is the author's allegorization of Ps. 118.19 f. ('Open to me the gate of righteousness', etc.) to mean the way of Christ (48.2–4).

In all the seven genuine epistles of Ignatius there is no allegory and virtually no typology.[1] But there is one remarkable passage where he may be referring to the practice of allegorizing. In *Philadelphians* 8.2 Ignatius says that he heard (when he was at Philadelphia) some people saying, 'Unless I find it in the charters I will not believe it in the gospel.'[2] He goes on, 'And when I said to them, "It is written," they answered me that that is begging the question. But to me the charters are Jesus Christ, the inviolable charters are his Cross and his Death and his Resurrection and the faith which is through him.'[3] Judaizing Christians have already been referred to in this Epistle (6.1). It is possible that these Christians were challenging the contemporary practice in the Christian church of allegorizing the Old Testament Scriptures so as to find Christ in them everywhere.[4]

The *Didache* shows no allegory and very few examples even of typology.[5] One of these is a phrase in the eucharistic prayer (9.2): 'We give thee thanks, our Father, for the holy vine of David thy Son which thou hast made known to us through Jesus thy Son' (παιδός σου). Another passage (14.2) applies Mal. 1.11, 14 to the Eucharist using it as a warning 'that your sacrifice be not profaned' (ἵνα μὴ κοινωθῇ ἡ θυσία ὑμῶν), an example which might be thought to lie on the frontier between fulfilled prophecy and allegory. But otherwise the simplicity

---

[1]Unless we are to count as typology the complicated picture of *Ephesians* 18.2, referred to already above, p. 72.
[2]ἐὰν μὴ ἐν τοῖς ἀρχείοις εὕρω ἐν τῷ εὐαγγελίῳ οὐ πιστεύω.
[3]καὶ λέγοντός μου αὐτοῖς ὅτι γέγραπται, ἀπεκρίθησάν μοι ὅτι πρόκειται. ἐμοὶ δὲ ἀρχεῖά ἐστιν Ἰησοῦς Χριστός, τὰ ἄθικτα ἀρχεῖα ὁ σταυρὸς αὐτοῦ καὶ ὁ θάνατος καὶ ἡ ἀνάστασις αὐτοῦ καὶ ἡ πίστις ἡ δι' αὐτοῦ.
[4]Ignatius refers to the prophets as witnessing to Christ on more than one occasion; e.g. *Philadelphians* 5.2 (where Kirsopp Lake's suggestion in the note *in loc.* to his translation that these are Christian prophets is most unlikely), 9.1–2; cf. *Smyrneans* 5.1; 7.2.
[5]I find it very difficult to believe that the *Didache* should be placed late in the second century, or even in the second century at all, and not in the first. The phrase Χειροτονήσατε οὖν ἐπισκόπους καὶ διακόνους (15.1) is pretty clear evidence that the writer does not know of monarchical episcopacy, and yet most scholars seem to think that the *Didache* emanates from Syria, where certainly after the career of Ignatius (ἐπίσκοπον Συρίας *Romans* 2.2) that institution would be known. The theology is primitive, the tone is intensely Jewish, the preoccupation with prophets argues an early period for the work. The difficulty that the *Epistle of Barnabas* also includes 'The Two Ways' is lessened if we assume that this Epistle is itself early.

of the typology and the absence of allegory support the argument in favour of an early date for this work.

The *Second Epistle of Clement*, perhaps because it is evidently later than the sub-apostolic works already considered, yields rather more material for those who are searching for allegory. That the writer is aware of the possibility of allegorizing appears from his reproducing the allegorization of some apocryphal *logion* of Christ, quoted perhaps from the *Gospel according to the Egyptians*. The words (12.2–5) are obviously enigmatic and intended for such treatment, and not at all reminiscent of the sort of words attributed to Jesus in the canonical Gospels. Earlier (2.1–3) the writer has quoted Isa. 54.1 as a prophecy applicable to the Church (as does Paul in Gal. 4.27), and he says that 'Cry aloud, thou that didst not travail!' is an exhortation to pray earnestly and not to lose heart like women in travail, an example which we may also classify as lying on the frontier of allegory. Towards the end of the work, however (14.1–5) we find a very interesting passage containing more than one example of allegorization. It is concerned with the spiritual Church. The 'den of robbers' of Jer. 7.11 is said to be figurative of the condition of those who do not perform the will of the Lord, a condition contrasted with that of being in the spiritual, primal, heavenly Church (14.1). 'I do not think that you are unaware,' says the author, 'that the living Church is the body of Christ, for the Scripture says: God made man male and female. The male is Christ, the female is the Church' (14.2). Next, having explained that the spiritual Church was manifested in the body of Christ, he says that if anybody 'keeps her in the flesh and does not corrupt her (τηρήσῃ αὐτὴν ἐν τῇ σαρκὶ καὶ μὴ φθειρῇ) he will receive her (ἀπολήψεται αὐτήν) in the Holy Spirit. For the flesh itself is the antitype of the spirit; therefore nobody who corrupts the antitype will partake of the reality (3).[1] And if we say that the Church is the flesh and Christ is the Spirit, then he who insults the flesh has insulted the Church. Therefore such a man will not receive the Spirit, which is Christ (4). Of so great a life and immortality can the flesh itself partake if the Holy Spirit be joined to it' (5). The treatment of the text about the 'den of robbers' and of Gen. 1.27 is unmistakably allegory, even though it is easy to see how it has grown out of typology.

---

[1] ἡ γὰρ σὰρξ αὕτη ἀντίτυπός ἐστιν τοῦ πνεύματος· οὐδεὶς οὖν τὸ ἀντίτυπον φθείρας τὸ αὐθεντικὸν μεταλήψεται. It is noteworthy that the author does not really use 'antitype' as the Epistle to the Hebrews uses it (*pace* Lundberg's remark, quoted above, p. 67), because for him the antitype is a means of achieving the reality, whereas this does not hold good for the use of the word in Hebrews.

The view of the Church as a sacrament of Christ is a remarkable one, showing how firm a grasp upon the truth of the Incarnation this writer has.[1]

The writers of the sub-apostolic period, then, with the exception of the author of the *Epistle of Barnabas*, show no signs at all of being influenced by Alexandrian, far less by Philonic, allegory, and even *Barnabas* has several examples of allegory that is not Alexandrian. They seem, when they use allegory at all, to be for the most part inheriting, and perhaps a little developing, the central Christian tradition of allegory which was in its turn influenced by Jewish Palestinian allegory, either of the Rabbinic or of what we might call the Messianic or prophetic sort, as evidenced by the *Habakkuk Commentary* and the *Damascus Document*. The reason for the comparative rarity of allegory of this kind in this literature (again with the exception of the *Epistle of Barnabas*) is no doubt because its authors in their surviving works did not have much occasion for interpreting the Old Testament. There is, for instance, absolutely no allegorization of the Old Testament, or of the New Testament, in the *Shepherd* of Hermas, though the book is full of allegories. It is obviously written by somebody of mediocre intellect and education and in a humble station of life.[2]

When we examine the works of Justin Martyr, however, we find an abundant development of this allegorical tradition. This is partly because the *Dialogue with Trypho*, which supplies us with most of our material, was written in order to show that the Old Testament pointed to Jesus Christ and therefore necessarily employs contemporary methods of scriptural interpretation; and partly because Justin was more of an intellectual than the authors of much of the sub-apostolic literature, and found allegory an important ally in providing an intellectual justification for the Church's retention of the Old Testament as its sacred literature, a task which was no small part of Justin's apologetic responsibility. Many of his scriptural interpretations would strike the reader as little

[1]Cf. Hermas, *Shepherd*, Similitudes V.7. Tertullian, *Adv. Marcionem* III.24, regards this 'Jerusalem from above' as the city destined to appear at the Millennial Kingdom.

[2]Neither is there any typology of the Old Testament. Hermas uses τύπος several times, in *Visions* III.xi.4 to mean the explanation of a vision, and in *Similitudes* II.2 to mean the parable of the elm and the vine given there; in *Visions* IV.i.1, ii.3 and iii.6 it means the 'type' of a coming persecution embodied in a vision; in *Similitudes* IX.x.1 the word means the marks left by stones when they are taken out of the ground. These uses are all quite untechnical. My text for Hermas is that of Kirsopp Lake in Vol. II of his *Apostolic Fathers*, but I have had the privilege of seeing in typescript the new edition of Hermas' text compiled by Miss M. Whittaker, B.D., my colleague on the Staff of the University of Nottingham, for the *GCS* series.

more elaborate than some of the typology to be discovered in the New Testament or in the Apostolic Fathers. He says, for instance, that just as Abraham obeyed the call to 'go out from the land in which he dwelt' (Gen. 12.1), so Christians have obeyed Christ's call to abandon their homeland (πολιτεία, but it could mean 'way of behaviour') and inherit the promised land.[1] And he deals with the flood in a manner which Lundberg has shown to be traditional. Relying on a text 'At Noah's flood I saved thee' (ἐπὶ τοῦ κατακλυσμοῦ τοῦ Νῶε ἔσωσά σε), which may be a version or a reminiscence of Isa. 54.8 f., he says that Noah's experience of salvation was a mystical sign (μυστήριον). Noah and his wife and his three sons and his three sons' wives made eight souls, symbolic of the eighth day on which Christ rose.[2] Then he goes on: 'Christ who was the first-born of all creation also became the beginning again of another race, reborn by him through water and faith and wood, since he brought the mystery of the Cross, just as Noah also was saved by wood, riding on the waters with his family.'[3] This particular observation seems to be added as an afterthought, as if he felt that this traditional piece of typology should be brought in somewhere, however awkwardly. But in other interpretations Justin goes much further than this. In particular, he is much more unrestrained than New Testament writers about reading back the presence of the pre-incarnate Christ into the Old Testament[4] and about allotting different passages of the same section to different alleged persons, a practice which we might call 'impersonation'. He makes an explicit avowal about this practice; 'But when you hear read passages of the Scriptures supposed to be said by various characters, do not imagine that they are said by the inspired people themselves, but by the divine Word who prompted them. For he sometimes speaks as one who foretells events that are to take place, and sometimes he makes utterances in the character of (ὡς ἀπὸ προσώπου) God the Master of all and Father, and sometimes in the character of Christ, and sometimes in the character of peoples who answer the Lord and his Father.'[5] Consistently with this principle, Justin is

---

[1]*Dial.* 119.5.   [2]*Dial.* 138.1.   [3]*Dial.* 138.2. Cf. above p. 69.
[4]E.g. in *Dial.* 57.2, after several chapters devoted to showing that a second god (δεύτερος θεὸς κατ' ἀριθμὸν ἀλλ' οὐ κατὰ γνώμην) is spoken of in Genesis under the description of a man, sometimes one of three, who appeared to Abraham, to Sarah, and to Lot, he counters Trypho's objection that this figure is described in Genesis as eating (and therefore cannot be the pre-incarnate Logos) by saying that 'eating' is only a metaphorical term, as one says that fire devours. He describes this explanation as τροπολογία.
[5]*Apol.* I.36.1 f.; the examples which Justin gives of the Father speaking in the Scriptures in this passage are Isa. 1.3 f.; 66.1; 1.14, 13b, 15, 13a, 11, 12; 58.6 f. (*Apol.* I.37.1–9). Examples of Christ speaking are: Isa. 65.2; 50.6–8;

ready to regard any passage in the Old Testament as spoken in the person of Jesus, or the Jews, or persecuted Christians, or the Holy Spirit, or God the Father. For instance, he refers Ps. 24 to Jesus, the questions and answers in the Psalm being regarded as a dialogue between angelic powers on the one hand and the Holy Spirit speaking in the character of God the Father, or in his own, on the other.[1] Ps. 47 is interpreted in a similar fashion, and Ps. 99 is taken to represent the Holy Spirit as rebuking the Jews for not recognizing Jesus as King and declaring that Samuel, Aaron and Moses did recognize him.[2] Many other such instances could be collected from the *Dialogue*, but such a practice is only a development of a tradition to be found in the New Testament, and indeed is perhaps even derived from an earlier tradition yet. We have already seen that a few examples of such 'impersonation' can be found in the Rabbis.[3] This is not the only exegetical point which Justin may have borrowed from contemporary Jewish scholarship. Justin frequently uses the verb 'shouts' (βοᾷ), usually with God as subject, to introduce a quotation from the Old Testament. Bonsirven notes that the Rabbis sometimes say that the Holy Spirit 'shouted' (*ṣawwaḥēt*) certain words found in the Bible.[4] This is not the first occasion for our finding reason to think that Justin has a special acquaintance with the Judaism of his day.[5]

There are also a number of interpretations in Justin where typology seems to be trembling on the verge of allegory. At one point he collects together indiscriminately all the instances of 'rod' (ῥάβδος) and of 'wood' (ξύλον) which he can find in the Old Testament (adding a few examples of anointing and a few references to the famous Stone to make weight) and applies them to Christ.[6] Moses throwing the stick into the water, Jacob crossing the river with his staff, Jacob's ladder, Aaron's rod, the 'tree by the water-side' of Ps. 1, the oak of Mamre, the 'rod and staff' of Ps. 23—all comes as grist to his exegetical mill. They all have

---

Ps. 22.19, 17; 3.6 (*Apol*.I.38.1–6). Examples of the 'prophetic spirit' speaking are: Isa. 2.3, 4 (*Apol*. I.39.1), by which Justin apparently means what we might call direct prophecy.

[1] *Dial*. 36.2–5. Cf. 30.2, where the word that Justin uses for Christ 'impersonating' in the OT in this way is σχηματοποιήσας.

[2] *Dial*. 37.1–4.

[3] See above, p. 1, where Bonsirven, *Exégèse Rabbinique*, pp. 172 f., is cited to support this point.

[4] *Op. cit.*, p. 32; the authorities cited by Bonsirven are *Mekhilta* on Ex. 15.2, p. 126; *Siphre* Deut. 32.26, 355, 148a. Cf. Aphraates, *Demonstratio* I (De Fide), 7, col. 17, where there occurs the phrase 'David of old proclaimed' (*dawīd qadem 'acrṣāh* (κηρύσσει)).

[5] See above, p. 12.

[6] *Dial*. 86.1–6.

A.E.–D*

reference to Christ's Cross. One of these types especially in the elaboration of its detail comes very close to allegory. Elisha threw a stick into the river and recovered the axe-head by means of which the sons of the prophets intended to make a house in which they could study the law. When we are baptized, Christ through his death on the Cross and his sanctifying us by water has rescued us and made us a house of prayer and worship.[1] Later, challenged by Trypho to say why his Christ should have died the death of one accursed, Justin replies that the Crucifixion was prophesied in the Old Testament. The passages he cites are Ex. 17.10–12 (Moses holding up his hands to secure victory for Joshua-Jesus who was leading God's people against Amalek);[2] Deut. 33.13–17, which mentions the 'wild-ox' (LXX 'unicorn', μονοκέρως) whose horns, Justin alleges, resemble a Cross; and Num. 21.9, the lifting up of the Serpent in the wilderness. Elsewhere[3] Justin cites a long series of proof-texts to demonstrate how Jesus was foretold by the prophets. The series begins with Gen. 49.10 f. ('The sceptre shall not depart from Judah . . . Binding his foal unto the vine, and his ass's colt unto the choice vine. He hath washed his garments in wine, and his vesture in the blood of grapes'). Jesus was descended from Judah, Justin says. The Gentiles believed in him. When he entered Jerusalem, the foal of an ass was waiting for him, 'tethered to a vine'.[4] The expression 'washing his robe in the blood of the grape' refers to the Passion of Jesus, for 'by his blood he purified those who believe in him'; the robe means those who believe in him; the blood of the vine means his blood, for it is not made by man and Jesus was 'not of man's seed, but of divine power'.[5] One of his interpretations provides us with an interesting piece of eucharistic typology. He quotes Isa. 33.13–19 as predictive of 'the bread which our Christ handed down to us to do in remembrance, and in order to make his body (σωματοποιήσασθαι) for the sake of those who believe in him,

[1]Dial. 86.6.
[2]Dial. 90.4. The next two examples are from 91.1–4; cf. 94.1.
[3]Apol. I.32.1–13. Cf. Dial. 3.1–4, where another list of the prefigurements of Christ's Passion is given: Moses holding up his hands during Joshua's battle with Amalek; the killing of the Passover lamb and the distribution of its blood; 'the goats sacrificed in the fast' (the Day of Atonement, cf. Epistle of Barnabas 7.11; 9.1–7); the scarlet thread given to Rahab the harlot (cf. I Clement 13.7 f.). Cf. too Dial. 112.2 where the Serpent in the wilderness is again referred to Christ's Passion.
[4]Here is a remarkable piece of oral tradition; independent of the Bible and wholly worthless!
[5]Other proof-texts are Isa. 11.1, 10, conflated with Num. 24.17 (Apol. I.32.12); Isa. 7.14 (Apol. I.33.1); Micah 5.2 (Apol. I.34.1); Isa. 9.6; 65.2; 58.2; Ps. 22.17, 19; Zech. 9.9 (Apol. I.35.1–11). For Origen's reproduction of this interpretation of Gen. 49.11, see below, p. 157.

THE DEVELOPMENT OF THE ALLEGORICAL TRADITION 107

for whose sake he became capable of suffering, and concerning the cup
which he delivered to us to do as we give thanks in remembrance of his
blood' (καὶ περὶ τοῦ ποτηρίου ὃ εἰς ἀνάμνησιν τοῦ αἵματος αὐτοῦ
παρέδωκεν εὐχαριστοῦντας ποιεῖν).[1]
From these examples of near-allegory we can turn to several instances
of full-blooded, well-developed allegory. The proof-text from Gen. 49.
10 f. which he cited in the *Apology* he later allegorized in a much more
thorough manner in his *Dialogue*.[2] This passage, said Justin, prophesies
the two advents of Christ, figuratively and enigmatically (ἐν παραβολῇ
καὶ παρακεκαλυμμένως). The colt is the previously untamed Gentiles
who have now come under the yoke of Christ, and the foal of the ass is
the Christian Jews who are already under the yoke of Moses. The
reference to 'washing his robe in wine and his garment in the blood of
the grape' is held to mean the Holy Spirit (the robe in which Christ's
people are clothed) and Christ's human nature which comes from God
and not from man (the blood of the grape). Earlier[3] he had allegorized
the twelve bells on the High Priest's garment as a symbol (σύμβολον)
of the twelve apostles. And later[4] he says that in the prophets Christ is
called (no doubt according to the allegorical interpretation) 'wisdom and
day and sunrise and sword and stone and rod and Jacob and Israel', a
statement which gives some idea of the range of Justin's allegory. More
than once he treats us to an elaborate allegorical exposition of a long
passage. He quotes, for instance, Micah 4.1–7 and interprets it.[5] The
passage, he says, refers to the two advents of Christ. The transformation
of warlike into peaceful instruments refers to the peace of mind and
heart which men of every race find in Christianity. Each man sitting
under his own vine refers to the Christians' insistence upon Christian
marriage (Ps. 127.3, 'thy wife shall be a fruitful vine'). The afflicted
woman of Micah 4.6 refers to the fact that all Christians will probably
be put to death in the Last Time. A similar exposition later on of
Jacob's matrimonial adventures makes out that Leah is the Synagogue,
and Rachel the Church; the variegated animals earned by Jacob's labour
for Laban represent the diverse virgins of the Gentile Christians; the
weak eyes of Leah represent the weakness of soul of Justin's Jewish
opponents.[6] Perhaps the most fantastic of all Justin's allegories is the
statement that the phrase in Lam. 4.20 ('The breath of our nostrils, the
anointed of the Lord', πνεῦμα πρὸ προσώπου ἡμῶν χριστὸς κύριος

[1]*Dial.* 70.2–5.　　　　　[2]52.1–2; 53.1–6; and 54.1–2.
[3]42.1–3.　　　　　[4]100.4.
[5]*Dial.* 109.1; 110.1–6; cf. the very similar exposition of Ps. 22 in *Dial.* 99–107.
[6]*Dial.* 134.3–6.

is Justin's version) means that man's upright stance and breathing
organs are a sign of the Cross.[1]

There are no signs at all in Justin of the influence of the Alexandrian
tradition of allegory. Mrs Flessemann-Van Leer points to two passages
where he speaks about the grace of understanding or knowing,[2] and
comments, 'We are here, quite clearly, in the neighbourhood of the
gnosis of Barnabas, though Justin himself does not employ the word in
this specific sense.' But this is a very insubstantial foundation upon
which to build a theory that Justin owes anything to the *Epistle of
Barnabas* or to the exegetical tradition of Alexandria. All the evidence
which we should expect for such an hypothesis is lacking. He does not
consistently claim nor boast of *gnosis*. He does not use the word *allegory*
or *allegorize*. He does not contrast the literal with the spiritual. He does
not allegorize the text of the Old Testament into speculative philosophy
nor into moral sentiments. He does not belittle the significance of history. His attitude to the Torah is quite different from that of the
Epistle of Barnabas.[3] The sources of his interpretation are evidently
Rabbinic allegory, the example of the writers of the New Testament, and
traditional typology, partly deriving from Jewish liturgy and partly from
Messianic and prophetical interpretation. All these are acted upon by
an eager desire to find Christ everywhere in the Old Testament. The
result is an allegory more elaborate and more remote from 'similar
situation' typology than any Christian interpretation before him. But
he has none of the smooth, confident efficiency of Origen, and in spite
of his vehemence his allegory is a little tentative.

Melito, Bishop of Sardis, from whose works a *Homily on the Passion*
and a few other fragments survive, in his interpretation of the Old
Testament shows no striking advance upon Justin. A fragment expresses
the suggestion that Absalom was a type of the devil, who rebelled against
the Kingdom of God.[4] In the *Homily* there is a vivid passage giving a list
of types of Christ in the Old Testament: 'Abel, murdered as he was;
Isaac, fettered as he was; Joseph, sold as he was; Moses, exposed as he
was; David, persecuted as he was; the prophets suffering for the sake
of Christ like him; the lamb sacrificed in the land of Egypt, which
smote Egypt and saved Israel through its blood.'[5] These do not suggest

---

[1] *Apol.* I.55.5.
[2] E. Flessemann-Van Leer, *Tradition and Scripture in the Early Church*, p. 80;
the two passages are *Dial.* 30.1, χάριν τοῦ γνῶναι, and 119.1, χάριν τοῦ νοῆσαι.
[3] For a tracing of the Christian attitude to the Torah, including Justin's, see
ch. 11 below, devoted to Origen's attitude to the law.
[4] Frag. 5, *Die Ältesten Apologeten*, p. 309.
[5] *Homily on the Passion* (ed. Campbell Bonner) 59 f., p. 127.

a very old traditional list of types, but a determination, like Justin's, to find Christ in any mention of personal violence in the Old Testament.[1] Melito goes quite as far as Justin in reading Christ into the Old Testament. Towards the end of his *Homily on the Passion* he chooses rhetorically to address an imaginary Jew: 'This is he who led you to Egypt and protected and fostered you there. This is he who gave you light in the pillar and shaded you in the cloud, who divided the Red Sea and led you across and destroyed your enemy. This is he who gave you the Law in Horeb, who gave you your inheritance in the land, who sent the prophets to you, who raised up your kings.'[2] Campbell Bonner remarks on this passage that Melito is probably transferring to Christ 'an ancient hymn of praise to the God of Israel for the benefits and blessings bestowed upon his people', and compares Justin, *Dial.* 131.3-6. The interesting point is that what may have started as a series of Jewish liturgical types of an *exauditi* sort, and then later become a series of Christological types, has now become a series of occasions when the pre-incarnate Christ was envisaged as present with his people under the old dispensation. Melito's handling of the Old Testament always seems to be trembling on the brink of allegory, but he never engages in it.

It is surprising and interesting to find Theophilus, Bishop of Antioch, whose *Three Books to Autolycus* were written not earlier than the death of Marcus Aurelius on 17th March, 180, indulging in allegory which has a clearly Alexandrian flavour. When Theophilus comes in the course of his apologetic work to discuss the creation, he takes the different acts of creation allotted to each day in the narrative of Genesis to be significant of various moral and spiritual things.[3] The creation of light, for instance, is 'an indication and a type of a mighty revelation' (δεῖγμα καὶ τύπον μεγάλου μυστηρίου); the sun is God, the moon, which waxes and wanes, man.[4] Harmless and predatory birds and fish are significant of different sorts of men, gentle and law-abiding or rapacious and cruel. This is, of course, a direct borrowing from Pseudo-Aristeas.[5] The

---

[1] On the other hand, Melito's list of passages predicting τὸ τοῦ πάσχα μυστήριον in the OT are: Deut. 28.66 (rendered as καὶ ὄψεσθε τὴν ζωὴν ὑμῶν κεκραμένην ἔμπροσθεν τῶν ὀφθαλμῶν ὑμῶν νυκτὸς καὶ ἡμέρας καὶ οὐ πιστεύσετε ἐπὶ τὴν ζωὴν ὑμῶν); Ps. 2.1 f.; Jer. 11.19; Isa. 53.7 (*ibid.*, 61-4, p. 129). These are probably traditional proof-texts.

[2] *Ibid.*, 84 f., p. 147.   [3] *Autolycus* II.14-17.   [4] *Ibid.*, II.15.

[5] *Ibid.*, II.16. Cf. above, pp. 43 f., 97 f.; *Letter of Aristeas*, 143-50, pp. 544 f. Bardy (*Autolycus*, p. 143 n. 1) compares Origen, *Hom. on Gen.* I.8 f., where the passage is expounded as referring to good and bad thoughts occurring in the mind. But the only parallel here is that Theophilus and Origen have in mind the same subject to allegorize. I cannot agree with R. M. Grant's surprising conclusion that Theophilus' exegesis is close to that of Palestinian Judaism and has no Alexandrian *traits* in it (*The Letter and the Spirit*, pp. 78-80).

beasts created on the sixth day are a type of various sorts of men too, and the birds mentioned in Gen. 1.26 represent men who repent from their unrighteousness and who, gaining wings for their souls, fly up to better things. The birds who do not fly are like wicked men who cannot escape from their sin.[1] The command to Adam to work the ground really means that he was enjoined to keep the commandment of God.[2]

That Theophilus was not prepared to indulge in wholesale allegory is evident from his account of the garden of Eden.[3] He shows no sign of specifically Philonic allegory, but at one point he does reproduce from Philo the thought that God judged only man fit to be created by his own hands.[4] But it is more likely that Theophilus found this sentiment in a contemporary *Reader's Digest*, of the sort that he used plentifully to supply him with philosophical opinions, than that he had read Philo or had been seriously influenced by him.

It would be beyond the scope of this brief survey to examine fully the use of allegory by Irenaeus, but it may be useful to record his use of this device in his *Demonstration of the Apostolic Preaching*, a work written about 190, later than the *Adversus Haereses*, as a short handbook to equip the Christian to give a reason for his faith.[5] It is likely that this work will represent, not the private allegorical fancies of Irenaeus, but as much allegory as in his opinion the average educated Christian could be expected to endure, and that the allegory will be traditional rather than individual. This conjecture is borne out by the many points of coincidence with Justin's work that the *Demonstration* exhibits. Armitage Robinson in his Introduction lists several of these,[6] the proof-texts from the Blessing of Jacob;[7] the suggestion that it was the Son of God who spoke to Abraham;[8] the association of Jacob's ladder with the Cross.[9] In his notes on the text Robinson adds several more coin-

[1]*Autolycus* II.17.   [2]*Ibid.*, II.24.
[3]*Ibid.*, II.19. For Philo, see *De Plantatione* 40 ff. and above, p. 51. For Origen, see below, p. 239.
[4]*Ibid.*, II.18, reading ἴδιον for ἀΐδιον; Philo, *De Opificio* 72-4. Bardy, *in loc.*, compares Irenaeus, *Adv. Haer.* IV.34.1.
[5]I quote the *Demonstration* from the translation from the Armenian by J. Armitage Robinson. There is also a German translation, *Des Heiligen Irenaeus Schrift zum Erweise der Apostolischer Verkundigung*, Εἰς "Ενδειξιν τοῦ 'Αποστολικοῦ Κηρύγματος in armenische Version entdeckt herausgegeben und ins Deutsche übersetzt, von Lic. Dr Karapet Ter-Merkerttschian und Lic. Dr Erwand Ter-Minassiantz, mit einem Nachwort und Anmerkungen von Adolf Harnack (Leipzig, 1907). Armitage Robinson claims that his translation is more accurate than the German version.
[6]*Op. cit.*, pp. 6-23.   [7]*Apol.* I.32; *Dem.* 57.   [8]*Dial.* 56; *Dem.* 44.
[9]*Dial.* 86; *Dem.* 45.

cidences: the emphasis upon Moses having changed his successor's name to that of Joshua;[1] the quaint idea that the X of the Cross is inscribed on all creation;[2] the reference to the Cross of Moses holding up his hands in order to ensure victory over Amalek;[3] the interpretation of Isa. 9.6 ('whose government is upon his shoulder') as a prophecy of the Crucifixion;[4] the allegorization of 'robe' in Gen. 49.11 to mean 'believers' and 'blood of the grape' to mean 'Christ's blood',[5] and the contention that Christians do not now need the law of the sabbath, for in Christ they enjoy a perpetual sabbath.[6]

In this work, therefore, Irenaeus was content in his handling of the Old Testament to follow the line laid down already by Justin. The greater part of the *Demonstration* consists of an adducing of proof-texts to prove that every part of the Christian dispensation was predicted in the Old Testament, precisely in Justin's manner and with several direct borrowings from him, using mainly the prophets (particularly Isaiah) and the Psalms as material. It is interesting to observe that there are two or three coincidences in Irenaeus' interpretation with the *Epistle of Barnabas*. Barnabas as well as Justin uses Moses' posture during the battle against Amalek as a prefigurement of the Cross;[7] both authors quote Isa. 45.1 as if for 'my anointed Cyrus' (Κύρῳ) they read 'my anointed Lord' (χυρίῳ) in their version of the LXX;[8] and both quote as a text from the Old Testament the sentence 'Spare my soul from the sword and nail my flesh', a conflation of Ps. 22.20 and Ps. 119.120, aided by a mistranslation of the LXX.[9] It is perhaps more likely that Irenaeus is using traditional material in common with the *Epistle of Barnabas* (though not a single common document) than that he is reproducing the Epistle's interpretation directly, as he probably is doing in the case of his coincidences with Justin. Certainly there is no trace at all of Alexandrian influence in the *Demonstration*, unless we count as Alexandrian influence the fact that he reproduces the attitude to the Torah of the Epistle to the Hebrews.[10] But there is no allegorization into general moral sentiments nor into philosophical speculation of a Philonic sort,

[1] *Dial.* 75, 113; *Dem.* 26. [2] *Apol.* I.60; *Dem.* 34.
[3] *Dial.* 91, 112, 131; *Dem.* 46, 79. [4] *Apol.* I.35; *Dem.* 56.
[5] *Apol.* I.32; *Dem.* 57; cf. above, pp. 106 f. Irenaeus reproduces the earlier allegorization of the *Apology* and not the later one of the *Dialogue*.
[6] *Dial.* 12; *Dem.* 96. [7] *Barnabas* 12.2; *Dem.* 46.
[8] *Barnabas* 12.11; *Dem.* 49. [9] *Barnabas* 5.13; *Dem.* 79.
[10] The tabernacle constructed in the wilderness was 'the visible form on earth of the things which are spiritual and invisible in the heavens, and a figure of the form of the church and a prophecy of things to come', *Dem.* 26. For a rather fuller treatment of the attitude to the Law to be found in the *Demonstration* see below, ch. 11.

and no attempt to undermine history by allegory. Chapters 10 to 29 of the *Demonstration* are a summary of sacred history, beginning at creation and going as far as David's reign in Jerusalem, without the slightest hint that the history is not to be taken literally.

Irenaeus does however introduce us in the *Demonstration* to a few new examples of allegory or of near-allegory. He takes the seven-branched candlestick, surprisingly, to be a pattern of the seven heavens.[1] He works out with some elaboration the correspondences between the tree of Eden and the tree of the Cross.[2] He allegorizes the passage in Isa. 11.6–9 describing the harmony of the animals in the Messianic age to mean the diverse and previously hostile and injurious sorts of men and women who have become reconciled in the Christian church.[3] Robinson (note *in loc.*) points out that in *Adversus Haereses* (V.23.4) Irenaeus had already discussed this passage, and while he recognized that it could have a spiritual interpretation, he himself inclined to refer it to a literal fulfilment yet to take place in the millennial kingdom. We can therefore trace a notable change of opinion in Irenaeus here; he has receded from the tendency to take eschatological imagery literally and instead allegorizes it into realized eschatology. This is a significant change, and we shall find it reflected in Clement of Alexandria and in Origen, though the results of their allegorization of eschatological passages are quite different. It is interesting also to observe that Irenaeus indulges in the *Demonstration* in quite an elaborate Christological typology of the Exodus, but that he does not explicitly connect it with baptism. Christ brings us out from the power of the Egyptians, that is from all idolatry and impiety, and from the Red Sea, that is from 'the deadly confusion of the Gentiles, and the grievous vexation of their blasphemy'. The stream of water from the rock in the desert is Christ himself; the twelve fountains are the twelve apostles. The Christian dispensation is the heritage into which Joshua-Jesus lead the people, 'who also delivers us from Amalek by the expansion of his hands and brings us to the Kingdom of the Father'.[4]

As far as the *Demonstration*, then, is concerned, we must characterize Irenaeus' allegory as conservative and showing no development on Justin's. But there is one point, not illustrated in the *Demonstration*, which we are bound to notice, and that is that Irenaeus is the first writer to allegorize the New Testament; we have already glanced at his elaborate exposition of the parable of the Good Samaritan as referring

---

[1]*Dem.* 9. [2]*Dem.* 34. [3]*Dem.* 61.
[4]*Dem.* 46.

to Adam, Paradise, the world, Christ's body, the Church, and so on.[1]
No doubt Irenaeus feels himself free to do this because he is among the
first writers to treat the New Testament unreservedly as inspired Scripture. Theophilus of Antioch takes the same attitude to the New Testament, but with more caution. He prefaces a quotation of the opening
words of the Fourth Gospel with the remark, 'That is what the holy
Scriptures and all the spirit-filled men teach us, and among them John
says . . .';[2] and later, 'On the subject of righteousness, too, about
which the Law spoke, the utterances of the prophets and of the Gospels
can be found to be of the same tenor, because all spoke inspired by the
same Spirit (πνευματοφόρους ἐνὶ πνεύματι) of God;'[3] and later he
calls the Epistle to the Romans 'the divine word' (ὁ θεῖος λόγος).[4] But
Bardy notes[5] that in spite of this Theophilus quotes the Gospels very
little, even when he is discussing Christian morality, and then only as
'the Gospels', never once in all his work mentioning the name of Jesus;
and he never allegorizes them. Irenaeus has no such reserve and will
when occasion arises (which is not very often) apply allegory to the text
of the New Testament without restraint. In spite of the efforts of some
modern French scholars to defend this practice, one cannot but feel that
Irenaeus is thereby placing his readers one stage further away from the
real meaning of the New Testament.

Before we consider the author who is nearest of all to Origen in his
use of allegory, and indeed in many respects his exemplar in the use of it,
Clement of Alexandria, it will be worth while to take a glance at one
who, though more nearly contemporary with Origen in time, was much
further from him in thought, Hippolytus. Taking as representative
pieces of Hippolytus' exposition two of his works, the *Commentary on
Daniel* and the *Commentary on the Song of Solomon*, we can with some
confidence pronounce that Origen was not in any significant way influenced by Hippolytus.[6] In the first of these works Hippolytus does not
allegorize the New Testament. Indeed it would be an overstatement to
say that Hippolytus when he wrote the *Commentary on Daniel* regarded
the New Testament as inspired Scripture in the same sense as the Old
Testament was; describing in the course of a commentary the unhappy

---

[1]*Adv. Haer.* III.18.2; see above, p. 76 n. 2.
[2]*Autolycus* II.22: ὅθεν διδάσκουσιν ἡμᾶς αἱ ἅγιαι γραφαὶ καὶ πάντες οἱ
πνευματόφοροι, ἐξ ὧν Ἰωάννης λέγει . . .
[3]*Ibid.*, III.12.   [4]*Ibid.*, III.14.   [5]*Ibid.*, p. 229 n. 4.
[6]Jerome, *De Viris Illustribus* 61 (*PL* 23.671-3), says that during Origen's
visit to Rome Hippolytus greeted Origen among his hearers during a lecture.
Many suggestions have been made about Hippolytus' influence upon Origen,
none of them, in my opinion, convincing.

career of a Syrian bishop who was led astray, he says 'he had not pains-takingly searched the Holy Scriptures, nor had he followed the voice of the Lord'.[1] But we can distinguish between Hippolytus' use of allegory in these two books. His *Commentary on Daniel* is an early work, written between 202 and 204, well before Origen had published anything.[2] Its scriptural exegesis is on the whole of a simple, primitive, literal type. He certainly does allegorize, but not in a very systematic way. He stands in much the same tradition as Justin, though perhaps he stretches allegory a little farther than Justin did. There is no trace at all of Alex-andrian influence in this work. At no point does he use ἀλληγορέω or its cognates. Hippolytus takes the same 'oracular' view of the Old Testa-ment as Justin, and many a Christian and indeed Jewish expositor before him: 'The divine Scriptures declare to us nothing irrelevant, but only what is for the instruction of us ourselves, and in order to enhance (πρὸς μακάρισμον) the prophets and to explain everything that was said by them.'[3] He takes quite literally, and defends on the ground that nothing is impossible to God, the going back of the sun on Hezekiah's dial and the arrest of the sun and moon for the benefit of Joshua and his army: 'And in the case of Hezekiah the moon as well as the sun turned back to avoid the collision of these two bodies taking place as they encountered each other in a disorderly way.'[4] The story of Susanna he allegorizes thoroughly. Susanna was ordained as a type (προετυ-ποῦτο) of the Church, Joachim her husband as Christ; the garden is the calling of the saints; Babylon is the world; the two elders are the two powers persecuting the Church, Jew and pagan.[5] The words 'they were parted from each other during the hour of dinner' (Susanna vv. 13 f.) mean that though the Jews do not agree with pagans about earthly food, in their outlooks (θεωρίαις) and in every practical matter (πράγματι κοσμικῷ) they agree.[6] Later in this work Hippolytus alle-gorizes the situation of Daniel in the den of lions: 'Today Babylon is the world, the satraps the power of the world, Darius their emperor, the den is Hades, the lions the angels who administer torment.'[7] This alle-gorization we shall later compare with Origen's allegorization of the same passage and find how great a difference divides the two scholars.

---

[1] μὴ ἐμπόνως ἐντυγχάνων ταῖς θείαις γραφαῖς μηδὲ τῇ φωνῇ τοῦ Κυρίου ἀκολουθήσας. *Comm. on Dan.* IV.18.2.
[2] *Ibid.*, Introduction, p. 10.   [3] *Ibid.*, I.7.2.
[4] *Ibid.*, I.7 f.   [5] *Ibid.*, I.14.5.
[6] *Ibid.*, I.15.5. For an account of Hippolytus' allegorization of Susanna's bath, see below, pp. 314 f.
[7] *Ibid.*, III.30.2. For Origen's treatment of this incident, see below, p. 278.

Later on[1] he allegorizes almost every detail of the description of the man clothed in linen in Dan. 10 so as to refer it to Christ. His habit of introducing through allegory futurist rather than realized eschatology is noteworthy. The sabbath, he tells us, is a type and image (τύπος and εἰκών) of the coming Kingdom of the Saints[2]—not of the present state of the Church, as Irenaeus would probably have interpreted it and as Hebrews does in fact interpret it. 'The things concerning the ark which took place of old under Moses in the wilderness were accomplished as types and images (τύποι καὶ εἰκόνες) of spiritual mysteries;'[3] and he goes on to show in the rest of the chapter that the dimensions of the ark of the covenant were indicative of the date of Christ's coming and of his Second Coming. And later he allegorizes the mysterious figurative references to old age in Eccles. 12.3–6 in an eschatological sense, referring them to the Last Time that is yet to be. It is significant that we can detect in Hippolytus a tendency to allegorize into futurist eschatology rather than realized eschatology; it is characteristic of the trend of thought of his time, as we shall see in the case of Clement of Alexandria and of Origen, that the theologians are losing their grip upon, and surrendering an interest in, the intense conviction that eschatology is now being realized evident, which was in the writers of the first century and, to a lesser extent, of the second.

Hippolytus' work on the *Song of Solomon*[4] must have been written later, perhaps much later, than his *Commentary on Daniel*. It is a remarkable fact that Hippolytus should have produced a work on the *Song of Solomon*. There were very few precedents for such a publication; the book does not provide any proof-texts in the early Church nor figure at all prominently in early patristic exegesis. It could, of course, be argued that Hippolytus had derived the idea from Origen. Origen wrote two books on the Song of Solomon; one, a short work, a fragment of which survives in the *Philocalia*, he composed perhaps about 225, certainly before he quitted Alexandria for Caesarea; the other he wrote much

---

[1] *Ibid.*, IV.37.   [2] *Ibid.*, IV.23.5.   [3] *Ibid.*, IV.24.2.

[4] It is uncertain whether we can class this as a Commentary, though as we have it today, surviving in a fragmentary condition in Slavonic, Armenian and Syriac versions, with a few sentences of the original Greek, it is in effect a Commentary. If the alternative Armenian version is to be trusted at one point (frag. 15, p. 355), reference is made to 'the Resurrection which we celebrate today,' and this part must therefore presumably have occurred in a Paschal Homily. Perhaps in Hippolytus' milieu no clear distinction was made between Commentary and Homily. Hippolytus' work on Daniel is in the form of a Homily. There is no evidence, internal or external, for the date of the work on the Song of Solomon, except that the more developed allegory suggests that it is later, perhaps much later, than the *Commentary on Daniel*.

later, probably in 244, and this survives in a Latin translation.[1] But it is wholly impossible that Hippolytus should have been influenced by Origen's later work, and highly improbable that he should have been inspired by the earlier. If we are to see any influence between these compositions, it is rather more likely that Hippolytus influenced Origen; but there is no need to adopt such an hypothesis. Probably both men were independently motivated by the fact, which by then must have been well known, that Jewish scholars had found it necessary to allegorize this work, and the Christian scholars were anxious to allegorize it in a Christian sense for the honour of the Church.[2] Anyway it is evident that nobody could have contemplated writing a Christian commentary on the Song of Solomon unless he was prepared to allegorize in a quite uninhibited manner.

Hippolytus for the most part allegorizes this book in a traditional, Christological manner, such as Justin might have used. The two breasts of the Bride in S. of S. 4.5 are the Old and New Covenants from which Christians suck as milk the commandments of Christ. The king of S. of S. 1.4 is Christ; the bridal-chamber is the Church. It is the Synagogue that cries, 'We will be glad and rejoice in thee.' The kids of S. of S. 1.8 are the souls of sinners, or the kids are Israel and the sheep Christians.[3] The little foxes of S. of S. 2.15 are heresies. At this point Hippolytus collects together all the references to foxes in the Bible which he can find and links them indiscriminately together, so that Christ's words to Herod (Luke 13.32) come next to Samson's adventure with the foxes (Judg. 15.4 f.), an incident which, impressed by its account of the burning of crops, Hippolytus considers to be a prefiguration of the Last Judgement.[4] He also applies S. of S. 3.1–4 to the women seeking the dead body of Jesus in the tomb. The watchmen (3.3) are the angels and the city is the New Jerusalem.[5] It is noteworthy that in this work Hippolytus is ready, during his indiscriminate searches of the biblical material, to allegorize the New Testament as well as the Old. With the age in which he lived, he is developing a respect for the New Testament great enough to place it on a level with the Old.

---

[1] See *Origen's Doctrine of Tradition*, pp. 13, 15, 26, 45 f.
[2] See above, pp. 33 f.
[3] Hippolytus *GCS*, Part I, pp. xxiii, xxiv; fragments 2 f. (p. 344); 6 f. (p. 346). Cf. frag. 19, pp. 359 f., where in S. of S. 1.5 Hippolytus recognizes Christ, angels, Christians, and sinners.
[4] Frag. 14, pp. 349 f. Cf. his equally indiscriminate heaping together of all references to beds that he can find, in connection with the mention of the litter of Solomon in S. of S. 3.7 (frag. 17, pp. 356 f.).
[5] Frag. 15, pp. 350 f.

In several places, however, Hippolytus produces in this work a different kind of allegory which we cannot exactly call new, for we have met it already in Philo; he allegorizes the biblical material, not into Christological, but into psychological statements.[1] The sixty warriors of S. of S. 3.7 are the six organs of sense; their swords are the desires of these organs.[2] The two breasts of S. of S. 4.5 are perceptions and sight, or soul and body; the mountain of myrrh of 4.6 means that when any persons crucify their bodies with their powers and desires, then they are at the 'hill of frankincense' and are glad.[3] This is a significant development. We cannot fail to see the influence of Philo here, and it signalizes the entry into the main stream of Christian exegesis of the Philonic tradition of allegorizing, an event which had been inaugurated by Clement of Alexandria and was to be fully established by Origen. Völker describes Origen's work on the Song of Solomon as interpreting the text 'soteriologically, ecclesiologically and referring it to the individual's mystical experience'.[4] We might say that Hippolytus had before Origen interpreted the same text soteriologically, perhaps ecclesiologically, and psychologically. This is some measure of the length to which the allegorical tradition had developed between the work of Paul and that of Origen.

With Clement of Alexandria we reach an author whose allegory is not only Alexandrian but openly and unashamedly Philonic; in fact he is more interested in allegorizing in a Philonic manner than in reproducing the traditional allegory arising out of a 'similar-situation' typology.[5] He does not merely see prefigurations in the Old Testament; he has reached the stage where he can see the text of Scripture as containing a hidden meaning everywhere. He is the first Christian scholar to formulate this doctrine, and he has borrowed it from Philo.[6] He tells us that mysteries have been inserted into the Scriptures in the first place to exercise the minds and wits of intellectual Christians and in the second to disguise the deeper and more upsetting doctrines from the simple

[1] For Philo's *penchant* for this sort of allegory, see above, pp. 48 f.
[2] Frag. 19, p. 368, lines 9–16.   [3] *Ibid.*, p. 370, lines 13–16.
[4] W. Völker, 'Die Verwertung des Weisheits-Literatur bei den christlichen Alexandrinern', *ZKG* LXIV, p. 30. The German language can express this sentiment in three words, 'heilsgeschichtlich-ekklesiologisch und individualistisch-mystisch', but I do not think that English writers who have to use ten words over it need envy their German counterparts.
[5] For another account of Clement's allegorization, see R. M. Grant, *The Letter and the Spirit*, pp. 84–9.
[6] Much of Clement's interpretation of Scripture will reveal itself as we trace Origen's and compare them. For Clement's attitude to the Law, see below, pp. 295–7. For his conception of the connection between allegorizing and the Church's rule of faith, see *Origen's Doctrine of Tradition*, pp. 58–65, 103–5.

Christians.[1] On the subject of the days allotted to creation in Genesis, a well-worn theme by his time, he reproduces in his own words the interpretation of Aristobulus and of Philo: this dividing of creation into days signifies that everything should keep its order for the future and that there was a hierarchy of value and importance among created things, even though in fact 'all things came into existence from one substance with one act of power'.[2] At one point in the *Stromateis* Clement maintains that as the ordinary education in the humanities of his day (τὰ ἐγκύκλια μαθήματα) is a preparation for studying philosophy, so philosophy is a preparation for Christianity.[3] This comparison between a popular and a higher education Clement had borrowed from Philo, even going so far as to quote a whole sentence from him about the danger of being so much occupied with the popular as to avoid the higher education.[4] In order to support this view Clement reproduces the allegorization of the story of Abraham, Sarah and Hagar which Philo had used in the same context: Sarah is wisdom; Abraham the faithful man; Hagar is the wisdom of the world (Αἴγυπτος δὲ ὁ κόσμος ἀλληγορεῖται). Before he can produce a child (Isaac, who is virtue) from Wisdom, Abraham has to be united to worldly wisdom, i.e. philosophy.[5] Clement even reproduces the allegorization of ἐγκρυφίας ('hidden' cakes) when it occurs in Gen. 18.6 (LXX), using it to prove the existence of secret doctrines in the Bible.[6]

But Clement can produce plenty of allegory of a Philonic character without being directly indebted to Philo. He allegorizes the turning of Lot's wife into a pillar of salt as the insensitive man who is in love with the atheism of idolatry.[7] He allegorizes the incident of Joseph being placed by his brothers in a pit; the sin of the brothers was not to allegorize the Torah! Their fault was to employ 'bare faith in the law'; this piece of exposition occurs in a chapter mainly devoted to a defence of allegorizing the Old Testament law.[8] He tells us that by the 'tree of life' in Gen. 2 and 3 Moses meant 'divine thought' (τὴν φρόνησιν θείαν)

[1] *Strom.* VI.15.129, *PG* 9.349.
[2] *Strom.* VI.16.142, *PG* 9.369. For this sentiment as voiced by Aristobulus see Eus. *PE* XIII.12.9-12 (667A–C) and above, pp. 42 f., and for Philo's version of it see *De Opificio* 13. Origen in his turn reproduces it (frag. on Genesis, *PG* 12.97).
[3] *Strom.* I.5.30, *PG* 8.721.
[4] *De Congressu* 77; he also reproduces a sentiment from 79.
[5] *Strom.* I.5.30-32, *PG* 8.724-8; Philo, *De Congressu* 20, 34-7.
[6] *Strom.* V.12.80, *PG* 9.120; Philo, *De Sacrif. Abeli et Caini* 59 f., etc. See above, pp. 47 f.
[7] *Protrept.* X.103, *PG* 8.220.
[8] *Strom.* V.8.53, *PG* 9.84; cf. the allegorization of Lev. 1.6 in *Strom.* V.11.67 (*PG* 9.104) which in fact owes much to Philo.

and that by Paradise the world could be intended.[1] And he is just as capable of inverting the true meaning of Scripture by an over-ingenious interpretation as is Philo: his comment on 'For the flesh lusteth against the Spirit and the Spirit against the flesh. Now these are contrary, the one to the other' (Gal. 5.17) is 'not contrary as evil is to good, but conflicting with each other for a good purpose'.[2] He is perfectly capable of allegorizing the New Testament too. In his little Homily, *Quis Dives*,[3] there occurs an interesting allegorization of the parable of the Good Samaritan, different from that of Irenaeus and Origen: Christ is the Good Samaritan, the good physician who heals the evil passions which the demonic powers inflict upon us as wounds; he pours 'wine, the blood of the vine of David'[4] into our wounded souls; he binds us with 'the unbreakable bonds of health and salvation . . . love, faith, hope'; he orders angels to look after us and gives them a great reward, because they too will be freed from the vanity of the world at the revelation of the glory of the sons of God.

Clement's language about Baptism will be dealt with later on.[5] Daniélou has an important chapter devoted to the typology of the flood in Clement of Alexandria and Origen.[6] He shows that Clement never goes beyond Philo's allegorical interpretation of this subject. The flood means purification, but not a specifically baptismal purification, and Clement's handling of this theme is, in Daniélou's view, no more than 'the mingling of the biblical flood, the Platonic flood, and the Stoic ἐκπύρωσις'.[7] Clement is much concerned to interpret Noah's Ark, and allegorizes it into moral qualities. The squared timber, for instance, denotes firmness. He is also greatly preoccupied with the meaning of the dimensions of the ark, whose numbers he imagines to denote various mysteries, but he makes no reference to Baptism. In all this interpretation he is indebted to Philo.[8] This is one example of Clement's tendency to ignore, perhaps even to reject, traditional typology in favour of a

[1] *Ibid.*, V.11.72, PG 9.109.
[2] *Ibid.*, IV.8.60, PG 8.1272: οὐχ ὡς κακὸν ἀγαθῷ, ἀλλ' ὡς συμφερόντως μαχόμενα. Cf. the description of Philo above, p. 48.
[3] *Quis Dives* 29, PG 9.634. In view of this and other passages, I cannot understand R. M. Grant's assertion (*The Letter and the Spirit*, p. 89) that Clement never allegorizes the New Testament.
[4] This phrase occurs also in *Didache* 9.2, in a eucharistic prayer; it is evidently traditional. It is not immediately obvious that Clement's use of it is eucharistic, but if the *Quis Dives* is a Homily given during the eucharistic rite, the association would be inescapable.
[5] See below, pp. 315–18.
[6] *Sacramentum Futuri*, book II, ch. III, 'Les Alexandrins et l'Allegorie de l'Arche', pp. 86–94.
[7] *Strom.* V.1.9, PG 9.21–4; *Sacramentum Futuri*, p. 87.
[8] *Strom.* VI.11.84 f., PG 9.305; *Sacramentum Futuri*, pp. 90–2.

(margin annotations: crossing water / strange as heretical baptism / problem with allegorical expositions)

Philonic variety of allegory. We can indeed find what might be called sacramental typology, but even this is remote from any traditional typology. He refers, for instance, the words of Prov. 9.16 f. ('Stolen waters are sweet, and bread eaten in secret is pleasant') to heretics who wrongly celebrate the Eucharist in bread and water.[1] In the same passage he allegorizes the words 'For thus shalt thou cross strange water' (Prov. 9.18a LXX) to refer to heretical baptism, which is no true baptism.[2]

Clement of Alexandria does not indeed show quite the same tendency to undermine historical narratives by allegory as Philo does, or as Origen does after him. He has, in fact, a stronger grasp upon the doctrine of the Incarnation than Origen. But in most other respects he has surrendered wholeheartedly to the Philonic tradition of exegesis. The temptation to use this tradition for much the same purposes as Philo used it, to introduce into the biblical text a philosophical system which is not there, was too great for him. He is the first Christian writer to use allegory for this purpose, and he provided an example which Origen followed with a deplorable eagerness. His indifference, perhaps his deliberate indifference, to traditional Christian interpretation meant that he forfeited the safeguards which it contained, weakened though they had been in the development of Christian exposition since New Testament times, against a gradual estrangement from the realities of history in interpreting Scripture.

That behind these known exponents of the art of allegory there were many other unknown allegorists in the Church cannot be doubted. Even as early as Justin's day the interpretation of Gen. 3.22 ('Behold, the man is become as one of us, to know good and evil') was a *crux interpretum*. Justin maintained that to describe the use of the plural number here as merely figurative language (τροπολογία) is the mark of 'sophists and those who cannot speak or understand the truth'.[3] In his Com-

---

[1] *Strom.* I.19.96, *PG* 8.813. For a consideration of Clement's eucharistic doctrine, see below, pp. 324 f.

[2] W. Völker, 'Der Verwertung des Weisheits-Literatur', *ZKG* LXIV, p. 12, n. 82, calls attention to these two passages.

[3] *Dial.* 129.2. Cf. the vigorous statement in Theophilus, *Autolycus* II.18, that the words 'Let us make man in our image' (Gen. 1.26) were addressed 'to nobody else but his own Logos and his own wisdom'. Bardy *in loc.* compares a similar statement in Irenaeus, *Adv. Haer.* IV.34.1. Perhaps both statements are implicitly directed against Tatian. Origen refers to Tatian as having declared that when God said, 'Let there be light', this was a prayer to light, and not an order, because God was in darkness. Origen indignantly refutes this view in *De* XIV.5 and *Contra Celsum* VI.51; Celsus apparently knew of this opinion.
  hall find many examples of previous allegorizing referred to in Origen's
  ; see below, ch. 5.

mentary on Daniel Hippolytus takes the view that the ten horns of the fourth beast in the visions of Daniel were a prefiguration of the ten kings destined ultimately to divide the Roman Empire between them. There is some reason to think that Hippolytus was here reproducing an older allegorization. Jerome says that 'all ecclesiastical writers reported' that this was the true interpretation, and that the pagan Porphyry stood alone in interpreting these ten horns as the successors of Alexander down to Antiochus Epiphanes.[1] It is interesting that the great majority of scholars today would support Porphyry's interpretation, and admire his perspicacity in preferring this one, although the history of the Roman Empire in the middle of the third century, when he was alive, must have suggested strongly that the ten destructive kings had already come on the scene. Elsewhere Hippolytus tells us that the 'seven times' which are to pass over the insane Nebuchadnezzar were interpreted by some as seven years, and by some as seven seasons.[2] It is rather more likely that these interpreters were Christians than that they were Jews. Clement of Alexandria gives five different contemporary interpretations of the text 'Where two or three are gathered together in my name, there am I in the midst of them' (Matt. 18.20).[3] Völker notes[4] that Clement has to oppose a school of thought within the Church which allegorizes the Book of Proverbs in order to disparage the study of philosophy and worldly science; this school evidently referred Prov. 5.3 (μὴ πρόσεχε φαύλῃ γυναικί) to 'Greek learning' (Ἑλληνικὴ παιδεία). It is a small but significant point that the formula deliberately inserted in the benedictions in the Jewish liturgy in order to debar Christians from taking part in it ran, 'who givest life to the dead, who humblest the proud, who dost build Jerusalem'.[5] By this time so much do Jews regard themselves as committed to the literal sense of the Old Testament, and Christians visualize themselves as the champions of allegory, that the literal interpretations of a prophecy inserted in the benedictions is enough to exclude Christians.

Before we attempt to draw conclusions about the development of Christian allegory up to the time of Origen from the material that we

---

[1] See Bardy's Introduction to Hippolytus, *Comm. on Dan.*, p. 24 n. 1; Jerome, *Comm. on Dan.* 7.7 f. (*PL* 25.530 f.). Incidentally, this is another example of the traditional interpretation of the Church proving rather a source of embarrassment.

[2] *Comm. on Dan.* III.10.2.

[3] *Strom.* III.10.68 f., *PG* 8.1169.

[4] 'Die Verwertung des Weisheits-Literatur', *ZKG* LXIV, p. 14.

[5] Simon, *Verus Israel*, p. 236. It is Rabbi Simon, speaking in the name of Rabbi Jehoshua ben Levi, who provides this information.

have surveyed, it is worth while considering two points of interest connected with this survey. The first of these is the typology of Eve in the
early Church. Justin takes Eve to be a type of the Blessed Virgin Mary.[1]
Commenting upon this passage, Daniélou suggests that this typology
'belongs to the oldest tradition of typology'.[2] Certainly this typology
reappears not long after Justin in Irenaeus[3] and in Tertullian[4] and
afterwards has a long history of elaboration and development in
Christian thought and devotion. But it is not the oldest tradition of the
typology of Eve, and in the early centuries is rivalled by the older
tradition. This older tradition sees Eve as the type of the Church. This
is the only type of Eve plainly discernible in the New Testament: 'I am
jealous over you with a godly jealousy, for I espoused you to one
husband, that I might present you as a pure virgin to Christ. But I fear,
lest by any means, as the serpent beguiled Eve in his craftiness, your
minds should be corrupted from the simplicity and the purity that is
towards Christ.'[5] This typology is reproduced in a writer who is probably contemporary with Justin, the author of *II Clement*. 'I do not
think you are unaware,' he says, 'that the living Church is the body of
Christ, for the Scripture says, "God made man male and female." The
male is Christ, the female is the Church.'[6] Hippolytus follows this typology once or twice. In his *Commentary on Daniel* he invariably takes
Susanna to be a type of the Church;[7] then, commenting on the elders'
attempt on Susanna, he says that as the devil hid originally in the serpent, so now, hidden in the elders, he stirred up their desire 'in order
that he might once again corrupt Eve'.[8] The same imagery reappears in
Hippolytus' work on the Song of Solomon. Christ, he says, at the Resurrection (to which he takes S. of S. 3.1–3 to refer) raises aloft Eve, who
does not now seduce (Adam), but desires to hold fast the tree of life.
As he has just said that Christ 'raises aloft a new race', it is likely that he
is taking the Church to be the New Eve. The passage later likens Mary
Magdalene and Martha to Eve, perhaps as firstfruits of the Church, for

[1] *Dial.* 100.5.
[2] *Sacramentum Futuri*, p. 32.
[3] *Adv. Haer.* III.32.1; V.19.1; *Dem.* 33.
[4] *De Carne Christi* 17.
[5] II Cor. 11.2 f.; cf. Eph. 5.22–33. The picture in Rev. 12 of the woman
crowned with the sun is so obscure that it can hardly be taken as unambiguous
evidence on this subject.
[6] *II Clement* 14.2. The Christians of Lyons and Vienne, in their letter describing the martyrdoms there, appear to regard the Church as the New Eve. See
Eus. *HE* V.1.45, p. 142.
[7] E.g. I.14.5; I.16.2–4.
[8] I.18.4: cf. I.22 (extant in Slavonic only; p. 113 in Lefèvre's edition).

Mary Magdalene as Apostle
to the apostles by virtue of
having announced the resurrection
THE DEVELOPMENT OF THE ALLEGORICAL TRADITION   123   to
the
Apostles

he describes them as 'the apostles of the apostles' inasmuch as they were sent to announce the Resurrection to the apostles.[1] In any case, he does not here show any inclination to envisage the Blessed Virgin Mary as the New Eve.[2] Origen, though he is perfectly ready to dispense with traditional typology and allegory when he thinks fit, also reproduces this typology of the Church as the New Eve, which surely has more right to be regarded as the original, traditional, imagery than the other.[3]

The other interesting point which we must at least take note of now, though we shall leave a full discussion of it till the end of this work, is that Daniélou claims that in the traditional typology of the early Church there is an element which constitutes original and trustworthy Christian tradition. In the third chapter of the fourth book of his work, for instance,[4] he produces a good deal of evidence to show, in his own words, that 'the theology of Baptism is not found in the individual teaching of the doctors, nor in the traditions of schools of thought, but appears in the official catechetical teaching given by the Church and by the magisterium. We are in the presence of ecclesiastical tradition itself. And it is virtually among the best authorized representatives of this tradition, among the bishops or the writers who reproduce official teaching, that we shall encounter our theme. This is true above all of the works where we catch an echo of catechetical teaching.'[5] We encounter among the Fathers who reproduce this 'ecclesiastical' tradition of typology not only the Scriptural types (such as those to be found in I Cor. 10 and 11, John 6 and 7) but also some non-scriptural figures; these latter could have derived from 'the pre-scriptural apostolic source'.[6] Another example of this is the typology of Joshua. It appears little in the New Testament; Daniélou can find only Heb. 4.8, 15 as evidence for it,[7] though he might have added Acts 7.45 had he looked a little further. But he devotes a whole chapter to showing that it survives abundantly in the Fathers as a piece of mainly non-scriptural traditional typology.[8] And at the end of his book he claims that the survival of this non-scriptural typology 'shows that we are in the presence of a reality which forms part of the deposit of tradition'.[9]

[1] Frag. 15, pp. 352 f.
[2] Cf. frag. 19, p. 369, lines 3–13, where, in commenting upon the phrase in S. of S. 3.11, 'with the crown wherewith his mother hath crowned him', he rejects what one would think an excellent opportunity of bringing the Blessed Virgin Mary into an allegorical scheme, and instead interprets the 'mother' as God.
[3] PA IV.3.7; Comm. on Matt. XIV.17.
[4] Sacramentum Futuri, pp. 152–76.
[5] Ibid., p. 154.
[6] Ibid., p. 176.
[7] Ibid., p. 205.
[8] Ibid., book V., ch. I, pp. 203–16.
[9] Ibid., p. 258.

This is obviously an important claim; it constitutes in fact one of the most important points raised by the investigation of the whole subject of allegory and typology, and it is one that we must keep in mind as we explore Origen's interpretation of Scripture. A few provisional observations will have to suffice at this point in our survey. In the first place, this train of argument may easily bring its user into the unfortunate position of having proved too much. Lundberg has shown that much of the typology of the New Testament derives from sources which are not only to be found in the very earliest strata of Christian tradition, but can be traced to pre-Christian milieux. Why should not this be true of this non-scriptural typology? The sources in which Lundberg finds traces of this very early typology are not always very satisfactory ones; some of them are Gnostic. Can we be sure that such origins as these have had nothing to do with this non-scriptural typology? *The Epistle of Barnabas* gives signs of having access to a version of parts of the Old Testament unknown to us, and unknown probably to the writers of the New Testament also, which it allegorizes freely. Are we to assume that this non-scriptural allegory 'forms part of the deposit of tradition'? Again, Theophilus of Antioch, a bishop who presumably would be well acquainted with the catechetical tradition of the Church of his day, in his apologetic work uses no typology at all (indeed he does not once mention the name of Jesus Christ) but does indulge in an Alexandrian kind of allegory which nobody could reasonably claim to belong to the earliest Christian tradition.

No doubt from a very early point in the history of the Church Christians used a number of contemporary categories—figures and types—as material with which they might interpret the significance of Jesus which seemed to them so unlimited and so manifold, and scholars today can trace the origin of these categories in periods and places which are sometimes pre-Christian. But to say this is not to say that all these categories, just because they are early, are part of the original Christian tradition and must be accepted as authoritative. This question is ultimately one of authority. What authority have we for believing that these non-scriptural types are authentic, have an apostolic if not a dominical origin? It is true that some writers even as early as the second century use some of these types for what may be official catechetical teaching. But then they use other categories in the same context which glaringly lack early authority. Irenaeus, for instance, uses Moses' posture during the battle of Israel against Amalek as a prefigurement of the Cross. This type is not found in the New Testament, and it is used before Irenaeus by Justin and before Justin by *Barnabas*.[1] Irenaeus is a bishop, and in the second century the bishop was pre-eminently the bearer of tradition. But this is a tradition which we cannot reasonably attribute to any early authentic source. Like all early non-scriptural traditions, this tradition is uncertain. We do not know with what authority it reaches us, precisely because it is *not* in the New Testament. It was simply because this uncertainty threatened to overtake all the Church's tradition that the Church collected together and guaranteed as authentic the books of the New Testament. To show that a tradition derives from a period before the recognition of the New Testament Canon (which is all that Daniélou can do in this case) is not to exempt that tradition from this uncertainty. Even if we were to show that it derives from a period before the writing of most of the books of the New Testament he would still not have obtained for it this exemption.

It seems reasonable, then, to look for the sources of Christian allegory not in Alexandria but in Palestine. Its origins are to be traced in the tendency to see situations described in the Hebrew Scriptures as fulfilled in events of the present or of the immediate past which we can discern in the literature associated with the Dead Sea Scrolls, a tradition of interpretation obviously influenced by Messianic interpretation. Other roots of allegory can be found in the practice of Rabbinic allegory, a practice which undoubtedly existed and indeed may have flourished quite strongly in the first century A.D., even though later generations of Judaism discouraged it and tried to efface its traces; it is likely that this early Rabbinic tradition of allegory did not hesitate to use allegory in order to deprive the Torah of its literal meaning. Christian allegory, derived from these roots and relying on these examples, was in addition supported and nourished by Christian typology, a kind of scriptural exegesis which was the natural consequence of the Christian conviction that with the coming of Jesus of Nazareth the Messianic Age and the Last Time had been inaugurated, and which itself had its roots in Jewish liturgy and Jewish exegesis. Indeed Christian allegory first appears as a by-product, rather tentative and sparse, of Christian typology. Allegory in the Christian tradition, however, soon becomes strongly developed and widely used by Christian theologians, who find it a serviceable instrument in their task of discovering references to Jesus Christ thickly scattered all over the Old Testament.[2] And when the

[1] See above, p. 111.
[2] I cannot quite agree with Mrs Flessemann-Van Leer in the distinction which she draws between the Apostolic Fathers on the one hand and Justin and the other Apologists on the other. She says of the Apologists, 'When we compare

documents of the New Testament begin to be recognized as authoritative and normative, it is natural that Christian writers should begin to allegorize them too.

But to the other tradition of allegory, the Alexandrian, we can attribute almost no influence upon the early development of Christian allegory. This tradition arose out of an imitation of Hellenistic, mainly Stoic, allegorizing which had had a long history in Greek literature and philosophy. It has distinctive and easily recognizable characteristics; its intention is to substitute for the literal meaning of the text another meaning, philosophical or moral or what we would now call scientific, which has only the faintest or most arbitrary connection with the literal sense. It is entirely unhistorical (we might almost call it anti-historical) and it has no connection at all with typology. We cannot find any significant traces of this sort of exegesis in early Christian allegory until we reach the *Epistle of Barnabas*, and even this work uses Alexandrian allegory only in its interpretation of the ceremonial enactments of the Torah. The two other documents representative of early Alexandrian Christianity, the Epistle to the Hebrews and Stephen's Speech in Acts, exhibit no specifically Alexandrian allegory at all and even *Barnabas* shows no sign of being influenced by Philonic allegory. It is only much later that Alexandrian exposition begins to reappear in Christian literature, with Theophilus of Antioch, and that Philo's exegesis begins to be influential, in Clement of Alexandria and perhaps in Hippolytus' work on the Song of Solomon. Philo's influence arrives in time to strengthen, we might perhaps think to strengthen disastrously, the tendency already being displayed by Palestinian allegory as developed by one and a half centuries of Christian use to move in exposition further away from the original meaning and the historical situation of the text.

This is not, however, the impression made upon others by the development of Christian allegory. Zöllig maintained that contemporary Protestantism felt the want of allegory in its teaching, and that 'in the Holy Scriptures besides the literal sense the mystical sense must come

---

them with the Apostolic Fathers, we perceive that the latter found in the Old Testament the persistently valid revelation of God, bringing the same message which Jesus Christ brought (Ignatius and Barnabas notably) . . . Justin, however, inaugurated a conception of the Old Testament which still more or less prevails in the theology of our own day, namely that its primary function is the prophecy of Jesus Christ' (*Tradition and Scripture in the Early Church*, p. 98). *Barnabas* is just as anxious to see Jesus Christ prefigured in the Old Testament as is Justin and the reason why in the other Apostolic Fathers so little allegory is evident is rather because they are not intellectuals and because in their extant works they have no occasion to expound the Old Testament; they do not seem to me to have a fundamentally different attitude to it.

into its own', and defined the modern conception of allegory as 'a figurative application of the language of Scripture with the intention of edifying'.[1] Bardy seems to approve highly of Hippolytus' allegorizing of the story of Susanna, and claims that beside the historical we must admit the allegorical way of interpreting Scripture. 'The first concentrates on showing the truth of the facts, the second on uncovering their mysterious meaning. Without preferring one to the other, it can be said that both of them have their validity.'[2] Daniélou, on the other hand, takes a very critical attitude to allegory, but welcomes typology with open arms. He boldly denies that there is a hidden sense in Scripture.[3] Typology, he says, is 'a relation between realities both of which are historical, and not between historical realities and a timeless world. . . . That is why nothing could be further from the truth than to reproach patristic exegesis with not taking history seriously.'[4] The oldest and ultimately the most important sort of typology is in Daniélou's view eschatological typology. In an earlier work he had elaborated upon this distinction between allegory and typology. The foundation of baptismal typology (and no doubt he would apply this to all Christian typology) is 'the unity of the divine plan, which does not only express itself by the unity of the creative and redemptive activity, but by the unity of a planned instruction which speaks an intelligible language and uses the same symbols, so that the sacred history is characterized by a certain style, by the use of certain terms, so that it is not a confused accumulation of events, like secular history, but an intelligible history, where the events present order and connection. The aim of exposition is to explain this language of history, to establish the similarities which connect the events and the institutions across the centuries. It is to explain the symbolism which makes a connection between the successive historical events. This of course assumes the reality of these events. But it assumes in addition that they constitute a certain intelligible language. The discovery of the "sacraments" (mysteries) contained in Scripture, that is the task to which the Fathers' exegesis addresses itself.'[5] In his *Sacramentum Futuri* Daniélou defines the typology of Irenaeus in words which obviously express for him the meaning of all typology: 'His master principle amounts to that of an imperfect order which prepares

---

[1]*Inspirationslehre*, pp. 124, 126 f., 129.
[2]Hippolytus, *Comm. on Dan.*, Introduction, pp. 45–7.
[3]'The Fathers and the Scriptures', *ECQ* X, pp. 265–73.
[4]*Ibid.*, p. 268.
[5]'Traversée de la Mer Rouge et Baptême aux Premiers Siècles', *RechSR* XXXIII, p. 429 (cf. pp. 416 f.). Compare the rather crude statement of the same position, quoted by Spicq from Javet, above, p. 89.

for but prefigures a perfect order. A conception of the world, like that of Irenaeus, which envisages it as a unique design, composed of two great consecutive stages, is essentially typological. Because the design is in fact unique, the two stages, while remaining in substance heterogeneous, are likely to present points of resemblance, analogies in which precisely typology consists; thus it is that one perceives the link which joins typology and theology in Irenaeus.'[1] And later he maintains that Hilary in his *Tractatus Mysteriorum* 'holds to the historical reality of the events, because typology consists precisely in showing that it is the history itself that is figurative, and not in substituting allegory for history.'[2]

We may readily endorse Daniélou's rejection of the attempt to see a 'mystical' or a 'spiritual' sense hidden everywhere under the literal text of Scripture. It is a concept derived directly from Philo, has no connection whatever with early Christian tradition and has been in the history of Christian exegesis a prolific parent of misunderstanding and folly. Whatever modern Protestantism may find lacking in its handling of Scripture, it is certainly not this. But it seems to me not nearly as simple a matter as Daniélou makes out to accept wholeheartedly Christian typology instead of allegory, even typology at a comparatively early stage in its development. In the first place, we have seen in many examples with what fatal facility typology slips into allegory. The assumption which Daniélou seems to make, that allegory is a wholly Alexandrian or Philonic phenomenon, is a quite false one. Allegory is a native growth of Palestinian Judaism and takes its place early on in Christian exegesis, even though quite a minor place, independently of Alexandria. If we reject allegory as a valid method in exposition we cannot help thereby casting doubt upon a great deal of Christian typology, even early 'catechetical' typology. In the second place, it seems to me that it is not enough to describe typology simply as 'a relation between realities both of which are historical', and leave it at that. We must ask, particularly in view of the perfectly legitimate development of historical criticism during the last century, any expositor to elucidate *a connection between the original meaning of any biblical text in its historical context and the typological meaning which he attaches to it* before we can be satisfied with his interpretation. Indeed the historical character of Christianity itself, whose central dogma is the Incarnation of the Son of God, must ultimately make this demand also. But this is a requirement of which, it seems to me, the Christian expositors of antiquity were very insufficiently aware; indeed our survey of the development of the alle-

[1]*Op. cit.*, p. 22.   [2]*Ibid.*, p. 41.

gorical tradition from the New Testament to the time of Origen has already suggested this conclusion. This is a point which we would do well to bear in mind as we begin to investigate the exegesis of the greatest Christian interpreter of the Bible between the age of St Paul and that of Jerome and Augustine.

PART TWO

Origen as an Exegete

5

Contemporary Exegesis

THE impression which we have already gained that allegory was a device already widely used when Origen began writing his expositions of Scripture is amply confirmed in the works of Origen himself. Harnack indeed says that Origen had already behind him an exegetical tradition which he was at pains to learn.[1] In a fragment of a commentary on Ps. 68.13 ('Will ye lie among the sheepfolds (LXX κλήρων, lots), as the wings of a dove covered with silver and her pinions with yellow gold?') Origen tells us that 'Some people say that the lots and feathers are the Old and New Testaments; others the practical and contemplative life; others knowledge of corporeal and incorporeal substances; others the knowledge of God and of Christ who was sent by him.'[2] Several such examples can be gleaned from the *Commentary on Matthew*. The 'little child' of Matt. 18.2 had been allegorized to mean the Holy Spirit.[3] Someone had also allegorized Caesar in the incident of the question about the tribute (Matt. 22.15–22) as the devil, a significant interpretation.[4] The Temple in Matt. 24.1 f. had already been interpreted as the Scriptures of the Old Testament, whose literal sense must be destroyed in order that the spiritual sense be built up.[5] Some people before Origen had wanted to allegorize Simon of Cyrene to mean the five senses, because he came from the Libyan Pentapolis.[6] Elsewhere Origen produces as the suggestions of his predecessors the interpretation of 'They have sown wheat and they have reaped thorns' (Jer. 12.13) as a reference to heretics;[7] the reference of Lam. 4.20 to Josiah as a type of

---

[1] *Der Kirchengeschichtliche Ertrag*, I, p. 22. For instances of previous allegorizing to be found in Origen's works see *ibid*. I, pp. 22–9, II, pp. 11–34.

[2] *PG* 12.1508. We have already seen one elaborate example of allegorizing the NT on the part of some predecessor of Origen to be found in his works, above, p. 76, n. 2.

[3] XIII.18; cf. the discussion of μίκρος and ἄγγελος in Matt. 18.10 in XIII. 26–30.

[4] *Ibid*., XVII.28.

[5] *Ibid*., Comm. Ser. 31; Harnack also cites this example, *op. cit*, II, pp. 24 f.

[6] *Ibid*., Comm. Ser. 126.

[7] *Hom. on Jer*. XI.3.

Christ;[1] the identification of Lot and his two daughters with Christ and the Old and New Testaments;[2] the interpretation of 'the dead' in Num. 16.48 as those who are dead in their sins and 'the living' as those who persevered in the works of life;[3] and this sentiment upon the story of Gideon and the fleece of wool (Judg. 6.36–40): 'On this subject I remember one of our predecessors saying in his commentaries (libellis suis) that the fleece of wool was the people of Israel, the rest of the earth was the other nations, and the dew which fell on the fleece was the Word of God, because favour was shown from heaven to that people alone; for upon Israel alone had the dew of the divine Law fallen.'[4] Origen also tells us that he knew that the writings and sayings of many people upon the subject of allegorizing the laws of the Pentateuch were in circulation.[5]

It is, however, equally obvious that there existed in Origen's day a large body of opinion hostile to allegory, both within the Church and outside it.[6] 'You could see the same state of belief even today,' says Origen of the unbelief described in the eighth chapter of St John's Gospel, 'in many people who are impressed by Jesus Christ when they read the narrative of what he did, but who cease to believe when the deeper meaning is unfolded to them and one greater than their capacity to understand, and suspect that it is untrue.'[7] We are reminded of the objection of the Philadelphian Christians to Ignatius, 'That is begging the question!'[8] Later in the same work Origen guards himself against the accusations of these sceptical folk: 'We have made these speculations, though we are not unaware that we have a reputation for superfluous inquiry and for explanation which is unable to convince the hearer, because we think it more important to examine every point than to pass over unexamined anything in the writings.'[9] A very similar pas-

---

[1]Hom. on Lam., frag. 116.
[2]Hom. on Gen. V.5.
[3]Hom. on Num. XI.5.
[4]Comm. on Judg. VIII.4; this expositor may have been a Jewish Christian.
[5]Comm. on Rom. II.13. I omit his reproductions of Philo's allegories, sometimes acknowledged, sometimes not, in, e.g. Hom. on Jer. XIV.5, 6; XVIII.4; XX.3; Hom. on Ex. IX.4; XIII.3; fragment on Genesis, PG 12.97.
[6]For information on this subject see de Lubac, Histoire et Esprit, ch. I; W. Völker, Das Vollkommenheitsideal des Origenes, p. 171; H. E. W. Turner, The Pattern of Christian Truth, p. 290; Eusebius' quotations in HE VI.19 of Porphyry's remarks about Christian allegorizing in general and Origen's in particular; and the many instances of opposition to allegory which will appear later in this chapter.
[7]Comm. on John XX.30; cf. XXXII.4, 8 where the same school of thought is mentioned.
[8]Ignatius, Philadelphians 18.2; see above, p. 101.
[9]Comm. on John XXXII.22.

sage in the *Homilies on Leviticus*[1] runs thus: 'Perhaps one of my hearers may say, what is this quibbler (*eurisologus*) doing? Why is he searching for words in every direction in order to evade the meaning of the passage?' And again we find this revealing remark: 'But if there is anybody of the number of those who appear to be believers and to accept the authority of the Scripture, who yet does not allow the device of this spiritual interpretation, but laughs at it and belittles it, let us try to instruct and persuade him from other parts of Scripture.'[2] It is evident, too, from the recently discovered report of a conference held between Origen and some bishops and others in Arabia, the *Conversation with Heracleides*, that throughout the proceedings Origen was hesitant and uneasy about introducing his allegorical explanations; 'I am troubled at the thought of speaking, and I am equally troubled at the thought of not speaking,'[3] he says during a long preface to his remarks on the main subject; he is afraid that he might be misunderstood by his crasser hearers because he is about to suggest a 'spiritual interpretation' (λόγον μυστικόν). Scherer, the editor of this text, points out that this fear of mockery and opposition when he used allegory was roused in Origen, not by captious Jews or Gnostics, but by Christian believers themselves.[4] Zöllig indeed, observing justly that allegory was in Origen's day both widely used and widely criticized, points out one place where Origen himself criticizes the use of it.[5]

We cannot read Origen's works for long without realizing that as he expounds Scripture he has constantly in mind several different schools of rival expositors of the text. These may be divided into three distinct groups, of whom the largest and the most dangerous was the Gnostics. Pre-eminent among the Gnostics, because their *forte* lay in a peculiar and in many ways attractive interpretation of the Bible, were the Marcionites.[6] Origen is on the whole more concerned about this school of exposition in his earlier works than in his later; we will find more references to them, for instance, in the *Peri Archon* and the *Commentary on John* (and in this latter more in the early books than in the later) than in the works written between 240 and 250; but even in the *Commentary*

[1]XVI.4.
[2]*Comm. on S. of S.* I, on S. of S. 1. 3 f.
[3]'Αγωνιῶ καὶ εἰπεῖν, ἀγωνιῶ καὶ μὴ εἰπεῖν, p. 152.17 (MS p. 15.7 f.).
[4]Introduction, p. 72, and Text, p. 151 n. 13.
[5]*Hom. on Gen.* XIII.3, *PG* 12.232. See Zöllig, *Inspirationslehre*, p. 119.
[6]For further information on Marcionite exegesis, see G. Salmon, article 'Marcion' in the *Dictionary of Christian Biography*; F. J. Foakes-Jackson, *Christian Difficulties in the Second and Twentieth Centuries*, chs. I–III; and E. C. Blackman, *Marcion and his Influence*.

on Matthew (246) and the *Contra Celsum* (248) and in some of the Homilies, most of which date from 246 or later, references to the Marcionites are not lacking.

It is quite clear that the Marcionites were among the fiercest enemies of allegory. The saying of our Lord recorded in Matt. 19.12, 'there are eunuchs which made themselves eunuchs for the Kingdom of heaven's sake, is one which Origen is quite convinced must be allegorized, and he says that this necessity puts the Marcionites in a quandary because Marcion taught that 'it is wrong to allegorize Scripture'.[1] And in the *Commentary on Romans* he refers to 'Marcion, who is not ready to allow any allegorical interpretation at all'.[2] That Marcion had strong Gnostic tendencies even though he cannot exactly be described as a characteristic Gnostic in his thought is shown by his rejection of the Virgin Birth; he declared the passages in the gospels referring to it to be spurious, because he thought such a birth inappropriate to Christ's divine nature.[3] But much more evident in Origen's polemic is the peculiar twist that Marcion gave to his system by his contrast between the God of the Old Testament and the God of the New Testament. 'They therefore assume,' says Origen of the Marcionites, 'that goodness is a certain impulse in which all should be rewarded with good, even though he to whom the good is done be unworthy and does not deserve to encounter good. . . . But justice they think to be an impulse of such a sort that it gives to everybody as he deserves. . . . For they think that that which is just does evil to those who are evil and good to the good, so that according to their interpretation the just man does not appear to wish well to the evil but rather to be moved by something approaching hatred towards them. And their argument relies on their finding occasional references in the narrative part of the Scriptures of the Old Testament concerning, for instance, the punishments of the flood and of those who are recorded as destroyed in it, or when Sodom and Gomorrah were laid waste by the catastrophe of fiery and sulphurous rain, or when they all perished in the desert because of their sins so that not one of those who had set out from Egypt can be found to have entered the land of promise except Joshua and Caleb. But from the New Testament they make a list of the sayings about pity and affec-

---

[1]*Comm. in Matt.* XV.3: μὴ δεῖν ἀλληγορεῖν τὴν γραφήν.

[2]II.13. See Harnack, *Der Kirchengeschichtliche Ertrag* II, pp. 67 f., for a fuller account of this passage and others of a similar tenor to be gleaned from Origen.

[3]*Comm. on John* X.6. Compare the equally significant statement in *Comm. on I Cor.*, frag. 34 (on I Cor. 7.7; *JTS* IX, p. 503), that the Marcionites forbid marriage, because the 'other god' (not the demiurge) has commanded chastity.

tion in which the disciples are instructed by the Saviour and in which it seems to be declared that "none is good, save one, even God the Father". And by this means they have dared to describe the good God as the Father of the Saviour Jesus Christ, but they say that the god of the world is another god, whom they choose to call just, yet not good.'[1] A quotation from the *Commentary on John* discloses another aspect of the same type of exposition: 'Some of the heretics claim to believe in Christ, yet because they have invented the fiction of another god besides the Creator, according to their theory, they do not hold that his advent was foretold by the prophets. They attempt to explain away the testimonies to Christ given through the prophets, and they claim that the Son of God has no need of witness since he provides enough ground of belief both in the health-bringing words which he used to preach, full as they were of power, and in the miraculous works which were capable of convincing anyone at all by their own credit alone. And they say, if Moses obtained belief through his word and his miracles, and had no need of any witnesses preceding him to foretell him, and moreover each of the prophets was received by the people as having been sent from God, why should not he who surpassed Moses and the prophets rather be able, without the prophets witnessing to the circumstances of his coming, to accomplish his purpose and benefit the race of men? They think therefore that it is misleading that he should be considered to have been foretold by the prophets since, as they would say, this was deliberately planned by those who did not wish believers in Christ to accept the newness of Godhead, but rather to fall back on the same god of whom Moses and the prophets taught before the time of Jesus.'[2]

In accordance with these convictions, the Marcionites picked out many characteristics of God as revealed in the Old Testament and branded them as peculiar to the inferior god of justice, not of mercy. They objected to the attribution to God of wrath and similar passions in the Old Testament.[3] They denounced the Jewish law as an evil system for administering justice, not goodness; they called it 'an evil root' and 'an evil tree'.[4] According to Clement of Alexandria some heretics (presumably extreme left-wing Marcionites) held that the law was so much corrupted and intermingled with evil by a deity who is the

---

[1] *PA* II.5.1.
[2] *Comm. on John* II.34; cf. *Philoc.* XI.1, 2, a passage from the twentieth book of the *Comm. on Ezek.*; and *Comm. on John*, frag. 49, where the demiurge is called κοσμοποιόν, and where John the Baptist is bracketed with the prophets as 'as of the earth'.
[3] *PA* II.4.4.   [4] *Comm. on Rom.* III.6.*

A.E.—E*

enemy of the true and original God that it is the Christian's duty to disobey, and not merely to ignore it, and where, for instance, the law says 'Thou shalt not commit adultery', the Christian should commit adultery.[1] They attributed 'fulness (*plenitudinem*, perhaps originally πλήρωμα) to Christ and to the Holy Spirit but imperfection and weakness to the God of the law'.[2] They identified the material promises made in the Pentateuch as the work of the god of the Old Testament and interpreted them literally.[3] On the question of the hardening of Pharaoh's heart, which as we shall see later was a very much vexed question,[4] they took the view that the god who did the hardening was the just but not merciful god of the Old Testament.[5] And they took our Lord's words concerning the mystery of the Kingdom (Mark 4.10-12) as his account of 'the vengeful intention retributing evil for evil' of the god of the Old Testament.[6]

We can go a little further in reconstructing Marcionite interpretation of Scripture by identifying in Origen's works a number of proof-texts upon which they apparently put particular reliance in propagating their doctrines. 'I will go down now and see whether they have done altogether according to the cry of it which is come unto me. And if not, I will know' (Gen. 18.21) they seized upon as an instance of the god of the law having to find out knowledge for himself and therefore being imperfect.[7] The action of Joshua in putting his feet on the necks of the five kings, killing them and hanging them on trees (Josh. 10.22-7) was picked out by the Marcionites (and by Valentinus and Basilides as well) as arguing the cruelty of the god of the Old Testament.[8] They plucked out of their context the words attributed to God in Deut. 32.39, 'I kill' and 'I have wounded' and described them as characteristic of the god of the Old Testament.[9] In Jeremiah, they pointed to the words, 'I will not pity nor spare, nor have compassion, that I should not destroy them' (Jer. 13.14), and said, 'You see what sort of a demiurge he is! How can he be good (ἀγαθός)?'[10] They were quite as ready to use the New Testament as a source of proof-texts. 'A good tree cannot bring forth bad fruits nor a bad tree good fruits, for a tree is known by its fruits' (Matt. 7.18) was a favourite text of theirs, for they interpreted the

[1]*Strom.* III.4.34 f., *PG* 8.1136-41.
[2]*Comm. on S. of S.* II, on S. of S. 1.11 f.
[3]*Comm. on Ps.* 4.6 (*PG* 12.1156) reproduced in *Philoc.* XXVI.4.
[4]See below, p. 143.
[5]*Philoc.* XXI.8-10, from *PA* III.1.9-11.
[6]*Philoc.* XXI.15, ἡ ἀμυντικὴ καὶ ἀνταποδοτικὴ τῶν χειρόνων προαίρεσις.
[7]*Hom. on Gen.* IV.6.   [8]*Hom. on Josh.* XI.3.
[9]*Contra Celsum* II.24.   [10]*Hom. on Jer.* XII.5.

tree as the law, apparently forgetting their prejudice against allegory.[1] They used the parable of the Unmerciful Steward (Matt. 18.23–35) to accuse the demiurge (presumably identified with the king of this parable) of having angry passions.[2] Taking the text 'No man hath seen God at any time' (John 1.18), they argued that since the god whom Moses spoke of was seen by Moses and before him by his ancestors, therefore Moses' god was not God the Father but the demiurge-creator.[3] Another proof-text of theirs from this gospel was 'Ye know neither me nor my father' (John 8.19), for they thought that this proved that the god whom the Jews worshipped (the demiurge) was not the Father of Jesus, because neither the Pharisees nor the people of Jerusalem knew the Father.[4] From the New Testament Epistles they selected Rom. 4.15, 'The law worketh wrath,' in order to discredit the law,[5] and Rom. 5.7, 'For scarcely for a righteous man will one die; for peradventure for the good man some one would even dare to die,' where they saw the contrast between the righteous ($\delta\iota\kappa\alpha\acute{\iota}ου$) and the good ($\grave{\alpha}\gamma\alpha\theta o\hat{v}$) as a reference to the contrast between the God of the law and Christ, an interpretation which suggests that Marcion did not have that profound understanding of Pauline thought which is sometimes attributed to him. They also interpreted a phrase in Ephesians, 'who hath blessed us with every spiritual blessing,' as implying a contrast with the material blessings mentioned in Leviticus and Deuteronomy, 'thinking that they would gain an opportunity from this interpretation to split up the Godhead'.[6] Finally it is interesting to observe that in Origen's day the Marcionites apparently accepted as authentic the First Epistle of John, for one of their favourite proof-texts was 'the whole world lieth in the evil one' (I John 5.19); they maintained that 'the evil one' was the world-creating demiurge.[7]

Marcionite doctrine in fact constituted a shrewd and unsparing exposure of the difficulties raised by the Old Testament, even though the Marcionite solution of them was a quite impossible one. The broad lines of Origen's reply to this attack will become evident as his whole attitude towards Scripture is unfolded in the later pages of this work, but it is profitable to look at some of his answers to particular charges. In many cases his simple and short reply was that the passage which scandalized the Marcionites must not be taken literally. The incident of

[1] *PA* II.5.4.
[2] *Comm. on Matt.* XIV.13.
[3] *PA* II.4.3.
[4] *Comm. on John* XIX.3.
[5] *Comm. on. Rom.* IV.4.*
[6] *Comm. on Eph.*, frag. 2, *JTS* III, p. 236.
[7] *Philoc.* XIV.2, from *Comm. on Gen.* III,

Joshua's brutal treatment of the five kings, for instance,[1] seemed to him
to demand allegory; the passage simply was unhistorical and was intended to be allegorized. To the Marcionite objection to the punishments inflicted by God in the Old Testament he usually replies that such
punishments were not vindictive or purely retributive but remedial and
reformatory. Those who perished in the flood were given a second
chance after death (I Peter 3.18–21). As for Sodom, God proposes to
restore even that, for Ezekiel says, 'And thy sisters, Sodom and her
daughters, shall return to their former estate' (Ezek. 16.55). Again, those
who fell in the desert were forgiven and restored after death; Ps. 78
says 'when he slew them, than they sought him', which means that they
sought God when they had been slain.[2] Origen has his own solution to
the problem raised by the hardening of Pharaoh's heart, which we shall
examine later;[3] to the Marcionites he is content to point out that even
on their account of the matter the god who hardened Pharaoh's heart
could not have been the just but not merciful demiurge, for what justice
is there in first hardening a man's heart and then condemning him for
having a hard heart?[4] His answer to the Marcionites' exclamations of
horror at the words in Jeremiah, 'I will not pity, nor spare, nor have
compassion, that I should not destroy them',[5] is a fine one: 'But if I
take as an analogy the juryman who withholds his pity for the common
good and the judge who rightly refuses mercy, I shall be able to convince you from this analogy that it is out of pity for the majority that
God refuses to pity the individual. And I shall take as analogy too the
surgeon and show that it is out of consideration for the whole body that
he has no consideration for a single limb.'[6] He did not find it difficult to
show that the New Testament does not in fact represent Christ or his
Father as unconditionally merciful to all men on all occasions. He points
out, for instance, that if we allow the repeated 'Woe unto you!' of
Matt. (23.13 ff.) it is inconsistent to reject the maledictions of the Old
Testament on the grounds that they were pronounced by the demiurge;[7]
and he observes how embarrassing to the Marcionites is St Paul's
statement that God gave up the Gentiles in the lusts of their heart to
uncleanness (Rom. 1.24).[8]

Certain other points raised by the Marcionites give Origen rather

[1]See above, p. 138.   [2]*PA* II.5.3.   [3]See below, pp. 214–7.
[4]*PA* III.1.9; here again Origen refers to the extreme left wing of the Marcionites who would describe the demiurge as positively evil (πόνηρος), and
not even just.
[5]See above, p. 138.   [6]*Hom. on Jer.* XII.5.
[7]*Comm. on Matt.* Comm. Ser. 13.
[8]*Comm. on John* I.35.

more trouble. The words of our Lord recorded in Mark 10.18, 'Why callest thou me good?' may have been used as a proof-text by the Marcionites, though it is hard to see exactly how. Origen explains the text rather lamely by saying that Jesus meant that he was preparing all things for the final confession of the goodness of the Father, and that time had not yet come.[1] His answer to the Marcionites' refusal to see any point in the witness of the prophets to Jesus, or any need for it, is an elaborate one. First of all, he says that God has provided many inducements to belief in Jesus Christ as the Son of God. Among these, the fulfilment by Christ of prophecies about the Messiah, such as those concerning the place of his birth and the land where he would be brought up, the effect of his teaching, his performing of miracles, and his suffering as man, are clearly the most influential today in bringing people to believe in him. Next, it is remarkable that the miracles of Christ, though sufficient in themselves to convince the men of his time, would now lose their power of conviction (τὸ ἐμφατικόν) and be suspect as fables were they not supported and guaranteed by Christ's fulfilment of prophecy. Thirdly, the prophets not only foretold Christ's coming, but they also set before us as much doctrine (θεολογίαν), and as frequently describe the mutual relations of the Father and the Son, as the apostles do. Finally, the prophets do not of course confer honour on Christ by witnessing to him, on the contrary they themselves receive honour by their witness. But the Marcionites already admit as much about the apostles; why should they not apply the same reasoning to the prophets?[2] Origen's confidence that the prophets tell us as much doctrine about Christ as the apostles do would not commend itself to the theologians of today, but it is very characteristic of his thought about the Bible, and in particular it evinces his determined emphasis upon the unity of scriptural thought. This was indeed the principle upon which all his defence of the Old Testament against the Marcionites was based, and appears over and over again in his works. To him St Paul's phrase 'according to my gospel' (Rom. 2.16) involved the assumption that there was only one gospel taught everywhere throughout the whole Bible.[3]

It is evident that whereas Origen found little difficulty in exposing the absurdity of the Marcionite interpretation of the Bible, he was less successful in meeting the difficulties which the Marcionites so ruthlessly exploited, even though he made a much better attempt at the task than

[1] *Comm. on John* I.35.   [2] *Ibid.*, II.34.
[3] *Philoc.* V.6 f., from *Comm. on John* III.

they. He was much more successful in countering the scriptural exegesis of another school of thought among the Gnostics whom we may justly call the Predestinarians.[1] Origen usually calls this school of thought οἱ φύσεις ἄγοντες, a phrase which literally means 'those who introduce (sc. into the argument) natures', but is perhaps best paraphrased as 'those who believe in determinism'. They believed that all men were born into the world with natures already so unalterably constituted that they were bound for either salvation or damnation, and that no conduct of theirs during this life could alter their destiny. Clement of Alexandria before him had remarked upon this opinion of theirs and had described them as the followers of Valentinus and Basilides.[2] The more extreme of them held that redeemed men are 'royal offspring' (βασίλειοι παῖδες) and therefore above law and morality and could behave as they liked without guilt.[3] Origen also identifies these heretics with the Valentinians.[4] They were therefore a peculiarly Alexandrian heresy, and it is not surprising that Origen pays more attention to them in his *Commentary on John* than in any other work, and more in the earlier books of this work than in the later.

This predestinarian doctrine of theirs Koch describes as one of the basic doctrines of Gnosticism;[5] the irrevocably saved they called the 'spiritual' (πνευματικοί) and the irrevocably damned the 'carnal' (χοικοί or ψυχικοί).[6] Their doctrine led them to decry the value of prayer,[7] but they had no objection to using allegory when it suited them.[8] Their doctrine has however some strong resemblances to that of the Marcionites, in spite of their use of allegory. Origen tells us that Valentinus as well as Marcion believed in the existence of a god of

---

[1]For further information on Gnostic interpretation generally, see C. Bigg, *The Christian Platonists of Alexandria*, p. 56; A. Cadiou, *La Jeunesse d'Origène*, ch. V; J. Daniélou, *Origène*, pp. 147 f.; W. Völker, 'Die Verwertung des Weisheits-Literatur bei den Christlichen Alexandrinern', *ZKG* LXIV, p. 5, n. 33; H. E. W. Turner, *The Pattern of Christian Truth*, pp. 232–8. For the Predestinarian school of thought, see Cadiou, *op. cit.*, pp. 308 f.; Harnack, *Der Kirchengeschichtliche Ertrag II*, p. 57 n. 3 and pp. 62 f.; H. Crouzel, *Théologie de l'Image de Dieu chez Origène*, p. 64. For Heracleon, see J. Armitage Robinson, *The Fragments of Heracleon*.

[2]*Strom.* II.3.10 f. (*PG* 8.941).

[3]*Strom.* III.4.34 f. (*PG* 8.1136–41).

[4]*Contra Celsum* V.61.

[5]H. Koch, *Pronoia und Paideusis: studien über Origenes und sein Verhältnis zum Platonismus*, p. 14.

[6]The χοικοί were the irrevocably damned, the ψυχικοί occupied an intermediate stage of being neither irrevocably bound for salvation, in contrast to the 'spiritual' people, nor irrevocably damned. But his contrast is more usually between the saved and the rest.

[7]*PE* V.2.

[8]*Comm. on Rom.* III.10;* they want to allegorize 'circumcision' in Rom. 3.30.

justice distinguished from the god of goodness;[1] that 'the Valentinians and other heretics' think that 'my Saviour speaks in the Gospel doctrines which are not in the old books' (i.e. the Old Testament),[2] and we shall find much evidence to the same effect when we consider the views of Heracleon.[3] They were particularly anxious to support their views from the Scriptures, and we can recover a number of proof-texts upon which they seem to have relied. The hardening of Pharaoh's heart described in Ex. 7.13–11.10 supplied them with an excellent testimony; God uncompromisingly pities whom he likes and hardens whom he likes, without having any reason.[4] Jezebel, again, they fixed on as an example of one who possessed a 'damned nature' (φύσις ἀπολλυμένη).[5] The parable of the Drag-net (Matt. 13.47–50) was one of their favourite passages, and so were several texts in the Fourth Gospel, 'If God were your Father, ye would love me', 'Why do ye not understand my speech? Even because ye cannot hear my word' (John 8.42 f.), and 'He that is of God heareth the words of God: for this cause ye hear them not, because ye are not of God' (John 8.47).[6] They relied particularly upon the Epistle to the Romans for proof-texts to support their doctrine.[7]

Origen has little difficulty in disposing of these arguments. Against their reliance upon the description of the hardening of Pharaoh's heart he reasons that if Pharaoh were of a determinately damned disposition, why did God have to *harden* his heart, and why does God have pity (Rom. 9.18 ff.) on certain people who should by the Predestinarians' theory possess determinately saved dispositions already?[8] But his main argument is to point out that there are innumerable examples in the Scriptures of people changing their dispositions and natures from being on the way to damnation to being on the way to salvation and vice versa. He adduces the remorse of Judas.[9] He points out that Peter and Paul were clearly of a 'spiritual' nature, and yet the one had denied his master and the other had persecuted the Church; their reply that it was not Paul who persecuted but *nescio quis qui erat in Paulo*, nor Peter who

---

[1]*PA* II.7.1; but in III.1.23 he says that the determinists believe that ἀγαθὸς ὁ ποιῶν οὐ μόνον πνευματικοὺς ἀλλὰ καὶ χοικούς, a passage contradicted by several other references quoted below.

[2]*Hom.* II.6 on Ps. 37, *PG* 12.1334, cf. frag. ex Catenis, *PG* 17.125, which looks like another version of the same passage.

[3]See below, p. 144.

[4]*Philoc.* XXVII.1, from the *Commentary on Exodus*.

[5]*Comm. on Rev.*, frag. 17, p. 28. Ps. 58.3 may also have been one of these proof-texts; see *Philoc.* XXV.1, from *Comm. on Rom.* I.

[6]*Comm. on John* XX.17, 20, 33.

[7]Origen's Preface to the *Commentary on Romans*.

[8]*PA* III.1.8.

[9]*Comm. on Matt.* Comm. Ser. 117.

denied, but *alius negavit in Petro,* demonstrated the futility of their position. And he observed how inconsistent with their assumptions was the text 'for ye were once darkness, but are now light in the Lord'.[1]

But we can gain a much more detailed picture of Valentinian exegesis when we examine the manner of expounding Scripture practised by a prominent Valentinian whom we meet in the pages of Origen, Heracleon. Clement of Alexandria mentions Heracleon once,[2] but almost all our information about him comes from Origen. Heracleon wrote his work on St John's Gospel long before any Christian commentary had appeared, perhaps before Irenaeus composed his work *Adversus Haereses;* he called it a Commentary ('Υπομνήματα). The predestinarian strain in his teaching is evident from what Origen tells us of him in his *Commentary on John.* He interpreted 'that which hath been made in him was life'[3] as 'that which was made for the spiritual people'.[4] He interpreted the Johannine account of Christ's entry into Jerusalem (John 12.12–19) allegorically; the entry into the Temple was Christ's journey from the material sphere (τὰ ὑλικά) to the 'psychic place' (τὸν ψυχικὸν τόπον), and he was in the Holy of Holies, not the outer court, to show that the 'pneumatic' souls enter the Holy of Holies, but the 'psychic' are left outside the *pleroma.*[5] The Samaritan woman at the well described in the fourth chapter of St John's Gospel served him as an example of an irrevocably saved nature: 'he praises the Samaritan woman for displaying that unwavering faith which was consonant with her nature, and not hesitating at what he said to her.'[6] And he claimed that the Jews were not able to hear the word of Jesus (John 8.43) because they were 'of the substance of the devil' (ἐκ τῆς οὐσίας τοῦ διαβόλου), the devil being of a different substance from either the 'pneumatic' or the 'psychic'.[7] Heracleon further shows his Gnostic leanings by interpreting the eating of the Passover lamb as a type of 'the rest that is in Marriage'.[8] He also believed that when the Samaritan woman referred

[1] *Comm. on John* II.20.
[2] *Strom.* IV.9.71–3, *PG* 8.1282 f.; see J. Armitage Robinson, *The Fragments of Heracleon,* p. 102.
[3] John 1.3b and 4a, as punctuated and interpreted by Heracleon, Origen and several others in the early Church.
[4] *Comm. on John* II.21.
[5] *Ibid.,* X.33.
[6] *Ibid.,* XIII.10; cf. XIII.15.
[7] *Ibid.,* XX.20. Incidentally in this passage Origen accuses Heracleon's fellow-Gnostics of 'revelling in allegories and referring narratives of healing to the healing of the soul'—a crime of which he was far from guiltless himself!
[8] *Ibid.,* X.18, τὴν ἀνάπαυσιν τὴν ἐν γάμῳ, presumably referring to some esoteric theory of a mystical marriage. Compare the next quotation.

to her husband she meant her *pleroma* and that when she said that she had no husband she meant that she had no 'cosmic' husband, or husband 'in the cosmos'; her husband was 'in the aeon'.[1]

But as Origen paraphrases or quotes Heracleon during his commentary in order to refute him we are struck by how much Heracleon, in spite of his *penchant* for allegory, has in common with the Marcionites. He is ready to add a phrase to the received text of Scripture: to the words in John 1.3 'without him was not anything made' he wanted to add the phrase, 'of the things in the cosmos and in the creation', because he believed that the 'aeon' and its contents were made before the Logos, and not by the Logos.[2] He decried the prophets and exalted John the Baptist in comparison with them. Christ was the Word (λόγος), John the cry (φωνή), the prophets merely the sound (ἦχος).[3] He suggests that 'the demiurge of the cosmos' was confessing his unworthiness through the mouth of John the Baptist when the latter said 'He that cometh after me, the latchet of whose shoe I am not worthy to unloose' (John 1.27).[4] He interpreted the words 'After that he went down to Capernaum' (John 2.12) as meaning that Jesus here began a new dispensation, descending to 'these lowest parts of the earth, these material parts (ὑλικά) to which he came'.[5] He uses the whole of the incident of the Samaritan woman at the well as an opportunity for contrasting the ephemeral and incomplete nature of the old dispensation with that of the new.[6] He takes 'this mountain' and 'Jerusalem' in John 4.21 ('Neither in this mountain nor in Jerusalem shall ye worship the Father') to mean either the devil (or the devil's world) and the creator (or creation) which the Jews worshipped, or the creation which was worshipped by those who lived before the law was given and by the Gentiles ('this mountain') and the creator who was worshipped by the Jews ('Jerusalem').[7] 'Ye worship that which ye know not' (John 4.22) he thought to refer, among others, to those who had wrongly worshipped the *demiurge*.[8] 'There is one that seeketh and judgeth' (John 8.50) he referred to Moses, to whom his master the *demiurge* had given judgement.[9] The Marcionite affiliations of Heracleon are unmistakable.

But it should not be thought that Heracleon was a mere wielder of proof-texts. He was a genuine commentator, who knew his business,

[1] *Comm. on John* XIII.12. [2] *Ibid.*, II.14.
[3] *Ibid.*, VI.20,21. W. Knox, *Saint Paul and the Church of the Gentiles*, p. 157, describes this contrast of λόγος and φωνή as belonging to popular philosophy. Cf. Ignatius, *Romans* 2.1.
[4] *Comm. on John* VI.39. [5] *Ibid.*, X.11.
[6] *Ibid.*, XIII.10. [7] *Ibid.*, XIII.16.
[8] *Comm. on John* XIII.19. [9] *Ibid.*, XX.38.

and it is likely that Origen learnt something from his technique. Several of his comments, indeed, show a capacity for commonsense interpretation of a passage where Origen fails to see the obvious meaning. He held, for instance, that John 1.15b–17 were intended to be the words of the Baptist, whereas v.18 was the comment of the evangelist, but Origen disagrees with this view.[1] On John 1.26–8, Heracleon remarks that John did not directly answer the Pharisees' question, but gave the answer he chose; Origen, as we would think irrelevantly, objects that this would be to convict John of gaucheness (ἀμαθία).[2] 'In the midst of you standeth one' (μέσος ὑμῶν στήκει, John 1.26) Heracleon takes to mean that Christ is already here, in the world and in man; to this Origen demurs, saying that Christ has been in the world always and has been in man always.[3] There is no doubt that most modern commentators would agree with Heracleon here. Again, Heracleon takes 'Hath any man brought him aught to eat ?' (John 4.33) of material food, comparing very reasonably John 4.11; Origen, very opaquely, dissents and suggests that the disciples thought that some angelic power had brought Jesus food.[4] The saying of Jesus, 'Say not ye, There are yet four months, and then cometh the harvest ?' (John 4.35), Heracleon does not allegorize, but takes as metaphorical much as a modern commentator would; Origen much prefers to allegorize it.[5]

But more often in his exegesis Heracleon reminds one, not of a modern commentator, but of Origen himself. 'The zeal of thine house shall eat me up' (Ps. 69.9, quoted in John 2.17) Heracleon desires to transfer from the person (πρόσωπον) of Christ speaking in the psalm to that of the powers defeated and cast out by Christ.[6] 'Forty and six years was this temple building' (John 2.20) both Origen and Heracleon agree must be allegorized; it occurs to neither of them that in its literal sense it could have referred to Herod's temple, though they debate as to whether it could have been Solomon's, the temple of Ezra and Nehemiah, or that of the Maccabean times.[7] Heracleon, with Origen, agrees to allegorize the story of the nobleman's son (John 4.46–54).[8] He expounds 'the lusts of your father it is your will to do' (John 8.44) by distinguishing between 'to wish' (ἐθέλειν) and 'to lust' (ἐπιθυμεῖν), between some who are sons of the devil 'by nature' (φύσει) and others who

---

[1] *Comm. on John.* VI.3.   [2] *Ibid.*, VI.30.   [3] *Ibid.*, VI.39.
[4] *Ibid.*, XIII.35.   [5] *Ibid.*, XIII.48.
[6] *Ibid.*, X.33.   [7] *Ibid.*, X.38.
[8] *Ibid.*, XIII.60; the nobleman is the *demiurge*, limited in power and acting wrongly, but not irredeemable, his servants are the *demiurge's* angels, with a cross-reference to Isaiah and a mystical interpretation of the seven days.

are so 'by choice' (θέσει); he collects a list of those who are sons of
Gehenna, of darkness, of lawlessness, and offspring of snakes and of
vipers; he distinguishes between those who are sons 'by nature' (φύσει),
'by conviction' (γνώμη), and 'by merit' (ἀξίᾳ). In short, he adopts very
much the methods that Origen did later in tackling the interpretation of
Scripture. 'Both extract the meaning they desire,' says Armitage
Robinson, 'by a violent system of metaphorical distortion.'[1] There can
in fact be little doubt that Origen owed something to Heracleon's
example, not only in general exegetical technique, but in some details
also. J. N. Sanders remarks that one feature of Valentinian exegesis, met
also in Heracleon, is 'a minute attention to grammatical detail, especially
in such things as the use of prepositions', and this is a feature very
evident in Origen's exegesis.[2] Armitage Robinson suggests that Origen's
identification of the nobleman in the incident of the healing of the
nobleman's son with Abraham may owe something to Heracleon.[3]
Origen also probably derived from Heracleon the odd idea that the
words 'other men have laboured' (John 4.36) referred to the ministry of
angels, perhaps in introducing men's souls into their bodies.[4]

Origen refers to the exposition of a few other Gnostic schools as well
as these. He mentions Basilides, who thought that the cryptic phrase in
Rom. 7.9, 'I lived without the law once,' meant that Paul had enjoyed a
previous incarnation.[5] And he refers to 'Apelles, the pupil of Marcion'
who was the leader of a heresy all on his own and who 'held the writings
of the Jews to be a fable (μῦθον)' and taught that Jesus alone had come
from God to dwell among men, in opposition to the demiurge.[6] He seems
to have specialized in violent attacks on the Old Testament; he pointed
out that all the animals could not possibly fit into the ark as it is described in Genesis, and thence glibly concluded, 'Therefore the story
is false; therefore the book does not come from God.'[7] Finally there were
the Ophiantes who will not admit any member till he has anathematized
Jesus and 'say blasphemies in praise of the Serpent who is cursed by

[1]The Fragments of Heracleon, p. 48. But he goes on to say that in contrast to
Heracleon Origen 'applies his method more consistently, and endeavours to find
a meaning which is based on a system formed from the study of the Fourth
Gospel as a whole, and of other books whose teaching is not alien to that of this
Gospel'.
[2]The Fourth Gospel in the Early Church, p. 62. Cf. Völker, Das Vollkommenheitsideal, p. 99, n. 8.
[3]The Fragments of Heracleon, p. 91; see Comm. on John XIII.59.
[4]Comm. on John XIII.50.
[5]Comm. on Rom. V.2.
[6]Contra Celsum V.54.
[7]Ψευδὴς ἄρα ὁ μῦθος· οὐκ ἄρα ἐκ θεοῦ ἡ γραφή. Hom. on Gen. II.2.

God',[1] but who are so outrageous as to need no reply. But these exegetical schools, if they can be dignified by this name, occupied Origen's attention very little compared with the Marcionites, the Predestinarians and Heracleon.

Some writers on Origen have claimed to see a considerable Gnostic influence both in his exposition and in some features of his theological system.[2] Daniélou believes that Gnostic allegory accounted for much of the use of allegory by Clement of Alexandria and Origen,[3] but this is a charge which can, I think, be dismissed out of hand. The same writer attributes to Gnostic influence Origen's habit of interpreting places as spiritual states, and his use of 'the perspective of an angelic history which repeats itself in human history'.[4] But the first of these suggestions encounters the difficulty that there is evidence that Origen derived from other sources than his own invention many, if not most, of the interpretations of biblical names which he quotes, sources which knew Hebrew and were probably Rabbinic, not Gnostic.[5] The second suggestion has more weight, as Origen is ominously fond of subordinating human history to 'heavenly' history, but I think this *penchant* of his can be accounted for on other grounds than a borrowing from the Gnostics.[6] Daniélou also suggests that Origen derived from the Gnostics 'the practice of bringing together all the passages in Scripture verbally referring to the same subject, whatever their context and whatever the traditional typology might be'.[7] This seems unjust to Origen, who is only carrying a little further the methods already visible in the *Epistle of Barnabas*, Justin, and, indeed, the Rabbis. Another Gnostic tendency in exposition which has been noticed is to give letters or numbers mystic meanings and to combine them to produce some point in an argument.[8] This is a habit which Origen occasionally, but not very

[1]*Comm. on I Cor.*, frag. 47 (*JTS* X, p. 30), Cf. *Contra Celsum* III.13; VI. 24–28; H. Chadwick's notes on this sect in his edition of *Contra Celsum* are full and informative, illustrated by diagrams. For lists of references to heretics in Origen's works see Harnack, *Der Kirchengeschichtliche Ertrag* I, pp. 30–38; II, pp. 54–81.
[2]For suggestions about Origen's doctrinal indebtedness to Gnosticism in general and Valentinianism in particular, see Völker, *Das Vollkommenheitsideal*, pp. 128 f., 143.
[3]'The Fathers and the Scriptures', *ECQ* X, pp. 265–73.
[4]*Origène*, pp. 191–3.
[5]See my article, 'The Interpretations of Hebrew Place-Names in Origen', *Vig. Chr.* X.
[6]This question is dealt with below, ch. 10.
[7]*Sacramentum Futuri*, pp. 243 f.
[8]See F. J. Badcock, *The History of the Creeds*, pp. 28 f.; E. Flessemann-Van Leer, *Tradition and Scripture in the Early Church*, p. 125, who refers to Irenaeus, *Adv. Haer.* II.37.1.

often, indulges, and he may have owed it, at least indirectly, to the example of Gnosticism, though it was probably not unknown to contemporary Judaism.[1] Two more small points have been attributed to the influence of the Gnostics on Origen. The imagery of the soul as the bride of Christ in Origen's works on the Song of Solomon is quite developed and is reminiscent of Gnostic, and especially of Valentinian, language. And the phrase used by Origen of the initiate receiving the highest communion with God, 'to admit the greatness' (τὸ μέγεθος χωρεῖν, *Comm. on John* XX.6) resembles a Valentinian phrase (τὸ μέγεθος αὐτοῦ καταλαβεῖν).[2] The first observation, though quite a weighty one, must be modified by the possibility that Origen knew something of contemporary Rabbinic allegorization of the Song of Solomon;[3] the second point may be based upon a mere coincidence of language. I am far from being convinced that a case has been made out for the suggestion that Origen owed any considerable debt to Gnostic exegesis.

Gnostic exegesis, however, was not the only rival to his methods of exposition that Origen had to face. There existed also a body of opinion which we can best describe as Literalist,[4] for their distinctive conviction was that the Bible must be taken literally, not allegorically, not even in most cases metaphorically. In Origen's words, 'they attack allegorical interpretation and want to teach that divine Scripture is clear and has nothing deeper than the text shows'.[5] They cannot be called a sect or even a school of thought, for they had nothing approaching a system of doctrine such as the Gnostics had. They were simply people who distrusted allegory and preferred a literal interpretation of the text, but they formed a recognizable body of opinion and they gave Origen a certain amount of trouble. We can recognize them already in Clement of Alexandria's mention of them: he quotes people as saying that if a number of precious stones are mentioned in Rev. 21, why should not Christians use these kinds of jewels to adorn themselves with.[6] This intense predilection for the letter of the Bible is a *trait* which we will find recurring in other accounts of them.

[1]See below, p. 207.
[2]See Völker, *Das Vollkommenheitsideal*, pp. 104 f. (and especially p. 104 n. 3 and p. 105 n. 1), pp. 114 f., p. 118 n. 5 and p. 119.
[3]See above, pp. 33–5.
[4]I prefer this word to the more common 'Fundamentalist', as it is more expressive and accurate. For more information on these Literalists, see Harnack, *Der Kirchengeschichtliche Ertrag* I, p. 49; II, p. 81; Koch, *Pronoia und Paideusis*, p. 20; C. Mondesert, *Clement d'Alexandrie*, pp. 39 f.; Crouzel, *Theologie de l'Image de Dieu chez Origène*, pp. 76, 154.
[5]*Comm. on Matt.* Comm. Ser. 15. Cf. *Hom. on Gen.* XIII.3.
[6]*Paed.* II.12.119, *PG* 8.541.

It is obvious that most of the Christians of this opinion were so not because they had an heretically-inclined mind or a taste for novelty and idiosyncrasy in doctrine, but because they were simple, unintellectual men and women who neither understood nor trusted the figurative ways of interpreting Scripture dear to the heart of the intellectual of that day. Origen calls them 'the simpler type of churchmen' (οἱ ἀκεραιότεροι τῶν ἀπὸ τῆς ἐκκλησίας), who in face of Marcionite attacks on the Scriptures refuse to separate the supreme God and the demiurge, but naïvely attribute cruelty and injustice to this supreme God.[1] When faced with the *locus vexatus* in Exodus about the hardening of Pharaoh's heart, they simply say that many other meanings of the Scripture are hidden from them, and that one of the hidden things is the right explanation about this passage.[2] But they cling obstinately to the literal meaning when they can. In order to explain without impairing the accuracy of the Bible the inconsistency between the statement of the Baptist in John I.21 that he is not Elijah and the words of our Lord recorded in Matt. 11.4, 'And if ye are willing to receive it, this is Elijah which is to come,' they were ready to resort to a theory of metempsychosis whereby John was shown to be a genuine reincarnation of Elijah but had forgotten the fact![3] They were disturbed by the suggestion that the command of Jesus in John 13.8, 12 to his disciples to wash each other's feet should not be taken literally, and seem to have made some effort to do so themselves, even though the Pedilavium, if it had ever existed, had long fallen into disuse as a custom of the Church.[4] It had even to be explained to them that the sentences 'all men come to him' and 'a man can receive nothing except it have been given him from heaven' (John 3.26 f.) cannot be taken as absolutely literal without qualification.[5]

Their worst fault, however, was a partiality for taking literally and in an anthropomorphic sense things said figuratively or analogically of God. They have to be warned against taking in a spatial sense the expression 'Our Father, which art in heaven', or 'any passages which by the simpler brethren are thought to state that God occupies a space'.[6] 'Though they are in the Church they say that the physical image of man is the image of God.'[7] For this perverse opinion they could quote as an

[1] *PA* IV.2.1.
[2] *Philoc.* XXVII.1, from a *Commentary on Exodus*.
[3] *Comm. on John* VI.10.
[4] *Ibid.*, XXXII.12. They admitted the figurative sense of this command, but thought that it ought to be taken literally too.
[5] *Ibid.*, frag. 44.   [6] *PE* XXIII.1.
[7] *Comm. on Rom.* I.19; cf. *Hom. on Gen.* I.13.

authority Melito of Sardis. According to Origen, he maintained in a book called 'God Incarnate' (Περὶ ἐνσωμάτου θεοῦ) that the text in Gen. 1.26, 'Let us make man in our image, after our likeness,' meant that man was like God in body and that God had a body, and he relied on references in the Bible to God's eyes and power of smell, hands, feet, fingers, and so on. Origen has a devastating answer to this sort of doctrine: 'We shall answer those whose understanding does not go beyond the literal sense with examples from the literal sense. From Zechariah, "the seven eyes of the Lord which look over all the earth" (Zech. 4.10). If God has seven eyes and we two, we are not made after his image. Again, we have no wings, but it says of God in the ninetieth psalm, "And under his wings thou shalt take refuge" (Ps. 91.4). If then he has wings and we are a wingless creature, man has not been made after the image of God.'[1] The phrase in Ps. 19.4, 'In them hath he set a tabernacle for the sun,' was taken by some to mean that at his Ascension Christ brought his body as far as 'that circle which is known as the zone of the sun', and there left it because it could not go any farther. 'But they hold this opinion only because they are unwilling to allow allegory in Holy Scripture and therefore they are tied to the bare literal narrative and invent legends and fictions such as these.'[2] It is in character that these people should, interpreting literally the promises and blessings in the Old Testament, argue that in the future life punishment will mean physical pain and reward physical pleasure.[3] They expect bodily enjoyment and even marriage after the resurrection. They rely on references in Isaiah and Revelation to the rebuilding and adorning of Jerusalem and to the destined subservience of other races to the Jews (Is. 54.12; 60.10–12; Rev. 21.18). They also cite in support of this view 'I shall not drink henceforth of this fruit of the vine' (Matt. 26.29) and the Beatitude that promises that those who hunger shall be filled (Luke 6.21). They believe too that the faithful will have offices and places of power in the resurrection world, citing 'Have thou authority over ten cities' (Luke 19.17).[4] Völker gives a concise summary of the creed of this type of what we might call *Chrétien moyen sensuel*: a belief in a Creator-God often thought of in a very material and corporeal way, in the resurrection of the flesh, in a judgement, fear of which is the main motive in ethical behaviour, in an historical Jesus who has destroyed by his Passion on the

[1]Fragment on Genesis, PG 12.93.
[2]Comm. on Ps. 19.4, PG 12.1243; this is a fragment quoted by Pamphilus in his *Apology for Origen*.
[3]Ibid., 4.6, PG 12.1152, reproduced in *Philoc.* XXVI.4.
[4]PA II.11.2; cf. Comm. on S. of S., Origen's Preface, PG 13.67.

Cross the power of demons and fate, and in the enjoyment of a hereafter envisaged materialistically.[1]

We cannot, however, dismiss this body of opinion as consisting purely of simple believers who clung obstinately to the literal interpretation of Scripture. There was obviously a Judaizing element among them. Origen constantly accuses them of Judaizing; he says that after becoming Christians they still favour 'materialist Judaizing' (τὸ σωματικῶς 'Ιουδαΐζειν)[2] and he associates Caiaphas the High Priest, as the representative of Judaism, with this literalism, saying that Caiaphas 'preferred the glory, associated with Judaism and fables, of the letter that killeth'.[3] This language may mean no more than that these Literalists were like the Jews in their attitude to Scripture, but there is other evidence that they were deliberate Judaizers. Origen knows of Christians in his day who do not agree to the 'spiritual' interpretation of the Mosaic law, but yet believe in Christ as spoken of by the prophets, and combine this belief with a literal observance of the law.[4] He refers to people who do not interpret the Scripture subtly enough, and among them are 'women who do not wash on the day of the Sabbath' and others 'who keep the Jewish fast'.[5] Others object when Origen ridicules the idea of circumcision as a permanent sign of a covenant between God and man, and when he points to the phrase 'circumcision of the heart' to be found in Scripture (Jer. 9.26; Ezek. 44.9; Rom. 2.28 f.) they reply, 'This makes things worse. It is impossible to imagine a literally circumcised heart.'[6] The same sort of people who deride what they call Origen's 'wordtricks and mist of allegory' refuse to allow that the History of Susanna is a canonical book.[7] Origen was therefore no doubt justified in classing these Literalists with Judaizers within the Christian Church, though it would probably be going too far to say that the two groups were identical.

We have already had some occasion to see how Origen answers this body of opinion. He shows how a literalist interpretation of the Bible

---

[1] *Das Vollkommenheitsideal*, p. 78.
[2] *Comm. on Matt.* XII.2
[3] *Ibid.*, Comm. Ser. 112: *gloriam aestimavit Judaicam et fabulosam litterae occidentis*.
[4] *Contra Celsum* II.3.
[5] *Hom. on Jer.* XII.13; these women did not however follow the absurd modern theory that Christians are bound to keep the Christian Sunday as the Jewish sabbath; some of the second class of people were probably among his hearers, for he puts the verb in the second person plural.
[6] *Hom. on Gen.* III.4; cf. the reference in *Hom. on Jer.*, frag. 4, to the people who are 'troubled about material sacrifice'.
[7] *Hom. on Lev.* I.I.

involves its exponents in hopeless contradictions. He produces some striking examples of this truth. In interpreting the text, 'My heart is inditing of a good matter' (ἐξερεύξατο ἡ καρδία μου λόγον ἀγαθόν, Ps. 45.1), the Literalists maintained that *logon* ('matter') needed no explanation, in contrast with Origen who held that this was an account of the relations between the Father and the Son (Logos). 'Is "my heart" then to be taken literally?' asks Origen, for both sides agree that the Father is the speaker in this psalm.[1] This opposition to Logos-doctrine among the Literalists, incidentally, is interesting, and may connect them with the Alogi known to have existed in Rome at the beginning of the third century.[2] A similar passage, referring no doubt to the same group of people, can be found in a fragment of the *Stromateis*, recovered by E. von der Goltz.[3] It is a comment on I Cor. 10.9 ('Neither let us tempt the Lord, as some of them tempted, and perished by serpents'), and it is designed to show that Christ must have been present with the children of Israel in the wilderness: 'Perhaps some ingenious explanation will be produced (εὑρησιλογήσουσιν) by those who do not desire that Christ should have engaged in these experiences (ἐκείνας τὰς οἰκονομίας ᾠκονομηκέναι) about the apparent allegory of the rock, but what will they say to this text? For some people did tempt him, that is, none but Christ, and therefore were they destroyed by serpents.' A disinclination to envisage Christ as present in a pre-incarnate state with the host of Israel in the Wilderness would be very characteristic of those who were anxious to belittle the Logos doctrine of the Church of their day. When in expounding the Epistle to the Romans Origen reaches the quotation of Ps. 69.22 f. in Rom. 11.9 ('Let their table be made a snare and a trap', etc.), he makes this an occasion of refuting 'those who deny the existence of allegories in divine Scripture and are wont to laugh at those who do not in all points follow the literal sense'. How are we to conceive, he asks, that their table could literally be made a trap for the Jews?[4] Though their protest at Origen's use of allegory may have had some substance in it, their own devotion to literalism at all costs was so irrational that they did not constitute a

---

[1] *Comm. on John* I.38.
[2] These may be the people accused by Origen of modalism in *Comm. on John* II.2, cited by F. Bertrand, *Mystique de Jésus chez Origène*, p. 32. It is, however, impossible to associate these people with the Ebionites, whose views are expressed in the pseudo-Clementine literature. The writer or writers of the Clementine *Homilies* and *Recognitions* accept the Fourth Gospel quite readily, and have little or no interest (as these Judaizers appear to have had) in the fulfilment of prophecy.
[3] Frag. 81, *TU* 17.4, p. 66.
[4] *Comm. on Rom.* VIII.8.

grave difficulty for Origen. He probably regarded them as nagging rather than dangerous.

Unintellectual Literalists, then, whose protest was mainly against the development and elaboration of Christian theology, were no very serious challenge to Origen, even though they showed some Judaizing tendencies. But Origen had also to face a counter-interpretation supported by a much weightier tradition of learning, and that was the interpretation of contemporary Jewish Rabbis. There is some evidence outside Origen's works that by the third century Judaism had begun to develop a deliberately anti-Christian exegesis. T. W. Manson points out that passages in the Old Testament claimed by early Christian authors as manifesting types of Christ and his Passion are also treated by Rabbinic writers but are by them deliberately given another meaning.[1] He parallels the treatment of the brazen serpent in the Fourth Gospel and in Justin with a treatment of the same incident, quite differently managed, in 'the Rabbinical commentary *Num.R.* 19',[2] and he compares the treatment of Aaron and Hur holding up Moses' hands, the Passover lamb, Rahab's scarlet thread and the brazen serpent again in Justin, Irenaeus and Cyprian, with the diverse treatment of these incidents in two other Rabbinic works.[3] He suggests that the Jewish interpretations of these incidents which appear so regularly in Christian apologetic are deliberately produced to counter the Christian interpretations of them. Support can be found for this conjecture, and confirmation of the early dating of such counter-interpretation, by a consideration of those passages in Justin's *Dialogue* where the author tells us what was the Jewish interpretation of those passages (mostly in the Psalms) where Christians saw predictions of Jesus Christ. Justin tells us that the Jews interpret Ps. 110 of Hezekiah, Ps. 72 of Solomon, Ps. 24 of Solomon at the dedication of the Temple and Ps. 99 also of Solomon.[4] Elsewhere he reveals that the Jews interpret Isa. 8.4 (a prophecy of the spoiling of Damascus and Samaria by the King of Assyria) of Hezekiah, and he again brings in Ps. 110, saying that the Jews take it of Hezekiah urged to sit at the right side of the Temple in order to overcome the

[1]'The Argument from Prophecy', *JTS*, XLVI, pp. 129–36.
[2]*Ibid.*, p. 130; the passages referred to are John 3.14 and Justin, *Dial.* 91 (Moses' hands held up and the brazen serpent).
[3]*Ibid.*, p. 131; the passages that he deals with are Justin, *Dial.* 91 (Moses' hands and the brazen serpent); Irenaeus, *Adv. Haer.* IV.4.2 and IV.50 (Moses' hands and the brazen serpent); Cyprian, *Testimonia* II.20–22 (brazen serpent, Moses' hands, Passover lamb); Mishna *Rosh-hashanah* III.8. (Moses' hands, brazen serpent) and *Mekhilta* on Ex. 17.11 (Moses' hands, brazen serpent, Passover lamb).
[4]*Dial.* 33.1 f.; 34.1–8; 36.2–5; 64.4–8.

King of Assyria, and Ps. 24, saying that the Jews see in it Hezekiah or Solomon or any Jewish King.[1] He tells us too that the Jews of his day apply Mal. 1.10–12 to the Jews of the Dispersion.[2] There can be little doubt that these interpretations are deliberately put forward as a defence against the ready use of Psalms and Isaiah by Christians to provide proof-texts for the claims that they are making for their Messiah.

Two more little pieces of evidence can be produced to strengthen the suggestion that even before Origen appeared on the scene Jewish scholarship was active in countering Christian exegesis. Strack-Billerbeck refer to a passage which represents Rabbi Eleazar of Modiim (obiit c. A.D. 135) as saying that 'whoever expounds meanings in the Torah which do not agree with the Halakah has no part in the age to come'.[3] Though Strack-Billerbeck are not very confident on the point, they think it possible that this may represent an original utterance of Eleazar condemning allegorizing of the Scriptures. Again A. Marmorstein suggests that Rabbi Johanan's prohibition of the Halakah being written down (though he suggested that the Haggadah should be written down) had an anti-Christian motive.[4] Rabbi Johanan lived during the third century.

Origen provides us with several examples of exegetical polemic on the part of Jewish scholars in his day. They objected, for instance, to the Synoptic Gospels' account of our Lord's Entry into Jerusalem. If the prophecy in Zechariah (9.9) applies to Jesus, as the Christians allege, how did Jesus 'destroy the chariot and horse from Jerusalem and destroy the bow of war' (Zech. 9.10)? And again, why use these animals for so short a journey, 'for those who seize upon the fifteen stades, a short distance only, will receive no very satisfactory justification for the journey'. And how did Jesus manage to sit on two animals?[5] The Jews also objected that Isa. 45.13, 'He shall build my city, and he shall let my exiles go free,' had not, as the Christians claimed, been fulfilled in Christ.[6] Origen mentions too that in one of his arguments with Jewish scholars about prophecy they maintained that Isa. 52.13–53.12 was written about the whole people which 'experienced the Dispersion and was afflicted, in order that many might become proselytes by reason

[1] Ibid., 77.2–4; 83.1–4; 85.1–4.
[2] Ibid., 117.1–5.   [3] SB III, p. 399.
[4] 'La Reorganisation du Doctorat en Palestine au Troisieme Siècle' REJ LXVI, p. 52. Presumably this is the R. Johanan of the Amoraic period who is described in Montefiore and Loewe, A Rabbinic Anthology (p. 697) as having died in 279 and (p. 706) as belonging to the Palestinian Second Division as reckoned by the authors.
[5] Comm. on John X.27.   [6] Comm. on Rom. VIII.8.

of the dispersal of the Jews among the other races.'[1] Origen points out, reasonably enough, how much more suitably the passage (and especially 53.8) could be applied to an individual and not to a people. The Jews, of course, asserted that 'there is no call for allegory'.[2] Into the same category we may put Aquila's deliberate translation of the Hebrew word for Messiah as *Elimmenos* ('Ηλιμμένος) instead of *Christ*, to avoid Christian associations with the latter word.[3]

Origen was in quite close touch with contemporary Rabbinic thought, and not merely by means of engaging with Jewish scholars in polemics; he obviously had friends among the Jews and not only among the Jewish Christians.[4] At the same time it is clear that Origen did engage in arguments with Jews. He frequently appeals to his knowledge of Jewish interpretation derived from such argument.[5] He realizes that the stock accusation of the Jews against Jesus is that he used sorcery to achieve his miracles and win his followers,[6] and has little difficulty in disposing of this argument. In return he accuses the Jews of putting their trust in myths and legends because they interpret the Bible 'superficially, assuming it to consist of fables'.[7] They look, for instance, to literal fulfilment of such prophecies as those of the Releasing of Prisoners in Isaiah (61.1), the Building of the Temple described in the later chapters of Ezekiel, the Destruction of the Chariot from Ephraim (Zech. 9.10), the Child Eating Butter and Honey (Isa. 7.15) and the Lion lying down with the Lamb (Isa. 11.6 f.).[8] Above all, they make the deplorable mistake of taking in a literal sense the ordinances of the Old Testament law.[9] They attempt, for instance, to explain away without resort to allegory the literal meaning of two ordinances which Origen frankly regards as ordaining what is impossible, the prohibition to leave one's house and the veto upon carrying burdens on the sabbath day; they allege that the house means a radius of two thousand cubits and that the burden means a certain kind of shoe or a sandal with nails in it, or that the burden is to be carried on one shoulder but not on two.[10] It is evident

---

[1]*Contra Celsum* I.55.
[2]*Hom. on Gen.* III.5: *allegoriae non superest locus.*
[3]*Comm. on John* XIII.26.
[4]See *Origen's Doctrine of Tradition*, pp. 146–56.
[5]E.g. *Contra Celsum* I.43, 55; II.32.
[6]*Ibid.* I.43 (μαγγανεία); III.1 (γοητεία).
[7]*Ibid.,* II.4: ἐπιπολαιότερον καὶ μυθικώτερον.
[8]*PA* IV.2.1.
[9]Cf. Harnack, *Der Kirchengeschichtliche Ertrag* II, p. 83 n.3.
[10]*PA* IV.3.2. The same passage tells us that 'Dositheus the Samaritan', among others, held that the prohibition against leaving the house meant that everyone was to remain in the same state of mind during the sabbath.

that Origen has no respect for the Halakah, and we see perhaps the motive of Rabbi Johanan's prohibition! In fact, 'the name of God is blasphemed among the nations, not only because of their most wicked activities but also because of the low and debased interpretation which they apply to the law and the prophets'.[1] The Jews also are at pains to explain away the passage in Gen. 49.11 which we have already seen Justin using as a Christian proof-text,[2] and which Origen interprets in a very similar way, either reproducing Justin or a traditional exegesis common to them both. For him the colt is the believing Gentiles; the ass's foal is the believing Jews; the vine is Christ because he took human nature, to which God attached his Word as a foal, that is he attached his people to Christ; the fruit of the vine is the future hopes of the people of God, supported by Christ. He rejects the literal interpretation of the passage and he quotes the interpretation of contemporary Jews, to the effect that the passage means that when the tribe of Judah was to inherit the portion of land allotted to it in Palestine the ground would bring forth so many vines that there would be no other trees to tie an animal to.[3] And they can give no intellectually respectable answers to Origen's strictures: when he discusses the passage in Leviticus, 'whosoever toucheth them (the offerings of the Lord) shall be holy' (Lev. 6.18), and points out that it is impossible to take this literally without outraging our moral sense, all they can find to reply is, 'That is what the Lawgiver determined; nobody argues with his Lord.'[4] Along with these Jewish exegetes he often mentions the Ebionites whom he defines as those of the Jews who accept Jesus as Christ.[5] They hold that Christ was sent primarily to the Jewish race.[6] They are strongly anti-Pauline.[7] With the Jews they accuse the Christians of ignoring the law in the Old Testament about unclean meats.[8] And they hold that every Christian should be circumcised.[9]

Finally, mention should be made of one group of biblical critics whose views were most hostile of all to Origen's convictions and with whom Origen had less in common than with any of the others. In all

---

[1]*Comm. on Rom.* II.9.   [2]See above, p. 109.
[3]*Hom. on Gen.* XVII.7 (*PG* 12.259 f). Origen of course rejects this Jewish interpretation.
[4]*Hom. on Lev.* IV.7.
[5]*Contra Celsum* II.1; cf. V.61, 65.
[6]*PA* IV.3.8; this is an opinion which Origen, of course, rejects. To him the Jewish race was only a temporary and material type of the 'spiritual' Israel consisting of redeemed people from every race and every aeon of existence to whom Christ was sent.
[7]*Hom. on Jer.* XIX.12.   [8]*Comm. on Matt.* XI.12.
[9]*Hom. on Gen.* III.4.

his exegesis Origen had to reckon with those contemporary philosophers and intellectuals who knew enough about the Bible to find it thoroughly unpalatable to their Hellenistic taste. Though, as we have seen, allegorizing was a well-established custom in pagan philosophy and theology of the time,[1] they objected strenuously to Christian allegory, and Origen is particularly sensitive upon this point. At one point in his work against Celsus he refrains from giving passages from Ezekiel which would illustrate his point because they are written 'very cryptically', and he does not want to expose his more far-fetched allegory to the attacks of 'those who are unworthy and irreverent', his pagan critics.[2] These are people who on the stock difficulty of the hardening of Pharaoh's heart object that 'actions unworthy of God are attributed to God'.[3] They brand the story of Moses breaking the tablets 'written by the hand of God' (Ex. 32.15-20) as a fable.[4] They laugh at the mention of Abraham's bosom,[5] and they accuse Jesus of showing cowardice at Gethsemane.[6] They deride the institution of circumcision as a sign of the covenant: 'So circumcision is to be a sign of something supernatural, and hold an allegorical meaning? So it was fitting that the visible sign of figurative things and the mysteries of the law were to be inaugurated to the accompaniment of children being brought to punishment and peril and of the torture of tender and still guiltless infants?'[7] This sort of criticism naturally made Origen even more anxious to allegorize away the literal meaning of the text of the Old Testament. Criticism of a rather more scientific kind was not lacking either. Speaking of the healing of the epileptic boy (Matt. 17.14-21), Origen says: 'Let the doctors then assign natural causes to it, giving their opinion that it is not an unclean spirit in this case but a bodily weakness, and give as the physical cause that the moist element in the head is disturbed by some sensitivity to the light of the moon, which has a moist nature.' But Origen refuses to believe them, holding that the epilepsy is caused by an unclean spirit anxious to have the moon, and therefore the moon's creator, God, blamed for the disease.[8] And the main motive for Origen's desire to allegorize the prediction of the cosmic portents which are to take place (Matt. 24.29 f.) is perhaps the knowledge that his more learned critics would declare that some of these portents (such as the

---

[1] See above, pp. 56-64.   [2] Contra Celsum VI.18.
[3] Philoc. XXVII.1, from the Commentary on Exodus: λέγεται περὶ θεοῦ τὰ ἀνάξια θεοῦ.   [4] Contra Celsum I.4.
[5] Comm. on John XXXII.20.   [6] Ibid., XXXII.23.
[7] Comm. on Rom. II.13. This was clearly a stock subject for attack. Philo calls it τὸ γελώμενον παρὰ τοῖς πολλοῖς, De Spec. Leg. I.1.
[8] Comm. on Matt. XIII.6.

stars falling on the earth) could not happen literally; probably Origen secretly agreed with them.[1]

The most violent critic of the Scriptures in this tradition was Celsus, the philosopher who wrote his *True Account*, a wholesale attack on Christianity, about 178 or 180.[2] Celsus constantly rejects the Christians' right to allegorize the Scriptures, though quite inconsistently he allowed pagan allegorizing.[3] 'You accept as your own,' he says, 'the cosmogony of Moses and the law of the Jews by some, as you call it, allegorization through types (τυπώδους ἀλληγορίας),'[4] but he regards this as mere chicanery. He complains that arguments in the Bible are not philosophically stated,[5] to which Origen replies very wisely that if they were they would be comprehensible only to the intellectuals. Celsus also attacks the historicity and accuracy of incidents in the Bible. He particularly objected that Moses' account of creation placed the creation of the world far too late.[6] He complained that the story of the ark was impossible and absurd and borrowed from the story of Deucalion in Greek myth, to which Origen's reply is to juggle with the dimensions of the ark in order to enlarge its size.[7] Celsus was, however, consistent enough to reject at the same time the historicity of the Greek myths.[8] He was specially derisive about the Christian argument from prophecy. The prophecies applied by Christians to Jesus could, he declared, be applied better to countless people and he spoke of the 'figures and equivocations and worthless pieces of evidence' (σύμβολα καὶ παρακούσματα καὶ ἀγέννη τεκμήρια) to be found in the prophetic passages.[9] And he suggests that if you take Isa. 52.14 seriously as a prophecy it follows that Jesus must have been mean-looking. Origen retorts that he can match prophecy against prophecy, citing Ps. 45.2 ('Thou art fairer than the children of men') and the accounts of the Transfiguration, and he adds that if Celsus admits that Isa. 52.14 is a prophecy of Jesus, then he is admitting something far more wonderful about him than could be discounted by the suggestion that he was ugly.[10] Celsus was very much of a rationalist in his attitude to Scripture. He threw doubt upon the reality of the angelic messages given to Joseph before and after the flight into Egypt,[11] and he ridiculed the account of the Resurrection,

[1] *Ibid.*, Comm. Ser. 48, 49.
[2] So de Faye, *Origène*, I, p. 141. For an account of Celsus' cricitism of the Bible see also the same work, I, p. 149; III, pp. 150–55.
[3] *Contra Celsum* I.20.
[4] *Ibid.*, VI.29. For other instances of Celsus' rejection of allegory, see I.17; IV.38, 48–51, 87.
[5] *Ibid.*, VI.1.   [6] *Ibid.*, I.19; cf. I.14.   [7] *Ibid.*, IV.41.
[8] *Ibid.*, I.67.   [9] *Ibid.*, II.28–30.   [10] *Ibid.*, VI.75.
[11] *Ibid.*, I.38.

adducing similar stories from pagan mythology and attributing the account to hallucination or deception on the part of the apostles.[1] Though the criticisms of the Bible which Origen had to meet from Gnostic quarters were shrewd enough, they were not the sort of objections that would arise in a modern mind. Celsus' attacks, however, sometimes remind us startlingly of the attacks launched by the critics of today, especially in his appeal to comparative religion and his determined scepticism. Some of these Origen was able to parry with confidence and firmness, but some found weak places in his armour, insufficiently protected by the shield of allegorization.

It is quite evident, then, that Origen, when he began producing his expositions of Scripture, was not writing in an exegetical vacuum. There existed before his day and during it a lively and varied world of scriptural exegesis. Gnostics had found their speculative adventures confirmed by Scripture; Predestinarians and Literalists had drawn their proof-texts from it; Marcionites had launched their attacks on the Old Testament; Jewish scholars were developing their defence of the Hebrew Scriptures against the Christian use of them; pagan intellectuals were sniping indiscriminately against Christian interpretation. All Christians, scholarly or uneducated, were interested in the interpretation of Scripture. We cannot even describe Origen as the first commentator on Scripture. Hippolytus had already written his work on Daniel before Origen had published a line, and several years before that Heracleon had produced his Commentary on the Fourth Gospel. There may well have been other commentaries written by orthodox Christians which have not survived. Indeed, so frequently do references occur in Origen's *Commentary on Matthew* to the comments or alternative interpretations of others that it is likely that Origen had before him a commentary by somebody else on the Gospel.[2] It is perhaps possible to distinguish two different ways of treating Scripture which had established themselves before Origen began writing, the method of using proof-texts and the method of writing a commentary. The first method was obviously the older, stemming from a tradition as old as Christianity itself and even perhaps older. We can trace it in those Testimonies which formed the subject of the studies of Rendel Harris and Dodd,[3] and we can follow it in the *Epistle of Barnabas*, Justin's *Dialogue* and Irenaeus' *Demonstration*. The Marcionites, the Predestinarians and the

---

[1] *Contra Celsum* II.55.
[2] Cf. *Comm. on Matt.* XIII.18, 26–30 *et passim*. Cf. also R. Cadiou, *La Jeunesse d'Origène*, p. 41.
[3] See above, pp. 73–6.

Literalists were only following a well-established tradition in compiling their proof-texts. But the second method of scriptural exposition had already appeared, in the hands of the Gnostic Heracleon. Origen adopted this method from Heracleon (for there is no evidence that he knew of Hippolytus' work) and developed it with such success that after his day the commentary-method was securely established as the more important and more satisfactory way of expounding Scripture.[1]

It is significant that it was a Gnostic writer who was the pioneer in commentary-writing. The Gnostics were on the whole the ablest of Origen's rivals in exposition, even though they were also the most perverse; Heracleon's comments are sometimes shrewder than those of Origen; the Marcionites' attacks upon the Old Testament were, at least on the Literalists' assumptions, devastating and unanswerable. The Gnostics may have contributed to the formation of the Canon of the New Testament; they certainly played a significant share (and not only by reaction) in moulding Christian exegesis. On their side the exegesis of contemporary Jewish Rabbis demanded a high degree of scholarship if it was to be satisfactorily answered, and the criticisms of pagan intellectuals forced into the foreground a question which had not hitherto been very prominent, that of the historicity of the biblical narratives.

So varied a field of exegesis demanded considerable ability from one who was to venture on it, and so manifold an attack on the integrity of the Bible called for versatility in the scholar who would defend that integrity. The confident but narrow approach which we find in Justin, the reliance upon second-hand philosophical sources which characterizes Theophilus, the somewhat wooden exposition of Hippolytus, would not suffice in this situation. Fortunately for the Christian Church, there came forward at this moment to encounter this difficult task a theologian who possessed all the ability and all the versatility which it demanded, Origen.

[1] It is possible that Origen refers to these two methods of expounding Scripture in a fragment of his *Commentary on I Corinthians*, written perhaps 232-3 (frag. 2, on I Cor. 1.4–10, *JTS* IX, p. 233): πάντι λόγῳ κεχρῆσθαι τῷ τε διεξοδικῷ καλουμένῳ (the commentary-method?) καὶ τῷ κατὰ ἐρώτησίν τε καὶ ἀπόκρισιν (the proof-text method?) καὶ παρεσκευάσθαι λέγειν καὶ κατὰ πάσης αἱρέσεως, καὶ τῷ τῆς ἀληθείας συνίστασθαι δόγματι.

6

Origen's Handling of the Text of the Bible

THE form of the Old Testament which Origen uses in the vast majority of his scriptural references is the LXX version. He follows this translation faithfully, even in its mistakes.[1] In his *Commentary on Hosea* he said that it is wrong to try to amend the text of the LXX even when the literal meaning seems to make nonsense; he was stimulated to make this remark by an inexplicable change of number visible only in the Septuagint text of Hos. 12.4.[2] There are many examples of his building arguments on mistranslations, in Job,[3] in Habakkuk,[4] and in Lamentations,[5] to take only a small selection. On several occasions he treats a word in the LXX text as if it were in fact the original word written by the author of the book concerned. Following Philo, he takes the ἐγκρυφίας ('hidden' cakes) of Gen. 18.6 to be symbolic of hidden mysteries.[6] He assumes that the word for 'matter' which occurs in the LXX version of Isa. 10.17 (ὕλη in Greek, *materia* in Rufinus' translation of Origen) is the original word, as it is in Wisd. 11.17.[7] And he regards the headings to the Psalms in the LXX version, some of which seem to bear little reference to the Hebrew original, as inspired.[8]

On three occasions in his *Commentary on Romans* Origen appears to

---

[1]Every Christian exegete of his day did this, of course, even the Literalists. See *Comm. on John* VI.10, where it is evident that the Literalists followed the LXX's πᾶσαν τὴν ἐξανάστασιν in Gen. 7.4 for 'every living thing'.

[2]*Philoc.* VIII.1.

[3]*Comm. on Ps.* 4.6, *PG* 12.1157, reproduced in *Philoc.* XXVI.5; Job.40.8b ('Wilt thou condemn me, that thou mayest be justified?') appears in the LXX (40.3) as οἴει δὲ με ἄλλως σοι κεχρηματικέναι ἢ ἵνα ἀναφανῇς δίκαιος; Also *Comm. on John* XX.22, where the LXX has in the nineteenth verse of the same chapter of Job 'made to be mocked by his angels', instead of 'He only that made him can make his sword to approach unto him'. Cf. *Philoc.* XXVII.9.

[4]*PA* I.3.4, where he follows the LXX mistranslation of בקרב שנים חייהו ('in the midst of the years revive it') as 'in the midst of two beasts'.

[5]*Hom. on Lam.*, frag. 79; in Lam. 3.38 the LXX takes 'Out of the mouth of the Most High cometh there not evil and good?' as a negative statement to the effect that evil and good do not equally come from God, and Origen follows it.

[6]*Hom. on Gen.* IV.1; for Philo's interpretation of this word, see above, pp. 47 f.

[7]*PA* IV.4.6.

[8]*Comm. on Psalms*, Preface, *PG* 12.1061.

quote St Paul's authority in appealing to the Greek of the LXX against the Hebrew text.[1] But it is a suspicious fact that all these examples occur in the *Commentary on Romans*, where, it is well established, Rufinus allowed himself peculiar licence in translating, and we cannot be sure, at least until the original Greek of parts of this work, which has been discovered among the find of papyri at Toura, is edited and published, that those passages do not owe their existence to Rufinus' hand.

Origen accepts almost without reserve all the books of the LXX extant only in Greek as canonical, though he is ready to confine himself quite cheerfully to the Hebrew Scriptures when arguing with Jews.[2] Field observes that though in the Hexapla where the LXX order differed from the Hebrew order Origen in every known case (except, for some reason, at the end of Proverbs) followed the Hebrew order, yet his theoretical admission of the priority of the Hebrew text in this work does not prevent him from treating the LXX text in it in a very conservative way. For instance, at Isa. 9.6, for the 'Wonderful Counsellor', etc. of the Hebrew text the LXX has a longish paraphrase, 'Angel of mighty counsel, for I will bring peace upon the rulers and health to him'; here Origen obelizes only the word 'angel'.[3] His attitude to the LXX is well illustrated by an interesting little note which he makes on the sentence tacked on in the LXX version alone to the end of the Book of Job. The sentence runs: 'And it is written that he will rise again with those whom the Lord will raise.' Origen's comment is: 'We accept these words also, even if they are not entirely in continuity with what precedes, yet (we accept them) on the grounds that one of the holy men attached them to the book: yes, in spite of this we accept it all, since we have received the book in this form from the Fathers.'[4] He knows perfectly well that this sentence is not part of the original book, but accepts it because it is respected as traditional by the Church of his day.

He acknowledges that the LXX is inspired, inasmuch as he often regards its divergence from the Hebrew text as divinely prompted. Commenting on the verse 'A virgin of his own people shall he take to

---

[1] VIII.6 (on Rom. 10.21); VIII.8 (on Rom. 11.9, where his aim is rather to show that St Paul could sometimes regard himself as not tied to the Hebrew text); and X.8 (on Rom. 15.9–12).

[2] E.g. *PE* XIII.2 and XIV.4. For a fuller treatment of Origen's attitude to the O.T. canon, see *Origen's Doctrine of Tradition*, pp. 133–7.

[3] F. Field, *Origenis Hexapla quae Supersunt*, Prolegomena, pp. lxi, lxiii.

[4] καὶ ταῦτα δὲ ῥήματα δεχόμεθα, εἰ καὶ μὴ ὡς τοῦ παντὸς ὕφους ὄντα, ἀλλά γε ὡς τινος τῶν ἁγίων αὐτὰ συνυφήναντος τῇ βίβλῳ· πλὴν ὅμως πάντα δεχόμεθα, οὕτως ἐκ τῶν πατέρων τὸ βίβλιον παρειληφότες. Pitra, *Analecta Sacra* II, p. 290. Cf. Origen's attitude to the Epistle to the Hebrews: see *Origen's Doctrine of Tradition*, pp. 141 f.

wife' (Lev. 21.14), Origen remarks that the Jews say that their texts do not have the phrase 'of his own people' though it appears in the LXX. He claims that it is by divine providence that their copies omit this phrase, because they are by their own disobedience no longer of the people of Christ.[1] Elsewhere Origen notes instances where the LXX translators render tenses as past which in Aquila or Symmachus are present or future. They usually refer to Christ, he says, and show that the LXX translators regarded their fulfilment as so certain in God's purpose that they could be regarded as past.[2] 'When their corn and their wine increased' (Ps. 4.7) appears in the LXX as 'from the fruit of corn' (ἀπὸ καρποῦ σίτου), but Origen tells us that the Hebrew text reads 'from the time of corn' (in Greek ἀπὸ καίρου σίτου), and then gives the reasons why the LXX made the change; they are purely doctrinal.[3] 'The king shall mourn and the prince' (Ezek. 7.27) does not, Origen points out, appear in the LXX, 'perhaps because the Saviour was not thought likely to mourn, or because [the translators] did not find the passage in the Hebrew'; he goes on, however, to admit honestly that these translators were not very accurate prophets, because Christ did weep over Jerusalem.[4] Ps. 2.12 has the phrase 'lest ye perish from the way'; the LXX reads 'from the right way', though the word for 'right' (δικαίας) appears neither in the Hebrew nor in any other version; it is therefore there either as a result of a 'divine device' (κατ᾽ οἰκονομίαν) or of a copyist's mistake; he then goes on to expound the meaning of the verse if either alternative be adopted.[5] A little later he reaches the phrase 'Thou hast smitten all mine enemies upon the cheek bone' (Ps. 3.7); here Origen points out that the LXX reads 'Thou hast smitten all mine enemies in vain' (ματαίως), though all other versions support the former reading. The most ancient copies, he says, probably read 'in vain', or else the LXX translators deliberately changed it, thinking 'on the cheek bone' too unworthy a reading; he then interprets the LXX reading.[6]

Such an attitude to a form of the Old Testament which could not possibly be the original form may strike modern readers as unreasonably credulous. But in fact it should be observed, even before we con-

[1]*Hom. on Lev.* XII.5.
[2]*Comm. on Ps.* 2.1, *PG* 12.1104.
[3]*Comm. on Ps.* 5.7, *PG* 12.1169.
[4]*Frag. on Ezek.* 7.27, *PG* 13.795.
[5]*Comm. on Ps.* 2.12, *PG* 12.1116.
[6]*Comm. on Ps.* 3.7, *PG* 12.1130. Cf. *Hom. on Jer.* XVI.5, where the LXX omission of the word 'first' in Jer. 16.18 is put down by Origen to inadvertence on the part of a copyist, 'or the Seventy omitted it deliberately'. After examining the other versions he found that the word was in the text.

sider Origen's attitude to the Hebrew text, that as concerns the LXX version he is remarkably restrained, and far more sober and scholarly than any of his predecessors and than most of his successors. We have seen Philo's uncritical admiration for the Greek version of the Pentateuch of his day.[1] Justin's account of the LXX is no less credulous, and he adds the remarkable detail that Herod was King of the Jews at the time that Ptolemy King of Egypt sent for the seventy translators![2] Hippolytus naïvely declares that the Jews only refuse to recognize the History of Susanna as authentic because they are ashamed of the behaviour of the two Jewish elders described in it.[3] Irenaeus reproduces the account of the *Letter of Aristeas* without question,[4] and Clement of Alexandria follows Philo's account and reproduces his attitude, merely applying what Philo had said of the Pentateuch to the whole Old Testament.[5] We find no childish accusations in Origen, and no credulous wonder at the thaumaturgy accompanying the making of the LXX translation. We might not inaptly describe his attitude to the question of whether the LXX or the Jews' Hebrew text should have priority as the attitude of a gentleman and a scholar. He never regarded the LXX text as normally a prior or a preferable text, but he thought of it as on occasion contributing, under inspiration, Christological nuances to the original text by addition or alteration. His treatment of it in the Hexapla reveals both his reverence for the LXX and his clear conviction that the Hebrew text must be regarded as the final court of appeal.

That this was his clear conviction can be shown by an abundance of evidence.[6] Origen believed that Hebrew was the original tongue of the human race left with the Jews when at the Tower of Babel the other races adopted other tongues.[7] He reminds his readers that the prophets wrote in Hebrew.[8] He can criticize the LXX rendering of Ezek. 16.4 ('They did not bind thy breasts' for Hebrew 'Thy navel was not cut') as 'one which sets out the meaning of the sentence rather than giving a word for word translation'.[9] Dealing with Lev. 4.27, he contemplates the possibility of the verse in the LXX version having a mistake due to the translator, though he finally rules out this possibility on the ground

---

[1]See above, p. 47.
[2]*Apol.* I.31.1–5; see above, p. 13, for his charge that the Jews deliberately mutilated the Hebrew text.
[3]*Comm. on Dan.* I.14.2.   [4]Eus. *HE* V.8.11–15, p.152.
[5]*Strom.* I.22.148, *PG* 8.893. See *Origen's Doctrine of Tradition*, p. 158.
[6]For more evidence on this subject see Field, *Hexapla*, Prolegomena, pp. liv and lxi.
[7]*Hom. on Num.* XI.4.   [8]*Contra Celsum* VII.59.
[9]*Hom. on Ezek.* VI.4.

that all the versions have the same reading.[1] In *Comm. on John* X.40 he
admits that the LXX translators did not know the meaning of the
Hebrew word *debir* in I Kings 6.16, and that he consequently was in the
dark as to its meaning.[2] Similarly he supports the reading in Ps. 11.7
'he has loved righteousnesses' (δικαιοσύνας ἠγάπησεν) by an appeal
to the most accurate copies, to other versions besides the LXX, and to
the Hebrew.[3] He points out, in a discussion of the proper forms of some
place-names in the Gospels, that in several places 'our copies' (i.e.
manuscripts used by Christians, in both Old Testament and New Testament display mistakes in names which can be discovered by comparing
them with the Hebrew and with Aquila's, Theodotion's and Symmachus' versions.[4] Even in discussing that *locus vexatus*, the 'Immanuel'
passage in Isa. 7, it is only with reluctance that he consents to argue with
those who do not recognize the Hebrew text as authoritative.[5] On Ex.
4.24–6 he remarks that the meaning in Hebrew, 'a bridegroom of
blood', is more correct than the LXX reading, 'the blood of circumcision stayed' (ἔστη τὸ αἷμα τῆς περιτόμης).[6] In tracing the meaning of
two words, Gehenna and Leviathan, he consults the Hebrew and
quotes it as more original and more likely to throw light on the question
than the Greek, which has 'ravine of the son of Ennom' (φάραγξ τοῦ
υἱοῦ Ἐννόμ) and 'dragon' (δράκων) for these two words.[7] In order to
explain an apparent inconsistency in the quotations of Ps. 118.25 by the
people at the Entry into Jerusalem described in Matt. 21.9, he appeals
to the original Hebrew text as final and to Aquila, not the LXX, as
normative in Greek.[8] He follows the opinion of a certain Jullus, 'the
patriarch, one who was held to be a wise man by the Jews', in attributing
Ps. 90 and the ten psalms following it to Moses, as the Hebrew text
does, although the LXX ascribes these psalms to David.[9] Origen's
attitude to both Hebrew and LXX text is well exemplified in his own
description of the policy he pursued in compiling the Hexapla in those

---

[1] *Hom. on Lev.* II.4.
[2] Ὅπερ οὐ δεδύνηνται ἑρμηνεῦσαι κυρίως οἱ μεταλαμβάνοντες εἰς Ἑλληνισμον
τὰ Ἑβραίων. For some reason Origen had not consulted Aquila or Symmachus
here, for they both have χρηματιστήριον here. Origen had certainly come in
contact with Aquila's and Symmachus' verions before he wrote these words (in
Caesarea, probably about 233).
[3] *Comm. on John* VI.6.   [4] *Ibid.*, VI.41.
[5] *Contra Celsum* I.35.   [6] *Ibid.*, V.48.
[7] *Ibid.*, VI.25: cf. frag. on Job 39.20, Pitra, *Analecta Sacra* II, p. 386.
[8] *Comm. on Matt.* XVI.19.
[9] *Comm. on Psalms*, Preface, *PG* 12.1056. 'Patriarch' here means an eminent
Jew chosen by the Romans to be the representative and ruler of the Jewish community. For his identity see *Origen's Doctrine of Tradition*, pp. 151 f.

cases where the LXX showed additions not in the Hebrew: 'Some passages we have obelized because they are not found in the Hebrew, though we did not dare to remove them entirely.'[1]

How great was Origen's own knowledge of Hebrew is a question which has occupied the minds of many students of Origen, but one on which, as far as I know, all the evidence has never yet been examined. Philo, as we have seen,[2] probably knew no Hebrew at all. Clement of Alexandria claims that one of his teachers was a 'Hebrew' in Palestine,[3] and he had picked up some Midrash,[4] but his translation of 'Hosanna' as 'light and glory and praise with supplication to the Lord'[5] does not reassure us, and it is better to assume that he was totally ignorant of Hebrew. Origen's case is obviously different. He certainly knew *some* Hebrew; he could not have compiled the Hexapla unless he had at least a working knowledge of the language, and this conclusion is confirmed by what we have seen already of his allusions to the Hebrew text, as well as by the statement in Eusebius.[6] We can indeed sometimes find him using his knowledge of Hebrew quite effectively to elucidate some point of exposition. In dealing with the 'Immanuel' passage in Isa. 7, he suggests that a Jewish scholar might argue that the Hebrew word for 'virgin' means 'young woman' (νεᾶνις) and not 'virgin' (παρθένος); he then quotes the original Hebrew word transliterated (ἀαλμά for עלמה) and produces two passages from Deut. (22.23–6) to show that the word in fact means 'virgin'.[7] And he can give quite a useful note on the word for 'and' in Hebrew, pointing out that the word is often used superfluously where we would leave it out in translation: 'For each language has its own peculiarity which seems awkward when translated into other languages. In this passage therefore the conjunction "and" must be thought superfluous and unnecessary.'[8]

A certain amount can be learnt about Origen's knowledge of Hebrew from a study of the transliterations of Hebrew into Greek which he

---

[1] *Comm. on Matt.* XV.14.

[2] See above, p. 47, n. 4.

[3] See his account of those who had taught him, *Strom.* I.1.11–13, *PG* 8.697–704.

[4] See *Strom.* I.23.154, *PG* 8.899.

[5] *Paed.* I.4.12, *PG* 8.264. Neither can we be favourably impressed by his statement that if you read the Greek for Eve, Εὔα, with a rough breathing, Εὕα, it forms the Hebrew word for a female serpent.

[6] *HE* VI.16.1, borne out by *PA* I.3.4 and IV.3.14.

[7] *Contra Celsum* I.34; see H. Chadwick *in loc.*, who points out that the MT does not in fact support Origen's argument.

[8] *Hom. on Num.* XIX.3; Origen has learnt something, since in the *PA*, written perhaps twenty years before, he asserted that not a single word of Scripture is superfluous!

makes in the course of his works.[1] Some of these may have been encountered by him in documents already existing, such as the transliterated column in the Hexapla, which Kahle thinks to have been taken from the transliteration of the Hebrew Scriptures into Greek in the Jewish synagogue at Caesarea; these can tell us little of his skill in the language. But other transliterations, to be found sporadically in Origen's books, may be his own work. In the course of his *Commentary on the Psalms*, for instance, he has occasion to reproduce some words from the original Hebrew of Pss. 75 and 76, and it is interesting to observe that he leaves out altogether the Hebrew letters א and ה, as he does in the transliterated column in the Hexapla.[2] In his *Commentary on Matthew* he chooses to quote the original Hebrew words for 'man' and 'male', 'woman' and 'female', three of which occur in Gen. 1.27; he reproduces the transliteration of 'and female' (all one word in Hebrew) as if it all meant merely 'female'.[3] In his *Letter to Africanus* Origen alleges that woman is called *Essa* (ἐσσά) in Gen. 2.23 because she is taken from man and that *Essa* is also the Hebrew for 'I have taken', perpetrating an elementary mistake; he compares Ps. 116.13 ('*I will receive* the cup of salvation').[4] Another fairly accurate quotation of the original Hebrew can be found later in the *Commentary on Matthew*, where Origen reproduces a verse and a half from Ps. 118.25 f.[5] The longest example of Origen's transliteration outside the Hexapla is the list which he gives us (reproduced in the table opposite) of the names given to the books of the Old Testament by the Jews, quoted in Eusebius (*HE* VI.25) from

[1]For full information on this subject see Field, *Hexapla*, Prolegomena, pp. lxxii–lxxiv; J. Halévy, 'L'Origine de la Transcription du Texte Hébreu en Caractères Grecs dans les Hexaples d'Origène', *Journal Asiatique*, series IX, vol. XVII, pp. 335–41; Kahle, *The Cairo Geniza*, pp. 86 f.

[2]*Comm. on Psalms*, PG 12.1060: he reproduces סלה as σέλ and עמודיהה as Ἀμουδᾶ (Ps. 75.3): ומלחמה appears as Οὐμαλαμά (Ps. 76.3); and ענר – ארץ is rendered as ἀνίη ἄρς.

[3]*Comm. on Matt.* XIV.16: ἀνὴρ μὲν γὰρ δηλοῦται τῇ ἲς φωνῇ (איש), ἄρσεν δὲ τῇ ζαχάρ (זכר), καὶ πάλιν γυνὴ μὲν τῇ ἐσσά (אישה) φωνῇ, θῆλυ δὲ τῇ ἀγκηβᾶ (ונקבה).

[4]*Letter to Africanus* 12: he reproduces Ps. 116.13 (כוס – ישועות אֶשָּׂא) as χῶς Ἰσουῶθ ἐσσά. Origen had Theodotion as a predecessor in this error, for he had translated אישה as λῆψις, and Symmachus had rendered Gen. 2.23 as αὕτη κληθήσεται ἐσσὰ ἀνδρίς, ὅτι ἀπὸ ἀνδρὸς ἐλήφθη αὕτη. See Field, *Hexapla* I, p. 15 n. 35.

[5]*Comm. on Matt.* XVI.19; here is the Hebrew and Origen's transliteration:
אנא יהוה הושיעהנא אנא יהוה הצליחהנא ברך הבא בשם יהוה
ΑΝΝΑ ΑΔΩΝΑΙ ΩΣΙΑΝΝΑ, ΑΝΝΑ ΑΔΩΝΑΙ ΑΣΛΙΑΝΝΑ ΒΑΡΟΥΧ ΑΒΒΑ ΒΣΑΙΜ ΑΔΩΝΑΙ.

THE NAMES OF THE BOOKS OF THE OLD TESTAMENT
transliterated by Origen
(Eusebius *HE* VI.25)

Greek Name	Hebrew Name Transliterated	Meaning
Γένεσις	Βρησίθ	ἐν ἀρχῇ
Ἔξοδος	Οὐελεσμώθ	ταῦτα τὰ ὀνόματα
Λευιτικόν	Οὐϊκρά	καὶ ἐκάλεσεν
Ἀριθμοί	Ἀμμεσφεκωδείμ[1]	—
Δευτερονόμιον	Ἐλεαδδεβαρείμ	οὗτοι οἱ λόγοι
Ἰησοῦς υἱὸς Ναυῆ	Ἰωσοῦε βὲν Νοῦν	—
Κριταὶ 〉 Ῥοῦθ	Σαφατείμ	—
Βασιλειῶν πρωτὴ δευτέρα 〉	Σαμουήλ	ὁ Θεόκλητος
Βασιλειῶν τρίτη τετάρτη	Οὐαμμέλχ Δαβίδ	Βασιλεία Δαβίδ
Παραλειπομένων πρωτὴ 〉 δευτέρα	Δαβρηϊαμείν	λόγοι ἡμέρων
Ἔσδρας πρῶτος δεύτερος 〉	Ἔζρᾶ	βοηθός
Βίβλος Ψαλμῶν	Σφαρθελείμ	—
Σολομῶντος Παροιμίαι	Μελώθ[2]	—
Ἐκκλησιάστης	Κωέλθ	—
Ἄσμα Ἀσμάτων	Σὶρ Ἀσσιρίμ	—
Ἡσάϊας	Ἰεσσία	—
Ἰερεμίας σὺν Θρηνοῖς 〉 καὶ Ἐπιστολῇ	Ἰερεμία	—
Δανίηλ	Δανίηλ	—
Ἰεζεκιήλ	Ἰεζεκιήλ	—
Ἰώβ	Ἰώβ	—
Ἐσθήρ	Ἐσθήρ	—
Τὰ Μακκαβαϊκά	Σαρβήθ Σαβαναιέλ[3]	—

an otherwise lost *Commentary on Psalms*. We may conclude that this is the transliteration of a list supplied to him by some Rabbinic source, especially in view of his version of the name of Numbers. It shows us

---

[1] Probably this is an attempt at חמש הפקודים ('fifth of the numbered men'), which is a title for Numbers to be found in the Talmud.

[2] This may be a copyist's error for ΜΕΣΛΩΘ or ΜΣΑΛΩΘ. The word is sometimes treated as feminine in Rabbinic literature.

[3] This probably represents an original ספר בית שבני חל ('book of the house of warriors').

A.E.–F*

Origen as, on the whole, anxious to achieve accuracy but in several instances badly puzzled and in at least one instance falling into error. This last list serves to remind us that Origen was in touch with contemporary Rabbinic sources, a fact which has been established by an abundance of evidence.[1] It is also highly probable that he had before him at least two types of lists of etymologies from which he derived his interpretations of Hebrew names, one type which we might call a List-etymology and the other an Onomasticon-etymology, some composed by those who knew Hebrew better than Greek, and some by people to whom Greek was more familiar than Hebrew.[2] It is likely that these lists come from purely Jewish, rather than Jewish Christian sources. A few other etymologies he derived from Philo.[3] Once or twice he seems to attempt an etymological venture himself, relying on his own knowledge of Hebrew. He interprets *Cush* in Gen. 2.13 as 'shadowing', but he cannot resist, in view of the likeness of the name in Greek to the Greek word for 'dust' (Χοῦς for *Cush*, χοῦς for dust), using the meaning 'dust' in expounding the text. Again, he interprets the complicated name *Zaphenath-Phaneah* (Gen. 41.45) as 'he revealed hidden things' (κεκρυμμένα ἀπεκάλυψε), perhaps because he guessed that the Hebrew for this word (צפנת–פנח) represented a hybrid of the Hebrew for 'go forth' (יצא) and the Greek for 'it has appeared' (ἐφάνη).[4] One more such example may appear in Origen's interpretation of *Sidon*, which he takes to mean 'the hunters' (θηρῶντες), deriving this meaning apparently from a mistaken reading of the Hebrew of Ps. 124.7.[5]

None of these attempts at interpreting Hebrew gives us much confidence in Origen's knowledge of the language, and we can glean from his works a few more examples of errors in Hebrew. He interprets 'Samuel' as 'There is God himself'.[6] In commenting on the heading of Ps. 34 in Hebrew and Septuagint, 'A Psalm of David, when he changed his behaviour before Abimelech', Origen concludes that by 'Abimelech' a mistake has been made, not for Achish which one would expect, but Ahimelech (I Sam. 21.1–6); he explains that the mistake could easily be

---

[1] See, e.g., *Origen's Doctrine of Tradition*, pp. 149–56.
[2] See 'Interpretations of Hebrew Names in Origen', *Vig. Chr.* X.
[3] *Ibid.*, pp. 103 f.
[4] These passages appear in the *Commentary on Genesis*, PG 12.100 and 136. See 'Interpretations of Hebrew Names in Origen', p. 104.
[5] *Hom. on Ezek.* XIII.4; he probably mistook כצפר for מצידן and translated 'our soul is escaped from Sidon, from the snare of the hunters'. See 'The Interpretation of Hebrew Names', p. 104. Origen repeats this odd interpretation of Sidon in *Comm. on Matt.* XI.16.
[6] *Ibi ipse deus*, *Hom. on I Sam.* I.5, presumably שם הוא אל.

made by a copyist, 'The letters in Hebrew, I mean the Caph and Beth, have so very similar a form that they differ from each other not at all or only by the least tittle'.[1] This statement is of course reasonably accurate of the letters Caph and Beth in the Aramaic script which Origen used and which we still use. But unfortunately, as Origen ought to have known, Ahimelech is spelt with a Heth and not a Caph, and he has here made an elementary mistake. Another piece of inaccuracy appears in his statement that the word for 'salvation' in Ps. 27.1 ('The Lord is my light and my salvation') is the same in Hebrew as the letters of the word for Jesus in Hebrew. Now the word for 'Joshua' in Hebrew (which Origen consistently renders as 'Jesus', 'Ιησοῦς) has one more letter than the word for 'salvation' in the Psalm (יהשע, Joshua; ישע, salvation).[2] It is therefore likely that Origen has made a mistake here, misled, perhaps, by his habit of omitting the Hebrew Hé in transliteration.

We have therefore a reasonable amount of evidence before us on the subject of Origen's knowledge of Hebrew, enough for us to make a fairly confident judgement. We can dismiss at once the extraordinary statement of Wutz that Origen did not dare to compare himself with Philo in this respect and knew less Hebrew than he.[3] There is very little evidence that Philo knew any Hebrew at all, whereas Origen certainly knew considerably more than merely the letters of the Hebrew alphabet, and could venture occasionally to expound the Hebrew text, even though he often made mistakes in doing so. He does not in fact pretend to know much Hebrew; he is modest about his knowledge and more often than not will refer the reader to the experts in Hebrew. In trying to determine whether the puns on the names of trees in the History of Susanna (πρῖνος and πρίειν, σχῖνος and σχίζειν) could be a reproduction of the same puns in Hebrew, he did not rely on his own knowledge of the language, which was insufficient for this point, but had to consult his friends among the Jews.[4] And in the vast majority of his interpretations of Hebrew place-names he relies on lists supplied to him by others and not on his own knowledge of Hebrew.[5] He often refers to the Jews as experts on the Hebrew text in phrases which suggest that he himself is

---

[1]*Comm. on Psalms*, PG 12.1068. Clement of Alexandria makes the same mistake, *Strom.* I.21.110 (PG 8.836).
[2]*Comm. on Ps.* 27.1, PG 12.1276.
[3]F. Wutz, *Onomastica Sacra*, pp. 37, 43, 51. Huet was apparently the originator of this strange view.
[4]*Letter to Africanus* 6.
[5]See 'The Interpretation of Hebrew Place-Names in Origen', *Vig. Chr.* X, p. 105.

not one. 'Those who can read Hebrew say' . . .[1] 'Those who are expert in Hebrew matters say' . . .[2] 'The Jews say that Kedar is interpreted as darkness.'[3] It is quite misleading to say that Origen knew virtually no Hebrew; he knew far more than any eminent Christian theologian for a century before him, or any of his own day. But his knowledge was very superficial and he had little confidence in it himself.[4] It was sufficient to enable him to use the information which he was able to procure from contemporary Rabbinic scholarship, but he could not use it critically.

We have already seen reason to believe that the LXX and the Hebrew text were not the only authorities to whom Origen appealed in his handling of the text. He knew and quite often used the versions of Aquila, of Symmachus and of Theodotion. For Aquila he has a particular respect. In his *Letter to Africanus* he describes Aquila as 'a slave to the Hebrew text[5]—a perfectly justified criticism—but adds that Aquila 'is believed by the Jews to have translated Scripture more carefully, and those who know the Hebrew language usually follow him on the grounds that he is the most successful of all translators'; incidentally this remark implies that Origen himself was far from skilled in the Hebrew language. In another place he observes with what faithfulness Aquila follows a variety in grammar between two synonymous terms in Gen. 1.16 ff. and characterizes him as 'Aquila who is anxious to translate as literally as possible'.[6] In endeavouring to find the correct version of Ps. 118.25 quoted by the people at our Lord's Entry into Jerusalem (Matt. 21.9), he quotes Aquila's translation of the Psalm to show what the correct Greek translation should be.[7] Commenting on Gen. 2.4 ('These are the generations of the heaven and of the earth') he corrects both the Hebrew text known to him and the LXX by reference to Aquila's translation,[8] and he notes that Aquila regards as

---

[1] *Hom. on Num.* XIV.1, *Aiunt ergo qui Hebraicas litteras legunt.*
[2] *Comm. on Ps.* 24.10, *PG* 12.1269: οἱ τὰ Ἑβραίων ἠκριβωκότες. In this case he probably means Jewish Christians, for they obviously believe that the LXX is prophesying about Christ.
[3] *Hom. on S. of S.* I.6.
[4] The verdict of G. Bardy is a sound one: 'We must simply conclude that if Origen had learnt enough Hebrew to read it and to transcribe it, yet he had never possessed more than a superficial knowledge of the language.' 'Les Traditions Juives dans l'Oeuvre d'Origène' (*Revue Biblique* XXXIV, pp. 217–52).
[5] Δουλεύων τῇ Ἑβραικῇ λέξει. Cf. Field, *Hexapla*, Prolegomena, p. xix.
[6] 'Ὁ κυριώτατα 'ερμηνεύειν φιλοτιμούμενος 'Ακύλας, *Philoc.* XIV.1, from the *Commentary on Genesis*, Book III. Compare *Comm. on Ps.* 4.4. (*PG* 12.1148) where he again appeals to Aquila as being the most accurate of translators.
[7] *Comm. on Matt.* XVI.19.
[8] *Fragment on Genesis, PG* 12.97.

apocryphal the addition in the LXX to Gen. 4.8, 'And Cain said to Abel his brother, Let us go into the field.'[1] And on Prov. 27.10 ('Go not to thy brother's house in the day of thy calamity') he says that where the LXX has 'unfortunate' (infelix, ἀτυχῶν) Aquila, 'correctly translating the Hebrew', has 'rustic' (ἀγροικός).[2]

He can also appeal to Symmachus' translation. When he reaches the text 'My children are desolate' (Lam. 1.16) he observes that the LXX translates 'my sons are destroyed' (ἠφανισμένοι) but that Symmachus here reads 'desolate' (ἔρημοι), and he expounds this last reading, and a little later in the same work he again cites a variant of Symmachus and interprets it.[3] Or he will quote the readings of both Aquila and Symmachus; he does so at least twice in the extant fragments of his *Homilies on Jeremiah* and *Homilies on Lamentations*, works in which he seems particularly to have relied on Symmachus' version.[4] He seems sometimes to have viewed the alternatives of Aquila and Symmachus as legitimate but not necessarily preferable variations, without asking which was the true text, theirs or that of the LXX. This attitude is illustrated in his handling of the heading of Ps. 45. Here the RV translates 'set to Shoshannim', to which the margin adds, 'That is, lilies'. The LXX reproduces the Hebrew as 'on behalf of those who are destined to be transformed' (ὑπὲρ τῶν ἀλλοιωθησομένων). Origen explains this translation according to his conception of the doctrinal teaching of the psalm, then admits that the Hebrew for these words means 'the lilies' or 'the flowers', and that Aquila reads 'on the lilies' (ἐπὶ τοῖς κρίνοις) and Symmachus 'concerning the flowers' (περὶ τῶν ἀνθεων). He then tries to reconcile the two interpretations by saying that flowers are things destined to change very swiftly.[5] He can also sometimes appeal to all three of these translators together, Aquila, Symmachus and Theodotion, against the LXX.[6]

[1] *Ibid., PG* 12.101.   [2] *Hom. on S. of S.* II.4.   [3] *Hom. on Lam.*, frags. 35 and 86.
[4] *Hom. on Jer.*, frag. 45 and *Hom. on Lam.*, frag. 116. Aquila and Symmachus are also quoted, and each version interpreted, in a fragment on Job, Pitra, *Analecta Sacra* II, p. 372.
[5] *Comm. on Psalms*, Preface, *PG* 12.1064.
[6] E.g. *Hom. on Jer.*, frag. 14, where he prefers their reading σφράγις to the LXX's ἀποσφράγισμα; perhaps *Hom. on Jer.* XVIII.6, where he remarks that in Deut. 1.31 some Greek MSS omit the phrase, 'The Lord thy God bare thee as a man doth bear his son.' This in fact looks like a theological omission by the LXX translators; but Aquila, Symmachus and Theodotion have the phrase, and Origen says that οἱ ἀπὸ ἑβραίσμου ἑρμηνεύσαντες (which probably means these three translators) not finding the reading παρ' Ἕλλησιν (which probably means the LXX), invented it, 'as they did in many other passages'. But Origen has no objection to using the phrase in his exposition; indeed he finds it very useful. Cf. too *Comm. on John* XXVIII.16 where the authority of these versions is invoked to reject a reading in Num. 23.16.

There is one other textual authority to whom Origen very occasionally refers, and that is 'the Hebrew' (ὁ Ἑβραῖος), an authority whom he occasionally cites for information of a midrashic type;[1] the same phrase occurs in the Hexapla as a source to which a number of readings are attributed. The identity of this authority has exercised the conjectures of many scholars. Kahle thinks that the readings attributed to this man in the Hexapla 'are taken from old Greek translations of Jewish origin'.[2] B. J. Roberts says that it has been assumed that 'the Hebrew' was Aquila.[3] This is a priori unlikely; Origen would not have described Aquila (whom he mentions by name openly several times elsewhere) as a Hebrew, because Aquila in fact was not a Hebrew by race, but a Jewish proselyte. I myself guessed that 'the Hebrew' might be Rabbi Simeon ben Lakish.[4] I have since observed a piece of evidence which puts both Aquila and Simeon ben Lakish out of court. In one place, where fortunately a Greek fragment has survived, Origen tells us that 'the Hebrew' identified the two Seraphim of Isa. 6 as 'the only-begotten of God' and 'the Holy Spirit'.[5] The man who could make this interpretation must have been a Christian and not a Jew. There is no reason at all to assume that 'the Hebrew' of the Hexapla is anybody else than the 'the Hebrew' of the Commentaries. Origen did not draw a hard and fast line between his two kinds of works. In the Commentary on Matthew, for instance, he makes constant references to the readings of Aquila, Symmachus and Theodotion, and occasionally to the Quinta and Sexta, all of which he must have derived from his Hexapla. Therefore we must conclude that 'the Hebrew' was a Jewish Christian, and our estimate of the origins of his readings in the Hexapla must be influenced by this conclusion. It is not easy to assume, as Kahle is perhaps anxious to do, that these readings come from ancient Greek translations owned by the Jewish synagogue in Caesarea, for some references to 'the Hebrew'

[1] See Origen's Doctrine of Tradition, pp. 142, 148, 154 f. My suggestion on p. 148 that this man might be Philo I now realize to be quite impossible.
[2] The Cairo Geniza, p. 165.
[3] The Old Testament Text and Versions, p. 133. If this book receives the second edition which, as an excellent text-book on a subject little furnished with text-books in English, it deserves, it would be well if some errors in the chapter devoted to Origen were corrected. Origen did not obtain his copy of Symmachus' version from one Julian (p. 126) but from a woman called Juliana; Pamphilus was not martyred in 300, but in 310 (p. 128) and the phrase on p. 129 referring to 'Origen's literary and exegetical works of this period' can only refer to the years 203–4 and shortly afterwards. But Origen did not publish anything till 218 at the earliest, and probably his first Commentaries did not appear till 220–25.
[4] Origen's Doctrine of Tradition, p. 155 n. 2. Cf. Field, Hexapla, Prolegomena, lxxvi–lxxvii.
[5] τὸν μονογενῆ τοῦ θεοῦ καὶ τὸ πνεῦμα τὸ ἅγιον, PA I.3.4.

appear in works of Origen written before he left Alexandria for Caesarea.[1]

We have already seen something of how Origen deals with variant readings. Though he had a perfectly good grasp of the discipline of textual criticism as it had been developed in his day, his attitude to variants in the text was sometimes disarmingly casual. That is to say, he will recognize a variant and interpret it unconcernedly as if both this reading and the other could be equally valuable and original. In the course of expounding Jeremiah he meets the verse 'I have not lent on usury, neither have men lent to me on usury'(Jer. 15.10). His comment is: 'There are two readings here, in the majority of manuscripts "I have not helped, nor has anyone helped me" (οὐκ ὠφέλησα, οὐδὲ ὠφέλησέ με οὐδείς), but in the most accurate, and those which agree with the Hebrew, "I have not lent on usury, neither has anyone lent to me on usury" (οὐκ ὠφείλησα, οὐδὲ ὠφείλησέ με οὐδείς). I must therefore comment on the version which is hackneyed and current in the churches, and not leave the version from the Hebrew Scriptures unexpounded.'[2]
In the next Homily (delivered perhaps the day after the last one) Origen recurs to this passage and decidedly prefers the reading of the Hebrew text, remarking, 'Even though this ("I have not lent on usury, etc.") is the reading we adopt, yet most of the manuscripts of the LXX version have not got this reading; but we later examined the other versions and decided that this (the LXX reading) was a scribal error. All the same, it is possible to expound the passage with either reading.'[3] In his Commentary on Romans he notes the existence at Rom. 12.13 of the reading 'the memory (μνείαις) of the saints' instead of 'the necessities (χρείαις) of the saints', and adds 'but we neither upset a settled usage nor make a hasty judgement about the truth, especially when either reading is useful for instruction'.[4] In his exposition of the Old Testament this ambiguous attitude to variant readings may be accounted for by his conviction that where the LXX differed from the Hebrew text and other

---

[1]E.g. Comm. on Ps. 1, PG 12.1080, reproduced in Philoc. II.3. Perhaps the Commentary on Genesis, PG 12.133.
[2]Hom. on Jer. XIV.3. For a good judgement on Origen's treatment of variant readings see E. Klostermann 'Formen der exegetischen Arbeiten des Origenes' (TLZ, 1947, pp. 203–8), and Daniélou, Origène, p. 141.
[3]Hom. on Jer. XV.4.
[4]Comm. on Rom. IX.12. The sentiment certainly sounds like Origen's but the expression may well be that of Rufinus, for he represents Origen as saying that he finds the variant in Latinis exemplaribus. In fact this reading appears in the first hand in D, in G and in some Greek fathers. Cf. Hom. on Num. XVIII.4, where Origen similarly expounds two different readings without deciding between them.

versions it might have been a deliberate and inspired alteration on the part of the Seventy translators. But this excuse cannot hold for his pursuing a similar policy with variants in the text of the New Testament.[1]

He is on the whole cautious about estimating the worth of variants in the New Testament. His comment on an alternative 'in him is light' for 'in him was light' in John 1.4 is that it is 'perhaps not unconvincing'.[2] In his *Commentary on Matthew* he says that he suspects that the phrase 'Thou shalt love thy neighbour as thyself' in Matt. 19.19 is a later addition to the text, not on textual evidence, but by comparing the passage with its parallel in other Synoptists, and he notes that the variety of readings prevailing throughout the Gospels makes this conjecture reasonable, and goes on to give a little note on the causes of this variety, and a description of his own Hexapla. The Latin version here adds a note not found in the Greek to the effect that Origen would not dare to do for the New Testament what he had done for the Old Testament in the Hexapla, but that he thinks it no harm to make a conjecture.[3] Variety from the LXX form of text displayed in quotations from the Old Testament in the New Testament always troubles Origen and he labours to explain it away. In the course of a minute comparison of quotations from Isaiah and Malachi in the accounts of John the Baptist given by Mark and John he notices that they do apparently alter their quotations; he accounts for this by saying that each evangelist 'abridges the literal words lying before him'.[4] He notes that in John 12.39 ff. the evangelist does not quote the exact words of the prophet in reproducing Isa. 6.10, and that this habit is frequently observable in the New Testament, but points out that the sense is the same.[5] And he recognizes that Stephen's account of Moses in Acts 7.22 owes something to Midrash.[6]

It is interesting to observe too that Origen is capable of conceiving that in some passages of the New Testament all the manuscripts existing in his day may have become corrupt. Of Matt. 5.45 ('That ye may be

---

[1]Daniélou, *Origène*, p. 142, notes this tendency in Origen to quote both the reading in his text and a variant reading and to expound both. He comments: 'He allows a double authority, that of Scripture and that of tradition. It is evident that this has remained the Church's position.' If this remark has any meaning, it seems to be that the tradition of the Church can supply acceptable readings which are not those of the original text—surely a very odd suggestion!
[2]καὶ τάχα οὐκ ἀπιθάνως, *Comm. on John* II.19; cf. *ibid.*, XX.23.
[3]*Comm. on Matt.* XV.14.
[4]ἐπιτεμνόμενος ὃ παρέθετο ῥητόν, *Comm. on John* VI.24; cf. 26.
[5]*Comm. on John*, frag. 92.
[6]*Contra Celsum* III.46.

sons of your Father which is in Heaven') he says, 'The reader will inquire whether this was said as it stands or whether the word "your" is there as a result of a mistake in the manuscripts.'[1] In his *Commentary on Matthew* he tries to explain how the quotation from Ps. 118.25 made by the people at our Lord's Entry into Jerusalem (Matt. 21.9) does not exactly tally with the version of this particular verse given in the LXX. His theory is that originally the evangelist had quoted the Hebrew of this psalm, but that it had been corrupted by copyists: 'So my opinion is that the Gospels in being written over and over again by people who did not know the language became confused at this point in their quotations from the psalm mentioned above.'[2] This is a remarkable, even though unacknowledged, modification of Origen's usual doctrine of the inerrancy of Scripture.

This survey of Origen's assessment of the relative merits of the LXX, the Hebrew text, the versions of Aquila, Symmachus and Theodotion, and of his handling of variant readings, should be enough to convince us of the error of those scholars who have maintained that Origen regarded the LXX text as alone inspired. Tollinton,[3] Harnack[4] and Koetschau[5] cannot have examined the evidence thoroughly to arrive at such a judgement. The more recent judgement of Kahle is a more satisfactory one:

'He was convinced that to the original a greater authority must be attributed than to a translation derived from it. . . . His aim is to repair the disagreements of the Greek Bible according to the authoritative Hebrew text. As his knowledge of Hebrew was not sufficient for doing this directly from the Hebrew text, he used all sorts of Greek translations of the Bible to which he had access, as a help in this task. He could, however, not speak frankly about these problems. He had to be cautious. The "Septuagint" was regarded as the canonical text, inspired by God. So we find in his works only occasionally a remark on these problems.'[6]

---

[1]*Comm. on John* XX.17.   [2]*Comm. on Matt.* XVI.19.

[3]R. B. Tollinton, *Selections from the Commentaries and Homilies of Origen,* Introduction, pp. xxxvi–xli.

[4]*Der Kirchengeschichliche Ertrag,* II, pp. 6 f., where he alleges that Origen insists that one must, in dealing with the Old Testament, always rely upon the 'inspired LXX text', even when other textual traditions are clearer. The exception is that apostolic writers have a right to alter or adapt the LXX text.

[5]Preface to his edition of the *Contra Celsum,* p.xxxiii, 'yet the Greek text of the Septuagint remains for him the inspired and predominant one'. The verdict of R. M. Grant (*The Letter and the Spirit,* p. 97) is also too sweeping.

[6]*The Cairo Geniza,* pp. 159 f. For a similar judgement see Field, *Hexapla,* Prolegomena, p. liv.

This verdict needs to be modified only in one direction. Origen did think the LXX inspired, but in a peculiar way. The translators had been prompted to make a number of additions and omissions and modifications of a deliberately Christological sort, but not in such a way as to allow Christians to conclude that the LXX had finally superseded either the Hebrew text or other versions.[1]

But when we have made all proper allowance for the fact that Origen was not wholly out of sympathy with the conventional view of the sanctity of the LXX prevailing in the Church of his day, we cannot but be impressed by the manner in which he handles problems of text and versions. He has a determined grasp of the main realities of the textual situation. He did not allow sentimentality nor polemical spirit to blur his vision. He makes large use of all the *instrumenta studiorum* available to him—alternative translations, the transliteration of the Hebrew text, Onomastica and name-lists and miscellaneous midrash from Rabbinic sources. He towers above all his predecessors, all his contemporaries and all his successors with the possible exception of Jerome. In his handling of the text Origen is at his best because here appears most lambently that quality of sweet reasonableness which was so characteristic of him (and so deplorably lacking in Jerome). It is the same sweet reasonableness which won the lifelong devotion of Ambrosius, evoked the eulogies of Gregory Theodorus,[2] and more than once enabled Origen to succeed in the task, which would have been considered impossible a century later, of winning large bodies of heretics back to the orthodox faith by argument alone without abuse or violence.

In expounding the text whose authenticity he endeavoured to establish by these means Origen employed methods which contrast notably with those of most of his predecessors, particularly Clement of Alexandria.[3] Clement's references to Scripture are, compared with Origen's, vaguer and much more often paraphrases. 'They shall be ashamed, and also confounded, all of them: they shall go to confusion together that are makers of idols' (Isa. 45.16), for instance, appears as 'For then, says some prophecy, the business that we have here will fare badly, whenever

---

[1]Kahle is therefore too sweeping when he says (*op. cit.*, p. 159), 'But he attributed to it (LXX) neither the miraculous origin nor the divine inspiration connected with that name,' though he is much nearer the truth than, e.g., Harnack.

[2]Later known as Gregory Thaumaturgus.

[3]For more information on Origen's exegetical methods see Bigg, *The Christian Platonists of Alexandria*, p. 169; Koetschau, Preface to his edition of the *Contra Celsum*, pp. xxxi–xxxvi; F. Prat, *Origène, le Théologien et l'Exégète*, p. 179; Cadiou, *La Jeunesse d'Origène*, pp. 73 f.; G. L. Prestige, *Fathers and Heretics*, pp. 114 ff.

they trust in statues.'[1] In comparison with this, Origen's methods are scholarly and almost scientific, even though the results produced are not what modern scholars could approve. Some examples will best illustrate this. In his *Homilies on Jeremiah* he reaches the passage 'Every bottle shall be filled with wine' (Jer. 13.12), part of a parable to illustrate the utterance, 'I will fill all the inhabitants of this land . . . with drunkenness.' Origen tackles this text thus:

i.   This statement could not be literally true; many bottles are not full of wine; such an interpretation 'appears to be not worthy of God'.

ii. Wine has various meanings in the Bible, sometimes bad (Deut. 32.32 f.), and sometimes good (Isa. 5.1 f.).

iii. 'And he poureth out of the same' (Ps. 75.8 RV) appears in the LXX as 'and he poured from this to that',[2] where the Greek has erroneously added 'to that'. Origen accepts this reading and says that the text means that God alternates between rewarding our good actions and punishing our bad. In this sense it is true to say that 'every bottle shall be full of wine'.

We might describe this interpretation as admirable in its general approach; Origen tries to see the text in its context in the whole biblical revelation (but not in the book of Jeremiah, an essential step which Origen invariably omits when dealing with the Old Testament). But his interpretation is vitiated by his reliance on a faulty translation and his determination to extort some immediately edifying meaning from the passage.[3] This passage is typical of his exegetical style. He weighs every phrase and nearly every word of each verse separately and minutely, explains its meaning by frequent and often fallacious references to other parts of Scripture, and then replies to difficulties and objections suggested by the verse. On John 8.23 ('Ye are from beneath; I am from above'), for instance, he rings the changes on the meanings of 'below' and 'above', ranging untrammelled through every part of the Bible, seizing material from Galatians, Matthew, Deuteronomy, I Corinthians, Ps.88, Ps. 6 and I Corinthians again with a noble lack of discrimination, making any one text have reference to the same subject as any other; one sentence slides subtly into another written centuries later with a completely different purpose. It is miscellaneous, but it is

---

[1]*Protrept.* X.98, *PG* 8.212.

[2]LXX: καὶ ἔκλινεν ἐκ τούτου εἰς τοῦτο; MT: רִיגַּר מִזֶּה; Vulgate: *et inclinavit ex hoc in hoc.*

[3]*Hom. on Jer.* XII.1, 2. Cf. *Philoc.* XXVII.8, where he says that exegetes should take into consideration τὸ πρὸς θεὸν εὐσεβές in their exposition.

magnificent.[1] Or again, he attempts to explain a grammatical variety
in two synonymous terms in Gen. 1.16 ff. by appealing to the chronology of the development of parts of speech, so elaborately will he
trouble himself to justify even the minutest points of the text.[2]

One of his most reiterated principles is that Scripture must be explained by Scripture. He quotes the saying of a Jew of his acquaintance
(in fact probably 'the Hebrew') to the effect that Scripture is like a house
which has inside it a series of flats, each with its front door locked, and
the keys in each door will not open the door each is in but will open one
of the others, and each key has on it signs indicating to the experienced
which door it will open.[3] Only the truly wise man can 'explain the whole
continuity of the statements made in a hidden way in the prophets,
comparing "spiritual things with spiritual" and establishing each of his
interpretations from the usual practice of the Scriptures'.[4]

We will illustrate this practice of Origen's by a single full example,
and one which on the whole shows him in a good light. It is a passage
which has already been selected by the fourth-century scholars who
compiled the *Philocalia*.[5] It consists of a discussion of a phrase in Ps.
4.6, 'Who will show us any good?' which takes up the question, What
are the good things promised and the bad things threatened in the
Bible? First he asks whether it is within our power to achieve or avoid
these things, and has little difficulty in showing that some at least are
within our power (quoting Matt. 25.21 ff. and Luke 6.45). He next sets
forth the case of the Literalists who hold that the promises and threats
of the Bible are promises and threats of outward, material good and
evil, and who quote Ex. 15.26, Deut. 28.1, 58 ff., Lev. 26.3, 16, and
also instance our Lord's healing of bodily infirmities and giving of
bodily relief. Origen in reply first points out the passages in Scripture
quite inconsistent with this view. Elisha, Isaiah and Jeremiah kept the
law; John the Baptist and Paul were righteous men; yet they all suffered
bodily evil, usually because of their righteousness. The prosperity
promised in Deut. 15.6, that the Israelites will lend to many nations
and borrow from none, is in flagrant contradiction to Ps. 15.5 and
Ezek. 18.8; fever, threatened to the Israelites in Deuteronomy, is
usually brought on by natural causes. Such words as 'health' or 'wealth'
or 'diseases' or words signifying material benefit or loss must mean

---

[1]*Comm. on John* XIX.20.
[2]*Philoc.* XIV.1 f., from the *Commentary on Exodus*.
[3]*Comm. on Ps.* I, *PG* 12.1080, reproduced in *Philoc.* II.3.
[4]*Contra Celsum* VII.11.
[5]*Philoc.* XXVI.1–8, from a *Comm. on Ps.* 4.

spiritual things. Next Origen points out what a low conception of duty and virtue and good living such an idea as the Literalists' implies. It means that virtue is pursued for the sake of material well-being, not for its own intrinsic worth. Finally Origen gives his own views on the subject. 'Good' and 'bad' never refer to material states or events, but they are sometimes within our power and sometimes not; Ps. 127.1, 'Except the Lord build the house', refers to God's prevenient grace (ἡ ἀντιλαμ-βανομένη τοῦ Κυρίου δύναμις); even when the farmer has done all he can to sow the grain, the crop is still dependent on the climate as well as the farmer's efforts. It is in our power, too, to determine whether or not we fall from God's grace by not persevering and relying on God's continual help. Paul's remark in Rom. 9.16, 'So then it is not of him that willeth, nor of him that runneth, but of God that hath mercy,' is made 'not as though God has compassion on us without our running and willing, but as if running and willing were as nothing in comparison with God's mercy, and therefore he quite rightly rather gave the title of "that which is good" to God's mercy than to man's part of willing and running'. The reasons for the mistake of the Literalists is that Scripture should sometimes be taken literally (κυριολεκτεῖν) and sometimes taken figuratively (καταχρῆσθαι). Sometimes because of the inadequacy of language (στενοχωρίαν τῶν ὀνομάτων) statements must be taken metaphorically. We must look for the allegorization (ἀναγωγή) of our Lord's miracles. They were a parable of his power as Logos to cure souls and they were also performed to impress people that they might believe at least 'for the works' sake'.

Origen in this exposition has been faced by two different ideas to be found in Scripture, one the less developed in Ps. 127, the other illuminated by the full light of revelation in Rom. 9. As always, he takes the more developed idea and tries to explain the other by it, even though he has in this process to resort to allegory. But his interpretation of the psalm is fundamentally right; in its words we find the seed or basis of that doctrine of God's anticipating grace which Paul was fully presenting. Further, the weight of Scripture is on Origen's side when he declares that God's blessings and punishments must not be identified with material well-being or injury. Again, his interpretation of our Lord's miracles as not simply and solely works of mercy, but as done partly with a semantic purpose, is of course correct and constitutes one of the chief points of the Fourth Gospel. Observe too Origen's rationalism evinced in his reference to fever as arising from natural causes, his conception of virtue for virtue's sake, and his careful removal of the

Interpreting scripture by scripture

sting of Paul's predestinarian doctrine. It was often this very rationalism that drove him into allegory. On the whole in this passage he does justify his claim to interpret Scripture by Scripture. He does not understand the outlook of the author of Deuteronomy and his interpretation of Paul is unpauline. But in spite of this his firm grasp of the fundamentals of the Christian faith has kept his interpretation of the passage sound.

There is no particular reason to think that he used concordances of either the Old or the New Testament, though his memory must have been a concordance in itself.[1] He expected his pupils when they were studying a Gospel to have copies of the other Gospels by them for purposes of comparison.[2] It is sometimes, but not very often, obvious that he is quoting from memory.[3] It is remarkable, too, how often Origen uses fabulous information about beasts to aid his exegesis in a manner reminiscent of a mediaeval bestiary. 'As the partridge that gathereth her young' (Jer. 17.11) taxes Origen's ingenuity severely.[4] He ignores the simile and turns the verse into an allegory. 'What sort of a bird is the partridge according to the naturalists?' he asks. Deceitful and licentious, is apparently Aristotle's answer. Then the partridge must be the devil; and so we find the richly comic suggestion, 'The partridge has spoken through Valentinus, the partridge has spoken through Marcion', etc. Later he gives us some highly inaccurate information about a lion, gathered from Aristotle's Natural History, and allegorizes it.[5] Elsewhere he gives us a long zoological note on the habits of the stork and the varieties of this bird.[6] As many writers have pointed out,[7] Origen uses the whole resources of contemporary knowledge in many fields, geography, physics and medicine, as well as zoology, to aid his exegesis.

He can sometimes exhibit a shrewdness on linguistic or critical points which would not be out of place from the pen of a modern commentator. He has observed, for instance, that in the New Testament the

[1]Cf. *Comm. on Matt.* XII.21, on ὁ δὲ στραφεὶς εἶπε τῷ Πέτρῳ, 'Now if you were to collect more examples of στραφείς (and particularly when they were applied to Jesus) and were to compare them with each other, you would find that this phrase was not set down just incidentally.' This comparison of many of the contexts in which the same word or phrase occurs is found again and again in Origen.
[2]*Comm. on Matt.* XVII.26.
[3]In *Comm. on John* II.25 he quotes Hos. 10.12 (LXX) three times and gives a reference only once, and then only in the words 'we find in one of the Twelve'. For the phrases which Origen uses to describe the Bible, OT and NT, see Koetschau's Introduction to his edition of the *Contra Celsum*, p. xxxii.
[4]*Hom. on Jer.* XVII.1, 2; the LXX version here runs ἐφώνησε πέρδιξ.
[5]*Hom. on Jer.*, frag. 3.
[6]Cadiou, *Commentaires Inédits des Psaumes*, on 104.17b, p. 87.
[7]E.g. de Faye, Klostermann, and Cadiou.

word translated 'wonder' (τέρας) never appears except in combination with the word for 'sign' (σημεῖον). On the well-known question whether, in the text 'this was the true light that lighteneth every man coming into the world' (John 1.9), the clause 'coming into the world' should be taken with 'light' or 'man', he recognizes that the clause could apply to either and says that it really should be taken to refer to both, first to 'light' and then to 'man'.[1] He realizes that the biblical meaning of 'knowing God' has some analogy to a man 'knowing' a woman, and cites Gen. 4.1; Eph. 5.22 and I Cor. 6.16 f.[2] He grasps the subtly portrayed advancing awareness of the Samaritan woman in her conversation with Jesus recorded in John 4, and says, 'But she does not yet think him to be greater than the prophets, nor the one who was prophesied, but only a prophet.'[3] And he will sometimes take trouble in establishing the historical context of a saying, as in the case of 'God is a spirit',[4] or try to determine the time that a book was written and the order in which it appeared, as in the case of the Epistle to the Romans.[5] He notes that the three evangelists who record the Temptation also record the Agony in the Garden, but that John records neither. The Synoptists, he says, portray Jesus 'more according to his human than his divine nature, but John rather according to his divine than his human nature'.[6] This shrewdness can however easily become misplaced ingenuity. Völker notes how readily Origen can exactly reverse the sense of a scriptural passage, as we have earlier seen Philo reversing the sense.[7] He interprets Eccles. 4.2, 'I praised the dead . . . more than the living' to refer to on the one hand those who have died to the world ('the dead') and on the other those who are still ensnared in the world.[8] But along with this occasional shrewdness and over-subtlety goes an unfailing humility. Origen is never dogmatic, never offensive; he advances his views with diffidence and constantly declares that if anybody has a more satisfactory interpretation he should be allowed to produce it.[9]

It is not easy to determine the exact difference between Origen's treatment of Scripture in the Homilies and his treatment of it in his

---

[1] *Comm. on John*, frag. 6.
[2] *Ibid.*, XIX.4.
[3] *Ibid.*, XIII.12.
[4] *PA* I.1.4.
[5] *Comm. on Rom.*, Origen's Preface.
[6] *Comm. on Matt.* Comm. Ser. 92. Cf. Clement's account of this Gospel as the 'spiritual' Gospel, Eus. *HE* VI.14.7; p. 190.
[7] See above, p. 48.
[8] *Hom. on Num.* VII.3; see Völker, 'Die Verwertung des Weisheits-Literatur', *ZKG* LXIV, pp. 24 f.
[9] Zöllig notes and praises this virtue, *Inspirationslehre*, p. 96. Whether the qualities in Origen's exegesis praised by Zöllig on pp. 126 f. of his work really are virtues is very doubtful.

Commentaries. Pamphilus in his *Apology for Origen* distinguished between the carefully orthodox statements contained in Origen's Commentaries which he regarded as private writings for the select few and those found in his Homilies which were statements made in public, when he might be bidding for popular support and less careful about orthodoxy.[1] Rufinus' translation does not permit us to distinguish the original Greek words used here for 'commentary' and 'homily'. Pamphilus is anxious to establish Origen's orthodoxy at almost any cost, and in fact experience of Origen's works suggests that almost the exact opposite is the truth, for Origen is careful not to upset the weaker brethren with daring speculations in his Homilies, but indulges in them more freely in his Commentaries. Klostermann points out that it is difficult to draw a hard and fast line distinguishing Origen's style and treatment in his Commentaries from those of his Homilies, for his Homilies are often learned and full of technical exegesis and his Commentaries are often edifying and designed to instruct the faithful.[2] Certainly if we compare Origen's Homilies with the scanty remains of homiletic works surviving from a period earlier than his, we do notice a difference. *II Clement* (which is probably a homily), Melito's *Homily on the Passion*, and Clement of Alexandria's *Quis Dives* (also perhaps a Homily) all quote Scripture frequently, the author of *II Clement* to enforce his moral lessons, Melito to enhance his rhetorical points, and Clement of Alexandria to adorn his miscellaneous arguments. But none of them handle Scripture with the same methodical thoroughness and rigorous pursuit of its meaning as Origen uses in his Homilies. He does not hesitate, for instance, to quote the versions of Aquila, Theodotion and Symmachus in his Homilies, nor to refer to the Hebrew text. It is obvious that Origen's Homilies were influenced by his Commentaries (which after all he must have always regarded as his main work) and not *vice versa*.

But in spite of this it is quite possible to detect in the Homilies signs that Origen knows that he is addressing a different kind of audience and expounding Scripture for a different purpose than those which he envisages in his Commentaries. C. W. Dugmore has shown how strong is the evidence for the view that in parts of the early Church at least daily public non-eucharistic prayer was held at which sermons

[1] *Apology for Origen, PG* 17.557.
[2] 'Formen der exegetischen Arbeiten', *TLZ*, 1947, pp. 203 f. De Faye makes the observation (*Origène*, III, ch. XI, pp. 150–55) that in treating of the life of Jesus in answer to the strictures of Celsus Origen holds firmly to the historicity of that life, the reality of its facts, and the truth of its miracles, especially the miracle of the Resurrection. He obviously did to some extent vary his treatment according to the public which he was addressing.

were delivered, in Origen's time and probably before it.[1] Klostermann[2] and de Lubac[3] have collected many details from the Homilies showing that they were delivered to Christians, many of whom were simple and unlearned, in a church, on passages of Scripture not chosen by Origen, and within a limited time. His exposition too shows occasional signs of simplification and restraint in the Homilies. At one point in his *Homilies on Jeremiah* he declares his intention of expounding 'the text and the literal meaning'[4] of a passage and of leaving the 'deeper meaning' on one side. In his *Homily on I Samuel* II he seems to be deliberately eschewing allegory. Generally in his Homilies, his style is simpler than in his Commentaries and far more directly edifying; he is at greater pains to emphasize his points and he goes into explanations of the context of passages more fully. Völker is justified in his insistence that the Homilies are good evidence for Origen's piety and for his skill as a pastor. He declares that in the Homilies we find a recognizably different Origen from the Origen of the Commentaries and of his other works. In the Homilies he is genuinely concerned as a psychologist and pastor with sin, with men and women's sinful actions. He treats these realistically with experience and understanding, even though it is often understanding based rather on third-century penitential practice than on the Pauline doctrine of grace. In his other works his attitude to sin is more that of the philosopher of religion who desires to fit sin into his whole picture of God's providential activity in the universe.[5]

But this point can be overemphasized, and in my opinion de Lubac has overemphasized it. It is superficial to claim that Origen's purpose in using allegory was purely a practical expedient to enable him to use Scripture satisfactorily in his sermons.[6] And it is ridiculous to claim that he was not in his Homilies, or elsewhere, in any significant way influenced by contemporary philosophy.[7] We cannot dismiss de Faye's

---

[1] *The Influence of the Synagogue upon the Divine Office*, pp. 46–9. But Dugmore's evidence derived from Origen's *Hom. on Gen.* X.3 (PG 12.383) will not hold as proof of the practice in the contemporary church at Alexandria, for these Homilies must have been delivered well after Origen had finally left Alexandria.

[2] 'Formen der exegetischen Arbeiten', pp. 203 f.

[3] *Histoire et Esprit*, pp. 131–5.

[4] τὴν λέξιν καὶ τὸ ῥητόν, XIX.11.

[5] *Das Vollkommenheitsideal*, pp. 16–18, 25–44.

[6] 'Such is the leading idea, as you can see, entirely practical, entirely apostolic, and at the same time entirely traditional, from which were born the greater number of Origen's Homilies', *Histoire et Esprit*, p. 135.

[7] 'Fully conscious of what his position as a teacher in the bosom of the Church requires, he desires no other source than the sacred Scriptures and never has recourse to philosophy except to express and illustrate a doctrine which philosophy does not inspire', *ibid.*, p. 153.

gigantic work in sentences such as these, and this judgement is contradicted by almost every page of Chadwick's monumental edition of the *Contra Celsum*. Origen began as a philosopher and never ceased to be a philosopher, though as a Christian priest he saw the necessity and usefulness of applying his philosophy to the personal problems of ordinary men and women. We must not forget that Clement of Alexandria and he formulated and openly professed a doctrine of Reserve; there were certain mysteries of the faith which could not be publicly declared to the unintelligent and uneducated, but only to the cultured Christian *intelligentsia*. And both theologians show a decidedly intellectualist cast of thought, which in Clement becomes almost Gnostic. Origen in his Homilies sincerely and carefully expounds Scripture for the ordinary man and woman in the pew, but we must not expect to find the full, the whole Origen there.

[handwritten note: what is heard in from the pulpit is only a portion of the understanding of the priest]

7

Inspiration

ORIGEN's frank recognition that the textual tradition of the Scriptures was open to deviation and error did not in the least affect his conviction that the Scriptures were not only inspired but verbally inspired.[1] Zöllig has pointed out that the word which Origen used for 'inspired' (θεόπνευστος) does not mean 'breathing the Spirit of God' in an active sense, but always, in a passive, 'inspired by God', and that most of his expressions for inspiration indicate this too: 'Holy Scripture has a divine nature, and this not simply because it contains divine ideas, nor because the breath of the divine Spirit breathes in its lines . . . but because it has God as its author.'[2] Origen declares that 'the holy books are not the compilations of men, but were written and have reached us as a result of the inspiration (ἐπινοίας) of the Holy Spirit by the will of the Father of all through Jesus Christ.'[3]

That every word of the Scriptures was carefully designed by God was in Origen's day no new doctrine. It is to be found in Philo. 'Observe carefully every subtle point,' he says, 'for you will find nothing spoken superfluously' (παρέργως).[4] And he tells us that Moses did not write a single unnecessary word.[5] This was no doubt part of Philo's debt to the Rabbinic tradition of exegesis; and no doubt Philo in his turn influenced Origen in this respect. But even Hippolytus, whose ideas, as far as we know, were quite independent of Origen's, can say, 'The Holy Scriptures declare to us nothing unnecessary (ἀργόν), but only what is for our own instruction, for the enhancement of the prophets and the exposition of what was said by them.'[6] Origen, anyway, goes quite as

---

[1] Zöllig devoted a treatise to this subject, *Die Inspirationslehre des Origenes*, in which he dealt with it fully and fairly, as long ago as 1902. But the work has never been translated from the German and is not very easy to obtain. For further information see F. Prat, *Origène, le Théologien et l'Exégète*, p. 187; R. B. Tollinton, *Selections from the Commentaries and Homilies of Origen*, Introduction, pp. xx–xxii; H. de Lubac, *Histoire et Esprit*, pp. 295–301; R. L. P. Milburn, *Early Christian Interpretations of History*, pp. 46 f., 49, 53.
[2] Zöllig, *op. cit.*, pp. 13–15.
[3] *PA* IV.9, cited by Zöllig, *op. cit.* p. 62; cf. p. 78.
[4] *De Leg. Alleg.* III.147; cf. above p. 46.
[5] *De Fug. et Invent.* 54.   [6] *Comm. on Dan.* I.7.2.

far as Philo in his theory of verbal inspiration, applying it, of course, both to Old and New Testaments. In a *Commentary on Psalm* 1 preserved in the *Philocalia*[1] he tells us that 'the wisdom of God has penetrated to all the inspired Scripture even as far as the slightest letter' (μέχρι τοῦ τυχόντος γράμματος). Elsewhere he says that we ought to believe that the holy Scriptures have no tittle void of the wisdom of God and that there is no jot or tittle in the Bible which will not achieve its effect on those who know how to understand it.[2] And in the *Commentary on Romans*, in noting the (totally imaginary) significance in the order of two nouns in Rom. 2.9, he takes the opportunity of declaring that he is one who 'believes that in the apostles' letters, through which Christ speaks, there is not one superfluous jot or tittle'.[3] And his meticulous care to explain every word of the biblical text in his exegetical works, perhaps most evident in his *Commentary on John*, amply confirms these statements. Indeed, to Origen, as Zöllig stresses throughout his thesis, inspiration *is* revelation.[4] Revelation means (and this is significant for Origen's thought) propositions, written or spoken, inspired directly by God. It is a little surprising that both Zöllig and de Lubac apparently regard this theory with satisfaction. Zöllig remarks that we can find in Origen's doctrine of verbal inspiration all the elements which compose the modern Roman Catholic theory of inspiration.[5] De Lubac observes that 'it is not against Origen that the accusation can be levelled that he conceives of inspiration or of true exegesis as an atomistic affair'; and he later maintains that though Origen's handling of Scripture was often uncongenial to our minds and even positively perverse, he is to be forgiven all because he held so firmly to the theory that there is a hidden sense in all the Scriptures.[6] As a matter of fact Origen's theory of inspiration very often drives him into exasperatingly atomistic exegesis, just because he is determined to believe that every verse, and sometimes every word, is an oracle in itself, independently of its context; this is indeed a result which the embarrassing theory of a hidden sense latent in all Scripture is eminently calculated to promote.[7]

[1]*PG* 12.1081; *Philoc.* II.4.
[2]*Philoc.* I.28 and X.1, from *Hom. on Jer.* XXXIX.
[3]*Comm. on Rom.* II.6; IX.41.
[4]Zöllig, *Inspirationslehre*, p. 77 *et passim*; Prat, *Origène, le Théologien et l'Exégète*, pp. 118 f., emphasizes this also.
[5]Zöllig, *op. cit.*, pp. 72 f.
[6]De Lubac, *Histoire et Esprit*, pp. 302, 307.
[7]An interesting example of the unhappy shifts to which champions of this theory are reduced is provided by *The Sensus Plenior in Sacred Scripture*, by R. E. Brown.

Origen does occasionally provide proofs of this inspiration. He is always inclined on this subject to argue in a circle; for half the time he is saying that the Scriptures are inspired because they contain divine oracles of a wonderful sort, and for the other half he is saying that because they are inspired they must contain divine oracles, even though they do not appear to. This ambiguity is the nemesis of this sort of theory. However Origen is far too accomplished a philosopher to allow this ambiguity to appear obviously. He does maintain that, in the words of a contemporary theological platitude, the Scriptures are inspired because they are inspiring. It was not, he says, easy to see that the Law and the prophets were inspired till Jesus came. But, now that the Advent has taken place, he who reads the prophetic books finds himself 'experiencing as he reads the phenomenon of inspiration'.[1] But immediately afterwards he adds that we cannot always see the inspiration of the Bible on the surface of the text, though we can be sure, in faith, that it is always there. Elsewhere he declares that 'that which is spoken possesses no power in itself, even if in itself it is true and most worthy of belief, for reaching the soul of man, if a certain power were not granted it from God and a charm blossoms upon what is spoken, and this very quality appears, not without divine inspiration, in those who speak without accomplished art.'[2] He ascribes a mysterious power of attraction to the words spoken by our Lord (and presumably to the same words written by the evangelists): God in Christ used 'a voice which because it was broadcast with power imported some inexpressible enchantment to those who heard it';[3] and a power was given by God to the words of sacred Scripture 'distinct from those who speak them,'[4] The work of Moses possesses the quality of 'automatically influencing those who hear it'.[5] The description of the recognition of Joseph by his brethren 'has a great conviction about it even without being allegorized'.[6] The very homeliness of the style of Scripture is an evidence of the honest intention of the writers and the lack of attractiveness is a sign of the 'more divine power' that invests the work.[7]

It is remarkable that the very passage where Origen represents this

---

[1] *PA* IV.1.6, παθὼν ἐξ αὐτοῦ τοῦ ἀναγινώσκειν ἴχνος ἐνθουσιάσμου; see Zöllig, *Inspirationslehre*, p. 12. The next passage referred to is IV.1.7.
[2] *Philoc.* XV. 3–4, from *Contra Celsum* VI.2.
[3] *Contra Celsum* II.70.
[4] Or possibly 'greater than those who speak them', διαφέρουσα τοῖς λέγουσιν, *Comm. on John* I.8.
[5] *Contra Celsum* I.18; 'automatically' translates αὐτόθεν.
[6] *Ibid.*, IV.47.
[7] *Ibid.*, III.39, reproduced in *Philoc.* XIX.2,

inspiring quality of the Scriptures in its strongest form is also one
where he betrays the ambiguity which lies behind it. He is exhorting
his hearers (for the passage occurs in a sermon) not to weary in
reading the Scriptures even if they find no obvious, immediate profit
in reading. Just as someone may be affected for good or evil by an incantation, without consciously realizing what is happening to him, 'even
so conceive that the pronunciation of the words in the holy Scriptures is
more powerful than any incantation. . . . Conceive, please, that
though our conscious selves receive no profit the powers that work with
the soul and the mind and our whole person are fed by the reasonable
food that comes from the holy Scriptures and those words.' Hearing
the reading of Scripture has the same effect on us as snake-charming has
on snakes; the metaphorical snakes in us are put to sleep by the reading.
It is as if one were to take some drug to improve the eyesight whose
immediate effect is imperceptible, but its activity is later recognized in
an increased power of seeing. 'Believe the same thing about the holy
Scripture, that, even if the mind does not perceive the result of the aid
that comes from the Scriptures, yet your soul is aided by means of the
bare reading itself.'[1] But in this very passage Origen lays bare the assumption that lies behind this theory: 'For you must accept one of
two conclusions about these Scriptures, either that they are not inspired
because they have no good effect, as the unbeliever would suppose; or,
as the believer would, you must accept that since they are inspired they
have a good effect.' The effect must therefore be subconscious where it
is not conscious. The argument has come full circle, but so skilfully has
Origen presented it that we are almost inclined to allow him to deceive
us without protest.

Origen does, however, supply two more arguments in favour of his
theory of verbal inspiration; they are both free from this ambiguity.
These are the effectiveness and swift spread of Christianity, and the
fulfilment by Christianity of prophecy in the Old Testament. The first
chapter of the fourth book of the *Peri Archon* is largely devoted to this
theme. The law of Moses and the revelation of Christ have proved
themselves divine by their effectiveness and their widespread acceptance,
unknown in any religion before. Again, the fact that our Lord's pro-

[1] All the quotations and paraphrases concerning this subject are from *Hom,
on Jer.* XX, reproduced in *Philoc.* XII.1 and 2. Zöllig comments on this passage.
Inspirationslehre, p. 22. Harnack, *Der Kirchengeschichtliche Ertrag*, I, p. 57,
observes it too, and comments, 'In this passage the crudest superstition of
antiquity, that is, magic, is justified'; this is the arrogance of liberal Protestantism
on the crest of its wave, but in 1918 psychoanalysis had not become widely
known. Crouzel, *Théologie de l'Image de Dieu chez Origène*, remarks upon it too,

phecies about the future career of Christianity have turned out true
suggests that 'God has really become incarnate and taught doctrines of
salvation to men'. Some of the prophecies fulfilled in Christianity are
Gen. 49.10 ('The sceptre shall not depart from Judah,' etc.) and Hos.
3.4 ('The children of Israel shall abide many days without a king',
etc.), which have been fulfilled in the destruction of the Jewish polity
and the cult at Jerusalem. Deut. 32.21 ('I will move them to jealousy
with those who are not a people') is a prophecy of the rejection of the
Jews at the coming of Christ. 'Grace is poured into thy lips' (Ps. 45.2)
is a prophecy of the effectiveness of Christ's teaching.[1] One of the proofs
of the truth of the incident of the dove alighting on Jesus at his Baptism
described in the Gospels is, he says elsewhere, the success of the faith
which Christ preached.[2] Origen suggests that Celsus should have been
convinced of the truth of Christ's divinity by the Christian account of
Jesus, the prophecies made about him and the moral improvement
effected in people's lives by faith in him.[3] Earlier he has said that the
way in which the Word commends himself is by the fulfilment of
prophecy and miracles which can be shown to have taken place, vestiges
of which are still preserved by Christians (i.e. some miracles are still
performed in the Christian Church).[4] Elsewhere in the same work he
says, 'That which characterizes divine inspiration is prediction of
things to come, declared in a supernatural manner, and their taking
place, so leading to the conclusion that it was a divine spirit which predicted them.'[5] And a little later he says, vindicating the superiority of
the Bible to the philosophy of the Greeks, 'But we have learnt from the
prophets finer utterances than these, once Jesus and his disciples have
revealed the intention of the Spirit who was in the prophets (who was
no other than the Spirit of Christ).'[6]

One of the consequences of the Scriptures being inspired in this way
is that they must be inerrant. Philo had already made this claim about
the Pentateuch. 'For the prophet [i.e. Moses],' he had said, 'is an interpreter of God who oracularly produces the words within him, and to

---

[1] *PA* IV.1.1–5, reproduced in *Philoc.* I.1–5. Origen is evidently giving here a
list of traditional proof-texts. He adds Ps. 72.7 f.; Isa. 7.14, 13; Micah 5.2;
Dan. 9.24; and Job 3.8.
[2] *Contra Celsum* I.43.
[3] *Ibid.*, V.3; cf. VIII.48.
[4] *Ibid.*, I.2; cf. VIII.9.
[5] *Ibid.*, VI.10.
[6] *Ibid.*, VI.19. Tollinton (*Clement of Alexandria*, II. p. 300) points out that
Clement used a similar argument from the swift extension of Christianity over
the world for the divinity of the Word. Zöllig notes these arguments in Origen,
Inspirationslehre, pp. 10 f.

God we can attribute no error.'[1] Similarly Origen says that the story of
the woman with the familiar spirit in I Sam. 28 cannot be false, however
painful it may be to think of a person like Samuel as under the control
of a demon: 'To say that it is not true encourages disbelief; this view will
return upon the heads of those who hold it.'[2] He deliberately rejects the
suggestion that when Jeremiah wrote the shocking words, 'O Lord,
thou hast deceived me and I was deceived' (Jer. 20.7), he might have
been making a mistake: 'It is not right to say this about a holy prophet.'[3]
He tells us that the faithful would believe 'that none of the evangelists
make mistakes or tell untruths.'[4] 'Are we to believe that the Apostle
contradicted himself?' he asks; 'This will be the suggestion of a first-
rate exegete!' He prefers to leave suggestions like this to the heretics
who concentrate only on those bits of Scripture where they can find
support for their fancies but ignore entirely those bits which contradict
them.[5] Consequently Origen is at great pains to explain away apparent
contradictions, mistakes or superfluities in the Bible. 'It was with the
greatest deliberation, and not because he did not understand the niceties
of the Greek language, that John sometimes used the articles and sometimes suppressed them.'[6] He approves the sentiment that John the
Baptist's answer in John 1.21, 'I am not' could not have been a mistake
on his part, on the grounds that a mistake of this sort would not be
appropriate to such a man.[7] When he reads in St Matthew's Gospel
(21.17), 'leaving them he went outside the city', he is impressed by the
fact that Jesus could not have gone there without leaving his interlocutors;
but a meaning must be found for this apparent superfluity; 'it is necessary to extract from what is said objects worthy of the wisdom of God
by which the Gospels have been written.'[8] Occasionally he will take
refuge in assuming a mistake in the textual tradition.[9] But very often
such meanings can be extracted only by resort to allegory. 'It must be
that the truth of these things lies in the allegorical understanding of
them (ἐν τοῖς νοητοῖς), or else, if the contradiction be not resolved,
belief in the Gospels is destroyed, on the grounds that they are not true
and not written in the divine Spirit, or else were merely haphazard
accounts'.[10] He sets out very fairly the contradiction between the
Johannine chronology of the cleansing of the Temple and the Synoptic,

---

[1]*De Praem. et Poen.* 55; see above, pp. 47.
[2]*Hom. on I Sam.* II, *PG* 12.1015.
[3]*Hom. on Jer.* XIX.15.   [4]*Comm. on John* VI.34.
[5]*Comm. on Rom.* III.7.
[6]*Comm. on John* II.2.   [7]*Ibid.*, VI.12 f.
[8]*Comm. on Matt.* XVI.27.
[9]E.g. *Comm. on Ps.* 8.2, *PG* 12.1184.   [10]*Comm. on John* X.3.

and then says: 'I for my part assume that it is impossible for those who admit in these matters no sense beyond that of straightforward narrative to establish that the apparent contradiction is really consistent. And if anybody thinks that we have interpreted unsoundly let him write in a reasonable way against our explanation.'[1]

Two theological convictions underlie this rigid theory of inerrancy. The first is that the Holy Spirit is ultimately the author of Scripture, whatever other names may appear as the authors. The account of the woman with the familiar spirit in I Sam. 28 must be true, he says, because the person who narrates it is the Holy Spirit; 'The composer in the case of these narratives is not believed to be a man, but the composer is the Holy Spirit who inspired men.'[2] Discussing Ps. 109, where he thinks that our Lord is speaking, although in Acts 1.16 Peter attributes it to the Holy Spirit through David, Origen concludes that the Holy Spirit speaks in each case, but takes personifications of Christ or God the Father or the prophet, as the case may be.[3] The other theological conviction is that the Incarnation of Jesus Christ the Word of God has a parallel in the indwelling (perhaps we might call it 'inscriptation') of the Word of God in the Scriptures. In a famous passage which is attributed to the Contra Celsum by the authors of the Philocalia but which does not appear in any known manuscript of that work, or in any other known works of Origen, he declares: 'We see in a human way the Word of God on earth, since he became a human being, for the Word has continually been becoming flesh in the Scriptures in order that he might tabernacle with us.' The well-instructed intellectual élite among the Christians will by means of allegory be able to see the Word transfigured on the mountain in the Scriptures, whereas the ordinary, superficial meaning of the Scriptures corresponds to the Jesus who appeared to the crowds.[4] A similar sentiment is displayed in the Commentary on

---

[1]Ibid., X.22. A fuller treatment of Origen's methods of harmonizing contradictions and difficulties in the Bible will be found below, pp. 259 ff.

[2]Hom. on I Sam. II, PG 12.1017.

[3]Philoc. VII.2, from the fourth of the lost Homilies on Acts.

[4]Philoc. XV.19. Though the passage from which these extracts are taken does not appear in the Contra Celsum, there can be no doubt that it is by Origen; vocabulary, style and thought alike assure us of that. Zöllig, Inspirationslehre, p. 17, and de Lubac, Histoire et Esprit, pp. 336–46, dwell on this point. J. A. Robinson in his edition of the Philocalia marks the passage as Unde?, and in his apparatus criticus, indicates that it does not appear in the direct tradition of the text of Contra Celsum. J. Scherer, Extraits des Livres I et II du Contre Celse d'Origène, likewise is silent about this passage, which does not appear in the extracts from Contra Celsum in the seventh-century papyrus edited by him. I can find no allusion to this passage in Chadwick's translation and annotation of the Contra Celsum.

Matthew, where Origen says that the Word 'is as it were incarnate in the Bible'.[1] Nothing could assure us more eloquently of Origen's conviction of the divine status and authorship of the Bible than this startling doctrine of the Bible as the extension of the Incarnation.

One would expect that, with such a doctrine of inspiration as this, Origen would have regarded the prophets and evangelists and other agents of the Holy Spirit speaking in the Scriptures as mere dictaphones, mechanically reproducing the words given to them without interference or modifications from their own individual personalities. This certainly is the doctrine of Philo. The genuine prophet, says Philo, 'declares nothing at all of his own, but is an interpreter of the promptings of another in all he proclaims, continuing in a state of ignorance all the time he is divinely possessed, and withdrawn from the citadel of the soul, where has come to dwell the divine Spirit, stimulating and producing sound in the entire mechanism of the voice so as clearly to reveal that which he predicts.'[2] The parallels to this type of inspiration are clearly pagan; the Delphic oracle and the oracle at Cumae described in the sixth book of the *Aeneid* spring to mind. 'More than once,' says H. A. A. Kennedy, 'he singles out as central for the prophetic state the falling into abeyance of reason (νοῦς) which is confined within definite limits of comprehension, and its replacement by the divine influence which opens up for the prophet a new realm of vision.' It is in accordance with this drastic theory that Philo can persuade himself that Moses prophesied the place and circumstances of his own death.[3] Justin probably held a similar theory of ecstatic possession in the prophets. In his *Apology* he writes, 'But when you hear read passages of the Scriptures supposed to be uttered by various characters, do not imagine that they are said by the inspired people themselves, but by the divine Word who prompted them. For he sometimes speaks as one who foretells events that are to take place, and sometimes he makes utterances in the character (ὡς ἀπὸ προσώπου) of God the master of all and

---

[1]*Comm. on Matt.* XV.3, ἐν βιβλίῳ οἱονεὶ σωματωθῇ. See H. von Balthasar, 'Le Mysterion d'Origène', *RechSR* XXVII, pp. 542, 545 f., and *Origen's Doctrine of Tradition*, p. 184, n. 3.

[2]*De Spec. Leg.* IV.49, quoted and translated by Kennedy, *Philo's Contribution to Religion*, pp. 226–33 (pages from which the quotation from Kennedy is also taken).

[3]*De Vita Mosis* II.29. See above, p. 11 and n. 4. Origen contradicts himself on this particular point. In *Contra Celsum* II.54 he alleges that Moses wrote Deut. 34.5 f., describing his own death. But in a fragment on the Book of Joshua (*PG* 12.824) he says that when Ezra rescued from oblivion and edited all the books of the Old Testament after the captivity he added all such passages as this one. It is impossible to be confident on the point, but probably the *Contra Celsum* represents his later judgement.

Father, and sometimes in the character of Christ, and sometimes in the character of peoples who answer the Lord or his Father.' And in his *Dialogue* he maintains that the prophet Zechariah saw Jesus 'in ecstasy' (ἐν ἐκστάσει).¹ Theophilus seems to subscribe to the same view when he calls the prophets 'inspired (πνευματόφοροι) by the Holy Spirit' and 'possessed (ἐμπνευσθέντες) and enlightened by God himself' and 'taught of God' (θεοδίδακτοι), and describes them as 'instruments of God' (ὄργανα θεοῦ).²

A few passages in Origen suggest that he too adopted this 'ecstatic' account of the method of the Holy Spirit's inspiring of his agents. He says that the Word of God used Jesus (that is, his body and rational soul) to say, 'I am the Way and the Truth and the Life', in the same way as the Jews admit that God used the prophet's soul and body as an instrument to say, 'Before me there was no God' (Isa. 43.10), and as the Greek god was supposed to speak through the Pythian oracle.³ And he suggests that the connection of Caiaphas with Jesus, however external, may have conferred upon him the capacity for some sort of prophetic ecstasy: 'It seems to me that ecstasy sometimes becomes a cause of prophesying, just as in this case his being high-priest of that year in which Jesus "should die for the people so that the whole race should not perish" was so to Caiaphas; because though there were other high-priests . . . none of them prophesies except the high-priest of the year in which Jesus should suffer.'⁴

But elsewhere Origen makes it perfectly clear that, wherever his speculations about Caiaphas or his desire to commend prophecy in terms of Greek religion might lead him, his considered opinion was that inspiration did not remove or paralyse the prophet's or evangelist's control of his rational faculties. He notes that the evangelists, as well as recording the titles which our Lord used of himself, expressed 'their own conceptions' (τὴν ἰδίαν διάνοιαν) in calling him by other titles.⁵ When the prophets spoke under the influence of the Holy Spirit, he explicitly declares, they were not 'in ecstasy' (ἐξιστάμενοι); 'voluntarily and consciously they collaborated with the Word that came to them.' They could refuse to speak if they chose, and he finds instances of this deliberate refusal in I Cor. 14.30, Num. 22.35, and Jonah's experience.⁶

¹*Apol.* I.36.1 f.; *Dial.* 115.1–4.
²*Autolycus* II.9. ³*Contra Celsum* II.9.
⁴*Comm. on John* XXVIII.20. See Zöllig, *Inspirationslehre*, p. 65.
⁵*Comm. on John* I.22.
⁶*Hom. on Ezek.* VI.1; the Greek comes from a fragment from Catenae, PG 13. 709; cf. *PA* III.3.4. Zöllig deals with this passage, *op. cit.*, pp. 69 f.; and Völker, *Das Volkommenheitsideal*, pp. 137 f.

This attitude is a little suprising in Origen. He may adopt it out of deliberate opposition to Philo, as Zöllig suggests, or just conceivably in order to dissociate himself from Montanism. But the very few passages in his works which overtly refer to Montanism do not particularly suggest that it was the Montanists' practice of prophetic ecstasy that repelled him,[1] and the theory of ecstatic prophecy was as much that of contemporary Judaism (as Origen himself says in the passage from *Contra Celsum* II.9 quoted above, p. 194) or of contemporary Christianity as it was Philo's. It is more likely that this rejection of ecstasy on the part of Origen is a natural corollary of his intense rationalism. He does not like any theory which tends to put reason into the background in an account of the relations between God and man.[2]

Consistently with this admission that the prophet's individual character and consciousness are preserved even when he is inspired, Origen admits that each prophecy has a local reference as well as a prediction of distant events in the future. At one point he specifies three audiences for and subjects for prophecy: some things the prophets spoke to their own contemporaries, others to those who lived later, but most of all they spoke concerning a certain Saviour who was to come to live among mankind.[3] In the same work he says, 'Now the prophets spoke whatever was to be understood directly as profitable to their hearers and conducive to the reformation of their characters without any concealment according to the will of God. But whatever was more mystical and rather for the initiated and entering the region of intellectual contemplation beyond what could be heard publicly, that they revealed through riddles and allegories and what are called dark words and things known as parables and proverbs.'[4] He has a long discussion, in treating Jer. 1.4–10, about whether these verses are applicable to Christ only or to Christ and Jeremiah, and if the latter view is taken which verses should apply to which person. He concludes that if the reader will allegorize dili-

[1]E.g. *Comm. on I Cor.*, frag. 74, on I Cor. 14.34 f., *JTS* X, pp. 41 f., where he mentions Priscilla and Maximilla and argues that they have no scriptural support for prophesying in the congregation. This particular distinction between conscious and ecstatic prophecy is in fact made by an anonymous late second or early third century writer quoted in Eus. *HE* V.17.2 f., and used against the Montanists.
[2]This is not to exclude the possibility that Origen may have envisaged a mystical union between the Christian soul and Christ. It seems to me that Völker has established this likelihood; the mystical state however was of a markedly intellectual sort (as far as this is consistent with mysticism), and I think that Völker's opinions should be modified by the considerations advanced in 'Interpretations of Hebrew Names in Origen', *Vig. Chr.* X, pp. 122 f.
[3]*Contra Celsum* III.3.
[4]*Ibid.*, VII.10.

gently enough he can make the argument between God and Jeremiah at his calling into a conversation between God the Father and the pre-incarnate Christ. The solution of the problem appears to be that the passage applies entirely to Jeremiah and entirely to Christ.[1] But these concessions are made largely in theory only. In practice his exegesis tends to ignore the local reference of prophecy altogether, and especially to sweep away with the broom of allegory all topographical references or anything obviously connected with the 'particularity' of the situation in which the prophecy was uttered. Dealing with the quotation from Hos. 1.9 f. by St Paul in Rom. 9.25 f., he says that the Jews may protest that Hosea did not speak this to the Christians or the Gentiles, but in Judaea, to those who were under the law. 'God should not necessarily be supposed to speak in mountains and crags and any earthly places, but God speaks in the mind of man, in the rational faculty, and in the depth of the heart' (*principali cordis*).[2]

One extravagant example of the operation of this theory of inspiration which frequently occurs is Origen's treatment of the Psalms. His assumption that the Psalms represented a number of prophecies about Christ in which different speakers and 'persons' might be discerned within the same psalm making predictions about the coming of Christ and even about the Christian Church had, of course, some support in the New Testament itself, and a great deal of support in later Christian writers, particularly in Justin. But Origen carried these principles to a greater length than anyone before him. For him the Psalms were in fact written by the Holy Spirit, who chose to impersonate, not the earthly author, David or Asaph or Solomon, who was too unimportant to be considered in this process of inspiration, but God the Father and God the Son.[3] He does, it is true, sometimes pause to reconstruct the circumstances in which the author, usually thought to be David, must have written the psalm originally; but where he cannot do this without doing violence to the sense[4] he allegorizes the passage and reads into it some meaning referring to Christian doctrine; and even those passages which he allows to reflect David's experiences are usually allegorized to refer to Christ as well. What troubles him is not the original historical context of the psalm, but the attribution of the inspired passage to different 'persons' within the Christological prediction conveyed by the psalm. The circumstances reflected in Ps. 69, for instance, do not fit

[1] *Hom. on Jer.* I.6–9.   [2] *Comm. on Rom.* VII. 18.
[3] *Philoc.* VII.2, a fragment from the *Homilies on Acts*.
[4] The word he uses to express this sentiment is ἀβιάστως, *Comm. on Ps.* 31, *PG* 12.1125; cf. his treatment of Ps. 30 in the same work.

anything historical in the life of either David or Jesus, and Origen is hard put to it to discover the proper 'persons' who should be thought to be speaking in the psalm; he finally inclines rather doubtfully to read it as referring to Christ's descent into hell.[1]

Within this framework of exegesis he ranges wildly and confidently. John 13.18 quotes Ps. 41.9 ('he that eateth my bread lifteth up his heel against me') of Judas. Origen of course accepts this application, strives to apply the preceding verse of the psalm to Judas, finds another reference to 'heels' in another psalm (49.5) and does his best to allegorize it in order to apply it to Judas too.[2] He believes that the Second Coming of Christ is foretold in Ps. 45.[3] In Ps. 13 he sees a dialogue between the Persons of the Holy Trinity,[4] and elsewhere he carefully divides the verses of a psalm among the prophet's own words, and the words which he was permitted to overhear God the Father saying to the Son.[5] 'I will open my mouth in a parable, I will declare hard sentences of old' (Ps. 78.2) is directly ascribed to Christ and said to apply almost especially to the parable of the Workers in the Vineyard (Matt. 20.1–15).[6] To the suggestion that our Lord showed weakness in his words at Gethsemane, 'Let this cup pass from me', Origen replies that the words of Ps. 27.1, 'The Lord is my light and my salvation, whom shall I fear?', are in fact the words of Christ spoken through the prophet in a contrary sense.[7] He often allegorizes the headings to the Psalms, as indeed Melito had done before him.[8]

A conception of inspiration such as this one rested necessarily upon a conviction of the inseparable unity of Scripture, and this is a theme of which Origen never tires. In fact what he is contending for is not so much the unity as the uniformity of Scripture. A modern theologian might think of the unity of the Bible as like the unity of a tapestry in which there are a multitude of different strands, and different colours and patterns woven by these strands into a single theme or picture. Origen's conception of the unity of Scripture is more like that of the steel shell of a ship, in which a number of different but uniform plates

---

[1]*Comm. on Ps.* 69, *PG* 12.1512.
[2]*Comm. on John* XXXII.14; cf. XXXII.19, frag. 98, *Contra Celsum* II.11, and many other passages.
[3]*Contra Celsum* I.56.
[4]*Comm. on Ps.* 13, *PG* 12.1204.
[5]Cadiou, *Commentaires Inédits des Psaumes*, on 110.1, p. 97.
[6]*Comm. on Matt.* XV.28.
[7]*Exhortation to Martyrdom* XXIX.
[8]*PE* XXIV.4; *Comm. on Rom.* II.14; *Comm. on Psalms*, Preface, *PG* 12.106; Melito is referred to in *Comm. on Ps.* 3.1 (*PG* 12.1120) as having identified Absalom in the heading of this Psalm with the devil.

of steel are welded into one. He contrasts philosophy with the Scriptures and says: 'But those who profess to undertake any discussion and statement of any sort whatever outside this, even if they are words supposedly concerning the truth (yes, I shall say something rather unexpected), not one of them is Word, but they are each words . . . so that according to this argument we would say that he who makes any utterance whatever foreign to the religion of God speaks a miscellany of words (πολυλογία), but he who speaks the things that belong to truth, even if he touches every subject so as to leave out nothing, always speaks one Word. . . . Consider whether on this reasoning we can call all the holy writings one Book, but the writings outside these many books.'[1] He compares the harmony of the different parts of Scripture to the harmony of the strings of a lyre.[2] He maintains that the unity and order of the Godhead is reflected in the unity and order of the Scriptures.[3] For him, now that Christ has come, all the Scriptures are evangelical: 'Before Christ's coming, the law and prophets, since he who elucidates the mysteries they contain had not yet come, did not possess that promise which was contained in our definition of the gospel. But when the Saviour came and caused the gospel to become incarnate, by the gospel he made everything, so to speak, a gospel.' But he admits that 'it is right that that gospel which brings into being the gospel which is thought to be contained in the Old Testament also should be especially called the gospel.'[4] Later in the same work he writes: 'For God first declared his gospel through the prophets, by the ministry of prophets and those who possessed the Word of the means of salvation; and later God gave grace and apostleship for the obedience of faith among all the Gentiles, Paul, and the rest, and he gave it through Jesus Christ the Saviour, who possessed the means of salvation.'[5] Elsewhere he defines prophecy as 'the revealed knowledge (σημαντικὴ γνῶσις) of invisible things attained through the Word, the knowledge concerning the structure of the world and of the function of elements and times'.[6]

We have already glanced at one list of proof-texts which Origen gives us to substantiate his grandiose claims for the fulfilment of prophecy.[7] In the *Commentary on John* he gives another list of proof-texts from the Pentateuch which he considers convincing. They are:

[1] *Philoc.* V.5, part of the only surviving fragment of *Comm. on John* V.
[2] *Philoc.* VI.2, from the lost second book of the *Commentary on Matthew.*
[3] *Philoc.* XXVII.3, from a *Commentary on Exodus.*
[4] *Comm. on John* I.6; cf. I.15.
[5] *Ibid.,* II.10.
[6] *Comm. on I Cor.,* frag. 55, on I Cor. 14.6, *JTS* X, p. 36.
[7] See above, p. 191.

1. Gen. 49.8, 10; Jacob's blessing of Joseph's sons.
2. Num. 24.7, 8, 17; Balaam's prophecy of Israel's greatness.
3. Deut. 33.7; Moses' blessing of Judah.[1]

Elsewhere he maintains that the clearest prophecy, and one of the most important, which Christ fulfilled was the prediction in Micah 5.2 that the Messiah would be born in Bethlehem. The next clearest is Gen. 49.10 ('The sceptre shall not depart from Judah, nor the ruler's staff from between his feet, until Shiloh come, and unto him shall the obedience of the peoples be'). Next after this come two quotations from Deutero-Isaiah (Isa. 42.4 and 49.9). The second of these is fulfilled by the wide extent of the Christian Church of Origen's day.[2] These passages are all no doubt inherited by Origen as traditional Christian proof-texts; we can find these, or proof-texts of much the same type, in Justin's *Dialogue*. In themselves they are, one must confess, to the mind of a modern scholar far from impressive. But through the alchemy of Origen's allegorizing theology they could be transmuted into the pillars of an irresistible system of prophecy, complete in every detail. They were in fact to Origen merely the paradigms of prophecy which he could use as his exemplars in discovering an innumerable host of predictions of a much subtler and more Alexandrian sort throughout the whole Old Testament. In the passage just quoted, where he gives the list of proof-texts from the Pentateuch he adds, 'On the other hand, among those things that are written in the law it is possible to find very many referring to Christ in types and riddles.' He is not content with a traditional list of proof-texts, highly though he does value this. He is determined to supplement this list by his own particular techniques of allegory.

One of the most remarkable examples of the application of this theory of Origen's of the unity of the Old and New Testament is his habit of reading the pre-incarnate Logos into the Old Testament. He had here a small amount of support in the New Testament itself. It is probable that in such passages as I Cor. 10.1–4 and II Cor. 3.16 f., St Paul envisaged Christ as being in some prefigurative manner present with his people in the Wilderness. And Christian literature before Origen had already taken considerable advantage of such authority as this. Justin, for instance, alleged that it was Christ who had appeared to Abraham at the incident of the Sacrifice of Isaac; he is called 'Angel' and 'Apostle' when his appearances are referred to in the Old Testament, and he

---

[1] *Comm. on John* XIII.26.   [2] *Contra Celsum* I.51, 53.

appeared to Moses; sometimes he appeared 'in the form of fire, and sometimes too in a bodiless image'.[1] And Clement of Alexandria had said that the Saviour 'talks through the Bush', i.e. it was he who had addressed Moses from the burning bush; he also spoke through the prophets, and finally in the Incarnation through his own flesh and blood.[2] He says elsewhere of the same incident, 'A divine vision (θεοείδης ὄψις) was manifested to him [i.e. Moses] of light which took shape at the burning Bush. . . . That Word which was first seen through the Bush was later exalted through the thorn' [i.e. in the crown of thorns on the Cross].[3] And he tells us that it was the Logos who spoke to Ezekiel, saying, 'I will bind up that which was broken, and I will heal that which was sick', etc. (Ezek. 34.16, 14).[4]

Origen drives this type of speculation to much greater extremes. Abraham was declared by Jesus to be alive because he had kept the word of Jesus, and the same is true of the prophets: 'For they too kept the word of the Son of God, when "the word of the Lord came to Hosea" or "the word came to Jeremiah", or "the word came to Isaiah", because there came no other word of God to any of these except him who was in the beginning with God, his Son the Word who was God.'[5] The words of Christ are, Origen says, not only the words of Christ incarnate: 'for before that, Christ the Word of God was in Moses and the prophets. How indeed could they have been able to prophesy about Christ without the Word of God?'[6] The words of Solomon's prayer in I Kings 8.39 he regards as addressed to God the Son.[7] It was Christ who was the Bridegroom of Israel under the old dispensation, even though he had to divorce her later.[8] The four separate agreements made by the owner of the vineyard in the parable (Matt. 20.1-16) are the covenants

[1]*Apol.* I.62.3 f.; 63.1-17.
[2]*Protrept.* I.8, *PG* 8.64. But Clement marks these degrees and emphasizes that the Incarnation is the climax. For all his vagueness in other respects, Clement had a firmer grasp upon the Incarnation than Origen.
[3]*Paed.* II.8.75, *PG* 8.488. The same comparison occurs in the *Epistle of Barnabas* 7.11; Clement has a particular fondness for this work; see *Origen's Doctrine of Tradition*, pp. 68 f.
[4]*Paed.* I.9.84, *PG* 8.349. Cf. Irenaeus, *Adv. Haer.* III.22 and 6.2; and Tertullian *Adv. Praxean* 16, where he says that the Son descended from time to time to have converse with men, 'in vision, in dream, "in a looking-glass, in an enigma" '.
[5]*Comm. on John* XXVIII.42; cf. Zöllig, *Inspirationslehre*, p. 50.
[6]*PA* I, Origen's Preface 1. Later in the same work (I.3.6) Origen says that he who said through Moses 'I am who I am' is clearly God the Father. But I do not think that this necessarily precluded Origen from envisaging the Father as speaking through the Son even here.
[7]*Comm. on Matt.* XII.6.
[8]*Ibid.*, XIV. 19.

A.E.—G*

made with Adam, Noah, Abraham, Moses, and Christ, and the owner
of the vineyard who made them is Christ himself.[1] Christ is of course
associated with the traditional theophanies of the Old Testament; it was
he who had said to Moses, 'Man shall not see my face and live' (Ex.
33.20).[2] The man with whom Jacob wrestled (Gen. 32.24) was the Word
of God: 'In this manner did the men of that time see the Word of
God, just as our Lord's apostles, who said, "That which was from the
beginning, that which we have heard, that which we have seen with
our eyes, that which we beheld and our hands handled, concerning the
Word of Life".'[3] In fact, it is wrong in Origen's opinion to distinguish
too sharply the Incarnation from other Advents of the Lord: 'There is
not only one Advent (*adventus*) of my Lord Jesus Christ in which he
came down to earth. He came to Isaiah and he came to Moses and he
came to the people, and he came to each of the prophets.'[4] The text
'The word that came to Jeremiah from the Lord' (Jer. 11.1) makes it
clear, he says, that there were three periods for our Lord's advents to
the world: first, 'even if not bodily, still in each of the saints' of the
Old Testament before the Incarnation, as in this passage; then bodily,
in the Incarnation, then after his visible Incarnation 'he will again dwell
among us'.[5]

So extreme is Origen's account of the relation of Old Testament to
New Testament that the reader is constantly tempted to conclude
that for him there is no fundamental distinction between the revelation
given in the Old Testament and that given in the New. He says, for
instance, that the Advent and Incarnation of Christ were known to
those 'for whom the spiritual fulness of the time came', such as Moses
and the patriarchs and the prophets.[6] The spirit of Sonship was poured
out on the prophets and Moses as well as on those who believed on
Jesus Christ when he came, but he admits that they did not anticipate
the grace of redemption.[7] The phrase 'in the midst of you standeth
one' of John 1.26 moves Origen to say that the Word has been in the
world always and has been in man always, and could not be said to
have come into the world for the first time at the Incarnation.[8] Jesus
did 'walk openly among the Jews' (John 11.54) when as the Word of
God he came among their prophets, but he ceased to do so at the point
where this phrase is used in the Fourth Gospel.[9] In one sense, therefore

[1] *Comm. on Matt.* XV.32.
[2] *Ibid.*, XII.43.
[3] Fragment on Genesis, *PG* 12.128.
[4] *Hom. on Isa.* I.5.
[5] *Hom. on Jer.* IX.1.
[6] *Comm. on John* I.7; cf. VI.4.
[7] *Ibid.*, XIX.5.
[8] *Ibid.*, VI.39.
[9] *Ibid.*, XXVIII.24, repeated *ibid.*, frag. 86.

Jesus is, according to Origen, more present in the Old Testament than in the New Testament. It is true, he says, that the prophets only perceived (ἐνόουν) the things which they predicted as destined to happen in the future, whereas the apostles had the privilege of 'witnessing its activity through the thing itself taking place'; but this does not mean that the prophets were inferior to the apostles.[1] The prophets in fact 'enjoyed in advance (προαπέλαυον) the advent among them of a greater One'.[2] The 'revelation of the mystery which hath been kept in silence through times eternal' (Rom. 16.25) was intended only for the select few capable of understanding it; among those were the prophets, who did not, however, teach it openly, but 'they covered it in silence according to the command of the eternal God until the time should come that "the Word should become flesh and dwell among us".'[3] He reaches his most daring and most shocking point of extravagance on this theme in a comment on the words, 'But now ye seek to kill me, a man that hath told you the truth, which I heard from God: this did not Abraham' (John 8.40). Some people, say Origen, would make the comment on this verse that it is obvious that Abraham did not seek to kill Christ, for Jesus did not live in Abraham's time; but they would be wrong. Christ, as 'a man that hath told you the truth which I have heard from God', *did* live in Abraham's time. Indeed in a spiritual sense as 'a man understood allegorically' (τροπικῶς νοούμενος ἄνθρωπος) Christ could be crucified in Abraham's day, even before the Incarnation, and in the same sense Moses and the prophets could say, 'I no longer live, but Christ liveth in me', and similarly these men could have been crucified with Christ and have risen with him, but 'not at all according to the bodily burial of Jesus or his bodily resurrection'.[4]

In accordance with these convictions, Origen will readily interpret any part of the Old Testament as intended for the edification of the contemporary Church, theologians, clergy, or people, not, as *I Clement* or the Pastoral Epistles or almost any writer of the sub-apostolic literature might have interpreted it, as providing examples of good or warnings of bad conduct, or moral exhortations, specific or general, but as positively and specifically predicting the point or the situation to which he applies it. The taunt-song of the king of Babylon (Isa. 14) is applicable to any person prominent among the churches who has

---

[1]*Ibid.*, VI.5, τὴν ἐνέργειαν διὰ τοῦ πράγματος ἐπιτελουμένου κατανοεῖν.
[2]*Contra Celsum* VII.4.
[3]*Comm. on Rom.* X.43; cf. VIII.6, where Origen says that Isa. 53.1 f. is spoken by the prophet in the character of the apostles.
[4]*Comm. on John* XX.12.

denied his faith during a time of persecution.[1] The words of Isa. 3.14 f.
refer to the conduct of presbyters in the Church of Origen's day.[2] The
words of Lam. 4.20, 'The breath of our nostrils, the anointed of the
Lord, was taken in the pits, of whom we said, Under his shadow we
shall live among the nations', are interpreted as a prophecy of the mode
of resting in the soul of Jesus taken by the divine Logos.[3]

Though we shall later see some evidence that Origen did a little
modify his extreme doctrine of the relation between the Old Testament
and the New, it must be confessed that his unqualified and confident
development of a theory which had been treated with some caution by
all his predecessors and had begun as little more than a speculation
cannot be justified by any argument. It in fact consists in turning the
Old Testament into an intellectual dress rehearsal for the New, not in
the sense that in the Old Testament are found conceptions of God which
achieve at once their focus and their embodiment in the New, but in
such a way that the Old Testament contains the whole gospel contained
in the New—Christology, ministry, sacraments, everything—only presented in the Old as a number of intellectual propositions apprehended
by the enlightened, instead of enacted on the stage of history and associated with an historical figure, as in the New Testament. This seems
to me not only a superfluous and indeed misleading piece of speculation
but a complete misunderstanding of what the Old Testament, and
indeed the whole Bible, conceives to be the method of revelation, the
way in which God meets man. Yet even this theory has found its defenders among reputable and even distinguished modern scholars. 'A
prejudice against patristic exegesis would have to be deeply rooted',
writes Daniélou, 'to prevent one attaching greater importance to this
part of (Origen's) work. In fact, far from being negligible, it appears to
us to be on the contrary the most important. Though he is the originator
of textual criticism of the Old Testament, Origen is much more the
great theologian of the relation between the two Testaments, where he
expresses the common tradition of the Church. Ephemeral cultural
elements borrowed from Philonic or Gnostic allegorism do not at all
reduce the permanent value of his biblical theology.'[4] It seems to me

[1] *Exhortation to Martyrdom* XVIII.
[2] *Comm. on Rom.* VIII.10.
[3] *PA* II.6.7; but later, in the *Hom. on Lam.*, frag. 116, Origen interpreted this
text differently. It was in fact, because of the LXX's translation of 'the anointed'
as Χριστός a traditional Christian proof-text, but Origen, in *PA* at least, gives
it a peculiar theologizing twist of his own.
[4] *Origène*, p. 304.

that in this instance this eminent theologian has permitted his enthusiasm to outrun his judgement.

One more aspect of Origen's theory of the inspiration of the Bible
remains to be noted, and that is his respect for the significance and
efficacy of names and numbers.[1] An interest in this subject had long
been evident in Christian theologians, inherited originally from Jewish
sources. We have already seen that the Rabbis tended to allegorize
proper names.[2] Marcel Simon has shown how widespread among Jewish
and Jewish-influenced circles was a belief in the magical power latent
in the pronunciation of the divine name or names, during the period
when Origen was writing.[3] Origen certainly derived the greater number
of the etymologies of Old Testament names from contemporary Jewish
(and probably not Jewish Christian) sources.[4] He also borrowed a few
of his etymologies from Philo,[5] and it may well be that Philo was one
of those who provided him with his theory about names. Philo tells us
that the names which Moses gives are identical with the things themselves, and that this characteristic is peculiar to the names in the Pentateuch.[6] Clement of Alexandria shows a lively interest in the meaning
of biblical names; he almost always follows Philo blindly in deriving
them.[7] Origen was therefore showing his usual enterprise in exploring
Rabbinic Jewish sources for his etymologies rather than resting content
with Philo.

On several occasions in his works Origen gives the *rationale* of his
belief in the power of names and their importance. He rejects Celsus'
claim that the name for God in any philosophy or religion refers to the
same God. The names for God in the Bible, he says, have not been
given at random, but have their own peculiar solemn meaning and
efficiency. 'Our Jesus too possesses a similar metaphysic of names since
his name is clearly to be seen driving out ten thousand demons from
souls and bodies, producing its effect upon those from whom they were
driven out.' And he concludes that 'it is not the meanings which signify

---

[1] For further information on this subject see Zöllig, *Inspirationslehre*, p. 113,
and Harnack, *Der Kirchengeschichtliche Ertrag*, I, pp. 52–8.
[2] See above, p. 29.
[3] *Verus Israel*, pp. 400–5.
[4] See 'Interpretations of Hebrew Names in Origen', *Vig. Chr.* X.
[5] For some examples, see *ibid.*, pp. 103 f.
[6] *De Cherubim* 56.
[7] E.g. in the etymology of Isaac, Rebecca and Abimelech (*Paed.* I.5.21, *PG* 8.
273, 276), and of Abraham, Sarah and Hagar and Israel (*Strom.* I.5.3, *PG* 8.724);
but Judah is in this last passage interpreted as δύνατος, whereas Philo interprets
this as Κυρίῳ ἐξομολόγησις; Abram and Abraham again as Philo (*Strom.* V.1.–8,
PG 9.20).

objects, but the qualities and peculiar properties of the sounds which have
some power in them for accomplishing various things.' He expressly
takes this view in order to defend the action of Christians who will
die rather than apply the name of God to Zeus, even than name him.
He claims that names such as Abraham, Isaac, Jacob, Israel, Sabaoth
and Adonai have no thaumaturgical effect when translated into their
meanings in other languages. It is the _sound_, not the meaning, that constitutes the power of a name.[1] He treats the subject also in his _Exhorta-
tion to Martyrdom_, very appropriately, for those to whom the work was
addressed were in a situation where they might at any moment be
required to name pagan deities in worship on pain of death. 'The subject of names is a deep and esoteric one,' he says, 'and if anybody is
acquainted with it he will see that if names were given conventionally
the demons invoked or other powers of any sort invisible to us would
not obey those who know them and pronounce their names as belonging
to them.'[2] 'Look for the interpretations of names,' he says elsewhere,
'for the names were given with power by the Holy Spirit. In fact you
ought to know that the names are indicative of tempers and constitutions and qualities, and from them it is possible to see the appropriate-
ness of the person named.'[3] ' "Name",' he says, 'is a summary title of
the very nature of the person named.'[4] One of the objections to the
theory that John the Baptist was a re-incarnation of Elijah was, in
Origen's eyes, the fact that this would have involved a change of name
given to the same soul, yet no reason for this change is given in Scripture, as it is in the cases of Abraham, Sarah, Jacob, and Peter.[5]

He refers very often to the fact that sacred names are used in contemporary Christian exorcism. This exorcism is effected 'by the power
of the invocations of the adorable Trinity,'[6] or in the name of Christ,
and Origen admits, somewhat reluctantly, that the efficacy of these
exorcisms seems to be to some extent independent of the character of
the person using them.[7] Even the Ophianites, heretics who indulge in a
worship of Satan travestying Christianity, use invocations.[8] And people

[1] _Philoc._ XVII.1-4, a _cento_ of passages from _Contra Celsum_ I and V.
[2] _Exhort. to Martyrdom_ XLVI.
[3] _Frag._ on Gen. 17.5, _PG_ 12.116.
[4] _PE_ XXIV.2.
[5] _Comm. on Matt._ XIII.2. Cf. _Comm. on John_ XX.27, 'It is the same thing for
us to share one and the same names and to share the action which is signified by
the name'. This is perhaps borrowed from Philo, who calls names 'the expressions of powers' (χαρακτῆρες δυνάμεων, _De Mutatione Nominum_ 65).
[6] τῆς δυνάμεως τῶν τῆς προσκυνητῆς τριάδος ἐπικλήσεων, _Comm. on John_
VI.33; cf. II.33 and Justin _Apol._ II. 6.6.
[7] _Contra Celsum_ I.6 and II.49.   [8] _Ibid._, VI.32.

without any connections with Christianity at all use the names of
Abraham, Isaac and Jacob in conjunction with that of God for the
successful exorcism of demons.[1] This practice savours to us today of
magic and of a mechanical, sub-Christian, religious conception, but we
should not judge Origen harshly on this point. He was uneasy himself
about the affinities of this practice with magic and tried to spiritualize
and rationalize it. And as long as both pagans and Christians chose to
make the naming of sacred names a test of whether a man was a pagan
or a Christian, and a test which was a matter of life and death, no
Christian theologian could afford to treat the subject lightly.

The *Epistle of Barnabas* shows a keen interest in the allegorical
significance of the letters of the name Jesus.[2] Clement of Alexandria
allegorizes the *iota* of the name Jesus, and imagines that the Decalogue
is significant because this letter *iota*, the first letter of the name Jesus,
stands for ten.[3] But Origen, as far as I know, never indulges in this sort
of futile speculation. Perhaps the discipline of textual criticism
had taught him how frail are arguments based on the letters of
Scripture.

On the other hand, Origen evinces a lively concern for the significance
of the numbers which he encountered in the text of the Bible.[4] Origen
professes to have derived this interest from Jewish sources.[5] If so, it is
on the whole not likely that Origen knew of the particular 'science of
numbers' known as *Gematria* which was beginning to be developed by
the Jews of his day (as Turner suggests), but that he was influenced in
this by the Bible itself and by Philo. The Book of Daniel and the
Revelation of St John the Divine both obviously display a belief in the
mystical significance of numbers, very often to the bemusement and
confusion of their later expositors. And Philo shows throughout his
work an intense preoccupation with the occult significance of numbers,
a preoccupation which was originally no doubt derived from the Pythagoreans.[6] In imitation of Philo, Clement of Alexandria will on occasion

[1] *Ibid.*, VI.34.
[2] 9.8; see above, p. 90.
[3] *Paed.* I.9.85, *PG* 8.352 and *Strom.* VI.16.145, *PG* 9.377. Cf. frag. 8 in *PG*
9.743.
[4] For some interesting information on speculation about numbers among
Christians, and its sources, see Bardy's Introduction to Hippolytus' *Comm. on
Dan.* pp. 48–50.
[5] Turner, *The Pattern of Christian Truth*, p. 281, calls attention to this statement, found in a fragment on Ezekiel, *PG* 13.800 f.
[6] So G. H. Whitaker, Introduction to Vol. I of the Loeb edition of Philo,
p. xvii. See also H. A. A. Kennedy, *Philo's Contribution to Religion*, pp. 48 f.
For examples see *De Opificio* 45–52, 89–106; *De Decalogo* 18–31; but these are
only a few out of many.

indulge in speculation about numbers, usually, but not always, derived from Philo.[1] And Hippolytus can make great play with the significance of the dimensions of Nebuchadnezzar's statue, including a reproduction of the statement of the *Epistle of Barnabas* that the I and H of the Name of Jesus represent the number eighteen.[2]

Certainly Origen took full advantage of these precedents. He sees significance in the fact that the books of the Old Testament are twenty-two in number;[3] in the six days of creation (an idea borrowed directly from Philo);[4] in the forty and six years that the Temple was a-building;[5] in the twenty-eight cubits comprising the length of the curtains of the tabernacle made by Moses;[6] in the four days that Lazarus was in the tomb and the four hundred years of the sojourning of the children of Israel in Egypt and the forty days' fast of Moses, Elijah and Jesus;[7] in the fifteen stadia of the distance of Bethany from Jerusalem (eight for the circumcision added to seven for the sabbath);[8] in the statistics of the Israelites in the wilderness (22,273);[9] in the five loaves and two fishes of the Miracle of the Feeding, and the twelve baskets and the five thousand men;[10] and in the six days between the Confession at Caesarea Philippi and the Transfiguration.[11] This belief in the occult significance of the numbers given in the Bible naturally tends to enhance for Origen its oracular aspect.

Such, then, is Origen's doctrine of the inspiration of the Bible. Like everything else that he devised, this doctrine is articulated with skill and ability and with a depressing thoroughness. It is in fact the starting-point of the classical or traditional Christian doctrine of inspiration. Nobody spoke of a 'special sense' in the words of the Bible before the Christian Platonists of Alexandria and no theologian since Origen's day has gone much further in developing this doctrine; indeed, after Origen there was little room left for development. It ought to be obvious that Origen's doctrine is not founded upon any secure foundations. It was very largely a theological expedient resorted to in order to justify his particular 'oracular' treatment of the Bible, and to place it securely

---

[1] E.g. *Strom.* IV.25.158 f., *PG* 8.1368; *ibid.* VI.11.84 f., *PG* 9.305. This is partly derived from Philo, and partly from the *Epistle of Barnabas*.
[2] *Comm. on Dan.* II.27.6–8.
[3] *Comm. on Ps.* 1, *PG* 12.1084, reproduced in *Philoc.* III.
[4] Philo, *De Opificio* 13; Origen, fragment on Genesis, *PG* 12.97.
[5] *Comm. on John* X.38.
[6] *Ibid.*, XXVIII.1.
[7] *Ibid.*, frag. 79.
[8] *Ibid.*, frag. 80.
[9] *Hom. on Num.* IV.1.
[10] *Comm. on Matt.* XI.2.
[11] *Ibid.*, XII.36.

beyond the reach of Marcionites, Gnostics and Literalists; and it was made possible only by the unlimited use of allegory. It is totally unscriptural, totally uncritical, totally unreal. It is as well that those who still seek in our day to retain this doctrine (in however rehabilitated a form) should understand on how ambiguous a basis the doctrine stands.

8

Accommodation

IN spite of his very strong doctrine of inspiration Origen does not entirely exclude from his system a distinction of revelation between the Old Testament and the New.[1] There is a famous passage in the first book of his *Commentary on John* which sets out this distinction in some detail: 'Of these Scriptures, then, which are current and are believed in all the churches to be inspired, it would be no mistake to say that Moses' law was the firstripe fruit (πρωτογέννημα) and the gospel the firstfruit (ἀπαρχή). For it was after all the crops of the prophets up to the time of the Lord Jesus that the perfect Word blossomed.' Then he compares the Epistles with the Gospels. The Epistles are full of profit and well worth public recitation, but cannot be put on a level with documents characterized by 'Thus saith the Lord Almighty' (II Cor. 6.8); and 'I say and not the Lord' and 'I ordain in all the churches' are statements which 'have apostolic authority indeed, but not the directness of the words derived from divine inspiration' (τὸ εἰλικρινὲς τῶν ἐκ θείας ἐπιπνοίας λόγων). The Old Testament cannot be called the gospel because it does not point out him who is coming, but heralds his coming beforehand. The apostolic writings can be called the Gospels, but only in a secondary sense: 'Every single passage in the Epistles will not be a Gospel when it is compared with the account of the acts concerning Jesus and his experiences and words'. Then comes the well-known statement that as the Gospels are the firstfruit of the Scriptures so the Gospel of St John is the firstfruit of the Gospels, since none of the other Gospels shows the Godhead of Jesus so uncompromisingly.[2]

On several occasions Origen makes a distinction between the gospel and the law. Moses and Elijah had not before seen the glory of Christ

---

[1] This subject has been treated by Bigg, *The Christian Platonists of Alexandria*, pp. 184–90; Zöllig, *Inspirationslehre*, pp. 26 n. 5, 45, 53, 57 f., 74–6; Völker, *Das Vollkommenheitsideal*, p. 53 n. 1; E. Molland, *The conception of the Gospel in Alexandrian Theology*, pp. 110 f.; and Daniélou, *Origène*, p. 131.
[2] *Comm. on John* I.2–4.

illuminated as they saw it at the Transfiguration. They had up till then been awaiting 'the fulness of the time in which it was fitting that at the unique advent of Jesus Christ things which were unique among anything in the world ever spoken or written should be revealed'.[1] Elsewhere he says, of Christ, 'He becomes great as time goes on in the prophets. In the law alone he is not yet great, in as far as it is covered by a veil,'[2] and he can speak of the law-books as 'the Old Testament of the Old Testament',[3] and points out that Jesus himself distinguished between the laws of Moses and the laws of God (Matt. 19.7 f.).[4]

Origen will even distinguish between degrees of revelation within the Old Testament. Speaking of the prophets, he says: 'they too attained, led by the Spirit according to the approach given through types, to the vision of the truth. Therefore not all the prophets but many desired to see what the apostles were seeing [Matt. 13.1]. For if there was a distinction of degree among the prophets, the fully graduated and outstanding did not *desire* to see what the apostles were seeing, for they had already beheld it; but those who had not attained in the same degree as these to the scaling of the height of the Word were in a state of striving after the things made known to the apostles through Christ.'[5] The book of Numbers, though full of mysteries, has fewer mysteries than Deuteronomy, and even Moses is a schoolmaster and represents childish beginnings compared with Joshua.[6] Prophets could even make a mistake. How was it, he asks, that God said that he would bring on a pestilence of three days to punish David's sin, and yet stopped it on the first day (II Sam. 24)? It was the fault of the prophet Gad, he answers, who made this promise on his own authority, and not of God; prophets do not always speak the words of God, 'and whatever is spoken by a prophet is not always to be taken as spoken by God.'[7]

The conception of a developing revelation can by the nature of the case find little room in Origen's doctrine of inspiration, but it is not completely excluded, and there are even a few hints that Origen could have made use of this thought had he found it profitable. Wise men (prophets and patriarchs) had the Spirit only in part, whereas Jesus gives not the Spirit by measure, being himself the fount of Spirit.[8] The Jews from their earliest days learnt 'the immortality of the soul and the

[1] *Comm. on John* XIII.47 f.
[2] *Hom. on Gen.* XII.5.
[3] τῶν παλαιῶν τὰ παλαιά, *Comm. on Matt.* X.15.
[4] *Comm. on I Cor.*, frag. 35, on I Cor. 7.8–12, *JTS* IX. p. 505. Cf. *Comm. on S. of S.* II, on S. of S. 1.4.
[5] *Comm. on John* VI.3.
[6] *Hom. on Num.* I.3.
[7] *Ibid.*, XVI.4.
[8] *Comm. on John*, frag 48.

judgement-hall below the earth and rewards of living rightly. These doctrines were imparted to them still in the form of a fable (μυθι-κώτερον) when they were children and lived in the world of childhood' (τὰ παιδίων φρονοῦσιν); but when they progressed further in the Word the things which once were fables were changed to hidden truth.[1] Origen is probably here speaking of the development of the individual Jew from childhood to maturity, and not of the development of the race. But this is a line of thought which might have brought him far. He admits too that the Jews of old could not have even continued in existence if they had obeyed the injunctions of the gospel.[2] The description of the Servant as marred in his appearance (Isa. 52.14 and 53.3) is interpreted as the words of those who under the Old Testament understood the Word 'in an indirect way' (ἐν εἰσαγώγῃ).[3] The grace of perfection was not given to the patriarchs and prophets before the Incarnation.[4] Noting that Ps. 82 describes anyone to whom the Word of God came as a god, Origen says, 'If we must make distinctions between the Testaments and say that these "gods" disagree with each other (which is of course a suggestion wrong even to entertain but one which we do make on the understanding that we are using words in a strained sense), I would boldly say that a much more human element is exhibited in the Old Testament than in the New'.[5] He sometimes refers to the Old Testament as 'watery' (ὑδαρῆς), and to Christ as turning the water of the old dispensation into wine;[6] and this same adjective 'watery' he frequently applies to the Jewish, literal interpretation of the Scriptures.[7] Origen will even on occasion admit that St Paul may have made a mistake. He notices the syntactical inconsistency in the first sentence of the second chapter of Ephesians and puts it down either to a mistake in the manuscript tradition, 'or it was not observed to be a mistake by Paul who was unskilled in writing'.[8]

The consequence of these concessions is that Origen very occasion-

[1] *Contra Celsum* V.42.
[2] *Ibid.*, VII.26.
[3] *Comm. on Matt.* XII.32.
[4] *Comm. on S. of S.* II, on S. of S. 1.11 f.
[5] *Hom. on Ezek.* I.9.
[6] E.g. *Comm. on John* XIII.6.
[7] Zöllig refers to this passage, *Inspirationslehre*, p. 38. I think that this is always the sense that Origen attached to this word. That is why the emendation ὑδαρῆ for the difficult οὐδεῆ in *PA* I.8.4, suggested by Delarue and Mansi, will not do; the word must mean 'insipid' and not (as the emendation would demand) 'aquatic'. Clement of Alexandria uses the word in exactly the same sense in *Paed.* II.2.29, *PG* 8.424. Crouzel, *Théologie de l'Image de Dieu chez Origène*, pp. 201–5, does not seem to have appreciated this.
[8] *Comm. on Eph.*, frag. 9, on Eph. 2.1–5, *JTS* III, p. 402.

divine significance
in hum or letter
the divine & human
element in scripture

ACCOMMODATION   213

ally speaks of the Bible in terms not very different from those which a
modern exegete, speaking from the other side of the revolution created
by the advent of historical criticism, would use. He speaks of the
Scriptures as composed of two elements, the divine and the human. He
sees this indicated in the account of the anointing by Jesus of the eyes
of the blind man with mud mixed with saliva: 'Consider then if you can
take the whole Scripture and the manner of the record given in it and
say that it is composed, as far as concerns the divine ideas in it, from the
saliva of Christ, but as far as the record given in apparently historical
narrative and in human affairs, from the clay of the earth.' But he adds
that we can eventually 'cast aside the mud in order that we may approach Jesus seeing'.[1] The phrase 'my cup runneth over' of Ps. 23.5 he
refers to the divine Wisdom 'mingling divine ideas with human diction'.[2] He expresses a very similar idea when he says that 'the treasure
of the divine significances of Scripture is kept shut within the frail
vessel of the humble letter.'[3] And he will very occasionally recognize
that we must allow for 'particularity' in interpreting a text. He says that
even if the Jews had always kept the law they would still have needed
prophets, because men have a natural curiosity about the future, and
this is why such apparently trivial things as lost asses (I Sam. 9.20) and
the illness of the king's son (I Kings 14.1) are made the subject of
prophecy.

Origen's exegesis is not exclusively for intellectuals. We have seen
that his sermons were intended partly for what we might call the average
man in the pew.[4] He can write a fine sentence like this, 'Rather let the
educated man and the wise and the intelligent come if he wish, but none
the less let any unlearned and unintelligent and uneducated and simple
person come. For the Word promises to heal people of this sort too
when they come, making them all worthy of God.'[5] Zöllig points out
that for Origen a considerable part of the difference between the Old
and the New Testaments lay in the effectiveness and popularity and
appeal which the New Testament had and which the Old Testament
lacked.[6] De Lubac has collected several similar passages from Origen's
works.[7]

[1]*Comm. on John*, frag. 63.
[2]*Comm. on Ps.* 23.5, *PG* 12.1264.
[3]*PA* IV.3.14: a similar interpretation of II Cor. 4.7 is made in *Hom. on Ex.*
VII.1.
[4]See above, pp. 183–5.
[5]*Contra Celsum* III.48, reproduced in *Philoc.* XVIII.19.
[6]Zöllig, *Inspirationslehre*, p. 39.
[7]*Histoire et Esprit*, pp. 83–5.

But this scholar is certainly going too far when he suggests that to Origen the difference between the intellectual and the simple believer is ultimately insignificant because both classes of Christian can be brought to the higher knowledge which is the greatest secret and reward of the Scriptures.[1] I know of no passage in Origen's works which suggests that the simple and uneducated believer can attain to the higher knowledge. Origen, as an orthodox Christian, of course admits that such people can be saved and, as we shall see, is quite firm upon the point that even the most intellectual Christian must start where the simple believer starts and go with him through the preliminary stages of his way. But he believes that the intellectual will outstrip the uneducated believer in his spiritual progress, and, as far as I can see, outstrip him, at least in this world, permanently. Origen is at heart a rationalist, and to his rationalism the intellectual is more interesting, more worth paying attention to, than the other.

This rationalism shows itself in a number of ways in his exegesis of Scripture.[2] Origen admits the necessity of in some sense accommodating Christianity to the intellectual temper of the philosophy of his day. He gives as one reason for the existence of different schools of thought within the Church a desire that the doctrines of Christianity should agree with the views of a majority of the Greek intellectuals who were attracted to Christianity.[3] And wherever he can, he reproduces the terms and reads into the biblical text the ideas of Greek philosophy.[4] The prime example of this desire to rationalize his theology is displayed in his treatment of that scandal to the rationalist, the biblical doctrine of the predestinating power of God. The passage which brings this doctrine to the fore in its starkest form is that passage which we have already found a *locus vexatus* debated in the argument with the Predestinarians and the Marcionites—the account of the hardening of Pharaoh's heart.[5] Irenaeus had already found this subject a difficulty,[6] and many are the struggles which Origen has with it. One of his ex-

[1] *Histoire et Esprit*, p. 86.
[2] For this subject see also Denis, *De la Philosophie d'Origène*, pp. 246–8, 261, 278 f.
[3] *Contra Celsum* III.12, reproduced in *Philoc.* XVI.1.
[4] E.g. *Contra Celsum* VI.7, where Celsus has analysed the problem of cognition into ὄνομα, then λόγος, then εἴδωλον, and finally ἐπιστήμη; Origen says that John the Baptist is the ὄνομα (or φωνή), coming before the λόγος; Christ incarnate is the λόγος, Christ-in-the-individual is the εἴδωλον and Christ as wisdom in the perfect is ἐπιστήμη. But the examples are innumerable.
[5] See above, pp. 138, 140, 143 f., 150, 158. On this subject see also de Faye, *Origène*, III, pp. 187–90, and Koch, *Pronoia und Paideusis*, pp. 114, 128–31.
[6] *Adv. Haer.* IV.45.1 f.; see J. Lawson, *The Biblical Theology of St Irenaeus*, p. 67.

[handwritten margin note at top: The belief that God's activity or requirement is unacceptable - rebellion against - hardening of heart]

planations is that the responsibility in this case lay with Pharaoh, whose only response to God's miracles performed through Moses was to harden his own heart.[1] Another is to suggest that the Word is a physician of souls, and as physicians often deliberately aggravate and worsen their patients' states, that they may eventually cure them, so God often deliberately leaves people in sin or hardens them that he may lead them more surely to final repentance in this world, or, as in the case of Pharaoh, in the next.[2] A third explanation was that just as the sun does not *make* people swarthy, but it is the nature of the swarthy person which produces the swarthiness, so God does not harden Pharaoh's heart, but Pharaoh's heart is of such a sort that the effect of God demanding the freedom of his people is to harden it.[3] Yet another explanation calls in the analogy of a slave-owner who puts to death one of the worst of his slaves, whose crimes most deserve death, in order by his example to bring about the reformation of the rest. In these circumstances he could say to the slave condemned to death what God in Exodus is recorded as saying to Pharaoh, 'For this purpose did I raise thee up, that I might shew in thee my power' (Rom. 9.17, quoting Ex. 9.16).[4] The other outstanding passage which presented a painfully predestinarian appearance was the account of the birth of Jacob and Esau, especially as it is handled by Paul in Rom. 9.10-13. God apparently destined the first to favour and the second to rejection before they were born, in fact in their mother's womb. Here Origen takes the same way of escape as in the case of Pharaoh, only in reverse order. Pharaoh was given his chance in the next life, Jacob and Esau had had their chance in the life before this one, as souls in a state of pre-existence.[5] Jacob's soul before his birth was perceived by God to be pure, and therefore God made him a vessel for honour; Esau's was impure, so he was made a vessel for dishonour.[6] Origen may well have learnt this device of calling in the future life to redress the balance of the present one from Philo, who employs it in the case of Nadab and Abihu. Far from their being the subject of exemplary divine punishment, Philo sees them as having been translated to immortality: 'It is thus that the priests Nadab and Abihu die in order that they may live, receiving an incorruptible life in exchange for mortal existence, and being translated from the

[handwritten margin note: God does not harden hearts; God's activity to unacceptable is the...]

[1] *Philoc.* XXI.9-10, preserving a fragment of the Greek of *PA*, III.1.10 f.
[2] *Philoc.* XXVII.4-8, from a *Commentary on Exodus.*
[3] *Comm. on S. of S.* II, on S. of S. 1.6, reproduced in *Philoc.* XVII.13.
[4] *Comm. on Rom.* VII.16.
[5] *Comm. on John* II.31; *Philoc.* XXIII.20, from book III of a *Commentary on Genesis*; *PA* II.9.7; III.1.22.
[6] *Comm. on Rom.* VII.17.

created to the uncreated.'[1] Philo indeed is Origen's predecessor also in shying away from the biblical doctrine of predestination; he insists that the text 'the iniquity of the Amorite was not yet full' (Gen. 15.16) implies no predestination on the part of God, and entirely changes the meaning of the passage by allegory.[2] But Origen uses the device of bringing in the future life in order to remove its sting from the biblical doctrine of predestination far more frequently than Philo. He applies it to those who perished in the flood, to the people of Sodom, and to those who fell in the wilderness.[3] Koch indeed prefers to see in this doctrine the 'Platonic-Stoic' theory of an endless series of world cycles, but the direct influence of Philo is more likely.[4] Origen's doctrine of pre-existence is not so much in evidence in his dealing with this subject, but the case of Jacob and Esau is not the only occurrence of it. He applies it to two other biblical characters who were said to have been chosen by God from their mothers' wombs, Jeremiah and John the Baptist,[5] and he uses it to explain the difficult phrase, 'Lead us not into temptation.'[6]

Philo was perfectly ready to believe in the pre-existence of souls, probably deriving this doctrine from Plato's *Timaeus*.[7] Clement of Alexandria had explicitly disavowed any such doctrine, and had attributed it to Basilides.[8] Origen here is no doubt following Philo and probably too Philo's master Plato. But we must not attribute to him the even wider influence of the Pythagoreans nor of Indian philosophy, both of which employ this doctrine of the pre-existence of the soul. Origen's motive in including such a doctrine in his system is not in order to account for the existence of suffering in this world, as it is in Indian philosophy, but in order to reconcile his conception of human freewill and moral responsibility with the predestinarian doctrine of Exodus and of Romans; and he more than once rejects the particular form of pre-existence believed in by the Pythagoreans, metempsychosis or the transmigration of souls from one body to another. He does indeed suggest that fallen angels inhabit the souls of animals and in this form exercise the power of prediction for evil,[9] and he hazards the speculation that

---

[1]*De Fug. et Invent.* 59; but in *De Vita Mosis* II.275–87 he represents the sons of Korah as punished for their wickedness.

[2]*Quis Rer. Div. Heres* 300–6.

[3]For the references of these last three instances, see above, p. 140.

[4]*Pronoia und Paideusis*, p. 92; cf. pp. 147 f. Anyway Koch has in fairness to Origen to modify his suggestion by so many qualifications that little cogency is left in it.

[5]*PA* I.8.4.   [6]*PE* XXIX.10.

[7]See Kennedy, *Philo's Contribution to Religion*, p. 80.

[8]*Strom.* IV.26.167 and 12.83, *PG* 8.1377 and 1292.

[9]*Contra Celsum* IV.92.

certain men become angels before the general resurrection.[1] But neither of these conjectures involves an acceptance of the doctrine of trans-\ migration. Origen is, indeed, careful to dissociate himself from this doctrine, which he calls by its proper name, *metensomatosis*.[2] He describes as 'strangers to the Church's teaching' those who hold it;[3] to regard John the Baptist as a reincarnation of Elijah is 'an opinion concerning transmigration alien to the Church of God.'[4] And when in order to illustrate a point he makes an imaginary case of a fish emerging from the sea and becoming something higher in the order of creation, he guards himself very carefully; 'I took an analogy; let no one seize on this as an excuse for alleging statements which he has not heard me use.'[5]

The reason why Origen is so emphatic in denying a belief in the transmigration of souls is because his own doctrine of the pre-existence of souls, though not identical with this doctrine, is embarrassingly like it. The connection of John the Baptist with Elijah brings up this question forcibly; and Origen discusses it at some length in his *Commentary on John*.[6] His conclusion is that John was an angel who had deliberately chosen to become incarnate in order to minister to Christ. This belief in the pre-existence of souls plays quite a prominent and indispensable part in Origen's theological system.[7] He thinks, for instance, that it is hinted at in the class of workers in the parable who stand all day idle till the eleventh hour (Matt. 20.9).[8] Long after his death others, notably Jerome and the Emperor Justinian, attributed to Origen this very doctrine of metempsychosis which he so carefully disavows. Crouzel has made the attractive suggestion that what misled these men (apart from sheer malice) was Origen's theory that men who allow different passions to master them become like different beasts.[9]

Along with the biblical doctrine of predestination Origen is anxious to rationalize any suggestion of God's having had foreknowledge of events. The passage which brings this subject to his notice particularly

---

[1]*Comm. on Matt.* XVII.30. On this subject see also Denis, *De La Philosophie d'Origène*, p. 191; Cadiou, *La Jeunesse d'Origène*, p. 200; Koch, *Pronoia und Paideusis*, pp. 93, 137 f.; Harnack, *Der Kirchengeschichtliche Ertrag* II, p. 77.
[2]*Contra Celsum* VI.36; VIII.30.
[3]*Comm. on Matt.* XI.17.
[4]*Ibid.*, XIII.1.
[5]*Hom. on Jer.* XVI.1.
[6]II.31 and VI.10–14.
[7]It is expounded in *PA* I.8.1 and II.3.1–4; cf. *Comm. on S. of S.* II, on S. of S. 1.8.
[8]*Comm. on Matt.* XV.34.
[9]*Theologie de l'Image de Dieu chez Origène*, pp. 201–5.

is Ps. 109, for this psalm was universally accepted in the Church of his day as a prediction of Judas' betrayal of Jesus. He wrestles with this passage in a quotation from the third book of a *Commentary on Genesis*.[1] He contends for the complete foreknowledge on the part of God as to what, in the circumstances, was bound to happen, the entire moral responsibility of Judas for the betrayal, and the entire absence of a relation of cause and effect between God's foreknowledge and Judas' sin. 'God knows moral certainties' is in effect Origen's explanation. He indignantly rejects the suggestion that God's foreknowledge of events precludes our influencing them by prayer. God knows what we shall will and how far we will it and answers our prayers as far as he sees good for us and in whatever way his foreknowledge knows to be best.[2] Again, God did not foreknow evil souls: 'It is not that anything can lie hid from that nature which is everywhere and lacking in nothing, but that everything which is evil is considered unworthy of his knowledge or his foreknowledge.'[3] Any other apparently predestinarian passages are explained away by similar devices. The well-known quotation of Isa. 6.9 f. ('Make the heart of this people fat', etc.), reproduced in Mark 4.12, Matt. 13.14 and John 12.39, is one such passage. It means, says Origen, either that these people were ordained not to understand the message because if they did hear it plainly they would turn too soon or superficially or in the wrong way, or that it is the devil who blinds these people and God's activity is confined to healing them.[4] And the text, 'For it is God who worketh in you both to will and to work' (Phil. 2.13) means no more than that all things can exist only in God and can use their wills only in God, though human beings determine the specific use of their wills themselves.[5]

Origen deals in a similar way with a wide range of similar difficulties which shock his conception of what is proper and reasonable. He refines anthropomorphisms, bowdlerizes improprieties and explains away whatever seems unphilosophical, in the process very often blunting the sharp edges and blurring the vivid lights of biblical thought. He explains 'The kingdom of God is within you' (Luke 17.21) as referring to the knowledge of God naturally implanted in every man's mind.[6] We are re-

---

[1] It is preserved in *Philoc.* XXIII.9–11; cf. *Comm. on Rom.* VII.8.
[2] *PE* VI.1–4.
[3] *Comm. on Rom.* VII.7.
[4] *PA* III.1.17 and *Comm. on John*, frag. 92.
[5] *PA* III.1.20. Cf. *Comm. on Rom.* VIII.8, where Origen's comment on 'Let their eyes be darkened, that they may not see' (Ps. 69.23) is, 'darkened to seeing perversity'.
[6] *PA* I.3.6.

minded of Clement of Alexandria's smooth paraphrase, 'It is easier for a camel to go through the eye of a needle than for a rich man to practise philosophy.'[1] Evil, Origen says, is no more than an inevitable consequence of creation, 'a few phenomena existing for the sake of the coherence of the whole appear as the consequence implied in (God's) works, just as the spiral shavings and sawdust appear as the consequence implied in the works of the carpenter and it is a necessity for housebuilders that they should appear to be making the incidental products of buildings such as dirt coming from the stones and the plaster.'[2] He explains the glory (δόξα) which the Old Testament states to have shone, for instance, on the face of Moses when he came down from Mount Sinai and which is described in the New Testament in such passages as II Cor. 3, as 'an intimate knowledge of God and a vision with the eye of the mind which is fitted for it by its exceeding purity'.[3] To him the mystical marriage of Christ with the Church alluded to in (e.g.) John 3.29 ('He that hath the bride is the bridegroom' etc.) means no more than the union of 'the rational being of which a part is the soul of man' with Jesus the 'sower of good things' so that the soul can bring forth 'practical and intellectual virtues'.[4]

The rationalism is inevitably suspicious of what modern theologians call the 'particularity' of God's revelation in the Old Testament, that is, its involvement with local, ephemeral and often apparently trivial or even improper details and situations, and Origen according strives to dissolve this 'particularity' into general truths and abstract principles. Samson's adventures with women described in the book of Judges were not sins on his part but 'dispensations' of God.[5] The children who reproached Elisha, saying, 'Go up, thou baldhead!' (II Kings 2.23) were only delivered over to spiritual bears, not real ones,[6] just as the 'pair of turtle-doves and two young pigeons' which were offered in accordance with the law at the Purification were only spiritual birds.[7] The more trivial ordinances of the law often evoke this response from Origen: 'Are we to imagine that Almighty God who was giving answers to Moses

[1] *Strom.* II.5.22, *PG* 8.953.
[2] *Contra Celsum* VI.55; cf. *Comm. on Ps.* 49.5 (*PG* 12.1444) where he says that the Psalmist does not fear the sin of Adam, for 'nobody is condemned for somebody else's wrongdoing'.
[3] *Comm. on John* XXXII.27.
[4] *Ibid.*, frag. 45.
[5] *Ibid.*, frag. 65, οἰκονομίας.
[6] *Hom. on Ezek.* IV.7.
[7] *Hom. on Luke* XIV, on Luke 2.24. Cf. *Hom. on S. of S.* II.4, where he denies the literal meaning of 'bed' in Matt. 9.6: 'The Son of God had not come down from heaven to earth for the purpose of giving commandments about beds!'

from heaven made regulations about an oven, a frying-pan and a baking-pan ?'[1] The polygamy of the patriarchs and other men in the Old Testament provokes him to a similar device; he apparently believed that it was not really polygamy that the Bible intended but what we might call *polyarety*—the more wives are recorded the more virtues the person in question had![2] The imprecations upon children in the Psalms draw out all his skill in order to explain them away. 'Let his children be fatherless and his wife a widow' (Ps. 109.9), means that 'the orphans are evil thoughts which have buried their own father Satan, and the soul which has not received seed from the devil is a widow', so that the Psalmist here is invoking blessing, not curses.[3] He epitomizes his whole attitude to 'particularity' in a comment on Gen. 18.8, 'Abraham . . . stood by them under a tree': 'We cannot believe that the intention of the Holy Spirit was exhausted in narrating in the books of the law where Abraham was standing. What profit do I receive when I have come to hear what the Holy Spirit is teaching the human race if I am to hear that Abraham was standing under a tree ?'[4] It is in the same spirit that he suggests that the words of Jesus at Gethsemane asking that the cup might pass from him referred, not to the avoidance of death altogether, but of the kind of death, in order that he might encounter some other, possibly more painful and precious, passion;[5] that he conjectures that the words of Matt. 18.6, 'It were better for him that a millstone were hanged about his neck and he were cast into the depths of the sea,' imply that the subject of such punishment would be reformed by it and would later emerge to be henceforward immune from such marine penalties;[6] and that he interprets the parable of the Wheat and the Tares (Matt. 13.24–30) to mean that it is evil thoughts, not evil persons, which are to be burnt, and that the persons will be left penitent and grieving.[7] It is not, after all this, surprising to learn that Origen discourages prayer to God about 'earthly things'.[8]

Typical too of this rationalism is Origen's extreme sensitiveness to the anthropomorphism of the Old Testament and his determination to do away with it. In this he had as his main exemplar Philo. 'Let us not

---

[1]*Hom. on Lev.* V.5.
[2]*Hom. on Gen.* XI.2.
[3]*Comm. on Ps.* 109.9, *PG* 12.1568; cf. *Comm. on Ps.* 137.9, *PG* 12.1660, where the curse against the children of Babylon is similarly explained.
[4]*Hom. on Gen.* IV.2.
[5]*Exhort. to Martyrdom* XXIX.
[6]*Comm. on Matt.* XIII.17.
[7]*Ibid.,* X.2.
[8]οὐδὲ περὶ ἐπιγείων προσευκτέον, *PE* VIII.1.

be filled with such silliness as to imagine that God uses the organs of the
mouth or the nostrils so as to breathe, for God is not only not in human
form (οὐκ ἀνθρωπόμορφος), he is without qualities' (ἄποιος).[1] And
Philo asks, dealing with Gen. 4.9 ('Where is Abel thy brother?')
whether God can really be said to ask a question, for this would imply
lack of knowledge on his part, and answers that God does so only in
order to elicit a response, for good or evil, from the person questioned.[2]
Origen can similarly declare that not only must references to God's
members, such as eye, hand and ear, be allegorized into powers in God,
but even the phrase 'soul of God' is to be interpreted to mean the only-
begotten Son of God.[3] Even the description of God as 'Spirit' or as
'light' is too anthropomorphic for Origen and he insists upon allegory
in these cases.[4] Even God's love must not be thought of in a human way.[5]
It follows from this that God does not hate anybody;[6] this is in fact a
conviction borrowed directly from Clement of Alexandria who says that
nobody can be said to be an enemy of God; the most that can be said is
that they act as enemies towards his covenant.[7] By a similar exegesis
Origen explains away references to God's repenting;[8] here he is borrowing immediately from Philo.[9] And Origen explains the attribution of
a memory to God by saying that 'the Lord remembers that man in
whom he is and does not remember him in whom he is not.'[10]

On the subject of miracles Origen shows a remarkable restraint and
indeed caution. It is not that he doubts the possibility of miracles or
questions whether those recorded in either the Old or the New Testament really took place. But he realizes the limitations of the evidential
value of miracles. He lived in a world where many people claimed to
perform miracles, people such as Apollonius of Tyana, and he knew
that mere miracle-mongering would make no appeal to contemporary
pagan intellectuals; it savoured of vulgar sorcery. So he approaches the
subject with care. He remarks that the miracles of Jesus, though sufficient in themselves to convince the men of his time, would now lose

[1]*De Leg. Alleg.* I.36; cf. *De Congressu* 115, where Philo makes a similar denial
about God smelling.
[2]*Quod Deterius* 57 f.
[3]*PA* II.8.5; cf. *Contra Celsum* VI.64.
[4]*Comm. on John* XIII.22.
[5]*Ibid.*, frag. 50.
[6]*Contra Celsum* I.71; cf. *Comm. on John* X.13.
[7]*Strom.* VII.12.69, *PG* 9.496.
[8]*Contra Celsum* VI.58; frag. on I Sam. 15.11, *PG* 17.44.
[9]*Quod Deus Immut.* 33–50, which discusses the same passage as that dealt
with in *Contra Celsum* VI.58.
[10]*Comm. on Ps.* 132.1, *PG* 12.1649.

importance not in the miracle, but in the truth it symbolizes

their power of conviction and be suspected as fables were they not supported and guaranteed by Christ's fulfilment of prophecy.[1] He contends for the necessity of exercising a critical faculty in accepting the miraculous (παράδοξα), and of neither indiscriminately allowing nor indiscriminately rejecting every recorded instance of it.[2] He insists that even miracles are no violation of natural law.[3] He regards the healing of the man at the pool of Bethesda (John 5.2) as largely accomplished by the man's faith.[4] And he insists over and over again that the chief value of a miracle is not that it happened but the truth symbolized by it, which is to be gained by allegory.[5] This conviction sometimes drives him into absurdities, as when, commenting on the incident of the stater in the fish's mouth (Matt. 17.24–27), he insists that the fish was improved by being caught.[6]

Finally, Origen is always aware that he must square the statements in the Bible with the theories of contemporary physics. He is just as anxious as a modern theologian would be to avoid any sort of physical interpretation of the Ascension. 'Consider incidentally whether you should not understand as mystically and not spatially spoken of Jesus' soul the text "having ascended far above all heavens" [Eph. 4.10]; for the intellectual ascent of that soul leapt beyond even all the heavens and, as it is possible to assert, in that moment reached God himself.'[7] Elijah's ascension is similarly treated;[8] and the descent of the Spirit on Jesus is carefully described as not spatial.[9] This sensitiveness to the danger of a spatial interpretation of any activity connected with God is influenced in part at least by Philo, who insists that to say that God dwells in a house does not imply that he is in a place but is only a way of referring to his providence and care for the place, and sedulously allegorizes the statement in Gen. 4.16 that Cain went out from the presence of God.[10] The accounts of divine visions or voices particularly exercises Origen. Where the Scriptures say that 'the heavens opened',

[1]*Comm. on John* II.34.
[2]*Contra Celsum* V.57.
[3]*Ibid.*, V.29.
[4]*Comm. on John*, frag. 61.
[5]E.g., *Comm. on John* I.36; *Contra Celsum* II.48; *Comm. on Matt.* XI.5, 17; XIII.3.
[6]*Ibid.*, XIII.10.
[7]*Comm. on John* XIX.22. Similar statements are to be found in *PE* XXIII. 1–4; *Hom. on Gen.* IV.5; *Comm. on Ps.* 18.7 f., *PG* 12.1228; and *Comm. on Matt.* Comm. Ser. 7.
[8]*Comm. on John*, frag. 75.
[9]*Ibid.*, frag. 20.
[10]*De Sobrietate* 63; *De Post. Caini* 1. Cf. the very similar attitude of Aristobulus before him, recounted above, p. 42.

he explains, they are really referring to a projection into a visionary
form of an objective but interior experience by the imagination of the
person who had such an experience. This applies to Ezekiel's visions, to
Isaiah's visions, and probably too to our Lord's vision of the dove at
his Baptism: 'Perhaps he who reads the Gospels wisely must similarly
interpret even the case of our Saviour, even though such an interpretation may form a difficulty for simpler people' who have very materialistic
ideas of the heavens.[1] It is quite clear that Origen had no intention at all
of involving his theological system with a three-storey universe!
Origen also has a careful discussion of the heavenly voice heard at
Christ's Baptism. He notes that it was not recorded to have been heard
by the crowds, and that God's voice is always heard only by those whom
he wills to hear it, and hints (though he refrains from asserting) that the
voice was not a physical voice produced by air-waves or any other
physical means.[2] Here too Philo had been before Origen, and Aristobulus before him, as we have already seen.[3] Similar problems of physics
are dealt with by Origen similarly. His allegory of Matt. 24.29 f. involves the assumption that the cosmic portents predicted there could
not happen literally.[4] He carefully explains the 'darkness over all the
earth until the ninth hour' of Matt. 27.45; he says that it only means
dark clouds interposing between the sun and the earth and that by 'all
the earth' the evangelist meant no more than all Judaea or all Jerusalem;
he admits freely that it is unlikely in the extreme that the sun should be
eclipsed at Passover time when the moon was full, and he is prepared
to regard the phrase of Luke 23.45, 'the sun being eclipsed' (τοῦ ἡλίου
ἐκλείποντος), as a gloss and to read instead the variant 'and the sun was
darkened' (καὶ ἐσκοτίσθη ὁ ἥλιος); he also admits that no contemporary non-Christian narratives or sources mention the darkness, except
Phlegon in his *Chronicles*, and even he did not state that it took place
when the moon was full.[5] The phrase in Ps. 136.6, 'to him that spread
forth the earth above the waters' stimulates Origen to a brief note on the
scientific problem which it raises when taken literally. If the earth is
founded on the waters, how can Job say (26.7), 'who stretcheth out the

---

[1] *Contra Celsum* I.48. The discussion of the significance of the dove at the
Baptism and the citing of the views of the followers of Basilides, of Valentinus
and of others in *Excerpta ex Theodoto* 5 and 16 (*PG* 9.656 and 665), show that
this was a passage which attracted particular interest in Origen's day.
[2] *Contra Celsum* II.72; in VI.62 he says that voice of God is not an audible,
physical voice.
[3] See the quotations from Philo and Aristobulus given above, p. 42.
[4] *Comm. on Matt.* Comm. Ser. 49.
[5] *Ibid.*, 134.

earth over nothing'? The solution is that the earth we live on is above
the waters, but the earth below 'the abyss', and therefore presumably
below these waters, is built on nothing.[1]

With much of this sort of exegesis a modern scholar will sympathize.
The rise of biblical criticism has introduced into all biblical exposition
a necessarily rationalistic element, and it is cheering to find Origen
exercising caution about accepting miracles and taking a sophisticated
attitude towards the Bible's presentation of scientific facts seventeen
centuries before we do. It is equally obvious that much of Origen's
rationalism is quite unnecessary and a positive hindrance to his exegesis,
the unhappy result of his determination to read into the text ideas that
are not there, and of his blindness to many aspects of biblical thought.
The line which it seems to me wholly inadmissible to take in this case is
to make the sweeping assertion, which de Lubac does make, that there
is no rationalism in Origen's thought at all.[2] I would venture to claim
that nobody who has read the evidence collected in these pages could
doubt that Origen, though a believing, devout and orthodox Christian,
was at the same time a prince of rationalists.

Origen then recognizes that in spite of the inerrancy and inspiration
of the Scriptures they do display a gradation of revelation, and that they
contain a number of features which demand skilful and sometimes embarrassingly complicated explanations. To account for these phenomena, which sometimes look painfully like imperfections in the book,
Origen produces a principle which exhibits at once the remarkable
flexibility and the strength of his thought, the principle of accommodation. It has been suggested that Origen derived this principle, which will
be illustrated in the following pages, from pagan literature and philosophy, and in particular from Maximus of Tyre.[3] But there is no need
to range so far afield to find the sources of Origen's thought here. The
principle of accommodation is well established in a rudimentary form in
Philo. On the phrase 'The Lord came down' (Gen. 11.5) Philo remarks:

<hr/>

[1] *Comm. on Ps.* 136.6, *PG* 12.1656.

[2] He says of Origen's thought, 'It is not at all esoteric. Even less is it a method
of expressing rash views or a rationalistic doctrine. It is to the light of day that
he brings out his interpretations' (*Histoire et Esprit*, p. 175). It is this sort of
wild distortion that makes the reader of his book regret that the author's learning
and acumen have been devoted to a partisan presentation of Origen's thought
instead of to the authoritative account of it which might have appeared from his
pen.

[3] So Daniélou, *Origène*, pp. 104 f. On this subject see also *ibid.*, pp. 274 f.; Cadiou,
La Jeunesse d'Origène, pp. 42 f.; Zöllig, *Inspirationslehre*, pp. 31, 34, 62; Turner,
The Pattern of Christian Truth, pp. 267 f.; Koch, *Pronoia und Paideusis*, pp. 60,
126 f., 141; Crouzel, *Théologie de l'Image de Dieu chez Origène*, pp. 141, 257–60.

'The lawgiver talks thus in human terms about God even though he is not a human being for the advantage of us who are being educated, as I have often said in other passages.'[1] And elsewhere he says that the resemblance of Jacob to Esau is said to have been confined to their hands, and then only 'by a divine condescension' (ἕνεκα τῆς οἰκονομίας).[2] Something of the same sort can be found in Clement of Alexandria, who solves the difficulty of reconciling God's goodness with his justice by saying, 'God is good in himself, but he is just for our sakes, and only that because he is good.'[3] And he expresses the same sentiment more fully when he says that God is spoken of in the Bible as if he experienced human passions, but we must not judge him by our own feelings: 'But in as far as it was possible for us to hear, burdened as we were with flesh, so did the prophets speak to us, as the Lord accommodated himself to human weakness for our salvation.'[4] But as Clement both regarded the revelation given in the Old Testament as less important than it was in Origen's eyes and, for all his Gnostic leanings, laid greater weight upon the Incarnation than Origen did, he found less need for this doctrine and used it sparingly. It is even possible that Philo (and Clement and Origen through him) ultimately derived this thought from Rabbinic exegesis. 'So great is peace,' said Rabbi Simeon ben Lakish, 'that Scripture speaks fictitious words in order to make peace between Joseph and his brethren. For it says, Thy father commanded before his death, saying, Forgive, I pray thee, the trespass of thy brothers. And we do not find in the Scripture that Jacob had given any such command.'[5]

Origen has a special word for this accommodation—*symperiphora* (συμπεριφορά). He applies it to the thought behind the words of our Lord describing Moses as giving the Jews a law 'for the hardness of your hearts'.[6] He almost exactly reproduces Philo's phrases on the

[1]*De Confusione* 135.
[2]*De Virt.* 208. I do not think that the editor of the Loeb edition of Philo has made out his case (Vol. VIII, p. 49, Appendix) that this passage is an interpolation. The word which I have translated 'condescension' is literally *economy*. Justin uses it of the condescension or accommodation whereby Jesus submitted to the Jewish law during his life on earth (*Dial.* 67.6).
[3]*Paed.* I.9.88, PG 8.356.
[4]συμπεριφερομένου σωτηρίως τῇ τῶν ἀνθρώπων ἀσθενείᾳ τοῦ Κυρίου, *Strom.* II.16.72, PG 8.1012.
[5]Quoted by Montefiore and Loewe (*A Rabbinic Anthology*, p. 532) from *Deut. Rabba* Shofetim, V.15. The biblical passage quoted is Gen. 50.16 f. Rabbi Simeon is described in this Anthology's 'List of Rabbis and their Generations' as living about 250, and as a Palestinian.
[6]*Comm. on Matt.* XIV.23. We have just seen Clement using the verb cognate with this word.

A.E.—H

subject when, in commenting on 'which is in the bosom of the Father' (John 1.18), he says, 'Because everything concerning the Godhead is unnameable, these things are shown to us who are human beings through human phrases. It is reasonable that the evangelist should have recorded this relation to the Father so as it should be indicated in terms of our own knowledge.'[1] Elsewhere he says, 'Why do you not realize that God handles for your sake even things which are least congenial to his nature?'[2] He expresses much the same doctrine in another passage 'For the Holy Spirit addresses our nature in a manner appropriate to its imperfection, only as far as it is capable of listening.'[3]

This doctrine of accommodation Origen expresses under a variety of images, all very ably managed and often beautifully expressed. One such image is that of a father accommodating his language to the understanding of his children. 'He condescends and lowers himself (συμ-περιηνέγχθη καὶ συγκατέβη) accommodating himself to our weakness, like a schoolmaster talking a "little language" (συμψελλίζων) to his children, like a father caring for his own children and adopting their ways.'[4] Again, in reply to Celsus' censures upon the anthropomorphisms of the Old Testament, he says: 'Just as when we are talking to very small children we do not assume as the object of our instruction any strong understanding in them, but say what we have to say accommodating it to the small understanding of those whom we have before us, and even do what seems to us useful for the education and bringing up of children, realizing that they are children; so the Word of God seems to have disposed the things which were written, adapting the suitable parts of his message to the capacity of his hearers and to their ultimate profit.' And later he uses the same simile of children being taught in order to explain references in the Scriptures to God punishing by fire; these harsh threats of punishment are an accommodation to the crude characters of those who could not otherwise be induced to obey God's will and who only think in these terms.[5]

This image finds it longest and most carefully worked out expression in a passage from the *Homilies on Jeremiah*, where he is endeavouring to explain how God can be said in the Bible to repent or change his mind:

'But when the providence of God is involved in human affairs, he assumes the human mind and manner and diction. When we talk

[1] *Comm. on John*, frag. 14.   [2] *Hom. on Gen.* IX.2.
[3] Pitra, *Analecta Sacra* II, p. 465, a fragment on Ps. 11.4.
[4] Frag. on Deut. 1.21 from Catenae, *PG* 17.24.
[5] *Contra Celsum* IV.71; V.16.

to a child of two we talk baby-talk because he is a child, for as long as we maintain the character appropriate to an adult age, and speak to children without adapting ourselves to their speech, children cannot understand us. Now imagine a similar situation confronting God when he comes to deal with the human race, and particularly with those who are still "babes". Notice too how we who are adults change the names of things for children, and we have a special name for bread with them, and we call drinking by some other word, not using the language of adults, which we use to people who are grown up and of the same age as we are, but a special childish and baby-language. And if we name clothes to children, we give other names to them, as if we were inventing a child's name for them. Do we suffer from arrested development when we do this? And if someone hears us talking to children, will he say, "This old man is losing his mind, this man has forgotten that his beard is grown, that he is a grown-up man"? Or is it allowable for the sake of accommodation (κατὰ συμπερι-φοράν) when we are associating with a child not to talk the language of older and mature people, but to talk in a child's language?'

A little later in the same passage he applies this illustration:

'Then, since we change our minds, when God talks to us who are liable to change our minds, he says, "I change my mind", and when he threatens us he does not profess to be able to foresee the future, but he threatens as if he were talking to children. He does not claim that he knew "all things before they be", but as if assuming the character of a child, if I may put it that way, he pretends not to know the future. . . . You could find many similar assumptions of humanity in Scripture, such as, "Speak to the children of Israel; it may be they will hearken and turn." God does not say "It may be they will hearken" because he was in uncertainty, for God is not in uncertainty so that he should say, "It may be they shall hearken and turn," but it was to make entirely clear your free choice and to prevent you saying, "If he foreknew my perdition I must perish, and if he foreknew my salvation I must assuredly be saved." He does not profess to know the future in your case, so that he may preserve your free will by his refraining from choosing or knowing beforehand whether you will turn or not. . . . You will find thousands of other statements about

God accommodating himself (τροποφοροῦντος) to man. If you hear of the wrath of God and his anger, do not think that anger and wrath are passions in God. They are accommodations in the use of language (οἰκονομίαι χρήσεως λέξεων) in order to correct and improve a child. We ourselves assume a frightening attitude to children, not because we have a disposition like that, but for an ulterior motive (κατ' οἰκονομίαν). If we keep in our countenance the benevolence towards the child which is our true feeling, and show the affection which we have towards it, we spoil it and make it worse. Similarly then God is said to be angry and declares that he is wrathful in order that you may reform and be improved.'[1]

In a quite different context, that of Rom. 8.26 ('And in like manner also the Spirit helpeth our infirmity') he can use the figure of a schoolmaster helping his pupil to illustrate this principle. 'Just as a schoolmaster who had taken on an ignorant pupil and one who knew nothing of reading, so that he can teach him and educate him, has to lower himself to the pupil's elementary stage and himself first tell him the name of a letter so that the pupil can learn it by repeating it after him, and in some respects the master himself becomes like a pupil in the first stage, and his words and thoughts are the words and thoughts suitable for a beginner: so also the Holy Spirit, when he sees our spirit troubled by the onsets of the flesh and not knowing how it should pray in the right way, himself like the schoolmaster first goes over the prayer which our spirit must repeat if it really wants to be a disciple of the Holy Spirit.'[2] We are reminded of the phrase of the sixteenth-century schoolmaster Roger Ascham in which he describes the master as, for the sake of his pupils, 'hanging clogs upon the nimbleness of his own soul'.

This doctrine reaches perhaps its most extreme form when Origen suggests that God may have deliberately deceived people in the Old Testament for their own good. When he wrote his *Stromateis*, at the very beginning of his literary output (about 222) he was tentative and uncertain about this conjecture. 'It is not to be thought that God sometimes tells a lie as a matter of accommodation' (*pro dispensatione*). But, if it is to benefit his hearers, he will sometimes use ambiguous words

---

[1] Both these long extracts come from *Hom. on Jer.* XVIII.6. A very similar explanation of God repenting and being angry occurs in a fragment on I Sam. (*PG* 12.992), dealing with God's repenting that he had made Saul king, and being angry with him (I Sam. 15.11).
[2] *Comm. on Rom.* VII.6; cf. *Contra Celsum* IV.12.

and cover with a veil what might do hurt if it were openly stated.'[1] Later
in his life, however, Origen grew bolder about this doctrine. The phrase
in Jer. 20.7, 'O Lord, thou hast deceived me and I was deceived', gives
him a great deal of trouble, and in this case he falls back upon the
principle of accommodation. We sometimes deceive children, he says,
in order to frighten them for their betterment. So God treats people
like children and has to deceive them for their own good. An example
of this is the men of Nineveh, to whom God said, 'Yet forty days, and
Nineveh shall be overthrown' (Jonah 3.4). By being led to think that
Nineveh would be destroyed they were induced to repent. And Origen
obviously thinks that this was particularly true of the Old Testament.[2]

Origen sometimes expresses this thought of God deceiving men in
the Scriptures for their own good by the illustration which strikes us
today as particularly modern, that of a doctor deceiving his patient. In
his *Homilies on Jeremiah* he presents his doctrine of accommodation first
under the figure of a father deceiving his own child for its good, and
then thus: 'If the doctor says to the patient, "You must be amputated,
you must be cauterized, you must endure even more painful treatment
than this," the patient would not submit himself to the treatment. So
sometimes the doctor makes some other pretext, and hides the instrument in question, the cutting steel, under the sponge, and again hides in
honey, if I may so express it, the true nature of the bitter medicine and
the unpleasant draught, with the intention not of hurting but of healing
his patient. The whole sacred Scripture is full of remedies such as
these.'[3] In this particular passage Origen claims this suggestion as his
own. But as a matter of fact he must have found it in Philo and Clement
of Alexandria, to whom it was almost a commonplace.[4] In order to
explain how the Pentateuch comes to describe God as having parts and
passions like a man, Philo resorted to this doctrine of God deceiving
men: 'Thus too in dealing with dangerous sicknesses of the body the
most approved physicians do not allow themselves to tell the truth to
their patients, since they know that this will but increase their dis-
heartenment and bring no recovery from the malady, whereas under the
encouragement which the opposite course of treatment gives they will

[1]Fragment of *Stromateis*, PG 11.101.
[2]*Hom. on Jer.* XIX.15.
[3]*Ibid.*, XX.3. On the use of medical language of this sort in Origen see also
Zöllig, *Inspirationslehre*, p. 22; Völker, *Das Vollkommenheitsideal*, pp. 61 n. 2,
74 f., 135 f.; Koch, *Pronoia und Paideusis*, pp. 74 f.
[4]It must however be admitted that in *Comm. on Matt.* XVII. 15–17 he does
acknowledge his indebtedness to Philo (though not by name) for a characteristic
statement of accommodation.

bear more contentedly their present trouble and at the same time the disease will be relieved. For what sensible physician would say to his patient, "Sir, you will be subjected to the knife, cautery or amputation", even if it will be necessary that he should submit to such operations? No one. . . . Whereas, if through the physician's deceit he expects the opposite, he will gladly endure everything with patience, however painful the methods of saving him may be.'[1] Clement of Alexandria uses the same image in much the same way, 'just as a doctor in treating sick people will tell a lie in order to heal those who are ill'.[2] Montdesert points out that this same illustration occurs several times in Plato.[3] This was no doubt the source from which Philo and Clement derived it.

The device of illustrating God's revelatory activity in the Bible by examples taken from medical practice was altogether a very well known one by Origen's day. Both Philo and Clement of Alexandria had used this device to suggest the widely different ways in which God deals with the different characters of men, as a doctor uses different treatments for different diseases.[4] And both explain the wrath or menace of God mentioned in the Bible by the illustration of the surgeon who has to use drastic surgery or amputate for the good of his patient.[5] Both show considerable interest in medicine, a feature which may well have been characteristic of Alexandrian thought.[6]

Origen therefore in using the figure of the doctor in a variety of other ways is not original, but he does sometimes achieve an effectiveness lacking in the others. He regards Christ as the 'Chief Physician'.[7] He illustrates (against the Marcionites) the function of the law in Paul's thought by comparing it to the art of medicine; by this art we can recognize a disease, but it does not follow that the art causes the disease.[8] And he borrows from Philo and Clement both the picture of the doctor applying different treatments to different diseases,[9] and the image of the

[1] *Quod Deus Immut.* 65 f. (Loeb editor's translation). The same image occurs in *De Cherubim* 15; *De Decalogo* 12; *De Sacrif. Abelis et Caini* 121–3.
[2] *Strom.* VII.9.53, *PG* 9.476; cf. *Paed.* I.1.3, *PG* 8.252.
[3] *Clement d'Alexandrie*, p. 166.
[4] Philo, *De Josepho* 33 f.; Clement, *Protrept.* I.8, *PG* 8.64. Theophilus of Antioch, too, can call God ἰατρός, *Autolycus* I.7: this is perhaps another instance of Alexandrian influence on Theophilus.
[5] Philo, *De Praem. et Poen.* 33: Clement, *Paed.* I.8.64, *PG* 8.328.
[6] Philo, *De Spec. Leg.* I.216–9; see Kennedy, *Philo's Contribution to Religion*, p. 13. Clement, *Paed.* I.6.39, *PG* 8.297; III.1.65 f., *PG* 8.640.
[7] ἀρχιατρός, *Hom. on Jer.* XVIII.5; cf. *PA* II.10.6, *medicus animarum nostrarum.*
[8] *Comm. on Rom.* III.6*; cf. *Comm. on John* XXXII, 24.
[9] *Hom. on Ezek.* III.8; cf. fragment on Proverbs, *PG* 13.32 f.

surgeon using drastic methods for the patient's good; 'it is as the Good Physician that he says, "My eye will not spare thee, nor will I pity" (Ezek. 7.4). It is just the physician who spares those people who need severer amputation and cautery, and who has compassion on those who need greater anguish and pains, who produces a less complete cure.'[1] Elsewhere he uses the analogy of the surgeon who uses a red-hot knife for cancer operations. God is the physician who knows the best cure for us: 'For he does not inflict punishments simply in order to torture, as some think, but like a father he knows all our sores. He knows what ulcer has risen and what its cause is, what is the festering of the unhappy mind and from what beginning it developes, what is the nature of our disease and what the sin from which it comes.'[2]

Even though in his use of examples from medical practice Origen is far from being an innovator, we may readily grant that in his employment of this principle of accommodation in his exegesis of Scripture he is at his best and greatest. At times we feel that he is very near indeed to the doctrine of progressive revelation and that had he found the need to use this doctrine he would not have been too much shocked by it to make use of it. But he is always inhibited from seriously contemplating such a line of thought by his conviction—reached by *a priori* and arbitrary presupposition—that the immaturity and imperfection must lie in the audience to whom the biblical message was addressed and not in the agent through whom the message was delivered. Still, when all has been said and done, this conception of accommodation was a noble principle nobly applied. It is the complement to his doctrine of inspiration. Together they form the two pillars of Origen's interpretation of the Bible. Upon these foundations he built an elaborate structure with the aid of his indispensable machinery of allegory.

[1]Frag. on Ezek. 7.4, *PG* 13.789; cf. another fragment of the same collection, on Ezek 8.18, where the analogy of the juryman who refuses to spare the criminal is added to this one.
[2]*Hom. on Ezek.* V.1.

PART THREE

Origen as an Allegorist

9

The Three Senses of Scripture

THE fact that Origen divided the interpretation of Scripture into three senses is almost as well known as the fact that Caesar divided Gaul into three parts.[1] He tells us in the *Peri Archon* that as man is divided into three elements, body, soul and spirit, so the Scriptures yield three meanings, literal (fleshly), moral (psychic) and intellectual or spiritual, the last sense only for the 'graduated' (τελειος) Christian. And he tries to support this view by a reference to Prov. 22.20 f., where in the first verse the LXX, for 'Have I not written unto thee excellent things ?', wrongly renders 'Have I not written unto thee in a triple way ?' (τρισσῶς).[2] But in the same passage he makes it clear that not all passages in Scripture must be supposed to bear all three senses; some passages contain only spiritual and moral senses, some all three senses; he believes that this theory is signified by the six water-pots of stone, containing two or three firkins apiece (John 2.6). He sees these three senses foreshadowed in the three storeys of the ark.[3] And in his Introduction to the series of *Homilies on Psalms* 37–39 he professes to intend to distinguish 'where there are prophecies and the future is spoken of, where various spiritual doctrines are implied, and where the passage is ethical'.[4] As examples of his following out this scheme in his exegesis we may take two passages. The first is his exposition of the healing of two blind men at Jericho by Jesus, described in Matt. 20.29–34. First comes the acceptance of the passage as literally true. Next follow the spiritual or intellectual interpretation: the two beggars are Israel and Judah, Jericho is the world, and so on. And finally there is the moral or psychological interpretation: our eyes too

---

[1] For further information on this trichotomy, see de Faye, *Origène*, I, pp. 75–82; Prestige, *Fathers and Heretics*, ch. III; Turner, *The Pattern of Christian Truth*, pp. 258–73.
[2] *PA* IV.2.4,5. Origen (as Völker points out, 'Die Verwertung des Weisheits-Literatur', *ZKG* LXIV, p. 21) uses the same argument from this text in *Hom. on Lev.* X.2; *Hom. on Num.* IX.7; and *Hom. on Josh.* XXI.2.
[3] *Hom. on Gen.* II.3.
[4] *Hom. on Ps.* 37, I.1, *PG* 12.1319.

must be opened by the Word of God, we too must come out of our Jericho, etc.[1] The other passage is his treatment of the story of Lot's daughter's lying with their father (Gen. 19.30–38). Origen does not attempt to deny the historicity of this incident. He produces a number of ingenious extenuations of the conduct of these young women. He then copiously allegorizes the story in a 'spiritual' sense. An allegorization of some predecessors or contemporaries, who identified Lot with Christ and his daughters with the two Testaments, he first rejects on the grounds that Lot's descendants, Moab and Ammon, are not respectable enough to fit Christ.[2] He prefers to think of Lot as the law, his daughters as Jerusalem and Samaria, and his wife as 'the people that fell in the wilderness'. Then he harks back to the 'moral' interpretation: Lot becomes the mind, his wife the flesh, his daughters vainglory and pride, and the whole is applied to the religious experience of contemporary Christians.[3]

Sometimes, however, Origen writes as if there were only two senses in Scripture, the literal and the spiritual. He draws an analogy with the Incarnation; just as when the Word came among us clothed in flesh there were two elements in him, that which was visible in him (the flesh) and that which was invisible and perceived only by a few (the Godhead), so the word brought forth by the prophets was clothed in the literal meaning, while the spiritual meaning corresponded to the hidden divinity.[4] This is no doubt because in practice Origen tended to ignore the moral sense or to fuse it with the spiritual, no matter how carefully he might distinguish it in theory. Zöllig has observed this tendency, and admits that for most purposes we can reckon that Origen saw only two senses, the literal and a higher one leading us beyond its limits.[5]

Daniélou suggests that Origen derived his idea that there were three senses in Scripture, corresponding to the body, soul, and spirit of human nature, from Philo,[6] but there is nothing precisely corresponding to this trichotomy in Philo's treatment of Scripture. Philo says that the Thera-

---

[1]*Comm. on Matt.* XVI.9–11; cf. XVI.23.

[2]These allegorizers were presumably quite recent students of the Bible, for few would have so confidently placed the New Testament on a level with the Old before about 170, and not Gnostics, for they would not have thought the Old Testament fit for allegory.

[3]*Hom. on Gen.* V.4–6; cf. XVII.1–2. It is interesting to note that Philo had already allegorized this incident. *De Post. Caini* 175 f.; see above, p. 48.

[4]*Hom. on Lev.* I.1; but Origen goes on to draw out the spiritual and the moral sense as well as the literal later in this Homily.

[5]Zöllig, *Inspirationslehre*, pp. 101 f.

[6]*Origène*, p. 164; he describes the trichotomy as 'Philonic' without giving a reference.

peutae believe that all the Pentateuch 'is like a living being, and that the literal meanings take the place of the body, but the invisible intention latent in the text takes the place of the soul'.[1] It was Origen's own enterprising invention to make out of this dichotomy of interpretation a trichotomy, assisted, one may conjecture, by Platonic psychology; there is no clear support for this threefold division in Clement of Alexandria.[2] That Origen found authentic support for this threefold scheme in Scripture itself is, however, a suggestion which we must emphatically deny, even when the very questionable statement is adduced in its support that the Bible itself divides the personality into body, soul and spirit.[3] What Origen in fact does with his triple division of scriptural interpretation is not to emancipate Scripture from Philonic exegesis, but to go one better than Philo. He out-Philos Philo.[4] The result, though it may be methodologically impressive, is to remove the reader one stage further from the original meaning of Scripture.

The literal sense is, as we have seen, one which Origen tends to associate with Judaistic tendencies, and with unintelligent Literalists and the simpler folk generally, but he does admit that it is useful in a humble and subordinate capacity.[5] Clement of Alexandria before him had used the word 'Jewishly' ('Ιουδαϊκῶς) to mean 'literally',[6] and his work Against the Judaizers may well have dealt with the importance of not taking the Old Testament literally; the only extant fragment of it would suggest this.[7] And Clement also associates literalism with the adverbs 'incompetently, boorishly and carnally'.[8] Origen tells us that those who interpret references to the life of the heavenly kingdom literally are expounding Scripture 'in some sort of Jewish sense'.[9] He admits, however, that 'those who follow the letter of the gospel (that is, its literal

[1] De Vita Contempl. 78.

[2] For Clement's very vague expressions about the anatomy of biblical interpretation, see Tollinton, Selections from the Commentaries and Homilies of Origen, II, pp. 210–12, and Montdesert, Clement d'Alexandrie, pp. 153–62.

[3] De Lubac, Histoire et Esprit, pp. 153, 155 f., advances both these conjectures. We must also dissent from this scholar's suggestion (p. 156) that Origen's conception of the πνεῦμα (and perhaps indirectly, of the 'pneumatic' interpretation) is genuinely founded upon St Paul's thought.

[4] 'It expresses the rhythm of the Mystery which all Scripture contains and reveals. . . . It obeyed a profound logic and it is very suitable for distinguishing Christian exegesis from Philonic exegesis, which could constitute a temptation for it.' De Lubac, op. cit., p. 159.

[5] For the literal sense generally see also Turner, The Pattern of Christian Truth, pp. 283–91, and for the terms that Origen uses to describe it see Zöllig, Inspirationslehre, p. 102 n. 4.

[6] E.g. Paed. I.6. 34, PG 8.292.

[7] Frag. 36, GCS III, p. 218; PG 9.768.

[8] Quis Dives 18, σκαιῶς, ἀγροίκως, σαρκίνως.

[9] PA II.11.3.

a different gospel for simple folks?

account) are saved, because even the bare literal narration of the gospel
is adequate for salvation to the simpler folk'.[1] Though the literal sense
should often be allegorized, even the literal sense of passages intended
for allegory was often intended to edify those who could understand
nothing beyond it.[2] Among the three interpretations of the parable of
the Workers in the Vineyard which Origen gives, one is expressly designed for those who find allegorization perplexing.[3]

Very occasionally Origen will even refuse to desert the literal sense
and allegorize. Discussing the command of our Lord given to the rich
young man to sell all and follow him (Matt. 19.21), Origen refuses to be
convinced by the argument that this should be allegorized because it is
an impossible command. There are instances of its being fulfilled in
Greek history and in the Book of Acts.[4] And similarly in handling the
text, 'And every one that hath left houses, or brethren, or sisters, or
father, or mother, or children, or lands, for my name's sake, shall receive a hundredfold' etc. (Matt. 19.29) he is not prepared to allegorize
'houses' and 'lands', though he is willing to do this in the case of 'father'
and 'mother'.[5] Generally throughout his *Commentary on Matthew*, his
last major work of exegesis, Origen shows an unusual respect for the
literal sense and tends to introduce allegory a little cautiously and
apologetically.

More often, however, Origen will insist that the literal sense must be
retained as well as the allegorical. He tells us that one of the functions
of the literal sense is to attract people to study the Bible so that they may
eventually venture upon the allegorical sense.[6] The retirement of Jesus
to a place called Ephraim (John 11.54) is, taken literally, a lesson to the
Christian to avoid unnecessary persecution; but the passage must be
elaborately allegorized also.[7] The reference to the Samaritan woman in
John 4.28, 'So the woman left her water-pot and went away into the
city', is worth interpreting literally because it shows how anxious the
woman was to proclaim Christ to her fellow-citizens; but allegorized it
means that she leaves the false and boasted water-pots of heresy for the
pure water of Christ.[8] Before he allegorizes the account of the healing

---

[1] *Comm. on Matt.* Comm. Ser. 27.
[2] *PA* IV.2.8.
[3] *Comm. on Matt.* XV.36 f.
[4] *Ibid.*, XV.15.
[5] *Ibid.*, XV.25; 'father' and 'mother' mean 'blameless bishops' and 'irre-
proachable presbyters'; the adjectives are significant of Origen's views on the
authority of ministers.
[6] *Contra Celsum* VII.60.
[7] *Comm. on John* XXVIII.23 f.
[8] *Ibid.*, XIII.29.

of the two blind men (Matt. 20.29–34) he takes care to explain that he believes in the literal sense also.[1] In one place he even says that it might be profitable for some to believe in the literal sense even though it is not true; so many people have fallen on evil ways when they find that the references to hell in the Bible are not to be taken literally that he is driven to this conclusion.[2]

But there are in Origen's works a number of instances, which have attracted the attention of many scholars, where he declares uncompromisingly that the literal sense cannot be true, and that the passage must be taken in a wholly spiritual (not even in a moral) sense. Many of such passages occur in the legislation of the Pentateuch. The law of the firstfruits (Num. 13), for instance, should be observed literally; but not all laws are to be so followed. There are distinctions between laws; some are called 'commandments', some 'judgements', some 'laws'. 'Commandments' are usually to be taken literally (e.g. the Decalogue); 'laws' are usually to be allegorized (e.g. the laws of the Passover or of unleavened bread). But some precepts are to be taken literally and also to be allegorized, for instance the commandment about marriage, which was confirmed as literally binding by our Lord but allegorically interpreted as a mystery by St Paul. Again, Abraham did literally have Sarah as his wife and Hagar as his concubine, but his actions were also allegorical.[3] Other examples of legal ordinances designed purely for allegory are 'Let no man go out of his place on the seventh day' (Ex. 16.29) and the commands in Lev. 13 and 14 about identifying leprosy on the skin or on the wall or in the warp of wool.[4] In the *Peri Archon* he has a long passage giving a much fuller list of texts which in his view cannot be taken literally. He begins with some incidents recorded in the Bible which he is confident nobody but a fool could ever imagine to have taken place literally: the existence of 'morning and evening' on the first three days of creation; the planting of the garden of Eden; God 'walking in the garden in the cool of the day'; Adam and Eve eating the apple. In the New Testament such an incident is the devil taking Jesus up to a high mountain and showing him all the kingdoms of the world and the glory of them. Then follows an interesting list of unreasonable or impossible ordinances in the law which are simply intended to be allegorized. Unreasonable commandments are the prohibition of eating the kite (Lev. 11.14), which nobody could want to eat anyway; and the command to

[1] *Comm. on Matt.* XVI.9.
[2] *Hom. on Jer.* XX.4.
[3] *Hom. on Num.* XI.1.
[4] *Comm. on Rom.* I.10; *Hom. on Gen.* II.6.

kill all Jewish children still uncircumcised after the eighth day, which
would, taken literally, entail irrational cruelty. Impossible commandments are represented by the command to eat the chamois (Deut.
14.5),[1] which Origen alleges to be a non-existent animal; and the prohibition against eating the gier-eagle (Deut. 14.12 LXX: γρύψ) which
Origen claims has never been caught or tamed by man; and the ban on
leaving the house or carrying a burden on the sabbath, an ordinance
which nobody can fulfil literally. Examples of such impossible commands designed only for allegory are to be found in our Lord's teaching
too. One of these is 'Salute no one by the way' (Luke 10.4); another is
the command to turn the left cheek when the right is struck (Matt. 5.39),
which is stigmatized as impossible on the odd ground that it is always
the left cheek that is struck; Alexandria must have been singularly
deficient in left-handed men of uneven temper! Another impossible
phrase is 'If thy right eye causeth thee to stumble' (Matt. 5.29), and
another the rule laid down by Paul, 'Was any man called being circumcised? Let him not become uncircumcised' (I Cor. 7.18). But Origen
adds that we must not think that no real historical events took place nor
that no law is to be observed literally, and gives some examples of literal
truth in both event and law.[2]

A few more examples of passages intended in Origen's view solely
for allegorical and not for literal interpretation can be gleaned from
Origen's works, taken both from the Old and the New Testaments. 'As
a thorn goes up into the hand of a drunkard' (Prov. 26.9) is one such,
and another is the statement that the sound of hammer and axe was not
heard in the making of Solomon's temple (I Kings 6.7),[3] and another is
the statement in Ps. 37.17, 'The arms of the wicked shall be broken.'[4]
Several more commands of our Lord are included in this category. The
command to forgive your brother unto seventy times seven (Matt.
18.21 f.) would be absurd if it were taken literally.[5] None of the reasons
given by Jesus for people becoming eunuchs (Matt. 19.12) can be taken
literally.[6] The same necessity applies to the command to the apostles to
have only one coat (Luke 9.3), where Origen believes that Jesus was

---

[1]LXX καμηλοπάρδαλιν, but Origen read τραγέλαφος.
[2]This long list of impossibilities destined solely for allegory is to be found in
PA IV. 3.1–4. The refusal of literal force to Matt. 5.29 is repeated in Hom. on
Num. XXV.3 and Comm. on Matt. XV.2.
[3]Hom. on Gen. II.6.
[4]Hom. on Ps. 37, III.9.
[5]Comm. on Matt. XIV.5.
[6]Ibid., XV.1; cf. XV.2, where three of the instances quoted from separate
passages here are bracketed together.

deliberately contravening the literal sense of Lev. 8.7 f.;[1] and to 'Let him that hath no sword sell his coat and buy one',[2] and to the injunction, 'But thou, when thou fastest, anoint thy head and wash thy face', etc. (Matt. 6.17 f.).[3]

Origen's attitude to the literal sense has caused some scholars to conclude that he gave it a wholly subordinate and insignificant place, and has instigated others to spring to his defence. 'When he mentions the literal meaning, he deals with it in a few phrases,' writes de Faye; 'he gives the impression of noticing it only to clear his conscience. But what is more serious, he overwhelms it with criticism. More often he declares it to be absurd; it is inconsistent with other passages of Scripture; it is unworthy of God. This sense is provisional; it is good enough for Jews; a Christian cannot be satisfied with it.'[4] Enough evidence has perhaps been already produced in these pages to show that this is a rather exaggerated presentation of Origen's depreciation of the literal sense. Bigg, on the other hand, claimed that Origen saw that the 'real and natural sense of the Bible . . . is the foundation of everything'.[5] Cadiou makes the same claim: 'The allegory is never without some relation to the literal sense.'[6] Prat, alleging the same justification, goes so far as to say that Origen never said that there were passages in the Bible devoid of any literal sense; the allegorical was always based upon the literal.[7] De Lubac (as perhaps might be expected) goes furthest of all and maintains that when Origen says that we cannot take any passage in its literal sense, or that because of its incomprehensibility, absurdity or inconsistency it is intended to have a spiritual sense, he means no more than that we cannot take this passage in *only* its literal sense, but must add the spiritual to the literal sense.[8] I cannot, I confess, see the force of any of these arguments in defence of Origen's treatment of the literal sense. De Lubac's contention is clearly wrong; Origen could not have made it plainer that, in the passages which he mentions as examples of places where the literal meaning is not intended, the literal sense cannot have any force at all, with or without the allegorical sense. As for the suggestion that in Origen's exposition the allegorical sense was based or built

---

[1]*Hom. on Lev.* VI.3.
[2]*Ibid.*, VII.5.
[3]*Ibid.*, X.2.
[4]De Faye, *Origène*, I, p. 110.
[5]*The Christian Platonists of Alexandria*, p. 170.
[6]*La Jeunesse d'Origène*, p. 46. Montdesert takes a similar attitude, *Clement d'Alexandrie*, pp. 143 f.
[7]*Origène, le Theologien et l'Exégète*, Introd., p. xvi.
[8]De Lubac, *Histoire et Esprit*, ch. IV, section 3.

on the literal sense, this argument seems to me either untrue or meaning-less. It is certainly true that when, for instance, Origen allegorized the Samaritan woman leaving the water-pot to mean the Christian soul leaving heresy he preserved enough resemblance between the text and its allegorical meaning to say that because *a* left *b* in the original therefore *x* left *y* in the allegory; he did not maintain that *a* leaving *b* was an allegory of *x seeking y*, or of something which had no connection at all with the original. But this is only to say that in his allegory he did not indulge in a positively surrealist irrationality. The same could just as well be said of all other allegory, Philonic, Hellenistic or any other sort at all. Indeed this is only to say that what Origen practised was allegory and not lunacy. If the contention of Bigg, Cadiou and de Lubac, how-ever, means that the allegorical sense in Origen's exposition has any necessary or justifiable connection with the literal sense, then any im-partial reader surveying the evidence in these pages will see that this is untrue. In fact I cannot see that any defence of Origen's treatment of the literal sense can be based on the connection which he establishes between the original text and the spiritual interpretation of it, because it is obvious that in the vast majority of cases such a connection exists only in Origen's imagination. Even if we ignore this obvious truth, however, we shall see that there are some allegorizations in Origen's works, those which we may call 'conventional', where even he abandons the attempt to see any connection between the original and its alle-gory, and explicitly pursues a purely arbitrary form of interpre-tation.

The 'moral' sense as articulated by Origen is almost exactly the sense into which Philo before him had allegorized the Bible, that is to say it is largely psychological and ethical.[1] Daniélou calls it '*ecclesial*' and liturgical,[2] because it is mainly applied to the conduct and the piety of the ordinary Christian. This too is why its appearances are more numerous in the Homilies than in the Commentaries. De Lubac aptly describes it as 'the application of the text made to the soul, without a Christian assumption being obviously introduced'.[3] The two disciples bidden to fetch the ass for the entry of Jesus into Jerusalem represent, in Origen's view, the 'moral' and 'spiritual' ways of allegorizing Scripture: 'for one applies the writings for the healing of the soul and allegorizes them for its benefit, and the other sets out the good things and true which are to come

[1] Cf. Zöllig, *Inspirationslehre*, pp. 110 f.; Prestige, *Fathers and Heretics*, p. 119.
[2] *Origène*, p. 166.
[3] De Lubac, *Histoire et Esprit*, p. 141.

through the medium of those things which lie in shadow.'[1] In short, the 'moral' sense deals with direct edification whereas the 'spiritual' consists of mystical and theological exegesis. He chooses as an example of the application of the 'psychic' or 'moral' sense to be found in the Bible St Paul's interpretation in I Cor. 9.9 f. of the text in Deut. 25.4, 'Thou shalt not muzzle the ox when he treadeth out the corn,' to mean that the Christian community is morally bound to support its apostle.[2] But though in some of his Homilies Origen does conscientiously complete his threefold interpretation by including the 'moral' sense of the passage under review, and though he does occasionally draw out this sense in his Commentaries, on the whole the 'moral' sense plays no significant part in Origen's exegesis, not because he had no occasion to draw edifying or devotional lessons from the text of the Bible but because in the practical work of expounding Scripture he found it impossible to maintain the distinction between the 'moral' and the 'spiritual' sense, and the former became absorbed in the latter.

We may therefore regard the 'spiritual' sense as the allegorical sense *par excellence*.[3] It is not easy to describe the characteristics of this sense because in Origen's hands it becomes so protean. Origen describes this sense as concerned wholly with the fulfilment of types and the shadows

[1] *Comm. on John* X.28.

[2] *PA* IV.2.6. Compare the treatment of this text above, pp. 78 f. W. den Boer, in an article in *Vig. Chr.* I, pp. 150–67, 'Hermeneutic Problems in Early Christian Literature', adverts to Origen's taking of this text in I Cor. as an example of the 'psychic' sense, and uses it to support his argument that there is no clear distinction between typology and allegory in the early Church and that no clear distinction between allegory and other sorts of interpretation was made by Clement and Origen. He says (p. 162) that in this case Origen describes as using the 'psychic' sense what we would call allegorizing, and points out that in *Contra Celsum* I.53 Origen describes the prophecy of the Suffering Servant in Deutero-Isaiah as προφητεία ἐνάργης and not as allegory. I do not think that den Boer has really understood the situation. Typology as Clement and Origen inherited it was obviously distinct from the Hellenistic, peculiarly Philonic type of allegory which they were using (Philo is scarcely mentioned in den Boer's article). Paul's allegory is in fact almost wholly typology, Origen's and Clement's a mixture of traditional typology and Philonic allegory. The 'psychic' sense was to Origen as much allegorizing as the 'pneumatic', but it was allegorizing to produce a moral rather than a doctrinal meaning. Both 'psychic' and 'pneumatic' senses are purely Philonic, and neither can be identified with primitive Jewish or Christian allegory. The Suffering Servant passage was not regarded as typological because Origen, with some justification, looked on it as direct prediction or prevision. Even today one hesitates to call it typology; it is not typology in the original Jewish-Christian sense.

[3] For a full account of the terms employed by Origen to describe this sense, see Zöllig, *Inspirationslehre*, p. 108 n. 1; de Lubac, *Histoire et Esprit*, ch. IV, section 3; and Cadiou, *La Jeunesse d'Origène*, p. 54 (a note on ἀναγώγη) and p. 96 (a note on γνῶσις); also see above, pp. 39–41, for Philo's vocabulary, from which Origen borrowed freely on this subject.

Interpretation must begin at lamb's head and end at its feet

of heavenly things to come. In support of his use of it he quotes I Cor.
10.1–11 ('These things happened to us by way of example'), Heb. 8.5
(the quotation of Ex. 25.40, 'See that thou make all things according to
the pattern shewn to thee on the mount'), St Paul's allegorization of
Sarah and Hagar (Gal. 4), and Col. 2.16 f. ('the shadow of things to
come').[1] The content of this allegorical sense he defined as knowledge
'concerning the secret mysteries of (God's) activities towards men',
which means in fact the speculative theology of Origen and his school.[2]
He gives a list too of the features in the Bible under which, as under a
veil, the allegorical sense is hidden: the account of 'material created
things' such as the creation of man, the biblical account of the beginning of history and the beginning of the chosen race, 'the wicked, lustful
and greedy acts of the lawless and irreligious', the accounts of 'wars, of
victors and vanquished', and 'through the written legislation the laws
of truth itself are foretold.'[3] To decide which bits of the Bible are literal
and which allegorical, demands, he says, great study and experience and
one should 'as far as possible search out from words which are similar
the meaning, scattered all over the Bible, of that part which is according
to the literal sense impossible'. Again, when we find a piece which is
purely 'spiritual' we must allegorize it along with the surrounding context of literally true narrative, because all Scripture has the "spiritual"
sense, but not all the literal'.[4] An elaborate allegorization of the Passover
lamb produces what is apparently another rule about this 'spiritual'
sense. It is feeble and insipid, Origen says, to interpret literally the
Passover lamb: 'He who takes the raw meat of the Scripture for cooking
must be careful not to take what is written in that insipid and watery
and tame sense.' Our interpretation must begin at the lamb's head, 'the
highest and leading doctrines concerning the heavenly things', and
finish at its feet, 'the most material or terrestrial things or evil spirits or
unclean demons'. The inward parts must not be omitted. 'And as we
must approach the whole of Scripture as one body, we must not break
or cut up the most sinewy and strongest joints of the harmony of its
whole system, as do those who as far as their own profit is concerned
break the unity of the Spirit in all the Scriptures.' This complicated
allegory ends with the enunciation of what looks like a general principle
for allegory. 'It must not be thought that historical narratives are allegories of historical events nor material features of material things, but

---

[1] *PA* IV.2.6.
[2] *Ibid.*, IV.2.7; see *Origen's Doctrine of Tradition*, pp. 78 f., 117 f.
[3] *PA* IV.2.8.   [4] *Ibid.*, IV. 3.5.

anagogical – referring to celestial things

the material features are allegories of spiritual things and the historical events of intellectual things.'[1]

Statements such as these suggest that Origen allegorized according to a regular and objective set of rules, however oddly these rules may have been conceived. But in fact no such rules can be deduced in Origen's application of allegory. His use of it breaks all rules and is unchartably subjective. He is determined to deduce his own theology from the Bible and though he does observe some limits in this process these limits are not imposed by any rules of allegory. Zöllig attempted to draw up such a set of rules, but their miscellaneous appearance and their insufficiency to cover all the examples of Origen's allegorization testify to the futility of such an attempt.[2] There is no difference between the 'spiritual' (πνευματικός) and the 'intellectual' (νοητός) sense in Origen's use.[3] And Zöllig himself agrees that though Origen often uses the word agoge (e.g. ἡ κατ' ἀγωγὴν ἀλληγορία), his use of it does not necessarily imply the sense in later, mediaeval, theology called the *anagogical*, referring to heavenly, celestial things in contrast to those which are spiritual in a general sense.[4] Whatever Origen's theory of allegory may have been, it is quite inaccurate to call his application of it systematic. We may give an account of the characteristics of his 'spiritual' sense, but we must not pretend that we can discern any rules that govern it.

We can sometimes discern within his use of the allegorical sense different levels of allegory. Some of these are illustrated in his treatment of the remark of Jesus about the Temple recorded in Matt. 24.1 f. ('There shall not be left one stone upon another which shall not be cast down'). The temple, says Origen, is the human race and the disciples implore Christ not to leave it; again, the temple is each individual, who can gradually fall into ruin if Christ is not in him; finally, the temple is the Scriptures of the Old Testament, whose literal sense must be destroyed in order that the spiritual sense may be built up.[5] When he has expounded the parable of the King's Supper (Matt. 22.1–14), treating it as an allegory, significant in every detail, he describes this as the obvious meaning of the parable and goes on to look for something even

---

[1] *Comm. on John* X.18. The last sentence runs: οὐ γὰρ νομιστέον τὰ ἱστορικὰ ἱστορικῶν εἶναι τύπους καὶ τὰ σωματικὰ σωματικῶν, ἀλλὰ τὰ σωματικὰ πνευματικῶν καὶ τὰ ἱστορικὰ νοητῶν.

[2] Zöllig, *Inspirationslehre*, pp. 115–17.

[3] Prat, *Origène, le Théologien et l'Exégète*, Introd., p. xvii, says that the νοητός is identical with the ψυχικός, but I do not think that this can be maintained.

[4] Zöllig, *op. cit.*, pp. 109 f.

[5] *Comm. on Matt.* Comm. Ser. 30 f. The last interpretation is somebody else's, which is interesting.

literal sense of OT must be destroyed in order ...

more profound (βαθύτερον) in it.[1] In his treatment of the incident of Jeremiah at the potter's house (Jer. 18.1–12) he has occasion to remark, 'Each reader interprets the words as best he can, he who reads superficially taking the meaning from them as it were from a spring flowing on the level, and the reader with the profounder understanding drawing it out as from a well. Certainly both can be edified, since the same passage is for one a spring and for another a well.' The superficial interpretation, he says, takes the passage as a reference to the resurrection of the body, the profounder as a statement of the destiny and possibilities of the two races, Christians and Jews.[2] The chief difference between the two methods of interpretation seems to be that the second is rather more complicated and less obvious an allegory than the first. They are both allegorical.

In a great many cases Origen resorts to allegory simply because he will not recognize an ordinary metaphor when he sees one, or, if he recognizes it, will not leave it alone, but in a heavy-handed way must rationalize it into an allegory. 'I came not to send peace, but a sword' (Matt. 10.34) means that Christ 'severs the injurious union of body and soul'.[3] He calls Ezekiel's metaphor of the king of Egypt as a dragon 'spiritual', pointing out carefully that the dragon could not be a literal one.[4] Discussing John 13.4, 'Jesus layeth aside his garments and took a towel and girded himself,' Origen sees in this act the symbolic enacting of the self-emptying which the act obviously signified, but he cannot leave the incident alone; he insists that the 'garments' must be allegorized.[5] He had, of course, to contend with a school of appallingly unimaginative literalists, as we have seen, but one often gains the impression that his answer to the literalists who cannot recognize metaphorical speech when they see it is an allegory which is almost equally unimaginative. The literalists insist upon taking literally references to bread and wine in the Bible, in such passages as Prov. 9.1–5, and the description of the adornment of Jerusalem with jewels in prophetic passages (such as Isa. 54.11 f.). Origen in reply asserts that, on the contrary, all these features must be allegorized, the bread, the wine, the sapphires, the carbuncles and all![6]

This determination to explain every conceivable figurative expression

[1] *Comm. on Matt.* XVII.15–17.
[2] *Hom. on Jer.* XVIII.4. The editor, Klostermann, points out that Origen derived the image of the stream and the well from Philo, *De Ebrietate* 112 f.
[3] *Comm. on John* I.32.
[4] *Ibid.*, VI.48; the passage referred to is Ezek. 32.2.
[5] *Ibid.*, XXXII.4.
[6] *PA* II.11.2 f.

and every difficulty by allegory sometimes causes Origen to see difficulties and figurative language where they do not exist. He accounts on
theological grounds for the difference between 'shoe' in John 1.27 and
'shoes' in Matt. 3.11.[1] Allegory can indeed become a devouring passion
with Origen, distorting all his exegetical judgement. He indulges in
elaborate and useless allegorization of every feature, every word, of the
Feeding of the Five Thousand.[2] On the phrase 'Thy truth reacheth unto
the clouds' (Ps. 36.5) he points out the 'clouds' cannot really mean
'lifeless clouds' incapable of receiving truth; 'clouds' must mean 'holy
people' and this transmutation applies also to the absence of clouds
producing a drought (I Kings 18) or to the clouds being commanded
not to rain on God's vineyard (Isa. 5.6).[3] The beautiful line in Lam. 1.2,
'She weepeth sore in the night', brings Origen against the striking use of
figurative language. He has no literary feeling and taste, unlike Clement
of Alexandria, and this phrase puzzles him. He first points out, labori-
ously, that a city cannot literally weep. Then he supposes that the city
is used metaphorically for its inhabitants, who could weep in the night.
All this he calls specifically the literal sense. Then he allegorizes the
passage to refer to the soul which weeps, exiled in confusion (Babylon)
away from its true home.[4] Origen is no poet and allegory is more often
than not the enemy of poetry.

On more than one occasion in his works Philo suggests that wherever
the word 'woman' occurs in the Scriptures it means 'sensible apprehension' (αἴσθησις).[5] Origen took full advantage of this hint. Not only does
he suggest that where 'woman' occurs it has a regular conventional
meaning;[6] but it is possible to gather from his works a long list of such
identifications, which we may call examples of conventional allegory.
'Horse' in the Bible usually means 'voice';[7] 'today' means 'the present
age';[8] 'leaven' means 'teaching';[9] 'silver' and 'trumpet' mean 'word';[10]

[1] Comm. on John VI.37.
[2] Comm. on Matt. XI.1.
[3] Hom. on Jer. VIII.3.
[4] Hom. on Lam., frag. 10. At one point Origen admits, perhaps a little shame-
facedly, that allegory can be indulged in quite unnecessarily, simply for the
pleasure of it: he distinguishes between allegorical explanation which is γυμνα-
σίας χάριν λογικῆς and that which is δογματικός (Comm. on Matt. XV.33).
[5] De Leg. Alleg. III.49; De Cherubim 41; De Spec. Leg. I.201.
[6] Comm. on Matt. XVII.31 and Hom. on Gen. I.15; 'woman' means the human
soul; Hom. on Ex. II.1, the flesh and the passion of the flesh. Zöllig, Inspirationslehre, p. 117, and Völker, Das Vollkommenheitsideal, p. 46, have noted
Origen's addiction to conventional allegory.
[7] Comm. on John II.5.
[8] Ibid., XXXII.32; cf. Comm. on Matt. XV.31.
[9] Comm. on Matt. XII.6.
[10] Ibid., Comm. Ser. 52; Hom. on Jer. V.16.

'clouds' (as we have already seen) mean 'holy ones';[1] 'feet' means 'the counsel by which we tread the journey of life';[2] 'well' means 'the teaching of the Bible';[3] 'linen' means 'chastity';[4] 'thighs' mean 'beginning';[5] 'unmixed wine' means 'misfortune';[6] 'bottle' means 'body';[7] 'secret' and 'treasury' mean 'the reason'.[8] In one or two of these instances Origen is following his usual habit of turning a metaphor widely used in the Bible into an allegory. But in the majority of them he is treating this allegory as purely or almost purely conventional; that is to say, the connection between the original word and the allegory rests on nothing but the arbitrary decision of the allegorist. This is the furthest stretch to which Origen pushes his device of allegory, and he could not have pushed it further without reducing it to palpable nonsense. It in fact, if pursued logically, transforms the Bible into a divine cross-word puzzle the solution to whose clues is locked in Origen's bosom.

The allegorical meanings which Origen extracts from his conventional allegories suggest that he is allegorizing very much in the tradition of Philo and of Philo's faithful disciple, Clement of Alexandria. There can be little doubt that Origen owes much to Clement in his doctrine of the secret teaching which he thinks he can extract from the Bible.[9] 'A common tradition, environment and philosophical background' is not enough to account alone for the resemblances between the two theologians.[10] Völker has shown that Origen follows Clement in appealing to Prov. 1.6 as a support for allegorizing Scripture; that Clement reads in Prov. 2.5 ('Then shalt thou . . . find the knowledge of the Lord') 'sensibility' (αἴσθησιν) for the 'knowledge' (ἐπίγνωσιν) of the Septuagint, and interprets it of the contrast between worldly and sacred knowledge,[11] and that Origen follows him in reading 'divine sensibility' (αἴσθησιν θείαν) and interprets it of 'the higher and not material sensibility' (Contra Celsum VII.34; PA I.1.9; IV.4.10); and that Clement

[1]Hom. on Jer. VIII.3; Comm. on Ps. 68.34, PG 12.1509; frag. on I Thess. 4.16 f., PG 14.1302.
[2]Comm. on Rom. III.4.
[3]Hom. on Gen. X.5.
[4]Hom. on Lev. IV.6.
[5]Frag. on S. of S., PG 13.212.
[6]Comm. on Ps. 60.3, PG 12.1480.
[7]Ibid., 119.83, PG 12.1601.
[8]Frag. on Ezek. 8.12, PG 13.797.
[9]See Origen's Doctrine of Tradition, chs. IV and V. For other views on the relationship between Origen and Clement, see Molland, The Conception of the Gospel in Alexandrian Theology, p. 166; Cadiou, 'Dictionnaires Antiques dans l'Œuvre d'Origène', REG XLV, p. 274, and La Jeunesse d'Origène, pp. 7, 12, 92.
[10]So Crouzel, Théologie de l'Image de Dieu chez Origène, p. 70.
[11]Strom. I.4.27, PG 8.717.

uses Prov. 10.17 ('He that forsaketh reproof erreth', παιδεία . . .
ἀνεξέλεγκτος πλανᾶται) as a proof of the necessity of the cultured
Christian being acquainted with philosophy, and Origen uses the same
text to show that the 'graduated' man must know dialectic (*Contra
Celsum* VI.7).[1] Origen knows Clement's exegesis and borrows from it
freely, though for reasons which it is not easy to conjecture he never
chooses to mention Clement by name.

But Clement's influence on Origen's allegorical treatment of the
Bible is slight compared with the influence of Philo upon Origen in this
particular. Some account of Philo's use of allegory has been given
already.[2] His whole tendency is to resolve the incidents and indeed the
words of the Bible into ethical sentiments or psychological analyses or
philosophical speculations, in contrast to the more conservative practice
of Jewish allegory or Jewish typology which tended either to relate all
scriptural passages to some point in the Torah or to see them typologically as foreshadowing events to take place in the Messianic age. Philo
will, for instance, identify Judah and Issachar with the bdellium and
onyx stone of Gen. 2.14 and then allegorize them into the man who is
thankful to God and the man who does practical deeds of virtue.[3] To
him Pharaoh is 'the atheistic and pleasure-loving disposition';[4] Egypt is
'the land of the body',[5] and so on. Clement of Alexandria is almost
wholly controlled by this type of allegory.[6] Völker says that in all the
instances of Clement's use of the Wisdom Literature he can find only
two examples of genuinely Christological interpretation; all the others
are Philonic and not even always recognizably Christian.[7] Origen is not
so entirely under the influence of Philo; but several direct borrowings
from Philo can be traced in his works (we have had occasion to note
several of them) and more impressive than occasional borrowings are
innumerable instances of Origen himself using allegorical interpretations
of a Philonic sort which are not to be found in Philo himself.[8] The thorn

[1]Völker, 'Die Verwertung des Weisheits-Literatur', *ZKG* LXIV, pp. 12 f.,
21, 23, 26.
[2]See above, pp. 46–53.
[3]*De Leg. Alleg.* I.80.
[4]*Ibid.*, III.212.
[5]*De Agric.* 88.
[6]See above, pp. 117–20.
[7]Völker, 'Die Verwertung des Weisheits-Literatur', p. 19 n. 133. The two
instances of Christological interpretation are *Strom.* I.17.81 and III.17.103,
PG 8.796 and 1208.
[8]'A well-known instance of his direct borrowings is his repetition of the
observation made by Philo that everybody who celebrates his birthday in the
Bible is a bad character, *Comm. on Matt.* X.22 (where Origen applies this observation to Herod Antipas) and frag. on Gen., *PG* 12.129. For further informa-

in the hand of the drunkard of Prov. 26.9 means wickedness in the fool's soul, and laws against setting fire to corn (Ex. 22.6) represent the Logos entering the soul of the wicked.[1] The cleansing of the Temple means Jesus driving unworthy thoughts of gain and unworthy traffickers in spiritual things from the souls of churchmen, or else his ejecting from the soul of the believer earthy things (the oxen), unintellectual things (the sheep), the dumb, unstable things (the doves).[2] 'My fatlings are killed' (Matt. 22.4) refers to a full and satisfying explanation of some theological problem.[3] The distinction that Moses established between clean and unclean foods means 'the different characters of rational beings',[4] an idea which we have traced back, through Theophilus of Antioch and the *Epistle of Barnabas*, to the *Letter of Aristeas*. The verse in Jeremiah (3.9), 'she committed adultery with stone and with stocks' elicits the comment, 'When we sin, we do nothing else but become stony-hearted and commit adultery with the stone.'[5] The veil which St Paul describes as lying on the hearts of those who will not accept Christ (II Cor. 3.12–18) Origen interprets in wholly moral terms; he urges his hearers to put away their sins and to 'turn to the Lord'; it is we who put the veil of wickedness over our wills.[6] The five kings of the Midianites killed by the children of Israel (Num. 31.8) are five vices exterminated from his life by the Christian.[7]

One peculiarly Philonic trait in Origen's allegory is his practice of representing the Bible itself as speaking of the necessity of speculative allegory. Wherever he finds a contrast drawn between 'spirit' and 'letter' in St Paul's letters he interprets this as the contrast between the 'spiritual' and the literal interpretation of Scripture.[8] The case of Levirate marriage cited by the Sadducean interlocutor of our Lord (Matt. 22.23–33) Origen allegorizes so that the woman is the human soul and two of the husbands represent the letter of the law (which dies)

---

tion on Origen's debt to Philo, see Daniélou, *Origène*, pp. 179–87, and de Lubac, *Histoire et Esprit*, pp. 146, 160 f. Zöllig, *Inspirationslehre*, pp. 121 f., discusses the same subject, but I cannot entirely agree with his conclusion that Origen 'placed the use of allegory as it was practised in his day on new and more solid principles, and impressed the stamp of his individuality on this art by means of many modifications and particularly a stricter regulation'.

[1]*Comm. on John* VI.58.   [2]*Ibid*, X.23 f.
[3]*Comm. on Matt.* XVII.22.
[4]*PE* XXVIII.12. Cf. the passage in *Hom. on Gen.* I.8 f. cited by Bardy, referred to above, p. 109 n. 3.
[5]*Hom. on Jer.* IV.6.   [6]*Ibid.*, V.8 f.
[7]*Hom. on Num.* XXV.3.
[8]E.g. *Contra Celsum* VI.70.

and the 'spiritual law' (which the soul marries).[1] The kingdom of God
often means the Scriptures, and to repent at the coming of the kingdom
means to change from the literal to the allegorical interpretation of
Scripture.[2] The bones or sepulchres of the prophets (Matt. 23.29–36)
signify the literal interpretation of the prophets' words in the Old
Testament; the soul and spirit of the prophets is the 'intellectual' interpretation of the Old Testament. The Pharisees, attending only to the
literal interpretation, kill the intellectual. In Zech. 9.9 f., for instance,
Christ is prophesied as entering Jerusalem on an ass and a colt and as
destined to 'cut off the chariot from Ephraim and the horse from Jerusalem'. These words were not literally fulfilled, but allegorically, in the
refutation of heretics.[3]

We can in fact see how this tendency to interpret passages in the
Bible as referring to the necessity of allegorizing has caused Origen to
revise in this Philonic sense in a late work his exposition of a passage
which he had in an earlier work treated in a traditional way. 'She is a
tree of life (LXX: ξύλον ζωῆς) to them that lay hold of her' he had
in the Commentary on John (XX.36) referred in a traditional manner to
Christ; but in the later Homilies on Exodus (VII.1) he interpreted this
image, along with a traditional Christological passage, the narrative of
the incident at Mara, thus: 'the bitterness of the letter of the law is
changed into sweetness of spiritual understanding.'[4] Both Hippolytus
and Origen interpreted the Song of Solomon in a way distinctly reminiscent of Philonic exegesis.[5] Origen professes to interpret this book
'either of the Church under the name of the bride or the bridegroom or
of the soul in union with the Word of God',[6] but with what we might
call a traditional typological interpretation he mingles much psychology
and philosophical speculation.[7] He interprets in his own characteristic

---

[1]Comm. on Matt. XVII.31.   [2]Ibid., X.14.   [3]Ibid., Comm. Ser. 27.
[4]Both these passages are noticed by Völker 'Die Verwertung des Weisheits-
Literatur', ZKG LXIV, p. 22 n. 142 and p. 28. But, rather confusingly, Völker
does not point out the contrast, and does not seem to realize that one passage
was written considerably later than the other. The text is Prov. 3.18.
[5]I cannot find any convincing evidence that Origen borrowed from Hippolytus in his work on the Song of Solomon. Cadiou (La Jeunesse d'Origène, pp. 65–
8) is confident that Hippolytus had an influence on Origen, relying on his exposition of this book for evidence. He also adduces Origen's imitation of Hippolytus
in expounding the headings of the Psalms. But Melito had already indulged in
this practice, and we can be sure that Origen had read Melito's works. See above,
pp. 115–17 for Hippolytus and pp. 108 f. for Melito.
[6]Comm. on S. of S. I, on S. of S. 1.1.
[7]See, for instance, this rather unpleasant piece of exposition, on S. of S.
5.14, 'His body (LXX κοιλία), is as ivory work': κοιλία ἐστὶ τοῦ Λόγου ὅτι
χωρητικοὶ τῶν μυστηρίων, τουτέστιν κοῖλοι πρὸς ὑποδόχην, frag. on S. of S.,
PG 13.208.

way the incident of Moses lifting up his hands during the battle between Israel Amalek (Ex.17.11), which as we have seen, was a traditional Christian type. 'The Amalekites and all the unseen enemies will be defeated, but the Israelite-principle in us will conquer', if we lift up our hands to God.[1] Or the hands are our deeds done according to godliness; if they are abundant we are raising our hands to God and we conquer the enemy; if our hands are down we must be conquered.[2] I have deliberately labelled this type of exegesis as Philonic, because it seems to me that it involves exactly the same mode of allegory as does Philo's psychological allegory or allegory into philosophical speculation. In it the correspondence between event and event is forgotten and a biblical incident is dissolved into a timeless analysis of good and evil impulses warring within the Christian's soul. Daniélou, in his masterly analysis of early Christian typology, *Sacramentum Futuri*, does not admit that this dissolution of typology by Origen is invalid. He is well aware of the dangers of allegory. He realizes, indeed he brilliantly analyses for us, how composite Origen's allegorical practice is. Referring to the treatment of this incident of Moses holding up his arms, he points out three passages in Origen, not yet mentioned here, where Origen interprets this passage in three different ways. Once he follows Philo in interpreting this incident as the elevation of the spirit above earthly things;[3] once he refers it to the Cross of Christ;[4] and once he takes it as foreshadowing the spiritual interpretation of the law.[5] But Daniélou finds this last sort of interpretation quite a legitimate one. For instance he draws a contrast which is favourable to Origen between Philo's interpretation of the basket daubed with pitch containing the infant Moses as the life of the senses, and Origen's reference of it to the involvement of the law in the literal meaning of Scripture.[6] On the other hand when Origen in his second Homily on Genesis treats the story of Noah and the ark first in a traditional way, as foreshadowing Jesus Christ bringing salvation at the consummation of the ages, Daniélou approves of his exegesis thus far, but regards him as abandoning the sound line of exposition when he goes on to interpret the three sorts of animals in the ark as Christians of three different spiritual

[1]*Comm. on John* XXVIII.5.
[2]Pitra, *Analecta Sacra* II, pp. 481 f., on Ps. 24.4.
[3]Philo *De Leg. Alleg.* III.186; Origen *Hom. on Ex.* XI.4; Daniélou, *Sacramentum Futuri*, p. 195. Daniélou has apparently not noticed the two interpretations of this passage just quoted above.
[4]*Hom. on Ex.* III.3.
[5]*Ibid* XI.4.
[6]*Hom. on Josh.* I.3; Daniélou, *op. cit.*, p. 194.

capacities, to regard the dimensions of the ark as indicating various sorts of mysteries borrowed from Philo and Clement of Alexandria, and to end with a 'moral' interpretation whereby the ark is the believing soul which must be covered with pitch inside and out, that is, made perfect in knowledge and in works.[1] It seems to me that it is much more difficult to distinguish between legitimate and illegitimate allegory in Origen's practice than Daniélou imagines. Once Origen abandons the fairly broad and recognizable path of traditional Christian typology and allegory he almost always indulges in an allegory of a basically Philonic, Hellenistic sort, and the fact that in this allegory appear the figures of Christ and the Church and the Christian soul does not make it less Philonic.

Origen's preference for this Hellenistic sort of allegory was probably strengthened by his often repeated conviction that with the coming of Christ types had been done away; though they might still foster the faith of the weaker brethren, they had in fact lost their significance.[2] Allegory, whereby the secret, original sense of any passage in the Old Testament was laid bare, was a more proper method of exposition for the enlightened Christian. But it would be quite inaccurate to suggest that Origen abandoned traditional Christian typology in his exegesis. We can detect a great deal of it, like the bones of his exegetical skeleton hidden beneath the flesh of allegorical elaboration. The temple in Jerusalem is the type both of the body of Jesus and of the Church;[3] the earthly Jerusalem has the same typology,[4] and so has Noah's ark.[5] Völker notes that in dealing with the Wisdom-Literature Origen, though he deserts the literal sense more readily than does Clement, shows a distinct preference for dogmatic and Christological interpretation, in contrast to Clement's psychological and ethical allegories.[6] Origen can indeed sometimes produce a really beautiful sentiment when

---

[1] *Ibid.*, pp. 89–93. Daniélou gives a fine analysis of the treatment of the figure of Isaac in Philo, Clement and Origen in pp. 112–28, and of the treatment of the Exodus in the same three, in pp. 154–76, 190–4. But he does not convince me that Origen's exposition is free from Philo's influence even where he is not reproducing Philo's interpretations.

[2] E.g. *Comm. on John* XIII.18; XXVIII.12.

[3] *Ibid.*, X.35.

[4] *Comm. on Rom.* VIII.8.

[5] *Hom. on Gen.* II.3. This subject is returned to below, pp. 321–3.

[6] 'Die Verwertung des Weisheits-Literatur', *ZKG* LXIV, p. 23. But Clement can occasionally include both Philonic and traditional Christian interpretation together; e.g. Isaac is σοφία τις ὑπερκόσμιος (borrowed from Philo *De Plantatione*, 169 f.) but also he represents Christ, especially as he carried the wood for his sacrifice just as Christ carried his Cross, and the divinity of Christ (brought to sacrifice but untouched by it), *Paed.* I.5.21–3, *PG* 8.276 f.

his preoccupation with Hellenistic allegorizing does not destroy with its baroque elaboration the effectiveness of the original image. On Ps. 118.24, 'This is the day which the Lord hath made, we will be glad and rejoice in it,' he comments: 'What then could be compared to this day, in which the reconciliation of God with men took place, and the long war was ended, and heaven was revealed to be earth, and men who were worthy of earth turned out to be worthy of the kingdom, and the first-fruits of our nature was raised far above the heavens, and Paradise was opened, and we received back our ancient native land, and the curse disappeared, and sin was broken?'[1] And on Matt. 27.28, 'And they stripped him and put on him a scarlet robe,' Origen says that this is a mystery foreshadowed in the scarlet thread of Rahab and the scarlet thread which Tamar bound on the hand of one of her twins, and adds, 'Therefore when now the Lord took the scarlet robe he took on himself the blood of the world.'[2]

One particular example of Origen's allegory has attracted the special attention of scholars, and that is his allegorization of the journey of the children of Israel through the Stations of the Wilderness as the journey of the Christian soul towards perfection. An allegorical treatment of this theme was not new in Origen's day. Heracleitus had allegorized the wanderings of Odysseus into an account of the various ills into which a man's life can fall.[3] Philo had allegorized some of the Stations of the Wilderness; Mara meant 'bitterness' and Elim meant 'gateways' (that is, entrances to virtue).[4] And Rabbinic scholars had drawn allegorical lessons from some of the names of these Stations.[5] In order to support his allegorization of these Stations of the Wilderness Origen used a document supplying the etymologies of the names of these places which he had certainly not compiled himself and which had probably been produced by Jewish scholars who were not Christians.[6] Völker has laid

[1] *Comm. on Ps.* 118.24, *PG* 12.1584.
[2] *Comm. on Matt.* Comm. Ser. 125. Origen refers to Rahab again in *Hom. on Josh.* I.4; III.4; VI.4; and VII.5, exciting thereby the enthusiastic admiration of Daniélou, who analyses exhaustively Origen's treatment of Rahab (*Sacramentum Futuri*, pp. 222–5); Origen's linking of Rahab with Hosea's prostitute wife and Mary Magdalene he particularly applauds: 'la chaine typologique déploie sur la registre légal, prophetique, évangelique, ecclésial, eschatologique; la thème unique de la Rédemption' (*ibid.*, pp. 224 f.; cf. *Origène*, p. 153). Nor is Daniélou at all disturbed when Origen applies this theme to the life of Christ in the soul of the Christian, saying that we must receive the spies of Jesus into our heart, etc. (*Sacramentum Futuri*, p. 224).
[3] Heracleitus, *Quaestiones Homericae* 70 ff., pp. 91 ff.
[4] *De Congressu* 163; *De Fug. et Invent.* 183; Daniélou, *Sacramentum Futuri*, pp. 184 f., calls attention to this.
[5] See 'Interpretations of Hebrew Names in Origen', *Vig. Chr.* X, pp. 121 f.
[6] *Ibid.*, pp. 115–23.

very great emphasis upon Origen's treatment of the Stations of the
Wilderness in his argument that Origen did believe in and openly teach
the possibility of the Christian soul attaining to a mystical union with
God in the fullest sense of the term.[1] He can only find very slight support for his contention that Origen spoke openly of what we would
today call a *unio mystica* in his works. This treatment of the Stations of
the Wilderness and a Latin version of a fragment on I Thessalonians
are in fact the sum of his direct evidence.[2] I do not think that Völker
has sufficiently realized how limited Origen was in his interpretation of
the Stations of the Wilderness by the necessity he was under of mani-
pulating into his system of gradual perfection thirty-eight etymologies,
none of which he had any hand in deriving himself.[3] Nor does he, in my
opinion, give enough weight to the fact that a large part of what Origen
appears to describe as mystical experience in fact consists of the characteristic theological and philosophical speculations of the Christian
Platonists of Alexandria.[4] But in spite of these qualifications, which might
have rendered Völker rather more cautious in drawing his conclusions,
we must admit that the general impression of the evidence collected by
Völker does suggest that Origen did conceive of the Christian soul as
attaining to mystical ecstasy.[5] What is most relevant to observe here is
that he achieved this by a characteristically Philonic allegorization of the
names of the Stations of the Wilderness.[6]

We have already had some opportunity of seeing the arguments by
which Origen defends his incessant use of allegory and his elaborate
extension of it to include sense on sense and depth below depth of
meaning. There is no other way of making sense of many passages of
Scripture which it would be disastrous to take in their literal sense. Only
by allegory can the Old Testament be defended against the attacks of
heretics. The practice of allegory is encouraged by Scripture itself.[7]
Almost all schools of thought, heretical and orthodox, except the Literalists and the Jews, were indulging in allegory in his day. 'But now there
are countless multitudes of believers who (though not all can expound the

---

[1]Völker, *Das Vollkommenheitsideal*, pp. 62–78, 139, 195.
[2]*Ibid.*, p. 124; the Latin passage runs thus: *Subitum ad meliora transcensum,
et idcirco raptum se voluisse dicere, ut velocitas transeuntis sensum cogitantis
excederet.*
[3]See 'Interpretations of Hebrew Names in Origen', pp. 122 f.
[4]Völker, *op. cit.*, pp. 91–8; but see *Origen's Doctrine of Tradition*, pp. 81 f.
[5]See especially, Völker, *op. cit.*, pp. 134–44.
[6]Lundberg, *La Typologie Baptismale*, pp. 117 f., is also impressed with the
Philonic character of this piece of allegory.
[7]One more example of this argument is to be found in *Contra Celsum* IV.44,
where Origen quotes Gal. 4.26 in support of the practice.

principles of spiritual interpretation systematically and thoroughly) are almost all persuaded that circumcision should not be understood literally nor the sabbath rest nor the pouring out of the blood of cattle, and do not believe that answers were given to Moses by God about these things.'[1] And Origen often claims that a licence to allegorize is an original part of the Christian tradition.[2]

A surprising number of modern scholars have joined their voice with Origen's in justifying the use of allegory in the manner in which he used it. Zöllig agrees that there was some ground in St Paul's writings for the use of allegory, though it should be employed 'always within the limits of apostolic authority or that of the Church taking the apostles' place', and he also uses the argument that the rule of faith sanctioned the practice of allegory; the Apologists had used it against the Jews; the pagans who were attracted by Origen's teaching found allegory congenial, and by its means Origen was able to read some of their ideas into the Bible. Zöllig believed that the Protestantism of his day felt the want of allegory in its teaching.[3] He accepted wholeheartedly the conception of a 'spiritual sense' latent in all Scripture: 'It is Origen's achievement to have demonstrated incontrovertibly that the Old Testament is a grand type of the New, and that in the Holy Scriptures besides the literal sense the mystical sense must come into its own.'[4] Klostermann is more half-hearted in his defence of Origen's use of allegory. He suggests that Origen had no other choice than to use it, that he only built upon what others had provided for him, and that allegory was sometimes the means of achieving a genuine understanding of the Bible.[5] De Lubac, one of the most recent expounders of Origen's thought, is far less critical than the others and far more ardent in his enthusiasm for Origen's use of allegory. On Origen's declaration that the allegorical interpretation must be used in order to render acceptable to his hearers passages in the Bible which in their literal sense are dull or purely 'Jewish' or indecent or irrelevant, de Lubac remarks, 'Such is the leading idea, as you can see, entirely practical, entirely apostolic and at the same time entirely traditional, from which were born the greater number of Origen's homilies.'[6] He defends in a spirited manner Origen's belief

---

[1] *PA* II.7.2.
[2] For the evidence that both Clement of Alexandria and Origen made this claim, see *Origen's Doctrine of Tradition*, pp. 63 f., 71 f., 82, 103–5.
[3] Zöllig, *Inspirationslehre*, pp. 123 f.
[4] *Ibid.*, p. 127.
[5] Klostermann, 'Formen der exegetischen Arbeiten des Origenes', *TLZ*, 1947, p. 206.
[6] De Lubac, *Histoire et Esprit*, p. 135.

in a 'spiritual sense' to be found in all Scripture and his particular interpretation of St Paul's contrast between the spirit and the letter.[1] After admitting freely that Origen's exegesis takes no notice of the context nor original meaning of the passages which it interprets and that his principle of collation and comparison is usually quite unsatisfactory, de Lubac writes: 'The principle which guides Origen is not usually the sense of a certain unity of the world of the Bible nor the perception of various influences. It is a principle of pure faith, which defies all empirical variety.' His method, 'deceptive for the historian, is often fruitful for the believer'. What he discovers in the Old Testament is always Christian doctrine, even though there may be no justification at all for discovering it there. 'The superficial contradiction does not always hinder the understanding in depth.'[2] Later in his book de Lubac asserts that the fathers, in spite of all their faults 'had a sort of natural sympathy (*connaturalité*) with the Scriptures, which our faith can only recover with difficulty'.[3]

I must confess that most of these arguments in defence of Origen's system of allegory seem to me most unconvincing. Origen's intentions in allegorizing may have been orthodox, admirable, and quite acceptable to modern scholarship. But to defend his intentions is not the same thing as to defend his methods in allegory. It seems to me that the account of Origen's threefold system of dividing allegory into literal, 'spiritual' and 'moral' given in these pages should persuade anybody that his method was ultimately self-frustrating. In an effort to distinguish objectively between three different senses of Scripture he only succeeded in reaching a position where all distinctions were dissolved in a 'spiritual' sense which was in fact governed by nothing but Origen's arbitrary fancy as to what doctrine any given text ought to contain. There is an historical sense of many passages of Scripture; many passages provide fit material for doctrinal statements and conclusions; and many are well fitted for edifying the faithful Christian.[4] But to maintain that all passages *must* yield, when allegorized or treated in any way any scholar likes to suggest, a 'spiritual' sense having direct relevance to Christian doctrine, and that many passages must not be taken in their literal sense because their literal sense, though not nonsense, is improper or irrelevant to Christian doctrine or in some way contains statements that ought not

[1] *Ibid.*, p. 307.
[2] *Ibid.*, pp. 314 f.
[3] *Ibid.*, pp. 430 f.
[4] I omit here the 'grammatical' sense, which seems to me to be merely an elaborate way of saying that the passage is not nonsense.

A.E.—I

to be in the Bible—these are suggestions which it is exegetical suicide to entertain. The best intentions in the world cannot redeem the expositor who adopts these principles.

Whether Origen in his adoption of this allegorical system had the best intentions is very much open to question. We have seen how deeply he was influenced by Philonic assumptions when he approached the text of the Bible. It is not really adequate in order to establish the character of Origen as an allegorist to confine oneself to an examination of his threefold scheme. That scheme, as we have seen, was largely a facade or a rationalization whereby he was able to read into the Bible what he wanted to find there. We must go on to explore the use which Origen made of this instrument of allegory. And if we are to test whether Origen's intentions in using allegory were as unimpeachable as de Lubac maintains we must pay particular attention to his attitude to history.

IO

Historicity

'IF we could weave together into a single system the accounts in the Gospels,' says Origen, it would be the most satisfactory method.[1] And in many instances he does endeavour to produce a harmony of the biblical passages which he has to deal with (very often of parallel accounts in the Gospels) much as all scholars up to the middle of the last century and a few very conservative ones today would have done.[2] On several occasions he writes as if the accounts of an incident given by all four evangelists, or at least by three of them, were deliberately designed to complement each other. He remarks, for instance, upon the various contributions of the four evangelists to the account of the baptism of Jesus, observing 'none of them made any addition to what Matthew had said, to avoid their repeating each other,' and so on in the same strain.[3] He speaks of 'the harmony of the three evangelists' in their description of the burial of Jesus.[4] And in reply to the suggestion of Celsus that the difference on the part of the evangelists about the number of angels appearing at the tomb at the Resurrection impugns the accuracy of their account he hints that the differences can all be harmonized (as well as allegorized).[5]

He has a variety of devices for harmonizing other inconsistencies in the Bible. He accounts for the discrepancy of sixty-five years in the

[1]*Comm. on John* VI.20. For further information on Origen's treatment of the historicity of the Bible, see Denis, *De la Philosophie d'Origène*, pp. 246–8; W. R. Inge, article 'Alexandrian Theology', *ERE* I, p. 316; Zöllig, *Inspirationslehre*, pp. 103 f.; J. Martin, 'La Critique Biblique chez Origène II : L'Allegorisme', *Anneles de Philosophie Chrétienne* CLI, 1905–6, pp. 231–58; Prat, *Origène, le Théologien et l'Exégète*, pp. 185, 187; and Millburn, *Early Christian Interpretations of History*, pp. 41 f., 46 f., 49, 53. For Philo's treatment of the subject, see above, pp. 48–52; Kennedy, *Philo's Contribution to Religion*, pp. 32–4, 36, 39; Bonsirven, *Judaisme* I, p. 261; for Clement's treatment of it, see Montdesert, *Clement d'Alexandrie*, p. 170.

[2]For further information on Origen's practice of harmonizing, see Bertrand, *Mystique de Jesus chez Origène*, p. 133.

[3]*Comm. on John* VI.50; cf. VI.27 f.

[4]*Contra Celsum* II.69: ἡ συμφωνία τῶν τριῶν εὐαγγελιστῶν.

[5]*Ibid.*, V.56.

Septuagint's figure for Noah's age on his begetting his sons (Gen. 5.28–32) by saying that the time which Noah lived before he 'pleased God' (Gen. 6.8) is not counted in one account and is reckoned in the other. It is a convenient explanation and reconciles discrepancies in the ages of Abraham, Enoch, Saul, Hezekiah and Methuselah.[1] The difficulty of tracing the descent of Jesus from David, when Joseph, who is apparently the figure through whom the descent is claimed, was not his real father, Origen meets by saying that doubtless Mary was legally married to Joseph and was of the same tribe as he, and in this sense Jesus could be described as 'born of the seed of David' (Rom. 1.3).[2] The divergence between the genealogies of Christ as given in the first and third Gospels, which was clearly a *locus vexatus* for contemporary biblical scholars, he reconciles by taking as his clue the fact that Luke inserts the genealogy immediately after his account of the Baptism of Jesus, whereas Matthew opens his Gospel with the genealogy. Matthew can therefore import into his genealogy such unmistakably sinful people as Rahab, Tamar, Bathsheba, Solomon and Rehoboam, whereas Luke's genealogy contains none of these; Matthew presents the Jesus who 'shall save his people from their sins', but Luke presents the Christ in whom his people who are cleansed by Baptism believe.[3] Origen will even explain a difficulty sometimes by blaming the imperfection of the evangelist. He points out that the accounts of Jesus' movements and the reasons for them given in John 4.43 are not very clear or well expressed and he elucidates their literal meaning, trying to show that though they are clumsily described they are consistent: 'and perhaps the intention of the phrase is as follows, but John, as an amateur in the word (ὡς ἰδιώτης τῷ λόγῳ) set down his meaning in a badly expressed way.'[4] Dealing with the two thieves crucified with Jesus, Origen says that Matthew, 'giving a general summary', said that both thieves reviled our Lord, whereas Luke, 'more accurately, as he had professed to write' (Luke 1.3) described one as penitent.[5]

But the most usual resort which Origen uses in order to reconcile inconsistencies in the Bible is to abandon the literal meaning of portions of the passages which cause the difficulty and to represent them as composed partly of literal and partly of purely allegorical meanings. There is one well-known chapter in which he sets out this method, and

[1]*Fragment on Genesis, PG* 12.100.
[2]*Comm. on Rom.* I.5.
[3]*Hom. on Luke* XXVIII, on Luke 3.23–8.
[4]*Comm. on John* XIII.54.
[5]*Comm. on Matt.* Comm. Ser. 133.

it must be quoted at some length. He is discussing the appearance of the dove at the Baptism of Jesus, to whose authenticity Celsus had taken exception:

'Against this point we must reply that to desire to make out that almost every narrative, even if it be true, actually took place, and to produce an acceptable theory about it, is an exceedingly difficult task, and in some circumstances impossible. Imagine somebody saying that the Trojan War had not taken place, chiefly because of the impossibility of fitting in the story about a certain Achilles having been born the son of a sea-goddess Thetis and a man Peleus, or about Sarpedon son of Zeus, or Askalaphos and Ialmenos, sons of Ares, or Aeneas son of Aphrodite? How could we make out such a case, if we were particularly troubled by the invention which had somehow or other been interpolated into the well-known story, accepted by everybody, narrating the war between the Greeks and the Trojans in Troy as having really happened? Again, imagine someone not believing the story about Oedipus and Jocasta and those who were born from them both, Eteocles and Polynices, on the grounds that the story of a Sphinx who was half a maiden had been interpolated into the narrative; how could we agree with such a theory? Rather, he who examines the narratives judiciously, and wishes to avoid leading himself into error in these also, makes distinctions, and will accept some parts and will take some figuratively, looking for the intention of those who composed such works; and some he will disbelieve on the ground that they were written in order to please certain people. We have made these prefatory remarks to apply to all the narratives about Jesus set forth in the Gospels, not challenging the more intelligent people to show a blind and unreasoning faith, but anxious to establish the fact that students must have judgement and a strong spirit of research, and, if I may call it so, a means of entering into the intention of those who wrote, in order that there may be discovered what was the state of mind in which each passage was written.'[1]

A similar passage declares: 'You will find in divine Scripture an admixture of that which is apparently not historical in order to exercise the intelligence (μίγμα τοῦ ὡς ἀνιστορικοῦ πρὸς τὸ γυμναστικόν), and especially in John's writings.' For instance, Jesus seats himself in a

[1]*Contra Celsum* I.42, reproduced in *Philoc.* XV.15.

physical sense by a material well, but he describes himself as 'living water'. So the miracle at Cana was as a 'spiritual work' the renewing of the old wine of the Old Testament by the New Testament, and the Cleansing of the Temple was the renewing of the Father's spiritual house.[1] Again, the account of David's wrong to Uriah must in part be allegorized and in part taken literally; if anybody thinks that he can provide a better explanation, let him do so. If we take the story literally, 'not only is David charged with incontinence but also with cruelty and inhumanity, for he dared to do against Uriah a deed which is inconsistent with the character of one who is even of moderately good behaviour.'[2]

A modern exegete may well sympathize with Origen in his candour in admitting that to endeavour to defend the historical truth of all incidents described in the Bible, and perhaps even in the Gospels, brings one into insuperable difficulties. But I think that de Lubac is going too far when he claims that 'in imagining that he sees in our Gospels a very flexible type of historicity united with an interpretation in depth of the reality of the task which they had of declaring to the people, he is not far from agreeing with the best of our recent historians, the believing ones as well as the others'.[3] There is, as far as I know, no evidence that the evangelists intended their accounts, or any part of them, of what purported to be historical events in fact to be treated as purely allegorical. Such a conclusion agrees more with the cast of thought of a Loisy than with that of a Hoskyns.

Origen is aware that this treatment of difficulties lays him open to the charge of abandoning altogether a belief in the historical truth of the Bible, and he guards himself against this charge. He declares that, though there are several irrational and untrue and impossible things in the Bible, we must not think that no real historical events took place and that no law is to be observed literally or that what was written about our Saviour was not literally true. For instance, Abraham was buried in a cave in Hebron, and so were Isaac and Jacob and their wives, and Shechem was given as a portion to Joseph, and Jerusalem, in which Solomon's temple was built, was the capital of Judaea, 'and a thousand

---

[1] *Comm. on John*, frag. 74.
[2] *Comm. on Ps.* 51, on the heading, *PG* 12.1453, reproduced in *Philoc.* I.29.
[3] De Lubac, *Histoire et Esprit*, p. 200. Even less are we in accord with his argument (pp. 203–6) that Origen's unsatisfactory methods of harmonizing the Gospels are extenuated by the fact that many recent and modern critics have used methods just as unsatisfactory and that several ancient writers, including St Ambrose (who, incidentally, was very much under the influence of Philo in this matter), took the same line.

other details'. 'For the incidents which are historically true are much
more numerous than the entirely spiritual interpolations.' Again, 'Honour
thy father and thy mother' and many other commandments are to be
observed literally, and so is our Lord's command not to be angry with
a brother and not to swear at all.[1] In accordance with this caution, we
can trace several passages in Origen's works where he deliberately
emphasizes the historical truth of an event or a detail. He will sometimes, for instance, invoke the authority of some non-Christian historian
to support a fact in the Bible. Josephus is appealed to as testimony for
John's practice of baptizing and for the martyrdom of James the
brother of the Lord,[2] and for the holiness of this James,[3] and for the
cannibalism practised during the siege of Jerusalem by the Romans and
some other details which Origen imagined to be predicted in Lamentations;[4] and Phlegon is adduced as a witness to the eclipse and the earth-
quakes which took place during the reign of Tiberius.[5] What is more
surprising is the fact, noted by de Lubac, that Origen accepts as historical the narrative of the sun and moon being stopped to enable
Joshua to win a complete victory over the five kings (Josh. 10.12 f.), in
spite of the fact that in the same homily he refuses to accept as historical
the massacre of the five kings by Joshua.[6] It is interesting to observe that
Hippolytus had before Origen's day defended the literal truth of the
story of the going back of the shadow on Hezekiah's dial and the stop-
ping of the sun and moon by Joshua on the ground that nothing is impossible to God.[7] Origen apparently accepts as historical the account
given in Genesis of the early history of the human race,[8] though, as we
shall see later, the story of Adam and Eve must not be included in this
statement. He claims that the veracity of the narratives in the Gospels
is evinced by the fortitude of those who wrote them and those who
believe them in suffering for the sake of the subject of the Gospels.[9]
He takes as literally addressed to John the Baptist the words of his father,
'And thou, child, shalt be called the prophet of the Highest' (Luke 1.76),

[1] *PA* IV.3.4.
[2] *Contra Celsum* I.47; incidentally Origen describes this James as brother only
διὰ τὸ ἦθος καὶ τὸν λόγον; cf. next reference.
[3] *Comm. on Matt.* X.17.
[4] *Hom. on Lam.*, frags. 105, 109, 114.
[5] *Contra Celsum* II.33.
[6] *Hom. on Josh.* XI.1, where he also allegorizes the passage; he allegorizes it
earlier, in I.5, and here too he apparently accepts the incident as historical, for
he declares that Moses is inferior to Joshua because he never succeeded in
arresting the sun and moon, as Joshua did. See de Lubac, *Histoire et Esprit*, p. 96.
[7] *Comm. on Dan.* I.7 f.
[8] *Contra Celsum* IV.80, reproduced in *Philoc.* XX.7.
[9] *Contra Celsum.* II.10.

for he believes that just as the child was wonderfully born and leapt in
his mother's womb so he was able a few days after his birth to understand what his father said to him![1] And Bertrand has called attention
to a passage where Origen betrays the fact that when he was in Palestine
he himself sought out the places visited by Jesus; presumably Origen
was not looking for allegories there.[2] He must have thought that Job
was a real person, for he is at pains to prove the accuracy of the statement that God restored to Job twice as much as he had lost, and to
render probable the record of the years of Job's existence (Job 42.10, 13,
16).[3] He believed in the reality of the enslavement of Joseph, as we can
infer from a comment full of pathos made in the course of expanding a
psalm, 'The literal meaning is designed to encourage slaves, and especially those who have been condemned to slavery because of their confession of the faith.'[4] He must have believed in the genuineness of some
of the genealogies in the Old Testament, for he wonders if Terah
(Gen. 11.26) was father of triplets.[5] And he defended the historicity of
the account of the making of the ark against the attacks of Apelles, maintaining that it is obvious that the measurements of the ark given in the
biblical account must stand for figures vastly bigger.[6]

On the other side, however, we must take into account the fact that
there were a number of details to be found in the Bible which Origen
quite certainly did not believe to have any basis in history at all. In the
first place, he held a theory that the Holy Spirit had deliberately inserted
into Scripture a number of obvious inconsistencies which could not be
taken literally and which were intended to startle the intellectual reader
into achieving their deeper sense by allegorizing them, much as G. K.
Chesterton represented a character in one of his 'Father Brown' stories
as leaving behind him in his journey through London streets a number of
small objects deliberately put out of place, as a trail for another to follow.
This was a theory the makings of which Origen had found in Philo.
Moses, Philo tells us, in his account of Joseph's career, suppresses
the detail of whose house Joseph fled to from the blandishments of
Potiphar's wife, 'in order that you may take the hint and allego-

---

[1] *Hom. on Luke* X, on Luke 1.76.
[2] γενόμενοι ἐν τοῖς τόποις ἐπὶ ἱστορίαν τῶν ἰχνῶν 'Ιησοῦ, *Comm. on John* VI.
24; see Bertrand, *Mystique de Jesus chez Origène*, p. 106.
[3] Pitra, *Analecta Sacra* II., 388–90.
[4] Cadiou, *Commentaires Inédits des Psaumes*, on 105.17 f., p. 89.
[5] Fragment on Genesis, *PG* 12.112.
[6] *Hom. on Gen.* II.2. But I cannot agree with de Lubac when he alleges that
this solitary instance proves that Origen argues regularly against those who
'were tempted to reject the letter when it appeared too improbable' (*Histoire et
Esprit*, p. 95).

rize'.[1] Another sentence of his runs, 'It must be declared that this is an example of doctrines conveyed in allegory, because the literal sense does not make very good sense.'[2] Again, he asks, Why should Moses speak of the river of Egypt alone as having a 'lip'? Some people, he says, might think it trivial to ask such things, but 'I hold that such matters are like condiments set as seasoning to the Holy Scriptures for the edification of its readers.'[3] Improving upon this type of theory, Origen asserts that in order to indicate the existence of the spiritual meaning the Holy Spirit provided 'things like stumbling-blocks and obstacles' (σκάνδαλα καὶ προσκόμματα), not fitting in with the ordinary narrative and context where they are found, to remind the reader that there is something diviner in the text. In some places Scripture wove into the narrative sometimes something which did not take place (τὸ μὴ γενόμενον) to indicate the deeper meaning, sometimes something which could have taken place, but did not, sometimes something impossible. The same principle can be applied to the legislation of the Old Testament, 'in which can often be found a law which is directly practical and suitable to the period of the legislation; but sometimes no practical principle appears in it. And sometimes even laws impossible of fulfilment are made, for the sake of the more skilful and inquiring.' We can also apply this theory to the New Testament. None of the Gospels and apostolic writings 'have a narrative entirely unmixed with incidents interpolated into the literal sense, which did not take place; nor have they legislation and commandments which in their entirety appear appropriate to their immediate context.'[4] There can be no question of these 'stumbling-block' passages being merely allegorizations built upon the substructure of an adherence to the literal sense; these are pure, unqualified allegorizations, as far as the literal sense goes, suspended in the air.

We have already seen in the last chapter what were the commandments and ordinances in both Old and New Testaments which Origen regarded as lacking in all literal force.[5] But we can also make a list of other things besides precepts in whose historical reality Origen had ceased to believe; we have had occasion already to examine the clear precedent which Philo had set him for such a theory.[6] It is not surprising to find in this list the account in Genesis of creation; in reply to

[1] De Leg. Alleg. III.238.
[2] De Plantatione 113.
[3] De Somniis II.301.
[4] PA IV. 2.9, reproduced in Philoc. I.16 f.; cf. Contra Celsum III.45 (Philoc. XVIII.16), Comm. on Romans VI.8 (Philoc. IX.3); see Zöllig, Inspirationslehre, pp. 32–4.
[5] See above, pp. 239–41.   [6] See above, pp. 51 f.

A.E.—I*

Celsus' objection that the author of Genesis refers to 'days' both before
and after the creation of sun, moon and stars, Origen determines to
allegorize the word 'day'.[1] It is probable that he did not believe in the
building of the Tower of Babel as an historical event. When he comes to
deal with it he dismisses the evidence from secular myth and history; he
says that the story is told only 'in the form of history' (ἐν ἱστορίας
τρόπῳ); he interprets the phrase 'as they journeyed east' (Gen. 11.2)
as a moving away from the true light; the bricks and slime (Gen. 11.3)
stand for greater or lesser sinfulness of a spiritual sort. On the other
hand he apparently regarded the dispersion (at the hand of angels) and
the multiplication of tongues (Gen. 11.8 f.) as historical events; he
summarizes the matter by saying that the author describes it 'as if in
the form of a story, which has some truth in itself but which also indicates some ineffable fact'.[2] He is doubtful of the historical truth of the
incident of Hagar at the well, where it is written 'And God opened her
eyes, and she saw a well of water' (Gen. 21.19). 'How can these words
be taken literally?' Origen asks, 'For where do we find it stated that
Hagar closed her eyes, and that they were afterwards opened?'[3] He
refuses to believe in the literal truth of accounts of massacres carried
out under God's orders; 'the righteous destroy every captured thing
of the enemy and of those who come from evil, so that not even an
infant and recently-grown evil is left', and this applies to Ps. 137.9,
'Happy shall he be that taketh thy children and throweth them against
the stones.'[4] Similarly the massacre of the inhabitants of Ai (Josh. 8.24)
he declares to be nothing more than a cutting off of demons inside the
people of Jesus, and not historical at all.[5] He implies that the array of
the High Priest described in Lev. 21 is so entirely a description of Christ
that it could apply to no literal Jewish priest.[6] The mention of the 'the men
of Anathoth' (Jer. 11.21) stimulates him to remark that 'the name of
Anathoth is here taken as a pretext. The whole mystery of the Jews is
allegorically spoken of in it. For Anathoth is translated "Obedience";'
and he goes on to say that there is no historical record of the men of
Anathoth seeking Jeremiah's life, either in Kings or in the book of
Jeremiah; he regards the whole episode as non-historical.[7] The references to the prince of Tyre in Ezek. 28 and to Pharaoh of Egypt in

---

[1] *Contra Celsum* VI.50; the same treatment of the matter appears in *Comm. on
Matt.* XIV.9. We have seen Philo abandoning the literal meaning in this passage, above, p. 51.
[2] *Philoc.* XXII.6–10, reproducing the third book of a *Commentary on Genesis*.
[3] *Hom. on Gen.* VII.5.   [4] *Contra Celsum* VII.22.
[5] *Hom. on Josh.* VIII.7.   [6] *Hom. on Lev.* XII.1.
[7] *Hom. on Jer.* X.4.

what Origen could not accept

Ezek. 29 could not, he believes, be intended to apply to the two historical kings, because things are attributed to them (such as Pharaoh
saying 'My river is my own' (Ezek. 29.3) and the residence of the king
of Tyre in Eden (Ezek. 28.13)) which were not true of these kings; the
words apply to demons connected with these regions.[1]

This entire dissolution of the historical reality of certain events and
details is not confined by Origen to the Old Testament. He applies it,
though with much greater caution, to the New also. There can be no
doubt that in his *Commentary on John* he declares, circumspectly but
explicitly, his entire disbelief in the historical reality of the Cleansing
of the Temple by Jesus and his Entry into Jerusalem as described by all
four evangelists. He sets out very clearly the contradiction between the
Johannine version of the Cleansing of the Temple and the Synoptic,
and then says, 'I for my part assume that it is impossible for those who
admit in these matters no sense beyond that of straightforward narrative to establish that the apparent contradiction is really consistent.'[2]
His own explanation is that St John's description of the incident is
purely allegorical. Jerusalem represents the souls of churchmen from
which Jesus drives out unworthy thoughts of gain and traffickers in
spiritual things; or it is an allegory of our Lord's superseding the law,
since he throws out the animals who were to be sacrificed.[3] He then
points out the difficulties of accepting the historical truth of the incident. The evangelist 'used an incident which had taken place' (that is,
the introduction of animals into the outer court of the Temple), but
Origen thinks it unlikely that Jesus would have been allowed by the
authorities to clear out the court as he 'was thought by them to be of
humble origin'. The only resource of 'the man who wishes to preserve
the historicity of the narrative' (τῷ τὴν ἱστορίαν σῶσαι θέλοντι) is
to imagine that Christ exercised a miraculous power of subduing the
souls of man. But Origen ends by preferring the purely allegorical interpretation.[4] In a similar manner he sets out many objections to taking as
an historical account the Matthaean version of the Entry into Jerusalem (Matt. 21.6–13). What was the need of recording such trivial
details as are described in this account? And even if Christ did fulfil
literally the details of the prophecy in Zech. 9.9, in what sense could he
be said to have fulfilled the words of the next verse about cutting off the
chariot from Ephraim and the war horse from Jerusalem?[5] Then he
reproduces the objections of the Jewish exegetes to the traditional

[1] *Hom. on Ezek.* XIII.1.   [2] *Comm. on John* X.20–22.
[3] *Ibid.*, X.23 f.   [4] *Ibid.* X.25.   [5] *Ibid.* X.26.

Christian interpretation of this passage, and adds some more of his own. Our Lord would act unworthily of the Son of God if he had need of an ass and a colt, and he would be stupid if he really was pleased by the disciples' putting their garments on the animals, and the people strewing branches in his way would only hinder his progress.[1] Origen prefers to take the whole incident as purely allegorical. 'Jesus is the Word of God who enters into the soul called Jerusalem, riding upon the ass loosed from its bonds by the disciples, I mean the unadorned writings of the Old Testament made clear by the two disciples who release its meaning; for one of them applies the writings for the healing of the soul and allegorizes them for its benefit, and the other sets out the good things and true which are to come through the medium of these things which lie in a shadow.'[2] By these two disciples he evidently means the 'moral' and the 'spiritual' senses of Scripture. It is quite clear in his whole treatment of the passage that he believes in the historicity of none of the evangelists' accounts of the Entry into Jerusalem and the Cleansing of the Temple. The differences in the evangelists' accounts of the Cleansing of the Temple are accounted for by assuming that the different accounts refer to different classes of people from whose souls Jesus cast out evil.[3] This particular exegesis lands him into extraordinary complications when later on he asks himself whether the things said to have happened to the Temple in the apparently historical narratives of the Gospels have also happened or will happen to the spiritual Temple which is the real meaning of the historical Temple.[4] In similar fashion he refuses historical reality to the dove recorded as descending at Jesus' Baptism; the story must be taken 'intellectually'; 'All these incidents, I mean the Spirit descending out of heaven on Jesus and remaining on him, were written for the sake of accommodation, and do not possess the qualities of an historical narrative, but of intellectual contemplation.'[5] The two young turtle-doves offered by Mary at the Purification (Luke 2.24) were no material birds: 'These birds were not like those which fly through the air, but something divine and too great for human observation was manifesting itself under the appearance of a dove and a turtledove.'[6] In view of these examples, we cannot agree

[1] *Comm. on John* X.27.
[2] *Ibid.*, X.28.
[3] See especially *ibid.* X.31 f.; in the last chapter he takes exception to Mark's phrase 'on which man never sat' (11.2). 'What thing except a man ever sat upon a colt?' says Origen.
[4] *Ibid.*, X.42.
[5] *Ibid.*, frag. 20.
[6] *Hom. on Luke* XIV, on Luke 2.23 f.

with the judgement that Origen sacrifices the literal sense entirely 'only in the smallest points which do not at all impugn the substantial historicity of the narrative' or only for the sake of symmetry.[1]

R. M. Grant has suggested persuasively[2] that Origen's theory that the evangelists had interwoven spiritual and non-historical statements with historical events was derived from a similar treatment of Greek traditional myths and of the narratives of Homer by Greek rhetorical and grammatical writers before him, Theon, Hierophilus and Strabo. Grant brings in tellingly Porphyry's accusation that Origen was always in the company of Plato, Numenius, Longinus and the Pythagoreans (Eus. *HE* VI.19.8), and suggests that Porphyry was referring to some such borrowings as these. In this respect, Grant claims, Origen was influenced less by Philo than by names such as these. But even if we concede this point, as we probably should, it remains broadly true that Philo was the chief influence upon Origen in his attitude to historicity.

The question of whether Origen regarded the story of Adam and Eve given in Gen. 2–3 as sober history or as what we would today call myth demands separate treatment. Opinions about this matter have differed widely. They range from the statement of Koch that 'Origen regarded the narrative of Genesis as an allegorical representation of the first sinful act, a representation of the first realization of the possibility of a fall given to men'[3] to Crouzel's declaration that Origen's allegorization of the story of Adam and Eve was never intended to destroy the literal sense.[4] We have seen how firmly Philo jettisoned the historical truth of these two chapters.[5] Christian opinion since the time of Philo had been decidedly in favour of the historical authenticity of the story of Adam and Eve. It is clear from Theophilus' references to Eden that he is not prepared to allegorize it away.[6] The summary of sacred history given by Irenaeus in his *Demonstration*, beginning at creation and going as far as David's reign in Jerusalem, gives no hint that the story of Adam and Eve is not historical,[7] and his doctrine of *anakephalaiosis* expounded in the *Adversus Haereses* must demand a belief in Adam as a real figure of history. Clement of Alexandria allegorizes the serpent in the garden

---

[1] De Lubac, *Histoire et Esprit*, pp. 102, 116; but he makes larger concessions on this subject on pp. 99–101.
[2] *The Letter and the Spirit*, pp. 99–102.
[3] *Pronoia und Paideusis*, p. 103 n. 1.
[4] *Théologie de l'image de Dieu chez Origène*, p. 150; cf. p. 148. See also Cadiou, *La Jeunesse d'Origène*, pp. 326 f.; N. P. Williams, *Ideas of the Fall and Original Sin*, pp. 215 f.; Daniélou, *Origène*, p. 120.
[5] See above, p. 51.
[6] *Autolycus* II.19.
[7] *Dem.* 10–29.

of Eden[1] but does not suggest that it was not a real serpent also, and certainly took as historical the account of the making of Eve from Adam's rib, because he argues that man's beard is 'older than Eve, and a sign of the stronger nature'.[2] Another reference is uncertain, but it is probably wiser to conclude that though he thought the allegorical meaning was more important than the literal he did believe the literal to be historically true.[3]

The evidence that Origen was anxious to allegorize the story of Adam and Eve into an entirely unhistorical parable is certainly strong. His doctrine of the pre-existence of souls and of a pre-mundane fall would seem to force him to adopt such a position. Celsus had complained that Genesis had represented God as forming man with his hands. Origen replies that you must not take literally either the forming or the hands; you might as well take literally the Bible's references to God's wings. The making of the woman from man's rib must similarly be allegorized; Celsus had said that out of shame at such stories as these the more respectable Jews and Christians had tried to allegorize them. Origen admits that they must of course be allegorized, just as parts of Hesiod must be allegorized. When Celsus objects to the story of the Fall in Genesis, Origen cites as parallel the myth of the conception by Penia from Poros of Eros in Zeus's garden in Plato's *Symposium*. He thinks this precisely parallel to the story in Genesis, and calls it a 'myth' (μῦθος), but a myth with an allegorical meaning for the intelligentsia; and he suggests that Plato may have picked the myth up from Jewish savants when he visited Egypt.[4] Then he says, more explicitly, that Adam is a single figure representing the whole human race: 'In the words which appear to refer to Adam Moses is making a scientific statement (φυσιολογεῖ) on the subject of the nature of man; because "in Adam", as the Word says, "all die", and they were condemned "in the likeness of the transgression of Adam", and the divine Word does not so much speak in these terms of some single person as of the whole race.' Similarly Eve means no single historical woman, but every woman.[5] Later in the same work he refers to the earth to which 'Adam, which means man', came after he had been cast out of Paradise.[6] Elsewhere he

---

[1]*Protrept.* XI.111, *PG* 8.228.   [2]*Paed.* III.3.19, *PG* 8.581.
[3]*Strom.* V.11.71 f., *PG* 9.109, where he says that Moses by 'the tree of life' meant τὴν φρόνησιν θείαν and by Paradise the world could be intended.
[4]*Contra Celsum* IV.37–9; this use (in 39) of μῦθος in a sense which is not pejorative and does not mean 'worthless legend' is, as far as I know, unique in Origen and not found in any other Jewish or Christian writer mentioned in this book.
[5]*Ibid.*, IV.40.   [6]*Ibid.*, VII.50.

interprets the verse, 'Fear not to go down into Egypt, for I will make
of thee a great nation' (Gen. 46.3) of 'the first-created . . . who goes
down into tribulations into Egypt when, cast out of the pleasures of
Paradise, he is brought to the toils and troubles of this world';[1] this is
a fairly plain reference to Origen's theory of a pre-cosmic fall and a clear
indication that the story of Eden cannot be placed on the plane of earthly
history. Again he writes, on the trees in the garden of Eden (Gen. 2.9),
'When, as we read, we progress from legends and the interpretation
according to the letter, let us ask what are those trees which God
planted; we say that there are no trees apprehended by the senses in
the place.'[2] In another fragment he declares that the coats of skins
(Gen. 3.21) must not be thought of as literal; to think this would be
'very silly and old-womanish (γραῶδες) and unworthy of God'. He also
suggests that Paradise in this context is not really a locality and that the
nostrils of Adam into which God breathed life must not be taken
literally.[3]

Against this very strong evidence that Origen did not see anything
historical at all in the story of Adam and Eve there can be set three
passages which suggest the contrary. In his *Defence of Origen* Pamphilus
quoted a passage from Origen's otherwise lost *Commentary on Philemon*
giving a list of people in whose existence the Christian believer must
believe, and some events attached to them. Among these are, 'that Adam
was the first man made . . . that God took Eve from Adam's ribs and
built her so as to become a woman.'[4] In his *Commentary on the Song of
Solomon* Origen said that Adam is to be numbered among the prophets
and ascribed to him Gen. 2.24 as well as Gen. 2.23.[5] In the *Commentary
on Romans* Origen seems to accept that all men were 'in the loins of
Adam' as Levi was 'in the loins of Abraham' (Heb. 7.1, 9 f.).[6] This
evidence should not be overlooked, but it has to be pointed out that the
Defence of Origen has come down to us in only one of its books, and that
in a translation by Rufinus; both Pamphilus and Rufinus after him were
perfectly capable of misrepresenting Origen in order to commend him to
their respective generations; the accusation of dissolving historicity into
allegory was one levelled against Origen in the time of both these

---

[1]*Hom. on Gen.* XV.5.
[2]Fragment on Genesis, *PG* 12.100; as the piece is quoted with indignation by
Eustathius, it is quite certain that Origen did not intend the trees to be taken
literally.
[3]*Ibid., PG* 12.101.
[4]Pamphilus' *Defence of Origen, PG* 17.591 f.
[5]*Comm. on S. of S.* II, on S. of S. 1.11 f.
[6]*Comm. on Rom.* V.1.

[handwritten annotation at top: Origin believed in the inspiration of the Holy Spirit and the importance of every word but not in the story being accurate]

writers. The same possibility of the original having been meddled with hangs over Rufinus' translation of the *Commentary on Romans*. We are left with only one passage (that from the *Commentary on the Song of Solomon*) where we can be quite confident about the meaning of the original, though it is quite possible that the other two passages may be faithfully reproducing the words of Origen. In the circumstances it seems to me wholly likely that Origen did not believe in the historical truth of the story of Adam and Eve, though he was quite capable of writing inconsistently in one or two passages of his works as if he did think the story historical.

One more example, a particularly startling one, of Origen's readiness to dissolve historical event into allegory must be mentioned. This is his theory of Jesus having in his earthly ministry appeared in a different *epinoia* to a number of different people. *Epinoia*, as Bertrand admirably defines it, 'means very precisely "point of view". An ἐπίνοια is, according to Origen, a particular relation (*saisie*) of the Son of God with a soul.'[1] During his earthly ministry, in Origen's view, Jesus, while still incarnate, continued to have different relationships with different souls and to appear to each soul in a different guise, so that the guise assumed for one soul might not be recognized by another. Let us hear Origen himself on the subject. He sets out in detail the difficulties and contradictions of the four different accounts of Jesus' movements after his Baptism given by the evangelists,[2] and frankly declares that allegory must be resorted to if the credit of the Gospels is to be preserved. 'It must be that the truth of these things lies in the "intellectual" understanding of them, or else, if the contradiction be not resolved, belief in the Gospels is destroyed, on the grounds that they are not true, and not written in the divine Spirit, or else were merely haphazard accounts.'[3] Later in the same paragraph he says that if anyone examines the Gospels carefully he will find several similar contradictions, and will either in bewilderment abandon a firm belief in the truth of the Gospels or will inconsistently cleave to one of them, not daring entirely to abandon belief in our Lord, or else conclude that their truth does not lie in their literal expressions. Then he gives his account of how the evangelists came to differ. They each have different acts or appearances of God to record designed for different people:

[1] *Mystique de Jésus chez Origène*, p. 21. See also Koch, *Pronaid oiund Paeusis*, pp. 65–74; and Völker, *Das Vollkommenheitsideal*, p. 99.
[2] *Comm. on John* X.1–3.
[3] *Ibid.*, X.3.

'Let us grant that there are people who perceive God in the Spirit and his words to the saints and his presence by which he appears in their presence to them at chosen moments in their spiritual development, even though these people are several in number and live in different places and are enriched with gifts which are not completely similar. Let us suppose that each of these on his own initiative describes what he sees in the Spirit concerning God and his words and his appearances to the saints in such a way that the record of one concerns the words spoken and things done by God to this righteous man in this place, whereas that of another concerns the prophecies delivered and things accomplished in the case of another righteous man, and another wishes us to hear about a third man besides the two already mentioned; and let us suppose that some fourth person does the same thing as the other three about someone else. Now let these four be collated as regards some of the things they were prompted to say by the Holy Spirit, and let them also give the narration of each of the others briefly, and the result is that their narratives will be of some such sort as this: "God appeared to such and such a man at such and such a time in such and such a place, in such and such a manner, if God appeared to him in the appropriate form, and he led him to such and such a place, where he did these things." The second writer might record that God appeared, at the same time as the events said by the first writer to have taken place in some city, to a man whom he himself knows, some second person, in a place far removed from the place of the first person, and might write that other words were said at the same time to him whom according to our supposition we have assumed to be the second person. And we can imagine just the same circumstances about the third and fourth writers.'

The result will be that if all these accounts are compared the writers will appear untruthful, as long as it is assumed that God cannot be in two different places, and cannot do two different things, at the same time.[1] Origen then applies this general description of his theory to the evangelists particularly:

'If therefore the meaning of the plain narratives is understood according to the principles which I have laid down, that is that from their historical character we were intended to understand

[1] *Comm. on John* X.4.

the things apprehended by their inner significance, the meaning would be found to have no contradiction, if the four writers were discerning men. It is thus that we must realize the matter to stand with the four evangelists, who use to the full many of the deeds done and words said according to the miraculous and amazing power of Jesus, but sometimes also interpolate into Scripture in a context which is apparently about things of the sense that which has been revealed to them in an entirely intellectual sense. I do not make the charge against them that for the advantage of the mystical purpose which exists in these accounts they change that which according to the plain narrative takes place in contradiction (to the accounts of others) in such a way as to say that something which happened in one place happened in another, or that what happened at one time happened at another, and that they set down narratives of this sort with any alteration. For their aim was, where it was possible, to tell the truth in a spiritual and a material sense, but where it was not possible to tell it in both senses, to prefer the spiritual to the material, since the spiritual truth is often preserved in what one might call the material un-truth. . . . And Jesus of course is many things in his different significances (*epinoiai*), and it is likely that the evangelists seized on different aspects (*ennoiai*) of these significances, and sometimes wrote their Gospels after conferring with each other on certain points.'[1]

St Paul's various methods of being all things to all men are suggested as a parallel to these *epinoiai* of our Lord, and so is Peter, who is recorded in John's Gospel as brought by Andrew to Jesus and as called Cephas, but is different in his *epinoiai* from the Peter of the Synoptists who was seen by Jesus with his brother walking by the sea-shore. Another example is John the Baptist, imprisoned, according to the Synoptists, before Jesus' Ministry, but according to John's Gospel preaching after the beginning of the Ministry. Another instance is Jesus baptizing; in the Synoptists he does not baptize at all, but in John's Gospel he bap-tizes through his disciples.[2] Bertrand calls attention to a passage where Origen says that Judas at the Arrest was obliged to kiss Jesus because a mark of recognition was necessary, *propter transformationes eius*, which no doubt means 'on account of his *epinoiai*'.[3] He notes that John's

[1]*Comm. on John* X.5.   [2]*Ibid.*, X.7 f.
[3]*Comm. on Matt.* Comm. Ser. 100; Bertrand, *Mystique de Jesus chez Origène*, p. 25 n. 1.

Gospel says that Jesus bore his own Cross, whereas the other evangelists say that Simon of Cyrene bore it; this means that there are two *epinoiai* of the Cross, the Cross which Simon bears and that which Jesus himself bears.[1] The Resurrection Appearances were only an extension of these *epinoiai*.[2]

At first sight it appears as if Origen were claiming that Jesus, and presumably Peter and Paul and John the Baptist too, were capable of appearing to two or more different people in different places at the same time, when he expounds his theory of *epinoiai*. But in fact closer inspection assures us that this is not so. All he means is that where the evangelists give apparently contradictory accounts of Jesus those details which are inconsistent with the rest of the narratives are not descriptions of the historical Jesus actually teaching or healing in Palestine but are parabolic ways of describing different significances of Jesus, allegories of his ultimate significance for different sorts of human souls. That he conceived that these *epinoiai* made it difficult for people to recognize Jesus in the flesh, however, suggests that to Origen the dividing-line between Jesus incarnate as a real man in a period of history, as a human individual, and the idea or understanding of Jesus in the minds and judgements of men, was very thin and uncertain; he does not maintain, as the Fourth Evangelist does, that the two are inseparably bound up together, but he conceives that the Jesus of history could during his life on earth occasionally dissolve into the Jesus of religious experience, leaving apparently no historical sediment behind. It is, however, going beyond the evidence to say, as de Faye says, 'Origen's philosophy owes nothing to Jesus who lived, spoke, and acted. Let us say, if it is preferable, that neither the picture of Jesus such as the earliest Christians drew it in the Gospels, nor his deeds nor words, had any influence on Origen's theology. The material of the Gospels was not one of the sources of his thought.'[3] On the other hand, it seems to me even greater exaggeration on the other side to claim, as Bertrand does, that Origen was profoundly concerned with 'the Christ of history, the Christ of the Gospels',[4] or to speak of his 'devotion to the humanity and to the

[1]*Comm. on Matt.* XII.24. Restatements of this theory appear in *Contra Celsum* IV.16 (as *ennoiai*); *Hom. on Luke* III, on Luke 1.11; and in a fragment on Luke quoted by Macarius, *PG* 13.1908.
[2]*Contra Celsum* II.63–6.
[3]De Faye, *Origène*, III, p. 160. But de Faye admits readily enough (pp. 150–5) that in the *Contra Celsum* Origen shows a surprising respect for historicity, and (pp. 160–3) that he does not entirely allegorize away historical truth.
[4]Bertrand, *Mystique de Jesus chez Origène*, p. 144; see also pp. 145 f.

Person of Jesus'.[1] Origen was not devoted to the *humanity* of Jesus, as his theory of *epinoiai* very clearly shows; he was devoted to the Logos whose activity as Logos (*not* as a human individual) in a post-incarnate existence was illustrated or enacted in parable or charade by Jesus incarnate as an individual. Bertrand, very surprisingly, nowhere in his work mentions the remarkable fact that Origen discouraged his pupils from addressing prayer directly to Jesus;[2] this is not characteristic of one who had a profound devotion to the humanity of the God-man. Origen certainly displays interest in every minute movement and gesture of Jesus recorded in the Gospels, but not because he is interested in the Jesus who lived as an individual in history but because he is interested in the theological or philosophical truths or the features of the religious development of the contemporary Christian of which he imagined these movements and gestures to be symbols. In history as event, in history as the field of God's self-revelation *par excellence*, Origen is not in the least interested. He is only interested in history as parable, and this fact is illustrated as effectively as anywhere else in his treatment of Jesus in his earthly ministry. 'What has this history to do with me?' Origen exclaims at one point; he is discussing the title of the book of Jeremiah (Jer. 1.2–3) with its record of the reigns in which Jeremiah prophesied.[3] It can be nothing more than tinder for the fire of allegory. The record of one Egyptian king succeeding another (Ex. 1.8) was, he says, recorded solely 'for our instruction and warning', so that we may not, having accepted Christ (Joseph means Jesus) as our king, fall away to the muddy business of spiritual brick-making, and so on.[4] 'In the year that King Uzziah died' (Isa. 6.1) cannot be merely a date; it means that

---

[1] *Mystique de Jesus chez Origène*, p. 153.
[2] See *PE* XIV.6 and *Origen's Doctrine of Tradition*, pp. 177 f.
[3] *Hom. on Jer.* I.2, τί οὖν πρὸς ἐμὲ αὐτὴ ἡ ἱστορία; cf. frags. 28 f. in the same work, where Origen recognizes that the two kings mentioned in Jer. 50.17 are historical (for they are to be met in the pages of II Kings), but their real interest to him is that they are types of Satan and the Man of Sin, and also warnings of the Satan within all of us. Incidentally, we may agree with de Lubac when he says (*Histoire et Esprit*, pp. 116–20) that ἱστορία means for Origen 'history without interpretation', but not when he asserts that for him μῦθος 'does not necessarily imply that it is a matter of false history, of facts which did not happen' (p. 118). We have seen only one example of μῦθος used in a favourable sense (see above, p. 270 n. 4) and even there the word does not imply that the facts did happen; I believe that hundreds of examples of μῦθος meaning 'worthless legend' could be collected from Origen's pages. All Christian writers before Origen who use the word use it in this pejorative sense; the example which de Lubac quotes from Justin to establish the favourable sense will not do: οὐ κενοῖς ἐπιστεύσαμεν μύθοις . . . ἀλλὰ μεστοῖς πνεύματος θεοῦ (*Dial.* 9.1) should be translated, 'we have not believed in empty legends . . . but in things full of a divine Spirit'.
[4] *Hom. on Ex.* I.5.

only when our leprous body is mortified can we see the Lord high and lifted up.[1] The statement of Ezekiel that it was in 'the thirtieth year' that he saw his vision (Ezek. 1.1) provokes the comment: 'What good does this numbering of years do me except this, that it was in the thirtieth year that the heavens were opened for the Saviour as well as for the prophet ?'[2] A reference in Ezek. 17 to Nebuchadnezzar besieging Jerusalem and taking away its chief men has an historical meaning, but more significant is its message that no spiritual Nebuchadnezzar should enter our Church, and that none can as long as a righteous king, a spiritual Hezekiah or Josiah, rules it; but if such a king does not rule, then Nebuchadnezzar may come up against our Church and any he takes captive he brings to Babylon, that is confusion.[3] Origen is no less insistent than Kierkegaard that the only history that concerns the Christian is history *for you*, but by history for you he means not the thirty years of God's self-disclosure in Christ but any history that can be turned into a parable conveying some sort of Christian truth. This is the only significance that he can see in history.

It is easy to see therefore that two wrong answers have been for long given to the old question, 'Did Origen completely dissolve history into allegory ?' It is as inaccurate to say that he had no belief in the historical truth of the narratives of the Old and New Testaments as it is to maintain that he had a deep respect for their historical truth. The fact is that he believed that most of the narratives were accounts of events which did happen (even though it is possible to compile, as we have compiled, a fairly long list of exceptions to this general rule), but he believed that what was significant about these events was not that they happened, but the non-historical truths of which they were parabolic enactments. A very large amount of evidence can be produced to prove this point. Answering Celsus's objection that Christ should have become invisible on the Cross, Origen contends that both the crucifixion and the burial, and all the details of both, had a symbolic meaning referring to mystical things which could not have taken place if the symbols of them had not taken place. 'These things which are recorded as having happened to Jesus do not yield the full view of their truth if they are understood according to the bare literal sense and narrative; for each of them is realized in the minds of those who search Scripture with understanding to be also a symbol of something. Just as his being crucified has the full

[1] *Hom. on Isa.* IV.3.
[2] *Hom. on Ezek.* I.4.
[3] *Ibid.*, XII.2.

explanation of its truth in "I am crucified with Christ" and in that which
is meant by "but God forbid that I should glory save in the cross of my
Lord Jesus Christ, by whom the world is crucified unto me and I unto
the world"; and his death was necessary because of "in that he died, he
died unto sin once", and because Paul calls the righteous man "conformed to his death", and "for if we have died with him we shall also
live with him"; so also his burial affects those who are conformed to his
death and those who are crucified with him, just as it is said in Paul's
writings, "We were buried with him through baptism" and we have
risen with him.'[1] Having in his *Peri Euches* cited as examples of
answered prayer Hannah, Hezekiah, Mordecai, Judith, the three young
men in the fiery furnace, Daniel in the den of lions, and Jonah, he proceeds to apply their cases, now allegorized, to the spiritual struggles and
deliverances of the contemporary Christian: 'Why should I enumerate
all those who have often fallen into almost irresistible temptations more
scorching than any flame, and yet have suffered no harm from them,
but have escaped these perils entirely unscathed, not even receiving
accidental injury from "the smell" of the hostile "fire"?'[2] He believed
that the adventures of each of his scriptural examples were historical,
though as historical events quite unimportant. The escape from 'invisible lions' was, for instance, more important for Daniel than the
deliverance from the material beasts.[3] Origen's treatment of this incident
in comparison with that of Hippolytus is at once more subtle and more
remote from the original text. He believes that the Entry into Canaan
took place really and historically, but the historical event was brought
about only in order to provide a type: 'They did these things with
visible weapons, but we do it with invisible. They conquered in material
battle, but we overcome in spiritual combat.'[4] On Ps. 66.6, 'He turned
the sea into dry land: they went through the river on foot,' he comments, 'looking at it historically, this happened once only, in Judaea.
But looking at it spiritually, this is always occurring, as God by his
teaching steers to virtue and knowledge souls which are tossed by the
salt waves of life and carried about with every wind.'[5] On the death of
Lazarus he says, 'As far as the symbol is concerned, grant that he
[Christ] is showing the death that took place in the story: but as far as
the allegory is concerned, we must allow him to set forth the death which

[1] *Contra Celsum* II.69.   [2] *PE* XIII.3.
[3] *Ibid.*, XVI.3. De Lubac, *Histoire et Esprit*, pp. 112 f., cites this passage with
what appears to me to be sentimental approval.
[4] *Hom. on Num.* VII.3.
[5] *Comm. on Ps.* 66.6, *PG* 12.1500.

they sometimes sleep who have not been enlightened in the eyes of their soul by God.'[1] The wrestling of Jacob with an angel did take place historically, but it was a spiritual, not a physical wrestling.[2] God deliberately ordained 'the narrative and account in their literal sense' of the birth, first of Ishmael from the handmaid and then of Isaac from the freewoman, in order that we might realize its allegorical significance, that fleshly thoughts must be cast out before spiritual and true ones.[3] 'The Church of God therefore interprets references to births in this way [i.e. allegorically], and in this way understands mention of procreations, upholds in this way the activities of the patriarchs by a respectable and decent interpretation, in this way refuses to stain the words of the Holy Spirit with futile and Jewish legends but regards them as full of decency and full of virtue and practical value. Otherwise what sort of profit will we derive from reading that so great a patriarch as Abraham not only lied to King Abimelech but also betrayed the honour of his wife?'[4] It is ridiculous to suppose that God really had respect to Moses' hands when he lifted them up during the battle against Amalek (Ex. 17.8–16), but in this incident (which did take place) God 'was foreshadowing mysteries to come'.[5] In a few fragments of his (otherwise lost) *Commentary on Galatians*, quoted by Pamphilus in his *Defence of Origen*,[6] he says, of the story of our Lord being asleep on a cushion in a boat (Mark 4.38), 'Although these events have a spiritual meaning, yet while the truth of the original event is unimpaired (*manente prius historiae veritate*) the spiritual meaning should be accepted;' and he contends that though Christ opens the eyes of the mind by his doctrine and allays the storms of the Church, yet he did actually heal blind men and did on that occasion still the storm. And again he says elsewhere, 'Christ once went to sleep in the disciples' boat, but when a storm arose the disciples woke him. The word here shows us that when a tempest of thoughts of anger or injustice or gluttony or pride occurs in the soul there awake out of sleep love, righteousness, temperance, continence, meekness, knowledge and wisdom.'[7]

[1]*Comm. on John*, frag. 79, on John 11.4.
[2]*PA* III.1.5.   [3]*Hom. on Jer.* V.15.
[4]*Hom. on Gen.* VI.3.   [5]*Hom. on I Sam.* I.9.   [6]*PG* 14.1293–6.
[7]*Comm. on Ps.* 44.23, *PG* 12.1428. It would be tedious to quote any more examples of this tendency of Origen's in the text, but many more could be produced, e.g. *Comm. on S. of S.* II, on S. of S. 1.6 (reproduced in *Philoc.* XXVII.13); *Comm. on John* II.29; VI.42; XX.3, 10; *Contra Celsum* II.16; IV.41, 43 f.; *PA* III.5.1; fragment on Genesis, *PG* 12.133; *Hom. on Gen.* VII.1. Clement of Alexandria sometimes displays tendency too, e.g. when he makes it clear that the theophany on Sinai was historical, though it could also be allegorized (*Strom.* VI.3.32 f., *PG* 9.252).

This is what Origen means when he so frequently insists that the reader cannot understand the literal sense unless he reads the spiritual sense into the passage too. This is a sentiment which has evoked admiration from some students of Origen.[1] History, according to this view, is meaningless unless a parable is derived from it, unless it is made into an allegory. This is not the same as saying that to history there must be brought an interpretation or it is a mere jumble. It is to say that history is a mere jumble unless there is brought to it *this* interpretation, this Philonic, allegorical, essentially anti-historical interpretation which dissolves particularity and ignores the possibility of revelation really taking place in event. In this treatment of the event by Origen history is not indeed abrogated, but it is dangerously externalized.

This 'externalizing' of history is emphasized by Origen's habit of resolving incidents and details in both Old and New Testaments into the religious experience of the contemporary Christian believer.[2] He says that, in every true disciple of Jesus, Jesus must be crucified between two thieves.[3] Jesus still speaks to some as to 'those who are without', in parables (Mark 4.11 ff.), to others 'in the house', to others on the mountain of Transfiguration, to others, who could not climb so high, below the mountain in order to heal them.'[4] The same is true of activities of others towards Jesus: 'In this way,' says Bertrand, 'every interior movement which the believer makes in his soul in respect of Christ living in the Church finds its appropriate symbol in an exterior movement made already in the presence of the historical Christ of the Gospels.'[5] The miracle of the stilling of the storm takes place in the experience of the Christian himself; he battles against the winds and waves of temptation; the Word comes to save him; the Peter in him attempts to be entirely master of the temptation and fails.[6] The parable of the Unmerciful Steward is applied to the Christian's experience; we have, spiritually, wives and children, we are spiritually debtors; we go, spiritually, out of the presence of our Lord.[7] For every faithful believer in his religious experience the veil is rent, the earth moves, the rocks are split, the tombs open, and so on to every detail of the Passion and Resurrection.[8] On the parable of the Good Shepherd he says, 'For when

---

[1]E.g. de Lubac, *Histoire et Esprit*, pp. 104–13, and especially p. 110.
[2]Bertrand treats of this tendency very fully in *Mystique de Jesus chez Origène*, Parts I and II.
[3]*Contra Celsum* II.44.
[4]*Ibid.*, III.21.
[5]*Mystique de Jesus chez Origène*, p. 44.
[6]*Comm. on Matt.* XI.5.
[7]*Ibid.*, XIV.13.   [8]*Ibid.*, Comm. Ser. 139.

the Saviour says, "I am the Good Shepherd", I do not understand it only in a general sense, as everybody understands it, that he is the Shepherd of the faithful (and this is of course a sound and true belief), but I ought also to have within me Christ in my soul, shepherding the irrational impulses within me.'[1] The same process is applied to Abraham's career; we must leave our home and our kindred and go into the land which God will show us, and we shall be made into a great nation.[2] The same spiritualizing tendency transmutes the text 'Wherefore ye must needs be in subjection not only because of the wrath, but also for conscience sake' (Rom. 13.5, which presumably means 'you must obey lawful authority not only for fear of punishment but also out of a sense of obligation') into 'Therefore you must be a slave to worldly (spiritual) powers not only because of the wrath which you have brought on yourself but also because you are accused by your conscience.'[3] His treatment of Lamentations and of the Song of Solomon is characteristic, for he sees far more references in both these books to the relations of the individual Christian soul to the Logos than to anything else. He is very uncertain in applying 'She weepeth sore in the night' (Lam. 1.2) to the city of Jerusalem, but he is quite confident when he applies it to the soul which weeps exiled in Babylon (confusion) away from its true home.[4] 'In Origen,' says Völker, 'the transformation of a great cosmic event into the inner life of the devout continually takes place, indeed with him both conceptions often lie side by side in the exegesis.'[5]

This tendency to dissolve historical events into religious experience has been defended as entirely legitimate by some modern scholars. De Lubac has described it as 'interiorizing history';[6] he distinguishes it from Philonic exegesis on the ground that Origen consistently adds the 'spiritual' meaning to the 'moral';[7] and he points out that Gregory of Nyssa and St John of the Cross shared with Origen the conviction that 'Scripture contains in fact, beneath the letter, the highest secrets of the spiritual life.'[8] Daniélou defends Origen's conviction that the controversy between Jacob and Esau and between Jew and Christian represents

[1] *Hom. on Jer.* V.6.
[2] *Comm. on Rom.* IV.7.
[3] *Ibid.,* IX.30.
[4] *Hom. on Lam.,* frag. 10.
[5] *Das Vollkommenheitsideal,* p. 110.
[6] *Histoire et Esprit,* p. 20.
[7] *Ibid.,* pp. 163 f., 165 f.
[8] *Ibid.,* p. 192 n. 333. Earlier (p. 43) he has said that many authors (and in particular he mentions those of the liberal Protestant school) are incapable of understanding Origen because their learning, however great, cannot compensate for the fact that they do not share in the life of the (Roman Catholic) Church, and that it is to be regretted that several Catholic writers have been influenced by them. So perhaps my failure to agree with this writer's arguments are attributable to this defect.

the controversy between spirit and flesh within each of us, saying that it 'rests upon the historical reality of the conflict of the two peoples, of which it is the legitimate development',[1] and describing it as 'a transposition to the history of the soul from the history of the people which is in one line of authentic typology',[2] and maintains that in Origen objectivity and subjectivity of interpretation are subtly woven together; from Philo he derives 'interiority' in his exegesis, the deriving of meanings concerning the ascent of the soul towards God, psychological and mystical, but from Christian typology he derived an objectivity, a respect for history; the two balanced each other, each compensating for the lack of balance in the other.[3]

I confess that I find these attempts to champion Origen on this point unconvincing. In the first place, de Lubac and Daniélou take rather different ground. What de Lubac describes as 'interiorizing history' and as adding the 'spiritual' to the 'moral' meaning Daniélou frankly labels as Philonic exegesis. Then this sort of exposition has no solid ground in St Paul and no vestige of support anywhere else in the New Testament. St Paul says that 'he that was born after the flesh persecuted him that was born after the spirit' and that this was also happening in his own day (Gal. 4.29) and several verses later on he says that the 'flesh lusteth against the Spirit and the Spirit against the flesh for these two are contrary to each other' (Gal. 5.17). He was claiming that the conflict of Ishmael and Isaac represented the conflict of Jew and Christian, of the man living under the Torah and the man living under grace in Christ, between two dispensations or states of relationship to God objectively established by him. And these states have, of course, their different effects in the religious experience and the behaviour of those who live under them. But to say this is very far indeed from saying that any figures in the Old Testament, Ishmael and Isaac, Esau and Jacob, or any other pair can legitimately be allegorized directly into descriptions of Christian religious or moral experience, further still from implying that any and every incident, movement and detail in Old or New Testaments is liable to yield such an allegorization. The step from Paul's allegorization to Origen's, a step into the non-historical world of Hellenistic allegory, can only be taken with the aid of Philonic exegesis. And that is precisely how Origen does achieve this step. The distinction between 'moral' (=Philonic) and 'spiritual' (=Christian)

---

[1]Daniélou, *Origène*, p. 167.
[2]Daniélou, *Sacramentum Futuri*, p. 121.
[3]*Ibid.*, p. 117.

interpretation (if it ever existed) disappears in Origen's exposition, and the balance between 'objective' and 'subjective' interpretation is never struck. All is merged in a morass of spiritualizing exposition which has no legitimate ground in historical reality. Origen certainly opened the way to the discovery in the text of the Bible of the deepest secrets of the spiritual life, but the only tools which he provided for the operation were those of theological fantasy.

Montdesert remarks that 'If we compare the Alexandrians with Irenaeus, we see the difference between the pure theology of the Incarnation and the theology where the Incarnation of Christ is not the only dominant idea.'[1] I am not sure that this is entirely fair to Clement. He can write a sentence like this: 'But that part of (divine) wrath which is akin to passion—if we should call his providence wrath—is inspired by benevolence, for God submits himself to experience passions for the sake of man, for whose sake the Word of God even became man.'[2] It is difficult to imagine Origen writing such a sentence; Montdesert's verdict is fully justified in his case. Behind Origen's treatment of historicity lies, not an abandonment of the dogma of the Incarnation of the Son of God, but an underestimation of it.

Each of our senses, says Origen, if we allegorize references to them in the Scriptures, can function in our relation to Christ; we can spiritually hear him and see him, and allegorically 'touch can make contact with the Word, as John says, "our hands have handled concerning the Word of life" ' (I John 1.1).[3] In a later work he says that nobody would be so silly as to imagine that this text should not be taken allegorically.[4] This is in fact to dissolve by allegory into spiritual experience one of the passages in the New Testament which insists most drastically upon the reality of the Incarnation: 'that which we have seen, that which we have heard' could perhaps be taken as figurative statements describing a spiritual experience, but not 'that which we have handled'; it may well be that this is why the author of the Epistle added this phrase. But Origen unconcernedly allegorizes it. Elsewhere he suggests that Christ's death and resurrection are a type (μυστήριον) of the crucifixion and burial with him of his body, the Church, reversing the conviction of Paul that the redemptive activity of Christ is that to which the Christian is to

---

[1]Montdesert, *Clement d'Alexandrie*, p. 188.
[2]'Ἀλλὰ καὶ τὸ ἐμπαθὲς τῆς ὀργῆς (εἰ δὲ ὀργὴν τὴν νουθεσίαν αὐτοῦ χρὴ καλεῖν) φιλανθρωπόν ἐστιν, εἰς πάθη καταβαίνοντος τοῦ θεοῦ διὰ τὸν ἄνθρωπον, δι' ὃν καὶ γέγονεν ἄνθρωπος ὁ Λόγος τοῦ θεοῦ, *Paed.* I.8.74, *PG* 8.340.
[3]*Comm. on Matt.* Comm. Ser. 64.
[4]*Contra Celsum* VII.34.

become conformed.[1] He says indeed explicitly that Christ became flesh
in order that he might first make his disciples conform to the Word-
made-flesh and then might lift them up to see him as he was before he
became flesh.[2] It is impossible to avoid the conclusion that the Incarnation was to Origen no more than a necessary device employed by God
as an important stage in the process of fully revealing himself.[3] He has
no favourite word for describing the Incarnation, but the word *economy*
is one which he does often use of it, in common with most of the pre-
Nicene Greek Fathers. In Origen's thought the word tends to mean
'device' or 'strategy' rather than 'dispensation'.[4]

This accusation has, of course, been levelled at Origen before and it
has sometimes been suggested in reply that, whatever Origen may have
thought about the Incarnation, the Cross was at the centre of his thought
and devotion. De Lubac and Bertrand cite a passage in which Origen
certainly does say that 'however far we may have reached in the highest
and most advanced contemplation of the Logos' we shall never forget
the Passion of Christ;[5] and Völker and Molland press the same point.[6]
On the other hand de Faye believed that fundamentally Origen found
the suffering and agony of Jesus a little hard to defend and a little difficult to understand; 'Origen was still too completely a Greek to share in
this sort of mysticism.'[7] And Koch says that in Origen's system for the
advanced Christians the Atonement of Jesus plays no essential part; they
only need the *epinoiai* of the discarnate Son.[8]

I think that the last two authors tend to ignore the fact that Origen
lived at a period when Christians were liable to be called upon to face
violent death for their faith and that he enthusiastically encouraged them
to endure this experience if it came upon them. In such circumstances
it would be amazing if the Cross made no appeal to Origen, and was as
remote from the centre of his thought as de Faye and Koch have sug-

---

[1]*Comm. on John* X.35. Compare the passage from *Contra Celsum* II.69 quoted
above, pp. 277 f.
[2]*Contra Celsum* VI.68.
[3]Compare Koch's words, 'The coming of the Logos into the world is only
one of the many other measures taken by Providence. It means—as does everything else which God does in other ways for the education of humanity—a step
forward, perhaps a very important step, but still only one among many' (*Pronoia
und Paideusis*, p. 31).
[4]E.g. 'fleshly economy', τὴν ἔνσαρκον οἰκονομίαν, Pitra, *Analecta Sacra* II,
p. 460.
[5]*Comm. on John* II.8; see de Lubac, *Histoire et Esprit*, pp. 86 f., 91 f.; Bertrand, *Mystique de Jesus chez Origène*, pp. 30, 32.
[6]Völker, *Das Vollkommenheitsideal*, pp. 102 f.; Molland, *The Conception of the
Gospel in Alexandrian Theology*, p. 153.
[7]*Origène* I, pp. 171 f.   [8]*Op cit.*, p. 77.

gested. But this does not necessarily affect the suggestion that Origen underestimated the centrality and importance of the dogma of the Incarnation, and even those authors who are anxious to stress how central was the Cross to Origen recognize this. Molland notices how Origen's spiritualizing tendency rivals and overpowers his belief in the Incarnation.[1] Völker admits that for the advanced Christian in his highest union with God Christ's mediation is, in Origen's thought, unnecessary.[2] Koch also points out that Origen's conception of education puts the love, the redemption and the forgiveness of God into the background; he even says that Origen's conception of God as Father and of God's love are in no way specifically Christian, and notes that his usual word for God's love is 'benevolence' ($\varphi\iota\lambda\alpha\nu\theta\rho\omega\pi\iota\alpha$).[3] And he is of the opinion that 'the Incarnation *per se* as an historical event does not play such a decisive part for Origen's spiritualizing conception as it does in other theological systems.'[4] Crouzel brings out clearly that to Origen the Incarnation was only a means of enabling people to reach the state whereby they could see God; the patriarchs had seen God through the Logos without the interposition of the Incarnation; the fact that in Origen's view the image of the invisible God apprehensible in Jesus is still itself invisible supports this point. 'We must not conclude from this,' says Crouzel, 'that the Incarnation has no place in his doctrine of the image, but this place . . . is secondary.'[5] Elsewhere in his work this scholar repeats the observation that the root-cause of Origen's subordinationism was that he envisaged the mediatorship of Jesus Christ as lying in his *divine* nature. quite apart from the Incarnation,[6] and illustrates effectively how entirely the Incarnation was to Origen a necessary part of a process and no more, a device adopted to transfer souls from involvement in matter to a post-material existence.[7] With this impressive chorus of testimony to Origen's underestimation of the Incarnation all that has been said in this work about Origen's attitude to the inspiration and the historicity of the Bible is in emphatic agreement.

We must therefore conclude, from our survey of Origen's estimate of the historical value of the Bible, that though he did regard most of the

[1] *The Conception of the Gospel in Alexandrian Theology*, p. 170.
[2] *Das Vollkommenheitsideal*, p. 191.
[3] *Pronoia und Paideusis*, pp. 34 f.
[4] *Ibid.*, pp. 63 f.
[5] *Théologie de l'Image de Dieu chez Origène*, pp. 75–83; the quotation is from p. 82.
[6] *Ibid.*, I, ch. I.
[7] *Ibid.*, II, ch. II.

narratives and accounts in it as historical, and does not deserve the strictures of de Faye on this point,[1] he only regarded this history as valuable because of the parabolic or symbolic significance which it contained, because, in short it could be allegorized, and that this view was simply a development of the Philonic attitude to history. I must therefore dissent from the judgement of H. E. W. Turner that 'the Christian estimate of history was already a stone of stumbling to Celsus, and here Origen, despite his fundamental sympathy with much of the Greek spirit and the priority which his theory of exegesis was to assign to the mystical over the historical, remains inflexible.'[2] Origen's estimate of history was essentially Greek. And we must characterize as absurd the statement made in an essay by Arseniev to the effect that 'Origen is very decisively a Christian realist, laying stress on the historic fact, on the concrete historical texture of life, on the concrete historical reality of our salvation;'[3] every single statement in this extraordinary sentence is contradicted by the evidence assembled in these pages.

A subtler and more elaborate attitude to this subject has been taken by two scholars, von Balthasar and de Lubac. To them the essential reality is, not the historical life of Christ, not some timeless philosophical interpretation of Christ's significance, but the life of the Church in the present world. 'This life of the mystical body, the μυστήριον τῆς ἐκκλησίας,[4] the great final symbol which gathers up the other two [the literal and moral senses] in itself, is already mingled with the eternal. The "pneumatic sense" which corresponds to it is not something abstract, wandering in unreality independently of history. It is the exterior history and the individual history which are "abstract" (in the Hegelian sense of the word) in comparison with this great "aeonian and numenal history" (Berdyaev) which unfolds itself at the border of time and eternity, between God and the world.'[5] This, in von Balthasar's view, is all that Origen is saying in his treatment of history. De Lubac takes substantially the same view. He claims that Origen's view amounts simply to this: what has happened in and to Christ must also happen in and to us who are in Christ. This truth justifies all Origen's exposition of a double sense, all his suggestions that the historical event is only a vehicle for a deeper meaning; his watchword is 'our Saviour

[1]See especially *Origène* I, pp. 75–82, and III, p. 115.
[2]*The Pattern of Christian Truth*, pp. 26 f.
[3]'The Teaching of the Orthodox Church on the relation between Scripture and Tradition', *ECQ* VII, Suppl., p. 17.
[4]Citing a fragment on Job, *PG* 12.1035.
[5]H. von Balthasar, 'Le Mysterion d'Origène', *RechSR* XXVII, p. 559.

who acted symbols of his own spiritual activities'.[1] This principle places Origen's interpretation 'in the centre of the Christian truth'; indeed this method 'results only in emphasizing evangelical realism, far from compromising it, for the reality of the history is the necessary guarantee of the mysterious reality which it signifies'.[2]

The New Testament says that Christ died and that because of this event we are redeemed when the redemptive event, which happened once for all, meets us in the sacraments of Baptism and the Eucharist. Origen says that Christ died at a point in history in order that we might timelessly be united to him in Christian meditation and experience, and that his other historical acts and sayings were performed (if they were performed at all) in order that we might now understand our relationship to him, our sanctification, our struggles against sin, and so on This is a very different belief, but it is one which apparently von Balthasar and de Lubac endorse. Such an attitude forces us back upon some larger questions: Is the Church really a higher stage after the Incarnation? Is the Church's relationship to Christ such that it is emancipated from the Incarnation? Is the Christian faith no longer vulnerable to history? Have the historical origins of the Christian religion, which are open to historical investigation, no essential bearing upon the Christian faith as the Church knows it and lives it today? And, more fundamental, did God really pour himself out, pledge himself and commit himself into history in the Incarnation, did he really move into history, or do such texts as John 1.14 and Phil. 2.5–11 and I John 1.1–4 only mean that God caused certain necessary eternal truths to be enacted in a parable or charade on the stage of history so that we, apprehending them, might be saved? It seems to me that, in their anxiety to justify Origen, von Balthasar and de Lubac come perilously near to saying that what the Church today believes and thinks about Christ is ultimately more important than what Christ did in those thirty years of revelation. Certainly Origen's theology is a halfway house to this position.

Finally, one question is left entirely unanswered by this defence of Origen, as it is by Origen himself. What is the connection between the original historical context of any passage in the Bible and the use of it

---

[1] ὁ καὶ σύμβολα ποιήσας τῶν ἰδίων πνευματικῶν πράξεων σωτὴρ ἡμῶν, *Comm. on Matt.* XVI.20, quoted by de Lubac, *Histoire et Esprit*, p. 206 n. 65.
[2] De Lubac, *op. cit.*, pp. 206–17; the quotations from de Lubac are from pp. 206 and 207; but it is scarcely possible to do justice to his viewpoint here; see also pp. 270, 278–94 (especially p. 288), and 363–73. Also see my article criticizing his viewpoint, 'History and Allegory', *Theology* LIX, pp. 498–503.

which the Church makes by allegory in Origen's time, or in our time?
In all his voluminous work de Lubac does not attempt, does not appear
to contemplate attempting, to answer this question. I cannot conceive
how anyone can satisfactorily defend Origen's attitude to historicity
until he has honestly faced this question.

II

The Law

WE have earlier had occasion to glance at Philo's attitude to the
Jewish law;[1] though he regarded its meaning as mainly symbolic, he did maintain that, with some exceptions, it ought to
be observed literally. According to Marcel Simon, this attitude to the
law was one which the Christians of the first few centuries would have
understood and approved in a Jew; they believed on the whole that the
Jews under the old covenant had been justified in taking the law literally,
though now that the Messiah had come they would expect the Jew to
abandon this literal observance.[2] Tertullian, for instance, uses the phrase
'to us, to whom sabbaths are alien, as are new moons and festivals which
were once favoured by God'.[3] On the other hand, Christians for the
most part entirely rejected the necessity for Jews or anybody else to keep
the Halakah, the 'tradition of the fathers', the fence for the law devised
by the Rabbis. Simon gives quotations from the *Didascalia*, Jerome and
Augustine, to show that it was a widespread custom in the early Church
to call the unwritten, oral, Halakic law the *deuterosis* (δευτέρωσις was
the name given to it by Greek-speaking Jewish communities at the time
when the Mishna was composed), and to identify it with the second law
described in the Pentateuch as re-written by Moses; this *deuterosis* was
'invested with a pejorative significance', indicating that this second law
was a temporary, man-made ordinance, now obsolete, in contrast to the
very high value set upon it by the Jews.[4] The Christians did not, as on
this theory they might logically have done, reject Deuteronomy as
uninspired.[5]

---

[1] See above, pp. 52 f.
[2] *Verus Israel*, p. 93.
[3] *Nobis, quibus sabbata extranea sunt et neomeniae et feriae a Deo aliquando
dilectae, De Idololatria* 14, quoted by Simon, *op. cit.*, p. 93 n. 4.
[4] *Ibid.*, pp. 115 f.
[5] But the Christian dialogue, *Timothy and Aquila*, did actually take this step:
'The fifth book is Deuteronomy, which was not dictated by the mouth of God,
but deuteronomized (δευτερονομηθέντα) by Moses; this is the reason why he
did not put it in the *aron*, that is, the Ark of the Covenant' (77A); see Simon,

But Simon also shows that the early Christians by no means entirely abandoned the observance of the law. They almost all agreed that the moral commandments could be distinguished from the ritual, and were in fact statements in a concrete situation of eternal moral laws: 'the natural parts of the law through which man is justified and which those who were justified by faith and pleasing to God used to observe even before the giving of the law', are the words of Irenaeus.[1] This distinction was indeed familiar to the Rabbis and was by them based on Lev. 18.4, and the synagogues had imposed on οἱ σεβόμενοι no more than the moral observances as essential. Arguments in the mouths of Christians against the ritual commandments include their being interpreted as a stigma branding the Jews instead of as a privilege distinguishing them; a demonstration of the contradictory nature of these ritual commandments; emphasis upon the fact that, with the destruction of Jerusalem and its being forbidden to Jews, some of the most important of the ritual ordinances cannot be carried out; and the suggestion that the ritual commandments were temporary, provisional, and designed to keep the Jews out of the mischief of idolatry.[2] Dugmore has also produced evidence to show that the normal Christian attitude to the Decalogue was to regard it as that part of the law which was still binding upon Christians, and has given an interesting account of the early Christians' observance of the Sabbath (i.e. Saturday); it was quite a widespread observance and continued in one way or another for at least five centuries.[3] We have already encountered some evidence that Sabbath-observance was quite a well-known phenomenon in Origen's day.[4]

It is probable in any case that, whatever the theologians might say, many of the commandments of the Jewish law were influential in the ordinary life of Christian people, for there was no sharp and decisive break between Judaism and Christianity, but a gradual drifting apart. But a consideration of some of the literature of the first two centuries of

---

op. cit., pp. 116 f. R. M. Grant, *The Letter and the Spirit*, pp. 52 f., has an interesting theory, which is not, however, altogether convincing, that Paul regarded Deuteronomy in much the same way, branding it as the law which 'was added because of transgressions' and treating it as a document intended only for allegorical and typological interpretation. If Paul did take this view, he was not followed in his singling out of Deuteronomy by any Christian for centuries after his death.

[1] *Naturalia legis per quae homo iustificatur, quae etiam ante legislationem custodiebant qui fide iustificabantur et placebant Deo, Adv. Haer.* IV.24.1.
[2] Simon, *Verus Israel*, pp. 196–203.
[3] C. W. Dugmore, *The Influence of the Synagogue upon the Divine Office*, pp. 29–36.
[4] See above, p.152.

Christianity suggests that the pattern of observance or rejection was more varied and miscellaneous than any generalization might lead us to expect.[1]

The *Epistle of Barnabas* evinces everywhere the conviction that not only is the old Jewish law no longer binding on Christians in its literal sense, but that it never should have been regarded as demanding a literal observance even by the Jews under the old dispensation. All the sacrifices of the Torah are now obsolete. 'He emptied these of force for this reason, that the new law of our Lord Jesus Christ, which is free from the yoke of necessity, might have an offering not made by man.'[2] When Moses broke the first tablets of the law, the people at that point broke the old law written on stone, in order that the new law of Jesus Christ might be sealed in our hearts.[3] There is, however, no evidence at all that the author regarded the second set of laws made by Moses as a mere *deuterosis*. He deprecates circumcision.[4] He allegorizes the laws about forbidden and permitted food in a way reminiscent of Pseudo-Aristeas.[5] He maintains that the Jews misunderstood the law: 'They went astray, because an evil angel deceived them.'[6] They misunderstood the purpose and significance of the Temple: 'Further, I will tell you about the Temple, how deceived were the miserable people who put their hope in the building, and not in their God who made them to be the real temple of God.'[7] On the other hand, Ignatius in three passages in his letters betrays the fact that contemporary Christians are observing the Torah,[8] though he tries to persuade them not to. Hermas makes several references to the law which Christ gave to his people, having received it from the Father, but it is almost certain that he does not in these refer to Jesus as the angel who mediated the law-giving on Sinai, but rather, in his characteristically moralistic way, he regards Christianity as a new law, and no doubt implies that it has superseded the old.[9]

Justin Martyr gives no sign that he believes any theory of the Halakah as a *deuterosis*, but he regards the law as for the most part a system imposed upon the Jews as a provisional preventative against sin. The commandment about the Sabbath and other ordinances were given because of the unrighteousness of the Jews, to restrain them, so that

[1]For some interesting material on this subject see Rendel Harris, *Testimonies*, Part II, ch. XIII, pp. 101–8.
[2]2.6   [3]4.7–9.   [4]9.6.   [5]See above, p. 99.   [6]9.4.
[7]16.1; the rest of the chapter develops this argument.
[8]*Magnesians* 9.1, σαββατίζοντες; 10.3, Ἰουδαΐζειν; *Philadelphians* 6.1, Ἰουδαϊσμόν.
[9]*Similitudes* V.vi.3, 4; VIII.iii.2, etc.

God's name might not be profaned among the Gentiles. God only ordained sacrifices in order to prevent the Jews' sinning; and the same was true of the building of the Temple.[1] Most of the enactments of the Torah, however, were intended to be reinterpreted in a non-literal or allegorical sense; the Jews have misunderstood the interpretation of the law, for it should be taken, not literally, but Christologically; every day is now a sabbath rest, there is a proper understanding of the unleavened bread, of cleanness of hands, of fasting, and so on.[2] There is no harm in keeping the enactments of the law, but when the purpose of them is known, the point of keeping them literally vanishes: 'We would be observing even this circumcision according to the flesh and the sabbaths and all the feasts literally, if we did not know the reason why they were commanded for you, that is, because of your lawless deeds and hardness of your heart.'[3] It was only by way of accommodation (οἰκονομία) that Jesus submitted to the Jewish law during his earthly ministry.[4] On the other hand, it is clear that Justin believes in the enduring validity of some commandments of the Jewish law, though he never makes clear which precisely these are. There are some things in the law of Moses which are 'good and godly and just' and they apparently have not been abrogated.[5] He divides the law into two classes of ordinances, one type which is 'permanent and suitable for men of all races, and a commandment and work which God enjoins', and another type which 'he ordained designing it to suit the hardness of the heart of your people' (i.e. Trypho's).[6] It is very probable that by these permanent ordinances Justin meant the moral commandments in the Torah, however he may have identified them.

We have already seen that Irenaeus believed that the law contained certain provisions which were 'natural' and apprehensible by and binding on all men even before the law-giving on Sinai.[7] His *Demonstration* gives us some more evidence about his attitude to the law. He certainly did not believe that the second law-giving was only a *deuterosis*; he describes Deuteronomy as a new summary of the law, with fresh legislation and many prophecies of Christ, given to the people before the attack on Jericho by Moses shortly before his death.[8] For the Jews of old, the law was a discipline: God is to those who believe Father, but

---

[1] *Dial.* 20.1; 22.11.
[2] *Ibid.*, 12.1–3; 14.1–3; 15.1; cf. also 20.1–4 (prohibition of foods); 23.4 (circumcision); 40.1–41.4 (a list of ordinances). For more examples of Justin's reinterpretation of points in the law, see above, pp. 103–7.
[3] *Ibid.*, 18.2.   [4] *Ibid.*, 67.6.   [5] *Ibid.*, 45.3 f.
[6] *Ibid.*, 67.10.   [7] See above, p. 289.   [8] *Dem.*, 28.

to the Jews Lord and Lawgiver, as a special dispensation for the times of man's disobedience.[1] The law was always intended to prefigure Christic even when its literal observance was obligatory upon the Jews. The tabernacle constructed in the wilderness, for example, was 'the visible form on earth of the things which are spiritual and invisible in the heavens, and a figure of the form of the Church, and a prophecy of things to come'.[2] Christians now do not need the law: 'There will be no command to remain idle for one day of rest for him who perpetually keeps sabbath.'[3] It is disconcerting to find, after all this evidence that the theologians insisted that the ritual law need not bind Christians, that Biblis, one of the martyrs of Lyons and Vienne, whose name and provenance do not at all suggest that she is a Jewish Christian, declares in refutation of the charges of cannibalism made against the Christians, 'How could people like the Christians eat children, for whom it is not even lawful to eat the blood of irrational animals ?'[4] This can only mean that Biblis and her fellow-Christians in a town in Gaul late in the second century were observing as part of their obligation the Jewish prohibition against eating the animal with the blood. One wonders how Irenaeus dealt with this practice when he encountered it in his own diocese.

Melito of Sardis has much to say about the law in his *Homily on the Passion*, all to the effect that though it was valid for the Jews before the coming of Christ it is no longer so now; he has no time or space for subtler distinctions concerning *deuterosis* or permanent moral commands. It is in this Homily that there occurs, as far as we know for the first time, the famous analogy that compares the law to the cast or model made by a sculptor or architect before he begins the work itself; it serves as a guide or foreshadowing of the real work, but when the work is completed, the model is no longer useful and can be cast away.[5] This analogy is also found in Pseudo-Justin, *De Resurrectione* 6, in Clement of Alexandria's work *Concerning the Passover*,[6] in Origen's *Hom. on Lev.*

[1] *Dem.*, 8.
[2] *Ibid.*, 26; for some more examples of this type of interpretation, see above, pp. 111 f.
[3] *Ibid.*, 96.
[4] Eus. *HE* V.1.26 (p. 140): πῶς ἂν παίδια φάγοιεν οἱ τοιοῦτοι, οἷς μηδὲ ἀλόγων ζώων αἷμα φαγεῖν ἐξόν; Tertullian, *Apology* 9.13 f., mentions Christians who refrain from eating meat strangled or with the blood in it. Cf. Minucius Felix, *Octavius*, 30.6.
[5] *Op cit.*, 36 f., pp. 109 f. Cf. Woollcombe, *Essays on Typology*, pp. 71 f.
[6] Frag. 33, *GCS* III, p. 218; but the application of the analogy is different here. Eus. *HE* IV.26.4 (p. 131) tells us that Clement's reading of Melito's περὶ τοῦ πασχά (not the surviving Homily) led him to write his own work with this title.

X.1, and in a Paschal Homily once attributed to Proclus of Constantinople but assigned by J. Martin to Hippolytus.[1] It may be that the shape of an Easter Homily was determined even before Melito's day, and that it was conventionally expected to contain some such treatment of the law as this, and also perhaps an attack on the Jews; but it is perhaps more likely that this Homily of Melito, couched as it is in very rhetorical and carefully composed Greek in accordance with the best models of contemporary oratory, was very influential in Christian antiquity. We shall be able to make a better judgement upon this point when Origen's Paschal Homily, which has been discovered among the find of papyri at Toura, appears in an edited form. Melito elaborates his conception of the law as a prefigurement of the gospel, now obsolete: 'And the law is the writing of a parable, but the gospel is the interpretation of the law and its fulfilment, and the Church is the receptacle of the truth.'[2] Again, 'the type is evacuated by the true substance (φύσει) and gives up its impression (εἰκόνα), and the parables are fulfilled when they are illuminated by the interpretation. Similarly the law was fulfilled when the gospel was illuminated, and the people was abrogated when the Church was raised up, and the type was broken when the Lord was manifested.'[3] The former institutions—the sacrifice of the sheep and the lamb, the temple, the physical Jerusalem—used to be valid (τίμιος), but now with the advent of their true fulfilments in Christ these are invalid (ἄτιμος).[4] Hippolytus in his exegetical works gives us little indication of his attitude to the Jewish law, beyond the fact that he regards it, along with the rest of the Old Testament, as predicting Christ; but at one point, commenting on S. of S. 2.9 ('He sheweth himself through the lattice'), he remarks: 'But the lattice is the law which

[1]PG 65.797. This Homily is much shorter than Melito's εἰς τὸ πάθος, but it reproduces the chiasmic style of Melito's work: 'For in one instance a lamb from the flock was sacrificed according to the law, and in the other Christ himself, the Lamb of God, is led on' and the ἐκεῖ . . . ἐνταῦθα rhythm continues for four more contrasts. The typology of the work is traditional and restrained, relating the circumstances of the Exodus to the atoning death of Christ with no sign of Philonic embroidery. It also contains an attack on the Jews, as Melito's does. It could well come from the early third century. Bonner in his commentary on Melito's work refers (p. 108) to this shorter Homily as inspired by Melito (or perhaps by Origen, who himself reproduced Melito's figure); but in his Introduction (p. 69) he says, 'I have seen nothing resembling Melito's comparison in the generally acknowledged works of Hippolytus, nor in the Paschal Sermon . . . which Martin has assigned to him.' I cannot understand this apparent contradiction. Was Bonner's Commentary written after his Introduction and not collated with it ?
[2]Homily on the Passion 40, p. 113.
[3]Ibid., 42 f., p. 113.
[4]Ibid., 44 f., pp. 113 f. For Melito's ideas of how Old Testament types are fulfilled, see above, pp. 108 f.

preached not only a single God, but also the Trinity in a hidden way, because they were children and not of age.'[1] This opinion probably implies a doctrine of the law as in its literal sense a provisional accommodation binding upon the Jews until the arrival of the Messiah.

Clement of Alexandria takes a considerable interest in the Jewish law. It is appropriate to his theory of the Logos as gradually educating mankind, both through the history of revelation to the Jews and through the achievements of Greek philosophy, that he should regard the law as both a schoolmaster and a policeman to the Jewish people under the old dispensation. The law both prepared the way for Christ and restrained the sinful impulses of the Jews. 'For the law is a course of education for disobedient children', and the use of fear as an incentive by God in connection with the law was 'for the restraint of sins and the encouragement of right conduct.'[2] Rather inconsistently (but consistency is never one of Clement's virtues), he can blame the Jews for regarding the law too narrowly as a policeman instead of seeing it as a prophet: 'For they did not recognize nor perform the intention of the law, but they thought that the law intended the very thing which they themselves imagined; they did not believe in the law as predicting, and they followed the literal meaning and menace, but not with the right presupposition and with faith.'[3] Still, there can be no doubt that Clement believed that the Jews were right to keep very much of their legislation literally, for he expresses the theory, a new and very convincing and attractive one, that the humanitarian laws were intended, taken literally, to prepare for the humane teaching of Christ. The laws governing the leaving of land fallow for a certain period had, he says, such a humane intention,[4] and several other laws of a humane kind, like that prohibiting the seething of a kid in its mother's milk, were designed to have a mollifying effect preparing for Christ's teaching.[5] Again, Clement regarded the moral part of the legislation as still valid for the Christian, as one would expect from so philosophically-minded a writer as he. He gleans precepts for the conduct of the Christian life freely from all over the Bible, especially from Isaiah, and in particular he commends the Decalogue (ἡ Δεκάλογος, whose number, he believes, is significant) because it 'comprises an exhortation which saves from

---

[1] Frag. 19, p. 365, lines 4–7.
[2] *Paed.* I.11.96 f., *PG* 8.365. For the attitude to the law of both Clement and Origen see also the chapter 'Law and Gospel' in Molland, *The Conception of the Gospel in Alexandrian Theology.*
[3] *Strom.* II.9.42, *PG* 8.977.
[4] *Ibid.*, II.18.86, *PG* 8.1028.
[5] *Ibid.*, II.18.87–9, *PG* 8.1029–33.

sins'.[1] The moral ordinances of the law coincide, in fact, with the moral convictions engraved on the hearts of all men, and both of these moralities are in harmony with what the apostles taught: 'These are the principles of the law, the ideals (παρακλητικοὶ λόγοι) not written on stone tablets by the finger of the Lord, but inscribed on the hearts of men, which alone are not capable of corruption. For this reason the tablets of the hard of heart were broken, in order that the beliefs of the little ones might be impressed upon receptive minds. Both laws ministered to the Word for the education of mankind, the former through Moses, the latter through the apostles.'[2] It is interesting to observe that though Clement shows no sign of regarding the second lawgiving as a deuterosis, he does take the breaking of the first set of tablets as symbolic of the abrogation of the law taken in its literal sense, or at least of the law as a way of righteousness in the sense that Paul attached to it. But Clement of course also agreed that the law must be allegorized. The man who understands the gospel will know how to allegorize the law: 'The esoteric (γνωστική) perfection of the man under law is the apprehension of the gospel, whose intention is that he who is under law should become perfect.'[3] By the miracle at Cana Christ signified his quickening of that which was watery (i.e. literal and insipid) in the intention of the law.'[4] The more embarrassing features of the legislation of the Pentateuch are explained away in this manner. Moses, in prohibiting Israel from eating pigs, really meant to prohibit them from keeping bad company. The animals with cloven hoof mean justice (which divides equally) and the chewers of the cud mean the spiritual meditation of the righteous man. All these are examples of allegory in the manner of Pseudo-Aristeas or Philo.[5] When he discusses the penalties of stoning and burning decreed in the law for the sin of adultery he is at pains to point out that the law does not conflict with the gospel. His solution is in fact (though he hints at it rather than stating it openly) to allegorize away the literal meaning of the law in this instance: 'The law is not of course inconsistent with the gospel, but agrees with it. How could it be otherwise, since one Lord is the provider of both? Observe that the woman who has committed fornication lives in her sin, but has died to the commandments. She who repents, as re-

[1]Paed. III.12.89, PG 8.668.
[2]Ibid., III.12.94, PG 8.673; the influence of Epistle of Barnabas, 4.7–9, is obvious.
[3]Strom. IV.21.130, PG 8.1340.
[4]Paed. II.2.29, PG 8.424; the word for watery is ὑδαρές; see above, p. 212, for a note on this word.
[5]Ibid., III.11.75 f., PG 8.652 f.

born in her manner of living, has rebirth of life; the former prostitute has died and the woman who was reborn by her repentance has returned again to life. The Spirit gives evidence to support what I have said when he says through Ezekiel, "I do not desire the death of a sinner, but that he may turn".[1] Clement of Alexandria, in short, accepted the traditional Christian attitude to the law in regarding its chief value as a prediction of Christ and in desiring to maintain its main moral principles as binding upon the Christian; but he modified this attitude in two characteristic ways; he allegorized the law in the manner of the Alexandrian tradition; and he envisaged the law as part of God's preparation of the chosen people for the coming of Christ, a concept which represents a new and useful contribution to Christian theology.

Before Origen's day, then, we can say with some confidence that the broad outlines of the traditional Christian attitude to the law had taken shape, though the details of interpretation varied considerably. Christians agreed that the Jews were right in observing the law literally under the old dispensation; for them it was an obligation, but from God's point of view it was a discipline. The *Epistle of Barnabas* is exceptional, along with Stephen's speech in Acts 7, in denying that the Jews ought to have kept the law literally. All Christians also agreed that though the ritual commandments were no longer binding on them, yet the moral commandments, defined with greater or lesser clarity, were still in force. And all were convinced that the law had a predictive or prefiguring function, to be operated either by typology or by allegory, which was intended by God who gave the law but which contemporary Judaism was stubbornly unwilling to concede. Preoccupation with the thought of the second law-giving as a *deuterosis* is a very secondary feature in Christian thinking about the law in the first two centuries, if it appears at all, but many would have agreed that the breaking of the first tablets of the law was significant of the transitory and provisional nature of most of its ordinances. Clement is alone in his fruitful concept of the law as a training for the Jews in humane conduct in preparation for the merciful precepts of Christ; and, as we shall see, this thought is not followed up by Clement's successor; Origen was too much intoxicated with allegory to take notice of this point.

But the evidence from Ignatius' letters and from the utterance of Biblis suggests that, in spite of the pointed periods of Melito and the curious explanations of Justin, some sort of observance of the other provisions of the Jewish law besides the moral ones was well rooted in

[1] *Strom* II.23.147, *PG* 8.1096 f.

A.E.–K*

the life of every Christian community. It would, after all, be surprising
if a society which had only recently emerged from Judaism and many
of whose members were deeply versed in the literature of the Old
Testament, as our inquiry into exegesis contemporary with Origen suggests, had been capable of abandoning the practice of the Jewish law as
totally as their intellectual leaders exhorted them to abandon it. How
far exactly the Christian should observe the Jewish law was no doubt
then, as it has been in most subsequent periods of Christian history, a
burning question.

Origen's treatment of the law is distinguished by his remarkable use
of the concept of natural law, a concept which is almost completely confined to his *Commentary on Romans* but which there appears again and
again. In one passage in this Commentary, which is extant in the original
Greek in the *Philocalia*, Origen gives an exhaustive list of the meanings
expressed in Scripture by the word 'law'. They are:

1. The law of Moses (e.g. Gal. 3.10, 19, 24).
2. The historical narrative written by Moses (e.g. Gal. 4.21).
3. The Psalms (e.g. John 15.25).
4. Isaiah's prophecy (e.g. I Cor. 14.21).
5. The more mystical and divine interpretation of the law (e.g. Rom.
   7.14).
6. The law 'disseminated in the soul according to universal concepts',
   the law of nature (e.g. Rom. 2.14 f.).[1]

Elsewhere in this work, Origen distinguishes three sorts of law as referred to in Scripture. These are:

1. The law of Christ.
2. The law of Moses.
3. Natural law, from which nobody is exempt.[2]

A Greek fragment of the *Commentary on I Corinthians* notes that in
I Cor. 14.21 St Paul calls the prophetic writings the law and this usage
is found 'in Aquila and the other versions',[3] but not in the LXX; and
a Greek fragment of the *Commentary on Romans* refers to 'the natural

---

[1] *Comm. on Rom.* VI.8, reproduced in *Philoc.* IX.1 f.; the phrase quoted under
the sixth division of law is νόμος ὁ κατὰ τὰς κοινὰς ἐννοίας ἐνεσπαρμένος τῇ ψυχῇ.
Cf.IV.4. For further information and references on this subject, see Koch,
Pronoia und Paideusis, pp. 51 f., and some of the Greek fragments of Origen's
Commentary on Romans, nos. 10 (*JTS* XIII, pp. 216 f.), 37 and 39 (*JTS* XIV,
pp. 13 f.).
[2] *Comm. on Rom.* II.8.
[3] Frag. 65, *JTS* X, p. 38.

law' (ὁ φυσικὸς νόμος).[1] And regularly throughout this Commentary, wherever St Paul's use of the word 'law' does not fit in with Origen's ideas of what St Paul meant by Moses' law, he interprets it to refer to this natural law.

The relation between this natural law and the moral commandments of the Jewish law are obviously in Origen's thought very close. Commenting on Rom. 2.14 f., he gives some example of this natural law. They are the prohibition of murder, adultery, stealing, and bearing false witness, the command to honour the father and mother, and the conviction that 'a single God is creator of all things'. And these principles are the principles of the gospel also:

> 'But such commands as these, which are said to be written in the heart, seem to me to fit in more with the laws of the gospel, where the universal standard is natural justice. For what is more consonant with our natural feeling than that men should not do to others what they would not have done to themselves? Natural law then can agree with the law of Moses according to the spirit, not according to the letter. What natural reasonableness will there be in this command, for instance, to circumcise a child on the eighth day, or not to weave wool with linen, or that no one should eat leavened bread on the day of the Feast of Unleavened Bread? When we have from time to time brought up those objections to Jews and asked that they should show us any practical purpose in these commands, we are aware that their custom was to reply simply that this was what the lawgiver decided. But we who think that all these things should be interpreted spiritually for this reason believe that "not the hearers but the doers of that law are to be justified", not the law according to the letter, which cannot of course have a doer because of the impossibility of fulfilling it, but according to the spirit, through whom alone the law can be fulfilled.'[2]

This is saying precisely the same thing as Clement of Alexandria said when he claimed that 'both laws ministered to the Word for the education of mankind, the former through Moses, the latter through the apostles',[3] but it is putting far more stress on the coincidence of this law common to Moses and the apostles with the natural law known to and binding upon all men. Origen identifies this natural law with the

---

[1] Frag. 14, *JTS* XIII, p. 220.
[2] *Comm. on Rom.* II.9.   [3] See above, p. 296.

'law of my mind' (Rom. 7.23) opposed by 'the law in my members', and also with the law 'written . . . with the Spirit of the living God /. . . in tables that are hearts of flesh' (II Cor. 3.3).[1] Whenever St Paul / refers to being without the law, or to a time before the law, as in Rom. 7.9 ('I lived without the law once'), he is in Origen's view referring to the natural law and not to the law of Moses, and means a man's childhood, before he had knowledge of right and wrong, that is, of the natural law. This assumption will work well enough to explain some texts (e.g. Rom. 7.9) but it becomes indefensible when in order to maintain it, Origen has to assume that the sentence, 'Until the law, sin was in the world' (Rom. 5.13), really means, 'Until the law, sin was dead in the world.'[2] Indeed, Origen carries this concept of natural law as far as to say, 'The Gentiles therefore, because they did not have the law written in tables or books, are said not to have followed after righteousness [Rom. 9.30]; but they had a righteousness implanted in them which the natural law taught them. They were therefore close to that righteousness which is of faith, that is, to Christ.'[3] And in one of his rare references to the natural law outside the *Commentary on Romans*, he suggests that Noah knew of the distinction drawn by the later Mosaic law between clean and unclean animals (Gen. 7.2) by the light of the natural law.[4] It is interesting, and perhaps significant, that the eminent Roman jurist Ulpian, who is distinguished from his predecessor Gaius in that, unlike Gaius, he emphasized natural law (*ius naturale*), was a contemporary of Origen's.[5] It is possible that in his doctrine of natural law Origen was displaying a sensitivity to one of the currents of thought of the pagan world of his day.

Origen does sometimes, a little reluctantly, admit that the Jews were justified in taking the law literally under the old dispensation. In reply to the derisive comments of heretics and heathen upon the Jewish practice of circumcision, Origen makes three points: Egyptian priests are circumcised, and so are people of many other nations; their circumcision cannot be allowed without allowing that of the Jews. This is a

---

[1]*Comm. on Rom.* V.6.
[2]*Ibid.*, V.1.
[3]*Ibid.*, VII.19.
[4]Fragment on Genesis, *PG* 12.105. Though almost all Origen's references to this natural law come from Rufinus' translation of the *Commentary on Romans*, there is no reason to suspect Rufinus of having inserted them or touched them up; the theme of Romans would naturally give rise to frequent mention of this subject; the subject of natural law was not a controversial one in Rufinus' day; and the Greek fragments in more than one passage bear out the integrity of the translation on this point.
[5]See E. Barker, *From Alexander to Constantine*, pp. 258–60.

type of Christ shedding his blood (giving it, Origen believes, to the devil); many shed their blood for God as a foreshadowing of this final bloodshedding, just as there were baptisms before the Baptism of Christ, purifications before the purification of the Holy Spirit and victims before the Victim. It is an advantage for a special race to have a special mark.[1] The prophets, he says, and any of their day who were wise knew that the law was spiritual, 'even though for the sake of the masses they appeared to keep the material observance of it also';[2] this argument admits the importance of the law at least for the Jew *moyen sensuel*. The distinction between clean and unclean foods was given in a series of commands by Moses from God to the Jews in order that the chosen nation might be marked out from others by such observances, although when the time came for the Gentiles to be brought into the Church the literal observance of these was automatically rendered unnecessary.[3] He admits that the laws about the Levites' rights of property (Lev. 25.32–4) taken in their literal sense 'look after the priestly and Levitical orders faithfully and devotedly enough'.[4] The law of retaliation was given to the Jews because of their infirmity,[5] but this statement involves the admission that the Jews were right to keep this law literally. Origen also admits that though the Gentiles at the time of their being called by God could not, under the Roman Emperor, have been governed by the law of Moses taken literally, yet the Jews of old could not have even continued existing if they had obeyed the injunctions of the Gospel. The Christians could not have properly enforced the capital punishments of the old law, nor could the Jews have defended themselves from extermination under the new.[6] And against the Marcionite description of the law as an 'evil root' and an 'evil tree' he justifies its function by an effective medical analogy; by the art of medicine we can recognize a disease, but this does not imply that the medicine causes the disease.[7]

Further, Origen allows that there are several points in which even the Christian of his own day ought to take the Jewish law literally. First of all, he gives an interesting classification of attitudes to the law in the contemporary Church:

---

[1]*Comm. on Rom.* II.13.
[2]*Ibid.*, VI.7.
[3]*Ibid.*, X.3.
[4]*Hom. on Lev.* XV.1.
[5]Fragment on Deuteronomy, *PG* 12.812.
[6]*Contra Celsum* VII.26. Zöllig (*Inspirationslehre*, pp. 43 f.) notes this fact, that Origen did not follow the *Epistle of Barnabas* in regarding the Jews as sinful for having kept the law literally.
[7]*Comm. on Rom.* III.6.*

1. There are those who have entirely abrogated the law because they
   interpret it spiritually.
2. There are those who interpret the law spiritually but still observe
   its precepts literally.
3. There are those who do not agree to the spiritual interpretation
   of the law but yet believe in Christ 'as the subject of prophecy' and
   keep the law, interpreting literally what Origen thinks is its
   spiritual meaning.[1]

The third class obviously comprises the Jewish Christians; the first
class probably includes the intellectual and cultured Christians; it may
well be that the second class is a rough description of the majority of
ordinary, unintellectual Christians like Biblis. Then, it is obvious from
what has already been said that a number of moral principles embodied
in laws would be regarded as binding on the Christian by Origen.
'Honour thy father and thy mother' is one clear example of this,[2] and
the commandment about married fidelity is another.[3] Origen would no
doubt have followed Clement in including the Decalogue in this list.

But there are also a number of specific provisions in the legislation
of the Old Testament, not obvious examples of general moral principle,
which Origen, surprisingly, insists are still binding upon the Christian.
The laws in the Old Testament which were expressly said to apply to
strangers and proselytes as well as to Jews are still in force for Christians; this, he says, is why the Council of Jerusalem decreed that
Christians should refrain from 'blood and things strangled' (Acts 15.20);
and Christians similarly might offer whole burnt-offerings as long as
the Temple was standing.[4] The warning against refraining from testi-
fying when you are a witness of somebody else's sin, conveyed in Lev.
5.1, serves as a warning to the Christian not to become involved in other
people's sins.[5] The regulations about fraudulently retaining deposits
and similar cases in Lev. 6.2 ff. apply, Origen says, literally to evildoers
and criminal people, on the ground that 'law is not made for a righteous
man, but for the unrighteous and unruly' (I Tim. 1.9); he assumes that
no Christian will come under this category, and so proceeds to allegorize the regulations.[6] The prohibition of wine (Lev. 10.8–11) is re-
affirmed and made valid by apostolic (I Tim. 3.8; Titus 1.7) and
dominical (Luke 21.34) command.[7] Dugmore has pointed out that when

---

[1] *Contra Celsum* II.3.
[2] *PA* IV.3.4; *Comm. on Rom.* II.9; see above p. 299.
[3] *Hom. on Num.* XI.1.   [5] *Comm. on Rom.* II.13.
[4] *Hom. on Lev.* III.2.   [6] *Ibid.*, IV.2.   [7] *Ibid.*, VII.1.

Origen has occasion to describe the proper way for the Christian to observe the sabbath (i.e. Saturday), he emphasizes that the Christian's observance should be a spiritual rather than a literal one, but it does include refraining from secular occupations and coming to church on that day.[1] Origen also shows an interesting tendency to find support for institutions and customs of the contemporary Church in some of the provisions of the Jewish law literally interpreted. He is, as far as I know, the first writer to equate the three orders of Christian ministry, bishop, priest and deacon, with three ministries in the Old Testament, high-priest, priest, and Levite.[2] In the *Conversation with Heracleides* Origen is represented as quoting Lev. 19.15 to support his contention that bishops celebrating the eucharist must 'keep to the conventions' in their prayers.[3] And he takes the calling of the congregation by Moses described in Lev. 8.4 f. as an indication that the people must be present at the election of a bishop.[4] The law of the first-fruits (Num. 18) should be observed in the form of a tithing to support the clergy.[5] And the law of restitution in the Old Testament applies especially to those who are in charge of the Church's finances.[6]

Origen's attitude to the sacrifices ordained in the legislation of the Pentateuch gives in miniature a picture of the whole of his attitude to the law. He says that the sacrifices of Israel of old were fed upon by angels.[7] He collects seven different sorts of sin-offering, the ram, the goat, the dove, etc. from Leviticus, and clearly believes that in themselves they did secure remission of sins for the Jew under the old dispensation, even though they now are only symbolic of the seven different ways in which the Christian can secure forgiveness of sins under the new dispensation.[8] Those sacrifices, too, had some mysterious power of

[1]*Hom. on Num.* XXIII.4; Dugmore, *The Influence of the Synagogue upon the Divine Office*, p. 31.
[2]*Hom. on Jer.* XII.3, but there are several other examples (see below, p. 330). The commonly held supposition that *I Clement* also displays this equation of NT and OT ministries is fallacious; anyone who reads the Epistle carefully should realize that though the author instances the OT ministry as an example of careful ordering of worship, to be imitated by Christians, it does not enter his mind that the ministries can be equated. On the contrary, it is clear that in *I Clement* bishops and presbyters are the same office.
[3]*Conversation with Heracleides*, p. 131 (MS pp. 4.33–5.1); see *Origen's Doctrine of Tradition*, pp. 179 f., and H. Chadwick's discussion of this passage in the notes on his translation of this work, *Alexandrian Christianity*, p. 440 n. 12.
[4]*Hom. on Lev.* VI.3.
[5]*Hom. on Num.* XI.1.
[6]*Ecclesiasticis dispensationibus*, *Hom. on Lev.* III.6. The last two examples are noted by Harnack (*Der Kirchengeschichtliche Ertrag*, I, p. 50), who observes that Origen takes a long step towards the transformation of Old Testament law into ecclesiastical institutions.
[7]*PA* I.8.1.   [8]*Hom. on Lev.* II.4.

rendering inefficacious the sacrifices made to demons until the coming of Christ did away with all sacrifices.[1] They acted, further, as a discipline upon the Jews. 'The Jews had been formerly accustomed to sacrifices in Egypt and used to like them, as their making the calf in the desert witnesses; so God permitted them to offer sacrifices to him, thereby restraining their undisciplined tendencies towards polytheism and intending to prevent them sacrificing to demons.'[2] One further practical advantage in sacrifices is mentioned when Origen says that 'the sacrifices were primarily a means of support for the priests and foreshadowing of true religion. There is a twofold advantage in sacrificing, both that honour is done to God and that whatever object anyone sacrifices he would not worship nor imagine to be God.'[3] But of course Origen holds just as strongly to the conviction that sacrifices are now not required and that their only purpose now is that, as they are recorded in the Old Testament, they provide (as in fact they always did provide, even under the old dispensation) material for allegory. The law is now dead, and the proof of it is the disappearance of sacrifices, altar, temple, purifications and Passover.[4] 'Present your bodies a living sacrifice' (Rom. 12.1) does not refer to the sacrifice of animals, but to the moral purity of Christians, to which the animal sacrifices ordained in Leviticus allegorically refer; the offering of a heifer meant the mortification of pride, of a ram the suppression of anger, of a goat the eradication of lust, and so on.[5] The phrase in Ps. 4.5, 'Offer the sacrifice of righteousness,' could not refer to material sacrifices; this conviction is supported by a wealth of quotation, Ps. 50.8; 51.16 f.; Jer. 6.20; 7.22; Matt. 12.6; Hos. 6.6. The sentence must be taken in a double sense, 'according to the symbolic and according to the more recondite and mystical sense'.[6] The former sense no doubt refers to the sacrifice of a broken heart and a contrite spirit, and the latter to the sacrifice of Christ.

It is interesting to observe that Origen knows that the Jews have writings which they call *deuteroseis*; he tells us that it is usual among the Jews for all their Scriptures to be opened to their children by their teachers and wise men, 'and at the same time these writings which they call *deuteroseis*'.[7] But he does not produce the theory that this *deuterosis*

---

[1]*Hom. on Num.* XVII.1.
[2]Fragment on Leviticus, *PG* 12.397; a precisely similar sentiment is found in a fragment on Numbers, *PG* 12.580.
[3]Fragment on Leviticus, *PG* 12.400.
[4]*Hom. on Gen.* VI.3.   [5]*Comm. on Rom.* IX.1.
[6]κατά τε τὸ συμβολικὸν καὶ κατὰ τὸ ἀπορρητότερον καὶ μυστικόν, *Comm. on Ps.* 4. 5, *PG* 12.1148.
[7]*Comm. on S. of S.*, Origen's Preface, *PG* 13.63.

is the second, inferior, law given to Moses after the breaking of the
tablets of the first law. On the contrary, he elaborates the attitude taken
by Irenaeus to Deuteronomy.[1] In Leviticus, he says, Moses is recorded
as hearing from God the laws which are written in the book, whereas in
Deuteronomy he teaches the people the laws that appear in it. This
means that Leviticus contains the 'first law', meant for the people of
Israel at that time, whereas Deuteronomy (as its name implies) is the
'second law', a law 'which is specifically handed on by Moses to Joshua
his successor, who is of course believed to have borne the appearance
of our Saviour by whose second law, that is by the ordinances of the
gospel, all things are brought to perfection'.[2] This passage is supple-
mented by a later one in which Origen maintains that the breaking of
the tablets of the first law demonstrated that the literal keeping of the
law was discouraged by God; the second law (presumably to be found
in Deuteronomy) was the superior allegorized law, referring to Christ.[3]
It is obvious, however, from the evidence already produced in these
pages alone that Origen was not consistent enough in this view to
allegorize only the legislation found in Deuteronomy. He allegorizes
indifferently all the Pentateuchal laws.

As we have already had occasion to see,[4] Origen identifies the Pauline
contrast between the 'letter that killeth' and the 'spirit that giveth life'
with the contrast between the law taken literally and the law allegorized.
In reply to Celsus' accusation about the inconsistency between Moses'
teaching and that of Jesus about wealth, Origen falls back on a doctrine
which he admits to be derived from Philo; 'The law is double, in one
sense literal, in another allegorical.' The literal law is described by
Ezekiel (20.25) as 'statutes that are not good'; this corresponds to St
Paul's 'letter that killeth' and 'the ministration of death'. But the
spiritual law Ezekiel calls 'good statutes' (20.11) and St Paul speaks of it
in the words, 'we know that the law is spiritual . . . so that the law is
holy and the commandment holy and righteous and good' (Rom. 7.12,
14).[5] The Christians' attitude to the Old Testament differs from that of

---

[1]See above, pp. 292 f.   [2]*PA* IV.3.12.
[3]*Comm. on Rom.* II.14; the same opinion is found in the passage already cited
from the Preface to *Comm. on S. of S.*, PG 12.63. Cf. the very similar passage in
Clement, *Paed.* III.12.94, PG 8.673, quoted on p. 296. The influence of the
Epistle of Barnabas 4.7–9 in both Clement and Origen is obvious. Simon,
Verus Israel, p. 114 n. 1 and p. 180, calls attention to the passage in *Comm. on Rom.*
[4]See above, pp. 300 f.
[5]*Contra Celsum* VII.20; Philo is referred to as τῶν πρὸ ἡμῶν τινες, and the
passage reproduced here is *Spec. Leg.* I.287. For more passages in Origen in a
similar vein not referred to below, see *Comm. on Rom.* VI.12; *Comm. on Matt.*
XI.12; and *Hom. on Num.* IX.4.

the Jews in this respect, that 'we both agree that the books are written by the divine Spirit', but in the opinion of the Christians 'the literal interpretation of the laws is not that which comprehends the intention of the giving of the law.'[1] As for the Jews, 'they have the books . . . the meaning of the Scriptures has been taken from them.'[2] Origen also often stresses that it was in fact impossible to fulfil the demands of the law. We have already seen several examples of the sort of ordinances which Origen considered to make impossible demands.[3] He adds a few more examples of these elsewhere; the passages about the Jews lending to many nations and borrowing from none (Deut. 15.6; 28.12) cannot be taken literally because as a matter of fact the righteous Jews never did lend to many nations and borrow from none, and they were never so inconsistent and lawbreaking as deliberately to refrain from these activities in order to flout the law. Again, the law may have promised that the Jews would rule other nations and be ruled by none, but this cannot be taken literally. The historical fulfilment of the promise that the Jews should fill all the earth was very inadequate. The command to destroy utterly all their enemies was clearly impossible of literal fulfilment, like the expressed intention of the Psalmist, 'Morning by morning I shall destroy all the wicked of the land' (Ps. 101.8).[4] The infirmity of the law is that 'it is weakened by the literal sense, so that it cannot be fulfilled.'[5] But it should be noticed that Origen's thought here is quite different from that of St Paul. St Paul maintained that the law made absolute moral demands upon the Jew which he could never perfectly comply with. Origen held that the law made demands which were either wholly irrational and purposeless or else physically impossible.[6] We suspect that his misunderstanding of Paul's thought is as great in his interpretation of the contrast between letter and spirit.

Consequently he allegorizes whenever he finds it convenient to do so every ritual ordinance, or indeed every ordinance that is not directly moral, that comes his way, and usually in a Philonic rather than a traditionally Christological sense. The parapet on the roof of a house enjoined in Deut. 22.8 means an injunction to take precautions against

---

[1]*Hom. in Num.* V.59 f. Simon, *Verus Israel*, p. 94, also adduces *Hom. in Num* II.58 on this point, as well as the passage next quoted in the text.
[2]*Hom. on Jer.* XIV.12.
[3]See above, pp. 239 f.
[4]*Contra Celsum* VII.18 f.
[5]*Comm. on Rom.* I.10.
[6]He does, however, acknowledge (*Hom. on Lam.*, frag. 113) that 'the law can save nobody, as Paul said. Therefore those who rely on the law shall not be able to help after the coming of grace.'

misunderstanding God's dispensations and so dying.[1] The laws about clean and unclean food really refer to spiritual purity and pollution.[2] Jewish feasts, even the Passover and Unleavened Bread which were continued in Christian observance, are significant only for their allegorical meaning.[3] Jewish fasts are to be taken as purely symbolical, though it is significant that Origen mentions that there are Christians who conscientiously keep them; even the command of our Lord concerning fasting (Matt. 6.17) is to be allegorized.[4] The ram offering is treated similarly: 'But if there was no secret meaning intended, what could be the sense of a bought ram being offered as a victim, and bought at a certain price? . . . So the good sense of the lawmaker ordains that a man's sin cannot be forgiven unless he have a fixed amount of money?' So of course the law must be allegorized.[5] So with the sabbath. Nobody before Christ really kept the sabbath, for nobody 'kept a sabbath from the works of the world'; when Christ came, he was 'our sabbath and our rest', and we are now called to keep a sabbath from 'the works of the world and carnal and harmful works', but not from works of righteousness.[6] Circumcision need not be taken literally; for the Christian, circumcision means not to use the member circumcised for more than its natural purpose, and that temperately.[7] The law of Levirate marriage really means the marriage of the human soul, first to the letter of the law and then to the spiritual law.[8] The Jewish priests who served the Temple knew such allegorizations of the law as these.[9] Jesus probably taught such allegorizations to the apostles during the forty days' interval between the Resurrection and the Ascension[10] (that Fortunatus' purse for theologians who cannot find historical evidence to support their speculations). Jesus and the disciples kept the Jewish law only as an accommodation to the Jews among whom they were living, though they knew its spiritual meaning.[11]

Origen sees Christ as the *telos* of the law in both the Pauline senses of the word, as its end and as its fulfilment, but he never approaches Clement's conception of the law as an immature preparation for Christ's teaching; he was too anxious to read Christ's teaching into the law by means of allegory to achieve such an insight. For him Paul's words,

<hr>

[1]*Comm. on Matt.* XVII.7.   [2]*Comm. on Rom.* IX.42.
[3]*Comm. on Matt.* Comm. Ser. 79; *Contra Celsum* VIII.22 f.
[4]*Hom. on Lev.* X.2.   [5]*Ibid.*, III.8.
[6]*Comm. on Matt.* Comm. Ser. 45.   [7]*Hom. on Gen.* III.6.
[8]*Comm. on Matt.* XVII.31.   [9]*Contra Celsum* V.44.
[10]*Contra Celsum* II.2.
[11]*Comm. on Matt.* XI.8; compare the statement in Justin, *Dial.* 67.6, quoted above on p. 292.

'nay, we establish the law' (Rom. 3.31) mean simply that 'whoever believes in Christ, about whom Moses wrote, establishes the law through faith, because he believes in Christ.'[1] This is certainly one of the meanings intended by Paul, and is indeed a somewhat embarrassing conviction to be found throughout the New Testament. The consequence is that as an obligatory code of behaviour the law is dead. Christ by his teaching of new opinions 'did away with the customs of the Jews even while he enhanced the teaching of their prophets', and at the same time he abolished the laws of the Greeks, especially on the subject of religion.[2] The law was only 'until the time of reformation' and passed away at the coming of the eternal teaching of the gospel.[3] Another way of putting this is to say that Christ is the law: 'He too is the law by which all are under law. Therefore he came for judgement, not as one who is under law, but as one who is the law. Indeed I believe that those who are now perfect and have been made one spirit with him themselves are not under law, but rather they themselves are the law.'[4] Origen therefore sees little necessity for regarding Christ's teaching as the perfection or consummation of the teaching of the law. 'On these two commandments hang all the law and the prophets' (Matt. 22.40) means that when you love God and your neighbour you understand the whole significance of the law and the prophets.[5] He can, speaking about forgiveness, say 'The law given by Moses used to punish those who did wrong, showing no forgiveness for things accomplished in contravention to it. And yet the law provided the fulfilments of mysteries by means of images and foreshadowings, conducting and preparing those who were led by them to the teaching of Christ, and for this reason the law is called a "tutor unto Christ". Now . . . the Saviour came, not to punish those who had sinned but to bring forgiveness for things done sinfully, and to bring fulfilment to the teaching and the understanding of images of the truth (by showing truth himself, or rather by himself being the truth).'[6] But what he means is probably, not that Jesus fulfilled the Jewish law's teaching on forgiveness, for Origen thinks that he almost contradicted this, but that he fulfilled the allegorical, spiritual, meaning, of the law. Again, discussing the text, 'Love worketh no ill to his neighbour. Love therefore is the fulfilment of the law' (Rom. 13.10), he agrees that if you apply love to each commandment you find that you are keeping law, for love will not kill, commit adultery, steal, bear false

---

[1] *Comm. on Rom.* III.11.   [2] *Contra Celsum* I.29.
[3] *Comm. on John*, frag. 56.   [4] *Comm. on Rom.* III.6.
[5] *Comm. on Matt.* Comm. Ser. 4.   [6] *Comm. on John*, frag. 9.

witness, and so on. But he adds that 'his neighbour' really means Christ: 'For if you carefully inquire who is our neighbour, you will learn that he is our neighbour who came and when we were wounded by thieves and stripped by demons laid us on the beast of his body and brought us to the inn of the Church and gave to the innkeeper to look after us and tend us (that is to Paul or to anyone who presides over the Church) the two pennies of the New and Old Testament, to cover the expenses of looking after us. If therefore we love this neighbour, we fulfil the whole law and all the commandments in loving him.'[1] Elsewhere he says, on 'The snare is broken, and we are delivered' (Ps. 124.7), 'The Old Testament breaks the snares of action, when it ordains, Thou shalt not commit adultery. The New Testament destroys the snares of thought, when it exhorts, Thou shalt not covet.'[2]

We can then see that Origen made no drastic innovation upon the traditional Christian attitude to the Jewish law which he inherited. Christians had from the very beginning maintained that the Jewish law predicted and prefigured Christ, and Origen made this his chief point, using for his elaboration of this point the Philonic tradition of allegory which he had found in Clement as well as Philo, and greatly enlarging and intensifying the use of it. He agreed that the Jews had been justified in observing the law literally before the coming of Christ, but he held that the breaking of the tablets of the first law was a sign that the second law was intended to be allegorized by Christians and not to be taken literally. There is no sign at all in Origen of a desire to identify the second law with the Halakah, as a *deuterosis*, and consequently to depreciate it. This particular theory, we must pronounce, cannot be found before the middle of the third century, when it appears in the *Didascalia*. It probably originated in Jewish Christian circles. Origen held firmly that the moral part of the Jewish law was still binding upon Christians. He identified the moral principles of the Torah, the moral precepts of Jesus and the originally Stoic and quite unchristian and un-Jewish conception of natural law, laying particular stress upon this last. And he showed a marked tendency to find support and analogies for the institutions of the contemporary Church in the details of the cultic system of the old dispensation. He regarded Christ as the fulfilment of the law, but much more because the law when allegorized can be made to yield Christian doctrine than because Christ's teaching completes or consummates the teaching of the law. It is interesting to observe how in his

[1] *Comm. on Rom.* IX.31.
[2] *Comm. on Ps.* 124.7 (*PG* 12.1637).

emphasis upon natural law and in his readiness to transform the details of the cult and ministry of the Jewish Church into a blueprint for the organization of the Christian Church Origen is helping to form the traditional Christian attitude on these subjects for the next twelve hundred years.

I2

Sacraments

ORIGEN's treatment of the sacraments is a subject which is not directly involved in a study of his interpretation of Scripture. But the importance of including in an account of his attitude to the sacraments an examination of his handling of baptismal typology and his interpretation of the sixth chapter of St John's Gospel shows that some exploration of the subject of this chapter will throw light on our central theme, and perhaps one chapter devoted to what might be called *marginalia* will be pardoned among the other thirteen.

We will begin by broaching a subject which in recent years has been very much to the fore in patristic scholarship, and that is the function of the Holy Spirit in the sacrament of Baptism. At what point, and in what authors, can we first trace the conviction that in Christian initiation the Spirit is conferred by some other rite than simple water-baptism, such as laying on of hands or chrismation, and in particular, can this conviction be found in the Christian Platonists of Alexandria? It can be said with some confidence that no such conviction can be found reflected in the writings of any author of the sub-apostolic period nor in those of any other second-century author until we reach Clement of Alexandria. It is almost impossible to prove beyond a doubt a negative in history; it cannot, to take a random instance, be demonstrated incontrovertibly that Julius Caesar was not assumed into heaven after his death; there is some evidence that a belief in his assumption was current in the Roman Empire not long after his death, and if someone was anxious to believe in this theory we could not absolutely forbid him to do so on historical grounds alone. But as far as negative evidence can go we can, I believe, rest assured that nobody in the Christian Church believed that the Holy Spirit was conferred in any rite apart from Baptism in water until at least the year A.D. 180. No such belief betrays itself in the copious language about Baptism of the author of the *Epistle of Barnabas*; indeed in one place he says, 'We go down into the water laden with sins and filth, and we come up bearing fruit in our heart, having reverence and hope towards Jesus in the Spirit'—a sentence which is incompatible with this belief.[1] Hermas in his *Similitudes* insists that it is not enough to bear the name of the Son, but that the Christian must also put on the garment of the maidens in the allegory of the tower-building: these maidens are 'holy spirits' and stand for 'powers of the Son of God'. And when Christians are 'clothed with these powers' they will be one with all others so clothed. The names of these maidens are 'Faith, Temperance, Power, Longsuffering, Singleheartedness, Innocence, Purity, Cheerfulness, Truth, Understanding, Harmony, Love'.[2] Is this an insistence that Baptism is not enough but that reception of the Spirit in another ceremony is an essential part of Christian initiation? It is much more likely that what Hermas means here is that Baptism is insufficient unless the fruits of Baptism are shown in the Christian life. Later he says that the righteous who died before Christ received 'the seal of the Son of God' and entered the kingdom. In the allegory of the tower-building, he here tells us, 'The seal therefore is the water; therefore we go down into the water dead and come up living.' He goes on to explain that 'the apostles and teachers' preached to the pre-Christian righteous the name of the Son (presumably after the death of the apostles and teachers).[3] A little later he is explaining the meaning of the mountains in the allegory of the tower-building. All these mountains, it is clear, mean fully initiated Christians whom he describes as 'having put on the holy spirit of these maidens', and they display characteristic moral qualities and attainments, obviously signified by their being clothed in this way.[4] Later still he refers to Christians as having received the Spirit whole and untorn, like a garment, and as obliged to return it intact to their Lord.[5] In short, though Hermas is much concerned that Christians should obtain the Spirit, there is no evidence that he regards that Spirit as conferred in a separate ceremony from that of water-baptism.

There is a similar absence of evidence in the Apologists. The only two who provide any material for discussion on the subject are Justin and Theophilus of Antioch. In his *Apology* Justin gives a long description of Baptism for the benefit of unbelievers.[6] He gives absolutely no indication that any other ceremony is involved except washing and invoca-

[1] *Epistle of Barnabas* II.II.
[2] *Similitudes* IX.xiii.I, 2, 5; xv.2. Cf. Lampe, *The Seal of the Spirit*, pp. 105 f.
[3] *Ibid.*, IX.xvi.3, 4.
[4] *Ibid.*, IX.xxiv.2.
[5] *Ibid.*, IX.xxxii.4; we cannot compare the language used in this passage with that used in the ones already quoted, as this one survives only in Latin.
[6] *Apol.* I.61.1–7.

tion of the name.[1] He describes Baptism as 'illumination'.[2] And in the *Dialogue* he interprets Baptism as a spiritual circumcision, contrasted with the fleshly circumcision of the Jews.[3] Theophilus maintains that God's blessing of the waters at the creation was a sign that men should receive repentance and forgiveness of sins 'through water and the washing of regeneration'.[4] There is no reference here to chrismation nor to any other ceremony, and no room for it in the prefiguration. But earlier in the work Theophilus has said, 'We are called Christians because we are anointed with the oil of God.'[5] We might take this as a reference to anointing in Christian initiation, but a careful consideration of the passage should make us hesitate before we come to this conclusion. In the first place, the most extraordinary thing about this passage is that Theophilus does not give the true reason why Christians are so called, namely because they believe in Christ. It must have been obvious to Theophilus, and to every other Christian of his day, that Christians were *not* called Christians because in their ceremony of initiation they were at one point anointed with oil, and there is no good reason why, writing for non-Christians, he should have fastened upon this one feature of Christian ceremonial and, quite erroneously, have represented it as the reason for Christians receiving their name. In the second place, we should have expected him to speak of the oil of the Holy Spirit, not the oil of God, if he was referring to a ceremony such as is suggested here. In the third place, a reference to material oil would be inconsistent with the context of Theophilus' remark. He points out examples of different sorts of anointing: a tower, a house, and an athlete are all at various times anointed with oil; in a sense the air is anointed with the light and the wind; so Christians are anointed with the oil of God. The sense seems to call for a third, different, sort of anointing, not by oil nor by light and wind. If we are to judge by Theophilus' *penchant* for Alexandrian methods of interpretation,[6] we should conclude that he was here referring to some sort of spiritual anointing without any reference

---

[1]Lampe, *The Seal of the Spirit*, pp. 109–11, effectively dismisses the argument of Ratcliffe, 'Justin Martyr and Confirmation', *Theology* LI, pp. 133–9, that Justin implies an additional ceremony, as 'pure speculation with no foundation in anything that Justin actually says'; and his summary (p. 111) runs: 'The important point for us to realize is that there is no evidence that Justin, or any other writer up to his time, had begun to identify any ceremony, other than Baptism in water, either with the sacramental medium of the gift of the Spirit or with the means whereby the believer was given the "seal for the last day".'

[2]*Apol.* I.61.12. [3]*Dial.*, 41.4; 43.2.

[4]*Autolycus*, II.16; cf. Lampe, *The Seal of the Spirit*, p. 114.

[5]*Ibid.*, I.12: καλούμεθα χριστιανοὶ ὅτι χριόμεθα ἔλαιον θεοῦ.

[6]See above, pp. 109 f.

to a material one at all. So once more we are left without satisfactory evidence in the literature of at least the first eighty years of the second century for the existence of a belief among Christians that the Holy Spirit is conferred in some ceremony apart from water-baptism.

Before we consider what the Christian Platonists of Alexandria have to say about this point it is worth while taking a brief glance at the evidence of Hippolytus. Hippolytus is usually regarded, along with his older contemporary Tertullian, as providing the first irrefutable evidence of the existence of such a belief about the conferring of the Holy Spirit as we have been considering. But to take this attitude would be to oversimplify the case. Lampe has argued that the Latin (Verona) text of Hippolytus' *Apostolic Tradition* is more original than the *Testament of our Lord* and the Sahidic, Arabic, and Ethiopic texts of the *Egyptian Church Order* which give a version of it. This Latin text does not separate the gift of the Spirit from water-baptism nor associate it with the bishop's laying-on of hands nor with anointing.[1] It is therefore interesting to note that, if we were to read Hippolytus' *Commentary on Daniel* and the fragments of his work on the Song of Solomon without having any preconceived notions on this subject in our minds, we would be likely to conclude that Christians were always thought to receive the Holy Spirit in water-baptism and that the ceremony of chrismation was gradually introduced as a fitting expression of this conviction. It would not be a difficult step to reach the point from this practice where it was generally believed in the Christian Church that the chrismation actually conferred the Spirit. When in his *Commentary on Daniel* he comes to allegorize the bath of Susanna, he tells us that the 'suitable day' is the Passover, on which a bath is prepared for these who would otherwise be destined to be burned. Susanna is the Church baptized; her two handmaidens are faith and love; the soap is 'the commandments of the Word'; the oil is 'the powers of the Holy Spirit with which [that is, with the powers] the believers after the bath are anointed as with myrrh . . . for whenever the Church desires to receive the spiritual bath, of necessity these two handmaidens [i.e. faith and love] must follow.'[2] This statement, preconceptions apart, suggests that Christians on Baptism receive the Holy Spirit and that oil or myrrh is thought of as a suitable symbol of this fact. Later in the same work he exhorts his hearers to 'imitate Susanna and enjoy the garden and wash in the perennial water and wipe off all dirt and be sanctified with heavenly

[1] *The Seal of the Spirit*, pp. 138–42.
[2] *Comm. on Dan.* I.16.2–5.

oil'.[1] The editor of this work, Lefevre, glosses this remark with the words, 'an allusion to the sacraments of baptism and confirmation'; but this does not seem likely, unless we are to make the difficult assumption that Hippolytus was addressing his Commentary to unbaptized Christians. If he was writing for already fully initiated Christians, then it would be futile to exhort them to become baptized and anointed, and this exhortation must refer to something else. Elsewhere he refers to Christians as 'bearing the trophy against death on their forehead', without actually referring to them as being anointed,[2] and, elsewhere, as 'bearing the seal of Christianity on the brow'.[3] And he interprets 'Stay me with raisins' (S. of S. 2.5), which he reads as 'anoint me with oil', to mean 'the power which teaches us all things and brings (them) to our remembrance, and establishes Christ in the inner man' (John 14.26); in other words, the oil means the Spirit.[4] It looks very much as if to Hippolytus in these works oil symbolized the giving of the Spirit. Two more comments on the same book, however, associate the Holy Spirit with baptism without mentioning anointing; 'the shield, however [S. of S. 4.4] is the power of the Holy Spirit which we experience through holy Baptism in faith;'[5] and he refers to the Holy Spirit as 'warning us through the water of Baptism'.[6] I suggest that the best conclusion to draw from this evidence is that when Hippolytus wrote these sentences which we have reviewed he knew of a ceremony of anointing in Christian initiation, that he regarded this ceremony as symbolizing the reception of the Holy Spirit, but that he never imagined that this ceremony *conferred* the Holy Spirit. In the language of a later day, Hippolytus regarded the ceremony as a symbol, but it was only later, or only by others, that it was regarded as a sacrament. It will be profitable to keep this hypothesis in mind when we examine the evidence in the Christian Platonists of Alexandria.

In Clement of Alexandria the evidence suggests that he too, like Hippolytus, associated the reception of the Spirit with anointing, but to say that Clement reveals a conviction that the Spirit is conferred in a ceremony of anointing, or indeed any ceremony, apart from water-baptism, is to press the evidence too far.[7] In one passage he points out that to adopt the views of Valentinus and Basilides that men are born

[1] *Ibid.*, I.33; the remark of Lefevre referred to below is on p. 127 n.*a*.
[2] *Comm. on Dan.* IV.10.3.　　　　　　[3] Frag. 13 on S. of S., p. 349.
[4] Frag. 19, *ibid.*, p. 363, lines 32–5.　　[5] *Ibid.*, p. 370, lines 28–30.
[6] *Ibid.*, p. 375, lines 14–16.
[7] The subject in Clement has been dealt with in a masterly fashion by Lampe in *The Seal of the Spirit*, pp. 153–7, though from a slightly different viewpoint.

into the world possessing natures already irretrievably damned or saved
is to make repentance and remission of sins in Baptism meaningless, 'so
that neither Baptism is any longer significant, nor the blessed seal, nor
the Son nor the Father'.[1] This certainly looks as if 'the seal', whatever
it is, is not Baptism; the whole phrase could mean 'neither Baptism nor
the invocation of the Trinity' (if we take the seal to symbolize the
Spirit), though this would admittedly be an odd way of expressing this
thought. On the other hand, he says elsewhere that the three days of
Abraham's journey to Mount Moriah signify 'the mystery of the seal',
by which he certainly means water-baptism and not a separate rite, for
he goes on 'the seal by which the true God is believed in'; probably the
three days suggest to Clement the profession of belief in the triune God.[2]
He also refers to someone who sinned deeply 'after the seal and the
redemption',[3] which, if order is significant, does not suggest that 'the
seal' refers to a ceremony of receiving the Spirit after water-baptism,
and there is one passage in the *Eclogae Propheticae* where 'seal' indubit-
ably means water-baptism.[4] And Clement can say that the Lord 'seals'
the Christian precisely as the hierophant in a mystery religion seals his
initiate.[5] The fact is that Clement's use of the concept of sealing in the
context of Baptism is altogether too loose and inconsistent to make it
compatible with the theory that he envisaged the anointing of Christians
in a ceremony apart from water-baptisms as the moment of their reception of the Spirit. It is much more likely that Lampe is right in saying
that for Clement 'the seal' meant, not a particular ceremony within
Christian initiation, but the effect of the whole rite, the marking of the
Christian's soul with the impress of God.

In one significant passage he says, 'When we are baptized, we are enlightened; when we are enlightened we are adopted as sons; when we
are adopted as sons, we are perfected; when we are perfected, we are
made immortal . . . this process is often called forgiveness (χάρισμα)
and enlightenment (φώτισμα) and perfection (τέλειον) and the bath
(λοῦτρον); the bath, through which we are cleansed of our sins; forgiveness, in that the punishments due to our sins are remitted; enlightenment, by which that holy light initiates into salvation, that is by
which we see clearly in divine things.'[6] It is evident that Clement is not

---

[1] *Strom.* II.3. 11, *PG* 8.941.   [2] *Strom.* V.11.73, *PG* 9.112.
[3] μετὰ τὴν σφραγῖδα καὶ τὴν λύτρωσιν, *Quis Dives* 39, *PG* 9.644.
[4] 12, *PG* 9.704.
[5] *Protrept.* XII.120, *PG* 8.211. It may well be that it was from the mystery
religions that the practice of chrismation was gradually adopted by Christianity.
[6] *Paed.* I.6.26, *PG* 8.281.

here expounding four successive stages in Christian initiation, but four different aspects of the same event. This impression is confirmed when in a series of passages from the *Eclogae Propheticae* he says that Israel's passing through the Red Sea, and also their passing through Jordan, are types of Baptism, and comments, 'the regeneration is through water and Spirit' and 'the Baptism takes place through water and Spirit;' he never keeps to a regular order in enumerating these two elements in Baptism, and specifically says, 'The heavenly water . . . is to be allegorized as Holy Spirit, as if it was the water of the spirit, just as (ordinary) water is of the body.'[1] Further, his references to chrism do not suggest that he regarded it as a medium of the Spirit apart from water-baptism. He speaks of the Lord's spiritual body, 'namely, that by which we are anointed;'[2] he speaks of Christ saying 'I anoint you with the unguent of faith.'[3] He objects to the additional ceremony added to Baptism by some (not necessarily heretics) of marking the ears of the baptized with fire.[4] And in a long passage,[5] a discourse on 'I fed you with milk, not with meat' (I Cor. 3.2), he discusses Baptism, making no mention at all of signing or chrismation, but regarding the ceremony only as concerned with water, though he speaks of 'the Word . . . illuminating the infants.'[6] And he describes the young robber whose story he tells in the *Quis Dives* as, in his repentance, 'baptized anew in his own tears'; in the same passage he has described Baptism both as an illumination and as a seal.[7] In the discourse on I Cor. 3.2, however, he does mention the giving of honey and milk to the baptized; Tertullian mentions this custom also.[8] The custom of signing the ears of the baptized with fire which called forth Clement's rejection was mentioned apparently by Heracleon, and therefore must go back as far as the seventh decade of the second century. It is clear that additional ceremonies, perhaps derived from the practice of the contemporary pagan religions[9] and

[1]*Eclogae* 6–8, *PG* 9.701. The last sentence runs: τὸ δὲ ἐπουρανίον ὕδωρ . . .
πνεῦμα ἀλληγορεῖται ἅγιον, οἷον τοῦ πνεύματος ὕδωρ, ὥσπερ ἐκεῖνο τοῦ σώματος.
[2]*Paed.* II.2.19, *PG* 8.409.
[3]*Protrept.* XII.120, *PG* 8.211.
[4]*Eclogae* 25, *PG* 9.709.
[5]*Paed.* I.6.34–51, *PG* 8.292–312.
[6]*Ibid.*, I.6.51, *PG* 8.312. I have refrained from giving any quotations from the *Excerpta ex Theodoto*, for we know that some of these extracts do not represent Clement's own thought, and we cannot be sure about the rest.
[7]*Quis Dives* 42, *PG* 9.648 f.   [8]*De Corona* 3.
[9]Plutarch tells us, for instance, that on the ninth and tenth day of the first month the Egyptians in their festival to Hermas eat honey and figs, saying 'Sweet is the truth' (*De Iside et Osiride* 68, 378B). The honey and milk in the case of the Christians would doubtless be thought to symbolize the baptized person having entered the promised land with Jesus, cf. Acts 7.4 f., 45 and above, p. 98.

probably associated with some traditional Christian symbol or type, were added at an early stage to the original rite of water-baptism, designed no doubt to emphasize some point of baptismal doctrine. It is very likely that the chrismation of the baptized person, in order to emphasize his reception of the Holy Spirit, had become a widespread practice in the Church by the year 200, and that Clement, along with Hippolytus, regarded this as the normal means of symbolizing the fact that *in the immersion of water* the Christian initiate received the Spirit. Or alternatively the ceremony of signing in Baptism may have been a very old one, adopted, as Rev. 7.3 f. suggests, to mark Christians as the chosen people, in imitation of the incident recorded in Ezek. 9.4;[1] in that case the association of the signing with the Holy Spirit is a development which we can trace taking place about A.D. 200. The one thing that is clear from the evidence is that in Clement we have no sure ground for seeing any other ceremony than water-baptism as the act which confers the Holy Spirit.

Lampe, in a very able handling of the evidence on this subject in Origen, has shown that in his anxiety to do justice to the incidents in Acts in which the gift of the Holy Spirit followed the laying on of hands after baptism, Origen does sometimes tend to divorce the reception of the Spirit from the experience of water-baptism, that he sometimes associates the Spirit symbolically with chrism, but that in spite of these facts it is very difficult indeed to conclude that Origen believed that the Spirit was given in a ceremony separate from the ceremony of water-baptism.[2] It is certainly noticeable that normally Origen seems to assume that the Spirit is conferred in water-baptism. 'Everybody who believes in Christ first dies and then after that is born again. . . . The plant is therefore first, the initial confession of a man in Christ. Next the leaves appear, when, being born again, he receives the gift of the grace of God from the cleansing of the Holy Spirit. Then he puts forth flowers, when he begins to make progress and to be adorned by beauty of behaviour;' there is no room for a separate gift of the Spirit here.[3] In another passage he sees in Ps. 23.1 f. an account of the instruction, Baptism, and communicating of the initiated Christian, without making any mention of a ceremonial unction. The omission is all the more marked because very shortly afterwards he comes to interpret the later verse (v. 5) 'he hath anointed my head with oil' and discourses long on it without referring at

[1] See *Origen's Doctrine of Tradition*, p. 151. But Origen does not mention signing with the cross as a ceremony of Christian initiation in this context.
[2] *The Seal of the Spirit*, pp. 164-70.
[3] *Hom. on Num.* IX.9.

all to baptismal unction. On the contrary, he stresses the inward nature of the initiation, speaking of 'the intellectual water of refreshment . . . a spiritual table'.[1] In another passage he speaks of the smearing of the doorposts at the time of the first Passover (Ex. 12.7), and remarks 'we anoint our house with blood', meaning by 'house' our bodies. But he interprets this anointing of our bodies in a wholly spiritual sense, to mean 'we believe in Christ'.[2] The reader is reminded of the words, already referred to, put into the mouth of Christ by Clement, 'I anoint you with the unguent of faith,'[3] and perhaps we have here some clue to the extraordinary statement of Theophilus that Christians are so-called because they are anointed with the oil of God.[4] On the other hand, Origen does clearly know of a ceremony in which the newly-baptized are anointed with chrism; Lampe reviews several passages which evince the existence of this custom, the most striking of which is the phrase, 'baptized in visible water and in a visible chrism'.[5] Again when he is interpreting the allegorical meaning of the experiences of the children of Israel in the wilderness he says, 'The sea is Baptism and the cloud is the Holy Spirit and the manna is the Word of God.'[6] This would fit appropriately into a reconstruction of three stages of Christian initiation, water-baptism, chrismation conferring the Spirit, and communicating, except for the characteristically Origenistic substitution of the Word of God for the Eucharist; he may therefore just as well in this passage be describing three aspects of the same single event of Christian initiation—water-baptism which includes reception of the Spirit and encounter with the Logos. The danger of reading into Origen's words a belief that the Spirit is received in a separate ceremony from water-baptism is well demonstrated by an examination of any of those passages in which Origen handles those texts in the Book of Acts which seem to support such a theory. In his *Commentary on John* he deals with Acts

[1] Pitra, *Analecta Sacra* II, pp. 478–81. Pitra himself here is anxious to see a reference to ceremonial unction, but, as far as I can see, without justification.
[2] Fragment on Exodus, *PG* 12.284.
[3] *Protrept.* XII.120, *PG* 8.241.
[4] *Autolycus* I.12. See above, p. 313.
[5] *Comm. on Rom.* V.8. Lampe deals with this passage (*The Seal of the Spirit*, pp. 165 f.); and Crouzel, *Théologie de l'Image de Dieu chez Origène*, p. 213, uses it to support a far-reaching, and to my mind far from justified, claim that this anointing had always been part of Baptism and that it was followed by 'confirmation then given according to the apostolic rite by the imposition of hands'. The first of these ceremonies (though not the second) may have been visible in the beginning of the third century; they are both invisible in the first two! It is even not impossible that the words '*et in visiblili chrismate*' may be due to Rufinus' sedulous desire to keep Origen's utterances abreast with the theological and ecclesiastical developments of Rufinus' own day.
[6] *Comm. on S. of S.* II, on S. of S. 1.11f.

8.16 ff. and 19.2 ff., and points out that 'the Baptism of regeneration did not rest with John but with Jesus through his disciples, and that which is called the washing of rebirth took place with the renewal of the Spirit which was in those cases "borne", since he was from God, "above the water" [Gen. 1.2] but it does not take place in every case along with the water.'[1] It is obvious here that Origen cannot be referring these passages in Acts to a contemporary practice of anointing separately from water-baptism to confer the Spirit, for then he would not have said 'it does not take place *in every case* along with the water'; presumably if such a custom existed Origen would have regarded the Spirit as being conferred in every case. It is much more likely that Origen is here expressing an emphasis which can be observed in the treatment of sacraments generally by the Christian Platonists of Alexandria; he stresses frequently the inward meaning of effect in moral life and spiritual development of the sacrament, and in this case he is insisting that regeneration must be completed by the fruits and the experience of the Spirit in the life of the regenerated person, and is using these passages in Acts to support this point. We have found a very similar emphasis in Hermas.[2]

This last passage dealing with the Spirit's part in initiation provides us also with a characteristic example of the two main points of Origen's baptismal theology. He says that just as our Lord's miracles, though they were symbols of the Word who rids us of every Spiritual disease and weakness, nevertheless healed the body, 'so also the washing through water, though it is a symbol of the cleansing of the soul which has washed away all stain coming from sin, is nevertheless intrinsically to him who exposes himself to the power of the adorable Trinity the source and fountain of divine graces.'[3] Origen believes firmly in the efficacy of Baptism, conceiving of it in an almost magical way, for it calls into play his doctrine of the power of names.[4] But he believes even more firmly in the inner moral experience and the doctrinal mystery of which Baptism is only an outward symbol. In another passage he says that the water in which we are baptized 'is no longer mere water, but is sanctified by a mystic invocation (μυστικῇ τινι ἐπικλήσει); and he adds 'For if we are first to become disciples after accepting the doctrines of truth, and then to observe the commandments given for the exercise of the moral virtues, and thus to be baptized into the name of the

---

[1] *Comm. on John* VI.33: 'in every case' (πᾶσι) could mean 'for everyone'.
[2] See above, p. 312.
[3] *Comm. on John* VI.33. Cf. J. G. Davies, *The Spirit, the Church, and the Sacraments*, p. 101.
[4] See above, pp. 205-8.

Father and the Son and the Holy Spirit, how can that water which is
received along with these any longer be "mere water", since it shares
as far as possible the power of the holy Trinity and is linked with virtue
both moral and intellectual ?'[1]

This juxtaposition of a traditional view of Baptism and a view which
tends to see its significance primarily as a symbol of some spiritual
experience or doctrinal truth is brought out clearly in Origen's treatment of baptismal typology. There are plenty of examples of Origen
reproducing traditional language about the typological significance of
Baptism. We have already seen one passage where, speaking of the
crossing of the Red Sea, Origen says, 'The sea is Baptism and the cloud
is the Holy Spirit.'[2] Lundberg notes several of these: in one passage a
fish with fins and scales is compared to a baptized Christian, 'who,
caught in the nets of faith, is called a good fish by the Saviour;'[3] in
Hom. on I Sam. II (about the woman with a familiar spirit) the old idea
appears of Jesus having blazed a trail through the kingdom of the dead
to Paradise for the faithful, and in the same Homily both the Red Sea
and the river Jordan are associated with the Waters of the Dead;[4] and
elsewhere Origen writes, 'But just as the water was to the Hebrews a
wall on the right and on the left, so also the fire will be a wall, if we do
what was said of those who believed in God and in Moses his servant',
a sentence which alludes to the old idea that Christians were after death
to cross through fire to Paradise.[5] J. H. Bernard gives several similar
examples.[6] And Daniélou has analysed a passage in the *Homilies on
Exodus*, showing that Origen here reproduces and refers to St Paul's
sacramental interpretation of the crossing of the Red Sea (I Cor. 10.1–4)
and also interprets it of Baptism; later in this homily Origen compares
the 'three days' demanded of Pharaoh by Moses and refused by Pharaoh
to the three days elapsing between Christ's institution of the Eucharist
and his Resurrection, applying this comparison to the necessity of
Christians dying and being buried with Christ in Baptism and rising
with him; and later still he identifies the Egyptians with demons who
try to detain the soul from Baptism and who in Baptism are brought to
nought. But Daniélou notes that in the same homily Origen suggests a
Philonic, allegorical, interpretation whereby the Egyptians are the

[1]*Comm. on John*, frag. 36.
[2]*Comm. on S. of S.* II, on S. of S. 1.11 f.; see above, p. 319.
[3]*Hom. on Lev.* VII.7; Lundberg, *Typologie Baptismale*, p. 50.
[4]*Ibid.*, p. 148; cf. p. 13 n. 1.
[5]*Hom. on Ps.* 37, III.1, *PG* 12.1337; see Lundberg, *Typologie Baptismale*,
p. 149.
[6]*Studia Sacra*, pp. 8, 12 f., 17 f.

A.E.–L

passions and the crossing of the Red Sea represents the battle of spirit against flesh.[1]

But there are also plenty of indications that Origen is ready to abandon or to modify traditional baptismal typology. One example of this is the well-known fact that Origen on several occasions produces an alternative typology of Baptism whereby the crossing of the Red Sea foreshadows admission to the catechumenate and the crossing of the Jordan prefigures Baptism, in accordance with his desire to interpret Joshua as a type of Jesus and to exalt him as superior to Moses, the representative of the law.[2] The children of Israel's crossing of Jordan under Joshua, he claims, was quite as significant as the crossing of the Red Sea in its Pauline interpretation, indeed it was more so, because Joshua, succeeding Moses, was a type of Christ, succeeding the old dispensation; the Jordan was a sweeter and more drinkable river than the Red Sea; the order of crossing Jordan explains the economy of the relations between the Father and the Son; and Christ proclaims his own pre-eminence in the text which proclaims Joshua's commanding position (Josh. 3.7). Elijah and Elisha were baptized in Jordan, and its outstanding virtue was illustrated by Naaman.[3] Again: 'Do not be surprised when these incidents which happened to the former people are referred to you, Christian man; to you who have crossed the streams of Jordan by the sacrament of Baptism the divine Word promises the journey and crossing through the air itself' (quoting I Thess. 4.17) . . .'You who have recently left the darkness of idolatry and desire to come to listen to the divine law, are now for the first time leaving Egypt. When you have been added to the list of catechumens and begun to obey the ordinances of the Church, you have crossed the Red Sea, and, living in the Stations in the Wilderness, you spend each day hearing the law of God and looking at the face of Moses unveiled through the glory of God. But if you shall have come to the mystical laver of Baptism, with the priestly and Levitical order standing by, and shall have been initiated into those holy and wonderful sacraments which those people know who are permitted to know, then also by the administration of the priests, with Jordan crossed, you will enter the land of promise in which Jesus receives you after Moses and himself becomes for you the

---

[1] *Hom. on Ex.* V.1 f., 5; Daniélou, *Sacramentum Futuri*, pp. 162–4; cf. *ibid.*, p. 147 and Lundberg, *op. cit.*, p. 119.

[2] This fact has been noted by several scholars. See Lundberg, *op. cit.*, pp. 117 f.; Daniélou, *Origène*, pp. 70 f.; *Sacramentum Futuri*, pp. 233–40; de Lubac, *Histoire et Esprit*, p. 192 n. 333.

[3] *Comm. on John* VI.44–7.

leader of a new journey.'[1] Incidentally this last passage appears to envisage instruction to catechumens, Baptism in water, and admission to the Eucharist, but not the conferring of the Spirit in a separate ceremony between Baptism and Eucharist.

The spiritualizing interpretation of Baptism, noticed already in Origen's tendency to introduce Philonic allegory into his handling of the sacrament, is observable in other ways too. Baptism, he often says, is spiritual circumcision, a cutting off from the heart of evil things.[2] He sometimes speaks of two 'washings of regeneration', one Baptism with water which is an outward and material Baptism, a Baptism 'through a glass, darkly', and the other the Baptism 'with the Holy Ghost and with fire', which is yet to be accomplished at the final regeneration.[3] And Völker notes how Origen converts the incident at Mara, which was often taken as a type of Christian Baptism, in his over-subtle and intellectualizing way, into a lesson about allegorizing the law; he links the stick which Moses threw into the bitter water with the 'tree of life' of Prov. 3.18, and comments, 'The bitterness of the letter of the law is changed into the sweetness of the spiritual interpretation.'[4] And we cannot describe as genuine sacramental typology his interpretation of the sentence, 'Let thy garments be always white' (Eccles. 9.8), as meaning that only by Baptism can purity be restored.[5] In short, Origen inherited and consciously used all the traditional types and figures and conceptions associated in Christian thought up to his day with Baptism, but he did not hesitate at the same time to expound his own characteristically spiritualizing and allegorizing re-interpretations of the sacrament, reminiscent of the rest of his Philonic inheritance, and was as ready to find scriptural support for those as for the others.

Very much the same observation can be made about Origen's handling of the Eucharist.[6] Origen certainly respected liturgical tradition and in some ways was conservative and conventional about this sacrament. The *Conversation with Heracleides* gives us a unique picture of

---

[1] *Hom. on Josh.* IV.1; cf. I.6 and XXVI.2, which reproduce the same pattern.
[2] *Comm. on Rom.* II.12, and often elsewhere.
[3] *Comm. on Matt.* XV.23.
[4] *Hom. on Ex.* VII.1; contrast Justin, *Dial.* 86.6; even Clement had given a Christological interpretation to this text in Prov. 3.18 (*Strom.* III.20.103, *PG* 8.1048). See Völker, 'Die Verwertung des Weisheits-Literatur', *ZKG* LXIV, p. 22 n. 142. But it must be added that in *Comm. on John* XX.36 Origen gives an entirely Christological interpretation of this text (noted by Völker, *op. cit.*, p. 28, though he does not contrast this passage in any way with that in the *Hom. on Ex.*).
[5] *Hom. on Ex.* IX.3; XI.7; see Völker, *op. cit.*, p. 22.
[6] For a general discussion of this subject, see Molland, *The Conception of the Gospel in Alexandrian Theology*, p. 136.

Origen, drawn, not by Origen himself and derived from his works, but by a sympathetic onlooker at a conference in which Origen was taking a leading part. In this conference Origen shows himself to be very anxious to secure right and consistent praying in the Eucharist on the part of the bishop who still in the middle of the third century was entitled to alter or vary the main prayer of the *anaphora* as he thought fit. Origen insists that the celebrant must address God as one God once in each prayer, as 'God through God', not twice, as two gods. And he exerts himself to exact a promise that the bishop shall 'abide by the conventions',[1] without innovating.[2] He tells Celsus that Christians 'have a symbol of our thanksgiving to God in the bread that is called "eucharist".'[3] He describes in a homily how carefully Christians avoid spilling any crumb of the bread 'when you receive the body of the Lord' at the Eucharist.[4] Elsewhere he says, 'And we eat loaves offered with thanksgiving and prayer for all that has been given to us, and become through the prayer a body which is holy in itself and sanctifies those who are associated with it with a wholesome intention.'[5] And he is entirely traditional in dissociating the Eucharist from any conception of the sacrifice of Christ being repeated there or elsewhere: Justin before him had said that God receives the sacrifices offered to him in the Christian Eucharist and that the only perfect sacrifices and well-pleasing to God are 'prayers and thanksgivings coming from those who are worthy'.[6] And Clement of Alexandria had written, 'There is indeed an altar on earth among us, in that spot where is the congregation of those who are intent on prayers, which has as it were one common voice and one mind. . . . For indeed the Church's sacrifice is the word sent up like sacrificial smoke from holy souls, whereby both the sacrifice and all the disposition (of the sacrificers) is simultaneously unveiled to God.'[7] Origen is probably expressing the conviction in the following passage: 'And indeed during the time of (God's) long-suffering, sacrifices (of the Jews) countered sacrifices (of the pagans); but when the perfect Victim came, and the immaculate Lamb who should take away the sin of the whole world, those sacrifices which used to be offered regularly to God

[1] For the meaning of this phrase, see above, p. 303.
[2] *Conversation with Heracleides*, pp. 129 f. (MS. pp. 4.30–5.10).
[3] *Contra Celsum* VIII.57; Chadwick (note *in loc.*) compares Justin, *Apol.* I.66.1, 'This food is called among us eucharist'.
[4] *Hom. on Ex.* XIII.3; Harnack, who calls attention to this passage (*Der Kirchengeschichtliche Ertrag*, I, p. 58), with characteristic arrogance, describes this as an encouragement of 'Christian superstitions'.
[5] *Contra Celsum* VIII.33.
[6] *Dial.* 117.1–5.
[7] *Strom.* VII.6.31 f., *PG* 9.444.

now appeared unnecessary, since all the worship of demons was driven out by a single victim.'[1] But Origen can also produce a sentiment like this: 'Moreover we are said to drink the blood of Christ, not only in the sacramental service (*non solum sacramentorum ritu*), but also when we receive his words, of which that blood consists, just as he said himself, "The words which I speak are spirit and life" ' (John 6.63).[2] Origen shows a strong tendency, not so much to regard the rite as symbolic and not sacramental, as to stress the symbolic aspect of it, sometimes to the detriment of the sacramental. This was not an entirely new emphasis in his day. Oulton collected four passages from Clement of Alexandria in which he interprets the 'eucharistic' words of John 6 in a non-eucharistic sense;[3] one is particularly striking: 'The Lord in the Gospel according to John said symbolically: "Eat ye my flesh and drink ye my blood," speaking in metaphor of the clearness of faith and of the eatable and drinkable properties of the promise; by which the Church, compounded as a man is of many members, is refreshed and increased, is welded together and compacted of both elements, of faith, which is the body, and of hope, which is the soul, even as the Lord was composed of flesh and blood.'[4] And in another passage Clement uses the figurative expression 'the wine, the blood of the vine of David' in a non-eucharistic sense, even though this must have been traditionally associated with the Eucharist, since it appears in a eucharistic context in the *Didache*.[5] This tendency Origen carries further. He hints at such a possibility in his treatment of the incident of Jesus giving the sop to Judas (John 13.26), which leads him to discuss eucharistic doctrine. He says that there is a power in the bread and the cup, and then adds, 'Let the bread and the cup be understood by the simpler folk according to the more usual interpretation concerning the Eucharist, but to those who have learnt to hear deeper things let it be understood also according to the more divine promise about the nourishing word of truth.'[6] The bread which has been blessed, he tells us elsewhere, is by itself nothing but bread; it is the Word blessing it which counts: 'The food consecrated "by the Word of God and by prayer" in as far as it is material "goeth into

---

[1]*Hom. on Num.* XVII.1.
[2]*Ibid.*, XVI.9.
[3]J. E. L. Oulton, *Holy Communion and Holy Spirit*, pp. 96 f.; the four passages are *Paed.* I.6.36, 38, 42 (*PG* 9.293, 296, 301) and *Excerpta ex Theodoto* 13, *PG* 9.664.
[4]*Paed* I. 6.38, Stählin's text, Oulton's translation.
[5]*Quis Dives* 29, *PG* 9.634; *Didache* 9. On the other hand, elsewhere Clement uses Melchizedek bringing bread and wine to Abraham as a eucharistic type in a conventional way (*Strom.* IV. 25.161, *PG* 8.1369).
[6]*Comm. on John* XXXII.24.

the belly and is cast out into the draught". But in as far as prayer has been made over it it becomes profitable "according to the proportion of faith" . . . and it is not the material (ὕλη) of the bread, but the word spoken over it, which is that which profits him who eats it not "unworthily" of the Lord.' And even this refers only to the 'typical and symbolic' body, the eucharistic elements. The 'bread of heaven' and 'true meat' and 'flesh' and 'blood' referred to in John 6 are apparently different and do not refer to the Eucharist.[1] He repeats this doctrine (which incidentally excludes transubstantiation) later in the same work: 'God the Word did not call his body that visible bread which he was holding in his hand, but the Word in whose mysteries that bread was to be broken. Nor did he pronounce that visible drink to be his blood, but the Word in whose mysteries that drink was to be poured out.'[2]

Similarly Origen seems deliberately to avoid interpreting passages in the Bible in a eucharistic sense, even where a passage seems to invite such an interpretation. 'The Lord is the lot of my inheritance and of my cup' (Ps. 16.5) provokes the comment, 'The Lord is also bread, as he provides instruction, and strengthens the heart of him who eats him; and he is a cup in respect of the truth, for he provides the cheerfulness of knowledge to him who drinks him by conforming to him.'[3] But the best illustration of this point is undoubtedly Origen's treatment of the 'eucharistic' passage in John 6. There is one passage where he quotes the words 'unless ye eat my flesh and drink my blood ye will not have life abiding in you' (John 6.53) in a plainly eucharistic context, but his explanation of the relation of the sacrament to what it symbolizes is so much intellectualized and spiritualized that we can scarcely set it against those passages where he interprets this Johannine passage in a wholly non-eucharistic sense.[4] These last are very numerous. Discussing the clause in the Lord's Prayer, 'Give us this day our daily bread,' he insists that the bread is entirely spiritual and that to eat it means to have contact with the Logos, an intellectual and spiritual apprehension of the Word of God, and he quotes to support this the 'eucharistic' passage in John 6.[5] In fact in his whole discussion of bread in this particular work he never suggests that it should be taken in a euchar-

---

[1]*Comm. on Matt.* XI.14. Cf. *Comm. on I Cor.*, frag. 34, on I Cor. 7.5, *JTS* IX, p. 502, 'those loaves which are greater than the shewbread, over which the name of God and of Christ and of the Holy Spirit is called'.

[2]*Ibid.*, Comm. Ser. 85.

[3]*Comm. on Ps.* 16.5, *PG* 12.1213.

[4]*Comm. on Matt.* Comm. Ser. 79, 86; we have seen an example of his language in this passage (Comm. Ser. 85) above.

[5]*PE* XXVII.1.

istic sense (*PE* XXVII.1–12). In one passage he even says that the words 'Except ye eat the flesh of the Son of Man and drink his blood ye have not life in yourselves. . . . For my flesh is meat indeed and my blood is drink indeed' (John 6.53, 55) must not be taken literally,[1] and on several occasions he interprets these words of the Christian hearing and assimilating the words of a preacher.[2] And again Origen can write, commenting on 'When the wicked . . . came upon me to eat up my flesh' (Ps. 27.2): 'If we eat the flesh of Christ (for, says he, "he that eateth my flesh and drinketh my blood") and the devils eat our flesh, then perhaps the devils eat the flesh of Christ, when they exert themselves to destroy the virtues and the true convictions that are in us.'[3] The part of Origen's *Commentary on John* which covered the sixth chapter of that Gospel is not extant, but there is no doubt about how he must have dealt with the 'eucharistic' passage in it.

In similar vein Origen occasionally allegorizes the actual accounts of the institution of the Eucharist. The Christian, he says, keeps every day as a festival; we must always eat the 'flesh of the Word' at a perpetual Passover, being always 'in the days of Pentecost', going always into the upper room and with the apostles praying and receiving the Spirit.[4] In a long passage allegorizing all references to upper rooms which he can find in the Bible, prompted by Jer. 20.3 ('put him in the stocks that were in the upper gate of Benjamin'), he reaches finally the upper room where the Eucharist was instituted, and he allegorizes this unconcernedly with the rest: 'And if you go up with him in order to keep the Passover, he gives to you the cup of the New Covenant,' and so on.[5]

This tendency of Origen, and in some degree of Clement also, to concentrate upon the symbolic meaning of this sacrament so much as to put its realistic or efficacious aspect into the background, or to interpret apparently sacramental language in an unsacramental way, has of course been noted by many writers. Von Balthasar points out that though Origen believes in a real sacramental presence (citing a Latin

[1]*Hom. on Lev.* VII.4.
[2]*Hom. on Num.* XXIII.6; XVI.9; *Hom. on Ex.* VII.8; XIII.3. The last three passages have been noticed by Dugmore, *The Influence of the Synagogue upon the Divine Office*, pp. 87–9.
[3]*Comm. on Ps.* 27.2 (*PG* 12.1277). Oulton has collected no less than eleven examples of similar rationalizing of statements in the New Testament of a sacramental nature, mainly from this passage in the Fourth Gospel, on the part of Origen (*Holy Communion and Holy Spirit*, pp. 97 f.). They include, besides four of those which have been already mentioned, *PA* I.1.9; *Hom. on Ps.* 37, I.2; *Comm. on Ps.* 78.25; *Hom. on Jer.* X.2; *Comm. on Matt.* XII.33; and *Comm. on John* I.30 and X.17 f.
[4]*Contra Celsum* VIII.22.
[5]*Hom. on Jer.* XIX.13.

translation of *Contra Celsum* VIII.33 quoted above, p. 324), yet he regarded the sacrament as primarily a sacramental means of achieving what it allegorically meant. 'The real and efficacious eating of the sacrament appears then to be for Origen the symbol . . . of another eating, more "divine" and more "true".'[1] Cadiou notes both Origen's preference for doctrine rather than ritual and his reserve and vagueness when speaking about sacraments.[2] But Koch goes altogether too far when he writes that in Origen the sacraments 'play an almost non-existent part'.[3] Daniélou expresses a more balanced judgement when he says that 'his whole work is orientated rather towards the sacrament of Scripture than towards the sacrament of the cult,' and that 'Origen, as a teacher, always insists much more upon the sacrament of preaching than on that of the liturgy . . .; the visible signs of the cult—and it is here that his Platonic cast of thought appears—only interest him as signs of spiritual realities. That is to say, he never denies the reality of the Eucharist, but it is easy to see that . . . he will be led to minimize it.' And he agrees that Origen put the eating of the Word in reading and studying Scripture on a parallel with the eucharistic assimulation of the Word.[4] De Lubac frankly accepts this statement of Origen's attitude to sacraments, and stoutly defends it as entirely orthodox and catholic. To Origen, he contends, Christ in taking our flesh took not only the body of flesh and blood, which people saw and touched, but also, as the same body, of which the flesh and blood was only a symbol, the 'mystical body', the Church, the redeeming organ of which all Scripture speaks, the organ round which the universe revolves, the dynamic centre of Origen's theological system. This body is more important. 'It is the reality, of which the other, even in its reality, is the "type", the symbol. . . . The historical life of Christ in his flesh and the mystical life in the Church are then one and the same life under two different aspects, in two "bodies", of which the first is symbolic and the second is symbolized.' In his apparently spiritualizing passages Origen is simply saying that the second body, symbolized in the Eucharist by the first, is more important; he is not denying the reality nor the significance of the first.[5]

---

[1]H. von Balthasar, 'Le Mysterion d'Origène', *RechSR* XXVII, pp. 549–52; the quotation comes from p. 552.
[2]Cadiou, *La Jeunesse d'Origène*, pp. 384–8.
[3]*Pronoia und Paideusis*, p. 78 n. 2.
[4]Daniélou, *Origène*, pp. 58, 74, 77 f.; on p. 79 he points out that in Origen's mystical theology 'the Eucharist marks the lower grade and mystical inebriation the highest'.
[5]*Histoire et Esprit*, pp. 355–63; the quotation is from p. 360. Cf. pp. 363–73, the section entitled 'Le Primat de la Parole'.

This is a clear and very able exposition of Origen's attitude to sacraments. What is startling is that de Lubac is apparently ready to defend this unconcernedly as orthodoxy. Not only does it make the very questionable assumption that the Church is Christ, apparently without qualification. But it suffers from the same shortcomings as does de Lubac's defence of Origen's attitude to history. It assumes that the Incarnation was no more than a symbolic means of achieving our salvation, an enactment upon the stage of history of eternal truths the understanding of which brings us salvation. In the thought of the New Testament God has poured and pledged himself into history, has committed himself into human nature, has moved into the circumstances of our life on earth, in the person of the Word who has become flesh; the Church is the place where this Incarnation has taken place and where the Word still is tabernacling among us, for salvation and for judgement; the sacraments of Baptism and of the Eucharist are the divinely-ordained means, or, better, moments or circumstances, in which men meet this incarnate Lord in the Spirit, in which the historical events by which our salvation took place become contemporary to us. In the thought of Origen, or at least of Origen interpreted by de Lubac, the Incarnation becomes a temporary sojourning of the Word in human form as a necessary but passing phase in the divine strategy, the Church becomes a further stage of revelation beyond the Incarnation, and sacraments are the symbols in handling which we enter that further stage and pay formal respect, but no more, to the earlier stage, the Incarnation. Logically this theory demands that we should regard the Incarnation as now over; and it is significant that in Origen's system the God-man, after his Ascension, has virtually abandoned his humanity. It is no coincidence that we should find the same defects in Origen's doctrine of sacraments that we have already found in his attitude to history; the two subjects are inextricably bound together.[1] In bidding farewell, politely but cheerfully, to the reality of God's activity in history, Origen is bidding farewell to the reality of the sacraments.

Origen takes a very similar attitude to the ministry. He accepts quite readily all the practices and doctrine which he has inherited, but he has his own peculiar contribution to make to the subject, and his allegorizing cast of thought inclines him to regard the ministry as ultimately a symbol. We have seen already that he recognizes the three orders of bishop, priest and deacon, and that he sees in them a fulfilment of the three ministries, of high priest, priest and Levite, under the Old

[1] See above, pp. 277 ff.

A.E-.L*

Testament.[1] He refers occasionally to an apostolic succession in the sense of a succession of bearers of authentic tradition; he claims, for instance, that he 'holds fast to the rule of Jesus Christ according to the succession of the apostles of the heavenly Church'.[2] And he remarks that it is necessary for a proper choice of a bishop that the people should be present at his election.[3] But, as with Baptism and the Eucharist, so also with the ministry; Origen cannot resist the temptation to allegorize this institution. Bishops, presbyters, and deacons are, he says, symbolic of spiritual things.[4] The bishop stands for Jesus, the priests for Abraham, Isaac, and Jacob, and the deacons for the seven archangels of God.[5]

As is well known, Origen has his own individual interpretation of the words recorded in St Matthew's Gospel as spoken by Christ to Peter at Caesarea Philippi (Matt. 16.17–19). 'The rock is every imitator of Christ, from whom they drank who "drank from a spiritual rock which followed them". And upon every such rock is built every principle of the Church and its constitution. For in each of those who are perfect and have the full number of the principles and acts and ideas which compose blessedness is the Church built by God.' He makes it clear, too, that he believes that what is said in the whole of this passage applies not to Peter only (that he specifically denies), but to the apostles as a whole.[6] Similarly 'the keys of the kingdom of heaven' (Matt. 16.19) were, in Origen's view, given not to Peter only, but also to every Peter who believes the confession which Peter made.[7] Peter, he says elsewhere, was taken by Jesus as a type of anyone who has the right disposition for the Church being built in him.[8]

It is while discussing this Matthaean passage, too, that Origen makes one of his most startling statements about bishops. Those who rely on this text 'to exalt the position of the episcopate' should know that authority to bind and loose depends upon moral and religious achievement in confessing Peter's confession, and not on any authority conferred by the episcopal office.[9] And, conversely, he holds that there are

[1]See above, p. 303. To the reference there given (*Hom. on Jer.* XII.3) we may add three more, *Hom. on Josh.* IV.1, VIII.7, and *PE* XXVIII.9 f.
[2]*PA* IV.2.2.
[3]*Hom. on Lev.* VI.3.
[4]*Comm. on Matt.* XIV.22.
[5]*Ibid.*, Comm. Ser. 10.
[6]*Comm. on Matt.* XII.10; cf. Comm. Ser. 139. Incidentally, a subsequent chapter (XII.12) suggests that Origen did not believe in the impeccability nor infallibility of the visible Church.
[7]*Ibid.*, XII.14.
[8]*Contra Celsum* VI.77.
[9]*Comm. on Matt.* XII.14. See *Origen's Doctrine of Tradition*, p. 109.

some people who are recognized by God as bishops, even though they have not been ordained.[1] It is in the same radical spirit that he maintains that, just as there were certain sins for which the priests under the old dispensation could not offer peace-offerings, so no one, not even bishops as successors of the apostles, can forgive idolatry nor adultery nor fornication in the Church of his day.[2] Origen had had unfortunate experiences with bishops and, though he is never bitter and never vindictive and never makes personal attacks, he does in several passages make it clear that bishops are not impeccable and can be very far from satisfactory in their behaviour and in their policy.[3]

His attitude to penance is, as we have already seen, inclined to be rigorist.[4] Baptism remits all sin, and after Baptism only comparatively light sins are capable of forgiveness. The method for these is contrition and confession to a priest. But Origen's views are not as much fixed and conventional as this account suggests. One interesting passage will reveal this. He emphasizes first (raising the point in the form of an objection by an imaginary interlocutor) that whereas for the Jews there was more than one opportunity for forgiveness, the case is different for the Christian; 'among us there is only one forgiveness of sins which is given at the beginning through the grace of the bath. After these there is no mercy for the sinner, nor is any forgiveness allowed.' In reply Origen says that discipline should be stricter for the Christians, for whom Christ died. But he adds that there are no less than seven ways of forgiving sin. These are:

1. Baptism.
2. Martyrdom.
3. Almsgiving (Luke 11.41).
4. Forgiving our brother's sins against us (Matt. 6.14 f. and 12).
5. Converting a sinner from the error of his ways (James 5.20).
6. Abundance of love (Luke 7.47; I Peter 4.8).
7. Contrition, repentance, tears, and confession to a priest of the Lord (Ps. 32.5; James 5.14). This is the hardest way of all.[5]

[1] *Comm. on Matt.* Comm. Ser. 12.
[2] *PE* XXVIII.10.
[3] See *Contra Celsum* III.9, 30; *Comm. on Matt.* Comm. Ser. 12; *Hom. on Lev.* XII.3; *Hom. on Ezek.* XII.2; Cadiou, *Commentaires Inédits des Psaumes*, 118.9a, p. 103; 119.161a, p. 118; 142, 4d, p. 130.
[4] See E. F. Latko, *Origen's Concept of Penance*; but this book should be approached with circumspection; see my criticism of it in *Origen's Doctrine of Tradition*, p. 47 n. 1, and my review in *Theology* LII, 1949, pp. 391 f.
[5] *Hom. on Lev.* II.4.

This should suggest to any reader that Origen's views on penance were neither stereotyped nor conventional. It should also be borne in mind that Origen sometimes suggests that the fully graduated (τελεῖος) Christian is in some sense an unordained priest and can even forgive sins.[1] The fact is that Origen's particular theological system, with its bias towards the intellectual, its disinclination towards taking history and event seriously and its allegorism twining like ivy round every branch of his theological structure, gives a peculiar and individual twist to every regular and traditional element in the Christian faith, and not least to the sacraments. We see the familiar features there, but we can perceive that they are blurred.

[1] See Völker, *Das Vollkommenheitsideal*, pp. 172–83, 187–9, and the references given there.

13

Eschatology

THE eschatological tradition which Origen inherited was a confused one. There is indeed a fundamental pattern in the eschatology of the New Testament, but it is presented in a number of different and not easily reconcilable forms, and the development of eschatological thought since the writing of the New Testament had not tended to bring about harmony among these forms or to produce a consistent interpretation of earlier eschatological material. The Apologists, for all their readiness to introduce Greek forms of thought into the presentation of Christian doctrine, had been markedly conservative in their eschatology, had seldom if ever strayed beyond the bounds of the literal interpretation of apocalyptic imagery, and had been, with a few exceptions, particularly preoccupied with a very literal presentation of the doctrine of the resurrection of the flesh. Irenaeus had seen no reason to extend to the region of eschatology that re-handling of traditional Christian doctrine which had proved on other subjects so effective and fruitful; his account of the Last Things had been conservative and almost naïve. The only hint to the contrary is contained in the *Demonstration*, where he maintains that the passage in Isa. 11.6–9 describing the harmony of the animals in the Messianic age should not be taken literally but allegorized—a view which he had rejected in his earlier work *Adversus Haereses*;[1] but this is no more than a hint. Hippolytus had been content to take eschatological imagery literally, though he expressed his dislike of a wave of chiliastic excitement which had caused a disturbance among Christians in Syria.[2] We have already seen that a confident expectation of a very crudely conceived millennium was one of the tenets of the type of thought among the less cultured Christians of Origen's day which we have called Literalist.[3] Tertullian had maintained in his usual trenchant manner a variety of

[1] *Dem.* 61; *Adv. Haer.* V. 33.4; see above, p. 112.
[2] *Comm. on Dan.* IV.18.2; see above, p. 114.
[3] See above, pp. 151 f.

eschatological views, not all of them consistent with each other. But, beyond attempts to justify the resurrection of the flesh which we would have to call ingenious rather than convincing, nobody had seriously attempted to reconcile traditional Christian eschatological beliefs with contemporary philosophical views or to work them into a homogeneous theological system.

The Christian Platonists of Alexandria make an entire break with this tradition of unreflecting conservatism. In the first place, they both resolutely reject the biblical doctrine of the wrath of God, and Origen goes to the length of holding the view usually called 'universalist', to the effect that all men will eventually be saved. He speaks of people moved 'apparently by fear of those punishments which are nominally (κατὰ τὸν λόγον) called eternal.'[1] He notes that the teaching of the parable of the Labourers in the Vineyard (Matt. 20.1-15) is that everyone shall be saved;[2] and in treating of the man cast into 'outer darkness' (Matt. 22.13) he makes it clear that he thinks that the man must eventually return from the outer darkness.[3] 'The Lord hath opened his armoury' (Jer. 50.25) means, he thinks, that the Church, which is now shut, shall be at the last opened by God, and God's wrath abolished.[4] Paul wrote in Romans (5.19) 'Even so through the obedience of the one shall the many be made righteous', not 'shall all be made righteous', because 'he wanted to leave the simpler and slacker an incentive for striving for salvation'; yet 'he does not keep the secrets of divine goodness from the more initiated'.[5] In other words, everybody will in the end achieve righteousness. There can be no such thing as eternal death. 'In fact, if the eternity of death is to be supposed to be the same as that of life, then death will not be the opposite of life, but its equal; for that which is eternal is not the opposite of that which is eternal, but the same. Now it is certain that death is the opposite of life; therefore it is certain that, if life is eternal, death cannot be eternal.'[6] Crouzel asserts[7] that on at least two occasions Origen explicitly denies universal salvation but the passages which he cites do not support this contention. In one of them[8] Origen's words run 'that they may be worthy to be found in the mystery of the resurrection, when God "will transform the body of humiliation" (Phil. 3.21), not of everybody, but of those who are

---

[1]*Contra Celsum* III.78.
[2]*Comm. on Matt.* XV.27.
[3]*Ibid.*, XVII.24.
[4]*Hom. on Jer.*, frag. 31.
[5]*Comm. on Rom.* V.2.
[6]*Ibid.*, V.7.
[7]*Théologie de l'Image de Dieu chez Origène*, p. 252.
[8]*Comm. on Matt.* XIII.21; the other passage in this work, XIII.27, referred to by Crouzel, is equally open to my interpretation.

genuinely disciples of Christ, so that it should be "conformed to the body of the glory" of Christ.' This statement, however, is not inconsistent with a doctrine of universal salvation, for, as we shall see, Origen believes that at the resurrection the bodies of those who are not numbered among the faithful will be raised, not yet to be 'conformed to the body of glory', but in order to undergo a long period of cleansing, whereas the bodies of the faithful will be thus conformed; inclusion in this glorious body is postponed but not eternally precluded for the others. The other passage cited by Crouzel[1] contains no clear denial of universalism at all, unless it be the statement that the Christian has been called to the hope from which Lucifer fell and to the place from which the rebellious angels fell. But this, in Origen's scheme, does not at all render it impossible for God eventually to recover even Lucifer and his angels. The fact is that universalism in Origen's thought is a necessary conclusion from his basic premises, and not, as it is in most modern thought, a 'larger hope' grounded on a strong belief in God's love and a kindly feeling toward all humanity, however degraded. In Origen's view for God to fail in reconciling into their original state as pure spirits wholly obedient to his will any beings at all, even only one or two, would be for God, the single, simple, primal, unalterable One, to compromise himself with change and becoming and corruption. This is inconceivable, and therefore all must be saved.

The whole conception of damnation or of anything analogous to wrath being displayed by God was alien to Origen's thought. Clement of Alexandria had set him an example here. God, Clement had said, is never angry; as for what the Scriptures call his wrath, 'This is a kindly device, to frighten us to prevent us sinning. . . . Each of us chooses his own punishments when he sins of his own accord; "the responsibility lies with the free agent; God is not responsible".'[2] In a later work he maintained that nobody can rightly be said to be an enemy of God; the most that can be said is that a man acts as an enemy towards God's covenant.[3] Origen abundantly elaborates this doctrine.[4] He defines wrath as 'the painful punishment of God inflicted for the benefit of the

[1]*Hom. on Ezek.* XIII.2.
[2]*Paed* I.8.68 f., *PG* 8.332 f.; the quotation is from Plato, *Republic* X.617E; it is a quotation much used by the Fathers, and occurs in Justin Martyr, Eusebius, Gregory Nazienzen and Theodoret. Earlier in the same passage Clement had quoted Plato, *Gorgias* 477A.
[3]*Strom.* VII.12.69, *PG* 9.496. Origen reproduces this sentiment in *Contra Celsum* I.71.
[4]For more information on this subject, see Koch, *Pronoia und Paideusis*, pp. 143 f.

sinner'.[1] Wrath, he says, is not a passion in God.[2] God's striking and punishing, his wrath (θυμός) and anger (ὀργή) are merely descriptions of his educative discipline. Elsewhere Origen distinguishes between wrath as 'anger blazing' and anger as 'a longing for revenge',[3] but he would not have applied either of these descriptions directly to God. Indeed he says, very finely, that wrath is precisely not to be angry: 'This is terrible, this is the last punishment, when we are no longer punished for sins, when we are no longer corrected in our faults. For that is the point when we have exceeded the limit of sinning and God in his wrath turns his wrath away from us.'[4] On several occasions he explains that wrath is something external to God and not part of his nature. God makes known his wrath, which is entirely alien from his nature, only in order to reform and educate men by fear of wrath.[5] Of Rom. 2.5, a passage referring to the sinner 'treasuring up' wrath, he says, 'This text has separated wrath from God. And in fact wrath is a different thing from God, and is not connected with him as if it was part of him. . . . So we by sinning provoke God so that he sends wrath which he does not possess in himself.'[6] Elsewhere during a long discussion of the wrath of God, he writes that it is 'external to God, but directed to supply the lack of those who need it, and they are given over to it as unworthy of God, in order that they might wish for God whom they have despised when they have come under the power of someone worse'; and he maintains that wrath can also mean the devil, comparing II Sam. 24.1 with I Chron. 21.1.[7] When therefore Origen encounters mention of God's wrath in the Bible he always dissolves it by a series of ingenious explanations. 'Every threat and toil and punishment brought on by God takes place, not *against* those who endure them, but for their good. And those which are thought to be the most unpleasant of the words which are applied to God, anger and wrath, are called correction and instruction.'[8] Or again: 'There is a wrath of God which burns slowly, when we have sinned in a less intolerable way and his bow is bent but he does not

---

[1]Pitra, *Analecta Sacra* II, p. 449.
[2]*Contra Celsum* IV.72.
[3]*Comm. on Ps.* 2.5, PG 12.1105. Cadiou, who calls attention to this passage, says that these definitions are taken directly or indirectly from rhetoricians' lexicons, and that they bear the mark of post-Aristotelian, and even Stoic, psychology, 'Dictionnaires Antiques dans l'Œuvre d'Origène', *REG* XLV, p. 281.
[4]*Hom. on Ex.* VIII.5.
[5]*Comm. on Rom.* VII.18.
[6]*Hom. on Ezek.* X.2.
[7]*Comm. on Rev.*, frag. 30, pp. 35 f.
[8]*Philoc.* XXVII.7, from a *Commentary on Exodus*.

shoot the arrow at us, and his sword is unsheathed but is not used. Rather by threat and by a demonstration he urges sinners to amendment';[1] or 'Consider whether benevolence may be the lot of those who follow the Word, but it will be expressed in a disciplining wrath. . . . There is indeed a certain benevolence of God, even when he disciplines, yes even when he disciplines by so-called wrath.'[2] The 'cup of the wine of the fury' of God, from which the nations are to drink (Jer. 25.15 ff.) is not an intoxicant liquor but a purgative medicine![3] 'The blasting of the breath of his displeasure' (Ps. 18.15) is explained thus: 'God does not immediately punish those who are sinners, but he gives warning of punishment before wrath, and this is his "blasting of the breath of his displeasure".'[4] 'But perhaps there is someone,' he says elsewhere, 'who is shocked by this word *wrath* and makes it an accusation against God. We will reply to him that wrath is not so much the wrath of God as a necessary strategy.'[5] On several occasions Origen explains wrath as a mere synonym for the punishment of God. This is how he explains John 3.36 ('the wrath of God abideth on him'): 'For we must not think that that which is called the wrath of God, is a passion on his part, for how could passion be attributed to the Passionless?'[6] On 'the wrath of God is revealed from heaven' (Rom. 1.18), he is careful to explain that the wrath of God is 'that power which directs the administrations of punishments and which inflicts chastisements on sinners'; it is often self-inflicted by sinners: 'they themselves become the judges who pronounce their own condemnation'; a little later in Romans (2.15) wrath means the pangs of conscience.[7] On Rom. 2.8 ('wrath and indignation') his comment runs, 'On the subject of wrath we have often observed that sometimes he who is troubled by being conscience-stricken by a knowledge of sin is "wrath", but "indignation" means an exasperation of that "wrath" which takes place and an intensification of it in certain cases.'[8] It is interesting to contrast with this fastidious refining away of the biblical doctrine of the wrath of God Theophilus' robust, though crude, acceptance of it: 'Is God angry? Yes, certainly. He is angry with those who do evil things. . . . He is an educator of

---

[1]Cadiou, *Commentaires Inédits des Psaumes*, on 2.12c, p. 73.
[2]*Ibid.*, 119.65 f., pp. 110 f.
[3]*PA* II.10.7.
[4]*Comm. on Ps.* 18.15, *PG* 12.1229; even the LXX had toned down 'nostrils' here to 'wrath'.
[5]*Necessariam dispensationem, Hom.* on *Ezek.* I.2.
[6]*Comm. on John*, frag. 51.
[7]*Comm. on Rom.* I.16.
[8]*Ibid.*, II.6.

the pious and a father of the righteous, but a judge and punisher of the impious.'[1]

But even on the subject of God punishing, Origen has many qualifications to make. Clement of Alexandria had set him a precedent here also. He had assigned three reasons for God punishing: that the victims of punishment may be reformed; that others open to reformation may be encouraged by the example; and that the victim of wrong done may not be neglected nor made liable to injury again.[2] Punishment in God's hands is 'like surgery applied to the passions of the soul'.[3] Fear is God's instrument for those who will not be persuaded by reason.[4] Origen takes up Clement's analogy of the surgeon and amplifies it. He has to deal with the Marcionites' quotation of Jer. 12.5 ('I will not pity, nor spare, nor have compassion, that I should not destroy them') to prove the cruelty of the demiurge. His answer runs: 'But if I take as an analogy the juryman who witholds his pity for the common good and the judge who rightly refuses mercy, I shall be able to convince you from this analogy that it is out of pity for the majority that God refuses to pity the individual. I shall take too as an analogy the surgeon and show that it is out of consideration for the whole body that he has no consideration for a single limb. . . . This is the reason why eternal fire was prepared, this is the reason why Gehenna has been established, this is the reason why there is such a thing as outer darkness; not only does the subject of punishment need these things but even more the common welfare.'[5] And he insists again and again that we punish ourselves and that the consequences of our sins often constitute our punishment. He would have agreed with the dictum, 'Nothing burneth in hell but self-will,' but he would have perhaps joined remorse to self-will.[6] 'God,' he says, 'is the agent of blessing, but each person who has done deeds worthy of cursing is himself the cause of the curse.'[7] God rewards those who deserve reward, but leaves the others to punish themselves.[8] 'God does not impose punishments, but we prepare for ourselves whatever we

[1]*Autolycus* I.3. For the wrath of God in the New Testament (a subject to which surprisingly little study has been given) see A. T. Hanson, *The Wrath of the Lamb*.
[2]*Strom.* IV.24.154, *PG* 8.1364; in *Paed.* I.8.70 (*PG* 8.340) he had defined punishment.
[3]*Paed.* I.8.64, *PG* 8.328.
[4]*Strom.* II.8.37, *PG* 8.971.
[5]*Hom. on Jer.* XII.5. *Eternal* fire is not of course for Origen everlasting, but aeonian. For a general treatment of the whole subject of punishment in Origen, see Koch, *Pronoia und Paideusis*, pp. 118, 123–36, 139 and ch. VII *passim*.
[6]*PA* II.10.6 (where there is also a long medical analogy) and II.5.3.
[7]*Comm. on Matt.* Comm. Ser. 72.
[8]*Comm. on Rom.* II.6 (where there is another illustration from medicine).

suffer. So we must now once more use the proof which we have so often used, "Walk ye in the flame of your fire and among the brands that ye have kindled" (Isa. 50.11). The fire is nobody's except your own, and it is you who have gathered the wood, the straw, and the material for the fire which shall break out.'[1] As might be expected, judgement is in Origen's view purely self-operating, the inevitable consequence of moral failure.[2]

Origen therefore summons all the resources of allegory to explain in this rationalizing sense all references to God punishing and judging in the Bible. The passages referring to God punishing people by fire, to which Celsus objects, are interpreted as simply the description of God bringing to repentance those whom nothing else could move; the fire is educative and purgative.[3] The parable of the Wheat and the Tares (Matt. 13.24–30) is ingeniously twisted round into a sense opposite to that intended by the evangelist; it is the evil thoughts, not the evil persons, which are burnt, leaving the persons penitent and grieving.[4] 'Happy shall he be that taketh thy little ones and throweth them against the stones' (Ps. 137.9) is treated similarly: we must take the children of the man of confusion (Babel) who are within us and dash them against the rock of Christ.[5] 'The soul that sinneth, it shall die' (Ezek. 18.4) refers to spiritual death only; 'I kill and I make alive' (Deut. 32.39) means 'clearly that death which brings life, that is, that a man should die to sin and live to God. . . . In the same way I understand the passage of Scripture, "God killed Er the son of Judah, because he was wicked" (Gen. 38.7). . . . For no evil thing is given by a good person; though it be unhappy, though it be full of pain, still it is brought about with the intention of curing, and with an eye to ultimate healing, that the hard discipline of severity might detach from sin that soul whom the lure and pleasure of sin had detached from God.'[6] This is how Origen deals with accounts of massacres in the Old Testament apparently commanded by God. The wholesale slaughter of Amalek, for instance, described in I Sam. 15.3, is dissolved in these words: 'Observe too whether such an interpretation does not aptly meet those who accuse the law of God on the grounds of its severity and cruelty because it declares that not only the nation of Amalek but also its seed is to perish. By this

---

[1]*Hom. on Ezek.* III.7. Koch, *op. cit.*, pp. 127 f., stresses particularly this aspect of Origen's doctrine of punishment: 'God punishes sins with sins'.
[2]See *Comm. on John* XXVIII.22, on John 9.39, 'For judgement came I into this world'.
[3]*Contra Celsum* V.15.
[4]*Comm. on Matt.* X.2.
[5]*Hom. on Jer.*, frag. 26.
[6]*Comm. on Rom.* VI.6.

interpretation the nation is to be referred to spiritual wickedness and its seed is to be interpreted as the teaching of the superstitions of the heathen and the worship of idols and every school of thought which induces a people to turn aside from God.'[1] Origen had learnt this smooth technique of explaining away awkward incidents such as this from Philo, who had written of the incident in which the sons of Levi were recorded as massacring three thousand men at the command of Moses, 'the priests of course do not, as some people think, execute men, rational creatures composed of soul and body, but they cut off from their own mind whatever things are peculiar and dear to the flesh.'[2] In similar vein Origen tones down the text 'The righteous will rejoice when he seeth the vengeance' (Ps. 58.10); 'The righteous man will rejoice when he sees the wisdom of the divine judgement directed towards punishing the unrighteous.'[3]

Origen, in fact, represents God's punishment as a benefaction, not a piece of retribution. The only form of punishment which he will recognize is deterrent and reformatory punishment. For him, as Koch emphasizes, 'punishment is blessing'.[4] Koch aptly puts his finger on the unscriptural nature of this doctrine of punishment when he says that for Origen, 'punishment has its origin, not in the holiness, but in the goodness of God.'[5] The same writer brings out how consistently Origen regarded God's punishment as educative,[6] as indeed most of the quotations on the subject already given have indicated. Once again we can find a Philonic precedent for this conception. On Deut. 8.2 ('The Lord . . . afflicted thee'), Philo says: 'This "afflicted" is equivalent to disciplined and instructed and made wise.'[7] It must however be admitted that there were plenty of other sources from which Origen could have derived ideas of this sort. Daniélou,[8] Koch,[9] and de Lubac[10] have pointed out analogies and precedents for this type of doctrine in Plato, in Plutarch, and in other Greek authors of Origen's day or before

---

[1] *Hom. on Num.* XIX.2; see above, p. 266.
[2] *De Ebrietate* 69.
[3] *Comm. on Ps.* 58.10, *PG* 12.1477.
[4] 'Eine Strafe ist eine Wohltat', *Pronoia und Paideusis*, p. 46. See *Contra Celsum* III.79 and IV.99 (reproduced in *Philoc.* XX.26).
[5] *Op cit.*, p. 133.
[6] *Ibid.*, pp. 28, 31, 62, 305. Cf. also Daniélou, *Origène*, p. 271: 'It could be said that Origen, himself a teacher, thought of his God as a teacher, as a master, to whom the education of children is entrusted, and his universe is a vast School where everything is subordinated to the education of free human beings.'
[7] *De Congressu* 172.
[8] *Origène*, p. 99.
[9] *Pronoia und Paideusis*, pp. 193–5, 203.
[10] *Histoire et Esprit*, pp. 239 f.

it; and Chadwick[1] has shown how the doctrine was continued by Iamblichus and others in the pagan world after Origen's day. In rationalizing and spiritualizing the biblical doctrine of God's wrath and God's punishment, Origen was obviously moving with the tide of contemporary sentiment.

To represent God's wrath as merely one aspect of God's education of mankind and as a disguised form of benevolence must have done much to reduce the urgency and tension of the original eschatological message of Christianity. But Origen's treatment of the Last Things of Christian tradition contributed even more to the reduction of this urgency. As one might expect, he never abandoned a formal belief in the conventional doctrines of the general resurrection, the last judgement, heaven, and hell; but he placed them in so extensive a vista of leisurely purgation and age-long spiritual adventure for the soul after death that they lost almost all their significance. Clement of Alexandria had suggested that there were grades of progress in heaven, first service, then enrolment in the heavenly 'presbytery', and that this was the meaning of St Paul's mention of different sorts of glory (I Cor. 15.40 f.).[2] Origen greatly develops this suggestion. The process of God becoming all in all, he says, 'is to be understood as not taking place suddenly, but gradually and by stages, in the course of infinite and immeasurable ages.'[3] He believes that the saints after death go to a 'paradise', where, gradually learning the 'reasons and principles' of everything on earth they gradually ascend to the 'kingdoms of heaven' through various spheres. This 'lecture-hall or school of souls', as Origen calls it, is not Purgatory but a sort of academic ante-chamber to heaven.[4] He does however at times indulge in speculation about a purgatory, not for the saints, but for those who are less than saints. The 'baptism with fire' (Luke 3.16), he says, is to take place after this life; it is to be administered by Jesus and to involve all those who need cleansing before they enter paradise.[5] He also made the following daring suggestion: 'I personally believe that even after the resurrection we need a sacrament washing and cleansing us, for no one could rise free from stains, nor could any soul be found which immediately lacked all

---

[1]See his edition of the *Contra Celsum*, p. 241.
[2]*Strom.* VI.13.107, *PG* 9.329.
[3]*PA* III.6.1. On the whole of this subject, see Molland, *The Conception of the Gospel in Alexandrian Theology*, pp. 145 f.
[4]*PA* II.11.6.
[5]*Hom. on Luke* XXIV, on Luke 3.16; cf. *Hom. on Ezek.* XII.2, and Crouzel, *Théologie de l'Image de Dieu chez Origène*, pp. 250 f. Clement of Alexandria had already sketched such a theory, *Strom.* VI.14.108 f., *PG* 9.329.

vices. Therefore at the regeneration a sacrament of Baptism is received, so that just as Jesus was cleansed as was consistent with the Incarnation (*dispensationem carnis*) by an offering, so we also should be cleansed by a spiritual regeneration.'[1] Incidentally, Origen denies the sinlessness (and therefore by implication the immaculate conception) of the Blessed Virgin Mary; he states that 'Mary, who was a human being, needed cleansing after her delivery.'[2]

Words of our Lord apparently suggesting a Second Coming to take place very soon he explains away: 'Henceforth ye shall see the Son of man sitting at the right hand of power' (Matt. 26.64) does not in his view imply a return of Christ in the near future, for in the first place Christ's disciples saw him 'sitting at the right hand of power' when they saw him risen from the dead, and in the second place an immense period of time is only a day in God's sight anyway.[3] And he reconciles the text, 'But now once at the end of the ages hath he been manifested to put away sin by the sacrifice of himself' (Heb. 9.26) with the other text 'that in the ages to come he might show the exceeding riches of his grace in kindness towards us in Christ Jesus' (Eph. 2.7) by saying that the 'end of the ages' was to be only the end of one cycle of ages, after which some of the 'ages to come' would begin.[4]

We have already noted Origen's tendency to use the next life as a useful dumping-ground for problems that cannot conveniently be solved within the limits of this life.[5] He employs it in order to reprieve those who were destroyed for murmuring about quails;[6] those who perished in the flood;[7] the people of Sodom;[8] and adulterers and adulteresses put to death by the law;[9] as well as to resolve the classic difficulty of the hardening of Pharaoh's heart. Koch says of Origen's eschatology,

[1] *Hom. on Luke* XIV, on Luke 2.22. A difficulty arises here, because earlier in the same homily Origen is represented as saying that it is 'a sacrilege' to maintain that the spiritual body rises polluted and stained. Either there is a corruption in the text (as the Migne editor maintains) or (as I think far more likely) Jerome has interpolated this last-mentioned sentiment, in order to maintain Origen's orthodoxy. See *Origen's Doctrine of Tradition*, pp. 43 f. We can be sure from *PA* II.10.2, 3, 8, that Origen found it perfectly possible to conceive of spiritual bodies rising not entirely pure. See below p. 347.
[2] *Hom. on Luke* XIV; similar statements are found in Hom. XVII and XX. The shocked Migne editor complains of Origen's *scandali, infidelitatis, ambiguitatisque!* Presumably Jerome, who translated these passages, shared the same scandalous scepticism.
[3] *Comm. on Matt.* Comm. Ser. 111.
[4] *PE* XXVII.15.
[5] See above, pp. 215 f.
[6] *PE* XXIX.10; cf. *PA* II.5.3 (the victims described in Ps. 78.34).
[7] *Contra Celsum* VI.59.
[8] *PA* II.5.3.
[9] *Hom. on Lev.* XI.2.

with some justice: 'There is no absolute distinction between this world and the next; the whole is an uninterrupted development which is in all circumstances directed by Providence in the way which is best for men.'[1]

In accordance with this view of eschatology Origen consistently allegorizes all eschatological imagery which he encounters in the Bible. Clement had given him some precedent in spiritualizing the fire of hell,[2] but Origen goes much further. He sets out, for instance, in his treatment of the apocalyptic discourse in Matt. 24, to see whether we are to take Matt. 24.30 ('And they shall see the Son of man coming in the clouds with power and great glory') literally or allegorically. After long discussion he comes to the conclusion that it would be quite possible to regard the text as either literal or spiritual, and equally possible to decide that 'clouds' meant 'holy and divine powers' or 'the most blessed prophets'. But anyone who concludes ('as a friend of God, as it were') that the truth lies only in the spiritual interpretation of the passage 'will say that those who take the passage literally must be excused on the ground that they are like children and little ones in Christ'. Anyway, he who can study the prophetic and apostolic writings properly already sees much of the glory which will be seen at the Second Coming of the Word.[3] The next verse ('And he shall send forth his angels with a great sound of a trumpet, and they shall gather together his elect from the four winds, from one end of heaven to the other') is similarly allegorized. The four winds are not material winds, heaven is the Scriptures, the trumpet is explained away in an exposition which collects references to trumpets from all over the Bible and concludes that the silver trumpet (Num. 10.1 ff.) means 'the mighty voice of the Word', because silver in the Bible often stands for the Word.[4] The passage in Dan. 9.24-7 describing the 'abomination of desolation' and the removal of sacrifice he refers, not to the Second Coming, but to the destruction of Jerusalem in A.D. 70.[5] The 'judgement-seat of God' (Rom. 14.10) and the open books of Dan. 7.10 are not to be taken literally.[6] The fragments that remain of his *Commentary on Revelation* are enough to establish that Origen allegorized all the eschatological language in that work. The 'door' of Rev. 4.1 was not of course literally opened in heaven (to maintain this

---

[1]*Pronoia und Paideusis*, p. 158; cf. pp. 89 f.
[2]*Strom.* VII.6.34, *PG* 9.449.
[3]*Comm. on Matt.* Comm. Ser. 50.
[4]*Ibid.*, 51 f.
[5]*Ibid.*, 40.
[6]*Comm. on Rom.* IX.41.

would be to invite the ridicule of the 'wise ones of this world') and the 'voice as of a trumpet' in the same verse means 'the magnitude of understanding with lucidity which came to him' (John), and so on.[1]

On the subject of what is usually called chiliasm, that is the belief that after the Second Coming the saints would reign for a thousand years with Christ on earth in a reconstituted Jerusalem, Origen is quite definite. Until his day chiliasm, while not a universally held doctrine, had apparently been quite a popular one. Eusebius gives us some information about views on this question held in the second century. He quotes Gaius as saying that Cerinthus the heretic particularly encouraged people to believe in an earthly kingdom after the resurrection in which people would enjoy the grossest pleasures.[2] Eusebius adds a little later some rather disparaging words about Papias (for Eusebius is anything but a favourer of chiliasm). He says that Papias reported some things as having come to him from unwritten tradition and also some odd (ξένας) parables and teaching of the Saviour and 'some other legendary stuff' (τινα ἄλλα μυθικώτερα). 'Among them he mentions that a period of a thousand years will take place after the resurrection from the dead while a material kingdom of Christ is set up on this earth.' But this, Eusebius thinks, is due probably to Papias' failure to realize the allegorical (μυστικῶς) meaning of what the apostles said.[3] Justin Martyr, very surprisingly, claims that chiliasm is a part of the catholic faith. 'I and any other Christians who are orthodox (ὀρθογνώμονες) in every point,' he says, 'understand that there will be a resurrection of the flesh, and a thousand years in a rebuilt and adorned and enlarged Jerusalem, as the prophets Ezekiel and Isaiah and the rest declare.'[4] A little later he enlarges on this theme. 'And next a man from our own number whose name was John, one of the apostles of Christ, in a revelation which was given to him, prophesied that those who have believed on our Christ would spend a thousand years in Jerusalem, and after that there would take place the general and, to speak summarily, simultaneous resurrection and judgement of all. This very thing our Lord also said, that "They shall neither marry nor be given in marriage, but they shall be as angels, being children of God of the resurrection".'[5] Irenaeus in his *Adversus Haereses* gave a literal interpretation of the

[1]*Comm. on Rev.*, frag. 25, p. 32.
[2]*HE* III.28.1, p. 89.
[3]*HE* III.39.11, p. 101.
[4]*Dial.* 80.5.
[5]*Ibid.*, 81.4; the Scriptural references in this passage are Rev. 20.4 and Luke 20.35 f.; cf. *ibid.*, 113.4.

Messianic banquet[1] and regarded the prophecy in Isa. 11.6–9 of the
harmony of the animals as destined to be literally fulfilled in the
millennial kingdom,[2] though as we have seen, in his *Demonstration* he
revoked this last opinion.[3] Tertullian was an enthusiastic, though not an
entirely consistent, champion of the millennial kingdom.

But Origen sets his face resolutely against chiliasm. He is well aware
that there are contemporary Christians who indulge in such hopes, but
he regards them with contempt. There are some misguided people who
expect in the future a literal fulfilment of promises. They expect after the
resurrection bodies capable of eating and drinking; marriage and pro-
creation of children; a literal Jerusalem adorned with precious stones;
the services of foreigners who may work as agricultural labourers, or as
builders to reconstruct Jerusalem; and an abundant supply of food and
wealth coming from the nations. They also expect that there will be
class distinctions in this restored state. 'But those who accept an interpretation of Scripture according to the apostles' meaning' refuse to
indulge in such gross fantasies and take every promise and hope suggesting such a picture in a spiritual way.[4] The contrast between Justin,
who regards a literal interpretation of the millennial kingdom as part of
Christian orthodoxy, and Origen, who regards in precisely the same
light an allegorical interpretation of the same subject, is striking, and,
for those who believe that the precise content of the Christian faith was
always well-known to faithful Christians, embarrassing. We have already
seen how Origen associated these chiliastic hopes with the narrow outlook and crude beliefs of the Literalists of his day.[5]

Yet Koch is not quite accurate when he says that Origen really has
no eschatology.[6] De Lubac is nearer the truth (though rather too
sweeping) when he says, 'Let us notice . . . that when he spiritualizes
the pictures of the apocalyptic discourse, he does not any the less believe
that they are speaking of a real event, the last act of the most real of all
dramas.'[7] The reader can sometimes catch a faint echo of the original
note of realized eschatology so strongly sounded in the New Testament,
as when Origen applies an eschatological passage in Isaiah (2.2–4) to the

---

[1] *Adv. Haer.* V.35.
[2] *Ibid.*, V.33.4.
[3] See above, pp. 151 f. and 333.
[4] *PA* II.11.2 f.; cf. *Comm. on Matt.* XVII.35, and for different ways of disposing of this promised kingdom see *PE* XXVII.13 and *Comm. on Rom.* X.1.
See also Turner, *The Pattern of Christian Truth*, p. 131 n. 4.
[5] See above, pp. 151 f.
[6] *Pronoia und Paideusis*, pp. 33, 89 f.
[7] *Histoire et Esprit*, p. 199.

contemporary Christian Church, saying that Christians now are 'in the last days'.[1] He expounds the apocalyptic motif of Anti-christ in a restrained way, stressing that this figure represents the power of evil personified, and that his coming is agreed by the Scriptures to be still in the future.[2] And he acknowledges two advents of Christ, one in humiliation, not recognized by the Jews, and the other in glory which both Jews and Christians regard as yet to take place.[3] He believes that in the end all the nations will be under one law, but hints that this will not take place till all men are freed from their bodies,[4] and he believes in a Last Judgement, though, as Chadwick points out, he does not think that it will take place within time.[5] And he believes that the martyrs are given special privileges in the unfolding of eschatological events.[6]

Origen also believes in the resurrection of the dead as in some sense an event to take place in the future. In the course of a comment on Isa. 26.19 ('Thy dead shall live, my dead bodies shall arise. Awake and sing, ye that dwell in the dust' [LXX 'tombs']), he says that everybody will rise, but there will be two resurrections (quoting Rev. 20.6) in the sense of two simultaneous but different resurrections, a glorious resurrection to a happy life for the good and a shameful resurrection to punishment for the bad. By 'tombs' the passage in Isaiah must mean any place where the body is laid, or a part of it; otherwise we would have to believe the absurd idea that only those who were buried in tombs in the strict sense of the word would rise. St Paul's phrase, 'It is sown in corruption; it will rise in incorruption' (I Cor. 15.42), must refer to the body and cannot possibly refer to the soul.[7] Elsewhere he gives a different interpretation of the two resurrections; these are 'one in which we rise with Christ from earthly things in mind and intention and faith so that we think upon heavenly things and look for things to come; and the other which is the general resurrection of all in the flesh. Therefore that resurrection which is according to the mind in faith seems to have been fulfilled already in those who mind "the things which are above, where Christ is

---

[1] *Contra Celsum* V.33.
[2] *Ibid.*, VI.43.
[3] *Comm. on John*, frag. 90.
[4] *Contra Celsum* VIII.72.
[5] *Comm. on Matt.* XIV.9; see Chadwick's ed. of *Contra Celsum*, p. 376 n.1.
[6] *Comm. on Rev.*, frag. 34, p. 39: the white robes of Rev. 7.9 and 13 are the bodies of the martyrs, 'already foreseen as risen incorruptible and spiritual'; and *Exhortation to Martyrdom*, XLII: the prophetic and eschatological 'acceptable time' (Isa. 49.8; 61.2) is the day of martyrdom. *Comm. on Matt.* Comm. Ser. 30: certain men may become angels before the general resurrection.
[7] Fragment of the *Commentary on Isaiah*, book VIII, preserved in Pamphilus' *Defence of Origen*, PG 13.217–20.

at the right hand of God". But the general resurrection of the flesh, which involves everybody, is still in the future; because the former was fulfilled at the First Coming, but the latter will be fulfilled at the Second Coming of the Lord.'[1] A long passage in the *Peri Archon* elaborates upon this view.[2] He maintains vigorously against heretics who deny the resurrection of bodies (*corporum*) that there will be a resurrection of bodies. This resurrection he describes in these words 'Out of the natural body that very power of resurrection and grace extracts a spiritual body, when it transforms it from humiliation to glory.'[3] But there will be different qualities of risen bodies. Those who come to the resurrection 'not yet cleansed in this life', that is, sinners, will have a different sort of body.[4] But we must not take this resurrection of the body in a mean and inferior way. There is a principle (*ratio*) in our bodies which the Word of God will take hold of and form from it a spiritual body at the resurrection. Even the wicked and those destined to punishment and everlasting fire will receive at the resurrection bodies which cannot be dissolved by punishment.[5] But these punishments, even the 'everlasting fire', will not consist of material fire. 'Each separate sinner lights the flame of his own fire for himself, and is not to be wrapped in any flame which will already have been lit by anybody else or which existed before him.' The 'fire' will consist solely of remorse, memory, and pangs of conscience.[6] Or it may consist of a distraction or dissipation of the soul.[7] The punishment of being cut asunder and having a portion appointed with the unfaithful (Luke 12.46) could mean the soul's being deprived of the gift of the Holy Spirit; or the removal of the corrupt part of the soul acquired since the Fall; or the removal of the guardian angel and consequent estrangement of the human (non-divine) part of the soul from God.[8] References to outer darkness mean that the (spiritual) bodies of the more wicked will be at the resurrection 'dark and black', that is presumably of grosser composition (though still spiritual) than the rest.[9] Exactly the same doctrine, though adapted for the pagan intellectual instead of the Christian student, and therefore rather less detailed, is found in a passage in the *Contra Celsum*.[10] In this passage occurs Origen's classic enunciation of what he means by the resurrection of the body: 'A certain principle is inherent in the body;

---

[1]*Comm. on Rom.* VI.9. I think it likely that Rufinus supplied the word *flesh* here for Origen's original *body*.
[2]*PA* II.10.1–5, 7 f.
[3]10.1; 'natural body' is *animali corpore*, perhaps originally ψυχικοῦ σώματος.
[4]10.2.   [5]10.3.   [6]10.4.   [7]10.5.
[8]10.7.   [9]10.8.   [10]V.18–24.

this is not corrupted and it is from this that the body is raised in incorruption.'[1] This passage, like the other one, leans heavily upon St Paul's analogy of the seed and the flower elaborated in I Cor. 15 for its exposition of the resurrection. It never refers to the resurrection of the flesh (σαρκός) but always of the body (σώματος), and it stresses even more than the other that the intellectual Christian will have to entertain a subtler and more refined doctrine of the resurrection than that held by the cruder and duller average believer. Elsewhere Origen, harping upon this same theme that the Christian can believe in the resurrection without believing in the resurrection of the flesh, describes this latter, cruder, doctrine as 'the resurrection as it is believed in the Church'.[2] He did not want to lay himself open to the charge of not believing in the resurrection, but he was equally anxious to avoid involving himself in the difficulties encountered by such writers as Athenagoras, Pseudo-Justin *On the Resurrection*, and Tertullian in defending a thoroughgoing doctrine of the resurrection of this flesh. The fact that he knew that the vast majority of the Christians of his day believed in this drastic version of the resurrection did not seriously influence him.[3] These are important qualifications made by Origen concerning the traditional doctrine of the resurrection of the body. But at the same time the evidence which we have surveyed makes it clear that Origen did believe in a resurrection; he did not allegorize it altogether away or refine it out of existence; he did regard it as in some sense an event yet to take place, and it would therefore be incorrect to say that he makes no serious allowance for eschatology in his theological scheme.

Origen, then, modified greatly the eschatological pattern which he had inherited. But two other features of his treatment of eschatological material also mark it out as unusual. In the first place he has a notable

[1] λόγος τις ἐγκεῖται τῷ σώματι ἀφ' οὗ μὴ φθειρομένου ἐγείρεται τὸ σῶμα ἐν ἀφθαρσίᾳ, V.23.
[2] *Comm. on Matt.* Comm. Ser. 29.
[3] W. L. Knox, in an article on 'Origen's Conception of the Resurrection Body', in *JTS* XXXIX, pp. 247 f., attempts to draw the conclusion from the tradition that Origen suggested that the resurrection body would be spherical (σφαιροειδῆ) that Origen believed that it is only the divine element in man that survives to take part in the resurrection, the ἡγεμονικόν in the soul of man. It might be replied that Origen's speculations about the nature of the soul's punishment after the resurrection, including the estrangement of the human part of the soul from God (see above, p. 347), exclude this possibility, for the non-divine part of the soul must survive if it is to be involved in punishment. But Dr Henry Chadwick, in a private communication, points out that the evidence that Origen made the suggestion that the soul after the resurrection will be spherical is very weak; it occurs only in the tenth anathema of the Council of 543 (Koetschau's ed. of *PA*, p. 176). In Dr Chadwick's opinion Origen never made any such speculation.

tendency, some instances of which we have already had occasion to notice, to interpret eschatological language in the Bible as applying directly to the religious experience of the individual Christian. The First and Second Comings of Christ, for instance, are (during the exposition of Matt. 24.3 ff.) dissolved into two entries of the Logos into the soul of the Christian, of which the Incarnation and the Parousia are only crude, though necessary, symbols.[1] The text 'For the Son of man shall come in the glory of his Father with his angels, and then shall he render unto every man according to his deeds' (Matt. 16.27) provokes a number of interesting comments. First he explains in an orthodox way that Christ's First Coming was not in glory, but that his Second Coming will be in glory. Then he proceeds by means of allegory to transmute this eschatology into religious experience. The Word appears to novices in the Christian faith with 'the form of a servant', so that they do not see his glory; but to the initiated he appears in 'the glory of his Father' so that they can say, 'and we beheld his glory, glory as of the only-begotten,' etc. In this case the 'angels' are the prophets of the Old Testament, whose words had 'no form nor beauty' (Isa. 53.2). Yet Origen ends with the cautious remark, 'But we say this without wanting to invalidate the literally interpreted Second Coming of the Son of God.'[2] Similarly, though he allegorizes the cosmic portents of Matt. 24.29 f. into various aspects of religious experience, he is careful not to deny that they may be fulfilled in a literal sense as well.[3] The eschatology of the kingdom coming 'in power' (Mark 9.1) he refines into different degrees of intellectual illumination on the part of those who see the Word.[4] The phrase 'Ye know not in what hour your Lord cometh' (Matt. 24.42) in its literal sense, he tells us, refers to the Second Coming, but in its 'intellectual' sense (which is clearly for Origen the more important one) to the full apprehension of his Lord by the intellectual Christian in his religious experience.[5] In expounding the Lord's Prayer he reaches the petition, 'Thy kingdom come'. He interprets the kingdom in this context as the intellectual and spiritual condition proper for the Christian. He does recognize that the fulness of 'Thy kingdom come' and of 'Hallowed be thy name' cannot be accomplished until Christ's Second Coming; but he believes that the individual soul can approximate

---

[1] *Comm. on Matt.* Comm. Ser. 32. For this whole subject see also Völker, *Das Vollkommenheitsideal*, p. 95; Bertrand, *Mystique de Jesus chez Origène*, pp. 101 f.
[2] *Comm. on Matt.* XII.29 f.
[3] *Ibid.*, Comm. Ser. 48.
[4] *Ibid.*, XII.32.
[5] *Ibid.*, Comm. Ser. 59.

closely to that fulness meanwhile by intellectual contemplation and by detachment, and characteristically he urges his readers now to put on 'holiness and incorruption' (I Cor. 15.53 f.), 'so that, as we are ruled by God, we are even now in the delights of rebirth and resurrection'.[1] This is the Pauline pattern of realized eschatology indeed; but it is the Pauline pattern turned upside down in the interests of a mystical idealism. Elsewhere he defines the kingdom of God as 'the contemplation of the ages which have been and which are to come'.[2] We are reminded of the significant sentence of Clement of Alexandria, 'It is easier for a camel to go through the eye of a needle than for a rich man to be a philosopher.'[3] Similarly Origen glosses the characteristic expression of the Epistle to the Ephesians, 'in the heavenly places' by 'in those things that are intellectual and beyond the senses'.[4] The expression 'we . . . shall together with him be caught up in the clouds' (I Thess. 4.16 f.) he interprets as meaning a sudden change to a better condition, comparable to St Paul's being caught up into the third heaven (II Cor. 12.2). And the 'clouds' mean the prophets or the apostles or both: 'If therefore anybody is caught up to Christ, he mounts up above the clouds of the law and the gospel, above the prophets and apostles.'[5] On 'The night is far spent, the day is at hand' (Rom. 13.12) Origen's comment is that there are two ways in which the day is at hand. The day of judgement naturally approaches nearer every day (though he does not seem to think that it is very near); and the more we receive Christ into our hearts the more day we let in on ourselves.[6] 'The God of peace shall bruise Satan under your feet shortly' (Rom. 16.20) causes him some trouble. If this refers to the devil, Satan has surely been already bruised, and we have no more reason to dread him. So he blunts the sharp edge of eschatology by assuming that Satan here means 'every spirit who opposes the faithful', and any temptation which they overcome.[7] The expression 'by reason of the present distress' in I Cor. 7.26, which most modern commentators take as referring to the crisis of the Last Time into which Christians have been precipitated, Origen refers to 'the sojourn in the body'.[8] And Daniélou has noted how in his treatment of the flood as a type Origen first produces an orthodox traditional eschato-

---

[1]*PE* XXV.1–3.
[2]*Comm. on Ps.* 145.13, *PG* 12.1673.
[3]*Strom.* II.5.22, *PG* 8.953.
[4]*Comm. on Eph.*, frag. 2, on Eph. 1.1, *JTS* III, p. 236.
[5]Frag. on I Thess. 4.16 f., *PG* 14.1297–1302.
[6]*Comm. on Rom.* IX.32.
[7]*Ibid.*, X.37.
[8]*Comm. on I Cor.*, frag. 39, *JTS* IX, p. 509.

logical explanation: Jesus Christ at the consummation of the times has
been commanded by God to make an ark and to give it dimensions full
of mysteries; of him Noah is a type, and the ark is the Church. Then he
introduces a new theme: the three rooms for three sorts of animals in
the ark are three sorts of Christians of varying spiritual capacities within
the Church.[1] He cannot resist moving from eschatology to the experience of the contemporary Christian.

There is very little precedent in previous orthodox Christian literature for this movement which is so common in Origen. The nearest
perhaps that we can find is the statement of Hippolytus that 'each man
knows that on the day when he quits this world "he is already judged"
(John 3.18), for the consummation has overtaken him.'[2] But this is not
very near. Völker points out that this movement is very common in
Valentinian systems, and believes that it is from Gnosticism that
Origen has derived this tendency.[3] I do not think that Origen is at all
likely to have borrowed this characteristic from the Valentinians, especially as we can find a source for it in an author whom we know Origen to
have studied and admired, namely Philo. The practice of dissolving the
eschatological language of the Bible into references to Christian religious
experiences represents the transmutation effected, by one who was both
a Platonist and a mystic, of Philo's practice of allegorizing the text of
the Old Testament into psychological or moral truths or descriptions of
the relation between the soul and God. The fact that the practice plays
so noteworthy a part in Origen's exposition shows how little congenial
to eschatology the bent of Origen's thought was.

In fact he has his own characteristic alternative to eschatology. This
is his use of what he calls the 'spiritual' or 'eternal' gospel,[4] and it constitutes the second unusual feature of Origen's treatment of the eschatological material in the Bible. Just as the law brought a shadow of good
things to come, so 'the gospel teaches us the shadow of the mysteries of
Christ, that gospel which is thought to be understood by everyone who
studies it'. The higher gospel shadowed forth by the ordinary gospel is
the 'eternal gospel' (Rev. 14.6), or, as Origen prefers to call it, the
'spiritual gospel'. To understand this gospel must be the aim of all serious students, but it can only be attained by some, and only by knowing

[1]Daniélou, *Sacramentum Futuri*, pp. 89 f., expounding *Hom. on Gen.* II.
[2]*Comm. on Dan.* IV.18.7.
[3]*Das Vollkommenheitsideal*, p. 126.
[4]On this subject see also Zöllig, *Inspirationslehre*, pp. 55 f.; Koch, *Pronoia und
Paideusis*, p. 88; Völker, *op. cit.*, p. 53 n. 2; 'Die Verwertung des Weisheits-
Literatur', *ZKG* LXIV, p. 31.

and believing in the ordinary gospel first. This ordinary gospel he calls 'sensible' (αἰσθητόν) in contrast to the spiritual nature of the other. It will be, he says, his business as an expositor to transmute the 'sensible' gospel into the 'spiritual' gospel and 'to penetrate into the depths of the gospel's intention and seek out in it the pure truth of the types'.[1] The phrase in S. of S. 2.3, 'I sat down under his shadow with great delight,' provokes the following comment: 'A man sets out to move from the shadow of the law to the shadow of Christ; so that because Christ is the life and the truth and the way, we are first placed in the shadow of the way and in the shadow of the life and in the shadow of the truth, so that we may understand in part, and in a glass darkly, so that after these things, if we walk by this way which is Christ, we may come to the point of understanding face to face what formerly we had seen as if in a shadow and darkly. . . . Therefore all who are in this life must necessarily be in some sort of shadow.'[2] The Jews had only 'the shadow of realities'. When Christ came he exhibited 'the picture of realities'. But we must realize that even Christ's work on earth gave us only 'pictures of spiritual things', and that 'by physical activities heavenly truths are indicated'. By 'picture' is meant whatever is apprehended for the moment and can be contemplated by human nature. 'But if you can in mind and soul reach heaven, there you will find those good things whose "shadow" the law had, and whose "picture" Christ exhibited in the flesh'.[3] At Christ's Second Coming the saints will live according to the principles of this spiritual gospel.[4] The Scriptures are composed of body, soul, and spirit, the body (the literal meaning) for the Jews under the old dispensation; the soul for us in this existence; the spirit for 'those who in the future will achieve the inheritance of eternal life', though we may be able to reach the 'spirit' of the Scriptures even now.[5] This eternal gospel, Origen suggests, was preached by Christ to angels.[6]

By the nature of the case it is difficult to determine exactly the contents of this 'spiritual' gospel, but we may safely assume that it would embody many of Origen's favourite theological speculations. His most daring suggestion in connection with it is that in order to fulfil this spiritual gospel Christ is crucified still in the heavenly places;[7] not only was he sacrificed in the earthly Jerusalem, but his blood was also shed

[1] *Comm. on John* I.7 f.
[2] *Comm. on S. of S.* III, on S. of S. 2.3.
[3] *Hom. on Ps.* 39, II.2, on Ps. 39.6, *PG* 12.1402-3. See above pp. 280 ff.
[4] *PA* IV.3.13.   [5] *Hom. on Lev.* V.1.
[6] *Comm. on Rom.* I.4.   [7] *PA* IV.3.13.

on 'the altar which is above in the heavens where also is the Church of the first-born'.[1] As we have seen, he envisages a fresh, 'spiritual', Baptism inaugurating or accompanying this 'spiritual' gospel.[2] Treating of the phrase 'in the regeneration' of Matt. 19.28, he maintains that there are two 'lavers of regeneration'; one is Baptism with water, which is Baptism 'through a glass darkly', and the other is Baptism 'with the Holy Ghost and with fire', destined to be accomplished at the final regeneration.[3] If Origen speaks occasionally of a Baptism with the Holy Ghost as if it were independent of Baptism with water, it is much more likely that he has in mind this Baptism associated with the 'eternal gospel' than a separate ceremony within Christian initiation supposed to confer the Spirit. The typological structure of Christian Baptism noted by Daniélou is therefore altered by Origen; Daniélou detects in traditional Christian baptismal typology three stages: first Noah in the Old Testament, prefiguring; second Christ in the New Testament, the reality, fulfilling; third the Christian, in sacramental initiation conformed to Christ, reproducing and enjoying the reality.[4] For this third stage Origen substitutes his conception of the 'eternal gospel' which the Christian can only fully encounter in the next life, and thereby upsets the whole traditional balance, for he shifts the reality from this life, in which Christ became incarnate and in which according to the traditional structure the sacraments bring us the reality of Christ to be apprehended and enjoyed here and now, to the next life, leaving us to regard this life, sacraments and all, as no more than a shadow of reality. It is, I cannot help thinking, a disquieting alteration. He applies the same treatment to the feasts mentioned in the Bible. He says that when Christ is called 'our Passover' (I Cor. 5.7), or when any reference is made to a Christian feast-day, then the future age is intended. We shall celebrate feasts in these 'heavenly places'; there existed a shadow of these feasts among the Jews who celebrated them in a material manner. We are now 'schooled in the true law under guardians and stewards until the fulness of the time in this case be upon us, and we

---

[1]*Hom. on Lev.* I.3. De Lubac, *Histoire et Esprit*, pp. 291 f., has not observed this passage, which corroborates the authenticity of the suggestion in *PA* IV.3.13; his suggestion therefore, that the passage in *PA* (which is derived from Justinian's letter to Mennas) is corrupt and does not represent Origen's real thought, cannot be entertained. He has anyway, as he himself admits, the judgement of Bardy against him here (Bardy, *Recherches sur l'histoire du texte et des versions latines du De Principiis d'Origène*, p. 187).
[2]See above, p. 323.
[3]*Comm. on Matt.* XV.23. Incidentally, this point is not realized by Daniélou when (*Sacramentum Futuri*, p. 78) he refers to this passage.
[4]*Sacramentum Futuri*, p. 76.

A.E.—M

shall reach the perfection of the Son of God'.[1] He applies words used by St Paul for the state of preparation and immaturity of the people of God under the old law to the state which Christians now enjoy in Christ. He believes too, that under this 'eternal gospel' there will be grades and distinctions among the faithful, foreshadowed by the divisions of the tribes articulated in Num. 34 and 35.[2]

This conception of the 'eternal gospel' to be found in Origen's exposition has been defended by some recent writers as both orthodox and satisfactory. Molland maintains that this concept represents a genuine eschatology on Origen's part, because it does envisage an end (ἔσχατον); it is, he admits, not the eschatology of the New Testament; it is Platonized eschatology, but still this is Platonism Christianized.[3] De Lubac is, in contrast, much warmer in his praise of this 'eternal gospel'; he regards it as highly satisfactory, quite unlike the extravagances of such later theological speculators as Joachim de Fiore; in contrast to this sort of theology, Origen is 'entirely eschatological'.[4] Daniélou agrees wholeheartedly with de Lubac. He describes Origen's suggestion that there is a new Baptism in connection with this 'eternal gospel' as the 'eschatological prolongation' of Baptism,[5] and thinks that Origen has here achieved a valid compromise between Christianity and Platonism.[6] And, discussing a passage in Origen where it is said that the first Parousia in the flesh is only a shadow and that we are not really risen with Christ and seated with him in the heavenly places, but that these things are foreshadowed by faith, Daniélou calls this doctrine admirable: 'We are at the heart of the Christian mystery of history, in the relationship which binds together the central event of the Resurrection, the present reign of Christ in the Church, the consummation of this reign at the end of the ages. . . . The key of this mystery is precisely the relation, at once symbolic and dynamic, of the first to the second Parousia.'[7]

I cannot share the complacency of these writers on this subject. This concept of the 'spiritual gospel' seems to me to be, not a Platonized form of genuine Christian eschatology, but an alternative to eschatology, indeed an evasion of it.[8] Origen sees the Incarnation, not as the crisis

---

[1]*Comm. on John* X.13–15 (the last quotation from 15).
[2]*Hom. on Num.* XXVIII.2.
[3]*The Conception of the Gospel in Alexandrian Theology*, pp. 156–8.
[4]*Histoire et Esprit*, pp. 217–27; quotations from pp. 220 f.
[5]*Origène*, p. 74.
[6]*Ibid.*, p. 157.
[7]*Sacramentum Futuri*, p. 250; the passage discussed by Daniélou is *Hom. on Josh.* VIII.4.
[8]Cf. Völker, *Das Vollkommenheitsideal*, pp. 184 f., where he gives several examples from Origen's works of the τελεῖος being represented as one who can

whereby God poured himself out into human nature and committed himself into history, but as merely one important stage in the long process of God's strategy of making himself known to human beings, preceded by other comparable though lesser stages, and followed by other more important stages of the process. Similarly, and working on the same assumptions, he sees the End and all that was traditionally associated with it as another of these stages, necessary indeed, but of minor importance compared with the new phase of God's strategy that was to follow it, the leisurely progress of souls over an immense period through a series of immaterial existences. Origen accepts *ex animo* all the apparatus of Christian doctrine—Incarnation, sacraments and eschatology. But so strong is the Platonic strain in his thought and so much intoxicated is he with the use which he can make of the literary expression of that Platonism—allegory—that he must regard this apparatus as no more than the outward expressions of eternal and unchangeable truths which are more important than those expressions. The writers of the New Testament conceive of God as having really *acted*, as having in truth brought about the last crisis in which all men are involved, by moving towards the world in Christ; and they believe that this was a real move, not just a shadow or picture showing what God was like, but an objective event in which men now in Christ encounter the reality of God. They believe that the crisis is to be consummated and the veil under which God even now approaches men torn away at the final development of this crisis, which they call the Parousia and Judgement. But they are nevertheless convinced that God is to be found in Christ really and effectively now, that he has decisively and uniquely approached and spoken to men in the Incarnation, which is made contemporary in the Holy Spirit and in the sacraments. The Christian writers of the second century held on to this conviction that God had encountered men in the last crisis, though they tended to change the emphasis from realized to futurist eschatology, that is to say to suggest that the crisis was about to break instead of saying that it had already broken. Origen does his best unobtrusively to remove any sense of crisis at all, and to shift the moment of encounter with the reality of God from this life to the next life, and to a next life conceived in idealistic and mystical terms. He does not think of God as moving at all; his theological concepts are, as far as God is concerned, all static rather

transcend even the Scriptures and anticipate eschatology through his knowledge of the 'eternal gospel'; in fact this seems to me to amount to a declaration on Origen's part that the τελεῖος can by-pass eschatology.

than dynamic; or rather, he has transferred the movement from God to man. It is man, it is the whole universe, which, in its unending *Sehensucht* towards the unchangeable God, displays movement in this scheme. God's vast plan of education (which is ultimately the image in which Origen conceives of salvation) cannot be called dynamic. It may well have been true that Origen came at a time when some bold step had to be taken by Christian theologians in dealing with the problem of primitive Christian eschatology. Origen's treatment of the problem was bold enough; indeed, it was revolutionary. But I do not think that anybody who has examined Origen's thought on this subject carefully could maintain that his eschatology was consistent with the eschatology of the New Testament.

CONCLUSION

14

Origen's Interpretation of Scripture

ORIGEN is the first father of the Church whose interpretation of Scripture we can survey and judge fully. The extent of his works which survive and his peculiar devotion to the Bible, so that he, more than anyone before him, is consciously expounding the whole Bible, make this full survey possible. It is clear that he was not the first Christian expounder of the Bible. As we look closely into his works we can see, appearing as insects appear under the microscope, a swarming world of varied and lively biblical interpretation. Indeed, we are driven to the conclusion that the average Christian in Origen's day knew his Bible well. It is true that not many Christians can have known how to read (though the proportion of literate Christians to illiterate must have been greater than during almost the whole course of the Middle Ages); it is true that books must in those days have been awkward things to handle and transport. But the intense interest that was taken in the Bible, even by people such as the Literalists who cannot have been educated, the wide diversity of biblical interpretation and the probability that daily services with reading of the Scriptures and preaching were held in several places, all suggest that the Bible was a powerful force and a familiar part in the lives of ordinary Christians. Several other pieces of evidence support this conclusion, such as the abundance of scriptural quotation in documents, such as Acts of Martyrs or the writings of Hermas, written by Christians who were neither particularly distinguished nor particularly well educated, and the prominence given to the destruction of Scriptures during Diocletian's persecution only fifty years after Origen's death. Further, the ease with which Origen's admirers were able to take down his sermons in shorthand during the later part of his life, and the, apparently reliable, transcript of the proceedings of the conference in Arabia attended by Origen and called the *Conversation with Heracleides*, suggest that the men of Origen's day did not find it very difficult to handle writing materials. In short, Origen's life covered a period when the Bible was widely known and widely discussed in the Christian Church. Only a church where the Bible is well known to the ordinary Christian can produce a great interpreter of the Bible.

But, though Origen was not an inventor in biblical exposition, he made a great difference to the development of this subject within the Christian Church. He brought the touch of a master to what had hitherto been nothing much more than the exercise of amateurs. The crude employment of proof-texts, which had been enough for Justin, for the Literalists and for the Marcionites, was as a result of Origen's work almost entirely superseded in favour of the carefully compiled commentary, equipped with a suitable apparatus of learning. In this sense we may say that Christian biblical exegesis begins with Origen; he is the first professional, because though Hippolytus had written works which we might call commentaries and Melito (and no doubt many others) had written Homilies on Scripture, and Clement of Alexandria had in his rambling way dealt with individual passages, none of these efforts could be called methodical or profound. In contrast to these, Origen brought the whole weight of contemporary scholarship—linguistic, critical, and philosophical—to bear upon the task of making the biblical commentary a permanent literary form for Christian writers, and he succeeded brilliantly. In fact all writers of commentaries today owe a debt to Origen as in this sense the great Founding Father of their activity. Unlike all Christian theologians before him, Origen was in his day a scholar of what we would now call world-wide reputation. He was known from Rome to Arabia, from Athens to Alexandria. His conversation was sought by the Empress Mammaea and feared by the philosopher Plotinus.[1] His reputation was enough to defy successfully the violent animosity of the Bishop of Alexandria and the remoter disapproval of the Bishop of Rome. Like Dionysius of Alexandria after him, he was called in to reconcile heretics, and succeeded in doing so. People came from far to hear his lectures; Gregory Theodorus was even lured from the law-school at Berytus and induced to embrace the profession of divinity instead of law by them. As a Christian expounder of Scripture, Origen towers like a giant above his predecessors and contemporaries.

One of the most important of the new contributions which Origen brought to Christian biblical exposition was his contact with streams

[1]I have seen no reason to withdraw or modify my conjecture that Origen met Plotinus in Athens in 244 or 245 and that the interview between them described by Porphyry took place then, though this conjecture has been eyed askance in several reviews of the book in which I made it. See *Origen's Doctrine of Tradition*, pp. 4–6.

of thought outside Christianity. He had established fertile contact with contemporary Judaism; his considerable acquaintance with Rabbinic scholarship is evident in his works;[1] he had learnt enough Hebrew to be able to read the Old Testament in its original language;[2] on the question of the rival authority of the LXX and the Hebrew text he decides in the ultimate resort for the Hebrew text;[3] and for his interpretation of Hebrew names in the Bible he relies on sources which are probably wholly Jewish, and not even Jewish-Christian. Again, he is deeply influenced by Greek or Hellenistic philosophy. To Plato he owes his whole bent of thought, his whole tendency to see all tangible and temporary phenomena as mere ephemeral symbols of a deeper, permanent, invisible reality, a tendency which shows itself throughout all his work, as much in his theory of the pre-existence of souls as in his treatment of historical events, of sacraments and of eschatology. From Philo he borrowed abundantly, far more abundantly than he acknowledged openly, though he does not deliberately conceal his debt to Philo, as (in my opinion) he does his debt to Clement of Alexandria. In the works of this great Alexandrian Hellenistic Jew Origen found the materials for his doctrine of the inspiration of Scripture, the tools whereby he was to overcome the stubborn particularity and reconcile the glaring inconsistencies of the Bible; here he found the means of reading into the Bible whatever non-biblical ideas were congenial to his own theological system, while professing (and no doubt sincerely imagining himself) to be a particularly enthusiastic and faithful interpreter of the thought of the Bible. From Clement of Alexandria and from several pagan writers of his own day he derived his conceptions of God's wrath, of punishment, and of judgement, which he found so useful in meeting the searching criticisms of the Old Testament made by the followers of Marcion. I do not agree with the suggestion frequently made by students of Origen's thought that he owed anything significant to Gnostic thought, with the possible exception that he derived the literary form of the commentary from Heracleon. Origen, unlike Clement, did not claim to be a Christian Gnostic; his allegory was allegory of a received text, whereas Gnostic allegory, with the exception of Heracleon's, could not usually be as strictly defined as this, and Origen's allegory owed its origins to other examples of allegory of a received text, such as those of Philo and of Heracleitus. But this openness to non-Christian intellectual influences

[1] See *Origen's Doctrine of Tradition*, pp. 148–56.
[2] See above, pp. 167–72.
[3] See above, pp. 165–71.

A.E.–M*

on the part of Origen meant that he was consciously endeavouring to reconcile the text of the Bible with contemporary philosophy and was under the necessity of finding in the Bible by some means or other his philosophical speculations. This had of course been attempted for Judaism by Aristobulus and Philo and for Christianity by Clement of Alexandria. But Origen essayed the task with a thoroughness, a subtlety and an effectiveness which nobody before him had approached. We may deplore the results of his enterprise of reading into the Bible conceptions which, we are bound to admit, are not there. But we could never describe the enterprise as crudely or inefficiently done.

One of the best illustrations of Origen's peculiar contribution to the exegesis of the Bible is his handling of the Old Testament law. The meticulous, miscellaneous, and far-ranging provisions of this legal code had embarrassed Christian theologians before Origen. The author of the *Epistle of Barnabas*, Justin Martyr and Theophilus of Antioch had all in their own way attempted to resolve this embarrassment. But the necessity of somehow retaining this law within his sacred Scriptures embarrassed Origen more acutely than the others; his characteristically Platonic aversion to particularity and the broad target which the law offered to Marcionite heretics and to pagan intellectuals made him especially sensitive on this point. Yet he made no very drastic or violent alterations in the traditional Christian attitude to the law. He allowed that some parts of the law were still applicable to Christian conduct, what we would today call the moral rather than the ritual precepts; and at the same time he found a method of making the large mass of legal material which neither he nor the majority of his fellow-Christians thought applicable to Christian life relevant; he transmuted this mass by means of the alchemy of allegory into reasonably orthodox Christian doctrine. And he retained a surprising amount of the literal sense of the law by suggesting that several of its enactments were directly relevant to the institutions of the Church of his day, inaugurating thereby a line of thought which was to have far-reaching consequences for many centuries afterwards. Very few theologians today would accept this particular solution to the difficulties raised by the presence of the Jewish law in the Christian Bible. But few solutions of the problem have been as ingenious, and unsatisfactory though Origen's answer to this question is, no alternative answers which are any less unsatisfactory seem at the moment to be available.

Competence, subtlety, ingenuity, symmetry—these are the leading qualities of Origen's interpretation of Scripture. He saw all the prob-

Literalists - naïve
reading into Biblical thought
one's own ideas
ORIGEN'S INTERPRETATION OF SCRIPTURE   363

lems; he had thought them out. He knew his material thoroughly; he knew exactly how to handle it in the most effective way for his purposes. To a degree unparalleled before his time and not often equalled after it, he was a *sophisticated* expositor. The manner in which he deals with Marcion, with the Gnostic predestinarians, with the naïve Literalists, and above all with Celsus; the fair-minded preference for the Hebrew text maintained in his controversies with Jewish scholars; the courteous yet confident unfolding of his argument which we find reported for us by the eye-witness in the *Conversation with Heracleides*; all these convince us that Origen was a master of the art of exposition as only a few have been masters of it. Why can we not go further? Why can we not call Origen a great interpreter of the Bible, in the same sense that Augustine and Luther and Westcott and perhaps Barth can be called great interpreters?

The answer in my opinion lies in the fact that in one important respect Origen's thought remained outside the Bible and never penetrated within it. Of the great interpreters (and indeed of several such as Hoskyns who are not usually called great) it is always evident that their minds were soaked in biblical thought; they give the reader the impression that they are speaking to him from inside the Bible; at least for purposes of exposition, they have successfully put themselves into the minds of the biblical author whom they are interpreting. Origen never quite conveys this impression, and on countless occasions gives the opposite impression, that he is reading into the mind of the biblical author thoughts which are really his own. The critical subject upon which Origen never accepted the biblical viewpoint was the significance of history. To the writers of the Bible history is *par excellence* the field of God's revelation of himself. The Jewish historians may not have achieved the accuracy of a modern historian, but they did believe that in the events of history God's will and purposes were made plain. The Jewish religious tradition re-interpreted all the primitive nomadic and agricultural festivals in order to attach them to critical points in the history of their race. The writing prophets saw God as judging and saving through historical crises, the menace of Rezin and Pekah to Judah, the threat of Sennacherib to Jerusalem, the collapse of the Assyrian Empire, the destruction of the southern kingdom by Nebuchadnezzar, the destined end of the Babylonian Empire at the hands of Cyrus. The apocalyptic and eschatological literature of later Judaism, grotesque and bizarre though it appears to us, was only a way of declaring God's control of history and his determination to manifest himself

God enters into our acts — even sinful ones

in history. The New Testament does not at all abandon or reduce this attribution of intense significance to history; on the contrary, the New Testament heightens it. The New Testament writers see God as having brought about a final crisis in history by means of the birth, life, death and resurrection of Jesus Christ. Further, they see this crisis as in effect God moving into history, into human existence; they see the significance of Jesus Christ as not merely an epiphany of divine truth, but as an *act* of God, *the* act of God, the consummating, decisive, final act, constituting in itself salvation and judgement.[1] In this world of corruption and sin the Church is the *locus* of this act; sacraments are the recreation, the making contemporary through God the Holy Spirit, of this act; eschatology is the mythological account of this act which at once explains and safeguards its significance. History is therefore an essential ingredient of revelation; it is an inseparable part of the manner in which God reveals himself. One might almost say that in the Incarnation God has in a sense taken history into himself.

God reveals God's self through his...

To this insight Origen is virtually blind. He does not, as he has been represented to do by some scholars, reject or abandon history; he does not deny any significance to sacraments; he does not dissolve eschatology entirely away. On the contrary, he defends the historicity of most of the events recorded in the Bible; he has an almost magical view of the efficacy of the invocation in Baptism, and his belief in the holiness of the consecrated bread provoked a supercilious protest from Harnack; and he undoubtedly looked for a resurrection of the dead in some form. He had too much respect for the Bible and for the rule of faith of the Church to abolish these traditional doctrines. But he perilously reduces the significance of history, and with history of sacraments and of eschatology. In his view history, if it is to have any significance at all, can be no more than an acted parable, a charade for showing forth eternal truths about God; it is not, as it is in the prophets, the place where through tension and uncertainty and danger and faith men encounter God as active towards them. To him the Incarnation is a necessary stage early in the long process of souls learning essential truths about God; it is not the final and unique event, contemporary to all men and women, whereby God speaks to them for salvation or ruin. To him the most important point about sacraments is that they are symbols of truths which are to be apprehended by the understanding. And in the process of demythologizing eschatology he removes what seems to me

---

[1] As a few examples of passages which seem to me to imply this conclusion I suggest Mark 1.14 f.; 14.62; John 1.14–18; I Cor. 1.30; Phil. 2.5–11; II Cor. 8.9.

*prejudice prevents
us from drawing
the right conclusions*

ORIGEN'S INTERPRETATION OF SCRIPTURE 365

the essential note of urgency and crisis conveyed by eschatological language. Such a mind as Origen's, in short, could never completely
assimilate biblical thought because it approached the Bible with one presupposition which closed to it many doors of understanding, the presupposition that history could never be of significance.

It may therefore be worth raising at the end of this study of Origen a
question which was in fact in my mind when many years ago I first
began to study Origen. Have modern interpreters anything genuinely
in common with Origen in their approach to the Bible? Anglican
scholars in particular have always claimed that their appeal is to the
Bible as interpreted by the early Fathers. But if the interpretation of the
Bible by one of the greatest of these early Fathers is radically different
from the interpretation which we would give of it today, and diverges
so drastically in its assumptions, what is left of this appeal to the early
Fathers?

We can begin by pointing out, in attempting to answer this question,
that Origen has in fact several characteristics in common with modern
biblical scholarship, characteristics which have been developed in
modern times mainly because of the revolution in biblical exposition
brought about by the advent of historical criticism. One such point is
obviously his treatment of the text of the Bible; here he is noteworthy as,
with the exception of Jerome, the sole Christian scholar in the ancient
world who recognized what we would now call the right facts and did
not allow prejudice to prevent him drawing the right conclusions from
them. Another point of contact is certainly his freedom from bibliolatry,
from a hampering and paralysing literalism. This literalism we have seen
to have constituted a real threat to honest and constructive thought
about the Bible in Origen's day, whether it was championed by Jewish
or by Christian teachers; and we are conscious that in our own day it
still constitutes, in a rather different form, a considerable menace. A
refreshing breath of freedom from fear blows through Origen's biblical
interpretation. He will not be bound by the proof-text method of interpretation which is always dear to the hearts of Literalists, and which had
in his day the authority of a venerable tradition attached to it. If he
thinks that an incident recorded in the Bible is unhistorical, he does not
hesitate to say so. If he finds an inconsistency, he recognizes it as such.
He is, moreover, remarkably free from concern about orthodoxy; this
is, in fact, the sad difference between Origen and his Latin translators.[1]
He has a genuine regard for the Church's rule of faith; he believes that

[1]See *Origen's Doctrine of Tradition*, ch. II.

not hypnotized not true ; interpretary
by true

it does represent in all important points a genuinely true interpretation of the Bible. But he is not hypnotized by it. It does not prevent him from indulging freely in speculation, and he is ready on occasion to recommend his pupils to ignore or transcend the rule of faith in the interests of scriptural truth. He does not have to keep an eye upon decisions of popes or of councils, upon theologians who have gone before him, or upon confessions of faith to which he is obliged to give lip-service. Here, too, he seems to me to be in harmony with the best of modern biblical scholarship. Again, we today are inclined to sympathize with much of Origen's exegetical rationalizing. To some extent we can follow him in his desire to mitigate the anthropomorphism of the Old Testament's descriptions of God. We are, as he was, particularly sensitive to the need of accommodating the statements of the Bible to the truths which have apparently been established by contemporary science. In particular we find it both surprising and refreshing that Origen seems deliberately to refrain from laying emphasis upon the evidential value of miracles. The reason was that in his day the climate of opinion was too friendly to miracles, whereas in our day it is not friendly enough to them. In the third century everybody believed in miracles and, perhaps as a consequence, all religious traditions could produce them in evidence. The effect on an intelligent third-century apologist for Christianity is to make him unenthusiastic about calling in miracles as evidence. The same result is produced on the twentieth-century apologist by the fact that almost nobody believes in miracles. But this abstinence from miracles in marshalling his arguments on the part of Origen makes embarrassing reading for those critics of Christianity who maintain (as some still do) that it was in the early centuries indebted for its success largely to its appeal to miracle. And above all we hail with surprise and note with pleasure the fact that Origen was a whole-hearted exponent of demythologizing. Not Rudolf Bultmann himself could be more anxious than Origen was to extricate essential Christian dogma from the belief in a three-storeyed universe, or from a literal interpretation of eschatological imagery. Indeed, a study of Origen should serve as a sharp and salutary reminder that the concept of demythologizing is no new one, and that it has appeared already, very early in the history of Christian thought, without involving the collapse of traditional Christian dogma or the searching reconstruction of the Christian creed. Origen was able to attempt nothing more or less than a revolution in Christian eschatology which had indeed far-reaching consequences but which could not possibly be described as making a complete break with the past, though it certainly is interesting for the historians of Christian doctrine that so drastic a remoulding of eschatology could be made within a little more than a century of the compilation of the New Testament. Finally, the modern interpreter of the Bible finds himself in entire accord with Origen's doctrine of accommodation. Here, in fact, Origen seems to stand upon the very threshold of the great change effected in biblical interpretation by the growth of historical criticism. Acted upon by pressures which had indeed different origins from those which influence modern scholarship but which moved in the same direction, Origen's agile mind conceived, or at least developed and elaborated, the conception of the Bible as a record of God's gradual revelation of himself to men, a conception which has had such a liberating and fruitful effect upon biblical scholarship during the last hundred years. Here undoubtedly Origen's exposition comes closest to ours.

These points of similarity provide an impressive extent of common ground between Origen and the modern exegete. But we must not ignore the wide differences between them. Origen's doctrines of the inspiration and of the inerrancy of the Bible, which had so controlling an influence upon his exegesis, are wholly unacceptable to most modern scholars, and from those who still accept them they demand so much explanation and modification that they disappear almost wholly into the realm of theological fantasy. That the Bible cannot be inaccurate or mistaken in any of the statements in it, and that every sentence, every word, every letter is (quite apart from the ambiguity that textual criticism must introduce into this theory) inspired inasmuch as it has God as its author —these are convictions which must in the light of modern scholarship be regarded as either meaningless or untrue. Again, Origen's use of allegory, with the exception of those few cases where he is confusing allegory with simple metaphor, is today widely regarded as wholly indefensible and as merely a process which caused Origen to mislead himself and others. At the best we might describe it as quaint and sometimes poetical; at the worst it is a device for obscuring the meaning of the Bible from its readers. Generally, Origen assumed that the Bible was an oracular book; that is to say, it consisted of a vast series of oracles which might or might not have some connection with each other, but which each in its own right had some divine or mysterious truth to convey. This is a conception which, since the arrival of historical criticism, has had to be entirely abandoned and is, as far as one can prophesy, never again likely to be revived. Origen also conceived of the Logos as active in the Old Testament in a manner which historical criticism has also made entirely unacceptable. Presumably responsible and honest scholars will never again maintain that the prophets of the Old Testament and its great men, such as Moses, Samuel, and David, were well instructed in Christian doctrine and knew nearly as much about it as the apostles did. Presumably the guiding principle in all exegesis of both Old and New Testaments will remain indefinitely the question of what any given text meant when it was first written or uttered to the first audience for which it was intended. All these presuppositions on the part of Origen, which had a profound influence upon his interpretation of Scripture, make his thought on biblical subjects appear alien to ours rather than akin to it.

The oracular view of the Bible was certainly held from a very early period by the early Church; indeed from the very beginning this must have been the Christian attitude to the Old Testament; and Christian writers such as Justin and Irenaeus had advanced some way towards the belief that the great men of the Old Testament foreknew Christian doctrine; perhaps it might be shown that the very beginnings of this idea can be traced to the New Testament. But Origen's doctrines of inspiration and inerrancy were derived directly from Philo. Those who today are anxious to champion these doctrines in a modified form, under the title of 'the catholic doctrine of inspiration' should realize that this doctrine derives from an Hellenistic Jew who, although he was a contemporary of Jesus of Nazareth, never knew of his existence and never met any of his apostles. It was from Philo, too, that Origen derived his use of allegory, and from Philo very largely his conception of the Logos as teaching divine truths to the men of the Old Testament which they assimilated by means of a partly mystical and partly intellectual apprehension, and it was in imitation of Philo that he turned traditional Christian typology into non-historical allegory. We can therefore reasonably claim that the particular parts of Origen's interpretation of Scripture which are irreconcilable with the assumptions of the scholars of today derive largely (but not solely) from sources extraneous to traditional Christianity, from a Platonic attitude to history and a Philonic attitude to Holy Scripture. What divides us from Origen is, for the most part, the presuppositions with which he approached the Bible, not his failure to realize the problems presented by the Bible nor the actual technique of interpretation itself.

Now, every generation of scholars approaches the Bible with a different series of presuppositions which have been largely supplied by contemporary thought quite independently of the Bible itself. It is obvious, for instance, that Anselm's interpretation of the Bible is conditioned by the hierarchical principle that governed mediaeval society. The later mediaeval exegetes relied on presuppositions supplied by Aristotelian philosophy. The eighteenth century exegetes were swayed by their belief in the sufficiency of natural theology and the power of reason, and the nineteenth-century scholars by their intense moralism and their rather shallow optimism. In the twentieth century our biblical exposition may well be distorted by the universally accepted and universally applied dogma of evolution and by an irrational fear of metaphysics. That Origen's interpretation of Scripture should have been deeply influenced by important presuppositions derived from contemporary non-Christian philosophy is, after all, only what we should expect, and is one of those circumstances for which allowance must be made in judging any ancient author. It means simply that if we appeal to Origen as one of the early Church Fathers, our appeal must be made with an intelligent discrimination. We shall appeal to his freedom, his flexibility, his honesty, his breadth, but we shall not attempt to find in him authority for the modern use of allegory or for a revival of an oracular view of the Bible. But before we can regard this question of the possibility of appealing to Origen as satisfactorily answered, we must ask how far Origen allowed his presuppositions to be modified by the Bible, and what it was that he derived from his interpretation of the Bible.

To ask these questions is in fact to broach the interesting subject of tradition in interpretation. Origen approached the Bible, we have found, with a series of presuppositions in his mind which had nothing particular to do with the thought of the Bible itself. Was he preserved from completely misunderstanding the Bible by the intractable and unmalleable material of the Bible itself, or was he kept on the right lines by a previously existing tradition of interpretation? This last question is answered in the affirmative by Daniélou, as we have seen.[1] He maintains that there was already current in the Christian Church, independently of the New Testament, a tradition of treating the Old Testament typologically which, though Origen sat more loosely to this than his predecessors, did exercise a restraining influence upon him. And he identifies this traditional interpretation with that elusive and unsubstantial concept 'the tradition of the Church', and tries to show thereby that Origen testifies to the existence of an unwritten tradition of the Church, independent of Scripture and interpretative of it, which derived historically from our Lord and his apostles.

[1] See above, pp. 123–5.

Having completed our survey of Origen's interpretation of Scripture, we ought to be in a good position to decide upon the justice of Daniélou's claim. We can first say with confidence that there *was* in Origen's day a previously existing tradition of interpreting the Old Testament by means of types in a Messianic sense, and that while this tradition is clearly marked in the New Testament it may well be that in Christian literature before Origen's day we can discern some examples of this tradition which do not appear in the New Testament. But two facts make it impossible to identify in this typological tradition an inter-pretative tradition independent of the Bible. The first is that this inter-pretative tradition appears unmistakably in the New Testament itself; in fact the number of examples of it to be discovered outside the New Testament is meagre, and the examples (such as the association of Joshua with Jesus) far from impressive. The other fact is that we can trace to some extent the pedigree of this typological tradition, and find that it is disconcertingly ancient; in fact it is pre-Christian! Not only has Lundberg shown that typological ideas similar to those which ap-pear in this tradition are to be found early in Gnostic thought and in other circles which are embarrassing for those who are anxious to see in this tradition 'the tradition of the Church'; but it is quite clear from the evidence of both Jewish and early Christian liturgy and from ancient Christian funerary art, from the remains of Rabbinic typology, and above all from the witness of the Dead Sea Scrolls, that typology was a Jewish phenomenon, which ante-dated the coming of Christianity and which was adapted by the Christians for their own purposes. A 'tradition of the Christian Church' which existed before the Christian Church did is an unusual one indeed. We may observe St Paul using Rabbinic allegory and several other devices of contemporary Palestinian exegesis in order to establish arguments in support of the Christian faith; but we would be rash indeed if we claimed for these the high status of an original tradition interpretative of the gospel which he had received and handed down parallel with it. This typological tradition of interpretation is in a precisely similar position. It is one of the accom-panying circumstances of the gospel of the Incarnation, like a belief in the activity of demons; but we have no right to claim that it is an original and necessary part of the Christian message, any more than we have a right to add a belief in demons to the articles of our creed.

Further, this typological tradition, though it was well-known to Origen, had very little influence upon his exegesis. He largely trans-muted it or deserted it for the (as it seemed to him) richer fields opened to him by allegory. He no doubt regarded it as a far from important part of the Christian faith. If we are to regard this typological interpretation as a tradition of the Church, we must admit that it exercised remarkably little restraint on Origen.

But if Origen was not restrained in his interpretation of the Bible by this previously existing typological tradition, were not his Platonic and Philonic presuppositions modified and limited in their operation by the material of the Bible itself? There are of course some obvious examples of such a modification. He could not deny the historical character of the life of Jesus. He could not present a Docetic Christ. He did believe in a resurrection of the body, and his refinement of this belief was grounded fairly enough upon St Paul's refinement of it in I Cor. 15. When he wants to refute the Marcionites' representation of the God of the Old Testament as cruel and just without being loving, it is to relevant passages in the Old Testament as well as in the New that he turns. He refutes the Literalists quite legitimately out of the Bible itself. He can almost always turn the tables on Celsus in argument because he genuinely does know his Bible and uses it properly; in fact, he knows the Jews' case better than Celsus does. He never disguised from himself or from his pupils that, however profoundly he might be concerned with making the gospel acceptable to the intellectual and however many theological privileges he might concede to him, Christianity was for all men and women of all stations and capacities, the unlearned and crude as well as the highly educated. Origen was not a Gnostic because the Bible forbade him to be one. But when we have made these necessary observations, we must confess that Origen was generally speaking not seriously restrained by the Bible; he knew very little about the intellectual discipline demanded for the faithful interpretation of biblical thought; his presuppositions were very little altered by contact with the material in the Bible, though he was perfectly willing to accept the ideas of the Bible where they did not conflict with his presuppositions. He had in his hand a panacea for all biblical intransigence, allegory. Where the Bible did not obviously mean what he thought it ought to mean, or even where it obviously did not mean what he thought it ought to mean, he had only to turn the magic ring of allegory, and—Hey Presto!—the desired meaning appeared. Allegory, in short, instead of ensuring that he would in his exegesis maintain close contact with biblical thought, rendered him deplorably independent of the Bible.

There was, however, one restraining influence upon Origen in his interpretation of Scripture. He always intended to interpret the Bible as the Church interpreted it. He was a loyal churchman, an encourager of martyrs, an adept in prayer, a constant preacher, and a reconciler of heretics. During the *Conversation with Heracleides* he begged the bishops present not to make liturgical innovations; he was a supporter of the old-fashioned rigorist policy in Church discipline. The whole life, custom and practice of the Church was very dear to him. He constantly declares the necessity of interpreting the Scripture according to the Church's rule of faith, and he carefully distinguishes the areas within which speculation is legitimate for Christians from the points upon which the Church's rule of faith is clear. It was, it seems to me, the belief and practice of the contemporary Church that exercised a more restraining influence upon Origen than any other pressure.

Does this mean that we must after all return to the view that Origen was restrained and influenced in his interpretation of Scripture by a 'tradition of the Church' independent of Scripture? The answer depends upon what is meant by 'tradition of the Church'. This phrase is one susceptible of widely divergent interpretations and many misunderstandings. It is exceedingly difficult to determine at any moment in church history what the 'tradition of the Church' is. Justin Martyr, for instance, says as plainly as possible that a literal interpretation of the Millennial Kingdom, described in Rev. 20.4, is an integral part of orthodox Christianity. Origen says that an allegorical interpretation of this prophecy is a piece of apostolic teaching. Gaius (quoted by Eusebius) attributed a belief very like Justin's to the heretic Cerinthus. Which of these authors is right about the 'tradition of the Church'? On the interpretation of one point in the book of Daniel, Porphyry the pagan is a sounder guide than all the tradition of the Church. Theophilus of Antioch, who as a Catholic bishop ought to have known what the 'tradition of the Church' was, makes the extraordinary statement that Christians are so-called because they are anointed with the oil of God.[1] Are we compelled to accept this as a genuine tradition? Clement of Alexandria believed in a tradition of teaching handed down unwritten, independently of the Bible, from our Lord and his apostles, which consisted of a number of speculations of a startlingly Philonic character, including the necessity of allegorizing the Bible.[2] Origen also included the command to allegorize the Bible in the Church's rule of faith. If we are to take all these statements at their face-value and endeavour to incorporate them somehow in a 'tradition of the Church' which is

[1]See above, p. 313.
[2]See *Origen's Doctrine of Tradition*, ch. IV.

original, unwritten and independent of the Bible, we shall find ourselves in deep waters indeed.

The rule of faith of the Church which exercised a restraining influence upon Origen was simply the version of Christianity which was preached, lived, and witnessed to by the Church of his day, as far as he knew it.[1] The Bible was a library of books, a vast mass of passages, which had no power of automatically preaching or summarizing themselves. The Church preached and summarized the Christian faith; its preaching could even be divided into articles, which would probably differ slightly according to the preaching of the Church in different places.[2] It would be inaccurate to describe this rule of faith as a creed, for a creed, certainly in Origen's time, would be a barer, austerer list of articles than the rule of faith, the irreducible iron rations of a Christian. The historical pedigree of the rule of faith must have been, formally, independent of the Bible, for the Church had been preaching its gospel and summarizing its message continuously from the very beginning. This is why Irenaeus and Tertullian can claim the rule of faith as an alternative to Scripture. But it would be entirely wrong to describe it as a source of doctrine independent of Scripture, because it had certainly by Origen's day and probably well before his day no other source, no other evidence, to draw upon except Scripture, and as far as I know no early Christian writer ever suggests that it had. Scripture was in fact the sources of the Church's preaching crystallized out into a written form at one point in their being handed down; and the New Testament was collected, read in the liturgy and recognized everywhere precisely because the Church needed the security of written, and not merely oral, sources for its rule of faith, and indeed for its whole life and witness. Besides Scripture the only sources for the Church's rule of faith were ordinary human common sense (including the rules of logic) and the Holy Ghost. The Church's rule of faith did not create or modify or supplement Scripture. It summarized, interpreted and preached it.

It seems to me, therefore, both accurate and honest to conclude that the chief restraining influence upon Origen's interpretation of Scripture was the Church's rule of faith. He did not, it should be added, regard this rule as infallible. On the contrary, he was ready to encourage his pupils to ignore it in certain cases. He teaches that they must learn a more advanced version of scriptural doctrine of the resurrection of the body than the Church's crude version of the resurrection of the flesh.

[1] *Ibid.*, ch. VI.
[2] For Origen's account of the rule of faith at Alexandria, see *ibid.*, pp. 116–18.

And in two places he directly contradicts what must have been by then the universal Christian practice of addressing prayer direct to God the Son.[1] But he clearly did hold the rule of faith in great respect, though he clearly gave even greater respect to the Bible. Perhaps it would be most satisfactory to conclude that what we see in Origen is an interaction between the Bible, the Church's interpretation of the Bible, and the insights of the individual scholar himself. We cannot describe him as an unqualified biblicist; we cannot say that he gave unquestioning assent to the *magisterium* of the church; we cannot describe him as a pure individualist in theology. To study the works of Origen is to witness an interesting and on the whole fruitful interplay between these three forces. Perhaps therefore in this sense the Anglican scholar can find in Origen a valuable ally. Perhaps in this sense it could be said that Origen is the best justification for the Anglican reliance on the Bible as interpreted by the early Fathers.

[1] *PE* XV.1; *Conversation with Heracleides*, pp. 129.13–130.9 (MS pp. 4.30–5.10).

ABBREVIATIONS

ARSV	American Revised Standard Version of the Bible
CQ	*Classical Quarterly*
CR	*Classical Review*
ECQ	*Eastern Churches' Quarterly*
ERE	*Encyclopaedia of Religion and Ethics*
Eus.*HE*	Eusebius: *Ecclestiastical History*
Eus.*PE*	Eusebius: *Praeparatio Evangelica*
GCS	*Die Griechischen Christlichen Schriftsteller der ersten drei Jahrhunderte*, Leipzig and Berlin 1897 ff.
JQR	*Jewish Quarterly Review*
JTS	*Journal of Theological Studies*
LXX	Septuagint Version of the Old Testament
MT	Masoretic Text of the Old Testament
NS	New Series
NT	New Testament
OT	Old Testament
PA	Origen, *Concerning First Principles* (*Peri Archon*)
PE	Origen, *Concerning Prayer* (*Peri Euches*)
PG	Migne, *Patrologia Graeca*, Paris 1857 ff.
PL	Migne, *Patrologia Latina*, Paris 1844 ff.
RechSR	*Recherches de Science Religieuse*
REG	*Revue des Études Grecques*
REJ	*Revue des Études Juives*
RV	Revised Version of the Bible
SB	Strack-Billerbeck: see Bibliography
TLZ	*Theologische Literarzeitung*
TU	*Texte und Untersuchungen zur Geschichte der altchristlichen Literatur*, Leipzig 1882 ff.
TWNT	*Theologisches Wörterbuch zum Neuen Testament*, ed. G. Kittel, Stuttgart 1933 ff.
Vig. Chr.	*Vigiliae Christianae*
ZKG	*Zeitschrift für Kirchengeschichte*

BIBLIOGRAPHY

I *The Works of Origen*

Philocalia ed. J. Armitage Robinson, Cambridge 1893; cited as *Philoc.*

The Eight Books against Celsus ed. P. Koetschau, *GCS* Origenes I and II, 1899; cited as *Contra Celsum.*

Concerning First Principles ed. P. Koetschau, *GCS* V, 1913; cited as *PA* (*Peri Archon*).

Concerning Prayer ed. P. Koetschau, *GCS* II, 1899; cited as *PE* (*Peri Euches*).

The Exhortation to Martyrdom ed. P. Koetschau, *GCS* I, 1899.

Entretien d'Origène avec Héraclide et les Évêques ses Collègues sur le Père, le Fils et l'Âme ed. J. Scherer, Cairo 1949; cited as *Conversation with Heracleides.*

Commentary on St Matthew's Gospel ed. E. Klostermann, *GCS* X–XII, (including the *Commentariorum Series*), 1935, 1933, 1941–55.

Commentary on St John's Gospel ed. A. E. Brooke, I and II, Cambridge 1896.

Homilies on Jeremiah, Commentary on Lamentations and Fragments on the books of Samuel and Kings ed. E. Klostermann, *GCS* III, 1901.

Commentary on the Epistle to the Ephesians: fragments ed. J. A. F. Gregg, *JTS* III, 1902, pp. 233–44, 398–420, 554–76.

Greek fragments of the Commentary on the Epistle to the Romans ed. J. Ramsbotham, *JTS* XIII, 1912, pp. 209–24, 357–68; *JTS* XIV, 1913, pp. 10–20.

Commentary on the First Epistle to the Corinthians: fragments ed. C. Jenkins, *JTS* IX, 1908, pp. 231–47, 353–72, 500–14; *JTS* X, 1909, pp. 29–51.

Commentaires Inédits des Psaumes: Étude sur les Textes d'Origène contenus dans le Manuscrit Vindobonensis 8, R. Cadiou, Paris 1936.

Die Scholien-Kommentar des Origenes zur Apokalypse Johannis, entdeckt und herausgegeben von Constantin Diobouniotis und Adolf Harnack, *TU* 38.3, 1911; cited as *Comm. on Rev.*

Fragments of Origen's Stromateis ed. E. von der Goltz, *TU* 17.4, 1899.

Analecta Sacra Spicilegio Solesmensi ed. J. B. Pitra, II, Tusculum 1884.

Extraits des Livres I et II du Contre Celse d'Origène ed. J. Scherer, Cairo 1956.

For all the other works or fragments of Origen which have survived in the original or in translation, I have used Migne, *PG* 11–14 and 17.

II *Other Ancient Authors*

APHRAATES *Demonstratio* I (De Fide), ed. R. Gräffin, *Patrologia Syriaca* I, I, 1894.

ARISTEAS, *Letter of* ed. H. St J. Thackeray, in H. B. Swete, *Introduction to the Old Testament in Greek*, Cambridge 1902.

376

BARNABAS, *Epistle of* ed. Kirsopp Lake, in *The Apostolic Fathers*, Loeb Classical Library, 2nd ed., Cambridge, Mass. 1945.

CLEMENT, *First and Second Epistle of* in *The Apostolic Fathers*, Loeb Classical Library.

CLEMENT OF ALEXANDRIA *Protrepticus, Paedagogus, Stromateis* (cited as *Protrept., Paed. and Strom.*), *Opera Minora*, ed. Otto Stählin, *GCS* I and II, 2nd ed., 1936, 1939; *GCS* III, 1909.

DEMETRIUS *On Style*, ed. W. Rhys Roberts, Cambridge 1902.

DIDACHE, THE in *The Apostolic Fathers*, Loeb Classical Library.

EUSEBIUS *Ecclesiastical History*, ed. W. Bright, 2nd ed., Oxford 1881; cited as Eus.*HE.*
Praeparatio Evangelica, ed. G. Dindorf, Teubner, Leipzig 1867; cited as Eus.*PE.*

HERACLEITUS *Quaestiones Homericae*, ed. F. Oelmann, Teubner, Leipzig 1910.

HERACLEON *The Fragments of Heracleon*, ed. J. Armitage Robinson, Cambridge 1891.

HERMAS *The Shepherd*, in *The Apostolic Fathers*, Loeb Classical Library; also ed. M. Whittaker, *GCS*, 1956.

HERMIAS *Irrisio Gentilium Philosophorum*, ed. H. Diels, *Doxographici Graeci*, 2nd ed., Berlin and Leipzig 1929.

HIPPOLYTUS *Commentary on Daniel*, ed. and tr. M. Lefevre, with an introduction by G. Bardy (Sources Chrétiennes), Paris 1947.
On the Song of Solomon, in *Exegetical and Homiletic Works*, ed. and tr. G. Bonwetsch and H. Achelis, *GCS* Hippolytus I, Part I, 1897, pp. 341–74.

IGNATIUS *Letters* in *The Apostolic Fathers*, Loeb Classical Library.

IRENAEUS *Demonstration of the Apostolic Preaching*, ed. and tr. J. Armitage Robinson, Cambridge 1920; cited as *Dem.*
Adversus Haereses, ed. W. W. Harvey, 2 vols., Cambridge 1857; cited as *Adv. Haer.*

JOSEPHUS *Antiquities* and *Contra Apionem*, ed. S. A. Naber, Teubner, Leipzig 1888; cited by book and section, and page of this edition.

JUSTIN MARTYR *Apology* (with Appendix) and *Dialogue with Trypho*, ed. E. J. Goodspeed in *Die Ältesten Apologeten*, Göttingen 1914; cited as *Apol.* I and II and *Dial.*

MELITO *Homily on the Passion*, ed. Campbell Bonner (Studies and Documents 12), London and Philadelphia 1940; cited by section, and page of this edition.
Fragments, ed. E. J. Goodspeed, *Die Ältesten Apologeten*, pp. 307–13.

PAMPHILUS *Apology for Origen*, book I tr. Rufinus, *PG* 17.615–32.

PHILO *Opera Omnia*, Loeb Classical Library; Vols. I–V ed. F. H. Colson and G. H. Whitaker, Vols. VI–IX ed. F. H. Colson.

PHILODEMUS *Volumina Rhetorica*, ed. S. Sudhaus, 2 vols., Teubner, Leipzig 1892 and 1896.

PLUTARCH *De Iside et Osiride* (from *Moralia* II. 3) and *De Audiendis Poetis* (from *Moralia* I), ed. W. Nachstädt, W. Sieveking and J. Titchener, Teubner, Leipzig 1935.

PSEUDO-PROCLUS *Easter Homily*, PG 65.796–800.
THEOPHILUS OF ANTIOCH *Three Books to Autolycus*, ed. with introduction and notes by G. Bardy, tr. J. Sender (Sources Chrétiennes), Paris 1948.
Τύποι 'Επιστολικοί ed. V. Weichert, Teubner, Leipzig 1910.

III   *Modern Authors*

A.   *Books*

ALLEGRO, J. M. *The Dead Sea Scrolls*, London 1956.
BADCOCK, F. J. *The History of the Creeds*, London 1938.
BARDY, G. *Recherches sur l'Histoire du Texte et des Versions Latines du De Principiis d'Origène*, Paris 1923.
BARKER, E. *From Alexander to Constantine*, Oxford 1956.
BERTRAND, F. *Mystique de Jesus chez Origène*, Paris 1951.
BIGG, C. *The Christian Platonists of Alexandria*, Oxford 1886, 2nd ed. revised, 1913.
BLACKMAN, E. C. *Marcion and his Influence*, London 1948.
BONSIRVEN, J. *Le Judaisme Palestinien au Temps de Jesus-Christ*, 2 vols., Paris 1934 and 1935.
Exégèse Rabbinique et Exégèse Paulinienne, Paris 1939.
BRIGHTMAN, F. E. *Liturgies Eastern and Western*, Oxford 1896.
BROWN, R. E. *The Sensus Plenior in Sacred Scripture*, Baltimore 1955.
BURROWS, MILLAR *The Dead Sea Scrolls*, London 1956.
BUTTERWORTH, G. W. *Origen on First Principles* (translated), London 1936.
CADIOU, R. *La Jeunesse d'Origène*, Paris 1935.
CHADWICK, H. *Origen: Contra Celsum* (translated with notes), Cambridge 1953.
CHARLES, R. H. *The Apocrypha and Pseudepigrapha of the Old Testament*, Oxford 1913; cited by chapter and verse, and page of this edition.
CROUZEL, H. *Théologie de l'Image de Dieu chez Origène*, Paris 1956.
DANIELOU, J. *Origène*, Paris 1948. (Eng. tr. by W. Mitchell, London 1955.)
Sacramentum Futuri, Paris 1950.
DAUBE, D. *The New Testament and Rabbinic Judaism*, London 1956.
DAVIES, J. G. *The Spirit, the Church and the Sacraments*, London 1954.
DE FAYE, E. *Origène, sa Vie, son Œuvre, sa Pensée*, 3 vols., Paris 1923, 1927, 1928; cited as *Origène*.
DE LUBAC, H. *Histoire et Esprit*, Paris 1950.
DENIS, J. J. *De la Philosophie d'Origène*, Paris 1884.
DODD, C. H. *According to the Scriptures*, London 1952.
DUGMORE, C. W. *The Influence of the Synagogue upon the Divine Office*, Oxford 1944.
DUPONT-SOMMER, A. *The Dead Sea Scrolls*, Eng. tr., Oxford 1952.
FIELD, F. *Origenis Hexaplorum quae Supersunt*, Prolegomena, Oxford 1875.

FLESSEMANN-VAN LEER, E. *Tradition and Scripture in the Early Church*, Assen, Holland 1955.
FOAKES-JACKSON, F. J. *Christian Difficulties in the Second and Twentieth Centuries*, London 1903.
FRITSCH, C. T. *The Qumran Community*, New York 1956.
GASTER, T. H. *The Scriptures of the Dead Sea Sect*, London 1957.
GRANT, R. M. *The Letter and the Spirit*, London 1957.
HANSON, A. T. *The Wrath of the Lamb*, London 1957.
HANSON, R. P. C. *Origen's Doctrine of Tradition*, London 1954.
II Corinthians (Torch Bible Commentaries), London 1954.
HARNACK, A. *Die Kirchengeschichtliche Ertrag der Exegetischen Arbeiten des Origenes*, *TU* 42.3, I and II, 1918.
HARRIS, RENDEL *Testimonies*, 2 vols., Cambridge 1916 and 1920.
JEREMIAS, J. *The Eucharistic Words of Jesus*, Eng. tr., Oxford 1955.
KAHLE, P. E. *The Cairo Geniza*, Oxford 1947.
KENNEDY, H. A. A. *Philo's Contribution to Religion*, London 1919.
KNOX, W. L. *Saint Paul and the Church of the Gentiles*, Cambridge 1939.
KOCH, H. *Pronoia und Paideusis*, Studien über Origenes und sein Verhaltnis zum Platonismus, Berlin and Leipzig 1932.
LAMPE, G. W. H. *The Seal of the Spirit*, London 1951.
LAMPE, G. W. H. and WOOLLCOMBE, K. J. *Essays on Typology*, London 1957.
LATKO, E. F. *Origen's Concept of Penance*, Quebec 1949.
LAWLOR, H. J. and OULTON, J. E. L. *Eusebius: Ecclesiastical History* (translated with introduction and notes), London 1928.
LAWSON, J. *The Biblical Theology of Saint Irenaeus*, London 1948.
LUNDBERG, P. *La Typologie Baptismale dans l'Ancienne Église*, Leipzig and Uppsala 1942.
MILBURN, R. L. P. *Early Christian Interpretations of History*, London 1954.
MOLLAND, E. *The Conception of the Gospel in Alexandrian Theology*, Oslo 1938.
MONTDESERT, C. *Clement d'Alexandrie*, Paris 1944.
MONTEFIORE, C. G. and LOEWE, H. *A Rabbinic Anthology*, London 1938.
NINEHAM, D. *Studies in the Gospels* (editor), Oxford 1955.
OULTON, J. E. L. *Holy Communion and Holy Spirit*, London 1951.
OULTON, J. E. L. and CHADWICK, H. *Alexandrian Christianity* (Library of Christian Classics), London 1954.
PAULY-WISSOWA *Real-Encyclopädie der Altertumswissenschaft*, Stuttgart 1896.
PRAT, F. *Origène, le Théologien et l'Exégète*, Paris 1907.
PRESTIGE, G. L. *Fathers and Heretics*, London 1940.
ROBERTS, B. J. *The Old Testament Text and Versions*, Cardiff 1951.
ROSE, H. J. *A Handbook of Greek Literature*, London 1934.
SANDERS, W. B. *The Fourth Gospel in the Early Church*, Cambridge 1943.
SCHOEPS, H. J. *Aus Frühchristlicher Zeit*, Tübingen 1950.
SIMON, M. *Verus Israel*, Paris 1948.

STANFORD, W. B. *Greek Metaphor*, Oxford 1936.
The Ulysses Theme, Oxford 1954.
STEUART, B. *The Development of Christian Worship*, London 1953.
STRACK, H. L. and BILLERBECK, P. *Kommentar zum Neuen Testament aus Talmud und Midrash*, 4 vols., Munich 1922–8; cited as SB.
SPICQ, C. *L'Épître aux Hébreux*, I, Introduction, Paris 1952.
TOLLINTON, R. B. *Clement of Alexandria*, 2 vols. London 1914.
Selections from the Commentaries and Homilies of Origen, London 1929.
TURNER, H. E. W. *The Pattern of Christian Truth*, London 1954.
VÖLKER, W. *Das Vollkommenheitsideal des Origenes*, Tübingen 1931.
WILLIAMS, N. P. *Ideas of the Fall and Original Sin*, London 1927.
WUTZ, F. X. *Onomastica Sacra*, *TU* 41, 1914.
ZÖLLIG, A. *Die Inspirationslehre des Origenes*, Freiburg 1902.

B. *Articles*

ARSENIEV, N. 'The Teaching of the Orthodox Church on the Relation between Scripture and Tradition', *ECQ* VII, 1947, Suppl., pp. 16–26.
BARDY, G. 'Les Traditions Juives dans l'Œuvre d'Origène', *Revue Biblique* XXXIV, 1925, pp. 217–52.
BATE, H. N. 'Some Technical Terms of Greek Exegesis', *JTS* XXIV, 1923, pp. 59–66.
BONSIRVEN, J. 'Exégèse Allegorique chez les Rabbis Tannaites', *RechSR*, XXIII, 1933, pp. 513–41; XXIV, 1934, pp. 35–46.
BÜCHSEL, F. ἀλληγορέω, *TWNT* I, pp. 260–4.
CADIOU, R. 'Dictionnaires Antiques dans l'Œuvre d'Origène', *REG* XLV, 1932, pp. 271–85.
DANIÉLOU, J. 'Traversée de la Mer Rouge et Baptême aux Premiers Siècles', *RechSR* XXXIII, 1946, pp. 402–30.
'The Fathers and the Scriptures', *ECQ* X, 1954, pp. 265–73.
DEN BOER, W. 'Hermeneutic Problems in Early Christian Literature', *Vig. Chr.* I, 1947, pp. 150–67.
HALÉVY, J. 'L'Origine de la Transcription du Texte Hébreu en Caractères Grecques dans l'Hexaple d'Origène', *Journal Asiatique*, series IX, vol. XVII, 1901, pp. 335–41.
HANSON, R. P. C. 'Moses in the Typology of St Paul', *Theology* XLVIII, 1945, pp. 174–7.
'Studies in Texts: Acts 6.13 f.', *ibid.*, L, 1947, pp. 142–5.
'History and Allegory', *ibid.*, LIX, 1956, pp. 498–503.
'The Interpretations of Hebrew Names in Origen', *Vig. Chr.* X, 1956, pp. 103–23.
INGE, W. R. 'Alexandrian Theology', *ERE* I, p. 316.
KAUFMANN, D. 'Sens et Origine des Symboles Tumulaires de l'Ancient Testament dans l'Art Chrétien Primitif', *REJ* XIV, 1887, pp. 33–48 and 217–53.

KLOSTERMANN, E. 'Formen des exegetischen Arbeiten des Origenes', *TLZ*, 1947, pp. 203–8.

KNOX, W. L. 'Origen's Conception of the Resurrection Body', *JTS* XXXIX, 1938, pp. 247 f.

LAUTERBACH, J. Z. 'The Ancient Jewish Allegorists in Talmud and Midrash', *JQR* (NS) I, 1910–11, pp. 291–333 and 503–31.

MANSON, T. W. 'The Argument from Prophecy', *JTS* XLVI, 1945, pp. 129–36.

MARMORSTEIN, A. 'La Reorganisation du Doctorat en Palestine au Troisième Siècle', *REJ* LXVI, 1913, pp. 44–53.

MARTIN, J. 'La Critique Biblique chez Origène: II, L'Allegorisme', *Annales de Philosophie Chrétienne* CLI, 77th year, 1905–6, pp. 233–58.

PERLES, J. 'Études Talmudiques', *REJ* III, 1881, pp. 109–20.

RATCLIFFE, E. G. 'Justin Martyr and Confirmation', *Theology* LI, 1948, pp. 133–9.

SALMON, G. 'Marcion', *Dictionary of Christian Biography*.

TATE, J. 'The Beginnings of Greek Allegory', *CR* XLI, 1927, pp. 214 f. 'Plato and Allegorical Interpretation', *CQ* XXIII, 1929, pp. 142 ff.; XXIV, 1930, pp. 1 ff.

VÖLKER, W. 'Die Verwertung des Weisheits-Literatur bei den Christlichen Alexandrinern', *ZKG* LXIV, 1952–3, pp. 1–33.

VON BALTHASAR, H. 'Le Mysterion d'Origène', *RechSR* XXVII, 1936, pp. 513–612.

INDEX OF REFERENCES

I BIBLICAL

A. Old Testament and Apocrypha

B. New Testament

A.E.–N

II PATRISTIC

A. Origen

B. Other Fathers

III OTHER ANCIENT AUTHORS

A. Jewish

B. Pagan

INDEX OF NAMES

Literalism - p 61, 62

See. p. 71 - Dying & Rising Savior

Look up epistle of Barnabus.

p. 74 - uses of Allegory

List of N.T passages that
   could be considered allegory. p 76, 78

SOS p. 78

Creation p. 9?

   security of written faith

cogent - adj. convincing, forcible
n. cogency
eschew = shun
abrogate - repeal or annul by
authorative act.

dispensation - that which is
dispensed by God to humans.

Typology - interpretation 4
recent event as the fulfilment
of a similar situation
recorded or prophesied
in scripture
Allegory - interpreting an object
or person or one or more
events meaning some
object of a later time
(or person) with an attempt
to trace a relation between
them. p2x

every time

Alexandrian Allegory. p 63 Also derivative
of Allegory, p 64 (a-historical)
Typology take into consideration
the intention of the original
— writer -
Allegory ignores intention of
original writer and is concerned
only with his or her own idea

Money 4 forgiveness of sins - p207
If Jesus is God - then Jesus
existed exists before his human birth

although - God inspired human
beings, the beings remain
human beings and not perfect.
Therefore the words though
inspired may not necessarily
perfect

prejudice prevents us from
drawing right conclusions p. 365
transcending rule of faith
by scriptural truth p. 366
mitigate to work against
erroneous usage. p. 366

anthropomorphism - attributing
a human shape to God p. 366
Being made in God's image -
not the same as making
God in our image. (exclusivity?) p. 366
security of written truth p. 373
Scripture - church's teaching
crystalized in written form, p. 373
study p. 190
the Word in the world p. 373

tendentious - opinionated or biased

naive - unsophisticated or artless

anthropomorphism - n. attribution of human form or character to an inanimate, object, animal or deity. adj. anthropomorphic.

hierophant - an interpreter of sacred mysteries

hierarchy - a series of terms of different rank.

aeon -

demiurge -

unworthy readings

credulous
obelize

Nemesis - agent of vengence

incantation - uttering of magical words.

Geneologies p-260
Wedding at Cana p-262

Hagar. p-264

8344 Jesus appearance as different points of view-344
Allegorizing Lot's daughter
Joseph & Tamar
[248]

look for inconsistencies in births of Isaac & Ishmael. p-242

LaVergne, TN USA
24 August 2009

155701LV00002B/10/A